"Sri Lanka is at the cross-roads on many fronts. The Routledge Handbook of Contemporary Sri Lanka comes at as a boon to researchers on these different fronts by identifying issues involved in the many problems that confront Sri Lanka. The problems of Sri Lanka reflect the conditions in many developing countries. It is befuddled with economic crises resulting from inability to service sovereign debts, unresolved ethnic crises fomented by chauvinist leaders, heavy corruption that depletes the national treasury, a political shift towards authoritarianism, environmental depletion, drug problems, pervasive criminal violence and other situations of social disruption. These different areas are covered by leading experts. This superbly written research handbook serves as a tool to study not only Sri Lanka but to compare its problems with other developing states with similar problems. It serves as an introduction to scholars new to the field and as a book that provides fresh insights into different aspects of social and economic life in the island to the established researchers. It will remain the best guide to research on aspects of socio-economic issues in Sri Lanka."

Muthucumaraswamy Sornarajah, *Emeritus Professor of Law, National University of Singapore*

"This excellent and important volume brings together a broad range of contemporary scholars in a hard-hitting, multi-disciplinary analysis of Sri Lanka's current political and economic malaise. Thirty-five original chapters carefully and critically delineate the multiple factors which converged in the 2022 anti-government "struggle" (aragalaya) and its subsequent repression, and cautiously point the way forward to greater political, economic, social and environmental justice in Sri Lanka. This unique collection will be valuable to everyone who wants to understand Sri Lanka's contemporary situation, and indispensable both to scholars who study it and to policy-makers who attempt to redress it."

Jonathan S. Walters, *Professor of Religion and George Hudson Ball Endowed Chair of Humanities, Whitman College, USA*

"This is a valuable reference book on a country that defies easy readings. Sri Lanka is today in flux navigating political turmoil, environmental degradation, ethnic tensions, and economic hardships due to an unprecedented collapse of the economy. This volume of 35 essays and reflections captures this moment in all its unevenness, shedding light on the ambiguities that lace Sri Lankan society. The book moves from chapters dissecting nationalism, politics, and institutions to more specific topics on the economy and political economy, labour, environmental tensions and social and cultural formations. The contributions are sharp, well researched, theoretically informed and seamlessly connected. While different approaches and positions are represented, they share a commitment to an equitable, just, and ecologically sensitive country to be forged in the future. This is an inspiring volume and a reliable source for anyone interested in Sri Lanka today."

Nira Wickramasinghe, *Chair and Professor of Modern South Asian Studies, Leiden University, The Netherlands*

ROUTLEDGE HANDBOOK OF CONTEMPORARY SRI LANKA

The Routledge Handbook of Contemporary Sri Lanka offers a comprehensive survey of issues facing the island country and an overview delineating some key moments in the country's contemporary polity, economy, and sociality.

This book outlines aspects and influences foundational to understanding a country defined by its economic and political turmoil, and rift with public distrust in today's shifting geopolitics. Chapters by various established scholars highlight this book's pivotal contribution in situating Sri Lanka's turmoil and deprivation in this current conjuncture.

The handbook is structured in seven parts:

- Nations and Nationalism
- Politics, State, and Institutions
- Economy and Political Economy
- Work and Life
- Environment and Environmental Politics
- Society, Social Systems, and Culture
- Moment of Flux, Looking Ahead

Each part includes on average six chapters covering the social sciences and humanities to survey emerging and cutting-edge areas of the study of Sri Lanka. Multi-disciplinary in focus, the book also includes an introductory section and concluding section, which creates the space and platform for senior, mid-ranking, and junior academics to engage in dynamic conversation with each other about contemporary Sri Lanka. Including scholarship from Sri Lankan experts, the handbook creates academic output, which chimes with broader calls in academia on decolonising the academic landscape.

An important reference work, this handbook will be of interest to scholars and students from wide-ranging academic disciplines and a focus on Sri Lanka, Asian and South Asian studies, sociology, environmental politics, development, labour, management, political economy, and anthropology.

Kanchana N. Ruwanpura is a Professor of Development Geography, the University of Gothenburg, Sweden, and an Honorary Fellow at CSAS, at the University of Edinburgh, Scotland.

Amjad Mohamed Saleem currently works at the International Federation of Red Cross and Red Crescent Societies in Geneva, Switzerland.

ROUTLEDGE HANDBOOK OF CONTEMPORARY SRI LANKA

Edited by Kanchana N. Ruwanpura and Amjad Mohamed Saleem

LONDON AND NEW YORK

Cover image: Gihan Mackay

First published 2025
by Routledge
4 Park Square, Milton Park, Abingdon, Oxon OX14 4RN

and by Routledge
605 Third Avenue, New York, NY 10158

Routledge is an imprint of the Taylor & Francis Group, an informa business

© 2025 selection and editorial matter, Kanchana N. Ruwanpura and Amjad Mohamed Saleem; individual chapters, the contributors

The right of Kanchana N. Ruwanpura and Amjad Mohamed Saleem to be identified as the author[/s] of the editorial material, and of the authors for their individual chapters, has been asserted in accordance with sections 77 and 78 of the Copyright, Designs and Patents Act 1988.

The Open Access version of this book, available at www.taylorfrancis.com, has been made available under a Creative Commons Attribution-Non Commercial-No Derivatives (CC-BY-NC-ND) 4.0 license.

Any third party material in this book is not included in the OA Creative Commons license, unless indicated otherwise in a credit line to the material. Please direct any permissions enquiries to the original rightsholder.

Funded by University of Gothenburg, Sweden/ Donation Funds at the University of Gothenburg for teachers' research and travel for scientific purposes 2024 (GU 2023/3001).

Trademark notice: Product or corporate names may be trademarks or registered trademarks, and are used only for identification and explanation without intent to infringe.

British Library Cataloguing-in-Publication Data
A catalogue record for this book is available from the British Library

Library of Congress Cataloging-in-Publication Data
Names: Ruwanpura, Kanchana N., editor. | Mohamed-Saleem, Amjad, editor.
Title: Routledge handbook of contemporary Sri Lanka / edited by Kanchana N. Ruwanpura, Amjad Mohamed Saleem.
Description: London ; New York : Routledge, 2024. | Includes bibliographical references and index.
Identifiers: LCCN 2023059355 (print) | LCCN 2023059356 (ebook) | ISBN 9781032293080 (hbk) | ISBN 9781032293097 (pbk) | ISBN 9781003300991 (ebk)
Subjects: LCSH: Sri Lanka--Politics and government--21st century. | Sri Lanka--Economic conditions--21st century. | Sri Lanka--Social conditions--21st century.
Classification: LCC DS489.84 .R68 2024 (print) | LCC DS489.84 (ebook) | DDC 954.9303/2--dc23/eng/20240227
LC record available at https://lccn.loc.gov/2023059355
LC ebook record available at https://lccn.loc.gov/2023059356

ISBN: 978-1-032-29308-0 (hbk)
ISBN: 978-1-032-29309-7 (pbk)
ISBN: 978-1-003-30099-1 (ebk)

DOI: 10.4324/9781003300991

Typeset in Times New Roman
by KnowledgeWorks Global Ltd.

Kanchana N. Ruwanpura gratefully acknowledges the generous grant given to her by Handelshögskolan, University of Gothenburg, Sweden, to make Open Access publishing of this volume possible. Grant details are as below: *Grant from the Donation Funds at the University of Gothenburg for teachers' research and travel for scientific purposes 2024 (GU 2023/3001)/ Bidrag ur donationsfonderna vid Göteborgs universitet för lärares forskning och resor i vetenskapligt syfte 2024.*

DEDICATION, IN THREE PARTS

I

Dedicated to the intellectual giants of Sri Lanka who continue to inspire us and to those who left us before their time in 2021 and on whose shoulders we stand:

Malathi de Alwis (Anthropology)
Qadri Ismail (English)
Pasad Kulatunga (Physics and Environmental Studies)

And to the doyen of feminist and critical thought:
Kumari Jayawardena as she enters her 90s.

Their imprint remains with us and their hopes for alternative and egalitarian futures to abide by Sri Lanka motivates this work in multiple ways.

II

Dedicated to those social activists who refuse to remain silent in the face of oppression and injustice despite the personal social costs that their activism brings. Many have passed away, especially since 2022 and who remain nameless but whose voices cannot be silenced.

III

Dedicated to the ordinary Sri Lankan, who is nameless and powerless, and has borne the brunt of the political, religious, ethnic, environmental, and economic challenges facing the country. Families, people, and communities forced to cremate when it went against their faith, were forced to sacrifice essential needs to make ends meet, and the victims and survivors of all the violence and repression that goes through in the country.

CONTENTS

List of Illustrations — *xiii*
List of Contributors — *xv*
Acknowledgements — *xx*

PART I
Introduction — **1**

If I was President — 3
Sarah Kabir

Slivers of Sri Lanka: Sways, Stability, and System Change? — 7
Kanchana N. Ruwanpura and Amjad Mohamed Saleem

PART II
Nations and Nationalism — **31**

1. Island Imaginaries: Insularity, Repetition, and the Spatial Politics of the National — 33
Tariq Jazeel

2. Authoritarian Politics and Gender in Sri Lanka: A Survey — 43
Rajni Gamage

3. Nationalism, Conflict, and Power-Sharing — 55
Bart Klem

4   Centring Conflict: Contemporary Sri Lanka in Perspective   68
    Shamara Wettimuny

PART III
Politics, State, and Institutions   81

5   Defining Sri Lanka's Identity: Reflections on Key Constitutional
    and the Legal Moments   83
    Bhavani Fonseka and Luwie Niranjan Ganeshathasan

6   Imagining the Nation: A Critical Overview of Sinhala
    Nationalism and Its Cultural Coordinates   94
    Harshana Rambukwella

7   Eastern Muslims of Sri Lanka: Developing an Identity
    Consciousness   106
    Aboobacker Rameez and Mohamed Anifa Mohamed Fowsar

8   Transitional Justice: State of Play in Sri Lanka   118
    Farah Mihlar

9   Contemporary Gender Activism: Engaging the Law and the State   130
    Kaushalya Ariyarathne and Kiran Grewal

PART IV
Economy and Political Economy   145

10 Sri Lanka's Foreign Debt Crisis: Deep Roots?   147
    Umesh Moramudali

11 The Sri Lankan Economy: Hope, Despair, and Prospects   162
    Prema-chandra Athukorala

12 Gender Equality in Sri Lanka's Economy: Persistent Challenges   176
    Dileni Gunewardena

13 Unveiling the Margins: Women, Caste, Class, and Post-War
    Development in Sri Lanka's North and East   194
    Narayani Sritharan

14 Higher Education in Contemporary Sri Lanka: Key Topics   207
    Kaushalya Perera

PART V
Work and Life — 219

15 Informality, Masculinity, and Agglomeration Imaginaries — 221
Nipesh Palat Narayanan

16 The Work and Lives of Agricultural Workers — 231
Cynthia M. Caron

17 The Gendered Political Economy of Work in Post-War Sri Lanka — 242
Jayanthi Thiyaga Lingham

18 Work and Life of Sri Lankan Garment Factory Workers: A Gendered Perspective — 253
Shyamain Wickramasingha

19 Microfinance, Debt and Indebtedness of Rural Sector Workers in Sri Lanka — 264
Nedha de Silva and Amali Wedagedara

PART VI
Environment and Environmental Politics — 275

20 Following Currents: Oceanic and Littoral Sri Lanka — 277
Rapti Siriwardane-de Zoysa

21 A Political Ecology of Sri Lanka's Urban and Regional Wetlands — 288
Missaka Hettiarachchi

22 Sri Lanka's Energy Transition: One Step Forward, Two Steps Back — 300
Gz. MeeNilankco Theiventhran

23 Environmental Protection in Sri Lanka: A Critical Legal Approach — 314
Kalana Senaratane

24 Ecological States: Nature, Militarization, and Nationalism in Sri Lanka — 325
Vivian Y. Choi

25 Sri Lanka's Environmental History — 335
Sujit Sivasundaram

PART VII
Society, Social Systems, and Culture — 347

26 Public Health System of Sri Lanka: Past, Present, and Future — 349
    Shashika Bandara

27 Politicizing 'the Virtual': Examining the Internet on the Intersections of Gender and Sexuality in Sri Lanka — 361
    Senel Wanniarachchi and Zahrah Rizwan

28 Feminist Pathways and Political Possibilities in Sri Lankan Plantation Studies — 372
    Mythri Jegathesan

29 Caste in Contemporary Sri Lanka — 383
    Dominic Esler

30 Dynamics of Low-Income Settlements in Colombo, Sri Lanka — 396
    Mohideen M. Alikhan

PART VIII
Moment of Flux, Looking Ahead — 407

31 COVID-19: Sri Lanka's Moral Test — 409
    Santhushya Fernando

32 People in the Palace — 416
    Dinesha Samararatne

33 After *Aragalaya*: Moving beyond the Status Quo? — 420
    Oliver Walton

34 Consolidating a Dangerous Consensus: The Failure of Sri Lanka's Public Policy Complex in 2019 — 423
    Kusum Wijetilleke

35 The 'Dreary Pillage of Privacy', Talking Economics in Colombo's Tower Blocks — 430
    Michael Collyer

Index — *434*

LIST OF ILLUSTRATIONS

Graphs

10.1	Debt to GDP ratio in Sri Lanka (Source: Author constructed based on CBSL data)	148
10.2	Concessionary vs non-Concessionary loans in Sri Lanka (Source: Author constructed based on data from the CBSL and ERD 2022)	149
10.3	Exports and external debt ratio (Source: Author compiled based on CBSL data)	151
10.4	Outstanding debt at the end of 2021 (Source: Author developed based on the data from ERD – Data includes State-Owned Enterprise (SOE) loans obtained through the Treasury)	153

Figures

1.1	Ptolemy's 12th Asian Map (*Tabula XII Asiae*) depicting 'Taprobane', from Michel Servet's *Ptolemy's Geography (Cosmographia)*, 1535 (Source: Wikipedia, public domain: https://commons.wikimedia.org/wiki/File:Ptolemy%27s_Taprobana.jpg)	38
11.1	Sri Lanka: current account balance and its domestic components, 1959–2021 (% of GDP)	168
11.2	Composition of external debt, 2005–2021 (%)	169
11.3	Sri Lanka: debt servicing, 1990–2021 (%)	170
13.1	War-affected districts	195
13.2	GDP, inflation, and the unemployment rate	196
13.3	Average economic indicators for war and non-war districts, 2009/2010 and 2012/2013	199
21.1	Encroachment of a marsh in the Kolonnawa area by informal settlements: (a) 1980 to (b) 2008 (Source: Survey Department of Sri Lanka)	294
21.2	Transformation of freshwater marshes to shrub wetlands in the Kolonnawa Marsh: (a) marsh habitat and (b) shrub habitat	295

List of Illustrations

22.1	Sri Lanka's primary energy by source (Source: Adapted from Energy Balance [Sustainable Energy Authority 2020])	301
22.2	Percentage loss in transmission and distribution (Source: ADB [2021])	302
22.3	Institutional matrix (Source: Adapted from Theiventhran [2022a])	303
22.4	Electricity generation mix. Data extracted from the CEB's annual reports NCRE – non-conventional renewable energy – sources including solar and wind power	305
22.5	Unit cost per electricity plant as of January 2022. (1) Biomass energy sources include waste-to-energy facilities. Since the CEB does not routinely report on all mini-hydro, wind, and solar power, these figures are not totals. (2) Fixed costs are the cost of equipment and construction of the power plant. Energy costs consist of fuel costs. (3) BMP is a Biomass plant, KPS (GT & GT7), Supplementary, WCP, Sojitz CCP, Sapu A&B, Uthuru Janani, KCCP and Barge are oil-fired power plants (Credit: Vidhura Ralapanawe)	306
22.6	District-wise breakdown of the capacities added as per approved loans (kW) as of 31 December 2021, under the rooftop solar power generation project (Source: Sustainable Energy Authority [2022])	307

Tables

10.1	Foreign debt repayment for different creditors	150
10.2	Maturity, grant element and interest rates of foreign debt – 2020	152
11.1	Key economic indicators, 1960–2021	166
12.1	Key indicators, Sri Lanka and comparator economies	178
12.2	Sri Lanka's relative position in relation to South Asia and emerging Asian economies	182
12.3	Unemployment rates by sex, age, education and province	186
12.4	Percentage distribution of the employed population by employment status and gender	187
12.5	Employed population by occupation and gender	187
13.1	Castes in Jaffna Peninsula, 1982	201
26.1	Sri Lanka's top ten diseases that causes most deaths in 2009 and 2019	352

CONTRIBUTORS

Mohideen M. Alikhan is a Senior Lecturer at the Department of Geography, University of Peradeniya, Sri Lanka. Alikhan has recently completed his PhD at the University of Sussex, UK. His research areas of interest include urban governance, housing, and migration with a special focus on displacement, relocations, and labour.

Kaushalya Ariyarathne, PhD, works at the Centre for the Study of Human Rights, Faculty of Law, University of Colombo. Her research interests are human rights, gender, queer theory, and subaltern studies. Her publications have appeared in the journals *Masculinities*, *Sri Lanka Journal of Humanities* and she is at the forefront of various activist initiatives in the country.

Prema-Chandra Athukorala is a Professor of Economics Emeritus in the Crawford School of Public Policy at the Australian National University, Canberra, Australia. He has published 11 books, 7 edited volumes, and over 200 papers in scholarly journals and multi-author volumes in the areas of international trade and economic development.

Shashika Bandara is a doctoral candidate focusing on global health policy and governance at McGill University. He holds a Masters in global health from Duke University. He has also worked in the humanitarian and human rights sector focusing on Sri Lanka and South Asia. His most recent publications include the editorial titled *"Sri Lanka's Health Crisis" in The BMJ*.

Cynthia M. Caron is an Associate Professor of Sustainability and Social Justice at Clark University in the United States at Clark University in the United States. Her research focuses on gender, land tenure relations, and climate change. She has active research projects in Sri Lanka and Mexico and has extensively published in journals and contributed to edited volumes.

Vivian Y. Choi is an Associate Professor of Anthropology at St. Olaf College and co-editor of the ethnography and photography collective Writing with Light. Her book, *Disaster Nationalism: Tsunami and Civil War in Sri Lanka*, is forthcoming. Her new research focuses on Indian Ocean warming, science, and climate change.

Contributors

Michael Collyer is a Professor of Geography at the University of Sussex, UK. He is a political geographer with an interest in people on the move and state institutions. He was a visiting researcher at the University of Colombo from 2006 to 2009 and has managed a series of research projects in Sri Lanka since then.

Nedha de Silva is a PhD candidate attached to the Global Peace and Security Center of Monash University, Australia and has experience as an educator in both Sri Lanka and Australia. Her research interests lie in women's work and security in the informal sector, violence, care, the digital economy, and religion.

Dominic Esler is an Assistant Professor of Anthropology at the Lahore University of Management Sciences. His research focuses on caste, Catholicism, and northern Sri Lanka, and recently appeared in *Multi-religiosity in Contemporary Sri Lanka: Innovation, Shared Spaces, Contestation* (Routledge, 2021), edited by Mark P. Whitaker, Darini Rajasingham-Senanayake, and Pathmanesan Sanmugeswaran, including in other outlets.

Santhushya Fernando is both a medical doctor and MD, with specialism in Public Health and a Senior Lecturer in Medical Humanities at the Faculty of Medicine, University of Colombo, Sri Lanka. She has co-authored *Montage of Sexuality in Sri Lanka* and *A Primer for Undergraduate Courses in Medical Humanities and Professionalism*, amongst her many other writings.

Bhavani Fonseka is a Senior Researcher and Attorney at Law with the Centre for Policy Alternatives, with a focus on research, national and international advocacy, and public interest litigation. She is the editor of the books *Elusive Justice and Emblematic Cases in Sri Lanka* (2023) and *Transitional Justice in Sri Lanka: Moving Beyond Promises* (2017).

Mohamed Anifa Mohamed Fowsar serves as a Professor in Political Science at the Department of Political Science at South Eastern University of Sri Lanka. As an academic, his primary research interests include Muslim minority politics, local governance, political economy, and peacebuilding. Professor Fowsar has an extensive publication track record.

Luwie Niranjan Ganeshathasan, LLB (Colombo), LLM (Notre Dame), is an Attorney at Law and a legal researcher. Since January 2012, he has been involved in public interest litigation cases on issues of constitutional law, administrative law, and human rights law and has published several articles and book chapters on Sri Lankan constitutional law.

Rajni Gamage is a Postdoctoral Fellow at the Institute of South Asian Studies (ISAS), National University of Singapore (NUS). She holds a PhD in Political Science and International Relations from the University of Queensland, Australia. Her research focuses on the politics of state formation in Sri Lanka, including political parties, elite politics, and development and inequality.

Kiran Grewal is a Professor in Sociology at Goldsmiths, University of London. She is the author of *The Socio-Political Practice of Human Rights* (2016) and *Racialised Gang Rape and the Reinforcement of Dominant Order* (2017). Kiran's current research focuses on subaltern conceptions of human rights and social justice in Sri Lanka. For more information, please visit https://www.decolonial.org.

Contributors

Dileni Gunewardena, PhD, American, is a Professor of Economics, the University of Peradeniya, a Non-Resident Fellow of Verité Research, and a PEP Research Fellow. She has been a Fulbright Research Scholar, a Brookings Institution Echidna Global Scholar, and a PGAE Scholar at American University. Her research is in gender, labour markets, and poverty.

Missaka Hettiarachchi is a Senior Fellow at the World Wildlife Fund (WWF) and an Adjunct Associate Professor at the James Cook University, Australia. He is an engineer by training and holds a PhD in environmental planning. He has published widely on wetlands management and disaster risk reduction.

Tariq Jazeel is a Professor of Human Geography and co-Director of the Sarah Parker Remond Centre for the Study of Racism and Racialisation at University College London, UK. Tariq has published on nationalism, modernity, postcolonialism, and the spatial politics of Sri Lanka.

Mythri Jegathesan is an Associate Professor in Santa Clara University's Department of Anthropology. She studies plantations, labour, gender, and minority politics. Her book, *Tea and Solidarity: Tamil Women and Work in Postwar Sri Lanka* (2019), details plantation life and work dynamics amidst ethnonationalist politics and civil war in Sri Lanka.

Sarah Kabir is a researcher and author who specialises in the areas of peacebuilding and reconciliation. She has an MSc in International Development and Humanitarian Emergencies from the London School of Economics. She has worked within a range of complex cultural contexts and her publication, *Voices of Peace*, gives insight into Sri Lanka's protracted conflict.

Bart Klem is an Associate Professor at the School of Global Studies, Gothenburg University. His research focuses on civil war, post-war transition, and contested sovereignty. His recent book *Performing Sovereign Aspirations* with Cambridge University Press adopts a performative perspective on the frictions and contradictions around the Tamil nationalist movement in Sri Lanka.

Jayanthi Thiyaga Lingham is a Research Associate at the University of Sheffield, UK. Her research interests are in feminist and critical historical approaches to the international political economy of development, violence, and conflict. Her PhD (SOAS 2019) examined women's working lives in the post-war Northern Province of Sri Lanka.

Farah Mihlar is a Sri Lankan/British academic and activist. She is a Senior Lecturer and lectures in human rights at the Centre for Development and Emergency Practice, Oxford Brookes University. Prior to this, she lectured in transitional justice at the University of Exeter. Farah's research is on justice for marginalised groups in post-conflict contexts.

Umesh Moramudali is a Lecturer at the University of Colombo focusing on public finance, Chinese loans, and political economy in Sri Lanka. His research has appeared in numerous media outlets, with engagement in broadcast media. He is a Chevening scholar and holds an MSc in Economics from the University of Warwick.

Nipesh Palat Narayanan is an Assistant Professor at the Centre Urbanisation Culture Société, of the INRS (Institut national de la recherche scientifique), Montreal, Canada. His research explores knowledge hegemonies by investigating everyday infrastructures, informal practices, and culinary cultures. His work is situated within the larger domain of southern theory.

Kaushalya Perera, PhD, is a Senior Lecturer at the Department of English, University of Colombo, Sri Lanka, where she teaches linguistics. Her primary area of research is discourses of higher education, on which she has published in scholarly.

Harshana Rambukwella is a Professor and a comparative literature and cultural studies scholar. His interests are in the intersections between literature, history, aesthetics, and nationalism in South Asia, which has also culminated in the book *The Politics and Poetics of Authenticity*. Harshana is currently Visiting Professor at New York University (NYU) in Abu Dhabi.

Aboobacker Rameez serves as a Professor in Sociology at the Department of Sociology at South Eastern University of Sri Lanka. His primary research interests include identity, ethnicity, and social issues. He has an extensive publication record and currently serves as the Vice Chancellor of South Eastern University of Sri Lanka.

Zahrah Rizwan is a feminist researcher with a multi-disciplinary academic background in gender and women's studies, English, economics, and business. Her research interests include exploring topics of leisure economies – sex work and night clubs; gender-based violence and technology. Zahrah also currently functions as an Advisor to FRIDA The Feminist Fund.

Kanchana N. Ruwanpura is a Professor at the University of Gothenburg, Sweden and an Honorary Fellow at the University of Edinburgh, Scotland. With a PhD from the University of Cambridge, England, she has published extensively on feminist, labour, and ethnic politics; *Garments without Guilt?* with Cambridge University Press is her most recent (2022) book.

Amjad Mohamed Saleem is a peacebuilding practitioner. He currently works at the International Federation of Red Cross and Red Crescent Societies in Geneva, Switzerland. He is ALSO a Research Fellow at the Universiti Malaya, Malaysia. Amjad has an academic interest in peacebuilding and reconciliation in Sri Lanka. This work extends his PhD from Exeter University, UK.

Dinesha Samararatne is a Professor at the Department of Public Law, University of Colombo. Her research interests include constitutional resilience, fourth-branch institutions, and judicial review. She has published extensively and her most recent publications include *Constitutional Resilience Beyond Courts: Views from South Asia* (2023), which she edited with Tarunabh Khaitan and Swati Jhaveri.

Kalana Senaratne is a Senior Lecturer at the Department of Law of the University of Peradeniya, where he teaches Public International Law and Constitutional Law. He is the author of several peer-reviewed journal articles, chapters in edited volumes and has recently published *Internal Self-Determination in International Law: History, Theory, and Practice* (2021).

Rapti Siriwardane-de Zoysa is an environmental anthropologist and an independent researcher. Her works include *Fishing, Mobility and Settlerhood: Coastal Socialities in Postwar Sri Lanka* (Springer, 2018), and co-edited volumes *Coastal Urbanities: Mobilities, Meanings, Manoeuvrings* (Brill, 2022), and *An Anthology of Non-conformism* (DIO Press, 2024).

Contributors

Sujit Sivasundaram is a Professor of World History at the University of Cambridge and a Fellow in History at Gonville and Caius College, Cambridge. His latest book is *Waves across the South: A New History of Revolution and Empire* (2020), which won The British Academy Book Prize. Histories of the Indian and Pacific oceans; race and racism; material cultures; sciences, empires, and environments are his research areas.

Narayani Sritharan is a Postdoctoral Fellow at AidData – a research lab at William & Mary, a Templeton Fellow at Foreign Policy Research Institute, a member of the Steering Group, and a Co-Founder of Diversifying and Decolonising Economics (D-Econ). Her research is on foreign aid by emerging donors and their impact in developing countries.

Gz. MeeNilankco Theiventhran holds a PhD in Human Geography at the University of Oslo. His research mainly concerns equity justice and geopolitical aspects of energy transitions in the Global South. He leads the International Development Studies Master Programme at the University of Oslo.

Oliver Walton is a Senior Lecturer in International Development at the University of Bath specialising in the political economy of war-to-peace transitions, NGO politics, conflict, and peacebuilding, with a geographical focus on Sri Lanka. His recent work has examined the role of borderlands and brokers in post-war transitions in Nepal and Sri Lanka.

Senel Wanniarachchi is a Doctoral Researcher at the London School of Economics and Political Science. His research is interested in how discourse on 'culture' and 'heritage' get co-opted to legitimise anti-imperialist but also nationalist, 'anti-gender', and anti-human rights frameworks. In Sri Lanka, Senel co-founded an activist organisation called *Hashtag Generation*.

Amali Wedagedara is a Senior Researcher at the Bandaranaike Centre for International Studies (BCIS), Colombo, Sri Lanka. She recently completed her PhD at the University of Hawai'i, Manoa. Her research interests are political economy of finance, development, and gender.

Shamara Wettimuny is the Junior Research Fellow in History at The Queen's College, University of Oxford. Her research focuses on ethno-religious violence and identity in Sri Lanka and recently appeared in *Modern Asian Studies*. Shamara was a Visiting Lecturer at the University of Colombo and is the founder of *Itihas*.

Shyamain Wickramasingha is a Research Fellow of the Department of Management at the University of Sussex Business School and a Visiting Fellow at the Copenhagen Business School. She obtained her PhD from the National University of Singapore and works on global apparel production networks and labour regimes in South Asia broadly, and Bangladesh and Sri Lanka specifically.

Kusum Wijetilleke is a freelance media presenter, researcher, and political commentator with a BA in Accounting and Finance from the University of Kent (UK), a Master's in International Relations from the University of Colombo (Sri Lanka), where he is also currently reading for a PhD. He has over 15 years of corporate and banking experience in Sri Lanka, Dubai, and UAE.

ACKNOWLEDGEMENTS

We want to use this opportunity to register our appreciation to several people who made this volume possible. First, Dorothea Schaefter for approaching the lead editor and entrusting her with this task, being open to the inclusion of other editors and working with us patiently, generously, and productively – even as the world, Sri Lanka, and everything about us seem to go astray.

Our next thanks go to all the authors who worked with us to bring this volume to a close. We faced several hiccups and delays, not only of world-making events. We particularly wanted to acknowledge the patience of early starters, who got all their chapters in place by the initial mileposts and then kindly waited for peers to get to their end goal – which extended beyond a few months. Similarly, given Sri Lanka's shifting situation, we appreciate the colleagues, who made possible the last section by coming on board towards the latter part of the project. We also, and mostly, want to acknowledge the authors who did not get their feedback on time and then for their forbearance with us (Amjad and I) to get up to speed with this lapsed work.

We want to thank our families for their patience during these last few years as we dealt with different crises whilst trying to deliver this project. Sincere thanks also go to friends who have been supportive of the editors during this project.

We then want to thank colleagues in India and Sri Lanka. T&F's team in India – Saraswathy Narayan and Mayank Sharma, and a whole host of others (whose names we do not even know) made this product possible through the various stages of copy editing, indexing, proofs, and production. Every layer of the publication process is tedious work and to do so remotely from faraway places is unlikely to be easy; so, we want to thank the team – inclusive of behind-the-scenes personnel – who makes our academic work possible.

In Sri Lanka, Gihan Mackay enthusiastically agreed to do our cover design within a limited budget to capture the spirit of the volume and the vast majority of the country's populace clamouring for system change. Thank you!

Our academic advisory board read multiple rounds of each chapter and offered detailed and careful review comments, especially where this was necessary. We are grateful for their input and diligence through a two-year process and for taking our constant nudging for review reports in an amicable way. Likewise, our thanks to the early endorses of this volume M. Sornarajah, Jonathan Walters, and Nira Wickramasinghe for unhesitatingly adding more work to their busy schedule

Acknowledgements

to read the entire volume towards the end of the process and agreeing to support it when T&F approached them.

Doing an exercise like this across different regions with different contributors in the best of times can be challenging, but we also faced the challenges of COVID (repeatedly for both of us), long COVID, draining work contexts, and bereavements. For the second editor, this meant personal bereavement as he lost his father (who was highly supportive of this project) during this period. We are also acutely aware that incidents in Sri Lanka also posed a personal and professional challenge to everyone who worked through this period. During this time, Amjad and I kept our sanity intact by constantly touching base with each other to manage our mental health by drawing on our humour to cope with the more than occasional diatribes that came our way or when authors went AWOL or simply pulled out at the end. This acknowledgement is also then to everyone for supporting each other in the best spirit of collegiality through months and years of ups and downs.

Finally, Kanchana is grateful to Handelshögskolon, University of Gothenburg, for generously facilitating open-access publication of this book by awarding a grant for this purpose: Tack så myket!

Kanchana and Amjad
Gothenburg, Sweden; and Geneva, Switzerland
March 28th 2024

International Advisory Board

Radhika Coomaraswamy, Former United Nations Special Rapporteur on Violence against Women and International Centre for Ethnic Studies, Colombo, Sri Lanka
Arjun Gunaratne, Professor of Anthropology, Macalster College, Saint Paul, MN, USA
Alan Keenan, The International Crisis Group, London, UK
Kanishka Jayasuriya, Professor of Politics and International Studies, Murdoch University, Perth, Australia
Jeanne Marecek, Professor – Emeritus, Swarthmore College, Swarthmore, USA
Camille Orjuela, Professor, School of Global Studies, University of Gothenburg, Gothenburg, Sweden
Vidyamali Samarasinghe, Professor, School of International Studies, American University, Washington, DC, USA

PART I

Introduction

IF I WAS PRESIDENT

Sarah Kabir

If I was President,
The first thing that I would do
Is to change the status quo.
So, it matters not where you pray, whom you love,
what you wear, or what you own.
A Sri Lanka, where every citizen can dare to dream the dream,
That one day! he or she, might be able to lead.

If I was President,
Your 'Sri Lankannes' will not be reduced to one aspect of your identity.
You can wear a pottu or a headscarf,
As a Sri Lankan you I will treat.
For diverse we are; in language, skin tone, gender, sexuality,
In the clothes we wear, how we pray, the food we eat,
In thought, in faith and beliefs.
And in this diversity comes an unparalleled unity,
Bound, 'if' the promise, to respect each other, we keep.

An apathetic citizen, other leaders might adore,
I will change to an engaged one, that is what I will implore.

One who makes it their aim to prioritise love over hate,
Truth over pseudo-nationalism,
Empathy over Apathy.
Then maybe, just maybe,
There can be a space that is safe and free,
For all Sri Lankan citizen's to be.

If I was President, my country wouldn't need a slogan to uphold the law,
The scales of the justice system – would work without flaw.
And every religion, every practice, and every culture, I will respect,
So long! as it doesn't force or take away from another, at your behest.

See… for me, I think of Sri Lanka as a Pol-Sambol
70% of coconut that fills up the bowl,
And 30% of flavour and colour,
That reminds you of 'home'.

If I was President,
I'd break the cycle where nationalism is used as a tool to divide,
Where it's ingrained in citizens, who then push leaders to inscribe.
Nationalism, will be a thing we ALL own;
A pride we wear and, with it, a past we must know.

The past, under the rug I would not sweep,
But address every injustice that made a mother weep.
Acknowledging these stains is not to bring mother-Lanka shame,
But to say, we are big enough as a nation, and true to our words when we say, 'never again!'

Where you have been discriminated, I will not deny,
As denial aims to encourage another conflict we cannot survive.
What led you to believe a weapon is all you had to wield,
I will rectify and heal, so my country will not bleed.

If I was President, I would respect the dead.
I wouldn't destroy cemeteries where you lay them to rest.
I would allow you to mourn, to light a candle in their name,
So, we remember as a nation, the cost of war that was in vain.

I'd push for an understanding and an acceptance of our past
As that is the only way, a positive peace would last.

If I was President, your freedom of speech I would not infringe,
For there is much I could learn from what rages within.
But I will remind you, that this freedom is not an end in itself,
But a means to protect the rights and lives of all – even those who are not your friends.
Sadly, I know there will always be racists and misogynists,
But a platform to amplify their views I will not facilitate.

And in this space,
Independence Day would be one all Sri Lankan's can celebrate with pride,
Where it matters not what language in which you recite –
The National anthem – would be sung with a sense of belonging,
Where the words ring true to your heart and have meaning.

If I was President

If I was President,
My pride, I would put aside,
And acknowledge my limitations.
That being President doesn't give me a PhD or a Major,
In economics, in law, in health, trade or diplomacy,
So, if I was President… I'd be open to learning!
And those accomplished I will find,
To consult,
With always the country's best interest in sight.

I wouldn't make my decisions based on a second term,
I wouldn't centralise, but my power I would devolve.
My committees would not be just for optics, or friends,
They would represent all
And to make this country better, a hand they would lend.

Of all the controversial things I might have said,
There's one in particular today I feel, surprisingly, scared to address.

A problem, that for centuries has divides us all,
Where 'class' has allowed a few to gain, and the rest left to fall.

This, today, remains unchanged,
As many of us privileged prefer class divisions to remain.
We enjoy our high-flying jobs, and our rich threads,
We enjoy our food cooked, plates cleaned, and our cosy beds.
So, threatened we are, by the thought of another,
Being able to climb up that ladder.

For this, If I was President,
Schools – urban or rural – well trained teachers I will provide.
Education or language, will not be a thing that divides.
The tools you need I will work hard, so you can access,
As equal opportunity is the key ingredient for a nation's success.

The homeless, would not be swept off the street,
But given shelter, a roof – under which to sleep.

I wouldn't press my foot,
Down on your throat,
Suppressing your breath,
Instead, I'd bend the knee.
Because it is you that I serve,
It is you, that allows me to lead.

Sarah Kabir

If I was President,
I would not fight the truth that we live in a globalised world,
Interconnected we are, as covid-19 has shown.
Geographical boundaries? are just lines on a map,
As the butterfly who flaps her wings in Sinharaja – might be felt all the way up on the alps.

If I was President,
The environment I will restore,
And be aware of the seeds we sow,
Nothing stands alone, in today's world that we know,
Not the past, not the present, nor the future we hold.

We are all interconnected by a single thread that weaves through,
And so, there must be unison for Sri Lanka to be more.
For her heart to beat with joy,
For our hearts to swell with pride,
To be proud of our nation! of where we came alive.

Now of course, you must be thinking, 'all of this is easier said than done,'
And the race to become President, is not mine to be won.

But in this space of being a citizen, I refuse apathy!
Even if I can't be President, I will – and I can – still lead,
To build a nation of unity, one that celebrates diversity,
A Sri Lanka where every little girl (or boy) … could not just dream,
but wake up! and say,
I am going to be President one day.

SLIVERS OF SRI LANKA

Sways, Stability, and System Change?

Kanchana N. Ruwanpura and Amjad Mohamed Saleem

If I was President, your freedom of speech I would not infringe,
For there is much I could learn from what rages within.
But I will remind you, that this freedom is not an end in itself,
But a means to protect the rights and lives of all – even those who are not your friends.

....

But in this space of being a citizen, I refuse apathy!

If I was President
(Sarah Kabir)

Introduction

We start our edited volume with a sense of hope through a poem by peace researcher Sarah Kabir that instils courage to face the dark and dismal times that have plagued Sri Lanka in the not-so-distant past and that continues to ask questions for the future. She recited this poem at International Women's Day (IWD) in 2021 amidst a global pandemic and long before the *aragalaya* (අරගලය)/அரகலய (Porattam)/the struggle of 2022 had taken form. In any given period, it is always difficult to write about Sri Lanka amidst its daily challenges. To start to put together an edited volume on Sri Lanka in June 2021, during the global pandemic, would have been seen by some as herculean. Yet we remained hopeful that in those dark days of lockdown, narratives of change and hope needed to be shared. So, in that spirit, we start with a few lines by Kabir because these stanzas capture the hope, fear, and our refusal to be apathetic despite the difficult and dark times that continue in Sri Lanka (see also Daily FT 2023).

Sri Lanka at that moment in time was in a dark place and continues in this vein. Recovering after the Easter Sunday bomb blasts of 2019, the global pandemic, and subsequent lockdowns created untold stresses and strains on the economy, politics, and the people. The change in government to a nationalistic right-wing one in 2020 incited by the 2019 bomb attacks prompted concerns about a return to a highly oppressive and securitized system of governance.[1] The forced cremation debacle during the pandemic justified the fears of minorities that their rights were no longer important.

Thus, the IWD in March 2021, where many feminists on the day were articulating their rage within an increasingly oppressive regime, could be seen perhaps even as giving early voice to the fury and hope, almost always entangled in bitter-sweet ways, which poured over to streets of Sri Lanka (and not just Colombo) by the latter part of 2021 (see also CPA 2023). The Xpress Pearl disaster, one of the worst environmental disasters to hit Sri Lanka in May 2021, further propelled the country to the precipice as citizens increasingly became frustrated at the situation (Withanage 2021). So, the protests started with the farmers in rural Sri Lanka, then spread to island-wide teacher strikes, before spreading to neighbourhoods, such as Kohuwala and Mirihana, on the outskirts of Colombo, before the larger-scale mass protests reached Colombo.

The *aragalaya*, as we know it and which captured the global imagination in April–July 2022, then has a longer precursor than is commonly acknowledged and should not be seen in isolation from other incidents plaguing Sri Lanka (Sathkunanathan 2022a; Thiruvarangan 2022; Skanthakumar 2023; CPA 2023; Senanayake 2023). They are all connected. However, its importance in Sri Lanka's long and convoluted history cannot be understated nor indeed its contribution to the country's proud history of collective protests (Senanayake 2022a, 2022b; Skanthakumar 2023; CPA 2023). So, our journey into exploring Sri Lanka in the current context must consider the incidents leading up to and following the *aragalaya*. We are fortunate to have many of those who were involved in the *aragalaya* in various forms writing for us.

Situating Sri Lanka in this current conjuncture is a fraught exercise, where at best one can do is to highlight slivers of a country in flux whether it is, political turmoil, environmental degradation, ethnic tensions, and cataclysmic economic deprivation. To be writing about Sri Lanka amidst the 2021/2022 history-making moments was and is challenging in manifold ways; capturing the complexities that led to the *aragalaya* and a peaceful overthrow of a corrupt and ruthless political family regime in staggered stages was often perceived to be a singularly improbable task. Yet, against the odds, it took place – and herein lies the hope. The best we can aspire to do in the introduction is to trace the contours of the country by admitting that we are not trying to frame or pin its instabilities on this or that issue but a confluence of interconnecting factors. Some facets and features of these interconnections of Sri Lanka and its intricacies are given greater thought and consideration by the contributors to this volume. Our aspiration in this introductory chapter is necessarily more modest: to offer an outline of Sri Lanka's political, political economy, and socio-cultural conditions.

We start by tracing and delineating some key moments in the country's contemporary polity, economy, and sociality. By doing so, we want to offer readers a sketch of some key aspects and influences foundational for grasping a country in turmoil, where public trust is under constant duress. The turbulence has been decades in the making; given an unresolved ethnic conflict and bloodied war since at least 1983; deepening economic inequalities; schisms within communities; and creeping authoritarianism, enmeshed in a highly inequitable global economic order with shifting geopolitics. All these factors obfuscate simple readings of Sri Lanka's instability and underline the need for system change and structural transformation towards an equitable, just, and ecologically sensitive country to be forged in the future. Fashioning Sri Lanka's future then requires redistributive and political justice to be at its core, as many of the chapters within the volume trace.

Betrayal of Public Trust: The Economy, Nation, and Society Intersect?

The nation has been at the heart of academic attention, civil society activism, and media debate since the 1983 ethnic violence and riots in Sri Lanka. The violence of July 1983 and the following internecine violent conflict and war for a nearly three-decade period (26 years to be precise if 2009 can be marked as an endpoint, which on its own is a moot point) continue to colour and haunt the country 40 years afterwards (see also Jazeel and Ruwanpura 2009; Wickramasinghe 2009). The commemoration of a violent and tragic day for the nation four decades later in 2023 continues to be ironically violently halted by politicians, inclusive of Ranil Wickramasinghe, in denial of their complicity in giving birth and perpetuating the violence, suppression, and oppression, which are hallmarks of Sri Lanka's polity (VOA 2023).

The ethnonationalism that started with the politicization of the Sinhala-Buddhist consciousness in the 1950s has permeated almost every significant minority community relationship (Tamils and Muslims) by now (see Abeysekera 2022; Saleem 2020). The nation is unmade recurrently by no less than a political regime that allegedly wants to uphold the national sovereignty, the nation as a unitary state and yet recurrently recreate the fissures that never allow us to confront our traumatic past, societal sins, or heal (Coomaraswamy 2022). The sinister presence of nationalist forces is so politicized by various political factions that Ambika Satkunanathan (2023) in a significant social media intervention noted how the religious right-wing nationalist forces within the Tamil-Hindu and Sinhala-Buddhist communities were joining hands to intimidate and unleash violence against the Muslim community. However, the layering of violence in the country is complex, as orchestrated violence by Sinhala communities against the Tamils in the East and North has started to resurface with a vengeance in 2023.

Violence is not new to Sri Lanka. The more terrifying prospect is that into an already potent mix that Klem and others have written about regarding influences by right-wing Muslim religious forces in eastern Sri Lanka (Klem 2011; Klem and Maunaguru 2017, 2018), Sathkunanathan (2023) is calling for tracing India's religious right and its presence. A new-fangled influence that the country can well do without. While apathy arises again, especially among the upper-income denizens of Colombo, the *aragalaya* and the spirit it infused – including anger and rage – refuses to go into slumber, despite the attempts at suppression by an unelected (and subsequently illegitimate) head of state, amidst scripts of stability that circulate in the mainstream and that are portrayed for an international audience (see also Daily Financial Times 2023). Indignation is often found among the working classes and informal sector workers, who seethe at their inability to vocalize their frustrations, because of the fear instilled by the current regime through heavy-handed policing tactics against mass protests. Torpor and rage simultaneously and not so strangely cohabit within Sri Lanka's polity. This cohabitation reflects class dynamics within the country as well as the fact that just over half (55.7%) of Sri Lanka's population face multiple vulnerabilities, which the United Nations Development Programme (2023) encapsulates in its multi-dimensional vulnerability index (UNDP 2023).

Contestations over the nation are then also melded with discord over resource distribution and allocation. Inequities in wealth distribution and resource misallocation, aside from entrenched corruption, have persisted in the past four decades but have received less attention in the media and policy circles until the start of 2022. When the severity of the economic crisis came to full view, with the differential impacts on display on television screens and broadsheet newspapers, shying away from the underbelly of Sri Lanka's economy was impossible. The economic underclass that propelled and kept the economy going and the challenges they faced was in full view. In Sri Lanka's case, the walking classes that Arundhati Roy (2020) speaks of were not walking home but sauntering in queues because they took so long, simply to get essentials – from kerosine to milk powder to gas cylinders – to enable daily life. The portal to Sri Lanka's sociality and polity was then also the economic crisis. The nature and shape of the economy and who it works for matters. This iniquitous tempo was glaringly made evident in 2022.

Although, the debt crisis and its impacts cut across almost all class, ethnic, and political groups, its most acute effects were felt by the working and the low-income across all ethnic groups. Nonetheless, many commentators underlined that economic crises and embargos were not new to communities living in war zone areas, where shortages of essentials and long power cuts, for instance, were the daily grind (Ruwanpura 2006; Kadirgamar 2009; Satkunanathan 2022a, 2022b). These were the ethnic minorities as well as the poor. Not all sections within Tamil and Muslim communities are the economic underclass even as the working classes also come from the majority community – and casteism, for instance, entrenches differentiation within minorities (Paramsothy 2019; Thiruvarangan 2019). The intersecting and overlapping class, ethnicity, and gender (to name a few social registers) identities in Sri Lanka are then as multifaceted and complex as in other parts of the world. It renders homogenized ethnic identities and ethno-nationalist politics tropes, unable to speak to the intricacies of the nation and its people, and the gendered and language politics therein (Ismail and Jeganathan 1995; Thiruvarangan 1995, 2019; De Mel 1996; de Alwis 1997; Abeysekera 2002; Thiranagama 2018; Jegathesan 2019; Gunaratne 2001; Silva 2001; Wanniarachchi 2023). Yet the continued focus on homogenized identity politics has made conversations on redistributive politics and economic inequality as inscribed across all ethnic groups, almost impossible until 2022 (see CPA 2023). The economic crisis then garnered focus – among the people themselves – that economic disenfranchisement and impoverishment along with political prejudice were a common lot for most of the Sri Lankans across the ethnic spectrum.

The identification of economic deprivation and political injustice as a shared struggle had its celebratory and symbolic moments during the *aragalaya*. Most significant of these were: the coming together of religious figures from all faiths in the country to protect protestors from state violence at the start; the standing together of clergy from various beliefs and *aragalaya* activists during a gathering to remember the Tamil civilians killed at the end of 2009; religious figures feeding *aragalaya* advocates across ethnic and spiritual divides, as made emblematic through symbolic and religious garbs; and *aragalaya* demonstrators across ethnic divides singing the national anthem in both languages and/or simply associating and expressing camaraderie; the first pride parade in Sri Lanka (see also de Silva, Dhammalage and Nilafdeen 2022; Krishnamoorthy 2022; Pathirana 2022; Srinivasan 2022; CPA 2023; Skanthakumar 2023). These occurrences and episodes were symbolically significant for a country ensnared in three decades of war and conflict, where ethno-nationalist politics was used, deployed, and mobilized by callous and corrupt politicians to keep economically disenfranchised communities apart.

The *aragalaya*, punctured the recurrent othering, which by 2023, as de Silva et al (2022) notes, is always contextually refracted (see also Soysa 2022; Srinivasan 2022; Daily FT 2023). More specifically, through their research, they observe which "… religious group (is) perceived as the 'other' varies by region … (as) the 'other' is also heavily reliant on locally constructed narratives, which are shaped by business or political relationships, as well as shared historical and cultural associations" (2022: unpaginated). Being attentive to such splinters, as Mishra (2014) quoting Clifford Geertz, notes is important because grasping the general, differences, variations, and particulars also offers a threshold to acknowledging a society in flux. In the case of Sri Lanka, the age of fury emerged with the optimism and imagination of a pluralist society, which nonetheless was not without its contradictions and antagonisms (Skanthakumar 2023). However, as Thiruvarangan (2019) states "counter-hegemonic imaginations of pluralism, coexistence and cultural resistance to violence, dispossession and exclusions perpetuated by nationalist, racist and neoliberal forces" are to be fêted for underlining the quest for justice (2019: unpaginated). The *aragalaya* did not sidestep questions of justice, even as ambiguities and animosities also coincided and punctured radical transformations of the plurality of polity, sociality, and political economy.

In underlining this tension, Skanthakumar (2023) primarily connects the antagonisms focused on the financial, economic crisis, debt, and socio-economic registers. Others have instead underlined an inability to acknowledge the long-standing grievance or struggles of Tamil communities calling for political justice or families (mothers and fathers) simply trying to locate abducted children over decades. Mothers' struggle that started in the 1980s continues decades later with different waves of state violence (de Alwis 1997; Soysa 2022; Satkunanathan 2022a). Likewise, the impossibility of gathering in collectives or mobilizing en masse to remember the dead and missing due to intensive surveillance in the north was seen as a reflection of the failure of southern protestors to acknowledge the scale and temporality of the struggles of the Tamil community (Satkunanathan 2022b). However, as Thiruvarangan (2022) underlines, ethnicity alone is an insufficient category to encapsulate dispossession and inequalities within minority communities. He underlines how caste, class, and gender refract ethnic groups and neglecting these social vectors in his estimation is a flaw with "serious social and economic ramifications for people...and their struggles for land, housing, livelihood and dignity" (2022: unpaginated; see also Maunaguru 2020; Paramsothy 2019).

The fractures and fault lines in the Sri Lankan polity then do persist, but not without filaments of optimism and hope, as a study CPA (2023) captures. They have done the only known systematic study of *aragalaya*, including interviewing 1,000 people across the country and across ethnic and religious groups in the immediate aftermath of the March–July 2022 period.[2] In its brief analysis, it underlines how contrary to the perception that the *aragalaya* was a space dominated by the majority community – it shows that even within the Galle Face area, one space among many, there was a healthy presence of all ethnic communities with almost one-third of all households joining the mobilization in various ways. Ethnic breakdown of protest participants varied from about a quarter of people consisting of Sinhala and Up-Country Tamils, one-fifth of Muslims and 16% coming from the Tamil community. And within this grouping, the Tamils that participated were predominantly older than 30 years while for the other ethnic groups, youth were the key participants. Nonetheless, as CPA (2023) notes, this "inter-ethnic solidarity (however, fleeting) is an extremely commendable achievement for the Sri Lankan democracy" (2023: 13). Likewise, the study rightly notes how the *aragalaya* "highlights struggles that were considered peripheral to the majoritarian core" (CPA 2023: 1). The organic, impromptu, and sometimes even chaotic nature of *aragalaya*, however, was pivotal for waking a civic consciousness in Sri Lankans on a large scale and the active citizenship it inculcated through these momentous months.

However, a year later, an unelected and illegitimate head of state (Ranil Wickramasinghe) has repeatedly resorted to state violence from the moment of his inauguration (Soysa 2022). He started by first brutally dismantling the protest site at the Galle Face Green. Subsequently, state violence was used to suppress any protests and rallies, as was the frequency of abductions, false labelling, and reprisals. This included fiercely frustrating the commemoration of the 40-year anniversary of Black July 1983 when communities across the ethnic divide came together. A President of a nation striving to heal and break out of four decades of repeated cycles of violence, Wickramasinghe is proving to be incapable of representing.

Nonetheless, the proposed Domestic Debt Optimization (DDO)/Domestic Debt Restructuring (DDR), and its pernicious targeting of the workers' pension fund, a meagre social security protection for the working poor, stirred labour rights activists and unions to come to the streets (Ghosh and Ruwanpura 2023).[3] While these protests were more scattered because of the fear of reprisals, intimidation, and fearmongering, the spirit of *aragalaya* – and the quest for system change – still percolates in the country, even if may seem diluted. It is both sombre and salutary that on August 29, 2023, a civil society collective had to call for ending state repression to push back on the President and remind him of the right to peaceful protest (Colombo Gazette 2023).

Sri Lanka's economy, polity, society, and nation at this conjuncture are then in a particularly entangled disarray because of the persistent betrayal of public trust. Democracy hangs by tattered threads and fascist forces grip their hold on political power, including attempts at stirring organized ethnic violence in various parts of the country becoming frequent. The country is at a crossroads and the global financial architecture that hinges on at least twofold global processes also has a bearing on the resolution of Sri Lanka's debt crisis. On the one hand, complex geopolitics between the USA, Europe, Japan, and China are being played out in the debt restructuring process. On the other hand, and less acknowledged, is also how multilateral institutions are held captive to predatory financial institutions and financier interests so that the economic sovereignty of Sri Lanka, as well as other countries, is being compromised.

The corruption of capitalism in the global economy and its deleterious consequences for indebted countries in the global South and the possibilities of odious debt are gaining increasing recognition (Standing 2017; Roos 2019; Martin 2022; Mattei 2022; Varoufakis 2022). Overlaying the financialising of global capitalism and its injurious bearing on people in the global South is also the corruption that takes place within the country, which malevolently continues and is openly acknowledged (Lindberg and Orjuela 2016; Arudpragasam 2022; Kuruwita 2023). Against this backdrop, calling out for odious debt has come from various quarters, including a debt justice statement issued earlier in 2023 by 182 academics from economics to development studies (Gunawardena 2022; Sornarajah 2022a, 2022b, 2022c; De Alwis 2023; Debt Justice UK 2023). However, this appeal to consider Sri Lanka's indebtedness is not novel. One of its early proponents Wickremasinghe, then holding the role of the premiership, in 2013 writing for the broadsheet *Sunday Times* in Sri Lanka had this to say:

> As a result, any loans raised under Section 2.1(b) of this Act are not valid.... an "unconstitutional act is not a law; it confers no rights; it imposes no duties; it affords no protection; it creates no office; it is in legal contemplation as inoperative as though it had never been passed." When it comes to repayment Parliament is not required to honour such debts.
>
> In fact, the next Parliament will not be legally bound by any obligation to respect the loan agreements with other nations, international organisations, and commercial institutions made under Section 2.1(b) of this Act, as they are not legally binding.
>
> (Wickramasinghe 2013: unpaginated)

Now in power as an unelected and illegitimate President behoved to both a parliament that has lost public trust and has no legitimacy, plus contending geopolitical forces, the President is keener to uphold the interest of external financiers, robber barons and a corrupt political class than the economic sovereignty and interests of people. And so, although he wrote about the betrayal of public trust a decade ago in 2013, from where the above quote is taken, the public perfidy to a nation and its people continues in manifold ways (see also Daily FT 2023). Consequently, both hope and disillusionment intermingle, where volatility, organized violence, and tension sit alongside people committed to promoting just futures.

Country and Its Crossroads

How Sri Lanka came to be at this conjuncture is what our volume hopes to capture, although without any bold claims that we have the definitive word. The volume is divided into eight sections, including the introductory section which consists of Kabir's powerful, incisive, and provoking poem.

Our other main sections include Nations and Nationalism, Politics, State, and Institutions, Economy and Political Economy, Work and Life, Environment and Environmental Politics, and Society, Social Systems, and Culture. After which we conclude with shorter reflective pieces that attempt to capture the tentativeness of Sri Lanka to acknowledge the flux that the country is going through – with a section called Moments of Flux, Looking Ahead. We turn to short summaries of these sections to guide the reader before we end with our reflections on what writing in academia increasingly means at this current juncture.

Nations and Nationalism

The concept of the nation and understanding what is meant by nationalism in Sri Lanka has been shaped by a unique set of historical, geographical, and socio-cultural factors. This section explores key themes and issues within this context, highlighting the islandness, spatial politics, and cultural coordinates that have contributed to the complex tapestry of Sri Lankan identity and nationalism.

Jazeel's chapter titled "Island Imaginaries: Insularity, Repetition, and the Spatial Politics of the National" contends that Sri Lanka's islandness constitutes a fundamental element of its national identity. Located in the Indian Ocean, the island's isolation has played a pivotal role in shaping its distinctive cultural and political landscape. It is imperative to delve into the historical context of Sri Lankan statehood, which has been profoundly influenced by the notion of island spatiality. Consequently, the nation's history is characterized by recurrent episodes of ethnic and religious tensions, frequently stemming from disputes over power sharing, social mobility, territory, and resource allocation. By juxtaposing the colonial conceptions and realizations of the island-colony, the contested trajectories of post-independence statehood, and the experiences of the Sri Lankan diaspora, this chapter posits that the post-colonial geography of the Sri Lankan Island nation has consistently remained subject to contingency, cultural factors, and fragility.

The spatial dimensions of the nation, encompassing issues, such as land ownership and resource management, have occupied and continue to occupy a central position within the discourse of nationalism. Concerns about authoritarian politics have also arisen in Sri Lanka, marked by instances of power consolidation, the erosion of democratic institutions, and constraints on freedom of expression and assembly. In her chapter titled "Authoritarian Politics and Gender in Sri Lanka: A Survey," Gamage investigates the enduring colonial legacies that facilitate authoritarian politics while undermining more inclusive models of power distribution and democratic governance. This analysis extends to examining the intersection of gender with authoritarianism. The utilization of emergency powers and the suppression of dissenting voices have triggered apprehensions regarding the state of democracy in Sri Lanka, with particular attention to its gender-specific consequences. While civil society organizations, activists, and international stakeholders have called for heightened respect for human rights and democratic values, underscoring the imperative of upholding the rule of law and safeguarding fundamental liberties, the author contends that the current dynamics run the risk of perpetuating Sinhala Buddhist nationalism and endorsing authoritarian styles of political leadership in tandem with the prevailing pattern of unequal development.

In the chapter titled "Nationalism, Conflict, and Power Sharing," Klem examines scholarly work related to Sinhala (-Buddhist) nationalism, Tamil nationalism (including separatism), and the politics of Muslim ethnic identity. These various forms of identity politics continue to maintain distinct and intricate relationships with the State. Throughout history, these differing aspirations of various ethnic and religious communities have frequently ignited violent conflicts. However, in the post-war era, the challenge lies in fostering reconciliation through power-sharing mechanisms and the decentralization of political authority. Despite the imperative of addressing Sri Lanka's 'national problem,' achieving a sustainable solution remains a formidable task. The path forward is marred by political discord, deep-seated mistrust, and historical grievances, all of which impede progress towards resolution.

The section concludes with Wettimuny's chapter titled "Centring Conflict: Contemporary Sri Lanka in Perspective," which delves into the extensive history of conflict in Sri Lanka, with a primary focus on the last century. Although contemporary Sri Lanka is notably marked by the enduring ethnic conflict between the majority Sinhala Buddhists and the Tamil minority, which culminated in 2009, the origins of this conflict can be traced back to historical grievances and the clash of competing nationalist ideologies. These factors have often resulted in violent confrontations and violations of human rights. Utilizing the perspectives of identity, ideology, and victim narratives, the chapter emphasizes significant historical events and underscores the importance of gaining a deeper understanding of these conflict histories. Such insight is deemed vital for preventing the recurrence of similar conflicts in the future.

Sri Lanka's history of nations and nationalism is deeply rooted in its islandness, the historical context, spatial politics, ethnic conflicts, and cultural dimensions. The contemporary challenge lies in finding a path towards reconciliation and power-sharing among its diverse communities. Understanding the complex interplay of these factors is essential to comprehending the dynamics of nations and nationalism – and to ascertain how these plays out in Sri Lanka, our next section turns to Politics, State, and Institutions.

Politics, State, and Institutions

Politics, state, and institutions in Sri Lanka have been the subject of intense scrutiny and debate, particularly in relation to the country's constitution and law. In the chapter titled "Defining Sri Lanka's Identity: Reflections on Key Constitutional and Legal Moments," Fonseka and Ganeshathasan delve into the series of constitutional and legislative reforms that carry significant implications for the structure of the state, fundamental rights, and the rule of law in post-independence Sri Lanka. The Sri Lankan constitution, which was ratified in 1978, introduced a presidential system of government, endowing the president with substantial executive powers. However, this period also witnessed the enactment of 21 amendments, raising concerns about the balance of power within the system and sparking contentious debates among various political factions. Additionally, the chapter addresses the impact of laws and their implementation, which have contributed to an executive-heavy governance model, thereby affecting democracy and reconciliation efforts in Sri Lanka. These moments in the nation's history are significantly shaped by identity politics and a legacy of activism, but questions also linger regarding the processes involved and their long-term ramifications. Fonseka and Ganeshathasan also further explore recent developments in Sri Lanka's constitutional and legal landscape within the context of the post-war and pandemic environment, shedding light on critical issues that warrant consideration – perhaps even underlining Ayesha Wijayalath's (2022) remarks that Sri Lanka is at a constituent moment.

In Rambukwella's chapter titled "Imagining the Nation: A Critical Examination of Sinhala Nationalism and Its Cultural Coordinates," he focuses on how Sinhala nationalism has exerted a significant influence on shaping Sri Lanka's political landscape. This influence is closely intertwined with the perception of the island as the ancestral homeland of the Sinhala people. He further explores the pivotal role played by cultural coordinates, such as language, religion, and historical narratives, in reinforcing this brand of nationalism throughout the 20th century. However, this approach has frequently marginalized other ethnic and religious communities, thus contributing to heightened tensions and conflicts. Moreover, in the chapter, he underscores the enduring significance of 'culture' as a key arena for the perpetuation of nationalist ideals. Nevertheless, it advises against the assumption that culture and the nation are self-evident categories, advocating instead for an approach that regards both culture and nation as categories of practice, rather than as inherent ontological truths.

The Muslims residing in Sri Lanka constitute a unique ethnic and religious minority, characterized by a considerable degree of diversity within their community. Notably, the Eastern Province is home to a substantial Muslim population, distinguished by its distinct cultural customs, religious traditions, and linguistic variety. In the chapter titled "Eastern Muslims of Sri Lanka: Shaping Identity Consciousness," authored by Rameez and Fowsar, a comprehensive examination is conducted into the multifaceted process of identity formation among the Muslim community in the eastern region of the country. This exploration presents a distinct facet of Sri Lanka's multicultural identity. These Muslims' experiences have been significantly influenced by their interactions with both the Sinhala and Tamil communities. However, their distinctiveness also arises from their unique experiences during the conflict and their close association with the Tamil community, setting them apart from the Muslim community in other regions of the country, where interactions with the Sinhala community are more prevalent. Over time, they have cultivated a distinct sense of identity, navigating the intricate web of ethnic and religious affiliations that characterize Sri Lanka. The intersectionality of being both Muslim and Eastern has thus played a pivotal role in shaping the community's identity and social dynamics. The complexities associated with how Eastern Muslims negotiate their identity, interact with other communities, and confront the challenges of coexisting in a multi-ethnic society are highlighted in this chapter. Their experiences serve as a testament to the intricate and diverse nature of the nation's overarching identity.

The issue of justice, accountability, and redress for victims of human rights violations that have marred Sri Lanka's post-independence history remains a source of deep-seated contention. In the wake of the conclusion of the civil war in 2009, the demands for accountability and justice concerning wartime atrocities have grown increasingly vocal. The Sri Lankan government has, at times, flirted with internationally recommended models for transitional justice mechanisms. However, progress towards achieving substantive transitional justice has been frustratingly sluggish, and the government's approach to addressing past human rights violations has come under fire for its lack of transparency and perceived absence of political will. Mihlar's chapter, titled "Transitional Justice: The Current State in Sri Lanka," delves into the national investigative commissions' efforts to uncover the truth, especially regarding forensic and narrative aspects, although these processes have been structurally flawed and subject to compromise. Judicial and reparative outcomes have been disappointingly minimal. While the establishment of bodies like the Office of Missing Persons and the Office for Reparations can be seen as initial steps, substantial challenges still loom on the path to achieving reconciliation and accountability. The chapter argues that several factors underscore the frailty of the transitional justice processes. Drawing on the recent 2022 protest movement, it concludes that peace and democracy in Sri Lanka hinge on accountability and structural reforms.

Gender, sexuality, and legal matters in Sri Lanka have emerged as areas of ongoing concern. While the country has made strides in advancing women's rights and fostering gender equality, substantial challenges persist. Challenges, such as gender-based violence, discrimination, transgender rights, and unequal access to economic opportunities, continue to confront society. As articulated by Ariyarathne and Grewal in their chapter titled "Contemporary Gender Activism: Engaging the Law and the State," significant progress has been achieved in broadening the comprehension of concepts such as intersectionality, human rights, feminism, and the very nature of politics itself.

However, endeavours aimed at reforming laws and promoting policies that are sensitive to gender-related issues still encounter resistance. This underscores the imperative for persistent advocacy and continuous legal reforms to effectively address these concerns. The chapter posits that gender and transgender activists must adopt an approach that scrutinizes the role of law and the State in facilitating social change. This approach should encompass explorations of emotions, aesthetics, and imaginaries while simultaneously confronting issues of power, hierarchy, and subalternity.

The pleas by Ariyarathne and Grewal for a multifaceted approach as crucial for addressing the complex challenges associated with gender and law in Sri Lanka also bring into the fold questions around redistributive economic justice. These concerns connect well to the section on the Economy and Political Economy, which provides broad brush strokes of the state of the economy, including accounting for gendered and ethnic bearings.

Economy and Political Economy

The spatial politics within Sri Lanka, with its gendered, ethnic, and class dynamics occur within a particular political economy context. The country's political economy for the past four and half decades has been oriented towards giving precedence to market exigencies and forces, adapting to neoliberal policies as elsewhere globally. This market fundamentalism, however, has not panned out as in economic textbooks, as the model version appearing in books that promote neoclassical economics had no historical precedence to start with (Chang 2014).

Economics itself is a vast and rich paradigm, with schools of thought that reflect the entire political ideological spectrum; from the right (Hayek, von Mises) to the left (Marx, Sraffa, Miliband, Lenin, Gramsci) and everything in between (Smith, Schumpeter, Robinson, Keynes, Veblen, Polanyi, and Galbraith). While mostly (dead) white men and their ideas circulate and continue to dominate and shape economic policies and ideas well into the 21st century, feminist, black, and post-colonial economists have been puncturing the colonial rootedness of economic thought (Matthaei 1996; Charusheela 2004; Banks 2008; Danby 2017; Hossein 2019).

Many traditions are inscribed and rooted in political economy, which at its most basic level is the notion that economic decisions and policies are also fundamentally political choices, with resource-distributive consequences that matter to people's lives. They were not meant to be models for boys (quite literally) to play around with by devising different scenarios based on assumptions that may or may not reflect grounded reality (Matthaei 1996; Chang 2014; Waller and Wrenn 2021; Piketty 2022). However, as many heterodox economists have underlined, the rich tradition of political economy has been usurped by a narrow clique of economic thinkers: neoclassical economics. This school of thought is promoted and presented as the prescriptive cornerstone for understanding how the economy should function. Consequently, economic policies promoted by multilateral institutions, such as the IMF (International Monetary Fund), the World Bank and the ADB (Asian Development Bank), come from this narrow economic framework, often resulting in a global economy dominated and shaped by neoliberal policies and increasing financialization of capitalism (Chang 2014; Standing 2016; Harvey 2005; Mazzacutto 2020; Varoufakis 2022). The upshot is that even economists and development economists who were once considered mainstream are rooting for change (Rodrik, Baqir and Diwan 2023; Stiglitz 2023).

It is against this backdrop of a rich tradition of political economic thought, where neoclassical economics dominate, that contributions to this section need to be read. Most economists writing on Sri Lanka do so broadly from a neoliberal perspective, occasionally drawing on institutionalist thought. The political economists' interventions in Sri Lanka often come from a Marxist perspective, although our efforts at drawing them in or keeping them aboard did not bear fruit (more in Writing in Academia below). We want our readers to be attentive to these economic and political economy debates, large and small, that may be missed out in economic readings of Sri Lanka – especially given its current economic crisis.

The first chapter of this section is by Umesh Moramudali. His work seeks to uncover the deeper roots of the debt crisis in the country, given that Sri Lanka defaulted on its sovereign debt for the first time in April 2022. Entitled "Sri Lanka's Foreign Debt Crisis: Deep Roots" Moramudali tries to capture the causes of the sovereign default as well as the potential foreign debt outlook of the country. He attributes how the transition of Sri Lanka to a middle-income country by relying excessively on foreign international finance markets and bilateral borrowers meant that the country did not address its structural weaknesses. This chapter alerts us to how these facets meant borrowing practices of the Sri Lankan government left immense room for corruption and overpricing, factors that persist to this date and even after default. His analysis also gives due consideration to the complex geopolitical tensions that are shaping Sri Lanka's debt restructuring process – and how the country's reliance on international money markets and bilateral loans has compromised the country's economic and political sovereignty.

While Moramudali's analysis draws on strands of institutionalist thought, the contributory chapter titled "The Sri Lankan Economy: Hope, Despair and Prospects" by Prema-chandra Athukorala takes a more orthodox approach to the analysis of the Sri Lankan economy. It offers "an interpretative survey of the economic policy and performance of the Sri Lankan economy," to quote him, going back to the immediate post-independence era. It then underlines in more detail recent policy failures from the time of the CoVID-19 pandemic to claim the need for combining the prescriptive IMF policies to establish stabilization. Structural adjustment is also seen to be key to restoring what Athukorala notes as an anti-tradable bias, given existing incentive structures. As a champion of the IMF, Athukrola negates how the IMF policies have been implanted 16 times in the country contending that it is the failure of multiple Sri Lankan governments and policymakers that have lapsed from following IMF policies. However, he does bring our attention to the need for democratic legitimacy, political stability, and social dialogues for popular engagement – all of which are in short order in the country.

These chapters, as important as they are to understand Sri Lanka's economic crisis, offer only a sliver towards understanding the political economy of the country and indeed the complex manoeuvrings in the global economy, the financialization, and corruption of capitalism globally too. Neither of these chapters then do the heavy lifting of connecting to global debates where once mainstream economists are calling for a drastic change of traction to how development is financed – nor indeed to the dangers and follies of being reliant on financialized capitalism (Standing 2016; Varoufakis 2022; Rodrik et al 2023; Stiglitz 2023). In Sri Lanka, these critiques have come from feminists, unions, left-political activists, and academics, who have brought attention to the social fallout for women and workers, and how returning to the IMF is unlikely to be the silver bullet as before (Ghosh 2021; Feminist Collective for Economic Justice 2023; Ghosh and Ruwanpura 2023; Gunawardena 2023; Gunawardena, Kadirgamar 2023; Nicholas and Nicholas 2023; Pathirana with Unions 2023; Chandrasekhar, Ghosh and Das 2024). We draw attention to another angle to offer the reader multiple interpretations of Sri Lanka's debt crisis and to highlight the globalized nature of the current waves of debt crisis (UNDP 2022). Sri Lanka is not on its own, despite the country's political and economic banes also needing prescriptive medicines.

The chapters that follow the initial interconnected, but not necessarily expansive readings of the debt crisis, tackle other critical aspects of the national economy. Sri Lanka consists of 52% women. This demographic balance is rarely, if ever, reflected in policy-level discourse and most certainly not in the political realm, recurrently occupied by geriatric men and increasingly with no legitimacy. Once considered an egalitarian haven for equitable human development, the Sri Lankan economy continues to face persistent challenges in the realm of gender equality as Dileni Gunewardena outlines in her chapter "Gender Equality in Sri Lanka's Economy: Persistent Challenges." Women workers underpin tea, garments, and migrant work; economic spheres that contribute most to earning foreign exchange for the country. However, women labouring in these sectors does not earn a living wage, which is in addition to the gender-earning pay gaps that persist. Her chapter also then goes on to cover the neglected dimension of unpaid labour of women, which for the first time was conducted in 2017. Using Sri Lanka's first National Time Use Survey, she illustrates how on any given day the average woman spends one hour and 54 minutes on food and meal preparation, and one hour and six minutes on childcare and instruction. In contrast, the men average time used by men for each of the domestic care activities is 12 minutes. Gunawardena goes on to associate the gender gap around time use as a reason for Sri Lanka's historically low FLFP (female labour force participation) rates, where women seek part-time or self-employment to enable the double burden of work. While she associates the double burden of work for poorly compensated jobs for women, this line of thinking neglects the fact that living wages are absent for most working-class men too. There needs to be more research to establish the extent to which living wages for the working classes are inflected by both patriarchal, class, and feudal norms, and as such continuously undervalue those labouring for foundational sectors of the Sri Lankan economy (some are covered in the Work and Life section of this volume).

The marginal status of women – as modulated by caste is the focus of Narayani Sritharan's chapter entitled "Unveiling the Margins: Women, Caste, Class and Post-War Development in Sri Lanka's North and East." Her chapter is pivotal for understanding not just the marginal status of women but also a contested area of Sri Lanka, which has been marginalized due to the ravages of war for over 30 years. In the post-war context, she outlines how the initial economic growth, there were no or limited inclusive opportunities for inclusive and sustained opportunities, where mobility is especially restrictive for women-headed households and lower-ranked caste groups who must confront heavily militarized regions and the surveillance that come with it. In these areas too, household-level indebtedness and low labour force participation compound and feed into exclusion, which propagates and intensifies both social exclusion and division. Sritharan's chapter is important to underscore how the global economic infrastructure that percolates to different parts of the country has differentiated outcomes for communities, often refracted by gender, class, ethnicity, and other social vectors, even within uneven regional development.

The unevenness of development in the higher education sector in the past few decades is covered in the title entitled "Higher Education in Contemporary Sri Lanka: Key Topics" by Kaushalya Perera. In this chapter, Perera argues that policy changes targeting the higher education sector have impacted university students in the areas of employment, governance restructuring and what she broadly terms conflict – that overviews a spectrum as wide as ragging/hazing, sexual harassment to student and faculty protests. This chapter shows how privatization measures in the higher education sector, which extend beyond the prevalence of private universities, created a contested landscape within existing public universities. The resultant changes in the structures and systems of management have tended to compound inequities and stresses within higher education rather than diminish. Partly this is due to the underfunding of education, inclusive of higher education, in Sri Lanka, where it now gets the lowest funding for education in South Asia. Quite a fall for a country that used to be held as a beacon for high social development with concomitant resource allocation, despite slow or low growth (Sen 1981; Humphries 1983). The multiple ways in which this resource misallocation coupled with an economy that poorly rewards work or is attentive to climate change and the environment are the focus of the other two sections in this volume.

Work and Life

The large-scale infrastructure development, which has been the primary post-war development strategy for Sri Lanka, rests upon agglomeration imaginaries that range from the 'ideal' village (for instance *gam udawa* of the 1980s) to the modern metropolis is the focus of Narayan's chapter. Within this broader obsession of Development with a D – i.e. large-scale infrastructure development, he looks at questions around informality and masculinity with a chapter titled "Informality, Masculinity and Agglomeration Imaginaries." Nipesh Palat Narayan's contention is that working life needs to be located within the socio-spatial context within which it unfolds; and the changing nature of informality and the gendered nature of work, he says needs to be framed within masculine agglomeration imaginaries that fail to account for grounded life.

Not accounting for how Sri Lankan people earn a living and the sectors in which they earn their livelihoods is also reflected in the chapter by Cynthia M. Caron, when she writes on "The Work and Lives of Agricultural Workers." She outlines how the World Bank estimated in 2022 that roughly 27% of people in the country worked in the agricultural sector, which is just below one-third of the population. Her chapter goes over not just the structural conditions that shape the lives of agricultural sector workers but also how risks increasingly associated with climate change, agrochemical usage and government policies affect them. We find then that it is not just wages and a fluctuating economy that affect agricultural workers but also policies that keep enforcing workers, including women, into export-oriented value chains that are often more and not less extractive (see also Senevirathna 2018). These exploitative conditions also have some bearing on rural indebtedness that De Silva and Wedagedara cover in their chapter (more below).

While Caron's chapter covers rural agricultural workers more broadly, Jayanthi Thiyaga Lingham's focus for her chapter is on "The Gendered Political Economy of Work in Post-War Sri Lanka." In locating the creation of employment activities in post-war areas of the country and framing it within the rubric of political economy, Lingham is keen to underline how job creation without attentiveness to decades of war and trauma also affects the working life chances of women workers. In this regard, she explores further the triumvirate between the state, military, and capital framed as a necessary analytical handle by Ruwanpura (2018), which otherwise often goes unremarked upon – or analysis is too often limited to the state-military nexus (Kadirgamar 2013; Ruwanpura 2022). Lingham shows how the military surveillance in the region circumscribes women's mobility and that self-employment is a scant survival mechanism. In her analysis, a running and critical theme is to appreciate the gendered experiences of women workers, it is also pivotal to acknowledge the relationship between the productive and social reproductive spheres.

The centrality of social reproduction for understanding the work of women is also examined in some detail in the two chapters that follow around garment sector workers and rural indebtedness. Shyamain Wickramasingha in her chapter titled "Work and Life of Sri Lankan garment factory workers: A Gendered Perspective" surveys the existing scholarship around the embodied experiences of women workers in the garment sector. Her chapter is framed around the interactions between global labour governance regimes and the agency of workers, and the pressure faced by workers across different spheres. These spaces include workers in post-war areas, Tamil migrant workers in the Economic Processing Zones (EPZs) away from their villagers, migrant workers and informalization, and how the pandemic and economic crisis are deepening already challenging work conditions – and threatening to take away their limited labour rights.

It is both the precarity of work conditions that Wickramasingha writes about and the double burden of work that Gunawardena outlines that may be contributory factors for women to seek and remain in self-employment rather than seek formal sector jobs. Seeking entrepreneurial activities, however, comes with another set of financial risks that are rarely acknowledged because livelihood creation is often considered a panacea. Nedha de Silva and Amali Wedagedara complete this section with their chapter entitled "Microfinance, Debt and Indebtedness and Rural Workers in Sri Lanka." Both newspaper reportage and studies done in Sri Lanka show how self-employment via microfinance has furthered poverty, led to dispossession and displacement, and increased violence. Their chapter looks at how microfinance has unfolded in rural communities over decades to underscore how instead of neoliberal tropes of entrepreneurialism and empowerment, the outcomes are entrenched and deepening poverty and inequality. To foreground these connections de Silva and Wedagedara draw on feminist writings on social reproduction that speak to Sri Lanka's current crisis moment in significant ways – given that the debt crisis is a masculine project while calls for debt justice are feminist. In other words, the debt crisis needs to be gendered because of the intimate and intricate connections between debt at the macro scale and indebtedness at the household level (Ruwanpura, Muchchala and Rao 2022).

Issues around exploitation and stresses on Sri Lanka also infiltrate the country's ecological fabric. The next section of the volume offers both the political, social, and historical understandings of the environment and environmental politics in Sri Lanka. In doing so the contributors to this section highlight how in an age of climate change to neglect environmental stresses is also to abandon people and communities who draw upon the socio-ecological world they inhabit. These chapters also reveal the increasing commodification and militarization of the environment result in environmental politics that are enmeshed in the larger political fabric that is both global, national, and local.

Environment and Environmental Politics

This section starts with a contribution by Rapti Siriwardane-De Zoysa that acknowledges the geographical entity of an island by giving prominence to the oceanic and littoral spaces of Sri Lanka. In her chapter titled "Following Currents: Oceanic and Littoral Sri Lanka," she assesses prevalent scholarship that focuses on the land and instead features formative writings on fishing communities and coastal politics. Her contribution brings in both wartime and tsunami-related scholarship to call for conceptually plural analysis that promotes the entanglements between people, species, and places to critically disentangle emergent forms of coastal urbanization that cause upheaval to fishing communities.

The disruption and disorder linked to our ecological world that comes with hyper-urbanity is a running theme in the chapter that follows entitled "A Political Ecology of Sri Lanka's Urban and Regional Wetlands." Missaka Hettiarachchi adopts a political ecology lens to illustrate how wetlands have increasingly come to the fore in socio-environmental conflicts due to penetrative infrastructure development and dense urbanization. While wetlands are evanescent ecosystems, low-income communities have lived adjacent to wetlands, learning to live with the environment and seasonal risks of inundation. The commodification of space without attentiveness to ecological harm is exemplified in the ways in which wetlands are reframed as prime land for urban regeneration. This is a far cry from wetlands, often considered perilous environmental spaces or the backyards of cities, which are now framed as potential spaces for urban real estate. The upshot is not just the dispossession and displacement of low-income communities and inhabitants but also the environmental risks and disasters compounded in the process. In this chapter, he traces the ecological trajectories of urban and regional wetlands and the socio-environmental politics shaped by this commodification process.

The perverse ways in which grappling with climate change in Sri Lanka is further elaborated and examined by Theiventhran in his chapter "Sri Lanka's Energy Transition: Once Step Forward,

Two Steps Back." He points out that for Sri Lanka to be secure in its energy usage, its future must depend on the adoption of renewable energy to redress financial and social challenges, although this requires adapting technologically too. However, the country's dependence on fossil fuels means that dislodging its usage needs to be cognizant of the socio-political and spatial politics, Theiventhran argues that energy justice and security need to be framed through the prism of public values. Rethinking energy security through public values instead of strategic national interests will help potentially re-localize the economy around communities and institutions oriented towards public action that democratizes and hence potentially make the energy transition just.

Justice, however, is increasingly elusive in Sri Lanka – and its gaps are evident in the legal sphere, as Kalana Senaratne traces for us in his chapter "Environmental Protection: A Critical Legal Approach." Senaratne adopts a critical legal lens to argue that reliance on the law brings with it mixed potential, and more laws and regulations in and by themselves may not protect the environment. He, for instance, notes how the existing legal enactments, regulations, and judicial decisions may camouflage attempts at protecting the environment. Even as Sri Lanka has a relatively well-developed legal and institutional framework, the chapter outlines how there is a need to be attentive and critically examine prevailing legal chronicles about environmental protection in the country. One of the concerns that Senaratne raises has to do with how narratives on environmental protection in Sri Lanka construct a mythical past that glorifies ethno-nationalist (Sinhala-Buddhist) tropes that negate tensions prevalent both historically and in contemporary times. He illustrates therefore the need to adopt critical legal reflection to not just protect the environment but to also be cognisant of how the nationalist political terrain is entangled with environmental politics.

Choi continues this theme of environmental entanglement with Sri Lanka's politics in her essay titled "Ecological States: Nature, Militarization and Nationalism in Sri Lanka." In this chapter, she traces the linkages between the militarization of nature and the environment in the country by accentuating three different historical periods. One is around how colonization schemes in the dry zone of the country intersected with both nationalist ideologies and environmental management and while the former is well-traversed ground by numerous scholars Choi offers a new angle by drawing out the linkages to the environment (Tennekoon 1988; Brow 1996; Klem and Kelegama 2020). She then turns her attention to the politics around the post-tsunami period and outlines how managing hazards and risks are constructed as national security threats that closely overlap with militarization that continue to resonate with the politics around post-war colonization in former war-torn areas. In wrapping up the chapter, Choi raises how existential threats of climate change ought to compel policymakers to rethink human and non-human connections to appreciate the island's ecological space differently – and reimagine the social and political.

Whether Sri Lanka will do the needed radical reimagination of its environment is up for debate. However, to motivate thinking in this direction, Sivasundaram ends this section with his chapter – and what he calls a prospectus – entitled "Sri Lanka's Environmental History." This chapter calls for Sri Lankan studies to be much more environmentally attentive by examining not just outsiders but also how indigenous communities narrated the island over the long duree. Sivasundaram draws on the cartographic, textual, and embodied to juxtapose colonial knowledge production against the ecology and intellectual culture of Sri Lanka in a bid to make more space for animal histories. One of his purposes in the chapter is to disrupt the boundary between the human and the non-human – and stretch and expand conventional understandings of the environment in the country. His prospectus is then a plea to turn away from limiting oneself to the plantation complex, deforestation, and nature – as important as these are – to much more pressing environmental emergencies that keep unfolding where we all face existential risks.

Society, Social Systems, and Culture

Sri Lanka's social systems, institutions, and social fabric is the penultimate section of the volume – and the last segment of full chapters. The chapters for this part of the book cover areas as diverse as the public health system in the country, feminist pathways on plantation studies, caste politics, and the digital sphere. It ends with an uplifting chapter on the low-income settlements in urban Sri Lanka and how these spaces are the archetype where pluriverse futures already exist – and how a closer look at these communities offers more than glimmers of hope.

Sri Lanka's public health system has encountered notable difficulties, particularly in the wake of the CoVID-19 pandemic and the recent debt crisis. In Bandara's chapter, titled "Public Health System of Sri Lanka: Past, Present, and Future," he delves into the various challenges and pressures faced by the country's healthcare infrastructure. Presently, the health system grapples with shortages in its workforce and essential medicines, among other pressing issues. Urgent measures are required to rectify these deficiencies in essential medicines and other critical areas. Looking towards the future, the chapter explores the necessity for Sri Lanka to prioritize the strengthening of its health system, focusing on policy and financing aspects. This proactive approach is deemed crucial to ensure the nation's healthcare infrastructure can meet the challenges it faces and provide effective care to its citizens.

Digital media has assumed a pivotal role in shaping the contemporary landscape of Sri Lankan society. The rapid proliferation of smartphones and the expansion of internet connectivity have ushered in a digital revolution, fundamentally transforming how individuals communicate, access information, and engage in public discourse. Nevertheless, it is imperative to acknowledge that digital media has also magnified existing gender dynamics. Women's interactions in online spaces frequently entail experiences of harassment, cyberbullying, and the reinforcement of patriarchal norms. In their chapter titled "Politicizing 'the Virtual': An Exploration of the Internet's Intersection with Gender and Sexuality in Sri Lanka," Wanniarachchi and Rizwan scrutinize how majoritarian politics, patriarchy, and heteronormativity manifest themselves in the digital realm and the implications for women and queer individuals in Sri Lanka. In response to these challenges, there exists a pressing need for innovative approaches to navigate and counteract these exclusionary power structures within these platforms. They underscore the intricate nature of the digital realm, which encompasses both violence, inequality, and injustice, as well as community, solidarity, resistance, joy, and pleasure. Addressing these issues will also necessitate a multifaceted strategy that includes the promotion of digital literacy, the advocacy for safer online environments, and the active challenge to gender stereotypes.

Plantation studies continue to play a pivotal role in illuminating the historical and social dynamics inherent to Sri Lanka's plantation communities, predominantly composed of Tamil-speaking estate labourers of Malaiyaka Tamil heritage who were brought to the country during the colonial period. These communities have grappled with entrenched marginalization and economic hardships. In Jegathesan's chapter, titled "Feminist Pathways and Political Possibilities in Sri Lankan Plantation Studies," a comprehensive examination is conducted of the literature and discussions within the English-medium scholarly discourse concerning Sri Lankan plantations in the post-war context over the past half-century. This review highlights the importance of comprehending and addressing the multifaceted challenges faced by plantation workers, which encompass labour rights, land ownership, and equitable access to education and healthcare. She concludes by advocating for a heightened emphasis on the regional and global linkages that Sri Lanka's plantations maintain with broader interdisciplinary dialogues encompassing the reproduction of gender, politics, labour, and development. This approach is seen as essential to fostering a more comprehensive understanding of the complexities inherent to plantation communities and their place within the larger socio-economic context.

Caste politics remain a significant and enduring factor in Sri Lankan society. Despite the official abolition of the caste system, its influence continues to shape social interactions, especially in rural areas and more prominently since the cessation of the conflict in 2009. In Essler's chapter titled "Caste in Contemporary Sri Lanka" the enduring relevance of caste is demonstrated across various domains, highlighting persistent gaps in the empirical research on caste. Discrimination and inequalities rooted in caste continue to persist, impacting individuals' opportunities and their potential for social advancement. To combat caste-based discrimination and foster social inclusivity, the chapter discusses the theoretical and methodological challenges that future researchers in the field of caste studies in Sri Lanka need to address. Presently, this research is divided into separate investigations focused on either Tamils or Sinhalese. The chapter advocates for the development of an integrated field that can comprehensively address the complexities of caste dynamics in Sri Lanka, transcending ethnic boundaries.

The *watta* culture stands as a distinctive facet of Sri Lankan society, particularly prominent within low-income settlements in Colombo. This culture is characterized by a profound connection with nature, traditional livelihoods, and unique cultural traditions. In Mohideen's chapter titled "Dynamics of Low-Income Settlements in Colombo, Sri Lanka," a comprehensive exploration is undertaken to understand how these settlements represent distinct geographic areas that foster mutually beneficial relationships among various groups in their daily interactions. However, despite the potential benefits of cultural diversity among the people, this way of life faces a multitude of challenges. The settlements' reputation for being problematic areas often obscures their valuable and noteworthy diversity. Additionally, the absence of proper documentation for property ownership places *watta* settlements amid complex socio-economic and environmental predicaments, perpetually haunted by the looming threat of eviction. It is imperative to prioritize efforts aimed at comprehending the *watta* culture, acknowledging its cultural significance, and advocating for sustainable development practices. Recognizing and preserving this unique aspect of Sri Lankan society is essential for fostering cultural diversity and pluralism, as it must be the basis for a redistributive and egalitarian political economy.

In conclusion, society and culture in Sri Lanka are shaped by a range of factors, including digital media and gender politics, plantation studies, caste politics, and the unique *watta* culture. These aspects highlight the complexity and diversity of Sri Lankan society, underscoring the importance of promoting inclusivity, social justice, and respect for cultural heritage in building a cohesive and harmonious nation.

Moments of Flux, Looking Ahead

Sri Lanka's current juncture is recurrently in flux – even as we finalize this volume, debates are raging about the pressures placed on the working poor in the country's debt restructuring programme. Equally, oppressive political pressures continue in the form of the Anti-Terrorism Bill, which in the name of remedying the defects of the country's draconian Prevention of Terrorism Act (PTA), infringes upon the political freedoms and rights of people with the proposed expansion of police powers in the new legislation, with less judicial oversight of intercepting telecommunications; provisions that weaken the legal basis to arrest individuals suspected of or 'possibly' engaged in, any offence under the legislation; limiting the right of access to lawyers for persons charged under the law. If the *aragalaya* offered a symbolic presence in the public imagination of the struggles that Sri Lankans face, the quest for political, economic, and social justice is still ongoing. While geriatric politicians – mostly men – hold onto (illegitimate) power with recurrent crisis cycles that are never grappled with in meaningful ways, kakistocracy, kleptocracy, and ethnocracy hold sway (de Votta 2022; see also Daily FT 2023). Sri Lanka's crisis, however, is of the political economy, where both economic and political failures matter as does the terms on which the country is integrated into the global economy – where finance capital enables and not disables localized corruption of the state, business elites, and the military. The triumvirate in the country shows no ready signs of disintegrating even as the edifice crumbles.

Within this backdrop to capture Sri Lanka's moment of flux, we conclude the volume not with an afterword but with a series of short interventions that aim to capture different moments of Sri Lanka – its uneven politics, its hope, and betrayals. These short writings capture how Sri Lanka failed its moral test during the pandemic at a policy level due to the widening of inequalities, yet at the same time stirred dormant consciousness around the politics of redistribution as Fernando outlines in "CoVID-19: Sri Lanka's Moral Test." The public expressions of this consciousness are captured by Samaratane in her chapter "The People in the Palace," where she profiles the manifestations of civic consciousness among Sri Lankans – and how peaceful and organic protests of the *aragalaya were* also an expression of re-democratization. Not without its lamentable lapses and the inability to connect economic and political injustice, she nonetheless records this unique historical moment in Sri Lanka for what it achieved: to peacefully overthrow a corrupt family regime. The ramifications and the spirit of the *aragalaya* are powerful and continue to stir hope that about 18 months later, the Supreme Court of Sri Lanka, with a majority judgement, held that the Rajapaksa regime had violated public trust (Al Jazeera 2023).

System change, however, is yet to come. Walton and Wijetilleke in their respective chapters summarize slivers of the political and economic topology that make it intangible for consequential transformation to take place. Despite the inspirational kudos generated by the *aragalaya*, the pushback from the political and vested business interest in the country is traced by Walton in his chapter "After Aragalaya: Moving Beyond the Status Quo?" In his appraisal, the very organic and chaotic political energy and imagination that came together engendered a divided response in the aftermath of Gotabhaya Rajapaksa's (the former President) resignation. The misinformation on economic policy options available to people led to divided positions on the post-family regime rule and a lack of an inclusive position on minority communities was a catalyst for the system change that is yet to transpire. Feudal and patriarchal debris in the political and business classes especially – often governed by geriatric men – appear fossilized in the political economy fabric.

This ossification in the public policy terrain over the long durée is captured by Wijetilleke when he sketches how political class and a politicized bureaucracy acted in consort with each other culminating in the debt default of 2022. His intervention especially focuses on the 2019 tax cuts as countering consensus held among international financial institutions. Wijetilleke's writing focuses on the internal contradictions that led to debt default due to external factors – namely the pandemic and seller's inflation (to quote Isabelle Weber). While his position reflects internal inequities, it is also important to bear in mind that imbalances within Sri Lanka are also enabled by a financialized uneven global development terrain, where risks are pushed onto developing countries without undertaking any responsibility – or even without calling out for odious debt when corrupt political regimes roost (Sornarajah 2022a, 2022b).

The implications of these glaring inequities on the ground are captured by Collyer when talking economics of the research process – or indeed academic work – is a fitting conclusion to this section and the volume. In his chapter "The 'dreary pillage of privacy', Talking Economics in Colombo's Tower Blocks" he delineates not just the residents and their informed take on the changing urban geographies of Sri Lanka and inequities therein but also the imbalances of the research process itself especially in terms of economy of research. His brief sketch is a telling reminder of the spirit and energy of *aragalaya* and the analysis that propelled the collective mobilization of people came from within. A collective consciousness borne out of everyday deprivation and struggles.

Conclusions: Writing in Academia

Academia too is a space of struggle and some of these difficulties transpired through the two-year process of putting this volume together. When we excitedly undertook to edit this volume in late 2020/early 2021, Sri Lanka was going through toughening political and economic conditions but not many of us anticipated the acute economic crisis that unfolded nor indeed the emergence of an inspirational *aragalaya*. Conditions in Sri Lanka affected and slowed down the process of writing and finalizing this volume. This is to be expected.

However, there were also other underlying facets of academia that we often gloss over and offer finessing touches in this way or that rarely call out by name the tensions and antagonisms within academic spaces. It results in, often idealistic students (we were once too) that treat academia as some hallowed space because academics reflect their ideological and political positions in this way or that – and engage in healthy debate. Academic spaces are far from the revered space they may have once been if it was ever that (Collini 2012; Bhopal 2016; Ahmed 2017). The intense corporatization of academic management results in not just unhealthy workspaces where time is taken from research and teaching but also where women and minority groups need to navigate racism, exclusion and marginalization and the disempowering effects on academics caught in these binds.

Stress and anxiety abound in academia, with the upshot that often there is a failure to be reflective and introspective of how we interact with each other – all caught in similar institutional dynamics. In putting this volume together, we had to contend with these undercurrents, which ranged from colleagues who went silent and non-responsive (standard one may say) to those who were antagonistic or dropped out at the very end after long and hard work on the part of reviewers and editors, despite acquiescing to requests for delaying delivering chapters. In writing in academia, we are most grateful for colleagues who were aware of combined and conflicting pressures and yet were graceful and patient in waiting for each other and us – especially those colleagues who made the original milestones and yet were graciously forbearing.

It is also easy to forget the effects of the pandemic from a personal perspective where many writers and editors suffered from CoVID-19, had family members also suffering and bereavements. The political and economic effects of this cannot be understated. The pandemic made many of us appreciate the small things in life we may have taken for granted, such as the ability to gather with friends, travel, or simply go about our daily routines without fear. It also meant that we need to rethink how we engage each other and how we understand the intersectionality of the complexity of people's lives.

From the smallest corners of our lives to the grand stage of Sri Lanka and globally, the continuum of struggles highlighted in this handbook and which we all face is a testament to our shared humanity. Each person's daily battles are the threads that weave the tapestry of our collective struggle, connecting smaller spaces to the vast expanse of our national and international challenges. The tussles faced by our authors in preparing for this are also a microcosm of what is faced by the wider society. The message of persistence and perseverance resonates through the continuum of struggles, reminding us that our common experiences unite us more than they divide us. This is the message of the *aragalaya* and comes out strongly from the chapters in this volume. The journey from smaller spaces to the national and worldwide stage is a reminder that the struggles of one are the struggles of many, and injustice in one place is injustice for all; and for Sri Lanka, togetherness, in acknowledging our collective trauma, is needed to curve just futures.

If there is a take-home message for us: As we navigate the intricate web of shared experiences and global challenges in this current conjuncture, let us remember that the message of unity and perseverance echoes through all our (internationalist) struggles, from the smallest to the largest spaces in our lives.

Notes

1. In a troubling Channel Four (2023) Dispatches exclusive, entitled *Sri Lanka bombings: Were 269 people killed for political power?*, the culpability of the terror and violence on Easter Sunday 2019 draws strong linkages between the man and family that subsequently returned to power in 2020.
2. Even as CPA's (2023) study is comprehensive, thorough, and insightful, it too misses the temporality of the *aragalaya* by limiting the start of the people's uprising to end March 2022 and Mirihana by emphasizing on scale. The smaller neighbourhood protests that preceded this period and indeed peaceful protests and struggles over the long durée are equally important catalysts to understanding the *aragalaya*. In late 2021, the protests initiated by farmers in the rural areas, island-wide teachers' marches in late 2021 as well and the Catholic community demanding justice for the Easter Sunday bombing and the much longer struggles of the mothers and families of the disappeared all matters – even as they may not have captured the imagination and political urgency of the people. Like with any organic struggle, the impetus and inspiration for broader-scale collective mobilization start elsewhere; and the rural and enduring political injustices were as critical for understanding 2022 as were the rural and urban communities and collectives.
3. EPF fund consists of pension savings for workers, who often earn less than Rs 100,000 per annum (equivalent to £250.00 per year); and any DDO will have particularly gendered, classed, and ethnic impacts as the bulk of workers in the garment and tea sectors are women (Ghosh and Ruwanpura 2023; see also Ghosh 2021).

References

Abeysekera, Ananda (2002) Colours of the Robe: *Religion, Identity and Difference* Columbia: University of South Carolina Press.

Ahmed, Sara (2017) ***Living a Feminist Life*** Durham: Duke University Press

Al Jazeera (2023) "Sri Lanka Top Court finds Rajapaksa brothers guilty of economic crisis". (15 November). https://www.aljazeera.com/news/2023/11/15/sri-lanka-top-court-finds-rajapaksa-brothers-guilty-of-economic-crisis#:~:text=Sri%20Lanka%27s%20Supreme%20Court%20has,crisis%20by%20mishandling%20the%20economy

Arudpragasam, Amita (2022) "How the Rajapaksa's Destroyed Sri Lanka's Economy" ***Foreign Policy*** (28 April). https://foreignpolicy.com/2022/04/28/sri-lanka-rajapaksa-protests-economy-corruption/

Banks, Nina (2008) "The Black Worker, Economic Justice and the Speeches of Sadie T.M. Alexander" ***Review of Social Economy*** 66(2): 139–161

Bhopal, Kalwant (2016) "British Asian Women and the Costs of Higher Education in England" ***British Journal of Sociology of Education*** 37(4): 501–519

Brow, James (1996) ***Demons and Development: The Struggle for Community in a Sri Lankan Village*** Tucson: University of Arizona Press

Centre for Policy Analysis (2023) ***A Brief Analysis of the Aragalaya 2023*** Colombo: CPA – Social Indicator

Chandrasekhar, C.P., Jayati Ghosh and Debamanyu Das (2024) *Paying with Austerity: The Debt Crisis and Austerity in Sri Lanka* PERI Working Paper series. Amherst: University of Massachusetts

Channel Four (2023) *Sri Lanka bombings: Were 269 people killed for political power?* (5 September). https://www.channel4.com/news/sri-lanka-bombings-were-269-people-killed-for-political-power-dispatches-exclusive

Chang, Ha-Joon (2014) ***Economics: The Users Guide*** London: Pelikan Books, Penguin

Charusheela, S. (2004) "Post-Colonial Thought, Postmodernism and Economics: Questions of Ontology and Ethics" In ***Postcolonialism Meets Economics*** S. Charusheela and Eiman Zein-Elabdin (eds) Oxford: Routledge, pp 40–58

Collini, Stefan (2012) *What Are Universities For?* London: Penguin

Colombo Gazette (2023) "Civil society calls for end to state repression in Sri Lanka" (29 August). https://colombogazette.com/2023/08/29/civil-society-collective-calls-for-end-to-state-repression-in-sri-lanka/

Coomaraswamy, Radhika (2022) "Introduction" In *Counting and Cracking* Edinburgh: Edinburgh International Festival, unpaginated.

Daily Financial Times – Sri Lanka (2023) "The non-existing agreement of May 2022" (27 November). https://www.ft.lk/ft_view__editorial/The-non-exciting-agreement-of-May-2022/58-755610

Danby, Colin (2017) *The Known Economy: Romantics, Rationalists and the Making of a World Scale* Oxford: Routledge

de Alwis, Malathi (1995) "Gender, Politics and the 'Respectable Lady'" In *Unmaking the Nation: The Politics of Identity and History in Modern Sri Lanka* Pradeep Jeganathan and Qadri Ismail (eds) Colombo: SSA, pp 137–157

de Alwis, Malathi (1997) "Motherhood as a Space of Protest: Women's Political Participation in Contemporary Sri Lanka" In *Appropriating Gender: Women's Activism and the Politicization of Religion in South Asia* Amrita Basu and Patricia Jeffrey (eds) London/New York: Routledge

De Alwis, Sarath (2023) "Odious Debt" *Daily Financial Times – Sri Lanka* (23 January). https://www.ft.lk/columns/Odious-debt/4-744401

De Mel, Neloufer (1996) "Statis Signifiers: Metaphors of Women in Sri Lankan War Poetry" in *Embodied Violence: Communalizing Women's Sexuality in South Asia* Kumari Jayawardena and Malathi de Alwis (eds), pp 168–98

de Votta, Neil (2022) "Sri Lanka's road to ruin was political and not economic" *Foreign Policy* (12 July). https://foreignpolicy.com/2022/07/12/sri-lanka-crisis-politics-economics-rajapaksa-protest/

Debt Justice UK (2023) "Ghosh, Piketty and Varoufakis among 182 experts calling for Sri Lanka's debt cancellation". https://debtjustice.org.uk/press-release/ghosh-piketty-and-varoufakis-among-182-experts-calling-for-sri-lanka-debt-cancellation

Feminist Collective for Economic Justice (2023) "World Bank and IMF's targeted discourse against working poor of Sri Lanka" *Daily Financial Times – Sri Lanka* (8 May). https://www.ft.lk/opinion/World-Bank-and-IMF-s-targeted-discourse-against-working-poor-of-Sri-Lanka/14-748032

Ghosh, Jayati (2021) *Gender Concerns in Debt Relief* Issue Paper – December 2021 IDRC-IIED https://www.iied.org/sites/default/files/pdfs/2021-12/20691iied.pdf

Ghosh, Jayati and Kanchana N. Ruwanpura (2023) "Sri Lanka's Dangerous Domestic Debt Restructuring" *Project Syndicate* (13 September). https://www.project-syndicate.org/commentary/sri-lanka-government-imf-austerity-deal-will-exacerbate-debt-crisis-by-jayati-ghosh-and-kanchana-n-ruwanpura-2023-09?barrier=accesspaylog

Gunaratne, Arjun (2001) "What's in a Name? Aryans and Dravidians in the Making of Sri Lankan Identities" In *The Hybrid Island: Culture Crossing in the inversion of identity in Sri Lanka* Neluka Silva (ed) Colombo: Social Scientists Association and London: Zed Books, pp 20–40

Gunawardena, Charith (2022) "Time for new solutions for Sri Lanka: Fight for private creditor debt cancellation" *Daily Financial Times – Sri Lanka* (28 July). https://www.ft.lk/columns/Time-for-new-solutions-for-Sri-Lanka-Fight-for-private-creditor-debt-cancellation/4-737981#

Gunawardena, Charith (2023) "IMF Deal: Facts behind the Hype" *Daily Financial Times – Sri Lanka* (23 March). https://www.ft.lk/columns/IMF-deal-Facts-behind-the-hype/4-746642

Gunawardena, Devaka, Niyanthini Kadirgamar and Ahilan Kadirgamar (2023) "The IMF Trap: Debt, austerity and inequality in Sri Lanka's Historic crisis" *Phenomenal World* (1 March). https://www.phenomenalworld.org/analysis/the-imf-trap/

Hossein, Caroline S. (2019) "A Black Epistemology for the Social and Solidarity Economy: The Black Social Economy" *The Review of Black Political Economy* 46(3): 209–229

Nicholas, Howard and Bram Nicholas (2023) "An Alternative View of Sri Lanka's Debt Crisis" *Development and Change* 54(5): 1114–1135

Humphries, Jane (1983) "Gender Inequality and Economic Development" in *Economics in a Changing World* Dieter Bos (ed) New York: St Martin's Press, pp 218–233

Jazeel, Tariq and Kanchana N. Ruwanpura (2009) "Dissent: Sri Lanka's New Minority" *Political Geography* 28(7): 385–387

Jegathesan, Mythri (2019) *Tea and Solidarity: Tamil Women and Work in Postwar Sri Lanka* Columbia: University of Washington Press

Kadirgamar, Ahilan (2009) "Sri Lanka's Post-War Political Economy and the Question of Minorities" *Economic and Political Weekly* 44(24): 72–77

Kadirgamar, Ahilan (2013) "The Question of Militarisation in Post-War Sri Lanka" *Economic and Political Weekly* 48(7): 42–46

Kadirgamar, Ahilan (2023) "Dispossession by Domestic Debt Restructuring" *Daily Financial Times – Sri Lanka* (23 July). https://www.dailymirror.lk/opinion/Dispossession-by-Domestic-Debt-Restructuring/172-262249

Klem, Bart (2011) "Islam, Politics and Violence in Eastern Sri Lanka" *Journal of Asian Studies* 70(3): 730–753

Klem, Bart and Thiruni Kelegama (2020) "Marginal Placeholders: Peasants, Paddy and Ethnic Space in Sri Lanka's Post-War Frontier" *The Journal of Peasant Studies* 47(2): 346–365

Klem, Bart and Sidharthan Maunaguru (2017) "Insurgent Rule as Sovereign Mimicry and Mutation: Governance, Kingship and Violence in Civil Wars" *Comparative Studies in Society and History* 59(3): 629–656

Klem, Bart and Sidharthan Maunaguru (2018) "Public Authority under Sovereign Encroachment: Community Leadership in War-Time Sri Lanka" *Modern Asian Studies* 52(3): 784–814

Kuruwita, Rathindra (2023) "IMF's package to Sri Lanka includes corruption fixing" *The Diplomat* (30 March). https://thediplomat.com/2023/03/imfs-package-to-sri-lanka-includes-corruption-fixing/

Krishnamoorthy, Priyanka (2022) "Sri Lanka's Next Test" (22 July). *Project Syndicate* https://www.project-syndicate.org/commentary/sri-lanka-rajapaksa-ouster-moment-of-ethnic-solidarity-by-priyanka-krishnamoorthy-1-2022-07

Lindberg, Jonas and Camilla Orjuela (eds) (2016) *Corruption in the Aftermath of War* London: Routledge

Martin, Jamie (2022) *The Meddlers: Sovereignty, Empire, and the Birth of Global Economic Governance* Cambridge: Harvard University Press

Mattei, Clara E. (2022) *The Capital Order: How Economists Invented Austerity and Paved the Way to Fascism* Chicago: University of Chicago Press

Matthaei, Julie (1996) "Why Feminist, Marxist, and Anti-Racist Economists Should Be Feminist–Marxist–anti-Racist Economists" *Feminist Economics* 2(1): 22–42

Maunaguru, Sidharthan (2020) "Sovereign Deities and Tiger Politics in Sri Lanka" *Current Anthropology* 61(6): 686–712

Mazzacutto, Mariana (2020) *The Mission Economy: A Moonshot Guide to Changing Capitalism* London: Allen Lane

Mishra, Pankaj (2014) "The Western Model Is Broken" *The Guardian – Long Read* (14 October). https://www.theguardian.com/world/2014/oct/14/-sp-western-model-broken-pankaj-mishra

Paramsothy, Thanges (2019) "Inter-Caste Marriage in Conflict Settings: War, Displacement and Social Conditions in Cross-Caste Kinship Formations in Jaffna, Northern Sri Lanka" *Journal of South Asian Studies* 7(2): 39–49

Pathirana, Dhanusha with unions (2023) "CBSL Chief disregards trade mis-invoicing; collaborates with corporate and political corruption" *Daily Financial Times – Sri Lanka* (13 February). https://www.ft.lk/opinion/CBSL-Chief-disregards-trade-mis-invoicing-collaborates-with-corporate-and-political-corruption/14-745237

Pathirana, Saroj (2022) "'Supreme power of people': Sri Lanka marks 100 days of protests" *Al-Jazeera* (18 July). https://www.aljazeera.com/news/2022/7/18/supreme-power-of-people-sri-lanka-marks-100-days-of-protests

Piketty, Thomas (2022) *A Brief History of Equality* Cambridge: Harvard University Press

Rodrik, Dani, Baqir, Reza and Ishac Diwan (2023) "Realizing new growth opportunities in developing countries" *Project Syndicate* (11 January). https://www.project-syndicate.org/commentary/realizing-new-growth-opportunities-in-developing-countries-by-dani-rodrik-et-al-2023-01?barrier=accesspaylog

Roos, Jerome (2019) *Why Not Default? The Political Economy of Sovereign Debt* Princeton and Oxford: Princeton University Press

Roy, Arundhati (2020) "The pandemic is a portal" *Financial Times* (3 April). https://www.ft.com/content/10d8f5e8-74eb-11ea-95fe-fcd274e920ca

Ruwanpura, Kanchana N. (2006) *Matrilineal Communities, Patriarchal Realities: A Feminist Nirvana Uncovered* Delhi: Zubaan Books and Ann Arbor: University of Michigan Press

Ruwanpura, Kanchana N. (2018) "Militarized Capitalism? The Apparel Industry's Roles in Scripting a Post-War National Identity in Sri Lanka" *Antipode* 50(2): 425–446

Ruwanpura, Kanchana N (2022) *Garments without Guilt? Global Labour Justice and Ethical Codes in Sri Lankan Apparels* Cambridge: Cambridge University Press.

Ruwanpura, Kanchana N., Bhumika Muchchala and Smriti Rao (2022) "Gendering the Debt Crisis: Feminists on Sri Lanka's financial crisis" *Daily Financial Times – Sri Lanka* (12 November). https://www.ft.lk/opinion/Gendering-the-debt-crisis-Feminists-on-Sri-Lanka-s-financial-crisis/14-741880

Satkunanathan, Ambika (2022a) "Aragalaya versus Struggles" *Economic and Political Weekly* 57(52): 24–26

Satkunanathan, Ambika (2022b) "The Tamil Struggle, the Aragalaya and Sri Lankan Identity" *Groundviews* (15 May). https://groundviews.org/2022/05/15/the-tamil-struggle-the-aragalaya-and-sri-lankan-identity/

Sathkunanthan, Ambika (2023) "Growing Hindu majoritarianism/nationalism in the Tamil community can't be ignored/Increasing anti-Muslim/anti-Christian rhetoric…" Twitter Thread *Twitter* (28 August). https://twitter.com/ambikasat/status/1693632208790073738

Saleem, Amjad (2020) "Re-Thinking Muslim Political Identity in Sri Lanka" *IIUM Journal of Religion and Civilizational Studies* 3(1): 84–112

Sen, Amartya (1981) "Public Action and the Quality of Life in Developing Countries" *Oxford Bulletin of Economics and Statistics* 43(4): 287–319

Senanayake, Devana (2022a) "First in four decades: Why Sri Lanka general strike matters" *Al-Jazeera* (29 April). https://www.aljazeera.com/news/2022/4/29/first-in-four-decades-why-sri-lanka-general-strike-matters

Senanayake, Devana (2022b) "Sri Lanka's Left Turn" *Foreign Policy* (12 September). https://foreignpolicy.com/2022/09/12/sri-lanka-left-politics-socialism-protest-movement-history/

Senanayake, Devana (2023) "Where does Sri Lanka's Protest Movement go from here?" *The Diplomat* (21 April). https://thediplomat.com/2023/04/where-does-sri-lankas-protest-movement-go-from-here/

Senevirathna, Priyan (2018) "Creating Shared Value through Partnerships in Agricultural Production in Sri Lanka" *Geoforum* 90: 219–222

Silva, Neluka (ed) (2001) *The Hybrid Island: Culture Crossing in the Inversion of Identity in Sri Lanka* Colombo: Social Scientist Association and London: ZED Books

Silva, Shashik, Kaushini Dhammalage and Amaraah Nilafdeen (2022) "Religious Freedom and Coexistence: Beyond the Aragalaya" *Groundviews* (20 October). https://groundviews.org/2022/10/20/religious-freedom-and-coexistence-beyond-the-aragalaya/

Skanthakumar, B. (2023) "Sri Lanka has a proud tradition of revolt against leaders who trample on its people" *Jacobin* (29 August). https://jacobin.com/2023/08/sri-lanka-hartal-aragalaya-protest-history-left

Sornarajah, Muthucumaraswamy (2022a) "Recovering the proceeds of political corruption" *The Sunday Island* (1 May). https://island.lk/recovering-the-proceeds-of-political-corruption/

Sornarajah, Muthucumaraswamy (2022b) "Are Sri Lanka's debts odious" *The Island* (29 May). https://island.lk/are-sri-lankas-debts-odious/

Sornarajah, Muthucumaraswamy (2022c) "July 9th: The Revolutionary changes and its aftermath" *The Island* (24 July). https://island.lk/july-9-the-revolutionary-change-and-its-aftermath/

Soysa, Minoli (2022) "D-Day for the Aragalaya" *Groundviews* (5 August). https://groundviews.org/2022/08/05/d-day-for-the-aragalaya/

Srinivasan, Meera (2022) "Sri Lanka War Anniversary: Tamil Victims remembered in Colombo" *The Hindu* (18 May). https://www.thehindu.com/news/international/sri-lanka-war-anniversary-tamil-victims-remembered-in-colombo/article65426268.ece

Stiglitz, Joseph (2023) "Fixing Global Economic Governance" *Project Syndicate* (23 October). https://www.project-syndicate.org/commentary/global-financial-economic-architecture-needs-an-overhaul-by-joseph-e-stiglitz-2023-10?barrier=accesspaylog

Tennekoon, Serena N. (1988) "Rituals of Development: The Accelerated Mahaväli Development Program of Sri Lanka" *American Ethnologist* 15(2): 294–310

Thiranagama, Sharika (2018) "The Civility of Strangers? Caste, Ethnicity, and Living Together in Post-War Jaffna, Sri Lanka" *Anthropological Theory* 18(2–3): 357–381

Thiruvarangan, Mahendran (2019) Being Together: Imaginaries of Coexistence and Resistance in Contemporary South Asian Writings. Unpublished dissertation. CUNY Academic Works. https://academicworks.cuny.edu/gc_etds/3368

Thiruvarangan, Mahendran (2022) "Contestations over land in Northern Sri Lanka" *Jamhoor* (30 March).

United Nations Development Programme (2022) ***Avoiding 'Too Little, Too Late' on International Debt Relief*** New York: UNDP

United Nations Development Programme (2023) ***Understanding Multidimensional Vulnerabilities: Impact on People of Sri Lanka*** Colombo: UNDP

Varoufakis, Yanis (2022) ***Another Now*** Bodley Head: Vintage, Penguin Books

VOA (2023) "Sri Lanka on alert as activists commemorate anti-Tamil riots" (23 July). https://www.voanews.com/a/sri-lanka-on-alert-as-activists-commemorate-anti-tamil-riots/7192875.html

Waller, William and Mary Wrenn (2021) "Feminist Institutionalism and Neoliberalism" ***Feminist Economics*** 27(3): 51–76

Wanniarachchi, Senel (2023) "Imagining the Nation as a 'Web' of Animals: Affective Entanglements between Animality and (Nation)alism" ***Cultural Politics*** 19(2): 219–240

Wickramasinghe, Nira (2009) "After the War: A New Patriotism in Sri Lanka" ***Journal of Asian Studies*** 68(4): 1045–54

Wickramasinghe, Ranil (2013) "Betraying the doctrine of public trust" (24 February). https://www.sundaytimes.lk/130224/news/betraying-the-doctrine-of-public-trust-34394.html

Wijayalath, Ayesha (2022) "Sri Lanka in a constituent moment" IACL-AIDC Blog (26 July). https://blog-iacl-aidc.org/new-blog-3/2022/7/7/sri-lanka-in-a-constituent-moment

Withanage, Hemantha (2021) "The X-Press Pearl Fire – A Disaster of Unimaginable Proportions" ***Groundviews*** (3 June). https://groundviews.org/2021/06/03/the-x-press-pearl-fire-a-disaster-of-unimaginable-proportions/

PART II
Nations and Nationalism

1
ISLAND IMAGINARIES

Insularity, Repetition, and the Spatial Politics of the National

Tariq Jazeel

Introduction

... what is this object, Sri Lanka, in the first place?

(Qadri Ismail 2005, p. xiv)

On 17 May, 2009, the then President Mahinda Rajapakse gave a speech to the Sri Lankan nation celebrating the Government's victory over the Liberation Tigers of Tamil Eelam (LTTE) and the formal end of the 26-year civil war. His speech made clear the importance he attached to restoring Sri Lanka's territorial and sovereign integrity:

For almost three decades the laws enacted by this legislature were not in force in almost one-third of our land. When I won the Presidential Election in 2005 there were LTTE police stations in the North and East. There were Tiger courts. What was missing was only a Tiger parliament. Today we have finished all that forever. Today, this session of Parliament opens in a country where the writ of this august legislature spreads equally throughout the 65, 332 sq. km of territory of Sri Lanka ...

(Rajapakse 2009)

After asserting the importance of Sri Lanka's modern territorial cohesion, Rajapakse went on to mobilize a putatively 'national' history to this modern island sovereignty wherein, as he put it, "Mother Lanka fought against invaders such as Datiya, Pitiya, Palayamara, Silva and Elara", before going on to assert the post-colony's experience of having fought Portuguese, Dutch, and British colonizers (ibid.). In a characteristically rhetorical flourish, he then stressed that:

No longer are there Tamils, Muslims, Burghers, Malays and any other minorities. There are only two peoples in this country. One is the people that love this country. The other comprises the small groups that have no love for the land of their birth. Those who do not love the country are now a lesser group.

(ibid.)

Mahinda Rajapakse's words have arguably set the tone for much of Sri Lanka's post-conflict era insofar as they convey a common sense understanding that a post-independent national polity, one which had become increasingly fractured since well before the war's onset in 1983, had finally been put back together in May 2009. What he also made clear in his speech was the primacy and primordial cohesion of the *object* that his Sri Lanka Freedom Party (SLFP) government had reassembled: that is to say, the nation-state Sri Lanka.

My concern in this chapter is to draw attention to the spatial predicates of that *object*, the islandness correspondent with the nation-state that Rajapakse is at pains to assert as a historical given. As I argue in what follows, if Rajapakse's discourse of post-conflict unified territorial cohesion aims at being politically persuasive, ideological, and *unifying* at a key moment in Sri Lanka's recent history, then it relies on, and is buttressed by, a much more historically consolidated geographical imagination of islandness that so often seems to be naturally interchangeable with the very sign of Sri Lankanness. Even if the civil war had fundamentally been about territory, about contested geographical imaginations and claims, and about the very integrity of the nation-state, Rajapakse's narrative draws upon a spatial logic of inviolable islandness that both precedes and buttresses assertions that can be made about the inviolability of the reassembled nation-state. It is precisely this spatial common sense, therefore, that enables Rajapakse to assert that those who would dispute the island-state's integrity, those who do not in fact *love* this reassembled territorial whole, were now outliers – traitors even – in this modern post-conflict pact with a reconstituted national polity. As I show in this chapter, this is a spatial common sense that is anything but natural. Instead, it is one that has a long discursive and visual history that is foundational to this object – Sri Lanka.

If Rajapakse were to answer the question that Qadri Ismail (2005) poses at the outset of this chapter then, there is no doubt he would conceive Sri Lanka as a geopolitical object, an empirical reality; a place to which the label 'Sri Lanka' unproblematically refers. However, Ismail's question is meant as a provocation to take us elsewhere in terms of how we think about the *object*ivity of the nation-state. For if places like nation-states are indeed objects, he reminds us that they are produced narratologically. In fact, Ismail's own answer to the question he poses is to suggest the possibility that Sri Lanka is precisely the kind of object that is produced textually, by the kinds of narrative in which Rajapakse's words participate (2005: xiv–xv). In other words, despite – and indeed in part because of – the geopolitical materiality of the nation-state Sri Lanka, Ismail stresses that the assumption that the national object is a cohesive, territorial integrity is in fact an assumption that itself has been historically and textually produced. In other words, he asserts that Sri Lanka is a discursive object as much as it is a geopolitical reality. Like all nations and nation-states, it is a spatial story as much as a geopolitical entity (see Bhabha 1990).

With particular reference to Sri Lanka's island geography then, this chapter is an elaboration on a particular 'way of seeing' the post-colony as the discrete, inviolable, whole island entity to which the term 'Sri Lanka' refers. To be a little more precise, it is an assertion of the importance of historicizing that way of seeing, one that reaches back through European and colonial histories of the inviolable island-shaped wholeness that the proper noun Sri Lanka cannot help but reiterate. The chapter intends quite deliberately therefore to situate *post-colonial* Sri Lanka. Indeed, I mobilize a key critical perspective that postcolonialism facilitates in order to draw attention to the narrative and historical production of Sri Lankan islandness. If the hyphenated 'post-colonial' designates the historical period in which Sri Lanka is no longer under any kind of colonial occupation or governance, then the 'postcolonial' (*sans* dash) can usefully draw our attention to the lingering effects of the colonial in the present. The 'postcolonial' conceived this way alerts us to the ways that that which was formed in the colonial period remains stubbornly with us in the present, in the period we know to be after-the-colonial (see McClintock 1992; Nash 2002: 220). In other words, this mobilization of the postcolonial is a way of drawing attention to the role that colonial modernity has played in producing the modern world. In terms of colonialism's constitutive relationship with the modern world, Edward Said (1993: 6) has reminded us that by 1914 Europe held roughly 85% of the earth as colonies, protectorates, dependencies, dominions, and commonwealths. What this stark statistic reveals is not just that the facts of colonialism were geographical, that is to say spatial facts, but also that much of the world as we know it has been fashioned, produced, written by colonial encounter and vision. Sri Lankan islandness, this chapter argues, is one such form of colonial vision that haunts political modernity in the modern era. To be clear though, my aim in this chapter is not to disavow the Sri Lankan island in favour of, for example, a counter-nationalist spatial imagination, such as the LTTE's Tamil Eelam. Instead, it is simply to draw attention to the historical production of Sri Lankan islandness and in so doing to historicize the geographical common sense that so forcefully suggests objective and empiricist understandings of Sri Lanka. I aim to show Sri Lankan islandness to be neither natural in any sense, nor primordial, but instead a cultural geography, a cultural mapping.

To this extent, this is a chapter that joins a growing chorus of critical scholarship that aims, in more or less explicit terms, to think spatially about Sri Lankan politics, or, to phrase it slightly differently, to 'spatialise politics' in any kind of discussion about Sri Lankan nationhood (cf. Jazeel and Brun 2009). As Nihal Perera (1998) asserts in his elaboration on the historical relationships between Sri Lankan society and space, the contention behind much of this work is that "[s]pace is a constituent part of the polities, economies, and cultures in a society, if not on a one to one basis; it is conditioned by them and, at the same time, conditions them" (1998: 1–2). In the context of the civil war, for example, Anoma Pieris (2019) has shown how conflict occurs "simultaneously across multiple intersecting spatial scales comprehended through different spatial registers and spatial units", which for Pieris includes such spatial categories as nation, home, and city, as well as geographical modalities like route, camp, and exile (2019: 5). Beyond reckoning with the civil war, the spatial turn in critical Sri Lankan studies scholarship has also usefully elaborated on the geographical registers through which the postcolonial nation-state and national sovereignty are themselves assembled, imagined, and reified; for example, histories of landscape, environment, and emparkment (Jeganathan 1995; Jazeel 2013), the imperial intimacies and global routes of material culture (Wickramasinghe 2009), even the discursive terrain of geographical scholarship itself (Korf 2009). In what follows, my incomplete excavation of the pre-history of the taken-as-given island imagination that stands in such close proximity to the sign of Sri Lankanness intends to articulate with this broader and growing body of work on spatializing Sri Lankan politics (on islanding and islandness, also see Sivasundaram 2013; Godamunne, Abdeen and Siriwardena-de Zoysa 2022; Woods 2022).

This Repeating Island

The very utterance 'Sri Lanka' cannot sidestep the island-shaped repetition that this chapter probes. For Edward Said (1983), repetition is the fundamental process through which facts are given their historical *factuality*, their accordance, and reality its existential sense (1983: 114–115). Repetition makes reason from experience, turning events into history as the present and emergent acquire the contours of the familiar in the imagination. Thought this way, narrative fiction is a "filial device of handing on a story through narrative telling" (Said 1983: 117). Stories depend on a repetition of sorts, even as a novel's hero or heroine distinguishes themselves, they must do so against an otherwise familiar backdrop repetitively inscribed in the imagination. Repetition precipitates the *naturalization* of the social. What falls away from view as this repetition gains momentum are real questions about origins. Not questions about the origin of an object, for as we can see from President Mahinda Rajapakse's very certain declarations about Sri Lanka's embattled history, assertions about those kinds of origins gain sway as we endlessly repeat an object's actuality. What falls away from view, rather, are real questions about how an object ever emerged *as an object* in the human imagination, questions about the origins of ideas (about the idea of 'the national' in this case), about our concrete assumptions around human and natural existence and the (con)textuality of that existence (Said 1983: 120).

As an utterance 'Sri Lanka' is a repetition that hands on a spatial story whose origins are often lost or at least obfuscated; it references a known object whose representational genealogy is often occluded. For 'Sri Lanka' (the nation-state's name since 1972) derives from the Sinhala language – which replaced English and superseded Tamil as Ceylon's official language in 1956 – and roughly translates as 'Venerable/Holy Lanka', where 'Lanka' was the Sinhala term used in Orientalized translations of Sinhalese scriptures to refer to the island territory. 'Sri Lanka' *is* insular and exclusive islandness, rewritten and repeated (see Carter 1987:. xiii–xxv), which is to stress how in language particularly the past weighs heavily on the present (Said 1983: 123).

It is a geopolitical fact that islandness remains the spatiality cognate with Sri Lankan nationhood. At the same time, islandness was historically a taken-for-granted, yet also heavily contested, geographical imagination in the context of Sri Lanka's 26-year civil war. As I have indicated, each time we utter the very word 'Sri Lanka' we cannot help but re-inscribe, repeat, the island form imaginatively and discursively. Subsequently it is unsurprising that to many, islandness seems so natural as to be interchangeable with the sign 'Sri Lanka'. Although in this context, we should remember that just over 200 years ago the physical island played host to a medley of coexisting colonies and kingdoms dispersed across its length and breadth. It was only in 1815 that British troops conquered the interior lying Kandyan Kingdom, thereby bringing the whole island under a single English-speaking administration and creating for the first time a (violently) 'unified' island polity, the colonial state that became the post-colony and nation-state. As Nira Wickramasinghe remarks, European colonization marked the transition wherein "Sri Lanka, from being a cluster of centre-based overlapping societies – galactic states, as it were – became a boundary-based society where the sea played the main role" (2006: 8). Islanding, as Sujit Sivansundaram (2013: 14) has put it, was an active process which included material efforts to separate the Ceylonese landmass from the Indian mainland by dredging the channel between colonial Ceylon and British India (also see Radicati 2019: 330). In other words, colonial Ceylon's physical disambiguation from British India was, in part at least, materially and deliberately engineered through the early 19th century. Administratively as well, Ceylonese islandness was accentuated by its governmental exclusion from the auspices and jurisdiction of British India. Unlike the latter, Ceylon was a Crown Colony, not under the administration of the East India Company. As Sivasundaram (2013: 14) writes, "the island was cast off from the mainland by the 1830s"; the administrative and physical processes of casting the island off from the mainland were, in fact, what made colonial Ceylon a different kind of laboratory for colonial state making than the British had at their disposal in the Indian mainland (ibid.). In addition, as Nihal Perera (1998) has shown, from 1815 through to the eve of independence, British rule in Ceylon was intent on physically instantiating control over the whole island to which it now lay claim, in ways that effectively and materially aimed at stringing together this newly assembled island territory (1998: 39–57). This included the establishment of a new communication infrastructure, as well as a connective island-wide network of roads and rest-houses, a putatively 'national' urban system centred on Colombo, and the organization of the island-colony into contiguous administrative divisions (ibid: 39). There was, of course, an economic logic behind these attempts to string the island-colony together: a networked colonial infrastructure with all roads leading to Colombo made it easier and quicker for the colony's valuable plantation commodities to reach imperial markets, just as it rendered transparent and accessible those plantations to the machinery of colonial administration.

However, to conceive of 1815 as an originary moment in spatial and administrative terms is only partially useful. As Sivasundaram (2013) convincingly argues, the Kandyan Kingdom's historical and territorial relationship with colonial power is best thought through the registers of recycling and movement rather than rupture and sudden change (2013: 11). If, Sivasundaram's thesis on this process of 'islanding' stresses that colonialism "set in motion a discursive and intellectual way of thinking and writing of this space as a romanticized and sexualized island, a lost Eden", part of the work of this chapter is to stress that these European geographical imaginations and fantasies in fact long pre-date the colonial encounter (ibid: 14). In other words, whilst we must recognize colonial encounter as the violent, spatially and materially transformative (not to mention contested) event that it was, the spatial/material result of 1815 had an imaginative and representational pre-history. In these terms, 1815 was less originary moment than the instantiation/inscription of a repeating European and imperial geographical imagination.

Writing of British India in ways that are just as useful for understanding the inception of colonial Ceylon, Matthew Edney (1997) remarks how "The creation of British India required the prior acceptance by the British of 'India' as signifying a specific region of the earth's surface" (1997: 3). 'Ceylon' – an existing island polity that emerged geopolitically in 1815 – was the production and articulation of an idea; it was an island *mapping* before it ever emerged as material colonial space. As such, beyond the economic competition between The Crown and the East India Company, and notwithstanding the clear mercantile benefits of colonial efforts to unify the island-colony, there were historical and imaginative reasons why it seemed like so much common sense for the British to physically, ideologically, and politically disambiguate the island-colony of Ceylon through the early 19th century.

The British establishment of island-wide rule was as much about realizing an imperial island-imagination whose roots lay variously in medieval European Mediterranean mappings and island fantasies (see Cosgrove 2001: 90–95), as it was about strategic and mercantile imperialism. It is not my intention to exhaustively piece together a European cartographic history of the island known as Ceylon, though I do want to point out that prior to the British arrival, Portuguese and Dutch colonizers controlled a varying array of fragments, chunks, and formerly autonomous kingdoms *across* island space. It is clear, for example, that Dutch colonizers never controlled the Kandyan Kingdom and, hence, did not govern the whole island. In fact, they brokered a treaty in 1766 that delineated political boundaries between the king of Kandy's territory and Dutch-controlled coastal areas (Barrow 2008: 1). Whilst this lays bare the fact that centralized island territoriality did not exist materially as Dutch possession, it is not to deny that islandness existed as a geographical imagination for the Dutch (and indeed, as Sivasundaram shows, for the Kandyans themselves). Imaginatively, the island existed as representational object, to-be-divided geopolitically. An early British minute on Ceylon by Hugh Cleghorn in 1799 reveals a similar imaginative cartography: "Two different nations [Sinhalese and Tamil], from a very ancient period, have divided between them the possession of the island …. These two nations differ entirely in their religion, language, and manners" (quoted in Rogers 2004: 633). Here Ceylon is conceptualized as a divided unity from the outset, just as the natural schema of Ceylon's cohesiveness as integrated whole island-body structures the way Cleghorn minutes the place.

This kind of singular and contained islandness is a representational and imaginative legacy that was not so much handed on baton-like to the British by the Dutch, but rather one that percolated

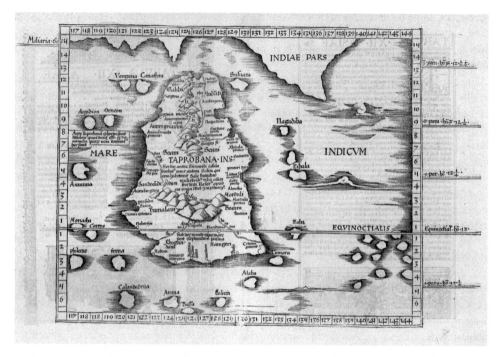

Figure 1.1 Ptolemy's 12th Asian Map (*Tabula XII Asiae*) depicting 'Taprobane', from Michel Servet's *Ptolemy's Geography (Cosmographia)*, 1535 (Source: Wikipedia, public domain: https://commons.wikimedia.org/wiki/File:Ptolemy%27s_Taprobana.jpg)

through the very fabric of European geographical knowledge since Iberian imperialism, which itself drew upon the maps of 'Taprobane' (Figure 1.1) that were based on Claudius Ptolemy's second-century BCE *Geography*. That Taprobane was believed to be the place of the Antipodes is of less interest in this context than the intense visual referentiality to an insular, self-contained island space that emerges from Ptolemy's *Geography*. Images of Taprobane use a simple whole page depiction of a space marked by one continuous yet heavily shaded line dividing land and sea. In the sea, scrawl-like waves are etched on the page and interspersed by a ring of satellite islands, all of which surround and contain the territory marked *Taprobana* that is positioned centrally on the page. In Ptolemy's *Geography*, and maps subsequently based on his books, regions of the earth were rendered chorographically. They were drawn without concern for their precise relationship in scale or location to larger geographical patterns, but instead with substantial visual attention and detail to be able to render what was thought was the character of a place. As Denis Cosgrove writes, chorographic images like Ptolemy's *Geography* sought to "give a visual impression of the actual look of the land" (Cosgrove 2008: 24). If chorographic images sought to depict, describe, and map, they did so impressionistically, through spatial stories. Taprobane's insular and introverted islandness was one such spatial story. It is one that has, as I show in the next section, through modern times been something of a prism through which Ceylonese and Sri Lankan history are typically refracted.

In his now classic examination of the formation of 'imagined communities' through the technologies of print culture, Benedict Anderson draws on Thai historian Thongchai Winichakul to elaborate on the process of *reversal* that is central to understanding the spatial and imaginative effects of early and pre-modern cartography. If today we reasonably assume that maps are a scientific abstraction of reality, a representation of that which exists objectively 'out there', maps the likes of those based on Ptolemy's *Geography* in fact "anticipated social reality, not vice versa. In other words, a map was a model for, rather than a model of, what it purported to represent ... a real instrument to concretize projections of the earth's surface" (Winichakul quoted in Anderson 1983: 173–174). It is, thus, with such spatial stories of islandness in mind that Vasco de Gama set sail east in the 16th century. These voyages themselves produced and consolidated vast geographical information systems from new Portuguese navigational and cartographical sciences and arts that Nihal Perera (1998) suggests were tantamount to *new* ways of seeing the world (1998: 16–33). Nonetheless crucially, if they were *new* ways of seeing – beginnings in terms of geographical knowledge – they were also repetitions that drew on a pre-history of chorographic spatial knowledge written by the likes of Ptolemy. The emergent ability to circumnavigate a land mass by sea, to co-ordinate eye and hand with imperial mastery, draw the coast*line*, and with Apollonian effort to plot geographic information from above, proved powerful. It effectively consolidated and (re)produced the chorographic and representational space of the Ceylonese island in the European imagination, a space contained by the line with which it was cartographically marked (also see Carter 1999).

A Very Modern/ist Trope

If European colonial encounters effectively materialized this kind of Ptolemeic island imagination geopolitically – particularly the ruthless 19th- and early 20th-century British ambition to create and maintain a unified Crown colony – then these spatial stories-cum-realities were handed on seamlessly into the modern period. Notwithstanding emergent Tamil nationalist contestations, anti- and post-colonial utopian aspirations for the future of the post-colony of Ceylon/Lanka were founded upon an unshakeable faith in a kind of island logic that by the 1940s had transcended historical memory or record to more or less achieve the status of 'pre-history'. In other words, even for mid-20th century anti-colonial nationalists, the "imperial duress" of what was effectively a historical and cultural island imagination had hardened around, and thus shaped from the outside in, emergent aesthetic and political dreams for a utopian post-colony (Stoler 2016). Ceylonese islandness had become more intractable than stone, apparently existing outside history to appear positively geological in its formation.

For example, for members of Ceylon's '43 Group – which comprised artists, photographers, and playwrights – the island was something of a taken-as-given spatial building block in their pursuit of a break with colonial aesthetic norms. They sought forms of modernist expression adequate to the task of forging an aesthetic break with the inherited Victorian academicism abundant in Ceylonese art schools in the early 20th century. The likes of George Keyt, Lionel Wendt, George Claessen, and Ivan Peries sought to bring Ceylonese folk culture into representation via formal modernist techniques and processes that effectively ruptured the colonial gaze on, and objectification of, Ceylonese culture. In so doing, however, they placed their faith in the inherited geological certainty of the island-shaped theatre of that folk culture. And their modernist faith in the island permeated the broader field of post-colonial artistic and cultural production in Ceylon.

The renowned architect Minnette de Silva (1918–98), for example, whose tropical style was key to the elaboration of a hybrid architectural modernism made to the measure of the tropics and whose work proved so influential for the tropical modernism of architects like Geoffrey Bawa, Valentine Gunasekera, and a whole generation of architects beyond, traces her own aesthetic influences through the '43 Group (see Jazeel 2017). In de Silva's posthumously published book

The Life and Times of an Asian Woman Architect (1998), she reproduces in its entirety a review essay written by artist George Keyt, a founding member of the '43 Group. de Silva had met Keyt through her mother's cousin, the photographer Lionel Wendt, also a founding member of the group. Keyt's essay is a review of a volume on *The Sinhalese Folk Play and The Modern Stage* by E. R. Saratchandra, and it begins:

> The survival of folk culture in a small country like Ceylon is astonishing when we take into consideration the later history of the Island. The occasional raids and invasions from Southern India in ancient times were not culturally destructive …, because the cultural structure of Ceylon was fundamentally an Indian extension. But destructive forces of an alarming nature made their appearance when, …, Ceylon began to stagnate and was finally subjugated by the sweeping domination of three successive powers from Europe …. Largely responsible for the survival of the Ceylonese folk and classical culture was the Buddhist religion, a faith which was somehow preserved through the centuries since Asokan times…
>
> *(Keyt in de Silva 1998: 144)*

Keyt articulates a historical refrain that was pervasive across the broader sweep of late- and post-colonial artistic, architectural, and literary modernism: foreign contamination of an idealized pre-colonial island polity that was unified all the way back. For the purposes of this chapter, it matters less that this assumed pre-colonial island unity was retroactively projected as the Sinhala-Buddhist *national*, itself a (fractured) national polity which was to begin to take shape in the mid-1950s. What is of interest here is simply the island shaped container for this imagined pre-colonial polity. For Keyt, the island is something like a geological certainty that exists beyond and outside the narrative arc of his schematic historical refrain. Whilst he conjures the island's cohesiveness narratively, Keyt imagines that cohesiveness to have nothing to do with narrative or political history. It is *pre*-historical and geological. Keyt's historical refrain is one of invasion from the seas and continents beyond, followed by defence from within, repeating and recycling through 2,500 years of history. His own narrative construction has no place for the slow, fractured, and contested set of processes over the longue-durée of history through which the complex territorial assemblage of island-wide governance was gradually and purposefully put together. In other words, for Keyt, for de Silva, and for Ceylon's anti-colonial modernists, there is little if any acknowledgement that a forcibly unified islandness was realized geopolitically and materially for the first time only in 1815. It is a retroactively projected islandness that frames their utopian aspiration for the recovery and modernization of Ceylonese folk culture. For the modernists, that utopian dream of a modern, post-colonial culture emerged seed-like from within the heart of an island that they assumed always was. Post-colonial Ceylonese culture was a manifest destiny entirely cognate with the spatial coordinates of this pre-historical islandness.

De-territorialization/Re-territorialization

Islandness, of course, is a spatial imagination that has not been without its contestations in the modern era. It is persistently in the process of being imaginatively de-territorialized and re-territorialized. Most notably Tamil separatist mappings, at the heart of Sri Lanka's civil war from 1983 through 2009, were geared towards securing a Tamil homeland. If achieved, it would have succeeded in fundamentally fracturing any material or political island-wide sovereignty. In this respect, 'Eelam' has been a countermapping that disavows the existence and historical legitimacy of the very islandness that this chapter has shown to be so ingrained in the imaginations of so many. If Eelam is a cartographic imagination that has historically aimed at fracturing the island imagination, it has affectively resonated with many across the country (and indeed beyond Sri Lanka's borders) who feel islandness to be an unhomely spatiality, one at odds with their sense of home, locality, security, and personhood. Anecdotally, in 2006 I recall a conversation with a Tamil man in the Eastern city of Batticoloa, which at various points through the civil war had been claimed by the LTTE. When asked by his German son-in-law whether he would ever consider leaving the island given how unsafe it had been in Batticoloa at various points through the previous 23 years, the man told me that his reply was that every time he returns to Batticoloa from the south and crosses the Kallady Bridge, he feels he has left the island! If the crushing military defeat of the LTTE in May 2009 brought an end to the bloody civil war, former President Mahinda Rajapakse's victory speech (with which this chapter began) aimed at re-territorializing those pieces of an island imagination that had been at risk of splintering away.

Nonetheless, separatism and the insecurities of civil war have not been the only existential threats to the island imagination that have emerged in modern Sri Lanka. In the context of the gargantuan Colombo Port City development project, which is currently rising out of the Indian Ocean at a rate only matched by the rapidity of Chinese overseas investment, real concerns over the deterritorialization of sovereignty have emerged in Sri Lanka (see Ruwanpura, Brown and Chan 2019; Radicati 2020). As Orlando Woods (2022) has written, the legal frameworks through which this Chinese investment has been ceded "create 'islands' of Chinese sovereignty through which the idea of Sri Lankan islandness is both being reimagined, and undermined" (2022: 8). As Woods argues, however, a recent shift and co-optation of the political discourse around the Port City development project in Sri Lanka has aimed at imaginatively seizing these existential threats that Chinese investment and its correspondent legal frameworks pose to Sri Lankan sovereignty and reframing this massive building project as an infrastructural gift that ultimately will extend the island. Islandness again repeats, reiterates, imaginatively consolidates upon itself.

The work of this chapter has been to de-naturalize Sri Lankan islandness, but in so doing to show how the cultural histories and stories that we tell about Sri Lanka are always also spatial histories. Building on Qadri Ismail's (2005) critical reflection on the production of knowledge *about* Sri Lanka, the chapter has aimed to show that the place (like any place) is not one that exists outside language and discourse (2005: xvi). In contemplating Ismail's provocative question, "what is this object, Sri Lanka, in the first place?", via the lens of islandness, the chapter has historicized that which can often appear to be pre-historical, geological, absolute. Sri Lankan islandness, I have argued, is a geography that inheres in the very sign 'Sri Lanka'; it is inalienable from its reiteration. It is, indeed, difficult to think outside those textual parameters to enliven the spatial imaginations that *could* circulate around modern Sri Lanka. And it follows logically from this that even in the production of this very Handbook, the reality of Sri Lankan islandness is reiterated in ways that have political and cultural effects. The implications of this kind of work to unsettle the histories of the spatialities we take for granted are towards creative geographical engagements with the sign of Sri Lanka that envisage it is as open, full with democratic, dynamic, and relational possibility.

References

Anderson, Benedict (1983) *Imagined Communities* London and New York: Verso
Barrow, I. J. (2008) *Surveying and Mapping in Colonial Sri Lanka* Sri Lanka: Vijatha Yapa Publications
Bhabha, Homi (ed) (1990) *Nation and Narration* London and New York: Routledge
Carter, Paul (1987) *The Road to Botany Bay* London and Boston: Faber and Faber
Carter, Paul (1999) "Dark with Excess of Bright: Mapping the Coastline of Knowledge" In *Mappings* Denis Cosgrove (ed) London: Reaktion, pp 125–147

Cosgrove, Dennis (2001) *Apollo's Eye: a Cartographic Genealogy of the Earth in the Western Imagination* Baltimore: Johns Hopkins University Press

Cosgrove, Dennis (2008) *Geography and Vision: Seeing, Imagining and Representing the World* London: I.B. Tauris

de Silva, Minnette (1998) *The Life and Work of an Asian Woman Architect* Colombo: Smart Media Productions

Edney, Matthew (1997) *Mapping an Empire: The Geographical Construction of British India, 1765–1843* Chicago, Illinois: Chicago University Press

Godamunne, Vichita, Azhar J. Abdeen and Rapti S. Siriwardena-de Zoysa (2022) "Shored Curfews: Constructions of Pandemic Islandness in Contemporary Sri Lanka" *Maritime Studies* 21: 209–221

Ismail, Qadri (2005) *Abiding by Sri Lanka: On Peace, Place and Postcoloniality* Minneapolis: University of Minnesota Press

Jazeel, Tariq (2013) *Sacred Modernity: Nature, Environment and the Postcolonial Geographies of Sri Lankan Nationhood* Liverpool: Liverpool University Press

Jazeel, Tariq (2017) "Tropical Modernism/Environmental Nationalism: The Politics of Built Space in Postcolonial Sri Lanka" *Fabrications: The Journal of the Society of Architectural Historians, Australia and New Zealand* 27(2): 134–152

Jazeel, Tariq and Cathrin Brun (eds) (2009) *Spatialising Politics: Culture and Geography in Postcolonial Sri Lanka* New Delhi: Sage

Jeganathan, Pradeep (1995) "Authorising History, Ordering Land: The Conquest of Anuradhapura" In *Unmaking the Nation* Pradeep Jeganathan and Qadri Ismail (eds) Colombo: Social Scientist's Association, pp 108–136

Korf, Benedict (2009) "Cartographic Violence: Engaging a Sinhala Kind of Geography" In *Spatialising Politics: Culture and Geography in Postcolonial Sri Lanka* Tariq Jazeel and Cathrin Brun (eds) New Delhi: Sage, pp 100–121

McClintock, Anne (1992) "The Angel of Progress: Pitfalls of the Term 'post-colonialism'" *Social Text* 31/32: 84–98

Nash, Catherin (2002) "Cultural Geography: Postcolonial Cultural Geography" *Progress in Human Geography* 26(2): 219–230

Perera, Nihal (1998) *Society and Space: Colonialism, Nationalism and Postcolonial Identity in Sri Lanka* Boulder, Colorado: Westview Press

Pieris, Ayoma (2019) *Sovereignty, Space and Civil War in Sri Lanka: Porous Nation* London and New York: Routledge

Radicati, Alessandra (2019) "Island Journeys: Fisher Itineraries and National Imaginaries in Colombo" *Contemporary South Asia* 27(3): 330–341

Radicati, Alessandra (2020) "The Unstable Coastline: Navigating Dispossession and Belonging in Colombo" *Antipode* 52(2): 542–561

Rajapakse, Mahinda (2009) [Full text of speech before Parliament on May 17, 2009, English translation], https://reliefweb.int/report/sri-lanka/sri-lanka-our-aim-was-liberate-our-tamil-people-clutches-ltte-president.Accessed on 23/05/2022

Rogers, Jonathan D (2004) "Early British Rule and Classification in Lanka" *Modern Asian Studies* 38: 625–647

Ruwanpura, Kanchana N, Benjamin Brown and Loritta Chan (2019) "(Dis)Connecting Colombo: Situating the Megalopolis in Post-War Sri Lanka" *The Professional Geographer* 72(1): 165–179

Said, Edward (1983) *The World, the Text, and the Critic* Cambridge, Massachussetts: Harvard University Press

Said, Edward (1993) *Culture and Imperialism* New York: Vintage Books

Sivasundaram, Sujit (2013) *Islanded: Britain, Sri Lanka, and the Bounds of an Indian Ocean Colony* Chicago, Illinois: University of Chicago Press

Stoler, Anne L (2016) *Duress: Imperial Durabilities in Our Times* Durham: Duke University Press

Wickramasinghe, Nira (2006) *Sri Lanka in the Modern Age: A History of Contested Identities* Colombo: Vijatha Yapa Publications

Wickramasinghe, Nira (2009) "The Imagined Spaces of Empire" In *Spatialising Politics: Culture and Geography in Postcolonial Sri Lanka* Tariq Jazeel and Cathrine Brun (eds) New Delhi: Sage, pp 24–43

Woods, Orlando (2022) "A Harbour in the Country, A City in the Sea: Infrastructural Conduits, Territorial Inversions and the Slippages of Sovereignty in Sino-Sri Lankan Development Narratives" *Political Geography* 92: 1–9

2
AUTHORITARIAN POLITICS AND GENDER IN SRI LANKA

A Survey

Rajni Gamage

Introduction: Colonial Legacies and Authoritarian Politics

In 2022, Sri Lanka experienced a national economic crisis with serious political and social ramifications. This crisis, although coming out of a particular context, has its roots in the structural conditions of authoritarian politics, historically consolidated in longer histories of European colonialism, the evolution of global capitalism including its neoliberal turn since the 1980s, and the uneven global and structural conditions that have followed.

This survey chapter critically examines the key themes of authoritarianism in Sri Lanka and its key developments. I do this by starting with an overview of the colonial legacies of authoritarian politics in this section. After that, I look at how the past three decades of ethnic war and post-war militarization came to be underpinned by authoritarian politics. I thereafter examine the politics of development which are central to authoritarian political practices. Additionally, throughout this chapter, I examine the intersection of gender and authoritarianism.

Feminist analyses of the colonial period examine the gendered role of women in society and how this was informed by both Western and Christian norms of patriarchy, as well as 19th-century Sinhala Buddhist nationalist thought. The latter nationalist leaders forwarded a notion of the ideal Sinhala Buddhist woman tasked with preserving the pristine, Sinhala Buddhist village (Silva 1997; Jayawardena 2002). Such analyses show how notions of gendered respectability in Sinhala Buddhism are influenced by colonial policies and ideas of Victorian morality aimed at producing submissive feminine subjects (Jayaweera 1990; De Alwis and Malathi 1997). Despite women becoming more ideologically and politically conscious and active during the lead up to independence, and middle-class women eventually seeing common cause with working-class women, their preoccupation with the nationalist struggle and lack of autonomy of women's organizations meant that the general patterns of patriarchy continued undisturbed after independence (Jayawardena 1986). These ideas then became part of popular culture through institutions, such as print media and school curricula (Silva 1997; Perera 2002). In the section Post-war Militarization and Authoritarian Politics, I discuss how these values continue to inform gendered norms in Sri Lankan society and the economy.

The imposition of colonial rule in Sri Lanka was a violent affair, and there are critical accounts on how local resistance and rebellion was repressed in an overtly militaristic approach (Jayawardena

2010; Wilson 2016; Sivasundaram 2018). This stands in contrast with imperial narratives, for example, which represented Britain's imperial rule in Sri Lanka as an invitation due to political discord and unrest and/or as a result of the political vacuum left by the withdrawal of other European colonial powers (Bassett 1929; Ludowyk 1967). Colonial authorities legitimized these violent crackdowns, citing a long tradition of native rebellion aimed at overthrowing the British government in Ceylon. This sought to undercut the challenges in establishing total dominion in a colonized society and, in doing so, obscured the nuanced nature of such resistance movements (De Silva 1997; Wickramasinghe 2009).

Despite growing criticism of the counterinsurgency methods used in the colonies, from the more progressive quarters of the colonial society, elements of autocracy endured (Sivasundaram 2018). The colonial administration in Ceylon rationalized authoritarian rule as necessary to introduce liberal developmental values, such as a free press and modern education, to a society that was ostensibly 'underdeveloped' and 'uncivilized'. One of the ways in which this was done was through reinforcing metropolitan understandings of 'heathenism' among the colonized peoples, through means such as the popular press (Rycroft 2006: 198). Even as disproportionate violence was meted out by colonial forces in subjugating the native, it was the native ontologies and epistemologies that were deemed 'inhuman' and 'backward' (Holden 1939). After the outbreak of WWII in Europe, British Emergency (Defence) Acts of 1939 and 1940 were applied to Ceylon. The Ceylon Defence (Miscellaneous) Regulations were framed under these Acts, in line with British defence regulations (Minattur 1982). Importantly, many of these emergency powers were used to break union strikes in the early 20th century.

Apart from counter-insurgency strategy, another key colonial legacy that features in Sri Lankan politics is the ethno-religious 'othering' of minority communities. During British colonial rule, ethnicity became the prevalent form of colonial social categorization. That is the issue of 'nativeness' and who 'belonged' became more rigidly defined along the lines of ethnicity after the 1830s due to the way in which colonial authorities sought to administer the colony (Jeganathan and Ismail 1995; Sivasundaram 2018; Wickramasinghe 2020). Sinhala Buddhist nationalist thought, which emerged in reaction to material injustices and discrimination under colonial rule, reproduced many of these tendencies (Gunawardena 1984; Harris 2006). Redressing this historical injustice thereafter became the core ideology of Sinhala Buddhist nationalism post-independence, violently imposing itself in the three-decade long ethnic conflict and spilling over into post-war military jingoism and nationalist politics.

Ethnic Conflict, Post-War Militarization, and Authoritarian Politics

Authoritarian politics involve the undermining of democratic institutions, norms, and processes, which happens with the concentration of power within a small group of decision-makers through the constitution and/or the mobilization of state security forces and laws. It can occur too due to the absence of adequate laws and proper functioning of institutions, which ensure transparency, accountability, inclusiveness, equity, and efficiency (Jayawardena and Kodikara 2003). Democratic institutions can also be destabilized through less formal means, such as a political culture of patronage, corruption, and nepotism (Jupp 1978; Jayawardena 2002; Bastian and Luckham 2003; Pieris 2022).

In Sri Lanka, power has been concentrated in the Executive Presidency through constitutional and electoral system reforms (Coomaraswamy 2015; Satkunanathan 2015; Senaratne 2019; Gomez 2022). This has subsequently resulted in an emphasis on personality-led politics, which in turn has sidelined the role and importance of parliament, judiciary, and a free and independent media (Welikala 2015). The resulting political culture has enabled a politics of populism and authoritarianism, which was exacerbated by the former President Mahinda Rajapaksa due to his success in wielding it to consolidate power (Gunawardena 2015; Gamage 2021; Jayasinghe 2021).

Several studies examine the resistance and agency of groups that push back on the state's hegemonic and violent thrust against minorities and other embodiments of 'difference' (Brun and Jazeel 2009; Seoighe 2018). This allows the opportunity to contextualize the Mahinda Rajapaksa regime against a history of state violence, especially since the 1980s when early authoritarian populist regimes faced two armed resistance movements from the North and the South. It prevents avoiding the accountability of the other main political party, the United National Party, also complicit in state violence, by playing up the spectre of the Rajapaksa regime. Such an approach also enables an understanding of insurgent movements, from the Liberation Tigers of Tamil Eelam (LTTE) to the Janatha Vimukthi Peramuna (JVP), as a response to state authoritarianism (Peiris 2000; De Votta 2002).

The mobilization of armed forces and emergency law to consolidate authoritarian rule has continued in the post-independence context (Coomaraswamy and De los Reyes 2004). Examples of disproportionate force used by the state include the military decimation of the largely rural-based communist JVP insurrections in 1971 and 1987–1989, and ending the civil war with Tamil insurgents through military means (Uyangoda and Bastian 2008). The Prevention of Terrorism Act (PTA), for example, was enacted in 1978 as a supplementary instrument to invigorate military operations in the North, where the Tamil insurgency was concentrated (Udagama 2015). In the post-war context, the protracted failure to repeal Emergency Regulations has been detrimental to democratic processes and has consolidated power within the Executive President and, by extension, the armed forces under its authority (Cave and Manoharan 2009; Rajasingham-Senanayake 2011).

The militant aspects to Sinhala Buddhist chauvinism, coupled with limited redistribution, resulted in a violent backlash in the form of the Marxist insurgency led by the JVP in the early 1970s (Kearney and Jiggins 1975; Gunasinghe 1980). It also marked the first instance of large-scale state crackdown post-independence. The ethnic conflict which started almost a decade later, fought between the LTTE and the Sri Lankan state, was the culmination of authoritarian politics. In the lead up to it and throughout the conflict, this phase was underlined by the official concentration of power through legal measures and armed force, not only within a group of political elite but also through the political leadership playing to (and being influenced by) a nationalist consciousness and the agenda of a unitary state (Dewasiri 2020).

Sivanandan's (1984) theorising on race and the politics of underdevelopment in Sri Lanka is particularly instructive for linking racialized logic of hierarchy and associated authoritarian politics of state rule during this period. He argues that the type of capitalism developed under British colonialism had a differential impact on social formations since and pronouncing uneven development. This consequently informed the violent social struggles and state authoritarianism around the ethnic conflict in the lead up to and since the 1980s.

The major rallying cry for Sinhala nationalists in the context of the ethnic conflict was defending the unitary nature of the 'Sinhala civilizational state'. Despite the country's pre-colonial history of social coexistence, majoritarian nationalism that emerged since the 19th century conceived of the state as under siege by colonial forces and 'Other' ethnic and religious groups allegedly intent on carving up the island and destroying its cultural and religious heritage (Amunugama 1991). Nationalist groups, such as the Jathika Chinthanaya, advocated for a 'return' to a state where the state was more explicitly the protector of a Sinhalese and Buddhist identity, and in this sense, to assume the paternalism and authoritarianism found within ancient Sinhalese kingdoms (Matthews 2004). These Sinhala nationalist movements strongly opposed power devolution as a solution to the ethnic conflict, as a result of which the issue underlying the ethnic conflict remains unaddressed even to the present day (Abeysekara 2002).

Post-war Militarization and Authoritarian Politics

The Rajapaksa family regime spans from 2005 to 2015 and again from late 2019 to 2022. Its rule was based on the support the family had marshalled through the final years of the ethnic conflict and the military victory against the LTTE in May 2009 (Grant 2014). With a high degree of popular legitimacy for 'winning' the war, the regime was able to consolidate a form of authoritarian rule through populist politics (Uyangoda 2011). This populist politics gave tacit or explicit support to othering ethno-religious minorities and political dissidents (Byrne and Klem 2015). In the post-war context, the authoritarian excesses of state rule heightened, following a politics of military triumphalism and jingoistic nationalism, that saw an almost total collapse of liberal and democratic exercise of the rule of law (Gunasekara 2013; Ruwanpura 2017).

Militarization in the post-war context, alongside extra-judicial state violence, enabled a climate of political impunity to silence the regime's critics and dissidents (De Mel 2007; De Votta 2014, 2017; Saravanamuttu 2014). This clamp down on democratic spaces, in the media and civil society, has further obstructed any challenges to the dominant political hegemonies (Spencer 2008; Jazeel and Ruwanpura 2009; Jazeel 2010). The Rajapaksa regimes 'populist authoritarianism' holds many continuities with state rule since independence, including around racialized politics (Goonewardene 2020).

Within many institutional-centric perspectives on authoritarian politics, it has been argued that this crisis of democratic governance escalated conditions towards the ethnic conflict in the 1980s, where state authoritarianism took on the form of military operations against a section of its own (dissenting) society (Wilson 1988; Wijesinha 2007). The 'cult of the personal' and power centralization within the Executive Presidency triggered resistance from excluded sections of society, in turn undermining the main goal of political stability (Obeyesekere 1984). The 1983 anti-Tamil pogrom ('Black July') is demonstrative of this, reaching the ubiquitousness of societal violence and with evidence of the state's involvement (Piyadasa 1984; Tambiah 1992; De Silva 2000).

The role of ideas and political discourse in regime consolidation is also highlighted in many of these analyses on authoritarian politics. Several critically discuss how sections of society are excluded from power-sharing, through elite discourses of 'patriotism', 'inclusive democracy', and 'liberal peace' which marginalize ethnic minorities (Stokke and Uyangoda 2011; Byrne and Klem 2015; Haniffa 2015). This includes the regime's dependence on pre-colonial myths to legitimize its Sinhala Buddhist nationalist, 'anti-elite' populism (Rampton 2011; Rambukwella 2018), where several of them also focus on the limits of the regime's exclusionary nationalist politics (Roberts 2015; Gunatilleke 2018).

Feminist scholarship proceeds to reveal Sinhala Buddhist nationalism and the nation-state to be a gendered project (De Mel 2001). Many of these feminist scholars examine how women from diverse backgrounds in Sri Lanka have engaged with and/or resisted the dominant Sinhala Buddhist nationalism but also militant Tamil nationalism (Hensman 1992; Thiranagama 2011; De Mel and Medawatte 2021). Within the prevailing power structures of these nationalisms, women are expected, in their personal and public lives, to embody, perform, and reproduce aspects fundamental to social constructs such as tradition, culture, community, and the nation (Hyndman and de Alwis 2004; Gunasekara and Nagaraj 2019). The gendered ways in which state violence is imposed and the strategies of agency in response are found in accounts of the (southern) Mother's Front protesting the disappearance of their male kin in the context of the late-1980s' communist uprising (Perera 1998; De Alwis 2009; Gunasekara and Nagaraj 2019). Some of these more contemporary writings grapple with the traumatic loss of loved ones in the context of state authoritarianism (Whetstone 2020; Buthpitiya 2022).

Political violence is shown to play out in gendered forms too, from the LTTE 'woman warrior' being valorized through invoking masculine traits and the female kin of enforced disappearances being viewed foremost in the roles of 'mothers' and 'wives' to the role of the feminist activist (Coomaraswamy 1996; De Mel 1996; De Alwis 2002, 2009). A dominant paradigm of 'masculinity' reproduces elements of criminality and violence, in the context of war recruitment campaigns and political violence (Ismail 1992; Jeganathan 2000; Coomaraswamy 2005). Other sites of how violence are gendered as a result of the protracted ethnic conflict are the women-headed household and war-affected women, including those with disabilities (Tambiah 2004; Ruwanpura 2006; Samararatne, Soldaic and Perera 2018; Höglund 2019). These dynamics have prevailed in a context of continued militarization of former conflict areas in the post-war years (Bandarage 2010; Satkunanathan 2018).

Authoritarian Politics and Capitalist Development

During British dominion, authoritarian rule was legitimized through the promise of development, modernity, and progress. Colonial policies on labour, race, and gender continue to have relevance, as they directly feature in post-independence politics, in response to struggles over rights by marginalized ethnic, gender, and class groups (Rogers 1987). These agitations are often responded to by the state in a heavy-handed authoritarian manner. These legacies are indicative of the global links of dependency that former colonies maintain even after 'independence', due to their immersion in a global capitalist system whose rules were established by former Western colonial powers (Ponnambalam 1981).

Early colonial policies tied to a model of capitalist development had gendered outcomes. For example, marriage laws established under British rule were considered as "a necessary prerequisite for a successful transition to the private initiative and ownership envisaged by the British" (Risseeuw 1992: WS52). The impact of these laws on land scarcity and gendered forms of labour are noted: women frequently occupied the lowest-paid sectors of paid labour and trade. Kumari Jayawardena analyses how the advent of colonial capitalism and attendant social reforms that were pursued by the state, in keeping with liberal ideas, were however class deterministic (Jayawardena 1986). While these reforms may have increased social mobility and education, among other things, the 'new woman' was observed to be subjected to continued and new patterns of subordination.

Many critical development studies attribute conditions of poverty and inequality to the process of development, during colonial times and in the post-1980s, with the ascent of neoliberal capitalism as the dominant development paradigm (Brow 1996; Korf 2006; Venugopal 2018). These studies link the discourse of official development to authoritarian politics and the maintenance and reproduction of racialized, gendered, and unequal outcomes, which include ethnic conflict. For those writing on economic liberalization since the late-1970s, material inequalities are shown to be managed by the ruling elite by doubling down on rural development discourse and policies in ways closely associated with Sinhala Buddhist nationalism (Tennekoon 1988; Woost 1993). The state also relied extensively on its repressive apparatus to manage resistance to the heightened inequalities of capitalist development. This involved the centralization of power and undermined power devolution and decentralization to rural areas, especially in the North and East (Matthews 1982). These developments contributed significantly to the official start of the ethnic conflict between the state and Tamil secessionists.

Analysts have commented on how contradictions of neoliberal economic reforms in the 1980s institutionalized authoritarian politics; or that neoliberal capitalist development required authoritarian political rule (Obeyesekere 1984; Peebles 1990; Tambiah 1996; Gunasinghe 2004; Winslow and Woost 2004). These contradictions spilled over, as the state coercive apparatus took on two fronts of armed resistance – militant Tamil separatists from the North and East led by the LTTE and the second communist insurgency (1987–1989) primarily from the rural South (but this time with a support base in urban and quasi-urban areas too) led by the JVP (Manor 1984; Moore 1993; Richardson 2005).

Here, it is important to note how 'national' economic growth accelerated during the war years, especially in the 1990s following market reforms and export-driven industrialization since the previous decade. The war economy provided employment for rural youth from the Sinhala South and formed a distinct political economy in itself (Perera 2016; Venugopal 2018). Some others, however, argue that neoliberal development did not require authoritarian politics, although the upshot has been ethnic polarization and loosening of the democratic fabric (Stokke 1997; Dunham and Jayasuriya 2001).

The gendered impact of this economic growth has been well documented. Feminist and development scholars have pointed out how joining the military for men and women becoming garment factory workers was a reflection of the ways in which the projects of nationalization aligned with the quest for greater integration in the global economy (Lynch 1999; Gunawardana 2013). These reveal how conflict generates new patterns of mobility and meanings of place, even as they contain many pre-existing forms of gender hierarchies and role-playing. Women workers, faced with the dual pressures of supporting the state's militarized nation-building and neoliberal development trajectory, were observed to negotiate multiple identities in response to cultural critiques and capitalist demands, in rural and urban spaces (Hewamanne 2009; Lokuge 2017; Ruwanpura 2017, 2022), in the plantations sector with mainly up-country Tamil women's labour (Kurian and Jayawardena 2014; Jegathesan 2019), and in foreign countries where many lower-middle class and working class women migrated to as domestic workers (De Alwis 2002). In the aftermath of the 2022 debt crisis, the gendered impact of widening social inequality such as in microfinance, and climate change, amidst heightened contestations over state power, have also been analysed (Wedagedara 2023; Attanayake 2024).

The war years meant increasing militarization and in the post-war context, the militarized landscape within which apparel sector emerged has also been brought under scrutiny for the unholy alliances between capital-state-military, which chapters by Lingham and Wickramasinghe outline further in this volume (Ruwanpura 2017, 2022). In the post-war context, issues of national significance, such as development, were 'securitised' by the leadership, thereby providing the military with the authority to lead the 'war' against poverty and underdevelopment (Keerawella 2013; Spencer 2016; Ruwanpura 2017, 2022). This witnessed the increasing role of the military in governance and in land occupation, especially but not limited to former conflict areas and in the context of the COVID-19 pandemic (Fonseka, Ganeshathasan and Welikala 2021). Conversely, power sharing and resolution of the 'national question' were framed in relation to overcoming poverty and 'under-development' (Byrne and Klem 2015). These actions were legitimized through populist discourse, which drew on a rural-centric, exclusionary Sinhala Buddhist nationalism, and was nostalgic for a pre-industrial society but which at the same time promised the best of capitalist development (Venugopal 2018).

Sri Lanka's authoritarian politics in the context of development has also been looked at from the perspective of international political economy and geopolitics. Given the 2007–2008 global financial crisis and Western political conditionalities linked to financial aid, especially in the context of geopolitics between the West (and its regional allies, India and Japan) and China for example, the adverse implications of a large military, international sovereign bond and foreign debt-funded mega-development projects on short-term regime consolidation have been raised (Bastian 2007; Athukorala and Jayasuriya 2012; Kadirgamar 2013). Along similar lines, others have documented the limits of such economic policies to contain public discontent over uneven dividends of economic growth (Goodhand 2013).

Conclusion

The prevalence of political patronage and military fiscalism and its connection to be the socio-economic base of the Rajapaksa regime have become the central themes of recent scholarship on Sri Lankan politics and development (Hensman 2010; Goodhand 2013; De Votta 2014; Byrne and Klem 2015). They all emphasize the role of dynastic/family politics in regime consolidation, but underline how this makes a regime vulnerable to resistance from those excluded from narrow networks of nepotism – as we have seen being played out in Sri Lanka during 2022.

The perspectives discussed in this chapter therefore have immediate resonance against the backdrop of Sri Lanka's current crisis, where authoritarianism and populist-nationalism of the Gotabaya Rajapaksa regime in power since 2019 were insufficient to maintain their power against large-scale public anger at economic mismanagement and corruption. Consequently, mass protests forced the Rajapaksa leadership to resign from political office. Nevertheless, authoritarian politics continue to intensify and require close and continued analysis alongside evolving attempts at emancipatory politics and politics of solidarity from the people.

References

Abeysekara, Ananda (2002) *Colors of the Robe: Religion, Identity, and Difference* Columbia: University of South Carolina Press

Amunugama, Sarath (1991) "Buddhaputra or Bhumiputra? Dilemmas of Modern Sinhala Buddhist Monks in Relation to Ethnic and Political Conflict" *Religion* 21(2): 115–139

Athukorala, Prema-chandra and Sisira Jayasuriya (2012) *Economic Policy Shifts in Sri Lanka: The Post-Conflict Development Challenge*. Working Paper No. 2012/15. Canberra: Australian National University

Attanayake, Dimuthu (2024) "In Sri Lanka, climate change traps women farmers in 'exploitative' cycle of economic violence" Retrieved from https://www.scmp.com/week-asia/people/article/3251582/sri-lanka-climate-change-traps-women-farmers-exploitative-cycle-economic-violence.

Bandarage, Asoka (2010) "Women, Armed Conflict, and Peacemaking in Sri Lanka: Toward a Political Economy Perspective" *Asian Politics and Policy* 2(4): 653–667

Bassett, R.H. (1929) *Romantic Ceylon: Its History, Legend and Story* Colombo: Asian Educational Services

Bastian, Sunil (2007) *The Politics of Foreign Aid in Sri Lanka: Promoting Markets and Supporting Peace* Colombo: International Centre for Ethnic Studies

Bastian, Sunil and Robin Luckham (2003) *Can Democracy Be Designed?: The Politics of Institutional Choice in Conflict-Torn Societies* London: Zed Books

Brow, James (1996) *Demons and Development: The Struggle for Community in a Sri Lankan Village* Tucson: University of Arizona Press

Buthpitiya, Vindhya (2022) "Absence in Technicolour: Protesting Enforced Disappearances in Northern Sri Lanka" *Journal of the Royal Anthropological Institute* 28: 118–134

Brun, Catherine and Tariq Jazeel (eds) (2009) *Spatialising Politics: Culture and Geography in Postcolonial Sri Lanka* Delhi: Sage Publications

Byrne, Sarah and Bart Klem (2015) "Constructing Legitimacy in Post-war Transition: The Return of 'normal' Politics in Nepal and Sri Lanka?" *Geoforum* 66: 224–233

Cave, Rosy and N. Manoharan (2009) "Resistance to Reform; Submission to Status Quo; Security Sector Reform in Sri Lanka" *South Asian Survey* 16(2): 291–314

Coomaraswamy, Radhika (1996) "Tiger Women and the Question of Women's Emancipation" *Pravada* 4: 8–10

Coomaraswamy, Radhika (2005) "Human Security and Gender Violence" *Economic and Political Weekly* 40(44/45): 4729–4736

Coomaraswamy, Radhika (2015) "Bonapartism and the Anglo-American Constitutional Tradition in Sri Lanka: Reassessing the 1978 Constitution" In *Reforming Sri Lankan Presidentialism: Provenance, Problems and Prospects* Asanga Welikala (ed) Colombo: Centre for Policy Alternatives, pp 32–54

Coomaraswamy, Radhika and Charmaine De los Reyes (2004) "Rule by Emergency: Sri Lanka's Postcolonial Constitutional Experience" *I.CON* 2(2): 272–295

De Alwis, Malathi (1997) "The Production and Embodiment of Respectability: Gendered Demeanours in Colonial Ceylon" In *Sri Lanka: Collective Identities Revisited* Michael Roberts (ed) Colombo: Marga Institute, Volume 1, pp 105–143

De Alwis, Malathi (2002) "'Housewives of the public': The Cultural Signification of the Sri Lankan Nation" In *Crossing Borders and Shifting Boundaries: Gender, Identities and Networks* Ilse Lenz, Helma Lutz, Mirjana Morokvasic, Claudia Schöning-Kalender and Helen Schwenken (eds) New York: Springer, pp 19–38

De Alwis, Malathi (2009) "Postnational Location as Political Practice" *Economic & Political Weekly* (7 March). Accessed on 25 March 2023. Available at https://www.epw.in/journal/2009/10/postnational-condition-special-issues-specials/postnational-location-political

De Mel, Neloufer (1996) "Metaphors of Women in Sri Lankan War Poetry" In *Embodied Violence: Communalising Women's Sexuality in South Asia* Kumari Jayawardena and Malathi de Alwis (eds) London: Zed Books, pp 168–189

De Mel, Neloufer (2001) *Women & the Nation's Narrative: Gender and Nationalism in Twentieth Century Sri Lanka* Lanham, MD: Rowman & Littlefield

De Mel, Neloufer (2007) *Militarizing Sri Lanka: Popular Culture, Memory and Narrative in the Armed Conflict* Delhi: Sage Publications

De Mel, Neloufer and Danushka Medawatte (2021) "Rural Women and Their Access to the Law: Gendering the Promise of Post-war Justice" In *In the Shadow of Transitional Justice* Guy Elcheroth and Neloufer de Mel (eds) London: Routledge, pp 125–137

De Silva, K.M. (1997) "Resistance Movements in Nineteenth Century Sri Lanka" In *Sri Lanka: Collective Identities Revisited* M. Roberts (ed) Colombo: Marga Institute, pp 145–164

De Silva, K.M. (2000) *Reaping the Whirlwind: Ethnic Conflict, Ethnic Politics in Sri Lanka* London: Penguin Books

De Votta, Neil (2002) "Illiberalism and Ethnic Conflict in Sri Lanka" *Journal of Democracy* 13(1): 84–98

De Votta, Neil (2014) "Parties, Political Decay, and Democratic Regression in Sri Lanka" *Commonwealth & Comparative Politics* 52(1): 139–165

De Votta, Neil (2017) "Civil War and the Quest for Transitional Justice in Sri Lanka" *Asian Security* 13(1): 74–79

Dewasiri, Nirmal Ranjith (2020) "Sri Lanka: The Buddhisization of Politics in the Sinhala-South" In *Religion and Politics in South Asia* Riaz Ali (ed) London: Routledge, Chapter 8

Dunham, David and Sisira Jayasuriya (2001) *Liberalisation and Political Decay: Sri Lanka's Journey from Welfare State to a Brutalised Society* The Hague, Netherlands: Institute of Social Studies

Fonseka, Bhavani, Luwie Ganeshathasan and Asanga Welikala (2021) "Sri Lanka: Pandemic-Catalyzed Democratic Backsliding" In *Covid-19 in Asia: Law and Policy Contexts* V.V. Ramraj (ed) Oxford: Oxford University Press, pp 349–362

Gamage, Rajni (2021) "Buddhist Nationalism, Authoritarian Populism, and the Muslim Other in Sri Lanka" *Islamophobia Studies Journal* 6(2): 130–149

Gomez, Mario (2022) "Constitutional Struggle in Sri Lanka" *Federal Law Review* 50(2): 174–191

Goodhand, Jonathan (2013) "Sri Lanka in 2012: Securing the State, Enforcing the "peace"" *Asian Survey* 53(1): 64–72

Goonewardene, Kanishka (2020) "Populism, Nationalism and Marxism in Sri Lanka: From Anti-Colonial Struggle to Authoritarian Neoliberalism" *Geografiska Annaler: Series B, Human Geography* 102(3): 289–304

Grant, Trevor (2014) *Sri Lanka's Secrets: How the Rajapaksa Regime Gets Away with Murder* Melbourne: Monash University Publishing

Gunasekara, Tisaranee (2013) "Militarisation, Lankan Style" *Economic and Political Weekly* 48(7): 33–38

Gunasekara, Vagisha and Vijay K. Nagaraj (2019) "The Construction of the "responsible Woman": Structural Violence in Sri Lanka's Post-war Development Strategy" In *The Political Economy of Conflict and*

Violence against Women: Cases from the South Kumudini Samuel, Claire Slatter and Vagisha Gunasekara (eds) London: Bloomsbury Publishing, pp 29–57

Gunasinghe, Newton (1980) "Land Reform, Class Structure and the State in Sri Lanka: 1970–1977" *Journal of Social Studies* 9: 28–57

Gunasinghe, Newton (2004) "The Open Economy and Its Impact on Ethnic Relations in Sri Lanka" In *Economy, Culture, and Civil War in Sri Lanka* Deborah Winslow and Michael D. Woost (eds) Bloomington, IN: Indiana University Press, Chapter 4

Gunatilleke, Gehan (2018) "The Constitutional Practice of Ethno-Religious Violence in Sri Lanka" *Asian Journal of Comparative Law* 13(2): 359–387

Gunawardena, Devaka (2015) "Contradictions of the Sri Lankan State" *Economic & Political Weekly* 50(9): 56–62

Gunawardena, R.A.L.H. (1984) "The People of the Lion: Sinhala Consciousness in History and Historiography" In *Ethnicity and Social Change in Sri Lanka* (Papers presented at a seminar organised by the Social Scientists Association December 1979), Colombo: Social Scientists' Association, pp 1–53

Gunawardana, Samanthi J. (2013) "Rural Sinhalese Women, Nationalism and Narratives of Development in Sri Lanka's Post-war Political Economy" In *The Global Political Economy of the Household in Asia* Juanita Elias and Samanthi J. Gunawardana (eds) London: Palgrave Macmillan, pp 59–74

Haniffa, Farzana (2015) "Competing for Victim Status: Northern Muslims and the Ironies of Sri Lanka's Post-war Transition" *Stability: International Journal of Security and Development* 4(1), p.Art.21, https://doi.org/10.5334/sta.fj

Harris, Elizabeth (2006) *Theravada Buddhism and the British Encounter: Religious, Missionary and Colonial Experience in Nineteenth-Century Sri Lanka* London and New York, NY: Routledge

Hensman, Rohini (1992) "Feminism and Ethnic Nationalism in Sri Lanka" *Journal of Gender Studies* 1(4): 500–509

Hensman, Rohini (2010) "Sri Lanka Becomes a Dictatorship" *Economic and Political Weekly* 45(41), 41–46

Hewamanne, Sandhya (2009) "Duty Bound? Militarization, Romances, and New Spaces of Violence among Sri Lanka's Free Trade Zone Garment Factory Workers" *Cultural Dynamics* 21(2): 153–184

Höglund, Kristine (2019) "Testimony under Threat: Women's Voices and the Pursuit of Justice in Post-war Sri Lanka" *Human Rights Review* 20: 361–382

Holden, Lord (1939) *Ceylon* London: George Allen & Unwin Ltd

Hyndman, Jennifer and Malathi de Alwis (2004) "Bodies, Shrines, and Roads: Violence, (Im)mobility and Displacement in Sri Lanka" *Gender, Place & Culture* 11(4): 535–557

Ismail, Qadri (1992) "'Boys Will Be Boys': Gender and National Agency in Frantz Fanon and LTTE" *Economic and Political Weekly* 27(31/32): 1677–1679

Jayasinghe, Pasan (2021) "Hegemonic Populism: Sinhalese Buddhist Nationalist Populism in Contemporary Sri Lanka" In *Populism in Asian Democracies: Features, Structures, and Impacts* Sook Jong Lee, Chin-en Wu and Kaustuv Kanti Bandyopadhyay (eds) Leiden and Boston: Brill, pp 176–196

Jayawardena, Janaki (2002) *Cultural Construction of the 'Sinhala Woman' and Women's Lives in Post-Independence Sri Lanka*. (PhD). University of York

Jayawardena, Kumari (1986) *Feminism and Nationalism in the Third World* London: Zed Books Ltd

Jayawardena, Kumari (2002) *Nobodies to Somebodies: The Rise of the Colonial Bourgeoisie in Sri Lanka* London: Zed Books

Jayawardena, Kumari (2010) *Perpetual Ferment: Popular Revolts in Sri Lanka in the 18th and 19th Centuries* Colombo: Social Scientists' Association of Sri Lanka

Jayawardena, Kumari and Chulani Kodikara (2003) *Women and Governance: Sri Lanka* Colombo: International Centre for Ethnic Studies

Jayaweera, Swarna (1990) "European Women Educators under the British Colonial Administration in Sri Lanka" *Women's Studies International Forum* 13(4): 323–331

Jazeel, Tariq (2010) "Sri Lanka Inside-Out: Cyberspace and the Mediated Geographies of Political Engagement" *Contemporary South Asia* 18(4): 443–449

Jazeel, Tariq and Kanchana N. Ruwanpura (2009) "Dissent: Sri Lanka's New Minority?" [Guest editorial] *Political Geography* 28(7): 385–387. https://doi.org/10.1016/j.polgeo.2009.08.002

Jeganathan, Pradeep (2000) "A Space for Violence: Anthropology, Politics and the Location of a Sinhala Practice of Masculinity" *Subaltern Studies* 11: 37–65

Jeganathan, Pradeep and Qadri Ismail (eds) (1995) *Unmaking the Nation: The Politics of Identity and History in Modern Sri Lanka* Colombo: Social Scientists' Association, pp 137–157

Jegathesan, Mythri (2019) *Tea and Solidarity: Tamil Women and Work in Postwar Sri Lanka* Washington: University of Washington Press

Jupp, James (1978) *Sri Lanka—Third World Democracy* London: Frank Cass and Co

Kadirgamar, Ahilan (2013) "The Quest of Militarisation in Post-war Sri Lanka" *Economic and Political Weekly* 48(7): 42–46

Kearney, Robert N. and Janice Jiggins (1975) "The Ceylon Insurrection of 1971" *Journal of Commonwealth & Comparative Politics* 13(1): 40–64

Keerawella, Gamini (2013) *Post-war Sri Lanka: Is Peace a Hostage of the Military Victory? Dilemmas of Reconciliation, Ethnic Cohesion and Peace-Building* Colombo: International Centre for Ethnic Studies

Korf, Benedikt (2006) "Dining with Devils? Ethnographic Enquiries into the Conflict-Development Nexus in Sri Lanka" *Oxford Development Studies* 34(1): 47–64

Kurian, Rachel and Kumari Jayawardena (2014) *Persistent Patriarchy: Women Workers on Sri Lankan Plantations* Colombo: Social Scientists' Association

Ludowyk, Eevelyn Frederick Charles (1967). *The Story of Ceylon*. London: Faber

Lynch, Caitrin (1999) "The "good Girls" of Sri Lankan Modernity: Moral Orders of Nationalism and Capitalism" *Identities Global Studies in Culture and Power* 6(1): 55–89

Manor, James (1984) *Sri Lanka: In Change and Crisis* London and Sydney: Croom Helm

Matthews, Bruce (1982) "District Development Councils in Sri Lanka" *Asian Survey* 22(11): 1117–1134

Matthews, Bruce (2004) "Tightening Social Cohesion and Excluding 'others' among the Sinhalese" In *Sri Lanka in an Era of Globalization: Struggling to Create a New Social Order* S.H. Hasbullah and Barrie M. Morrison (eds) Delhi: Sage, Chapter 4

Minattur, Joseph (1982) "Emergency Powers in Sri Lanka, 1817–1959: A Historical Perspective" *Journal of the Indian Law Institute* 24(1): 57–83

Moore, Mick (1993) "Thoroughly Modern Revolutionaries: The JVP in Sri Lanka" *Modern Asian Studies* 27(3): 593–642

Obeyesekere, Gananath (1984) "The Origins and Institutionalisation of Political Violence" In *Sri Lanka in Change and Crisis* James Manor (ed) New York, NY: St. Martin's Press, pp 153–174

Peebles, Patrick (1990) "Colonization and Ethnic Conflict in the Dry Zone in Sri Lanka" *The Journal of Asian Studies* 49(1): 30–55

Peiris, Gerald H. (2000) "Insurrection and Youth Unrest in Sri Lanka" In *Millennium Perspectives – Essays in Honour of Kingsley de Silva* G.H. Pieris and S.W.R. de A. Samarasinghe (eds) Colombo: International Centre for Ethnic Studies

Perera, Nihal (2002) "Feminizing the city: Gender and Space in Colonial Colombo" In *Trans-Status Subjects: Genders in the Globalization of South and Southeast Asia* Durham, NC: Duke University Press, pp 67–87

Perera, Sasanka (1998) "Beyond the margins of a failed insurrection: The experiences of women in post-terror Southern Sri Lanka" *Edinburgh Papers in South Asian Studies*, No. 11

Perera, Sasanka (2016) *Warzone tourismTourism in Sri Lanka: Tales from darkerDarker placesPlaces in paradiseParadise*. Delhi: Sage Publishing

Pieris, Pradeep (2022) *Catch-All Parties and Party-Voter Nexus in Sri Lanka* Singapore: Palgrave Macmillan

Piyadasa, L. (1984) *Sri Lanka, the Holocaust and after* London: Marram Books

Ponnambalam, Satchi (1981) *Dependent Capitalism in Crisis: The Sri Lankan Economy, 1948–1980* London: Zed Press

Rajasingham-Senanayake, Darini (2011) "Lanka @ 63: The 'military business model' of post-war economic development" *Groundviews* (27 February). Accessed on 25 March 2023. Available at https://groundviews.org/2011/02/27/lanka-63-the-%e2%80%98military-business-model%e2%80%99-of-post-war-economic-development/

Rambukwella, Harshana (2018) *The Politics and Poetics of Authenticity: A Cultural Genealogy of Sinhala Nationalism* London: UCL Press

Rampton, David (2011) "'Deeper hegemony': The Politics of Sinhala Nationalist Authenticity and the Failures of Power-Sharing in Sri Lanka" *Commonwealth & Comparative Politics* 49(2): 245–273

Richardson, John (2005) *Paradise Poisoned: Learning About Conflict, Terrorism and Development from Sri Lanka's Civil Wars* Kandy: International Centre for Ethnic Studies

Risseeuw, Carla (1992) "Gender, Kinship and State Formation: Case of Sri Lanka under Colonial Rule" *Economic and Political Weekly* 27(43/44): WS46–WS54

Roberts, Michael (2015) "Mahinda Rajapaksa as a Modern Mahāvāsala and Font of Clemency? The Roots of Populist Authoritarianism" In *Reforming Sri Lankan Presidentialism: Provenance, Problems and Prospects* Asanga Welikala (ed) Colombo: Centre for Policy Alternatives, pp 642–655

Rogers, John D. (1987) "Social Mobility, Popular Ideology, and Collective Violence in Modern Sri Lanka" *The Journal of Asian Studies* 46(3): 583–602

Ruwanpura, Kanchana N. (2006) *Matrilineal Communities, Patriarchal Realities: A Feminist Nirvana Uncovered* Ann Arbor, MI: University of Michigan Press

Ruwanpura, Kanchana N. (2017) "Militarized Capitalism? The Apparel Industry's Role in Scripting a Post-war National Identity in Sri Lanka" *Antipode* 50(2): 425–446

Ruwanpura, Kanchana N. (2022) *Garments without Guilt? Global Labour Justice and Ethical Codes in Sri Lankan Apparels* Cambridge: Cambridge University Press

Rycroft, Daniel J. (2006) *Representing Rebellion: Visual Aspects of Counter-Insurgency in Colonial India* Oxford: Oxford University Press

Samararatne, Dinesha, Karen Soldaic and Binendri Perera (2018) *Out of the Shadows: War-Affected Women with Disabilities in Sri Lanka* Sydney: Western Sydney University

Saravanamuttu, Paikiasothy (2014) "Deepening Democratic Structure in Sri Lanka" In *Democracy, Sustainable Development, and Peace: New Perspectives on South Asia* Akmal Hussain and Muchkund Dubey (eds) Oxford: Oxford University Press, Chapter 5

Satkunanathan, Ambika (2015) "The Executive and the Shadow State in Sri Lanka" In *Reforming Sri Lankan Presidentialism: Provenance, Problems and Prospects* Asanga Welikala (ed) Colombo: Centre for Policy Alternatives, pp 371–398

Satkunanathan, Ambika (2018) "Sri Lanka: The Impact of Militarization on Women" In *The Oxford Handbook of Gender and Conflict Fionnuala Ní Aoláin* Naomi Cahn, Dina Francesca Haynes and Nahla Valji (eds) Oxford: Oxford University Press, Chapter 45

Senaratne, Kalana (2019) "The Executive and the Constitutional Reforms Process in Sri Lanka" *The Round Table* 108(6): 625–638

Seoighe, Rachel (2018) "Nationalistic Authorship and Resistance: Performative Politics in Post-war Northeastern Sri Lanka" In *Culture and Politics in South Asia: Performative Communication* Dev Nath Pathak and Sasanka Perera (eds) London and New York, NY: Routledge, Chapter 4

Silva, Neluka (1997) "'Mothers, Daughters and "Whores" of the Nation': Nationalism and Female Stereotypes in Post-Colonial Sri Lankan Drama in English" *Journal of Gender Studies* 6(3): 269–276

Sivanandan, Ambalavaner (1984) "Sri Lanka: Racism and the Politics of Underdevelopment" *Race & Class* XXVI(1): 1–37

Sivasundaram, Sujit (2018) "Cosmopolitanism and Indigeneity in Four Violent Years: The Fall of the Kingdom of Kandy and the Great Rebellion Revisited" In *Sri Lanka at the Crossroads of History Zoltán Biedermann and Alan Strathern* (eds) London: UCL Press, pp 194–215

Spencer, Jonathan (2008) "A Nationalism without Politics? The Illiberal Consequences of Liberal Institutions in Sri Lanka" *Third World Quarterly* 29(3): 611–629

Spencer, Jonathan (2016) "Securitization and Its Discontents: The End of Sri Lanka's Long Post-war?" *Contemporary South Asia* 24(1): 94–108

Stokke, Kristian (1997) "Authoritarianism in the Age of Market Liberalism in Sri Lanka" *Antipode* 29(4): 437–455

Stokke, Kristian and Jayadeva Uyangoda (2011) *Liberal Peace in Question: Politics of State and Market Reform in Sri Lanka* London: Anthem Press

Tambiah, Stanley J. (1992) *Buddhism Betrayed? Religion, Politics, and Violence in Sri Lanka* Chicago, IL: University of Chicago Press

Tambiah, Stanley J. (1996) *Leveling Crowds: Ethnonationalist Conflicts and Collective Violence in South Asia* Chicago, IL: University of Chicago Press

Tambiah, Yasmin (2004) "Sexuality and Women's Rights in Armed Conflict in Sri Lanka" *Reproductive Health Matters* 12(23): 78–87

Tennekoon, Serena N. (1988) "Rituals of Development: The Accelerated Mahaveli Development Program of Sri Lanka" *American Ethnologist* 15(2): 294–310

Thiranagama, Sharika (2011) *In My Mother's House: Civil War in Sri Lanka* Pennsylvania, PA: University of Pennsylvania Press

Udagama, Deepika (2015) "An Eager Embrace: Emergency Rule and Authoritarianism in Republican Sri Lanka" In *Reforming Sri Lankan Presidentialism: Provenance, Problems and Prospects* Asanga Welikala (ed) Colombo: Centre for Policy Alternatives, pp 286–332

Uyangoda, Jayadeva (2011) "Sri Lanka in 2010: Regime Consolidation in a Post-Civil War Era" *Asian Survey* 51(1): 131–137

Uyangoda, Jayadeva and Sunil Bastian (2008) *State Responsiveness to Public Security Needs: The Politics of Security Decision-Making* London: King's College London

Venugopal, Rajesh (2018) *Nationalism, Development and Ethnic Conflict in Sri Lanka* Cambridge: Cambridge University Press

Wedegedara, Amali (2023) "'Community-led development: Solution for microfinance crisis'" Retrieved from https://www.themorning.lk/articles/lo7MbwbxYRMumhKIksgD

Welikala, Asanga (2015) "Nation, State, Sovereignty, and Kingship: The pre-Modern Antecedents of the Presidential State" In *Reforming Sri Lankan Presidentialism: Provenance, Problems and Prospects* Asanga Welikala (ed) Colombo: Centre for Policy Alternatives, pp 499–546

Whetstone, Crystal (2020) **Nurturing democracy in armed conflicts through political motherhood: A comparative study of women's political participation in Argentina and Sri Lanka**. (PhD). University of Cincinnati

Wickramasinghe, Nira (2009) "Many Little Revolts or One Rebellion? The Maritime Provinces of Ceylon/Sri Lanka between 1796 and 1800" *South Asia: Journal of South Asian Studies* 32(2): 170–188

Wickramasinghe, Nira (2020) *Slave in a Palanquin: Colonial Servitude and Resistance in Sri Lanka* New York, NY: Columbia University Press

Wijesinha, Rajiva (2007) *Declining Sri Lanka: Terrorism and Ethnic Conflict* New Delhi: CUP

Wilson, A. Jeyaratnam (1988) *The Break-up of Sri Lanka: The Sinhalese-Tamil Conflict* London: C. Hurst & Company

Wilson, James (2016) "Reappropriation, Resistance, and British Autocracy in Sri Lanka, 1820–1850" *The Historical Journal* 60(1): 47–69

Winslow, Deborah and Michael D. Woost (eds) (2004) *Economy, Culture, and Civil War in Sri Lanka* Bloomington, IN: Indiana University Press

Woost, Michael D. (1993) "Nationalising the Local Past in Sri Lanka: Histories of Nation and Development in a Sinhalese Village" *American Ethnologist* 20(3): 502–521

3
NATIONALISM, CONFLICT, AND POWER-SHARING

Bart Klem

Introduction

Sri Lankan nationalism features predominantly as an absent presence in the scholarship on identity politics and conflict in Sri Lanka. Arguably, the island's modern history has not yielded an all-Sri Lankan sense of nation. To the degree that a "national" or "civic" nationalism has taken root in Sri Lanka, it has always remained a feeble contender to ethnic or ethno-religious manifestations of nationalism. What is sometimes presented as Sri Lankan nationalism is by and large an articulation of *Sinhala* nationalism or – more particular yet – Sinhala-*Buddhist* nationalism. This political orientation is then rivalled by ethnic minority stances, most obviously Tamil nationalism, but also Muslim ethnic chauvinism. In addition, these ethnic orientations become embroiled with Leftist ideologies as well as different forms of Buddhist, Islamic, Hindu, and Christian revivalism. The lines between nation, race, ethnicity, religious group, language community, and other social identity categories, such as caste and class, can be quite blurry and there tends to be some slippage between the different labels.

Given the difficulty of establishing clear boundaries around ethnonationalism and conflict – and the formidable tradition of scholarship on these issues – this chapter is at risk of embarking on an elusive pursuit of crafting a comprehensive overview, thus sacrificing a coherent analytical narrative. I have sought to grapple with this by condensing the vast established literature on the civil war and its prior history into the first section. The subsequent sections then discuss literature that has emerged after the 2009 end of the war. In short, I will review: new retrospective analyses of the war; recent scholarship on the Sri Lankan constitution and democratic backsliding; the writing on post-war ethnic subjectivity and contested memorial practices; religious revivalism and the ascendence of extremist political Buddhism; and reflections on the influence of the COVID-19 pandemic on these dynamics.[1]

Nationalism, Conflict, and Constitutional Order

The contested and contingent delineations of ethnicity and ethnonationalism match well with the constructivist perspective that prevails in the academic literature. To be Sinhala, Tamil, Muslim, or part of another group, so the reasoning goes, is not about having a set of essential characteristics but being part of a lived reality of producing and reproducing collective identities (Abeysekere and Gunasinghe 1987; Rogers 1994; Wickramasinghe 2006; Rasaratnam 2016). Ethnicity is the central element for the two main competing ideologies in Sri Lanka – Sinhala nationalism and Tamil nationalism – but ethnicity it is itself heavily shaped by political contestation (Spencer 2008; Uyangoda 2011). It has become entangled with conflict, both with the Leftist uprisings of the Janatha Vimukthi Peramuna (JVP) of the 1970s and 1980s and with the Tamil separatist conflict (Chandraprema 1991; Moore 1993; Wickramasinghe 2006; Uyangoda 2011). Ethnic identity, in short, features as both cause and consequence of conflict. And ethnicized accounts of history are as much the result of the present conflict as the other way around (Hellmann-Rajanayagam 1994a; Wickramasinghe 2013; Harris 2018).

The dominant academic diagnosis of Sri Lanka's ethnopolitical conflict centres on the problem of state formation combined with the throes of ethnic majoritarianism in a democratic arena (Spencer 2007; Uyangoda 2011; Venugopal 2018). Unlike most of its neighbours, Sri Lanka transitioned out of the colonial era through a sequence of deliberative constitutional reforms, which yielded a unitary democratic state and a Sinhala majority community that sought to redress the perceived privileges of the Tamil minority and the anglicized elite (De Silva 2005; Wickramasinghe 2006). The subsequent electoral dynamic of "ethnic outbidding" to vie for Sinhalese votes resulted in majoritarian state measures: redrafting of the constitution, pro-Sinhala language policy, affirmative action in education and state employment, land allocation programmes for the Sinhala peasantry, and a range of symbolically charged measures protecting Sri Lanka's supposed cultural character – a purportedly Sinhala-Buddhist island imperilled by a region and a world dominated by Christianity, Islam, and Hinduism (Rogers 1994; Wilson 2000; De Votta 2004; De Silva 2005; Schonthal 2016a).

In the mid-19th century Tamil identity had been premised on caste (the land-owning Vellalas), religion (Saivism), and language (Tamil), not (yet) on being part of an ethnic group or a nation (Arasaratnam 1994; Cheran 2009). In the dynamic of post-Independence ethnic politics, Tamil identity coalesced around Tamil ethnonationalism. Yet, when a political campaign for the advancement of Tamil rights and aspirations gathered pace in late colonial and early postcolonial times, the precise demarcation of the Tamil collective remained contentious (Wickramasinghe 2006; Cheran 2009; Vaitheespara 2009). At its narrowest, it effectively catered to the Vellala elite in Jaffna and Colombo; at its broadest it encompassed not only the category now known as Sri Lankan Tamils but all Tamil-speaking populations, thus including the Muslims (historically considered "Islamic Tamils") and Tamils of recent Indian origin (often referred to as "Indian", "Plantation", or "Upcountry" Tamils).

The ethno-political conflict then escalated in the 1970s. The Tamil parliamentarian leadership adopted an explicitly separatist position and a welter of armed youth militias sprung up (Wilson 2000). Prompted by the anti-Tamil pogroms of 1983, political violence intensified in the 1980s (Tambiah 1996; Bremner 2004; Spencer 2007). In this decade, the Liberation Tigers of Tamil Eelam (LTTE) coercively positioned itself as the dominant Tamil movement (Hellmann-Rajanayagam 1994b, 1994c; Wilson 2000; Thiranagama 2011). A sequence of peace attempts and military re-escalations finally resulted in the comprehensive military defeat of the LTTE, and the Tamil nationalist movement more widely, in 2009.

Matching the diagnosis of the ethno-political conflict as a problem of a majoritarian state, the focus of Sri Lanka's conflict resolution literature has long rested on constitutional reform, regional autonomy, and democratic power-sharing (Bastian 1994; Thiruchelvam 2000; Coomaraswamy 2003; Welikala 2012; Wickramaratne 2014: 137–250). The central keyword in this debate is: devolution, a term signalling a shift of state power from the national to the sub-national level to accommodate divergent ethnic aspirations. Scholars have grappled with the parameters of devolution – the unit (the whole northeast or smaller entities), the degree (regional self-government or merely decentralizing public service provision), and the question of symmetry (a uniform island-wide system or a special arrangement for the northeast) – as well as the legal status of a power-sharing arrangement (an interim arrangement, an act of parliament, or a constitutional settlement), which affects its credibility and robustness.

Sri Lanka has had a turbulent constitutional history. The 1931 Donoughmore constitution, a British imposition based on limited consultation, steered clear of regional or ethnic power-sharing (Edirisinha et al 2008: 54–97). The 1947 Soulbury that enshrined independence bolstered the unitary character of the state, though it encoded of minority protection in a clause known as Section 29 (Edirisinha et al 2008: 128–204; Welikala 2012). Subsequent bargaining between Sinhala and Tamil elites yielded compromise solutions that remained unimplemented (Wilson 2000; Edirisinha et al 2008). The 1972 Republican constitution, which was established despite explicit protest from the Tamil leadership, expanded executive prerogatives at the centre and corroborated Sinhala nationalist aspirations by affording a "foremost place" to Buddhism. The second Republican constitution (1978) endowed Sri Lanka with an exceptionally powerful executive presidency and a change-resistant electoral system.

The 1987 Indo-Lankan Accord comprises the historical counter-cadence to this gradual centralization of power. India's military intervention, legitimized with a self-assigned role as regional hegemon and guardian of Sri Lanka's Tamil minority, coerced a constitutional amendment that implanted quasi-autonomous provincial governance into an otherwise unitary constitution with an enormous central concentration of executive power. However, this 13th Amendment constrained and fudged key issues, and the ability of the provincial council system to enact a meaningful form of self-government was thwarted by subsequent administrative concoctions, and legal hoodwinking (Shastri 1990; Coomaraswamy 1994; Thiruchelvam 2000). As a result, Sri Lanka has emerged from the war with a system of devolved government that none of the belligerents want, but that it cannot get rid of without incurring India's wrath and unleashing a constitutional quandary over subsequent reforms.

Revisiting the Historiography of Ethno-Political Conflict

Some of the most insightful work on the armed conflict has appeared after the end of the war. Complementing the prior scholarship, recent works have shed unprecedented light on lived realities during the war. This includes the publication of diaries and authors revisiting their old field notes to produce ethnographically informed historical work (Bavinck 2011; Harris 2018, 2019). This has also yielded new conceptual interpretations of the Tamil militancy, most saliently Thiranagama's (2011) *In My Mother's House*. She offers a retrospective study of Tamil and Muslim subjectivity through the experience of conflict and war, thus problematizing the canonical tendencies in the existing historiography of the Tamil separatist conflict. Thiranagama unsettles the categories, phases, and key actors of the established analytical framework. She highlights how the experience of being Tamil or Muslim has transformed through the war years and how ethno-political narratives became entangled with a welter of social contentions around generation, caste, class, locality, and ideology. "War" Thiranagama posits (2011), "grounds life even as it takes it away – producing new people, new possibilities of voice, forms of heroism" (2011: 12). This becomes especially clear in relation to young Tamils who joined one of the militant groups. Alongside their separatist fervour, she highlights the sociological significance of escaping the confines of caste, gender, and gerontocracy of Tamil family life. The militancy, she argues, offered an alternative "horizontal form of kinship" (2011: 198).

A related body of work has ventured to study the LTTE state-making experiment of the 1990s and 2000s, a known phenomenon that had not previously received detailed empirical or theoretical attention (Mampilly 2011; Terpstra and Frerks 2017). Klem and Maunaguru (2017, 2018) posit that the creation of a de facto Tamil Eelam with a demarcated territory, population, an expanding array of LTTE departments and the co-optation of existing institutions as well as legal frameworks must be understood as a form of "sovereign mimicry". In pursuit of its separatist aspirations, the movement started crafting an institutional landscape that people could recognize as state-like, but these institutions always remained capricious. The god-like cult around the LTTE leader and his ability to change the rules or unleash sublime violence never let off, and the movement adulated the violent sacrifice of martyrs, and suicide cadres (see also Schonthal 2018). These commemorative practices, cemeteries, and transcendental depiction stood in sharp contrast to the movement's attempt to emulate secular state conduct with bureaucratic finesse but simultaneously compounded its enigma (Klem and Maunaguru 2017).

The religious dimensions of nationalist conflict in Sri Lanka have long been recognized, particularly in relation to the complex interface between Buddhism and Sinhala nationalism (Senivaratne 2000). The role of religious institutions and leaders in the multifarious landscape of the war received much less attention, but this aspect has received closer scrutiny in recent years (Klem 2011; Spencer et al 2015; Maunaguru 2018; Johnson and Korf 2021). The religious sphere, these authors point out, may afford a measure of insulation from politics and thus some form, however minimal, of protection against political violence. Churches become spaces of refuge, Hindu oracles offer transcendental forms of solace, mosque societies become humanitarian advocates, and inter-religious bodies reach out across ethnic and military fault lines. It also becomes clear that there are vast differences between religions and their many sub-dominations in terms of their institutional set-up and the kinds of leadership they spawn.

Taking issue with the simplified interpretation of the war as a bipolar conflict between Sinhala-dominated government and a Tamil insurgency, there has also been renewed interest for protagonists that eschew such categories. This includes ground-breaking work on the figure of the so-called traitor. Thiranagama (2011) highlights the discursive significance of traitors to ethno-nationalist repertoires of legitimating violence. She points out that traitors, unlike enemies, are defined by intimacy. It is their personal relationships and their intimate knowledge that makes them both dangerous and hard to identify, and it is this familiarity that warrants exceptional kinds of violence (Thiranagama 2010). The relentless and profoundly disturbing consequences to the lives of these outcasts and their family – in Sri Lanka and in exile, at the moment of rupture and for decades after – reverberate in the public consciousness, not least through literary writing that grapples with the "unnarratable" lived impact of these social fissures (Satkunanathan 2016; Kailasam 2021).

Dissenting voices do not only challenge the seam-sealed narratives of dominant political protagonists. They also bring into purview the historical contingencies and the messy chain of events that occurred before retrospective interpretations tidied up dominant historical narratives. They remind us how things could have been different, how one master cleavage prevailed over another, how one set of injustices gave birth to the next, and how heroes and saviours may transform into villains or henchmen. As part of a volume on dissidents, recent contributions reflected on the life stories of Joe Senivaratne (Amarasuriya and Spencer 2021), "Ranjan" and "Murali"– remarkable Sri Lankans who defy straightforward categorization, precisely because they resisted the rubrics that have come to be central to the established conflict script (Maunaguru 2021). And as such, they caution us to revisit the contingent origins of ethnonationalism and political violence and engage with the interstitial space between ethnic communities, the peculiar morphing of Leftist revolutionary energy into two disparate ethnonational uprisings and the complex symbiosis of violence and justice.

Scuttled Constitutionalism and Illiberal Democracy

For readers interested in Sri Lanka's long history of demanding and debating different constitutional and political models to mitigate ethnonationalist conflict, the volume by Edirisinha et al (2008) offers an unrivalled repository. It encompasses a meticulous archive of all major manifestos, proposals, and pacts since the 1920s (some of which have become difficult to trace) and curates these with commentaries to attend the reader to the finer nuances, revisions, and omissions placed within the political context of the time.

Constitutional scholarship, though less established in Sri Lanka than elsewhere in South Asia, has burgeoned in recent years. Combining insights from legal theory, the troubled interface between constitutional law and ethno-nationalist politics, and the everyday realities of legal and administrative practices, this literature has reached a degree of consensus about the key strengths, weaknesses, and unresolved dilemmas in Sri Lanka's constitutional order. *The Sri Lankan Republic at 40* comprises a comprehensive anthology of Sri Lanka's constitutional antecedents since the first Republican Constitution of 1972 (Welikala 2012). Apart from enlisting problematic issues, the volume offers insider accounts of the promulgation of different constitutional texts as well as theoretical engagement with the tensions and paradoxes around a constitutional architecture for plural democratic politics, the safeguarding of fundamental rights, the interface between law and religion, and the legal codification of shared sovereignty in a pluri-national society. It also highlights the peculiar rifts between constitutional design and empirical realities, which often diverge from the intended outcomes. For example, the constitutional clauses aimed at protecting Buddhism have arguably precipitated new forms of conflict *within* the Buddhist community about the correct interpretation and delineation of Buddhism and exposed new tensions in the uneasy relationship between Buddhism and politics (Schonthal 2016c).

Complementing these constitutional reflections, a joint effort by the Institute for Constitutional Studies provides a more focused analysis of the 13th Amendment and the resulting experiment of power-sharing through devolved government (Amarasinghe et al. 2019). The volume reviews the evolution of the one power-sharing arrangement that was implemented in Sri Lanka: the provincial council system, created under Indian duress in the late 1980s. The authors suggest that this system is reminiscent of a "white elephant": an impractical gift that one cannot refuse, which then leaves the recipient with a string of hazards and disfunctions. With focused essays on oft-ignored aspects, such as the compromised legislative and fiscal prerogatives of the provinces, the authors reveal the many ironies manifest in Sri Lanka's experience with devolved government. The system was created for the northeast but mostly worked in the rest of country because the North-Eastern Provincial Council was placed on hold for most of its history. Also, what was created as an explicitly political platform to assuage demands for self-government degenerated into an administrative layer within a centralized pyramid of government resource distribution.

While the contributions to the above volumes zoom in on meticulous details, a growing body of comparative work zooms out to establish overall patterns. Several initiatives scrutinized broader Asian (or global) trends to glean comparative lessons about constitutional design, power-sharing and federalism, electoral systems, or post-war settlements (Shah 2017; Breen 2018; O'Driscoll, Costantini and Al 2020). Rather adding new empirical insight about Sri Lanka, these volumes draw on contrasting experiences elsewhere to generate questions about the island's legal and political history and possible alternative trajectories.

The increased centralization of executive power under the Rajapaksa government after the 2009 defeat of the LTTE has received ample scholarly attention. The prevalent interpretation centres on the notion of victor's peace, which yielded an illiberal democratic settlement, where an initially high degree of electoral support was coupled with an increasingly authoritarian form of government (Ruwanpura 2016; Keethaponcalan 2019; Lewis 2020). In effect, De Votta (2021) argues, Sri Lanka has become an "ethnocracy": a system where resilient democratic institutions coexist with Sinhala-Buddhist majoritarianism. The further strengthening of presidential power through the 18th Amendment, the erosion of the independent judiciary, the shrinking space for media scrutiny, the militarized approach to post-war reconstruction and urban planning and the problems around patronage politics and corruption have all been well publicized (Satkunanathan 2016; Spencer 2016; Klem 2018).

The "good governance" government under President Sirisena was an interlude to these dynamics. The spectacular rise of this rainbow coalition in 2015 was followed by an even more spectacular collapse in 2018, through what has been coined "auto-coup", which then precipitated a constitutional crisis with an absurd constellation of two parallel claimants to the position of Prime Minister (Welikala 2020). Though the coup was curbed, the government never recovered from its sundering impact. Official consultations about a new constitutional settlement, which had raised high hopes in the early days of Sirisena's government, were side-tracked, but they gave impetus to the continued academic debate about fundamental constitutional issues in Sri Lanka. These are perhaps best captured in a special issue in the *Round Table*, with reflections on the abolishment of the executive presidency, the constitutional classification of the state itself, the creation of a Bill of Rights, and the implementation of the Right to Information Act (Jayasinghe 2019; Rajasingham 2019; Samararatne 2019; Senaratne 2019; Welikala 2019).

Post-War Transition and Rearticulated Subjectivity

The May 2009 defeat of the LTTE in the northern scrublands of Mullivaikal marks a pivotal turning point in Sri Lanka's modern history, arguably even surpassing independence. It fundamentally reshaped Sri Lanka's ethno-national conflict, it recalibrated the state and the political arena, and it had enduring impact on Sri Lankan society and the global expanse of its diaspora. Tamil nationalism lost its recourse to coercive authority, and the humanitarian massacre in the final months of the war left indelible scars in the social and political fabric of Tamil society. While there is no credible doubt about the large numbers of civilians who were trapped, targeted, and killed, as a result of blatant violations of humanitarian law by both sides, controversies remain over the exact sequence of events and their interpretation (University Teachers for Human Rights (Jaffna) 2009; Weiss 2011; Harrison 2012). Demands for further investigation and retribution – typically referred to with the euphemistic term accountability – have not let off.

Post-war memorial practices and politics also have received ample scholarly attention. In the Tamil community, not least in its diaspora networks, Mullivaikal has become a central reference point for Tamil subjectivity. The experience of defeat and victimhood, widely referred to as genocide among Tamil nationalists, now defines what it means to be part of the Tamil nation and share its disabled aspirations (Amarasingam 2015; McCargo and Senaratne 2020; Orjuela 2021; Thurairajah 2021). This is manifest in struggles over war memorials and the ceremonial commemoration of victims, heroes, and martyrs (Satkunanathan 2016; Seoighe 2017). It is also evident in Tamil political manifestos and in the repertoires of Tamil activism to vie for international attention and redress, such as in the UN Human Rights Council (Thurairajah 2020).

Post-war transition comprises a disorienting process of societal recalibration, where boundaries are redrawn, new connections are made and intensified circulation and exposure create both opportunities and anxieties (Klem 2014, 2018; Ruwanpura et al 2020). Arguably, the heightened moral stakes of defining the Tamil community and the demise of the LTTE as the despotic self-asserted custodian of the Tamil struggle have instigated renewed animosity over *intra*-Tamil divisions. This includes struggles over gender norms, adequate youth conduct and gerontocratic hierarchies, but it is perhaps most palatable in the renewed vigour of disputes over caste hierarchies. Following suit with other Tamil militant groups, the LTTE had embraced a modern revolutionary outlook that rejected caste but the group simultaneously harnessed Tamil cultural tradition and never persisted in eradicating the caste system. After their defeat, caste-based discrimination and associated rivalry over land claims, water use, temple boards, and social hierarchies came back out in the open, in both old and new ways (Thanges 2008; Silva, Sivapragasam and Thanges 2009; Bremner 2013; Kuganathan 2014; Thiranagama 2018; Silva 2020).

The Ascendence of Political Buddhism and Anti-Muslim Violence

The end of the war gave renewed impetus to religious revival movements in all the island's communities. Space opened for Pentecostal churches to intensify their proselytization; Sufi sects and moderate Islamic movements like Tableegh Jamaath lost ground to more radical groups, like Tawheed Jamaath; and the Hindu community experienced increased exposure to extremist influences and right-wing groups from India (Woods 2013; Mahadev 2015; Spencer et al 2015; Bastian 2016). Among these revivals, the ascendence Buddhist extremist was most pronounced because it conjoined with the radical Sinhala nationalist outlook of the Rajapaksa government. The phenomenon of political Buddhism, long spurned as inherently transgressive, transformed into a formidable electoral force, both within Jathika Hela Urumaya (JHU), a party of Buddhist monks, and among acolytes of the Rajapaksa government (Deegalle 2004; Holt 2016a; Lehr 2019). These trends contributed to a significant rearticulation of Sri Lanka's landscape of communal conflict: to some degree the ethno-*national* conflict morphed into an inter-*religious* conflict, and in the process the Muslim community replaced the Tamils as the primary antagonist for Sinhala-Buddhist majoritarianism (Haniffa 2015; Spencer et al 2015; Holt 2016b; Silva 2016; Mahadev 2019).

The delineation of the Muslim community as an ethnic group reflects the convolutions of national, linguistic, ethnic, and religious identities in Sri Lanka. Historically, they were a religious group that largely overlapped with the Tamil community in terms of language and cultural custom, but after the soaring of Sinhala and Tamil ethnonationalism (with the LTTE violence against Muslims and the 1990 Muslim "eviction" from the north as the definitive breakpoint) the Islamic community increasingly defined itself as a distinct ethnic group (McGilvray and Raheem 2007; Mihlar 2019). This resulted in the emergence of a distinct ethno-nationalist outlook and concurrent political parties, but these groups have invariably served as kingmakers in the national government to secure a measure of influence and access to patronage (Klem 2011; Spencer et al 2015). With the rise of Buddhist extremism in recent years, however, the widely felt anxieties among Muslims have put this pragmatic positioning under increased strain (Mihlar 2019).

Sinhala-Buddhist extremism has been spearheaded by the rise of Bodu Bala Sena (BBS), a militant group that vilifies Sri Lanka's minorities and the Muslim community in particular. Several authors have pointed to the similarities with anti-Muslim Buddhist movements in Myanmar (Holt 2016a; Lehr 2019; Orjuela 2020). BBS uses hate speech and rumours on social media, it advocates a boycott of Muslim shops, and it agitates against Halal certification, Islamic veiling, slaughter practices, and the status of customary Islamic law (Silva 2016). The group is known for its ability to instigate violence and deploy vigilante style thuggery. It incited attacks on Muslims in a sequence of skirmishes that reminded of Sri Lanka's pre-war riots and pogroms, including in Aluthgama in 2014 and Digana in 2018 (Haniffa 2016; Fowsar, Rameez and Rameez 2020). In both cases, the government and police stood accused of idling and condoning these escalations. Among many smaller disputes over places of worship, the *azan* (call for prayer), land claims and newly erected Buddha statues, Buddhist extremism precipitated heated tensions around the Daftar Jailani shrine (a Sufi pilgrimage site), the Dambulla mosque, a string of Buddhist sites along the east coast, as well as a complete military take-over and Buddhification of Kantadorai, a multi-religious but historically predominantly Tamil site in Jaffna (Heslop 2014; Spencer et al 2015; McGilvray 2016; McGilvray 2016; Schonthal 2016b; Harris 2019).

Several authors have explored the gendered nature of religious revivalism, purification agendas, and inter-religious conflict (Haniffa 2008, 2020; Malji 2021). Religious narratives have become entangled with notions of male virility, female chastity, and the policing of gendered dress, conduct, and piety. Protagonists on all sides have depicted women as custodians of tradition who are in special need of protection, spawning agitation around marriage-related conversion, fertility, and concurrent apprehension over forthcoming demographic shifts. This has added a patriarchal, arguably even misogynist, tinge to religious dispute, and plausibly it has also given rise to a more wide-ranging conservative impact on Sri Lanka's historically egalitarian gender disposition.

The dynamics of Islamophobia, religious conflict, post-war militarization, economic downturn, and constitutional crisis converged in the dramatic tragedy of the Easter Sunday suicide bomb attacks in 2019. This coordinated attack by an extremist Muslim outfit on churches and hotels killed over 250 people and sparked international alert. A previously little-known group National Tawheed Jamaath claimed responsibility for the bombings. Islamic State, facing defeat in the Middle East, vied to take credit with the unsubstantiated assertion that the bombers were operating in their name and with their support (Amarasingam 2019; Imtiyaz 2020). The crisis was aggravated by the ineptitude of the government to act on available prior intelligence, which was in turn caused by the fracturing within Sirisena's government after his auto-coup several months earlier (Welikala 2019). As a result of these dramatic events, the Tawheed movement, which had hitherto been a marginal subject of study (Spencer et al 2015; Mihlar 2019), suddenly stood in the spotlights for a raft of blog authors, pundits, terrorism experts, and other scholars. Though readily interpreted in transnational terms, as a new terrorist juncture conjoining Sri Lanka's conflict pathology with a globalized Islamist discourse (Amarasingam 2019; Imtiyaz 2020; Mahoharan, Chatterjee and Ashok 2021), the Easter attacks thus far appear to be a historical outlier. No escalating dynamic of asymmetrical violence occurred, but the securitized political blowback of the event has had severe adverse effects for the Muslim community and arguably for Sri Lanka at large (Haniffa 2020).

The Political Dynamics of the Covid-19 Pandemic

In loose reminiscence to the social and political turmoil after the 2004 tsunami (McGilvray and Gamburd 2010), the pandemic has become a lightning rod for pre-existing societal anxieties, tensions, and trends. Many of the above-described dynamics around ethno-nationalism, post-war conflict, and state conduct have become rearticulated through the coronavirus emergency, thus adding new meaning and significance to otherwise familiar dynamics. There are religious dimensions to the pandemic, including new spiritual conduct under social distancing regulation, transcendental interpretations of the pandemic, coping mechanisms, and ritual forms of salvation (Schonthal and Jayatilake 2021). The pandemic offers new discursive ammunition to depict another group's cultural practices as harmful or irresponsible, which has fortified anti-Muslim sentiments among Sinhala extremists.

The government response to the pandemic has aggravated concerns about democratic backsliding, constitutional erosion, and the routinized deployment of emergency powers (Fonseka, Ganeshathasan and Welikala 2021; Peiris 2021; Klem and Samararatne 2022). As in other countries, government-imposed restrictions, curfews, travel bans, and full lockdowns promulgated societal opposition. In Sri Lanka, concerns over "executive aggrandisement have an especially deep-seated character, though, considering the prior erosion of the rule of law and democratic norms and the authoritarian inclinations of the Rajapaksa government" (Fonseka et al 2021: 362). Alarm has been raised about the bypassing of government departments, the abolishment of checks and balances, the curtailment of rights and freedoms, the continued expansion of special authorities under the presidency, the routine dissolution of parliament, and the further expansion of military routines and personnel into public office (see Peiris 2021). On the one hand, Sri Lanka's past teaches us that these trends do not bode well: the expansion of executive has often proven difficult to roll back. On the other, it reminds us that every centripetal force ultimately creates its own counterforces and that no government or political dynasty, however formidable its political muscle, ultimately manages to last.

Note

1 I wrote this chapter in the first weeks of 2022 and I have used that date as a cut-off point. The crisis, protest, and turmoil around the "aragalaya" (struggle) of 2022 and beyond are thus not discussed in this chapter.

References

Abeysekere, Charles and Newton Gunasinghe (eds) (1987) *Facets of Ethnicity in Sri Lanka* Colombo: Social Scientists' Association

Amarasingam, Amarnath (2015) *Pain, Pride and Politics: Social Movement Activism and the Sri Lankan Tamil Diaspora in Canada* Athens: University of Georgia Press

Amarasingam, Amarnath (2019) "Terrorism on the Teardrop Island: Understanding the Easter 2019 Attacks in Sri Lanka" *CTC Sentinel* 12(5): 1–10

Amarasinghe, Ranjith, Asoka Gunawardena, Jayampathi Wickramaratne, A. Navaratna-Bandara and N. Selakkumaran (2019) *Thirty Years of Devolution: An Evaluation of the Workings of Provincial Councils in Sri Lanka* Colombo: Institute for Constitutional Studies

Amarasuriya, Harini and Jonathan Spencer (2021) "Intimate Commitments: Friends, Comrades and Family in the Life of One Sri Lankan Activist" In *The Intimate Life of Dissent: Anthropological Perspectives* Harini Amarasuriya, Tobias Kelly, Sidharthan Maunaguru, Galina Oustinova-Stjepanovic and Jonathan Spencer (eds) London: University College London Press, pp 90–111

Arasaratnam, Sinnappah (1994) "Sri Lanka's Tamils: Under Colonial Rule" In *The Sri Lankan Tamils: Ethnicity and Identity*, Chelvadurai Manogaran and Bryan Pfaffenberger (eds) Boulder, CO: Westview Press, pp. 30–53

Bastian, Rohan (2016) "Recognizing the Spatial and Territorial Nature of Religious Communities in Colombo, Sri Lanka" In *Religion and Urbanism: Reconceptualising Sustainable Cities for South Asia* Yamini Narayanan (ed) London: Routledge, pp 97–114

Bastian, Sunil (1994) *Devolution and Development in Sri Lanka* Colombo: ICES

Bavinck, Ben (2011) *Of Tamils and Tigers: A Journey Through Sri Lanka's War Years* Colombo: Vijitha Yapa Press

Breen, Michael (2018) *The Road to Federalism in Nepal, Myanmar and Sri Lanka: Finding the Middle Ground* London: Routledge

Bremner, Francesca (2004) "Fragments of Memory, Processes of State: Ethnic Violence Though the Life Histories of Participants" In *Economy, Culture, and Civil War in Sri Lanka* Deborah Winslow and Michael Woost (eds) Indianapolis, IN: Indiana University Press, pp 137–150

Bremner, Francesca (2013) "Recasting Caste: War, Displacement and Transformations" *International Journal of Ethnic & Social Studies* 1(2): 31–56

Chandraprema, C.A. (1991) *Sri Lanka: The Years of Terror. The JVP Insurrection 1987–1989* Colombo: Lakehouse

Cheran, Rainford (ed) (2009) *Pathways of Dissent: Tamil Nationalism in Sri Lanka* Thousand Oaks, CA: Sage

Coomaraswamy, Radhika (1994) "Devolution, the Law, and Judicial Construction" In *Devolution and Development in Sri Lanka* Sunil Bastian (ed) Colombo: ICES, pp 121–142

Coomaraswamy, Radhika (2003) "The Politics of Institutional Design: An Overview of the Case of Sri Lanka" In *Can Democracy Be Designed? The Politics of Institutional Choice in Conflict-Torn Societies* Sunil Bastian and Robin Luckham (eds) London: Zed Books, pp 145–169

De Silva, Kingsley (2005) *A History of Sri Lanka* Colombo: Vijitha Yapa Publications

De Votta, Neil (2004) *Blowback: Linguistic Nationalism, Institutional Decay, and Ethnic Conflict in Sri Lanka* Stanford, CA: Stanford University Press

De Votta, Neil (2021) "Buddhist Majoritarianism and Ethnocracy in Sri Lanka" *Sociological Bulletin* 70(4): 453–466

Deegalle, Mahinda (2004) "Politics of the Jathika Hela Urumaya Monks: Buddhism and Ethnicity in Contemporary Sri Lanka" *Contemporary Buddhism* 5(2): 83–103

Edirisinha, Rohan, Mario Gomez, V.T. Thamilmaran and Asanga Welikala (2008) *Power-Sharing in Sri Lanka: Constitutional and Political Documents 1926–2008* Colombo and Berlin: Centre for Policy Alternatives and Berghof Foundation for Peace Support

Fonseka, Bhavani, Luwie Ganeshathasan and Asanga Welikala (2021) "Sri Lanka: Pandemic-Catalyzed Democratic Backsliding" In *Covid-19 in Asia: Law and Policy Contexts* Victor Ramraj (ed) Oxford: Oxford University Press

Fowsar, Mohamed Anifa Mohamed, Mohamed Abdulla Mohamed Rameez and Aboobacker Rameez (2020) "Muslim Minority in Post-war Sri Lanka: A Case Study of Aluthgama and Digana Violences" *Academic Journal of Interdisciplinary Studies* 9(6): 56–68

Haniffa, Farzana (2008) "Piety as Politics amongst Muslim Women in Contemporary Sri Lanka" *Modern Asian Studies* 42(2/3): 347–375

Haniffa, Farzana (2015) "Competing for Victim Status: Northern Muslims and the Ironies of Sri Lanka's Post-war Transition" *Stability: International Journal of Security and Development* 4(1): 21

Haniffa, Farzana (2016) "Stories in the Aftermath of Aluthgama" In *Buddhist Extremists and Muslim Minorities: Religious Conflict in Contemporary Sri Lanka* John Holt (ed) New York, NY: Oxford University Press, pp 164–193

Haniffa, Farzana (2020) "Sri Lanka's Anti-Muslim Movement and Muslim Responses: How Were They Gendered?" In *Buddhist-Muslim Relations in a Theravada World* Iselin Frydenlund and Michael Jerryson (eds) London: Palgrave Macmillan, pp 139–167

Harris, Elizabeth (2018) *Religion, Space and Conflict in Sri Lanka: Colonial and Postcolonial Perspectives* London: Routledge

Harris, Elizabeth (2019) "Contested Histories, Multi-Religious Space and Conflict: A Case Study of Kantarodai in Northern Sri Lanka" *Religions* 10: 537

Harrison, Frances (2012) *Still Counting the Dead: Survivors of Sri Lanka's Hidden War* London: Portobello Books

Hellmann-Rajanayagam, Dagmar (1994a) "Tamils and the Meaning of History" In *The Sri Lankan Tamils: Ethnicity and Identity* Chelvadurai Manogaran and Bryan Pfaffenberger (eds) Boulder: Westview Press, pp 54–83

Hellmann-Rajanayagam, Dagmar (1994b) "The 'Groups' and the Rise of Militant Secessionism" In *The Sri Lankan Tamils: Ethnicity and Identity* Chelvadurai Manogaran and Bryan Pfaffenberger (eds) Boulder: Westview Press, pp 168–207

Hellmann-Rajanayagam, Dagmar (1994c) *The Tamil Tigers: Armed Struggle for Identity* Stuttgart: Franz Steiner Verlag

Heslop, Luke (2014) "On Sacred Ground: The Political Performance of Religious Responsibility" *Contemporary South Asia* 22(1): 21–36

Holt, John (ed) (2016a) *Buddhist Extremists and Muslim Minorities: Religious Conflict in Contemporary Sri Lanka* New York, NY: Oxford University Press

Holt, John (2016b) "A Religious Syntax to Recent Communal Violence in Sri Lanka" In *Buddhist Extremists and Muslim Minorities: Religious Conflict in Contemporary Sri Lanka* John Holt (ed) New York, NY: Oxford University Press, pp 194–210

Imtiyaz, A.R.M. (2020) "The Easter Sunday Bombings and the Crisis Facing Sri Lanka's Muslims" *Journal of Asian and African Studies* 55(1): 3–16

Jayasinghe, Pasan (2019) "Significant in Isolation: Sri Lanka's Right to Information Regime in Enactment and Operation" *The Round Table* 108(6): 679–693

Johnson, Deborah and Benedikt Korf (2021) "The Predicament of Pastoral Sovereignty" *Political Geography* 87: 102368

Kailasam, Vasugi (2021) "Reading Sri Lankan Tamil Nationalism: Unnarratability in Shobasakthi's Traitor" *The Journal of Commonwealth Literature* 56(2): 265–282

Keethaponcalan, S.I. (2019) *Post-war Dilemmas of Sri Lanka: Democracy and Reconciliation* London: Routledge

Klem, Bart (2011) "Islam, Politics and Violence in Eastern Sri Lanka" *Journal of Asian Studies* 70(3): 730–753

Klem, Bart (2014) "The Political Geography of War's End: Territorialisation, Circulation, and Moral Anxiety in Trincomalee, Sri Lanka" *Political Geography* 38(1): 33–45

Klem, Bart (2018) "The Problem of Peace and the Meaning of 'Post-war'" *Conflict, Security & Development* 18(3): 233–255

Klem, Bart and Sidharthan Maunaguru (2017) "Insurgent Rule as Sovereign Mimicry and Mutation: Governance, Kingship and Violence in Civil Wars" *Comparative Studies in Society and History* 59(3): 629–656

Klem, Bart and Sidharthan Maunaguru (2018) "Public Authority under Sovereign Encroachment: Community Leadership in War-Time Sri Lanka" *Modern Asian Studies* 52(3): 784–814

Klem, Bart and Dinesha Samararatne (2022) "Sri Lanka in 2021: Vistas on the Brink" *Asian Survey* 62(1): 201–210

Kuganathan, Prashanth (2014) "Social Stratification in Jaffna: A Survey of Recent Research on Caste" *Sociology Compass* 8(1): 78–88

Lehr, Peter (2019) *Militant Buddhism: The Rise of Religious Violence in Sri Lanka Myanmar and* **Thailand** London: Palgrave Macmillan

Lewis, David (2020) "Sri Lanka's Schmittian Peace: Sovereignty, Enmity and Illiberal Order" *Conflict, Security and Development* 20(1): 15–37

Mahadev, Nina (2015) "The Maverick Dialogics of Religious Rivalry in Sri Lanka: Inspiration and Contestation in a New Messianic Buddhist Movement" *Journal of the Royal Anthropological Institute* 22: 127–147

Mahadev, Nina (2019) "Post-War Blood: Sacrifice, Anti-Sacrifice, and the Rearticulations of Conflict in Sri Lanka" *Religion and Society: Advances in Research* 10: 130–150

Mahoharan, N., Drorima Chatterjee and Dhruv Ashok (2021) "The New 'Other': Islamic Radicalisation and De-radicalisation in Sri Lanka" *India Quarterly* 77(4): 605–621

Malji, Andrea (2021) "Gendered Islamophobia: The Nature of Hindu and Buddhist Nationalism in India and Sri Lanka" *Studies in Ethnicity and Nationalism* 21(2): 172–193

Mampilly, Zachariah (2011) *Rebel Rulers: Insurgent Governance and Civilian Life during War* Ithaca, NY: Cornell University Press

Maunaguru, Sidharthan (2018) "Vulnerable Sovereignty: Sovereign Deities and Tigers' Politics in Sri Lanka" *Current Anthropology* 61(6): 686–712

Maunaguru, Sidharthan (2021) "Friends with Differences: Ethics Rivalry and Politics among Sri Lankan Tamil Former Political Activists" In *The Intimate Life of Dissent: Anthropological Perspectives* Harini Amarasuriya, Tobias Kelly, Sidharthan Maunaguru, Galina Oustinova-Stjepanovic and Jonathan Spencer (eds) London: University College London Press, pp 132–150

McCargo, Duncan and Dishani Senaratne (2020) "Victor's Memory: Sri Lanka's Post-War Memoryscape in Comparative Perspective" *Conflict, Security and Development* 20(1): 97–113

McGilvray, Dennis (2016) "Islamic and Buddhist Impacts on the Shrine at Daftar Jailani, Sri Lanka" In *Islam, Sufism and Everyday Politics of Belonging in South Asia* Deepra Dandekar and Torsten Tschacher (eds) London: Routledge, pp 62–76

McGilvray, Dennis and Michelle Gamburd (eds) (2010) *Tsunami Recovery in Sri Lanka: Ethnic and Regional Dimensions* London: Routledge

McGilvray, Dennis and Mirak Raheem (2007) *Muslim Perspectives on the Sri Lankan Conflict Policy Studies 41* Washington, DC: East-West Center Society of Environmental Economics and Policy Studies

Mihlar, Farah (2019) "Religious Change in a Minority Context: Transforming Islam in Sri Lanka" *Third World Quarterly* 40(12): 2153–2169

Moore, Mick (1993) "Thoroughly Modern Revolutionaries: The JVP in Sri Lanka" *Modern Asian Studies* 27: 593–642

O'Driscoll, Dylan, Irene Costantini and Serhun Al (2020) "Federal versus Unitary States: Ethnic Accommodation of Tamils and Kurds" *Nationalism and Ethnic Politics* 26(4): 351–368

Orjuela, Camilla (2020) "Countering Buddhist Radicalisation: Emerging Peace Movements in Myanmar and Sri Lanka" *Third World Quarterly* 41(1): 133–150

Orjuela, Camilla (2021) "Navigating Labels, Seeking Recognition for Victimhood: Diaspora Activism after Mass-Atrocities" *Global Networks* 22(1): 166–179

Peiris, Pradeep (ed) (2021) *Is the Cure Worse than the Disease? Reflections on COVID Governance in Sri Lanka* Colombo: CPA

Rajasingham, Sanjayan (2019) "Federal or Unitary? The Power Sharing Debate in Sri Lanka" *The Round Table* 108(6): 653–666

Rasaratnam, Madurika (2016) *Tamils and the Nation: India and Sri Lanka Compared* London: Hurst

Rogers, John (1994) "Post-Orientalism and the Interpretation of Premodern and Modern Political Identities: The Case of Sri Lanka" *Journal of Asian Studies* 53(1): 10–23

Ruwanpura, Kanchana (2016) "Post-War Sri Lanka: State, Capital and Labour, and the Politics of Reconciliation" *Contemporary South Asia* 24(4): 351–359

Ruwanpura, Loritta, Benjamin Chan, V. Brown and Kajotha (2020) "Unsettled Peace? The Territorial Politics of Roadbuilding in Post-war Sri Lanka" *Political Geography* 76: 102092

Samararatne, Dinesha (2019) "Proposals for a New Bill of Rights in Sri Lanka: Narrow Debates, Unmarked Challenges" *The Round Table* 108(6): 667–678

Satkunanathan, Ambika (2016) "Collaboration, Suspicion and Traitors: An Exploratory Study of Intra-Community Relations in Post-War Northern Sri Lanka" *Contemporary South Asia* 24(4): 416–428

Schonthal, Benjamin (2016a) *Buddhism, Politics, and the Limits of Law: The Pyrrhic Constitutionalism of Sri Lanka* Cambridge: Cambridge University Press

Schonthal, Benjamin (2016b) "Environments of Law: Islam, Buddhism, and the State in Contemporary Sri Lanka" *Journal of Asian Studies* 75(1): 137–156

Schonthal, Benjamin (2016c) "The Impossibility of a Buddhist State" *Asian Journal of Law and Society* 3(1): 29–48

Schonthal, Benjamin (2018) "The Meanings of Sacrifice: The LTTE, Suicide, and the Limits of the "religion question"" In *Martyrdom, Self-Sacrifice, and Self-Immolation: Religious Perspectives on Suicide* Margo Kitts (ed) pp 226–240

Schonthal, Benjamin and Tilak Jayatilake (2021) "Religion Amid the Pandemic: A Buddhist Case Study" In *Covid-19 in Asia: Law and Policy Contexts* Victor Ramraj (ed) Oxford: Oxford University Press, pp 265–278

Senaratne, Kalana (2019) "The Executive and the Constitutional Reforms Process in Sri Lanka" *The Round Table* 108(6): 625–638

Senivaratne, H.L. (2000) *The Work of Kings: The New Buddhism of Sri Lanka* Chicago, IL: Chicago University Press

Seoighe, Rachel (2017) *War, Denial and Nation-Building in Sri Lanka: After the End* Basingstoke: Palgrave Macmillan

Shah, Dian (2017) *Constitutions, Religion and Politics in Asia* Cambridge: Cambridge University Press

Shastri, Amita (1990) "The Material Basis for Separatism: The Tamil Eelam Movement in Sri Lanka" *Journal of Asian Studies* 49(1): 55–77

Silva, Tudor (2016) "Gossip, Rumor, and Propaganda in Anti-Muslim Campaigns of the Bodu Bala Sena" In *Buddhist Extremists and Muslim Minorities: Religious Conflict in Contemporary Sri Lanka* John Holt (ed) New York, NY: Oxford University Press, pp 119–138

Silva, Tudor (2020) "Nationalism, Caste-blindness and the Continuing Problems of War-Displaced Panchamars in Post-war Jaffna Society" *CASTE* 1(1): 51–70

Silva, Tudor, P. Sivapragasam and Paramsothy Thanges (2009) *Caste Discrimination and Social Justice in Sri Lanka: An Overview* New Delhi: Indian Institute of Dalit Studies

Spencer, Jonathan (2007) *Anthropology, Politics, and the State: Democracy and Violence in South Asia* Cambridge: Cambridge University Press

Spencer, Jonathan (2008) "A Nationalism without Politics? The Illiberal Consequences of Liberal Institutions in Sri Lanka" *Third World Quarterly* 29(3): 611–629

Spencer, Jonathan (2016) "Securitization and Its Discontents: The End of Sri Lanka's Long Post-War?" *Contemporary South Asia* 24(1): 94–108

Spencer, Jonathan, Jonathan Goodhand, Shahul Hasbullah, Bart Klem, Benedikt Korf and Tudor Silva (2015) ***Checkpoint, Temple, Church and Mosque: A Collaborative Ethnography of War and Peace*** London: Pluto

Tambiah, Stanley (1996) ***Leveling Crowds: Ethno-Nationalist Conflicts and Collective Violence in South Asia*** Berkeley, CA: University of California Press

Terpstra, Niels and Georg Frerks (2017) "Rebel Governance and Legitimacy: Understanding the Impact of Rebel Legitimation on Civilian Compliance with the LTTE Rule" ***Civil Wars*** 19(3): 279–307

Thanges, Paramsothy (2008) "Caste and Social Exclusion of IDPs in Jaffna Society" ***Colombo Review*** 1(2): 1–27

Thiranagama, Sharika (2010) "In Praise of Traitors: Intimacy, Betrayal and the Sri Lankan Tamil Community" In ***Traitors: Suspicion, Intimacy and the Ethics of State-Building*** Sharika Thiranagama and Tobias Kelly (eds) Philadelphia, PA: University of Pennsylvania Press, pp 127–149

Thiranagama, Sharika (2011) ***In My Mother's House: Civil War in Sri Lanka*** Philadelphia, PA: University of Philadelphia Press

Thiranagama, Sharika (2018) "The Civility of Strangers? Caste, Ethnicity, and Living Together in Postwar Jaffna, Sri Lanka" ***Anthropological Theory*** 18(2–3): 357–381

Thiruchelvam, Neelan (2000) "The Politics of Federalism and Diversity in Sri Lanka" In ***Autonomy and Ethnicity: Negotiating Competing Claims in Multi-Ethnic States*** Yash Ghai (ed) Cambridge: Cambridge University Press, pp 197–215

Thurairajah, Kalyani (2020) "Who Are We without the War?": The Evolution of the Tamil Ethnic Identity in Post-Conflict Sri Lanka" ***Ethnicities*** 20(3): 564–586

Thurairajah, Tanuja (2021) "Performing Nationalism: The United Nations Human Rights Council (UNHRC) and Sri Lankan Tamil Dasporic Politics in Switzerland" ***The Geographical Journal*** 188(1): 28–41

University Teachers for Human Rights (Jaffna) (2009) ***A Marred Victory and a Defeat Pregnant with Foreboding*** Special Report 32, 10 June 2009. Accessed on 10 January 2011. Available at http://www.uthr.org/SpecialReports/spreport32.htm>.

Uyangoda, Jayadeva (2011) "Travails of State Reform in the Context of Protracted Civil War in Sri Lanka" In ***In Liberal Peace in Question: Politics of State and Market Reform in Sri Lanka*** Kristian Stokke and Jayadeva Uyangoda (eds) London: Anthem Press, pp 35–62

Vaitheespara, Ravi (2009) "Towards Understanding Militant Tamil Nationalism in Sri Lanka" In ***Pathways of Dissent: Tamil Nationalism in Sri Lanka*** Rainford Cheran (ed) Thousand Oaks, CA: Sage, pp 33–54

Venugopal, Rajesh (2018) ***Nationalism, Development and Ethnic Conflict in Sri Lanka*** Cambridge: Cambridge University Press

Weiss, Gordon (2011) ***The Cage: The Fight for Sri Lanka and the Last Days of the Tamil Tigers*** London: The Bodley Head

Welikala, Asanga (2012) ***The Sri Lankan Republic at 40: Reflections on Constitutional History, Theory and Practice*** Colombo: Centre for Policy Alternatives

Welikala, Asanga (2019) "Constitutional Reforms in Sri Lanka – More Drift?" ***The Round Table*** 108(6): 605–612

Welikala, Asanga (2020) "The Dismissal of Prime Ministers in the Asian Commonwealth: Comparing Democratic Deconsolidation in Malaysia and Sri Lanka" ***The Political Quarterly*** 91(4): 786–794

Wickramaratne, Jayampathy (2014) ***Towards Democratic Governance in Sri Lanka: A Constitutional Miscellany*** Colombo: Institute for Constitutional Studies

Wickramasinghe, Nira (2006) ***Sri Lanka in the Modern Age. A History of Contested Identities*** London: Hurst

Wickramasinghe, Nira (2013) "Producing the Present: History as Heritage in Post-War Patriotic Sri Lanka" ***Economic & Political Weekly*** 47(43): 91–100

Wilson, Jeyaratnam (2000) ***Sri Lankan Tamil Nationalism: Its Origins and Developments in the 19th and 20th Centuries*** London: Hurst

Woods, Orlando (2013) "The Spatial Modalities of Evangelical Christian Growth in Sri Lanka: Evangelism, Social Ministry and the Structural Mosaic" ***Transactions of the Institute of British Geographers*** 38(4): 652–664

4
CENTRING CONFLICT
Contemporary Sri Lanka in Perspective

Shamara Wettimuny[1]

Introduction

Violent internal conflict has pervaded Sri Lanka for much of the last century, where complex and multi-dimensional facets have factored in. Identity, ideology, and narratives of victimisation, however, appear to emerge as common themes. This chapter offers a chronological account of Sri Lanka's history of conflict during the latter part of its colonial experience and throughout the post-independence period. It explores several types of conflict, including ethno-religious conflict in the early 20th century, ethno-linguistic conflict in the mid-20th century to the early 21st century, recent class conflict in the 1970s and 1980s, and a recurrence of ethno-religious conflict in contemporary times.[2] This chronological account is not meant to be an exhaustive telling of Sri Lanka's history of conflict. Instead, it aims to centre contemporary conflict in Sri Lanka by exploring causation and highlighting some of the shared drivers of violence that have recurred throughout this period.

Unequal access to resources due to class, gender and ethnicised lines of political patronage, and elite interests that exploit identity, ideology, and victim narratives for personal gain have all played pivotal roles in creating conditions for conflict. This chapter focuses on how these and other factors intersect and overlap with identity, ideology, and victim narratives in both driving and mobilising conflict and how this affects contemporary Sri Lanka.

Ethno-religious Conflict in the Early 20th Century

The year 1915 marked the first major episode of ethno-religious violence in colonial Sri Lanka. Although minor episodes of inter- and intra-religious violence had previously taken place throughout the 19th century, the scale and intensity of the anti-Moor pogrom of 1915 were entirely unprecedented (Somaratna 1991). The violence can only be fully understood considering various strands of identity formation that took place in the preceding decades.

Until the mid-19th century, ethno-religious identity in Sri Lanka was relatively fluid. Various aspects of identity, such as caste or region – for example, belonging to the Low-Country or the Kandyan regions – gained salience at different points in history (Guneratne 2002: 22). Importantly, Arjun Guneratne (2002: 26) observes that 'groups we identify today as Sinhala, Tamil or Muslim' crystallised from the 'successive movements of people from India' over centuries, suggesting a broadly common stock or origin. He accordingly argues that the idea of a 'pure' Sinhalese or Tamil race (or culture) is mere fiction. Nevertheless, conceptions of a distinct 'Sinhalese' identity expressed through language and religion can be traced as far back as to the 10th century (Strathern 2017: 221–223). As contact with European colonialism increased and 'new forms of control' – detailed below – were arbitrarily imposed on the island's populations, ethnic and religious identities also shifted (Sivasundaram 2013: 156).

Taxonomical initiatives by the British colonial administration included the categorisation of populations into more fixed categories through censuses and political representation. The British were preoccupied with classification primarily based on 'race' (Rogers 2004). The preoccupation with 'race' and ethnicity in Sri Lanka/Ceylon can be contrasted with the British prioritisation of religion as the key organising principle in India. Between 1833 and 1889, indigenous groups were represented by one of three Members in the Ceylon Legislative Council: a Sinhalese Member, a Tamil Member, and a Burgher Member in Council. Smaller groups, such as Muslims, were often collapsed into the ethno-linguistic category of 'Tamil' and thus were assumed to be represented by the Tamil Member in Council. However, from 1889, the Muslim community increasingly distinguished themselves as a distinct ethno-religious group (primarily comprising Moors who belonged to the Islamic faith) and resisted being classified as 'Tamil'. Such classifications contributed towards heightened local identity consciousness along racial lines both in terms of strengthening identities within groups and emphasising ethnic difference across groups (ibid). As Nira Wickramasinghe (2014) observes, some 'colonised peoples' realised that 'by claiming to belong to one or another group recognised by the colonial rulers one could obtain certain entitlements' (2014: 47). The attempt in the late 1880s by the then Tamil Member in Legislative Council, Ponnambalam Ramanathan, to claim that Moors were Tamil converts to Islam, and therefore adequately represented by the Tamil Member, is an example of deploying ethnic and cultural identities to maintain power. By contrast, Muslim elites attempted to highlight their Arab origins (and thus their distinction from Tamils) to 'safeguard [their] economic and other interests' (Ismail 1995: 58).

It is worth recognising that while religion became the organising identity marker for Muslim political representation vis-à-vis other communities in the Legislative Council, geographical and occupational identities were the crucial markers of power and influence *within* the Muslim community. Qadri Ismail, in his essay on 'Unmooring Identity' (ibid), argues that Southern, male, bourgeois, Moor traders tended to dominate the 'Muslim social formation', a claim that is reflected in the figures appointed by the British to the role of the Mohammedan Member in Legislative Council from 1889 onwards.

The 19th century was also a period of intensifying religious revival in Sri Lanka, as members of the Buddhist, Hindu, and Muslim communities became more conscious and assertive of their religious identities, largely as a confrontation with Christian missionaries. Anne Blackburn (2001) traces the Buddhist revival back to the 18th century but the revival reached a high point in the final third of the 19th century. This high point was signified by events such as the Panadura Debate of 1873 in which Ven. Migetuwatte Gunananda, a fiery orator from Balapitiya, successfully challenged Christian priests in front of an audience of many thousands (Malalgoda 1976; Amunugama 2019). The Hindu revival was driven by Saivite revivalists, such as Arumuga Navalar from the 1840s onwards in Jaffna, and aimed to counteract aggressive Christian proselytisation and publications that carried insults to Hindu beliefs (Hudson 1992; Wilson 2000). The Islamic revival heightened from around the 1880s as a response to local religious revivals and to global Islamic revivals in South Asia and beyond and focused on education for the Muslim community (Samaraweera 1997).

Within this overarching context of increased consciousness around 'race' and 'religion', fault lines between Muslim Moors (the majority ethnic group within the Muslim population) and other ethno-religious groups emerged. Perception that Moors controlled economic markets, particularly in the petty retail sector, and gained unfair advantage over traders and consumers of other communities was one divisive factor (Ali 1987). Contestation over religious space increased during this period, exacerbated by perceptions that the colonial administration sympathised with Moorish demands for the regulation of Buddhist 'noise worship' (Roberts 1994). In May 1915, these perceptions caused violence to erupt in Kandy, in the central province of Sri Lanka, against Moors gathered at a local mosque during a Buddhist procession that was observing Vesak Poya. Violence quickly spread to five out of the nine provinces and assailants included Sinhalese Christians as well as Tamils (Roberts 1994).

Importantly, the instigation and participation in the violence – mainly by Sinhala-Buddhists, but also by other communities, including Sinhalese Christians, and Tamils – were predicated on a narrative of victimisation whereby the Moor was framed as a competitor, usurper, and aggressor (Ismail 1995: 82; see also Wettimuny 2019). For example, Moors were viewed as competitors of Sinhalese traders in the desire to supply growing consumer demands in retail markets and were portrayed as aggressive moneylenders and debt collectors who exploited peasants and poor labourers (Dharmapala and Guruge 1965: 207). This victim narrative was further amplified when the colonial state eventually responded to the violence in the harshest of terms. Between June 1915 and August 1915, the British colonial state imposed martial law across several provinces in the island and arrested, imprisoned, and even executed several innocent Sinhalese who were assumed to have participated in the pogrom (De Souza 1919). The state's response was so brutal that it prompted Sinhalese and Tamils to shift towards campaigning for greater self-government.

Ethno-Linguistic Conflict in the Post-independence Period

Partially in response to the colonial state's ruthless repression of the 1915 pogrom, multi-ethnic nationalist organisations, such as the Ceylon Reform League (founded in 1917) and the Ceylon National Congress (founded in 1919), emerged. These organisations negotiated with the state to introduce changes to the electoral system in Sri Lanka. Thus, in the 1920s, a different form of identity politics took centre stage and relegated (physical) ethno-religious conflict to the background. However, this process of constitutional reform and devolution of power for greater self-governance in Sri Lanka eventually created concerns for the Tamil minority, which saw its electoral position weakening vis-à-vis the numerically dominant Sinhalese (Wickramasinghe 1991). Furthermore, ethnic and religious minorities viewed provisions contained within the 1947 Soulbury Constitution (Sri Lanka's first post-independence constitution) on legal protections for minorities in Parliament as inadequate (Schonthal 2012: 177). Nevertheless, and despite growing fears about insufficient minority representation, this period of negotiation and compromise was not marked by violent conflict. It was only in the post-independence period that Tamil political aspirations – particularly in terms of the use of the Tamil language – were blatantly suppressed by the government of the day. Within this overarching context, violent conflict in Sri Lanka emerged along ethno-linguistic lines.

In 1956, S.W.R.D. Bandaranaike swept to power as prime minister following a chauvinistic campaign that hinged on replacing English with Sinhala as the island's official language. Sinhalese nationalists believed the majority community had been disadvantaged during the period of British rule and were disproportionately (under)represented in employment within the civil service. In this context, a 'Sinhala Only' language policy was proposed to reverse the prioritisation of English that marginalised Sinhala speakers and prioritised English speakers, mainly Burghers and certain Tamils, that contributed to the feelings of victimisation by the Sinhalese – 'the "authentic" inhabitants of the island' (Rambukwella 2018: 78).

In the post-colonial period, the Sinhala Only campaign was supported by various groups in the rural and urban Sinhalese heartlands of Sri Lanka, including by Buddhist monks (Vittachi 1958: 19). The Official Language Act, which was passed in Parliament in 1956, was an ethno-linguistic policy that received support from the Sinhalese majority in the country. The Act was vehemently opposed by Tamil (and other non-Tamil) members of the public. Tamils of all classes were affected by the Act, as were English-speaking groups including the Burghers. Such opposition and 'counter-opposition' from Sinhalese groups triggered the first major 'ethnic riot' targeting Tamils in Sri Lanka in June 1956 (Rambukwella 2018: 78).

Considering the violent backlash caused by the Official Language Act, Bandaranaike attempted to diffuse the situation by devolving greater power to Tamil-majority areas in a negotiated compromise with the leader of the Tamil Federal Party, S.J.V. Chelvanayagam. The 1957 Bandaranaike-Chelvanayagam Pact, as it was known, also promised to introduce Tamil as the administrative language in the Northern and Eastern Provinces of Sri Lanka in a partial reversal of 'Sinhala Only'. However, the 'ethnicization' of Bandaranaike's electorate prevented lasting reform (Wilson 1993: 154). The Pact came under protest by many Sinhalese (including powerful Buddhist monks), who succeeded in disrupting the Pact. Bandaranaike, in his attempts to appease his core constituency, also proscribed the Federal Party (Manor 1989: 286–289). He was then assassinated in 1959. The conspirators allegedly involved in the assassination plot were known to have opposed the Bandaranaike-Chelvanayagam Pact.

S.W.R.D. Bandaranaike was replaced as prime minister by his widow, Sirimavo Bandaranaike – the world's first woman head of state. In Mrs. Bandaranaike's first term of power, she had to contend with escalating socio-economic grievances and failed to address the growing ethnic conflict (Weerakoon 2004: 106). The moderate cooperation and consensus that had existed between Sinhalese and Tamil political elites from the pre-independence period frayed during the 1960s and had virtually broken down completely by 1970 (Wilson 1993: 155).

Tamil nationalism thus emerged during this period and drew heavily from narratives of historical indigeneity and legitimate entitlement of Tamils on the island (Vaitheespara 2009). It was also influenced, to some extent, by Tamil nationalism in south India (Hellmann-Rajanayagam 1990: 118) Yet it also emerged as a reaction to the discriminatory policies of a post-colonial state that was preoccupied with appeasing Sinhala-Buddhist nationalist demands. A spate of anti-Tamil pogroms during the 1950s and 1960s enlarged the cleavages between Sinhalese and Tamils and introduced violence as a feature of the ethno-linguistic conflict (Tambiah 1992). These egregious episodes reinforced the victimhood of the Tamils, shaping a victim narrative of the post-independence Tamil struggle for greater autonomy, and eventually fed into the birth of Tamil militancy in the 1970s.

Class-Based Conflict

During the late colonial period, class-based conflict manifested through limited protests, such as boycotts and the Tramway Strike of 1929 (Jayawardena 1972; Roberts 1994: 128–134). However, such protests never threatened the stability or security of the state in the way post-independence class-based conflict did. The 1970s marked yet another turning point in Sri Lanka's conflict landscape. During this period, class politics that were submerged by the ethno-nationalist conflict would recurrently reappear.

In April 1971, a youth insurrection led by the Janatha Vimukthi Peramuna (JVP) rocked certain rural parts of the South, during which insurgents secured control of 'territory and populations for a few days or weeks' (Moore 1993: 600). The JVP were a group of individuals from the Sinhalese community, inspired by Marxist ideology and, ultimately, committed to the idea of revolution. Despite the centrality of its political ideology across the movement, the JVP were united by other identity markers. Mick Moore observes that this youth movement was 'almost exclusively Sinhalese Buddhist' (Moore 1993: 608). As Rajesh Venugopal (2010: 593) observes, the JVP represented 'a corporeal fusion of Marxism and Sinhala nationalism that exhibits both characteristics in seamless combination'. When the insurrection was launched, several police stations across the island were targeted for simultaneous attack. The JVP failed, however, to achieve much of their military objectives, including the capture of Colombo and the abduction of the prime minister and senior government figures.

The government of the day violently put down the uprising in 1971. The death toll of JVP cadres ranged between 2,000 and 3,000 (Moore 1993: 493). The insurrection was the first episode of violent class-based youth conflict, but it was not the last. Between 1987 and 1989, a second JVP insurrection took place. Like in 1971, the state's armed forces, as well as para-military groups, bloodily suppressed the uprising in 1989, leaving 'tens of thousands' of JVP cadres dead or missing (Venugopal 2010: 568).

Both insurrections featured identity, ideology, and victim narratives as the underlying mobilisers of violence. In the first insurrection, the JVP used class-based identity and Marxist ideology to appeal to Sinhalese youth who felt largely marginalised and disenfranchised by state policy on education and employment. Youth discontent was reflected in the participation of those who had 'relatively advanced educational qualifications, who felt excluded from the (state) employment rewards that they believed themselves to merit' (Moore 1993: 608). The parallels between the underlying causes in the call for a Language Act in 1956 and the motivation behind the JVP uprising suggest that socio-economic grievances connected to state education/employment were not adequately addressed in the intervening decade and a half. Significantly, such grievances were also shared by Tamil youth. Nira Wickramasinghe (2012) observes that the 'failure of the state to guarantee social mobility through education and the unequal distribution of education entitlements were central issues in the Southern ... and the Tamil insurrection in the North and East in the 1970s' (2012: 93). However, these shared grievances failed to translate into solidarities across the island as ethnic identities and religio-cultural ideologies became more charged and divisive in the 1980s (Abeysekara 2002).

The second JVP insurrection also featured identity and ideology as motivating forces. Resentment for caste-based oppression following the Sirimavo Bandaranaike/Sri Lanka Freedom Party (SLFP) government's 'slaughter' of suspected JVP insurgents in areas where the oppressed *Vahumpura* and *Batgam* castes inhabited during the 1971 insurrection lingered throughout the 1980s (Moore 1993: 609). The continued sense of 'alienation and exclusion by the *Vahumpura, Batgam* and other minority "low" castes' thus fed into support for the JVP's second insurrection (ibid: 626). Furthermore, Moore notes that Sinhala-Buddhist nationalism was a 'centrepiece' in the JVP's programme (ibid: 618). At the time, India had intervened in the ethno-linguistic conflict that prevailed in the North and East of the country. The intervention led to the Indo-Lanka Accord of July 1987, the promulgation of constitutional amendments to enable limited power sharing arrangements with the Tamils, and the deployment of the Indian Peacekeeping Force (IPKF) to enforce the terms of the Accord in October 1987 (Hoole et al 1992). The JVP used this context as a platform to oppose international intervention and devolution of power and to 'pose as the only truly patriotic force willing to combat a formidable coalition of enemies of Sinhalese Buddhism' (Moore 1993: 618).

Meanwhile, the second JVP insurrection contained class-based inequities that resulted in exclusion, both perceived and real, resulting from the advent of open economic policies. Between 1955 and 1977, Sri Lanka maintained a 'state-regulated economic system', during which the public sector drastically expanded, and political patronage determined who would be uplifted through education and employment (Gunasinghe 1996: 184–185). Following the landslide victory of the United National Party at the 1977 parliamentary election, the government decided to open Sri Lanka's economy to the world. Open economic policies dismantled state regulation, ended the system of quotas and permits that were distributed through Sinhalese networks of patronage, and de-nationalised ownership and management of enterprise (Gunasinghe 1996: 186). Various special concessions to Sinhalese were abolished. Significantly, youth aspirations in the rural South for instance were likely raised following liberalisation, in part due to access to information on 'alternative lifestyles' through advertisements for example (De Silva 2005: 534). However, these aspirations were not met, leading to a 'marked increase in social despair and rising political tensions' (Dunham and Jayasuriya 2000: 98–99).

In this context, the 1987–1989 insurrection resembled the 1971 insurgence in terms of 'educated unemployment' being one of the major victim narratives that drove the violence (Moore 1993: 616). Interestingly, the narrative resonated with both men and women. Between the 1940s and 1960s, women's enrolment in higher education in Sri Lanka had increased proportionate to men's enrolment from around 10% in 1942 to 42.5% in 1965 (Gunawardena 2003: 439). In this context, both men and women were frustrated by the lack of employment opportunities available to them after university. Thus, notably, both men and women participated in armed combat against the state (in both JVP insurrections), including in street battles and in the jungles, marking an irrevocable shift in gender relations in the sphere of conflict (De Mel 2001: 211).

Unlike the state's response to Tamil demands, the state demonstrated some sympathy towards Sinhalese grievances. In 1972, the second Sirimavo Bandaranaike government passed an Act that offered a 'standardisation' of university admissions that sought to address regional inequalities in access to education. In practice, this Act created an ethno-linguistic quota system designed to offer a larger number of university places to Sinhalese men and women (Perera 2001: 11). Following the 1987–1989 insurrection, the state launched a Youth Commission to inquire into the root causes of the conflict and to recommend structural changes to ensure non-recurrence (Sri Lanka Presidential Commission on Youth 1990). The Commission critiqued the district quota system of student recruitment to universities and found that the poor quality of university-level teaching and the equally weak performance of students – underscoring the under resourcing of public institutions – were major causes of youth discontent at universities (ibid). It meanwhile recommended the implementation of 'youth quotas' to improve youth representation in local authorities. This recommendation was premised on the Commission's conviction that the youth were 'substantially united in the belief that the [electoral] system does not give them the opportunity to represent and act upon the views' of the youth (ibid: 14). The eventual withdrawal of the IPKF from Sri Lanka in 1990, the establishment of disappearances commissions to investigate the disappearance of thousands of youth during this period, and the re-entry of the JVP into mainstream politics in 1994 marked the end of class-based violence on the scale of the two insurrections (Venugopal 2010: 596).

The Continuation of Ethno-Linguistic Conflict

By the late 1970s, Tamil militant groups constituted numerous social forces, classes, and ideologies, including but by no means restricted to the Liberation Tigers of Tamil Eelam (LTTE) (Vaitheespara 2009). At the same time, anti-Tamil attacks and pogroms were taking place more regularly. Like earlier anti-Tamil attacks in 1956, 1958, and 1965, Tamils were attacked in 1977 and 1981 (Wilson 1993: 145). Women were targeted in the violence, and widespread reports of abduction and rape emerged (Leary 1983; Pavey 2008). The 1983 anti-Tamil pogrom marked the worst of these excesses.

This new phase of the ethno-linguistic conflict contained strong identity-based and ideological elements. The LTTE emerged as the primary Tamil militant force by the 1980s and promoted a clear separatist ideology. The fact that it enjoyed de-facto control over territories previously occupied by the IPKF enabled it to administer a de-facto government in certain areas of the North and East (Hoole et al 1992). Interestingly, religion was not central to the LTTE's struggle – although caste and politics were – and thus the LTTE consisted of both Hindus and Christians (Hoole and Ratnajeevan 1996: 125; Frydenlund 2018). Due to this diversity, the LTTE appeared to deprioritise the influence of Hinduism in its separatist struggle.

Narratives of victimhood remained crucial to the continuation of armed conflict between the state and Tamil militants. These groups saw themselves as legitimate victims deliberately marginalised in instances, which arguably deepened inter-communal mistrust, fear, and political intransigence. Tamil narratives drew on state-sponsored repression and human rights abuses throughout this period to highlight their victimhood, such as the Trincomalee massacres, the 1995 Navaly Church bombing, the 1999 shelling of the Shrine of Our Lady of Madhu, and the destructions of Hindu temples between 1977 and 2009 (Fernando 2020; Sangam n.d.). The Sinhala-Buddhist victim narrative meanwhile focused on LTTE atrocities against civilian targets in the South, and sacred symbols of Sinhala-Buddhist culture, including the 1985 Sri Maha Bodhi Shrine massacre in Anuradhapura, the 1987 Aranthalawa massacre, and the 1998 bombing of the Temple of the Tooth in Kandy (Coningham and Lewer 1999). Other identity groups, including Muslims, were also victimised. A particularly egregious period of anti-Muslim persecution took place in the early 1990s when the entire Muslim community in the Northern Province was forcibly evicted by the LTTE (Commission on the Expulsion of Muslims, 2012) and in the Eastern Province, worshippers at mosques were gunned down. However, these experiences were often subordinated to Tamil and Sinhalese victim narratives within a 'hierarchisation of victimhood' (Haniffa 2015). Regardless, the continuation of ethno-linguistic conflict has depended greatly on perpetuation of victim narratives – both real and imagined – alongside identity-based politics and powerful nationalist ideologies.

The Re-emergence of Ethno-Religious Conflict

Despite the end of the armed conflict in 2009, insecurities and existential fears with respect to the 'agendas' of minorities have persisted among the Sinhala-Buddhist population (Saleem 2016: 173–174; Gunatilleke 2018). These include suspicion about minority control over the economic marketplace, and the dilution of Sinhala-Buddhist culture due to 'foreign' practices including the adoption of certain dress codes by the Muslim community. In this context, ethno-religious violence, particularly targeting Muslims, has re-emerged. Muslims have increasingly been targeted by hate campaigns (including conspiracy theories of unethical sterilisations of the Sinhalese in favour of Muslim procreation), discrimination (such as forced cremations during COVID-19), and physical violence against places of business and worship (Haniffa 2016). Often, militant Buddhist monks and organisations, such as the *Bodu Bala Sena*, were at the forefront of these campaigns. The participation of such militant monks fit into a longer history of rhetoric (and action) about the 'role and place of the monks who safeguarded the religious and national values of the country' that dated back to at least the 1980s (Abeysekara 2002: 207). In a speech that incited anti-Muslim mob violence in Darga Town and Aluthgama in June 2014, the monk Galgodaaththe Gnanasara Thero claimed 'Hereafter, if a Moorman or a person of another race even touches a Sinhalese or a yellow robe, that would be the end of this village … It is not enough to keep standing behind the temple gate to protect Buddhism. The Sinhalese are the ones who protect Buddhism … Your duty is to provide protection for the Sinhalese from all crises' (Speech made by Galagodaatte Gnanasara Thero in Aluthgama).

It is possible to see parallels in the discourses of grievance articulated by Sinhala-Buddhists against Muslims in post-war Sri Lanka, and the anti-Moor rhetoric that pre-dated the 1915 pogrom a century ago. In some sense, Sri Lanka appears to have come full circle, where ethno-religious conflict has once again been foregrounded in Sri Lanka's conflict landscape. The anti-Muslim rhetoric on social media in the 2020s echoes the propaganda in Sinhala newspapers of the early 20th century: that Muslims are threatening the economic and physical spaces of Sinhalese (Roberts 1994; Ismail 1995; Samaraweera 1997; Wettimuny 2020; Hattotuwa 2021). In this context, like in 1915, violence targeting Muslims has ensued, and such violence has drawn from the identity-based entitlement of Sinhala-Buddhists, and narratives of Sinhala-Buddhist victimisation (Gunatilleke 2018). Violent episodes against Muslims have taken place throughout the country in places such as Aluthgama and Darga Town in 2014, Gintota in 2017, Ampara in 2018, Digana and Teldeniya in 2018, and Gampaha and Kurunegala in 2019.

The targeting of Muslims has also revolved around ideological pre-occupations surrounding Islam. The process of Islamic revival that began in the 19th century went through several more waves in the 1970s and more recently in the post-war period. Followers of contemporary Islamic piety movements have asserted their identity through orthodox forms of attire and religious observance in a bid to signal religiosity and purity (Haniffa 2008). Moreover, funding from Middle Eastern sources have also incentivised this ideological shift towards ultra-conservatism (Faslan and Vanniasinkam 2015: 22). While the discussion on piety and attire is a complex one, the adherence to orthodox Islamic practices has raised concerns that certain segments of the Muslim community, particularly in the Eastern Province, have become 'radicalised' (McGilvray 2011). Within this overarching context, a violent and intolerant teaching of Islam has also emerged as an outlier within the broader Muslim polity. This outlier came to the fore on Easter Sunday, 21 April 2019, when a local group known as the National Thowheed Jamath (NTJ) perpetrated one of the most heinous terrorist attacks to have taken place on Sri Lankan soil. On Easter Sunday, the group launched coordinated suicide attacks on several churches and hotels, killing over 260 civilians. The anti-Muslim violence that predated these attacks are widely understood as having contributed to a victim narrative that propelled young Muslims to join militant Islamist groups such as NTJ and perpetrate violence against 'the other' (Imtiyaz 2020: 7).

Assertions of identity, ideology, and victim narratives have brought Muslims and other communities into the present day ethno-religious conflict in Sri Lanka (Saleem 2020). At its core lie identities galvanised by and fixated on authenticity, entitlement, and purity. Such identities appear to be further entrenched through ideologies and narratives of victimhood. Whichever identity group one considers, the same themes appear, thereby highlighting both the commonalities and the intransigence in their positions and struggles.

Importantly, the violence targeting Muslims in the post-war period was at a relatively smaller scale compared to the JVP insurrections. Meanwhile, class-based struggles including protests staged by farmers, workers, and students have continued to take place (Jayawardena and Kurian 2015). However, at the time of writing, Sri Lanka's conflict landscape has not witnessed major class-based violence on the scale seen in the 1970s and 1980s. Nevertheless, the widespread 2022 'Aragalaya' (struggle) against the Sri Lanka Podujana Peramuna-led government and the severe state repression of anti-government protestors contained elements of class-based violence that escalated in a deteriorating economic context. Vindhya Buthpitiya (2022) compares the state violence unleashed against anti-government protestors in July 2022 with the repression of 'anti-state subversion' in the 1980s. While the state resorts to familiar tactics to suppress youth and left-wing protestors, identity, ideology, and victim narratives may once again feed into future cycles of violence in Sri Lanka.

Conclusion

Centring conflict in Sri Lanka requires a close reading of the deep-rooted and multidimensional factors that drive its various forms. This chapter has offered an account of three forms of conflict and has teased out some of the major themes that appear to recur in each of them. First, identity has played a major part in the history of conflict in establishing fault lines, and in creating and maintaining the 'other'. Ethnic, religious, linguistic, and class-based identities have pervaded several conflicts in Sri Lanka over the past century. Second, ideology, by giving structure to discontent, has proved to be a powerful force in crystalising issues and in recruiting supporters for struggles. Such ideologies have included nationalism, religious dogmatism, and political thought, including Marxism. Finally, all conflicts have featured multiple victim narratives that have lent distinct identity-based and ideological struggles their moral legitimacy.

For Sinhala-Buddhist nationalists, their victim narrative is founded on historical grievances under colonial rule, and the existential threats that are constantly posed by minorities in the form of religious conversion, terrorism, and market dominance. For the historically marginalised class of Sinhalese youth, their narrative of victimhood was centred primarily around exclusion from education and employment, and caste-based oppression. For Tamils, their persecution by the Sri Lankan majoritarian state has shaped a powerful victim narrative that has propelled the call for autonomy and self-rule. For Muslims, the prevalence of hate speech, violence, and discrimination, particularly in the post-war period, underlies a compelling victim narrative. While Sinhala-Buddhists have looked to the state, and to some extent, militant nationalist groups, to promote their interests, some segments of disenchanted minorities have gravitated towards militancy as a means of furthering their interests. Meanwhile, the youth have repeatedly found themselves in violent conflict with the state's security apparatus. Such militancy on all sides has enabled a cycle of conflict that appears to recur in Sri Lanka.

What is true of conflict in Sri Lanka is perhaps true of all conflicts around the world and should not be treated as somehow special to the Sri Lankan case. However, these recurring themes need to be acknowledged and grappled with by both scholars and policymakers looking to understand conflict in Sri Lanka and to work towards its non-recurrence.

Notes

1 I am grateful to the editors of the *Handbook* and the anonymous reviewer of a draft of this chapter for their insightful comments and suggestions. Any mistakes contained in this chapter are my own.
2 Class conflict did not emerge in the 20th century and has a long history that can be traced back to the final years of Dutch colonial rule. For instance, Kumari Jayawardena (1972, 2010) examines peasant rebellions against the state and other landowners in the late 18th and early 19th centuries and explores the earliest origins of trade union action in the late 19th century.

References

Abeysekara, Ananda (2002) *Colors of the Robe: Religion, Identity and Difference* Columbia, SC: University of South Carolina Press

Ali, Ameer (1987) "Muslims and Capitalism in British Ceylon (Sri Lanka): the Colonial Image and community's Behaviour" *Journal of Muslim Minority Affairs* 8(2): 311–344

Amunugama, Sarath (2019) *The Lion's Roar: Anagarika Dharmapala and the Making of Modern Buddhism* New Delhi: Oxford University Press

Blackburn, Anne (2001) *Buddhist Learning and Textual Practice in Eighteenth-Century Lankan Monastic Culture* Princeton, NJ: Princeton University Press

Buthpitiya, Vindhya (2022) "The Heavy Footed State, Which Made a Mess" *Urban Violence*. Accessed on 5 September 2022. Available at https://urbanviolence.org/the-heavy-footed-state-which-made-a-mess/

Coningham, Robin and Nick Lewer (1999) "Paradise Lost: The Bombing of the Temple of the Tooth – A UNESCO World Heritage Site in South Asia" *Antiquity* 73: 857–866

De Mel, Neloufer (2001) *Women and the Nations Narrative: Gender and Nationalism in Twentieth Century Sri Lanka* Lanham, MD: Rowman & Littlefield Publishers, Inc

De Silva, Jani (2005) "Globalisation and the Besieged Nation: The Effects of Collective Violence on Sociological and Anthropological Research in Post-colonial Sri Lanka" *Sociological Bulletin* 54(3): 533–550

De Souza, Armand (1919) *Hundred Days in Ceylon under Martial Law 1915* Colombo: Ceylon Morning Leader

Dharmapala, Ananda and Ananda Guruge (1965) *Return to Righteousness: A Collection of Speeches, Essays and Letters of the Anagarika Dharmapala* Ceylon: Ministry of Education and Cultural Affairs

Dunham, David and Sisira Jayasuriya (2000) "Equity, Growth and Insurrection: Liberalization and the Welfare Debate in Contemporary Sri Lanka" *Oxford Development Studies* 28(1): 97–110

Faslan, Mohamed and Nadine Vanniasinkam (2015) *Fracturing Community: Intra-Group Relations among the Muslims of Sri Lanka* Colombo: International Centre for Ethnic Studies

Fernando, Ruki (2020) "Navaly Church Bombing – 25 Years On" *Groundviews* (7 July)

Final Report of the Commission on the Expulsion of Muslims from the Northern Province by the LTTE in October 1990 (2012) "The Quest for Redemption: The Story of the Northern Muslims" *Law and Society Trust*. Accessed on 14 March 2022. Available at athttps://www.lstlanka.org/publications/reports/the-quest-for-redemption-the-story-of-the-northern-muslims

Frydenlund, Iselin (2018) "Tamil Militancy in Sri Lanka and the Role of Religion" *Oxford Research Encyclopedia of Religion* Accessed on 14 March 2022. Available at https://oxfordre.com/view/10.1093/acrefore/9780199340378.001.0001/acrefore-9780199340378-e-629

Gunasinghe, Newton (1996) "The Open Economy and Its Impact on Ethnic Relations in Sri Lanka" In *Newton Gunasinghe: Selected Essays* Sasanka Perera (ed) Colombo: Social Scientists' Association, pp 183–203

Gunatilleke, Gehan (2018) *The Chronic and the Entrenched: Ethno-religious Violence in Sri Lanka* Colombo: Equitas and International Centre for Ethnic Studies

Gunawardena, Chandra (2003) "Gender Equity in Higher Education in Sri Lanka: A Mismatch between Access and Outcomes" *McGill Journal of Education* 38(3): 437–451

Guneratne, Arjun (2002) "What's in a Name? Aryans and Dravidians in the Making of Sri Lankan Identities" In *The Hybrid Island: Culture Crossings and the Invention of Identity in Sri Lanka* Neluka Silva (ed) London: Zed Books, pp 20–40

Haniffa, Farzana (2008) "Piety as Politics amongst Muslim Women in Contemporary Sri Lanka" *Modern Asian Studies* 42(2–3): 347–375

Haniffa, Farzana (2015) "Competing for Victim Status: Northern Muslims and the Ironies of Sri Lanka's Post-war Transition" *Stability: International Journal of Security and Development* 4(1): 21

Haniffa, Farzana (2016) "Stories in the Aftermath of Aluthgama: Religious Conflict in Contemporary Sri Lanka" In *Buddhist Extremists and Muslim Minorities* John Clifford Holt (ed) Web: Oxford University Press, pp 164–193

Hattotuwa, Sanjana (2021) "Sri Lanka: Digital Blooms in Social Media and Violence" In *Social Media Impacts on Conflicts and Democracy: The Tectonic Shift* Lisa Schirch (ed) London: Routledge, pp 183–193

Hellmann-Rajanayagam, Dagmar (1990) "The Politics of the Tamil Past" In *Sri Lanka: History and the Roots of Conflict* Jonathan Spencer (ed) London and New York, NY: Routledge, pp 107–122

Hoole, Rajan, Daya Somasundaram, K.A. Sritharan and Rajani Thiranagama (1992) *The Broken Palmyra: The Tamil Crisis in Sri Lanka, An Inside Account* Claremont: Sri Lanka Studies Institute

Hoole, S. and H. Ratnajeevan (1996) "The Ethnic Conflict in Sri Lanka: The Christian Response and the Nationalist Threat" *Dharma Deepika* 2(2): 122–150

Hudson, D. Dennis (1992) "Arumuga Navalar and the Hindu Renaissance among the Tamils" In *Religious Controversy in British India: Dialogues in South Asian Languages* Kenneth W. Jones (ed) Albany, NY: State University of New York Press, pp 27–51

Ilankai Tamil Sangam (n.d.) "Destruction of Hindu Temples in Sri Lanka". Accessed on 15 March 2022. Available at https://sangam.org/destruction-hindu-temples-sri-lanka/

Imtiyaz, A.R.M. (2020) "The Easter Sunday Bombings and the Crisis Facing Sri Lanka's Muslims" *Journal of Asian and African Studies* 55(1): 3–16

Ismail, Qadri (1995) "Unmooring Identity: The Antinomies of Elite Muslim Self-Representation in Modern Sri Lanka" In *Unmaking the Nation: The Politics of Identity and History in Modern Sri Lanka* Pradeep Jeganathan and Qadri Ismail (eds) Colombo: Social Scientists' Association, pp 55–105

Jayawardena, Kumari (1972) *The Rise of the Labor Movement in Ceylon* Durham, NC: Duke University Press

Jayawardena, Kumari (2010) *Perpetual Ferment: Popular Revolts in Sri Lanka in the 18th and 19th Centuries* Colombo: Social Scientists' Association

Jayawardena, Kumari and Rachel Kurian (2015) *Class, Patriarchy and Ethnicity on Sri Lankan Plantations: Two Centuries of Power and Protest* New Delhi: Orient Blackswan

Leary, Virginia A (1981–1983) "Ethnic Conflict and Violence in Sri Lanka: Report of a Mission to Sri Lanka in July–August 1981 on Behalf of the International Commission of Jurists" *International Commission of Jurists*. Accessed on 14 March 2022. Available at https://www.icj.org/wp-content/uploads/1983/08/Sri-Lanka-ethnic-conflict-and-violence-fact-finding-mission-report-1983-eng.pdf

Malalgoda, Kithsiri (1976) *Buddhism in Sinhalese Society 1750–1900: A Study of Religious Revival and Change* Berkeley, CA: University of California Press

Manor, James (1989) *The Expedient Utopian: Bandaranaike and Ceylon* Cambridge: Cambridge University Press

McGilvray, Dennis (2011) "Sri Lankan Muslims: Between Ethno-Nationalism and the Global Ummah" *Nations and Nationalism* 17(1): 45–64

Moore, Mick (1993) "Thoroughly Modern Revolutionaries: The JVP in Sri Lanka" *Modern Asian Studies* 27(3): 593–642

Pavey, Eleanor (2008) "The Massacres in Sri Lanka during the Black July Riots of 1983" *Sciences Po: Mass Violence and Resistance – Research Network* (13 May). Accessed on 14 March. Available at https://www.sciencespo.fr/mass-violence-war-massacre-resistance/en/document/massacres-sri-lanka-during-black-july-riots-1983.html

Perera, Sasanka (2001) "The Ethnic Conflict in Sri Lanka: A Historical and Socio Political Outline" *World Bank Background Paper* Accessed on 14 March 2022

Rambukwella, Harshana (2018) *The Politics and Poetics of Authenticity: A Cultural Genealogy of Sinhala Nationalism* London: UCL Press

Roberts, Michael (1994) *Exploring Confrontations: Sri Lanka – Politics, Culture and History* Reading: Hardwood

Rogers, John (2004) "Early British Rule and Social Classification in Lanka" *Modern Asian Studies* 38(4): 625–647

Saleem, Amjad (2016) "Muslim-State Relations in Sri Lanka: A Challenge for Post-Conflict Resolution" In *Muslim Minority-State Relations: Violence, Integration, and Policy* R. Mason (ed) New York, NY: Palgrave, pp 173–209

Saleem, Amjad (2020) "Re-Thinking Muslim Political Identity in Sri Lanka" *Journal of Religion and Civilisational Studies* 3(1): 84–112

Samaraweera, Vijaya (1997) "The Muslim Revivalist Movement, 1880–1915" In *Sri Lanka: Collective Identities Revisited* Vol. 1 Michael Roberts (ed) Colombo: Marga Institute, pp 293–322

Schonthal, Benjamin (2012) "Buddhism and The Constitution: The Historiography and Postcolonial Politics of Section 6" In *The Sri Lankan Republic at 40: Reflections on Constitutional History, Theory and Practice* Asanga Welikaka (ed) Colombo: Centre for Policy Alternatives, pp 202–218

Sivasundaram, Sujit (2013) *Islanded: Britain, Sri Lanka, and the Bounds of an Indian Ocean Colony* Chicago: University of Chicago Press

Somaratna, G.P.V. (1991) *Kotahena Riot, 1883: A Religious Riot in Sri Lanka* Nugegoda: G.P.V. Somaratna

Speech made by Galagodaatte Gnanasara Thero in Aluthgama (2014), *Readable*. Accessed on 5 April 2023. Available at https://si.allreadable.com/6a74FaQK

Sri Lanka Presidential Commission on Youth (1990) "Report of the Presidential Commission on Youth" *Sessional Paper No. 1 of 1990* Colombo: Government Publications Bureau

"Sri Lanka cabinet approves proposed ban on burqas in public" *Al-Jazeera* (28 April 2021) https://www.aljazeera.com/news/2021/4/28/sri-lanka-cabinet-approves-proposed-ban-on-burqas-in-public

Strathern, Alan (2017) "The Digestion of the Foreign In Lankan History, c. 500–1818" In *Sri Lanka at the Crossroads of History* Zoltán Biedermann and Alan Strathern (eds) London: UCL Press, pp 216–238

Tambiah, Stanley (1992) *Buddhism Betrayed?: Religion, Politics and Violence in Sri Lanka* Chicago, IL: University of Chicago Press

Vaitheespara, Ravi (2009) "Towards Understanding Militant Tamil Nationalism in Sri Lanka" In ***Pathways of Dissent: Tamil Nationalism in Sri Lanka*** R. Cheran (ed) New Delhi: Sage Publications

Venugopal, Rajesh (2010) "Sectarian Socialism: The Politics of Sri Lanka's Janatha Vimukthi Peramuna (JVP)" ***Modern Asian Studies*** 44(3): 567–602

Vittachi, Tarzie (1958) ***Emergency '58: The Story of the Ceylon Race Riots*** London: Andre Deutsch

Weerakoon, Bradman (2004) ***Rendering Unto Caesar: A Fascinating Story of One Men's Tenure Under Nine Prime Ministers and Presidents of Sri Lanka*** Colombo: Vijitha Yapa Publications

Wettimuny, Shamara (2019) "A Brief History of Anti-Muslim Violence in Sri Lanka" ***History Workshop Online*** (22 July). Accessed on 15 March 2022. Available at https://www.historyworkshop.org.uk/a-brief-history-of-anti-muslim-violence-in-sri-lanka/

Wettimuny, Shamara (2020) "A Colonial History of Islamophobic Slurs" ***History Workshop Online*** (7 September). Accessed on 15 March 2022. Available at https://www.historyworkshop.org.uk/colonial-history-islamophobia/

Wickramasinghe, Nira (1991) ""Divide and Rule" in Ceylon (Sri Lanka) during the Period of Transfer of Power" ***University of Colombo Review*** 10(Special Issue): 75–93

Wickramasinghe, Nira (2012) "Democracy and Entitlements in Sri Lanka: The 1970s Crisis over University Admission" ***South Asian History and Culture*** 3(1): 81–96

Wickramasinghe, Nira (2014) ***Sri Lanka in the Modern Age: A History*** New York: Oxford University Press

Wilson, A. Jeyaratnam (1993) "Ethnic Strife in Sri Lanka: The Politics of Space" ***Regional and Federal Studies*** 3(1): 144–169

Wilson, A. Jeyaratnam (2000) ***Sri Lankan Tamil Nationalism: Its Origins and Development in the Nineteenth and Twentieth Centuries*** Vancouver: UBC Press

PART III

Politics, State, and Institutions

5
DEFINING SRI LANKA'S IDENTITY

Reflections on Key Constitutional and the Legal Moments

Bhavani Fonseka and Luwie Niranjan Ganeshathasan

Introduction

The Sri Lankan State's political identity has been forged by contestation; repeated cycles of violence have confronted the nature and structure of the State. Armed insurrection predominantly mobilized by youth, the States' brutal response to these insurrections, including fortifying and entrenching security laws, and the search for justice and accountability by victims of this violence recur in Sri Lanka's post-independence history.

In 2023 Sri Lanka marked 75 years of independence from colonial rule. This was amidst daunting economic, governance, and political challenges. Decades of impunity, centralized decision-making, and systemic corruption characterized by politicized and ad-hoc processes and institutions have resulted in an unprecedented economic crisis that has contributed to shortages of essential items, long power cuts, high inflation, rising cost of living, and inequalities. In 2022, this economic crisis caused massive country-wide protests that called for "systemic changes" with people demanding for political and governance reforms. Despite the months-long protests and the departure of the incumbent president, meaningful reforms are yet to materialize. This is amidst a highly centralized and militarized governance model that has entrenched corruption, cronyism, and impunity with significant implications for governance, fundamental freedoms, and democracy.

Any reflection on Sri Lanka's post-independence period must entail an examination of events and developments that have defined the Sri Lankan State: identity politics, the rule of law, and socio-economic conditions. Sri Lanka's rich history of activism and debate has shaped these moments though questions about their process and implications loom large. On the constitutional front – the focus of this chapter – the 1978 Constitution witnessed the passage of 21 amendments whose core architecture remains unchanged despite attempts to retrofit horizontal and vertical systems of accountability with limited success. Laws and its implementation have also compounded an executive-heavy governance model, with implications for democracy and reconciliation in Sri Lanka.

Our chapter discusses contemporary moments in Sri Lanka's constitutional and legal landscape that have shaped the identity of the Sri Lankan State. We will discuss several key constitutional and legal amendments in Sri Lanka's post-independence period, examining how political debates and developments have influenced and shaped the law. The issues are salient in the context of an unprecedented economic and governance crisis, linked to several factors inclusive of the pandemic, global financial crisis, unsustainable debt, and unresolved cycles of violence. The first part examines debates and political contestations that have informed constitutional reform in Sri Lanka. We then proceed to discuss recent developments around the legacy of Sri Lanka's civil war, including demands by victim communities and others for accountability and reconciliation, and on legislative and structural reforms introduced in the post-war years. The chapter concludes by examining security laws, attempts at reforms, and setbacks.

Many of the key legal and constitutional changes have been focused on the contestation of the nature of the Sri Lankan State between the Sinhala and Tamil peoples. This could be misconstrued as framing the contestations regarding the identity and nature of the Sri Lankan State as a binary problem. As such it has to be remembered that this chapter is not an exhaustive exposition of all important constitutional and legal moments in Sri Lanka's post-independence period. Space constraints do not allow us to deal with several important legal and constitutional amendments, such as those that rendered much of the Up-country Tamil population stateless and subsequent changes which restored their citizenship or the complexities associated with the role of the Muslims in Sri Lanka's ethnic conflict (McGilvray and Raheem 2007; Vijayapalan 2014).

The Constitutional Dimensions of a Contested Sri Lankan Identity

Contestations about the identity, nature, and structure of the State pre-date its independence from colonial rule in 1948. From the disintegration of the Ceylon National Congress to undermining the "communally mixed Board of Ministers", complex ethnopolitical relations were a common theme in Ceylon's journey towards independence (Jennings and Tambiah 1952).

In 1926, S.W.R.D. Bandaranaike put forward the first serious political articulation of a federal Ceylon, with his articulation signalling complex relations between different constituent elements of the "Sinhalese" community (Edrisinha et al 2008). These federal ideas, however, did not see fruition, and Bandaranaike himself would later champion the controversial "Sinhala only" language policy, which established Sinhalese as the only official language of Sri Lankan in 1956. The language policy is widely considered a trigger point for the ethnic conflict between Sinhala and Tamil-speaking peoples initially, which also ended reverberating for Muslims too (Loganathan 1996; Thiranagama 2013).

In the lead up to independence Tamil nationalist leaders were not convinced about the idea of a federal State and instead, starting from 1926, preferred advocating for political power-sharing mechanisms in the central government. The "50:50" claim by Tamil political leaders, such as G.G. Ponnambalam, was the most prominent demand before the Soulbury Commission appointed by the British colonial government, to draft Ceylon's independent constitution. The claim was to share the representation in Parliament in such a way that Sinhalese would obtain 50% of the seats and all other minorities would obtain the balance 50% of the seats. This was however not acceptable to the Sinhala leaders and importantly to the Soulbury Commission as well, and the demands by G.G. Ponnambalam and others did not materialize in Ceylon's independence Constitution (Kumarasingham 2015). While the Soulbury Commission recognized the fear of minorities of majoritarian rule, they adopted other mechanisms which they claimed as more "effective and fairer" in conceptualizing a constitutional framework.

Despite claims for 50:50 and strong objections to political power sharing not being included in the independence constitution, G.G. Ponnambalam joined the first post-independence government (Edrisinha et al 2008). The Independence Constitution established a unitary form of government modelled on the United Kingdom, although an explicit provision proclaiming

Ceylon to be an "Unitary State" was absent. One of the first acts of this government was to enact the "Citizenship Act of 1948". This legislation effectively rendered stateless a large part of the Tamil population living and working mainly in plantation areas (Vijayapalan 2014). Ideological differences with Ponnambalam relating to the Citizenship Act of 1948 were cited as one of the reasons for a group of Tamil politicians to break away from Ponnambalam's political party, the All Ceylon Tamil Congress, in order to form the Federal Party of Sri Lanka in 1949.[1] The Federal Party claimed as its founding ideal the goal of establishing a Federal/Ceylon Sri Lanka (Edrisinha et al 2008).

The first mainstream political demand for secession was articulated by two prominent Tamil politicians – C. Suntharalingam and V. Navaratnam – during the late 1960s. These demands arose in the aftermath of the "Sinhala Only Act" and were primarily a response to the failure of agreements between Sinhala and Tamil leaders to address the inequality created by the operationalizing of the Act (Welikala 2013). These demands for secession were resisted by the Federal Party, which argued that "division of the country" would not benefit the country or the Tamil-speaking people. This was made explicitly clear in the Federal Party's election manifesto in the 1970 election, wherein they called for a new constitution based on a federal structure of government and requested the people to vote against all candidates who campaigned for secession (Welikala 2013). The Federal Party won 13 of the 16 seats contested in the Northern and Eastern Provinces and established itself as the dominant political party among the Sri Lankan Tamil community (Loganathan 1996).

The drafting of Sri Lanka's first Republican Constitution between 1970 and 1972 was another key flash point in the country's history, which saw the unitary nature the Sri Lankan State contested and ended up dominating the constitutional reform debate. The Federal Party submitted the "Model Federal Constitution" to the Constituent Assembly. This proposal was defeated by an overwhelming majority of the Constituent Assembly and the Federal Party discontinued its engagement with the process shortly thereafter (Edrisinha et al 2008). The First Republican Constitution and article seven in particular further entrenched the "Sinhala Only" policy by introducing cosmetic measures recognizing the "reasonable use of the Tamil Language in the Northern and Eastern Provinces". Much to the consternation of the Federal Party, the First Republican Constitution also gave Buddhism "the foremost place" in the new Republic and placed a duty on the State to "protect and foster" Buddhism while assuring the right of thought conscience and religion to all citizens.[2]

In response to the passage of the First Republican Constitution, the Federal Party joined with the All-Ceylon Tamil Congress and the Ceylon Workers Congress to form the Tamil United Liberation Front (TULF). The Federal Party and subsequent political formations led by the Federal Party have continued to deny the legitimacy of the First Republican Constitution (Loganathan 1996). Their objections were primarily based on the explicit entrenchment of the unitary state in the Constitution, the continued discrimination of the Tamil-speaking people of Sri Lanka based on constitutional recognition of the "Sinhala Only" policy, and the foremost place granted to Buddhism.

During the first national convention of the TULF in 1976, delegates adopted a resolution calling for the creation of a "Free, Sovereign, Secular and Socialist state of Tamil Eelam" within the territory of Sri Lanka (Edrisinha et al 2008). This was the first instance in which secession became a central focus of the political platform of a major political party. The resolution, which came to be known as the *Vaddukoddai* Resolution, went beyond a mere aspirational statement and called on the TULF to establish a political plan to achieve secession (Edrisinha et al 2008). It also called on Tamil youth to "fully throw themselves to the struggle of establishing the separate state of Tamil Eelam" (Edrisinha et al 2008: 254).

The aftermath of the *Vaddukoddai* Resolution saw a wave of non-violent protests by the TULF and other Tamil youth organizations. These protests were repressed by the government through various means, including the introduction of an emergency regulations that made it an offence to advocate for a separate State (Edrisinha et al 2008). The repression of these protests saw the rise of several Tamil youth-led militant organizations in the late 1970s and the early 1980s. Concurrent to fighting the Sri Lankan State, these militant groups subsequently engaged in a bloody and brutal contest to claim dominance over each other (Hoole et al 1992; Loganathan 1996). The widespread and systematic racial pogrom against Tamils in July 1983 saw increased support for these militant organizations from among the Tamil community, particularly towards the Liberation Tigers of Tamil Eelam (LTTE), who operated quickly to brutally crush other militant organizations and absorb their cadres.

The First Republican Constitution was replaced in 1978 by the Second Republican Constitution, which created significant changes to the Sri Lankan constitutional system. The most notable change was the transition from the Westminster model of a Parliamentary executive towards an elected Executive President. This Constitution continues to operate to date and has been amended 21 times. In its original form, the Executive President had broad ranging powers including control over Parliament and the judiciary, and immunity from legal suit for all official and private acts.

Soon after the July 1983 racial pogrom, the government introduced the sixth amendment to the Second Republican Constitution, with article 157A prohibiting citizens from advocating for the creation of a separate State within the territorial limits of Sri Lanka. It also prohibited any political party or association from having as its aims and objectives the establishment of a separate State within Sri Lanka's territory. These were made criminal offences triable directly by the Court of Appeal and the Supreme Court, and upon conviction, a person could be deprived of civic rights for seven years and be liable to forfeiture of property (ibid). The new amendment also mandated all public officials and persons holding office under the Constitution to subscribe to an oath that they will not, "directly or indirectly, in or outside Sri Lanka, support, espouse, promote, finance, encourage or advocate the establishment of a separate State within the territory of Sri Lanka".[3]

In addition to the prohibition on advocating for secession, the constitutional recognition of Sri Lanka as a "Unitary State" has also been touted by many Sinhala nationalists as a protection against secession thereby ensuring the territorial integrity of the State.[4] The term "Unitary State" first appeared in the First Republican Constitution, though the reason for its inclusion remains contested and unclear, as neither of the two Republican Constitutions defined the meaning of the term "Unitary State" (Jayawickrama 2013). However, over a period of time the significance of this term has grown as both a normative principle of Sri Lankan Constitutional law and as a political symbol (Welikala 2016).

Understandings of the term, however, are divided and mixed. The Public Representations Committee on Constitutional Reform, which was appointed in 2015 to gather opinions from the citizens of Sri Lanka on constitutional reform, identified a significant divergence of opinions expressed by citizens on the meaning of "Unitary State" (PRCCR 2016). A survey conducted in 2015/2016 (at the beginning of the constitutional reform process) found that 49.3% of the total respondents and 58% of Sinhala respondents understood the term to mean "one united and indivisible country" (Social Indicator 2016). This is indicative of the strong belief among the Sinhala community that the "Unitary State" label acts as a deterrent against secession. This political understanding of the term has been further complicated by the conflation of the terms "federalism" with "separatism" by those who oppose the devolution of power (Rajapaksa 2019). The basis of their argument is that when the unitary character of the State is not recognized by the constitution, it will automatically amount to a federal constitution and thus lead to secession.

This understanding of the unitary state as a *sine qua non* of protecting the territorial integrity of the Sri Lankan State has led to several complications in constitutional reform debates in

Sri Lanka. Firstly, it prevents a debate and discussion over the extent to which power can and should be devolved to subnational territorial entities to fulfil the aspirations of the Sri Lankan Tamil community and other minorities. Leaders of both main political parties have repeatedly pledged to allow maximum possible devolution in the country but have never explained what this means. Unfortunately, any debate on this issue seems to begin with the "unitary state" label and, therefore, does not move towards any meaningful deliberation or resolution.

Secondly, Tamil nationalists strictly resist the unitary label of the State, as they perceive it to be a means by which even the limited power that has been devolved can be taken back through judicial interpretation. This is primarily due to the legal interpretation of the term "unitary state" adopted by the Sri Lankan Supreme Court, when deciding the constitutional validity of the Thirteenth Amendment to the Constitution in 1987.[5,6] This interpretation by the Court resulted in entrenching a hierarchical relationship between the subnational entity to which power had been devolved to and the institutions of the central government. It also created limitations on any further devolution of power to subnational entities (Welikala 2016).

This intractable position between the Tamil nationalists and Sinhala nationalists on the unitary label has led to a stalemate in negotiations on the form and structure of the Sri Lankan State in a future constitutional order. It has also been a stumbling block for several subsequent constitutional reform efforts and a central reason for the failure of repeated attempts to negotiate a political settlement on the question of the nature of the Sri Lankan State (Edrisinha et al 2008).

Transitional Justice and Reforms

Sri Lanka's past cycles of violence have resulted in persistent demands by victims for reckoning, accountability, and redress with debates ranging on the merits of transitional justice and the different modalities encompassing restorative and retributive justice and whether its national and international (Bala 2017; Fonseka 2017; Medewatte 2017). Victims who have experienced violence at the hands of the State and non-State actors over the decades have continued their demands for truth and justice by way of mobilization, court challenges, vigils, and campaigns that has kept the issues alive (Samuel 2006; Kodikara 2022). This has resulted in successive governments promising domestic mechanisms for redress and accountability, with limited tangible results in obtaining truth and justice (Jayawardena and Pinto-Jayawardena 2016; Medewatte et al 2022). Amidst countless failures at seeking truth and justice in Sri Lanka, demands for international action grew among some sections of the victim communities, civil society, and the diaspora. This resulted in tensions and other dynamics within these groups as to whether truth and justice should be domestic, hybrid, or international (Bala 2017; Cronin-Furman 2020). This was in a post-war context of increasing ethno-nationalism and triumphalism that impacted debates about Sri Lanka's future, within the country and outside it (Wickramasinghe 2009).

Despite the pushback from various sections on truth and justice, there is increasing recognition that genuine reckoning for violence over the decades has been elusive but imperative. In a survey conducted by Social Indicator in 2019, a majority of Sri Lankans (72.4%) believe that it is important to know the truth about alleged crimes against humanity committed by all parties during the three-decade-long conflict (CPA/SI 2019c: 27). This view was largely attributed to the minority community with 75.4% of the Tamil community and 68.1% of the Muslim community indicating that it was "very important" to know the truth about alleged crimes against humanity committed by all parties, during the three-decade-long civil conflict in Sri Lanka. Among those who felt it was "not important", 21.2% were from the Sinhala and 15% from the Muslim community. On questions of redress for victims affected by civil unrest in the past, 49.3% of Sri Lankans believe that it was "extremely necessary", while 22.5% believe that it was "somewhat necessary" to investigate and hold those accountable before the law. It is notable that 76.5% of youth felt that investigating and holding those accountable before the law was "important".

Sri Lanka's post-war period witnessed several legislative reforms introduced because of commitments internationally as discussed below. In adherence to the commitments made with the United Nations Human Rights Council Resolution 30/1 in 2015, the then government of Sri Lanka established two of the four mechanisms promised via the enactment of law. In 2016, the Government of Sri Lanka enacted the Office on Missing Persons (OMP) Act, which provided the legal framework to establish the first independent and permanent office to investigate into the thousands of cases of enforced disappearances and missing persons in Sri Lanka (Fonseka 2017). Despite repeated calls by victims and civil society to independently investigate enforced disappearances, successive governments over the decades have taken the easy route by establishing countless commissions of inquiry or committees with limited to no progress made, with victims being unable to find out the whereabouts of their missing loved ones or being able to get closure (Kodikara 2021).

The Government of Sri Lanka's co-sponsoring of Resolution 30/1 itself was a significant step in the government's own recognition of Sri Lanka's legacy of past abuses and the need for structural reforms, with a wide range of commitment made from institutional and legislative reforms, to addressing ongoing violations and intimidation. It was also the first time in the post-war context, when the Government of Sri Lanka (GOSL) recognized the need for wide-ranging reforms, in an international forum (Bala 2017; Fonseka 2017). Despite the ambitious promises, the implementation faced numerous setbacks, from a lack of political will to take key reforms forward amidst mounting opposition from nationalist groups within Sri Lanka, to a lack of a comprehensive plan, and practical issues of the lack of capacity and expertise.

The enactment of the OMP Act faced robust push back from the then opposition and sections of victim groups, the former opposing any moves to investigate past abuses that could be attributed to those linked to the former regime, and the latter claiming that the OMP would shut the door to justice. For example, the debate on the OMP Act in 2016 witnessed heated exchanges and disruptions by the opposition that led to the subsequent delay in operationalizing the OMP, which only commenced in 2018. Despite the OMP now being in place for several years, the office continues to face setbacks, with the present regime seemingly inclined to speed through claims and offer compensation rather than pursue genuine truth and accountability (Kodikara 2021).

Another mechanism established as part of Resolution 30/1 was the Office for Reparations in 2018, which provided for a permanent office for the provision of reparations. Addressing one of the pillars of transitional justice, this office built on the work done by Rehabilitation of Persons, Properties and Industries Authority (REPPIA) with the objective of introducing a reparations policy and addressing grievances of the community. The opposition to the legislation was witnessed when it was challenged by some citizens in the Supreme Court, which resulted in weakening some proposed provisions. Concerns were also raised that the reliance on the Cabinet and Parliament to approve reparations would dilute the independence of the Office resulting in a politicization of the process.

Sri Lanka's large case load of enforced disappearances has resulted in decades of activism and mobilization of victims and civil society who have called for truth, accountability, and justice but with limited success. Despite the appointment of several commissions of inquiry on the issue and publicly available reports indicating the significant cases of enforced disappearances, the law to recognize the enforced disappearances as a crime and administrative steps to assist victims were long overdue. The first step to address the practical difficulties faced by victims of enforced disappearances was taken in 2016 when the then government introduced the concept of "Certificates of Absences", a temporary administrative measure, to assist victims who refused to proceed with obtaining death certificates via the Registration of Deaths (Temporary Provisions) (Amendment) Act No 16 of 2016. Certificates of Absence were like measures introduced in Nepal and other comparative contexts. Yet, some victims rejected the offer of death certificates as some perceived it as closing the door in their quest for justice. The attention on enforced disappearances also resulted in the enactment of legislation in 2018 titled the "International Convention for the Protection of all Persons from Enforced Disappearances Act No 5 of 2018", which criminalized enforced disappearances and provided procedural safeguards in preventing them.

Despite these few moves, much of what was promised in terms of transitional justice reforms have yet to materialize or have been extremely slow in implementation. This includes the widely debated hybrid justice model and the Truth and Reconciliation Commission both promised in Resolution 30/1. The brief period of 2015–2019 that witnessed some movement with transitional justice initiatives including legislative and institutional reforms was short-lived due to internal tensions within the *Yahapalanaya* government including a constitutional crisis in 2018, the deadly Easter Sunday attacks, and an effective campaign by the then opposition that de-legitimized transitional justice and other reforms. Narratives that portrayed transitional justice being pushed by "western NGOs" and that it threatened Sri Lanka's sovereignty, among others, found fertile ground among nationalist sections of society (Fonseka and Ganeshathasan 2016).

These narratives and conspiracy theories must be considered in a context when many were disillusioned with a government who had failed to deliver on its campaign promises. This was compounded by rising levels of fear and suspicion created in the wake of the Easter Sunday attacks in 2019 that exposed a complete breakdown of governance and security. The Easter Sunday attacks not only shut down any hope of progressive reforms including in the area of transitional justice but also witnessed increased ethnonationalist rhetoric and violence, with violence and intimidation especially against the Muslim community intensifying (Saroor 2021).

Security Laws

Sri Lanka's use of security laws continued unabated during the post-war years with the continued reliance on the Public Security Ordinance (PSO) and the Prevention of Terrorism Act (PTA). The PSO has been used on several occasions, including declaring a state of emergency and the use of Section 12 to call out the troops. While this section is not an exhaustive examination of security laws in post-war Sri Lanka, it is imperative to examine recent developments and the continued reliance on security laws during the period in focus. The section first examines the PTA and related issues and then examines the continuing use of emergency regulations.

Wide-ranging calls for the repeal and reform of the PTA resulted in the introduction of a Counter Terror Act in 2018 to repeal the PTA and bring in a new law. This move saw diverse groups including political parties, trade unions, civil society, and others mobilize to critique and challenge a draft law that many perceived as not addressing the fundamental problems entrenched in the PTA (HRW 2018; CPA 2019a). As with several other instances, the drafting of the Bill was shrouded in secrecy with most stakeholders left out of discussions. A leaked draft of the Bill raised serious concerns on the implications to fundamental rights and the rule of law. A subsequently released new draft saw some changes to the proposed Bill but continued to face opposition from various actors. Diverse calls opposing the Bill included some parties opposing the existence of any anti-terror laws and urging authorities to rely on existing criminal laws to address security challenges. Other local and international groups called for a more nuanced approach of improving the draft law to meet international standards and having adequate safeguards including judiciary and parliament oversight on its implementation.

After several months of discussions with two committees in Parliament deliberating on its contents, an improved version of the Bill that reflected contemporary international standards was produced in Parliament in 2019. This process, despite its delays, provided a Bill that was to replace the draconian PTA, removed some of its most problematic provisions, such as the admissibility of confessions and provided safeguards. Despite this, debates around national security and terrorism witnessed a major shift post Easter Sunday attack, with proponents for a stronger security law using the opportunity to call for stronger laws and measures even at the cost of due process safeguards and checks and balances. More recently, the Government of Sri Lanka has attempted to introduce the proposed Anti-Terrorism Act which is presently before the Parliament of Sri Lanka.

These discussions resurfaced yet again in 2021–2022, amidst international attention on Sri Lanka via the UNHRC sessions and EU GSP+ trade preference, which culminated in the adoption of the Prevention of Terrorism (Amendment) 2022 in March 2022. This, like the 2018–2019 Counter Terror Bill, witnessed diverse debates ranging from support for the need for strong security laws to sections calling for the complete repeal of the PTA, once again reinforcing the centrality of national security in contemporary politics and the reliance of security laws by state actors for different purposes. Amidst the massive public protests (widely known as the *Aragalaya*) in 2022 and the use of the PTA to detain three protesters, there was an increased awareness across sections of society about the legacy of the PTA to target dissent, resulting in increasing demands for its repeal. This is at a time when the government gazetted the proposed Anti-Terrorism Act in March 2023 which has witnessed many of the debates surrounding the Counter Terror Bill in 2018–2019 and the amendment to the PTA in 2022 resurface.

Notably, while the debate to repeal or reform the PTA continued with some in government promising to bring in new laws in adherence to international standards, the government also introduced regulations under the current PTA with significant implications to rights and the rule of law. At the time of writing, the regulations are being challenged in the Supreme Court with the outcome of the cases defining whether the regulations will be in force or struck down (The Morning 2022). This is in a context when some in government were engaging on reforming the PTA seemingly to meet international standards and due process safeguards, while others were drafting regulations that if implemented could be used to target individuals and communities, thereby undermining the limited due process safeguards available.

Declaration of emergency and regulations: After the Easter Sunday attacks in 2019, the government swiftly introduced emergency regulations, defending it as necessary in the face of unknown security threats (CPA 2019b). Some provisions were challenged in the Supreme Court with the government giving an undertaking in court for not proceeding with certain provisions, such as the disposing of dead bodies. Emergency was imposed again in 2021 on the pretext of addressing essential supplies and services in the wake of the COVID-19 pandemic (CPA 2021). This was met with vigorous opposition as to the validity of the need for emergency at a time when regular laws provided for the provision of essential services and supplies and for perpetuating militarization by appointing a retired military official as the competent authority.

Amidst increasing protests across Sri Lanka in 2022, then President Gotabaya Rajapaksa declared a state of emergency on 1 April, which saw the imposition of curfew across Sri Lanka for 36 hours seemingly to prevent a nation-wide anti-government protest from taking place (Jayasinghe 2022). Despite the curfew, thousands took to the streets to peacefully protest the government, the largest civil disobedience seen in recent years in Sri Lanka. Due to public and political pressure, the state of emergency was revoked within a few days. The same year saw two more instances when the executive president issued proclamations declaring a state of emergency, seemingly in response to the protests in May and July. The legality of all three instances is presently being challenged in the Supreme Court (Sooriyagoda 2022).

These recent incidents vividly demonstrate the willingness by some in government and state institutions, to naturally revert to a state of emergency as a panacea in the face of challenges ranging from national security to the maintenance of essential services and supplies, to preventing citizens using their democratic right to protest. Despite over 14 years having passed since the end of the war, the continued use of the PTA, the resorting to emergency regulations and push back on progressive reforms demonstrate the multiple challenges facing Sri Lanka. The entrenched nature of security laws and the natural reliance of them by different stakeholders, despite evidence of abuse, is telling as it illustrates how many continue to perceive national security as a key defining concept.

Conclusion

The chapter captures key moments that has defined Sri Lanka's constitutional and legal amendments, examining how political debates and developments influenced and shaped the law. The chapter notes that constitutional and legal frameworks cannot be examined in a vacuum and must be understood in context of the social and other factors that informed these legal proposals.

We demonstrate that identity politics, security considerations, socio-economic conditions and other issues define and condition narratives and with it influence the law and its implementation. Thus, future attempts at constitutional and legal reforms must take into consideration the various issues that have had an impact on the law-making process, the law, and implementation. Failure to identify and address these underlying political and social considerations has undermined reform efforts and further entrenched the centralized and militarized State, which has proven its inability to deliver on its promises of stability and economic prosperity.

Notes

1. The Tamil name of this party is "*Illankai Tamil Arasu Kachchi*" which translates into "Tamil State Party of Sri Lanka."
2. Article 6 read with Article 18(1)(d) of the First Republican Constitution.
3. Seventh Schedule of the Second Republican Constitution (as amended by the Sixth Amendment).
4. Article 2 of the First Republican Constitution and Article 2 of the Second Republican Constitution.
5. *In Re the Thirteenth Amendment to the Constitution and the Provincial Councils Bill* (1987) 2 SLR 312 at page 319.
6. The 13th Amendment was enacted in 1987, pursuant to the Indo-Sri Lanka accord. It created a second tier of governance known as Provincial Councils and devolved executive and legislative power to them. The 13th amendment is textually similar to the provisions on devolution found in the Indian Constitution; however in practice they operate very differently. One reason for this is the interpretation adopted by the Supreme Court, but more importantly mostly all the governments that have been in power since 1987 have actively tried to undermine the provisions of this amendment.

References

Bala, Mytili (2017) "Where Justice Is Non-Negotiable: Pragmatic Engagement for Accountability in Sri Lanka: Transitional Justice in Context" ***Harvard Human Rights Journal*** Accessed on 5 September 2022. Available at https://harvardhrj.com/2017/10/online-symposium-on-transitional-justice/

Centre for Policy Alternatives (2016) "Opinion Poll on Constitutional Reform – Topline Report" ***Social Indicator***. Accessed on 3 March 2024. Available at http://www.cpalanka.org/wp-content/uploads/2016/10/Opinion-poll-on-Constitutional-Reform_Final_Oct-16.pdf

Centre for Policy Alternatives (CPA) (2019a) *Q&A Proposed Counter Terror Act 2019* Accessed on 20 January 2023. Available at https://www.cpalanka.org/wp-content/uploads/2019/04/CTA_QA.pdf

Centre for Policy Alternatives (CPA) (2019b) *Understanding Emergency: Easter Sunday Attacks 2019.* Accessed on 20 January 2023. Available at https://www.cpalanka.org/wp-content/uploads/2019/04/QA_SoE.pdf

Centre for Policy Alternatives (CPA) (2021) *The Declaration of a State of Emergency and Regulations for the Maintenance of Essential Supplies and Services 2021.* Accessed on 20 January 2023. Available at https://www.cpalanka.org/wp-content/uploads/2021/09/Initial-Comment-CPA-Essential-Food-Serivces-ERs-2021-1.pdf

Centre for Policy Alternatives/Social Indicator (2019c) *Values and Attitudes Survey on 70 Years' of Independence in Sri Lanka* Colombo: Centre for Policy Alternatives

Cronin-Furman, Kate (2020) "Human Rights Half Measures: Avoiding Accountability in Post War Sri Lanka" *World Politics* 72(1): 121–163

Edrisinha, Rohan, Mario Gomez, V. T. Thamilmaran and Asanga Welikala (2008) *Power-Sharing in Sri Lanka: Constitutional and Political Documents, 1926–2008* Colombo: Centre for Policy Alternatives. Available at https://www.cpalanka.org/power-sharing-in-sri-lanka-constitutional-and-political-documents-19262008/

Fonseka, Bhavani (2017) *Transitional Justice in Sri Lanka: Moving Beyond Promises* Colombo: CPA

Fonseka, Bhavani and Luwie Ganeshathasan (2016) *Hybrid vs. Domestic: Myths, Realities and Options for Transitional Justice in Sri Lanka* Colombo: CPA

Hoole, Rajan, Daya Somasundaram, K.A. Sritharan and Rajani Thiranagama (1992) *The Broken Palmyra, the Tamil Crisis in Sri Lanka, An Inside Account* Claremont: The Sri Lanka Studies Institute

Human Rights Watch (2018) "Sri Lanka Draft Counter Terrorism Act of 2018" Accessed on 20 January 2023. Available at https://www.hrw.org/news/2018/10/21/sri-lanka-draft-counter-terrorism-act-2018

Jayasinghe, Uditha (2022) "Sri Lanka imposes curfew after president declares state of emergency" *Reuters* (April 2022). Accessed on 20 January 2023. Available at https://www.reuters.com/world/asia-pacific/tight-security-sri-lankas-capital-shops-open-after-state-emergency-order-2022-04-02/

Jayawardena, Kumari and Kishali Pinto-Jayawardena (eds) (2016) *The Search for Justice: The Sri Lanka Papers* Delhi: Zubaan

Jayawickrama, Nihal (2013) "Reflections on the Making and Content of the 1972 Constitution: An Insider's Perspective" In *The Sri Lankan Republic at 40: Reflections on Constitutional History, Theory and Practice* Asanga ed and Welikala (eds) Colombo: Centre for Policy Alternatives

Jennings, Ivor and H.W. Tambiah (1952) *The Domininon of Ceylon* Stevens & Sons Limited

Kodikara, Chulani (2021) "The Office on Missing Persons post-2020: Who and What Is It for?" *SSA Polity* (November 2021). Accessed on 30 December 2021. Available at http://ssalanka.org/office-missing-persons-post-2020-chulani-kodikara/

Kodikara, Chulani (2022) "Dissident Memory and Democratic Citizenship: Sandya Ekneligoda and Her Struggle for Justice" *SSA Polity* (January 2022). Accessed on 7 February 2022. Available at http://ssalanka.org/dissident-memory-democratic-citizenship-sandya-ekneligoda-struggle-justice-chulani-kodikara/

Kumarasingham, Harshan (2015) *The Road to Temple Trees Sir Ivor Jennings and the Constitutional Development of Ceylon: Selected Writings* Colombo: Centre for Policy Alternatives

Loganathan, Ketheshwaran (1996) *Sri Lanka; Lost Opportunities, Past Attempts at Resolving Ethnic Conflict* Colombo: Centre for Policy Research and Analysis

McGilvray, Dennis and Mirak Raheem (2007) *Muslim Perspectives on the Sri Lankan Conflict* Washington: East-West Center Washington

Medewatte, Danushka (2017) "Walking on a Tight Rope: Sri Lanka's Fragile Transitional Justice Process" *Harvard Human Rights Journal* Online Symposium. Available at http://harvardhrj.com/wp-content/uploads/sites/14/2017/10/Medawatte.pdf

Medewatte, Danushka, Neloufer De Mel, Sandani N. Yapa Abeywardena and Ranitha Gnanaraj (2022) "Conjunctures of Silence: Aphonias in the Prosecution of Conflict Related Sexual Violence in Sri Lanka – the Vishvamadu Case" *The Gender, Justice and Security Hub* 1–24

Public Representations Committee on Constitutional Reform (2016) *Report on Public Representations on Constitutional Reform.* Accessed on 03 March 2024. Available at https://constitutionnet.org/sites/default/files/sri_lanka_prc_report-english-final.pdf

Rajapaksa, Mahinda (2019) "A Draft Constitution to Destroy Sri Lanka" *Colombo Telegraph* (23 January). Accessed on 20 January 2023. Available at https://www.colombotelegraph.com/index.php/a-draft-constitution-to-destroy-sri-lanka/

Samuel, Kumudini (2006) *A Hidden History: Women's Activism for Peace in Sri Lanka 1982–2002* Colombo: Social Scientists' Association

Saroor, Shreen Abdul (2021) *The Muslims in Post War Sri Lanka: Repression, Resistance & Reform* Colombo: Alliance for Minorities

Sooriyagoda, Lakmal (2022) "SC nods for petitions challenging Proclamation of State of Emergency" *The Daily Mirror* (April 2022). Accessed on 20 January 2023. Available at https://www.dailymirror.lk/print/front_page/SC-nods-for-petitions-challenging-Proclamation-of-State-of-Emergency/238-234763

The Constitutional Assembly of the Eighth Parliament of Sri Lanka (undated) "Constitutional History". Accessed on 29 April 2019. Available at https://english.constitutionalassembly.lk/constitutional-history

The Morning (2022), "SC grants leave to proceed with case against PTA Deradicatlisation Regulations" *The Morning* (March 2022). Accessed on 20 January 2023. Available at https://www.themorning.lk/articles/186255

Thiranagama, Sharika (2013) "Claiming the State: Post-war Reconciliation in Sri Lanka" *Humanity: An International Journal of Human Rights, Humanitarianism and Development* 4(1): 93–116

Vijayapalan, Yogeswary (2014) *Endless Inequality: The Rights of the Plantation Tamils in Sri Lanka* Mayan Vije Limited

Welikala, Asanga (ed) (2013) "The Ilankai Thamil Arasu Katchi (Federal Party) and the Post-Independence Politics of Ethnic Pluralism: Tamil Nationalism before and after the Republic: An Interview with R. Sampanthan" *The Sri Lankan Republic at 40: Reflections on Constitutional History, Theory and Practice* Colombo: Centre for Policy Alternatives

Welikala, Asanga (2016) *The Sri Lankan Conception of the Unitary State: Theory, Practice, and History*. CPA Working Papers on Constitutional Reform. Accessed on 3 March 2024. Available at https://www.cpalanka.org/wp-content/uploads/2016/06/CPA-Working-Paper-1.pdf

Wickramasinghe, Nira (2009) "After the War: A New Patriotism in Sri Lanka?" *The Journal of Asian Studies* 68(4): 1045–1054

6
IMAGINING THE NATION
A Critical Overview of Sinhala Nationalism and Its Cultural Coordinates

Harshana Rambukwella

Introduction

In the novella *Inimage Ihalata* (*Up the Ladder* 1992) by Gunadasa Amarasekara – a prominent 20th-century Sri Lankan Sinhala-language writer – the main character Piyadasa engages in a literal and symbolic journey of nationalist self-discovery. As Piyadasa travels from the southern town of Galle further into the 'deep south' of the country he experiences an epiphany. In the town of Tissamaharama in the southeast corner of the island, Piyadasa sees manifest in the physical landscape the *weva, dagoba and ketha* (the irrigation lake, Buddhist stupa and paddy field) – the symbolic triad of Sinhala Buddhist nationalism that captured the imagination in the 1950s and maintained a hegemonic grip well into the 1980s (Spencer 1990b; Tambiah 1992). This symbolic triad signifies a vision of a grand pre-colonial past fashioned in the encounter between orientalist knowledge production and its appropriation by local intelligentsia. Amarasekara is considered an iconic Sinhala writer and a prominent nationalist ideologue. He is also part of a long line of 20th-century Sinhala creative artists who saw their role as a historical mission to craft a national cultural form.

In stark contrast, writing several decades after Amarasekara, Liyanage Amarakeerthi, a prolific and award-winning contemporary Sinhala novelist, presents a very different vision. In *kurulu hadawatha* (*The Bird's Heart* 2013), Amarakeerthi ironically deconstructs the narrative of nationalist authenticity nurtured by writers like Amarasekara. In *kurulu hadawatha* he reduces the vision of pastoral nationalist authenticity to fiction – a giant simulacrum sustained by an insidious nexus between expedient nationalist politics, neo-liberal capital and the marketing and media industries; marking what I call the 'death of authenticity' (Rambukwella 2018). His satiric treatment of authenticity underscores how the cultural coordinates of post-independence Sinhala nationalism go into crisis, with the welfare state withering in the late 1980s. However, while it marks the death of one kind of 'authenticity', arguably, culture remains a key site of Sinhala ideological reproduction.

I begin by referencing the cultural-aesthetic dimension of Sinhala nationalist discursive reproduction for several reasons. At one level it points to the central role culture and cultural reproduction plays in generating and disseminating a nationalist imaginary. At another it points to the dynamic nature of nationalist discourse, underlining that it is neither homogenous nor static.

For many decades 'liberal' scholarship on Sri Lanka has taken nationalism in general, and Sinhala nationalism, as its primary 'other'. In doing so critical scholarship has 'flattened' a multi-layered discourse into a singularly named phenomenon and framed nationalism in Sri Lanka as a 'bipolar' Sinhala-Tamil conflict, at the expense of other political-identity formations, such as Muslim identity (Rajasingham-Senanayake 1999; Ismail 2005; Wickramasinghe 2006). Politically, Sinhala nationalism is ascribed an ahistorical ontology. This standpoint also prevents us from seeing how Sinhala nationalism must be read against Tamil and Muslim nationalisms that form its ideological others (see also Klem, Gamage, this volume). From a conceptual and methodological perspective, it results in the 'naturalization' of nationalism, where it becomes a framework within which sociological and humanities research is entrapped (Brubaker 1996).

I also want to argue for a methodological approach where nationalism is an ontological fallacy, which is nevertheless important as a category of social practice and a category of analysis (Wimmer and Schiller 2003). While we conceptually deconstruct the nation, we must be critically cognizant of the ways in which it impinges upon social life. I start with some methodological and conceptual clarifications regarding nationalism and its normalization. Thereafter, I discuss a body of scholarship that implicitly and explicitly placed culture as a site from which to explore nationalism, without critical self-reflexivity and thus creating a narrative that normalizes and legitimizes Sinhala nationalism. Next, I discuss responses in the aftermath of the 1983 anti-Tamil pogrom, where the cultural formation of Sinhala nationalism was seen as a significant obstacle to 'peace'. Finally, the recent scholarship that coincided with the conclusion of the military conflict in 2009 – that self-consciously sought to break with the nation-centred approaches – is discussed.

Methodological Nationalism and the Early Period

The nation functions as a common-sense epistemic receptacle in social sciences and humanities everywhere, where the nation is taken as a given and 'natural' analytical category. Wimmer and Schiller (2003) call this methodological nationalism. Resisting methodological nationalism is remarkably difficult due to the deep-seated normativity the nation has acquired. In the Sri Lankan context this tendency is particularly marked in pre-1980s scholarship which was implicitly and explicitly shaped by a national agenda, informed by the euphoria of decolonization and political independence. For historians, for instance, the natural protagonist of history became the nation and followed a tradition of history writing 'inherited' from colonial historiography. As John Rogers (1990) has observed colonial historians crafted a history for Sri Lanka where they mapped a three-stage model of European historiography to the Sri Lankan context. According to this historical template, Sri Lanka had a classical golden age which then declined with the end of the Anuradhapura and Polonnaruwa kingdoms. A middle period like the European middle ages follows, and the arrival of European colonialism marks the third stage and a kind of economic and national renaissance. Some local intelligentsia, such as Anagarika Dharmapala, appropriated this narrative and interrupted its colonial teleology by proposing a hybrid third stage in which Western scientific rationality is combined with local cultural values (Rambukwella 2018: 48–72).

This national cultural form is evident when one looks at historiographies by Knighton (1845) and Tennent (1860[1977]), where these texts serve a 'colonial purpose' in how they compile and summarize knowledge to make the island 'knowable' for colonial governance. However, they also treat the island as a 'nation' and project this national imagination onto Sri Lanka's past as well. In doing so they implicitly normalize a national frame where the country becomes 'islanded' (Sivasundaram 2013; see also Jazeel, this volume). This kind of national framing contributes to methodological nationalism by generating a territorially bounded imagination delimited by

Sri Lanka's natural island borders congruent with scholarly analysis. One impact of this approach is that it has tended to downplay how the nationalist imagination is dialogic. This is manifested in Anagarika Dharmapala, who is identified as a one-dimensional nationalist both in anti-nationalist 'liberal' scholarship as well as nationalist scholarship (Rambukwella 2018: 48–72). Yet others have argued that the world Dharmapala inhabited was 'cosmopolitan' and his religious, social, and political entanglements extended well beyond Sri Lanka (Kemper 2015). What is also significant is that by using categories like 'nation' and 'nationalism' for the late 19th and early 20th centuries, one can inadvertently project today's relatively more hardened sense of nationalism onto a period in which these categories were still negotiated and debated. Therefore, terms, such as Sinhala Buddhist nationalism or Tamil nationalism, need to be used with caution to describe political mobilization in the late 19th and early 20th centuries because it risks historical anachronism.

This approach has bearing on how national cultural identity becomes defined after independence. Throughout the first half of the 20th century, a range of 'revivalist' movements emerged in Sri Lankan society, with the 'Buddhist revival' being the most influential (Malalgoda 1976; Gombrich and Obeyesekere 1988). In Tamil society, a slightly earlier 'Hindu revival' was led by Arumugar Navalar (Hudson 1992). The Buddhist revivalist movement is seen to have played a significant role in enabling a middle-level village-based intelligentsia – comprising Buddhist sangha, school teachers, and Ayurveda physicians – who played a critical role in the 1956 Sinhala nationalist electoral victory of the Mahajana Eksath Peramuna (MEP) (Rambukwella 2017; Dewasiri 2020). However, what such a reading occludes is that the revivalist activity in the early 20th century was not necessarily segregated along ethnic or religious lines. For instance, in the early 1900s, the Ceylon Reform Society initiated a programme to 'revive' indigenous medicine, with local elites from all communities contributing to this initiative (Abeyrathne 2015).

Emergence of a Sinhala National Cultural Form

The post-independence period and the period immediately leading up to and following the MEP victory of 1956 were the periods in which the Sinhala cultural national form begins to take concrete form and establish itself as a structure of feeling (Williams 1985). The political economy of this historical 'moment' is complex. Historians such as G.C. Mendis saw the 1956 MEP victory as a 'sudden' eruption of populist forces (Mendis 1963 [1957]) and a reversal of a historical trajectory set in motion by the colonial encounter in which Sri Lanka's future lay in the 'modernization' of the polity and a loosening of people's filial bonds to their ethnic, religious, and cultural identities. However, later historical assessments, particularly by historians such as K.M. de Silva (1981), saw it as the 'natural' outcome of representative democratic politics and the numerical superiority of the Sinhala community – an ideologically loaded assessment that rationalizes the narrative of Sinhala dominance in post-independence Sri Lanka as the inevitable outcome of representative democracy (Scott 1999; Ismail 2005). There is ideological convergence between the latter scholarly assessment of 1956 and Sinhala nationalist views about this historical 'moment'. For instance, Martin Wickramasinghe, Gunadasa Amarasekara's literary precursor, writing about the 1956 victory dubs it as 'bamunu kulaye bindawetima' or the 'fall of the comprador class' (1961). Many Sinhala intellectuals of the period saw it as a popular democratic revolution in which the 'common man' signified by the so-called five great forces or *pancha maha balawegaya* comprising *sanga, weda, guru, govi, kamkaru* or Buddhist priests, ayurvedic doctors, teachers, farmers and workers displaced an anglophile elite political culture. Another dominant theme that emerges in this period within Sinhala nationalist discourse is a sense of beleaguerment. Sinhala nationalists begin to see themselves as a beleaguered community and become what scholars have called a 'majority with a minority consciousness' (De Votta 2004: 62). Sinhalese begin to consider themselves the prime victims of colonialism and see minorities, particularly the Tamil minority, as those who enjoyed a privileged position under colonialism – a position that is also subtly upheld by historians like K.M. de Silva (1981), who rationalize the collective fears of the Sinhala community.

However, this narrative of the democratic promise of 1956 is informed by several ideological and political tensions. At one level the promise of decolonization failed to materialize in economic terms and with Bandaranaike's assassination in 1959 it faced a crisis of legitimacy. At the same time implementing Sinhala as the sole official language alienated the Tamil community resulting in inter-ethnic clashes – a short-sighted policy driven by insecurities of Sinhala beleaguerment (Bandaranaike 1963: 394–395). Bandaranaike's later attempt to undo the damage caused through political devolution via the Bandaranaike-Chelvanayagam pact alienated him from nationalist forces and led to the anti-Tamil pogrom of 1958 (Vittachi 1958). Social justice reforms by coalition partners of the MEP, such as the 1957 Paddy Lands Act promoted by leftist Philip Gunawardena, met with stiff resistance from the more 'middle-class' elements of the *pancha maha balawegaya*, such as Ayurveda doctors and teachers, because it threatened their land ownership privileges by transferring lands to tenant farmers. While the *pancha maha balawgaya* is invoked as a romanticized decolonizing social force, there were competing class interests within this seemingly homogenous nationalist political lobby.

In political-economic terms, the immediate historical context surrounding 1956 is characterized by competing class and ideological interests, but within the Sinhala cultural imagination, this period continues to have an ideological resonance. The significant Sinhala cultural output in diverse genres, such as literature, theatre, and film, is ascribed to approximately the decades of the 1940s and 1950s. In literature, the Sinhala novel begins to take a distinct postcolonial form, particularly with the publication of Martin Wickramasinghe's (1981 [1941]) *Gamperaliya* (*Uprooted*) an iconic realist novel about the 'modernization' of the Sinhala polity. This novel and its sequels *Kaliyugaya* (*Age of Kali* 1957) and *Yuganthaya* (*End of an Era* 1965), a trilogy exploring the rural to urban transformation of Sinhala identity, can be read as a rendering of an imagined community (Anderson 1983). The same kind of cultural imaginary was being replicated in other artistic domains as well. In theatre, the work of Ediriweera Sarachchandra with its invocation of the mythic past of the Sinhala people or the cinema of Lester James Pieris with its exploration of Sinhala village life was also shaped by this desire for a national cultural form.

This national cultural form and its implications also extend to the political economy of the country. Mick Moore (1985) has argued Sri Lanka's heavy post-independence investment in paddy cultivation – at the expense of more commercially oriented agriculture – can be attributed to the grand vision of a pre-colonial hydraulic civilization. R.L. Brohier, a member of the board of the *Gal Oya* irrigation development scheme initiated by D.S. Senanayake, independent Sri Lanka's first Prime Minister, expressed this vision succinctly.

> Ceylon has always mainly been an agricultural country. Hence, the parent earth was, and ever will be, the heart of Ceylon life. Truly the original decree that sent man forth a "tiller of the ground", is perhaps even truer in its natural than its metaphysical sense, when reviewed in the comprehensive landscape of agriculture in Ceylon from the early years of Aryan settlement 2500 years ago, through 23-centuries of Sinhalese kingship.
>
> *(Brohier 1953–56: 68)*

Post-independence Sri Lanka's political elite saw themselves as continuing the 'work of kings' and had a custodial relationship with the peasantry, where they projected themselves as moral and cultural guardians (Seneviratne 1999). This developmental vision, shaped by a Sinhala nationalist vision of pre-colonial authenticity, extended well beyond the 1950s into the 1980s. Even President J.R. Jayawardena, who instituted radical neo-liberal economic reforms in the 1980s, imagined himself within this pre-colonial legacy and styled himself like an ancient king (Kemper 1991; Krishna 1999).

The 1983 Anti-Tamil Riots and Sinhala Nationalism

In the aftermath of the 1983 riots progressive scholars from a range of ideological persuasions began to interrogate Sinhala nationalism and particularly its cultural dynamics intensely. An early expression of this line of scholarship was the volume *Sri Lanka, the ethnic conflict: Myths, realities and perspectives* (Committee for Rational Development 1984). This followed close on the heels of Newton Gunasinghe (1996 [1984]), considered an important leftist political economist, arguing in that 'ethnicity' will supersede 'class' as the most important factor in understanding Sri Lankan society. Following 1983, therefore, one sees a distinct 'identarian' and 'culturalist' turn in the scholarship on nationalism in Sri Lanka as scholars begin to interrogate history and culture as sites from which to understand Sri Lanka's troubled polity.

One outcome in scholarly activity is that Sinhala cultural identity and its relationship to nationalism become a dominant concern. The 1983 anti-Tamil violence generates a situation where the critical scrutiny of Sinhala nationalism becomes an ethical imperative, resulting in at least two unintended consequences. One is that identity politics and culture assumes a disproportionate significance in the study of nationalism in Sri Lanka. The other is that the scholarly inquiry becomes fixated on the nation-state and nationalism. While producing a rich and varied body of scholarship, this results in nationalism becoming an 'over-determining' category in the study of Sri Lanka.

History and the Roots of Conflict (Spencer 1990a) and *Unmaking the Nation* (Jeganathan and Ismail 1995) illustrate this focus. The first volume gathered a range of scholars from different disciplines to probe different aspects of nationalist myth-making and attempted to document multi-cultural alternatives to polarizing nationalist visions of history and community (Spencer 1990a). Similar in intent, though methodologically different, was the second volume, which noted 'we are not enamoured by the possibilities of the nation and nationalism, rather we are deeply suspicious of its claims and consequences. Not simply because the nation has failed – a viable claim in the Sri Lankan context; … it [is] untenable as an idea and as a form of social organization' (Jeganathan and Ismail 1995: 2). One commonality in both collections was a deep suspicion of nationalist ontologies. While Tamil nationalism was also critically interrogated much of the scholarship contained in these two volumes concentrated on Sinhala nationalism because of its dominance.

There was also a Sinhala nationalist ideological reaction to this scholarship, which was both scholarly and populist. The 'people of the lion' debate, between historian R.A.L.H. Gunawardana and literature scholar K.N.O. Dharmadasa, was a significant instance of this reaction. Gunawaradana argued that the term 'Sinhala' as a signifier of collective identity can only be traced to the 12th century and that ethnic identity formation was shaped by racial thinking introduced by Orientalist scholars, such as Max Muller. Dharmadasa refuted this revisionist thesis and argued that Sinhala collective identity could be traced at least to the 5th-century A.D. (Rogers 1994: 12).

The political stakes of this argument are evident when one looks at the timing of the rebuttal; as Dharmadasa's rebuttal appeared in 1989, ten years after the initial publication. In the mid-1980s the historical provenance of Sinhala identity became a matter of public intellectual debate. Following 1983 Sinhala nationalists attempted to rationalize violence as a product of a hoary historical enmity between the two groups. The post-1983 period also witnessed a sense of existential insecurity about Sinhala identity and culture, as international sympathy for the Tamil cause gathered force (Tennekoon 1990: 205). Debates on Sinhala identity often spilled over into public spaces, such as newspapers, where amateur 'historians' jostled with those with academic authority. The debates were battlegrounds on which nationalist scores were to be settled. They were also polarizing discussions where voices critical of standard wisdom about Sinhala cultural and linguistic antiquity were painted as 'unpatriotic'.

While Sinhala nationalism arguably remained the primary focus of liberal scholarship in the aftermath of 1983, Tamil nationalism also came under critical scrutiny. As the Liberation Tigers of Tamil Elam (LTTE) became more repressive and violent in its agenda, questions about their representativeness of the Tamil people were raised. *The Broken Palmyra* was an early example of such scholarship (Hoole, Somasundaram and Thiranagama 1990). Thereafter, critics, such as Qadri Ismail, have argued that Tamil nationalism failed to build an ethical alternative to Sinhala nationalism and reproduced the same kind of majoritarian logic on which Sinhala nationalism was based on (Ismail 2005). Other scholars, such as Rajasingham-Senanayake (1999), have argued that this led to a discourse of 'bi-polar' nationalism with scholarship and political discourse being framed by a Sinhala versus Tamil dichotomy, obscuring other fault-lines and social realities in Sri Lankan society (see also Klem, Gamage, this volume).

The ideological implications of this 'moment' in Sri Lankan scholarship still resonate, with the *jathika chintanaya* (JC: loosely translating as national thought) movement proving influential. Emerging in the late 1970s and associated with the writer Gunadasa Amarasekara and physicist Nalin de Silva (Dewasiri 2020), *JC* is based on fashioning an 'alternative' epistemology that sees 'western' thought as incompatible with Sinhala/Sri Lankan reality. *JC*'s influence is wide-ranging and Amarasekara and de Silva's ideas attracted a significant following, which has popularized these ideas in different domains (Goonewardena 2020). For instance, indigenous cures for COVID-19, such as a purportedly divine-inspired syrup, which was promoted in Sri Lanka during the height of the pandemic, were backed by medical professionals whose worldview is shaped by *jathika chintanaya* ideology (Rambukwella 2020). These groups have also been able to influence state policymaking and even the disastrous overnight switch to organic farming that took place in 2021 can be traced back partially to how professionals and politicians who were fellow-travellers of *jathika chinatnaya* were able to successfully mainstream a view that pesticide-derived arsenic in soil was the main cause in Chronic Kidney Disease of Unknown Etiology (CKDU) – a theory that has been hotly contested by the scientific mainstream in the country (Paranagama, Bhuiyan and Jayasuriya 2018). Nalin de Silva played a key role in 2012 in popularizing this view with a controversial research study in which he claimed that the 'god Natha' (part of the Sinhala-Buddhist pantheon of deities) directed him to look for arsenic in the soil. However, as scholars like Nari Senanayake (2020) point out the impact of the high profile *vasa visa nethi ratak* (a country rid of toxins) campaign, which was at least partially shaped by *JC* influence, has been ambiguous because it was poorly attuned to the consumption patterns, local economies and embodied practices of the rural farming communities most impacted by CKDU and was instead more focused on gentrified health food discourses.

Post-war Sri Lanka

The next temporal marker is what can be considered a 'post-nationalist' turn in scholarship on Sri Lanka in general, which coincides with the end of the war in 2009. A global shift in scholarship towards analytical frameworks that extend beyond the nation and place the study of cultures and societies in broader regional and international frames contributed to reorientation in scholarly works. Another factor was that the conclusion of the war created an 'ideological breathing space', which lessened the ethical compulsions to address nationalist excesses explicitly. This 'post-nationalist' scholarship about Sri Lanka was important because it allowed a different set of questions to be asked about society and culture and reassess received wisdom. An early outcome was a conference held at Cambridge University in 2011 with a primary focus on history and historiography but also included scholars from other disciplines. *Sri Lanka at the Cross-roads of History* was the outcome, which was explicitly framed in terms of addressing questions about how the study of Sri Lanka can benefit from a perspective that is not necessarily delimited by the boundaries of the nation-state (Biedermann and Strathern 2017).

Following on were several publications that share a similar critical spirit. Sujit Sivasundaram's *Islanded* (2013) critically interrogates how an 'island imaginary' emerged in Sri Lanka through the British colonial project and its experimentation in governance and knowledge production. Nira Wickramasinghe's *Metallic Modern* (2014)'s furthers this angle when she revisits late 19th- and early 20th-century Sri Lankan history for a 'history from below' and explores how everyday objects of consumption, such as the Singer sewing machine, embody peoples aspirations and worldviews. Her analysis demonstrates that 'ordinary' people participated in global material culture and thought and felt beyond a national frame.

Steven Kemper's (2015) reassessment of Anagarika Dharmapala also follows this 'post-nationalist' trajectory by reading Dharmapala's life and career outside the frames of reference imposed by the nation-state. The scholarship on Anagarika Dharmapala is a clear instance of how the complexity of a historical figure and a historical period is reduced by the imposition of a national or 'nationalist' imaginary. The multi-dimensionality of this man, who spent much of this adult life outside Sri Lanka and whose dying wish was to be reborn in India, is reduced to a singular national dimension bounded by the contours of the nation-state (Rambukwella 2018: 67–71). He is either seen as an intolerant chauvinist nationalist or an ardent national hero. A similar attempt at re-reading the scholar monk Hikkaduwe Sri Sumangala is evident in Anne Blackburn's *Locations of Buddhism* (2010). Not only does the book reassess Sri Sumangala as a complex figure whose identity was shaped by caste debates, Buddhist scholarship, struggles over the control of Buddhist property and monastic politics but also as a figure whose worldview was shaped by a 'Buddhist cosmopolis' that extended to parts of contemporary Southeast Asia. Another study that contributes to this general trend is *Colors of the Robe* by Ananda Abeysekara (2002) which traces the fraught political battles over 'ownership' of Buddhism in the 1980s and argues for an optic that does not frame Buddhism as a singular, ahistorical and unchanging category.

This body of post-war scholarship marks an important shift from that which preceded it. However at least implicitly this scholarship is also responding to nationalism and particularly to the claims of Sinhala nationalism. While it is not explicitly revisionist, as in the scholarship on Sinhala nationalism that dominated the 1990s and 2000s, it provides a subtle critique of nationalist assumptions about Sri Lanka's past. This body of knowledge, however, invites us to rethink and reimagine Sri Lanka as a cultural, physical, and political space.

Contemporary Life of Sinhala Cultural Nationalism

The war concluded in 2009. While a decade has passed, despite the 'post-nationalist' turn, Sinhala nationalism and its cultural articulation remain influential. The war ending was a significant turning-point in the postcolonial history of the country but its meaning, both symbolic and political, is sharply divergent for the Sinhala community and minority communities. Mahinda Rajapaksa, the former President, declared on May 19, 2009 in an address to parliament that the term 'minority' is removed from the national vocabulary. Instead, he proposed there are those who 'love' the country and those who do not, which is a politically expeditious definition of patriotism allowing the political elite to create a self-serving discourse (Jazeel and Ruwanpura 2009; Wickramasinghe 2009). It is also a darkly ironic statement, given that the conclusion of the war was marked by a distinct sense of Sinhala nationalist triumphalism, both societally and symbolically for the state. Popularly the war-victory was a second independence, with explicit references to the 2nd-century BCE Sinhala king Dutugemunu who defeated the Tamil/Chola king Elara (Wickramasinghe 2009). This is a narrative that has animated Sinhala nationalist thinking during postcolonial period. However, for many Tamils, the war victory was a moment of somber reflection. The human cost was felt keenly in the Tamil community and thousands were incarcerated in camps for Internally Displaced People in the north, although some Tamils also welcomed the defeat of the LTTE. While the military conflict ended and the perception in society at large was that 'peace' had been achieved, it was essentially a 'victor's peace' within which there was a little space for a meaningful discourse of reconciliation (Höglund and Orjuela 2011).

In cultural terms the end of the war saw a sharp increase in popular narratives about the Sinhala past. A glut of post-war films celebrated the martial history of the Sinhala community and critics coined the term 'yuda vindana' or 'war-derived pleasure' cinema to describe this trend (Kannangara 2011). Many post-war films revisit the Sinhala past to reconstruct heroic narratives of Sinhala kings and princes celebrating their achievement in battle and can be read as an obvious expression of the 'pride' within Sinhala-nationalism about the military victory over the LTTE (Karunanayake 2014). These artistic expressions of triumphalism were also complemented by a popular trend in large numbers of Sinhala tourists visiting the north of the country (De Alwis 2021). Some went to see physical remains of structures, such as bunkers, left behind by the 'vanquished' LTTE while others performed pilgrimages by visiting Buddhist sites in the north – long inaccessible due to the war. However, these pilgrimages also had a more insidious dimension, with an underlying strain of establishing Sinhala claims over territory that Tamil nationalist groups had long claimed as their 'territorial homelands' (Dewasiri 2013; Hyndman and Amarasingam 2014). There were also more institutionally sanctioned initiatives that fed the post-war narrative of Sinhala nationalism. For instance, while limiting the space for memorializing Tamil victims, each year an ostentatious state-sponsored ceremony was held to celebrate the conclusion of the war. At the same time military officials, monks and some intellectuals with a Sinhala nationalist proclivity engaged in an aggressive attempt to reclaim religious sites with a multi-religious history as exclusively Buddhist sites – such as the disputed Kuragala site where a Muslim mosque was forced to relocate (Tamil Guardian 2015). The post-war period has also seen an intense upsurge in islamophobia in the country as the Muslim community has come to represent the internal-other of Sinhala nationalism following the 'defeat' of Tamil nationalism. Various narratives about Muslim expansionism and an Islamic threat to Sinhala existence have circulated widely within Sinhala society (Haniffa 2015). These discourses also came to a head in 2019 with the 'Easter Sunday Bombings' and led to a mass consolidation of an existential threat to Sinhala identity that translated into a political triumph for Gotabhaya Rajapaksa who recorded an unprecedented electoral win in the presidential election of 2019.

However, while there was a sudden sharp rise in Sinhala nationalist sentiment and activism in the post-war period, the cultural content that informed this nationalist narrative also underwent some significant changes. To reiterate, the cultural coordinates of post-independence Sinhala nationalism were based on a pastoral cultural aesthetic symbolized in the *weva, dagoba, yaya* (irrigation tank, Buddhist stupa and paddy field) symbolic triad, which in turn derived its inspiration from the belief in a grand pre-colonial hydraulic civilization. However, in post-2009 Sri Lanka rather than this narrative a different narrative about the demon-King Ravana became popular and received institutional sanction, with the Civil Aviation Authority of Sri Lanka appointing a 'scientific committee' to study the physics of Ravana's flight. The Ravana story also de-links Sinhala history from that of India because the dominant Sinhala nationalist narrative holds that Sinhala identity has allochthonous Indian origins. However, as Witharana (2018) speculates, in post-war Sri Lanka there appears to be a necessity for a 'better story' or one that upholds the Sinhalese as an exceptional people with endemic origins. The resurrection of the Ravana narrative, which had limited popularity in the work of the *hela havula* (the collective of the *helas* or locals) in the 1920s (Coperahewa 2011), provides a pre-existing cultural trope to articulate a 'superior story'. The Ravana myth can be seen as serving several different purposes in post-war Sri Lanka. At one level it provides a historical narrative about a technologically advanced Sinhala past with a martial mythic hero – which aligns well with how the 'Sinhala nation' militarily vanquished the LTTE, a feat that many 'experts' believed impossible. At the same time Ravana allows Sinhala identity to be disconnected from that of the Indian subcontinent – which could be seen as ideologically desirable because of Indian sympathy for the Tamil nationalist cause and a history of providing material and other aid to the LTTE.

Conclusion

The cultural politics of Sinhala nationalism have undergone significant changes in post-war Sri Lanka. However, one could argue that these changes are more to do with the 'content', rather than the 'form' of Sinhala nationalism. Arguably the cultural history that sustained the Sinhala nationalist imagination has begun to shift from a pastoral aesthetic to a more technocratic and even urban one – and the Ravana myth complements this shift. At the same time the ethnic 'other' that defined Sinhala nationalist consciousness has also shifted from perceiving the Tamil community as an existential threat to the Muslim community. However, both these changes are shifts in 'content'.

The form of Sinhala nationalism which has derived its inspiration from a romantic notion of a pre-colonial past and a desire to resurrect selected elements of this past in the present and the perception that Sinhala identity is beleaguered and remains under constant threat remain. These concluding thoughts on the current form of Sinhala nationalism are, however, offered largely as provocations for further research. The moment we inhabit now is a fluid moment in the social, cultural, economic and political history of the nation-state. Indeed, the nation-state itself is under severe stress and the allure of the nation-state as a space that can fulfill the aspirations of its people is fast-eroding as the mass public protests during April–July 2022 revealed. It is, therefore, difficult to map or speculate with any certainty what form or shape Sinhala nationalism or its cultural imaginary will take in the near future.

References

Abeyrathne, M. Rathnayake (2015) "The Role Played by the Ceylon Reformed Society and the Oriental Medical Science Fund in the Revival of Traditional Medicine in Ceylon/Sri Lanka" *Social Affairs: A Journal for the Social Sciences* 1(2): 33–46

Abeysekara, Ananda (2002) *Colors of the Robe: Religion, Identity, and Difference* Columbia: University of South Carolina Press

Amarakeerthi, Liyanage (2013) *Kurulu Hadawatha [the Bird's Heart]* Kalubowila, Sri Lanka: Vidarshana Publishers

Amarasekara, Gunadasa (1992) *Inimage Ihalata [Up the Ladder]* Boralesgamuwa, Sri Lanka: Visidunu Publishers

Anderson, Benedict (1991[1983]) *Imagined Communities: Reflections on the Origin and Spread of Nationalism* London: Verso

Bandaranaike, S. W. R. (1963) *Speeches and Writings* Colombo: Information Division of the Department of Broadcasting and Information

Biedermann, Z. and A. Strathern (eds) (2017) *Sri Lanka at the Crossroads of History* London: UCL Press

Blackburn, Anne (2010) *Locations of Buddhism: Colonialism and Modernity in Sri Lanka* Chicago, IL: University of Chicago Press

Brohier, R.L. (1955) "D. S. Senanayake as Minister of Agriculture and Lands" *Ceylon Historical Journal* 5(1–4): 68–80

Brubaker, Rogers (1996) *Nationalism Reframed: Nationhood and the National Question in the New Europe* Cambridge: Cambridge University Press

Committee for Rational Development (1984) *Sri Lanka, the Ethnic Conflict: Myths, Realities and Perspectives* New Delhi: Navrang

Coperahewa, Sandagomi (2011) "Purifying the Sinhala Language: The *Hela* Movement of Munidasa Cumaratunga" *Modern Asian Studies* 46(4): 857–891

De Alwis, Malathi. 2021. "Divine Eyes on the Sorrows of Lanka: Post-War Devotion to Pattini-Kannaki" In *Multi-religiosity in Contemporary Sri Lanka: Innovation, Shared Spaces, Contestations* (1st ed.) M.P. Whitaker, D. Rajasingham-Senanayake and P. Sanmugeswaran (eds) Routledge. https://doi.org/10.4324/9781003029229

De Silva, K. (1981) *A History of Sri Lanka* Chennai: Oxford University Press

De Votta, Neil (2004) *Blowback: Linguistic Nationalism, Institutional Decay, and Ethnic Conflict* Stanford: Stanford University Press

Dewasiri, Nirmal (2013) *History after the War: Historical Consciousness in the Collective Sinhala Buddhist Psyche in Post-War Sri Lanka*. ICES Research Paper 09. Colombo: International Center for Ethnic Studies

Dewasiri, Nirmal (2020) "*Sanskarakawarayage Hendinweema* (Editor's Introduction)" In *Lankawe Nawa Prathi Jaathikawaadi Chintanaye Dasa Wasak (Ten Years of Sri Lanka's New Anti-Nationalist Thought)* Nirmal Dewasiri (ed) Kalubowila: Vidarshana Publishers, pp 1–28

Gombrich, Richard and Gananath Obeyesekere (1988) *Buddhism Transformed: Religious Change in Sri Lanka* Princeton, NJ: Princeton University Press

Goonewardena, Kanishka (2020) "Populism, Nationalism and Marxism in Sri Lanka: from Anti-Colonial Struggle to Authoritarian Neoliberalism" *Geografiska Annaler: Series B, Human Geography* 102(3): 289–304

Gunasinghe, Newton (1996 [1984]) "May Day after the July Holocaust" In *Newton Gunasinghe: Selected Essays* Sasanka Perera (ed) Colombo: Social Scientists Association, pp 204–205

Haniffa, Farzana (2015) "Fecund Mullas and Goni Billas: Gendered Nature of Anti-Muslim Rhetoric in Post-War Sri Lanka" *The South Asianist Journal* 4(1): 2–22

Höglund, Kristine and Camilla Orjuela (2011) "Winning the Peace: Conflict Prevention after a Victor's Peace in Sri Lanka" *Contemporary Social Science* 6(1): 19–37

Hoole, Ratnajeevan, Daya Somasundaram and Rajini Thiranagama (1990) *The Broken Palmyra: The Tamil Crisis in Sri Lanka, an Inside Account* Claremont, CA: The Sri Lanka Studies Institute

Hudson, Dennis D (1992) "Arumuga Navalar and the Hindu Renaissance among the Tamils" In *Religious Controversy in British India: Dialogues in South Asian Languages* Kenneth W. Jones (ed) Albany, NY: State University of New York Press, pp 27–51

Hyndman, Jennifer and Amar Amarasingam (2014) "Touring 'Terrorism': Landscapes of Memory in Post-War Sri Lanka" *Geography Compass* 8: 560–575

Ismail, Qadri (2005) *Abiding by Sri Lanka: On Peace, Place and Postcoloniality* Minneapolis, MN: University of Minnesota Press

Jazeel, Tariq and Kanchana N. Ruwanpura (2009) "Dissent: Sri Lanka's New Minority?" *Political Geography* 28(7): 385–387

Jeganathan, Pradeep and Qadri Ismail (1995) "Introduction" In *Unmooring the Nation: The Politics of Identity and History in Modern Sri Lanka* Pradeep Jeganathan and Qadri Ismail (eds) Colombo: Social Scientists Association

Kannangara, Vidarshana (2011) "*lankawe cinemawa yuda vindana sinemawak bawata pathwemin thibenawa* [Sri Lanka's cinema is turning into one based on was-pleasure]" *Vikalpa* (10 December). https://www.vikalpa.org/article/8565

Karunanayake, Dinidu Priyanimal (2014) "Militant Buddhism and Post-War Sri Lankan Cinematic Memory Work" *South Asian Review* 35(3): 79–94

Kemper, Steven (1991) *The Presence of the Past: Chronicles, Politics and Culture in Sinhala Life* Ithaca, NY: Cornell University Press

Kemper, Steven (2015) *Rescued from the Nation: Anagarika Dharmapala and the Buddhist World* Chicago, IL: University of Chicago Press

Knighton, William (1845) *The History of Ceylon from the Earliest Period to the Present Time* London: Longman, Brown, Green & Longmans; Smith, Elder & Co.; and Madden and Malcolm

Krishna, Sankaran (1999) *Postcolonial Insecurities: India, Sri Lanka, and the Question of Nationhood* Minneapolis, MN: University of Minnesota Press

Malalgoda, Kithsiri (1976) *Buddhism in Sinhalese Society 1750–1900: A Study of Religious Revival and Change* Los Angeles, CA: University of California Press

Mendis, G.C. 1963 [1957] *Ceylon Today and Yesterday: Main Currents of Ceylon History*. Colombo: The Associated Newspapers of Ceylon Ltd

Moore, Mick (1985) *The State and Peasant Politics in Sri Lanka* Cambridge: Cambridge University Press. New York, NY/Oxford: Berghahn Books

Paranagama, D.G.A., M.A. Bhuiyan and N. Jayasuriya (2018) "Factors Associated with Chronic Kidney Disease of Unknown Aetiology (CKDu) in North Central Province of Sri Lanka: A Comparative Analysis of Drinking Water Samples" *Applied Water Science* 8: 151. https://doi.org/10.1007/s13201-018-0792-9

Rajasingham-Senanayake, Darini (1999) "Democracy and the Problem of Representation: The Making of Bi-polar Ethnic Identity in Post/Colonial Sri Lanka" In *Ethnic Futures: The State and Identity Politics in Asia* Joanna Pfaff-Czarnecka, Darini Rajasingham-Senanayake, Ashis Nandy and Edmund Terrence Gomez (eds) New Delhi: Sage Publications, pp 99–134

Rambukwella, Harshana (2017) "Locations of Authenticity: S.W.R.D. Bandaranaike of Sri Lanka and the Search for Indigeneity" *The Journal of Asian Studies* 76(2): 383–400

Rambukwella, Harshana (2018) *The Politics and Poetic of Authenticity: A Cultural Genealogy of Sinhala Nationalism* London: UCL Press

Rambukwella, Harshana (2020) "Patriotic science: The corona virus pandemic, nationalism and indigeneity" Zurich University, Department of Geography Blog. https://www.geo.uzh.ch/en/units/pgg/Blogging-political-geography/Pirit-Pan-Ceremony.html

Rogers, John D. (1990) "Historical Images in the British Period" In *Sri Lanka: History and the Roots of Conflict* Jonathan Spencer (ed) London: Routledge, pp 87–106

Rogers, John D. (1994) "Post-Orientalism and the Interpretation of Premodern and Modern Political Identities: The Case of Sri Lanka" *Journal of Asian Studies* 58(1): 10–23

Scott, David (1999) *Refashioning Futures: Criticism after Postcoloniality* Princeton, NJ: Princeton University Press

Senanayake, Nari (2020) "Tasting Toxicity: Bodies, Perplexity, and the Fraught Witnessing of Environmental Risk in Sri Lanka's Dry Zone" *Gender, Place & Culture* 27(11): 1555–1579

Seneviratne, H.L. (1999) *The Work of Kings: The New Buddhism in Sri Lanka* Chicago, IL: University of Chicago Press

Sivasundaram, Sujit (2013) *Islanded: Britain, Sri Lanka and the Bounds of an Indian-Ocean Colony* Chicago, IL: University of Chicago Press

Spencer, Jonathan (1990a) "Introduction: The Power of the Past" In *Sri Lanka: History and the Roots of Conflict* Jonathan Spencer (ed) London: Routledge, pp 1–18

Spencer, Jonathan (1990b) "Writing within: Anthropology, Nationalism and Culture in Sri Lanka" *Current Anthropology* 31(3): 283–300

Tambiah, Stanley J. (1992) *Buddhism Betrayed?: Religion Politics and Violence in Sri Lanka* Chicago, IL: The University of Chicago Press

Tamil Guardian (2015) "New government, old BBS" *Tamil Guardian* (12 February). Accessed 15 October 2023. https://www.tamilguardian.com/content/new-government-old-bbs

Tennekoon, Serena (1990) "Newspaper Nationalism: Sinhala Identity as Historical Discourse" In *Sri Lanka: History and the Roots of Conflict* Jonathan Spencer (ed) London: Routledge, pp 205–226

Tennent, Emerson (1977) [1860] *Ceylon, an Account of the Island: Physical, Historical and Topographical with Notices of Its Natural History, Antiquities and Productions* Dehiwala: Tisara Praskashakayo

Vittachi, Tarzie (1958) *Emergency '58: The Story of Ceylon Race Riots* London: Andre Deutsch

Wickramasinghe, Nira (2006) *Sri Lanka in the Modern Age: A History of Contested Identities* Honolulu, HI: University of Hawai'i Press

Wickramasinghe, Nira (2009) "After the War: A New Patriotism in Sri Lanka?" *The Journal of Asian Studies* 68(4): 1045–1054

Wickramasinghe, Nira (2014) *Metallic Modern: Everyday Machines in Colonial Sri Lanka* New York, NY: Berghahn Books

Wickremasinghe, Martin (1961) *Upan Da Sita (From the Day I Was Born)* Colombo: Tisara Publishers

Wickremasinghe, Martin (1965) [1949] *Yuganthaya (End of an Era)* Maharagama: Samantha Publishers

Wickremasinghe, Martin (1981) [1941] *Gamperaliya (Uprooted)*. Dehiwala: Thisara Publishers

Wickremasinghe, Martin (2001) [1957] *Kali Yugaya (Age of Kali)* Rajagiriya: Sarasa Publishers

Wickremasinghe, Nira (2006) *Sri Lanka In the Modern Age: A History of Contested Identities* Honolulu, HI: University of Hawai'i Press

Williams, Raymond (1985) *Keywords: A Vocabulary of Culture and Society* New York, NY: Oxford University Press

Wimmer, Andreas and Nina Glick Schiller (2003) "Methodological Nationalism, the Social Sciences and the Study of Migration: An Essay in Historical Epistemology" *International Migration Review* 37(3): 576–610

Witharana, Dileepa (2018) "Technical Education in the Imagination of the Ceylonese Development State" *Review of Development & Change* XXIII(2): 162–182

7
EASTERN MUSLIMS OF SRI LANKA

Developing an Identity Consciousness

Aboobacker Rameez and Mohamed Anifa Mohamed Fowsar

Introduction

The narrative of Islam in Sri Lanka is one of cultural, economic, and geographical diversity, which has contributed to developing a heterogeneous Muslim community with diverse interests and political aspirations at local levels (McGilvray and Raheem 2007). Numerically, Muslims are the second largest religious ethnic minority on the island, accounting for more than 9% of Sri Lanka's total population (Mihlar 2019). The other main minorities are Tamils, Burghers, and Malays (Mohan 1987). The Muslim community is scattered throughout the country, and no district has Muslims constituting more than 50% of its total population. Due to this fact and their historical claims to a different identity, the ethnic identity of the community has evolved in opposition to the Sinhalese nor Tamil identity formation, leading to an 'anomalous position in Sri Lankan ethno-nationalist identity politics' (McGilvray and Raheem 2007: 1). This is even though the vast majority of the Muslim community speak Tamil but reject their linguistic identity in favour of religious identity of Islam as their ethnic marker (Nuhman 2007).

Although there has been much debate about the origins of Sri Lankan Muslims, most of them view themselves as descendants of Arabs or Moors (Asad 1993).[1] Due to the fact Islam came to Sri Lanka, through Arab merchants, the concepts of faith and ethnicity have become fused over time, ascribing a racial homogeneity to a community perceived as the 'Sri Lankan Muslim'. This perception, however, is not reflective of other ethnic communities within the Muslim community. For example, Malays were brought to Sri Lanka from Java by the Dutch. Additionally, a fair amount of Indian Muslims migrated from Tamil Nadu, India and settled in Sri Lanka for trade purposes, alongside small communities of the Memon and Bohra Ismailis, all of whom have contributed to the heterogeneity of the Muslim community (McGilvray 2008, 2011a).[2] Thus, Sri Lankan Muslims are a distinctive socio-cultural ethnic community.

Although there has been much published on Sri Lankan Muslims, we expand their contents and in-depth focus from a new perspective, in particular highlighting the critical division between Southern Muslims and Eastern Muslims (Azeez 1956; Phadnis 1979; de Silva 1986; Ali 1997; Knoerzer 1998; McGilvray 1998; Nuhman 2007; Imtiyaz and Hoole 2011; McGilvray 2011a; Imtiyaz 2012; Saleem 2019, 2020a; Imtiyaz and Saleem 2022). We contend that existing literature on Sri Lankan Muslims has avoided focusing on the two distinctive groups, Southern Muslims and Eastern Muslims, in favour of the broader category of 'Sri Lankan Muslims'. In effect, the Muslim community has been treated as a homogeneous entity, which does a disservice to understanding the lived experience of the communities living across the country (Saleem 2019). Much more focus has been aligned with the socio-political interests of Sri Lankan Muslims within Sinhala nationalism, which has also contributed to such avoidance of intra-group identity consciousness among Sri Lankan Muslims.

Ismail (1995) argues that the division and scattered residence of Sri Lankan Muslims into the South and East disturbs the unity of Sri Lankan Muslims in general and the construction of Sri Lankan Muslims nationhood in particular. Consequently, scholars have made little effort to focus on these divisions and separations among Sri Lankan Muslims. Even the few studies that have appeared on Eastern Muslims have attempted to bring out some of their distinctive features, but failed to highlight the distinctiveness between Southern and Eastern Muslims and have ignored the consciousness of Eastern Muslim identity (McGilvray 2003, 2008; Ismail, Abdullah and Fazil 2005; Imtiyaz 2009; Hussein 2011; Klem 2011).

However, Qadri Ismail's (1995) interventions have laid a foundation to extensively study this neglected area within Sri Lankan Muslim scholarship. As he argues, Muslim social formation consisted of two distinct groups, Southern and Eastern Muslims. Southern Muslims refer to Muslims living in other Provinces of Sri Lanka except for the Eastern Province, and Eastern Muslims refer to Muslims living in the Eastern Province. Thus it is not only a geographical differentiation, but socio-cultural and political reasons also contribute to such differences. Southern Muslim political elites and middle and upper-class men expressed Muslim social formation in their own way. They tended to identify themselves as a peaceful trading community descended from the Arabs, opposed the Tamil link to the Muslims dating back to medieval times, and traditionally maintained cordial relations with the Sinhalese. Eastern Muslims have tended to maintain good relations with Tamils too. Representations of Muslims were also gendered and classed (Ismail 1995; Haniffa 2016). They tended to exclude other segments of the society, including Eastern Muslims, who did not see themselves as traders in the Sri Lankan Muslim identity formation (Ismail 1995).

Thus, the intra-groups dimension of Sri Lankan Muslim identity is a crucial aspect to be studied to better understand their identity formation. This paper explores how Eastern Muslims' socio-cultural and political life differs from Southern Muslims. By living with Tamil communities, Tamil cultural traits have been infused into the life of Eastern Muslims. For example, they distinguish themselves from other Muslims in the country by adopting matrilineal practices inherited from the Tamil community (McGilvray 1989; Ruwanpura 2006; Imtiyaz and Hoole 2011). With the intensification of ethnic conflict in the 1980s and 1990s, they have also become more attentive to their separate identity (McGilvray and Raheem 2007). In more recent times, the emergence of religious and cultural revivals among Eastern Muslims has also affected the identity consciousness of the wider Sri Lankan Muslim identity and those outside of the community. For example, the targeting, vilification, and stigmatization of Muslims which become widespread, especially after the 2019 Easter Sunday Attacks, has often been attributed as a reaction against the conservatism and religious orthodoxy of Eastern Muslims (Saleem 2019). Hence, we highlight the importance of re-visiting Eastern Muslims' socio-cultural and political dynamics, but we also argue that understanding Sri Lankan Muslim identity cannot be done without an in-depth study of Eastern Muslims.

The History of the Sri Lankan Muslim Identity

Genesis of Identity

The Portuguese were the first to call the Sri Lankan Muslims, 'Moors', to denote Arab descent as well as refer to the religious identity of Sri Lankan Muslims (Imtiyaz 2009; McGilvray 2011b).

However, it would be under British colonial rule that a separate Muslim identity was established as the Muslim elites of that time recognized an opportunity to gain political representation as a distinct ethnic group in the legislature based on their religious convictions. In the early 20th century, as the British proposed a system of communal representation, the elite sought to distinguish the Sri Lankan Muslim identity along political lines (Ismail 1995; Imtiyaz and Saleem 2022). In 1889, when the Tamil representatives at the legislature, including Sir Ponnambalam Ramanathan, sought to include the Muslims within the identity of 'Tamil-speaking' people, there was immediate pushback from Muslim representatives. Ramanathan argued that the Sri Lankan Muslims were not a separate identity group from the Tamils but were ethnically and linguistically Tamil who believed in another religion (Ramanathan 1888; Ali 1997). Consequently, he believed a separate representation of Sri Lankan Muslims in the legislature was unnecessary. However, a Muslim scholar, I.L.M. Abdul Azeez, disagreed with Sir Ponnambalam Ramanathan's suppositions, rejected giving the Tamil identity to Tamil-speaking Muslims and instead argued that the Muslims had a different faith and culture and spoke a dialectic of Tamil (Azeez 1956; Saleem 2020a). The British rulers granted the first Sri Lankan Muslim representation in the legislature, significantly weakening Sir Ponnambalam Ramanathan's attempt to give a Tamil identity to Sri Lankan Muslims.

A separate representation of Sri Lankan Muslims in the legislature was also tantamount to recognizing the religious identity of Sri Lankan Muslims. As Azeez (1956) argues, the distinctiveness of the Muslims' identity as separate from the Tamils was also due to the religious distinctiveness of Islam. Thus, the Islamic religious faith played an essential role in the struggle for Sri Lankan Muslim political representation (Imtiyaz and Saleem 2022). With the shaping of the Sri Lankan Muslim identity from this time, political leaders were involved in initiating several legislations that incorporated Muslim religious traditions, including the marriage and divorce act, and education reforms.

Language, Religion, and Culture

Like ethnicity, language was also a crucial factor that contributed to the identity formation of an ethnic community (Nuhman 2016). In the Sri Lankan context, the language difference between Sinhalese and Tamils significantly influenced their distinct identity formation. However, in the case of Sri Lankan Muslims, religion also took precedence over the language factor (Ali 2004). Although Sri Lankan Muslims are native speakers of Tamil, most Sri Lankan Muslims living outside the Northern-Eastern Provinces also use the Sinhala language extensively. Additionally, Muslim elites in the metropolitan areas, including Colombo, use English daily – partly denoting class cleavages that cut across all ethnic communities in the country. In that sense, linguistic-based identity has not traditionally been applied to the Sri Lankan Muslim community (Nuhman 2007). Thus, instead of a linguistic platform, Sri Lankan Muslim elites were more concerned with religious and cultural elements to define their identity (Imtiyaz and Hoole 2011). As the Ramanathan-Azeez debates of 1889 show, the Muslim political elites of that time were committed to forming a separate Sri Lankan Muslim identity based on their Islamic religious and cultural values above their linguistic affiliations with Tamils (Hussein 2011).Moreover, the debates highlighted that Muslim political elites emphasized the linguistic differences caused in pronunciation as a way of further distinguishing itself from Tamils (Nuhman 2007).

As Klem (2011) pointed out, the cultural values associated with religion were and remain a significant drive for developing a unique identity among Sri Lankan Muslims. However, some cultural identity trends have also emerged among Sri Lankan Muslims, due to mixed marriages.

According to Imtiyaz and Hoole (2011), Sri Lankan Muslim men have married Tamil women as well as Sinhalese women and vice versa, thus indicating a meshing of cultural values over time.

Furthermore, the Madrasa education system, which is used as an instrument to teach Islamic religious values, Arabic language to the younger generation and produced a massive amount of Islamic preachers, has also played a vital role in forming the Sri Lankan Muslim identity. As Imtiyaz (2021) argues, during the British colonial rule, the Muslim elite used the Madrasa education system as a tool to bring about a renaissance of Islamic knowledge in the community. The intensified Madrasa education system has also dramatically affected the contemporary social dynamics of Sri Lankan Muslims, especially as 'Local Madrasas often target economically weaker sections of Muslims, who are very proud of their Arab culture and the Middle Eastern background' (Imtiyaz 2021: 9). Thus, a section of the Muslim community who have learnt their Islamic values through Madrasa education try to follow it as their way of life. They show a deep commitment to the values learnt, especially with regard to dress code and the distinctness between different Islamic ideological thinking and the intra- and inter-group conflicts. In a way, the idea of distinguishing Muslims from other religious and ethnic groups is a consequence of Madrasa education in Sri Lanka (Imtiyaz 2021).

Nonetheless, distinctions between Eastern Muslims also persist. With the onset of the Iran revolution and the oil crisis of the 1970s, there was a revival of global Islamic propagation support from the Middle East. With a greater influence from the Middle East coming in the form of migrant workers and financial support for mosques and Madrasas, this helped to boost the Madrasa education system. This in turn contributed to the growth of many religious-based intra-group divisions and the development of a more conservative identity (Imtiyaz 2021). Such intra-religious groups include Tablighi Jamaat, Jamaat-e-Islami, Tawheed Jamaat, Sufis, etc.[3] Some of these groups have promoted a more austere and conservative interpretation of Islamic religious practices in terms of ritual practices, dress code, and relations with others. In some parts of the East (and other parts of the country), these ideological differences have led to clashes between different groups, especially those influenced by Saudi Arabia and those belonging to Sufi or more 'traditional' spiritual sects (Imtiyaz and Hoole 2011).

A Separate Political Identity

In the first four decades since Sri Lanka's independence, the Muslim political elites succeeded in forging pragmatic, self-interested, and flexible alliances with the two main Sinhalese majority political parties, United National Party and Sri Lanka Freedom Party (Mohan 1987; Ameerdeen 2006; Imtiyaz 2012). They gained political benefits for the community by supporting the majority government, even though some of this would be to the detriment of minorities. For example, in 1956, Sir Razik Fareed, a prominent Muslim political elite at that time, supported the Sinhala Only Bill, which later was capitalized on by Muslim politicians to establish Muslim schools to promote Muslim education and the appointment of Muslim teachers to teach Arabic and Islam, as a reward for their support (Ameerdeen 2006). Thus, the political elite of that time fulfilled Sri Lankan Muslims' socio-economic and political interests to some extent in exchange for being a part of the successive ruling governments. Although anti-Muslim incidents erupted in Tamil and Sinhala majority areas throughout this period, these did not receive much broader community concerns and were dismissed as localized community problems (Ameerdeen 2006).

With the outbreak of the civil war with the Liberation Tigers of Tamil Eelam (LTTE) in the early 1980s, the Sri Lankan government tried to prevent Muslims' support for the Tamil nationalists' agenda by focusing on the security of the community (McGilvray and Raheem 2011).

During this period, conflicts between Tamils and Muslims had intensified in the Eastern region, with Tamil militants targeting Muslims and their places of worship throughout the Eastern Provinces, including the massacre of more than 1,000 Muslim civilians from Kattankudy, Eravur, and other Muslim areas (Ameerdeen 2006; Hasbullah and Korf 2009). As a result, Muslim security was highly uncertain, which led the government of the day to recruit Home Guards to work with military forces to mitigate the violence that had flared up in Eastern Province. The frustrated Muslim youths mostly joined Home Guards to ensure the safety and security of their community, but the government tactically used Home Guards against the Tamils in response to the LTTE brutalities. This led to a decline in trust between the Tamils and the Muslims reinforcing the cycle of violence committed by the LTTE against the Muslims (Haniffa 2016).

As a result of this decline, Eastern Muslims actively sought out political efforts to establish a Muslim political identity with the sole aim of preserving the security of the Muslims in the East (Knoerzer 1998). Thus, a separate Muslim political party, the Sri Lanka Muslim Congress (SLMC), was established with a broad popular support base in the East, marking a shift in Sri Lankan Muslim identity discourses. It was in stark contrast to the political elites' tendencies of the South, who were members of national parties, contested elections under those symbols and were not interested in forming a separate Muslim political party.

Placing Eastern Muslims: Socio-cultural Dimension and Political Dynamics

The Eastern Province is important for the country's stability in terms of its geography, society, culture, and natural resources. The Eastern Province, consisting of three districts, namely Ampara, Batticaloa, and Trincomalee, occupies an important place in the political geography of the Sri Lankan Muslim community. One-third of Sri Lanka's total Muslim population lives in the Eastern Province, and two-thirds of Muslims live outside the Eastern Province (Jameel 2011). In the Eastern Province, Ampara and Trincomalee are Muslim majority districts, and a significant number of Muslims also live in the Batticaloa district. In the Trincomalee district, Kinniya and Muttur areas are mostly populated by Muslims. Trincomalee town also has a significant Muslim population. In Batticaloa district, Kattankudy, Ottamavadi, Valaichenai, and Eravur are Muslim majority areas. In the Ampara district, Muslims are concentrated in the coastal areas from Maruthamunai to Pottuvil. It has an ethnically heterogeneous social structure where the three main ethnicities of the country, namely Sinhalese, Tamil and Muslims, live as per the country's diversified nature (Jameel 2011). It includes large amounts of agricultural land and marine resources, such as the natural harbour of Trincomalee and tourist sites. The East was also integral to the Tamil nationalists' claim for the so-called Tamil Ealam state, and it was a strategic part of the final phase of Sri Lanka's civil war where the government forces first defeated the LTTE in 2008 (Klem 2011).

The East has also been seen once as a symbol of the Tamil-Muslim socio-political combination and later the Tamil-Muslim rift (Ismail et al 2005). Nonetheless Eastern Muslims through the conflict years attempted to cordial relations with the Sinhala ethnocratic state and nationalist forces, thereby safeguarding their economic interests and seeking protection for themselves against threats from other dominant ethnic communities.

Eastern Muslims' customs, traditions, culture, and politics are unique among the Sri Lankan Muslim community as their way of life has been entangled with Tamils. Language is a significant part of this intertwining for Eastern Muslims; in particular, Tamil is the common vernacular. However, despite this, McGilvray and Raheem (2011) note that Eastern Muslims have not assimilated themselves into the Tamil identity while still identifying themselves as Tamil-speaking people. Moreover, as they argue, both ethnic groups also have matrimonial and residential bonds but share trading, agricultural activities, and working places (McGilvray 1989; Ruwanpura 2006).

Socio-cultural Dimension

McGilvray and Raheem (2011) point out that Southern Muslims were entrepreneurs and gem traders, thereby giving the impression that trade has been identified as the main livelihood of Sri Lankan Muslims. However, Muslims living in the East have a variety of trades, including rural farmers, fishermen, and petty traders (Nuhman 2007).

Since Muslims are scattered throughout the country, their way of life has been influenced by their non-Muslim neighbours. Hence, Tamil cultural influence was seen in the lifestyle of Eastern Muslims, and Sinhalese Buddhist cultural influence was seen in the lifestyle of Southern Muslims (Samaraweera 1986). Thus there is no commonality across the country regarding the way of life of Muslims, and the community is divided based on class, lifestyle, and regional differences.

This fragmentation also meant that there was a vacuum of national leadership for all Muslims in the early 20th century, which meant that this was dominated by a male, bourgeois, commercial Muslim elite centred in the South (Ismail 1995). According to Nuhman (2004), it was not until the 1930s that Eastern Muslims became interested in seeking a strong ethnic identity, despite there being no socio-political context in which they could pursue such aspirations. Due to the variety of largely agricultural trade that they pursued, Eastern Muslims were not integrated into the modern education system, and there was no educated 'middle class' among them at that time. Modern educational revivalism emerged among the Southern Muslims at the end of the 19th century, and thus Southern Muslim elites were seen as pioneers of the educational revival among Sri Lankan Muslims. However, Eastern Muslims were not notably inducted into this new system of education. No schools were established to bring about the revival of education among Eastern Muslims until the 1950s (Samaraweera 1986).

For a variety of reasons, Islamic faith rituals and traditions have historically played an important role in forming a sense of identity among Eastern Muslims forming the backbone of the distinctiveness of Eastern Muslims and developing a set of unique cultural values associated with Islamic beliefs. Despite the closeness of the Tamil cultural influence, Eastern Muslims have refused to accept cultural notions that were seen to be contrary to Islamic principles. Moreover, mosques and Islamic revival movements have consistently warned Eastern Muslims from the dangers of such cultural assimilation (McGilvray 2008). This has resulted, for example, in the areas of Kattankudy, Eravur, and Oddamavadi in the Batticaloa district in increasing the trend in wearing long robes covering the whole body of Muslim women as opposed to the convention of wearing the traditional sari of the Tamil community or the custom of veiling their heads as in the past or among Muslim women in other areas of Eastern Province (Imtiyaz and Hoole 2011). While the latter practice is much less common in other parts of the East, the principle is about developing a Muslim identity by assimilating certain cultural practices of countries, including the Middle East, as a way of showing distinctness (Imtiyaz and Saleem 2022). This distinctness of identity was further exacerbated during the conflict, where a Muslim 'religious' identity was developed to distinguish the Muslim Tamil speakers from the Tamil community, as a sense of security and safety (Nuhman 2007).

The religious focus among Eastern Muslims became more intense with the emergence of Islamic movements emerging from the late 1970s and supported in principle by a global upsurge of the propagation of Islam from the Middle East (Saleem 2019). Thus, different Islamic ideologies have influenced Eastern Muslims' way of life. In particular, the activities of the group Tablighi Jamaat have dramatically increased in the East in order to enable Muslims to become fully involved in Islamic theological activities. As such, the Tablighi Jamaat is still active in the Muslim-majority regions in the Eastern Province (Klem 2011). In contrast, Sufi Muslims live in areas including Akkaraipattu, Kalmunai, and Kattankudy (Faslan and Vanniasinkam 2015). Moreover, the Jamaat-e-Islami and Tawheed Jamaat groups are also active in these areas (Faslan and Vanniasinkam 2015). The different ideological approaches professed by these movements have led to tensions between those who profess Sufi/spiritual adherence which has been seen as one of the earliest traditions of Islam in Sri Lanka and the more recent ones, influenced by places like Saudi Arabia, which profess a more austere and hard-line adherence that is at odds with the Sufi practices. This has led, in the most extreme cases, to violent clashes between members of different groups (Faslan and Vanniasinkam 2015). In addition, since a lot of Eastern Muslims are also employed in the Middle East, this has influenced the development of the religious and cultural identities of communities (Imtiyaz and Saleem 2022).

Political Dynamics

In the post-independence period, Eastern Muslim political elites initially collaborated with Tamil mainstream politics (Imtiyaz and Saleem 2022). In the first parliamentary election post-independence, four representatives were elected on behalf of Eastern Muslims (Ameerdeen 2006). The Southern Muslim political elites also contested elections in the Eastern Province. However, during this time, concerns about Tamil nationalism and Sinhala language policy surfaced. When the Sinhala Only Act was passed in 1956, Southern and Eastern Muslims held opposing views. In the South, there was strong support for the Sinhala Only Act, but in the East, there was strong antagonism towards the act. As a result, Eastern Muslims feared Southern Muslims would abandon the Tamil language and claim a separate class from Eastern Muslims (McGilvray and Raheem 2007). These tensions highlighted the linguistic differences between Southern Muslims and Eastern Muslims. When Sinhala was made the official language, the Southern Muslims began to accept Sinhala as the language of education, administration, and business. In contrast, Eastern Muslims never gave up using the Tamil language in their entire mainstream activities, and they continued to adhere to the Tamil language and tradition.

Despite this affinity, clashes between the Tamils and Muslims in the East gradually emerged in terms of political representation, land, economy, administration, and political power in the post-independence context (Nuhman 2007). The rivalry created suspicion between the two communities in the Eastern Province, subsequently leading to the outbreak of violence between Tamils and Muslims in the 1950s and 1960s, which exacerbated the polarization between the two communities and created the impetus to pursue divergent political paths (Ismail et al 2005; Nuhman 2007). As Imtiyaz and Saleem (2022) point out, Eastern Muslims were also hard hit by the post-independence colonization schemes of the Sri Lankan government. The government's resettlement plans brought about changes in the demographic composition of Eastern Muslims and marginalized them in the irrigation and distribution of agricultural land.

During the 1980s, with the uprising of Tamil militants, including the LTTE in the East, the security of Eastern Muslims was also called into question by Tamil militants with their activities against Muslims intensifying to weaken the socio-economic and political strength of Eastern Muslims. Tamil militants killed Muslim home guards, civil servants, and parliamentarians, while Muslims who lived in border villages were also under attack. Many Muslims who had earlier joined the Tamil armed movements, including the LTTE, abandoned them due to their actions against Eastern Muslims. Muslims were also compelled to flee their homes with the intensification of Tamil militants' atrocities. There were bombings targeting Muslim areas, and subsequent attacks were launched on the Eastern Muslims' worship places. Even after the signing of the Indo-Lanka Accord in 1987, Eastern Muslims had to face various catastrophes (Ameerdeen 2006).

After the Indo-Lanka Accord, the LTTE started the second phase of the Eelam struggle, intensifying attacks against the Muslims in the Northern and Eastern Provinces. Consequently, in 1989, 41 Muslim police officers were killed by Tamil militants, and several Muslims were kidnapped and murdered. In the late 1990s, 75 Muslims from the East who returned to the country after fulfilling their holy pilgrimage in Makkah were massacred by the LTTE in the Kurukal Madam in the Batticaloa district (Ameerdeen 2006). Meanwhile, within two hours, more than 90,000 people from the North were forcibly evicted from their habitations by the LTTE. Around 123 Muslims were shot dead while offering prayers in mosques in Kattankudy in the East (Ameerdeen 2006). A similar number of Muslims were massacred in Eravur. The LTTE also carried out massacres of Muslims in Sainthamaruthu, Akkaraipattu, and other Muslim regions throughout the East (Ameerdeen 2006).

The LTTE frequently targeted the Muslims' economic establishments and cultural and religious symbols. Extortion was taken from Muslim traders, and a large amount of Muslim land was confiscated in the East. All these acts were designed to weaken the Muslims politically and economically (Ameerdeen 2006). Neither the Sri Lankan government nor the Southern Muslim political elite could ensure the security of Eastern Muslims. Consequently, the Eastern Muslim political elite believed their concerns were being overlooked and felt the Southern Muslim politicians did not give more attention to the grievances of Eastern Muslims (Imtiyaz and Saleem 2022).

As Haniffa (2016) argues that 'Muslim minority politics in the country as a whole became Eastern-centric with the escalation of the conflict. In the 1980s, the security concerns of the northern and Eastern Muslims became more urgent; however, the political elite of the South was quite inept at recognizing these concerns or addressing them' (2016: 200). This renewed a sense of a separate identity among Eastern Muslims who realized that a lack of a solid political foundation to articulate their political identity was tremendous, and they saw the need for a determined political leadership to advance their socio-economic and political interests. In this context, the idea of establishing a separate political party was propagated to give a new political identity to Eastern Muslims, and thus, the SLMC was born. The party's founder, M.H.M. Ashraff, had initially been involved with Tamil National Politics, but when he saw that such Tamil parties were not able to meet the socio-economic, political, and security goals of Muslims, he founded the SLMC. He believed that Eastern Muslims could secure their security and gain political advantage through his party. He also saw it as a way of ensuring that Muslim youth would not join the LTTE and thereby risk breaking up the county (Ameerdeen 2006). A considerable proportion of Eastern Muslims thus gave him the popular mandate that was required to address this political identity issue. The party grew in a short period to gain opposition status in the North-East Provincial Council established in 1988 (Knoerzer 1998). The party recognized the realities and heightened the sense of a national Muslim ethnic identity to defeat the Muslim political leaders who had joined the national parties. The party's leader successfully used Islamic principles as party slogans, took a stand against LTTE, and mobilized Muslim youth politically, using mosques as a base for his political efforts (Imtiyaz 2007). Thus, as Imtiyaz (2009) claims, the SLMC emerged as the most significant political force in the Eastern Province. Its campaign appealed to many politically marginalized Eastern Muslims, sowing the seeds of Muslim nationalism with anti-Tamil nationalism. By 1994, the SLMC had joined the Sinhala governments.

Post-war Complexities

After the war's end in 2009, Sinhala-Buddhist nationalism resurfaced in the country, making anti-Islamic rhetoric as the main agenda of Sinhala-Buddhist extremist forces. Activities that undermine Muslims' religious and cultural values were carried out by Sinhala-Buddhist extremist forces (Farook 2009). There have also been attacks targeting Muslim places of worship and businesses. It is notable that Muslim areas in the South (in 2014) and Central Provinces (in 2018) have been largely attacked by Sinhala-Buddhist extremist forces causing casualties and economic loss to Muslims (Fowsar, Rameez and Rameez 2020). The pretext of these attacks has been the questions of Muslim cultural issues, including Muslim women's clothing, slaughtering animals for food, and halal recognition. In 2018, Anti-Muslim extremist forces also rioted in the urban area of Ampara in the Eastern Province (Fowsar et al 2020). While this post-war trend has largely affected Muslims living outside the North and East, the link is drawn with the conservative/extreme manifestations of identity coming from places in the East, such as Kattankudy (Faslan and Vanniasinkam 2015).

The rise of anti-Muslim violence and the reticence of the state to act against perpetrators have subsequently led to the development of extremist ideologies among some Muslim youth, particularly in the East. With the rise in ISIS-related influences and past memories and trauma of youth developed from the LTTE brutalities against Muslims in the late 1980s and at the beginning of 1990s, young people on the whole have become more vulnerable to these issues trying to mobilize themselves against these negative forces. It eventually resulted in the Easter Sunday attacks in 2019 (Saleem 2019), where a young Muslim extremist preacher from Kattankudy led the suicide group, and a few other suicide bombers were also from the East. The region hence is also host to different Islamic ideologies and where variations are more prevalent.

Following the Easter Sunday attacks, Sri Lankan Muslims were viewed with suspicion, and the government also imposed bans on Islamic religious and charity organizations and restricted Muslims' cultural and religious activities. Sinhala-Buddhist extremists also spread anti-Muslim sentiment for political reasons, and many Muslim youths were imprisoned without solid evidence. Thus, the Easter Sunday suicide attacks became a historical stain posing massive challenges to the Sri Lankan Muslim identity (Saleem 2019). The attacks significantly affected Eastern Muslims and negatively impacted their socio-political dynamics, as many of those who led the attacks and those involved in the attack were from the East. After this catastrophic incident, there is a growing concern to make reformations in various matters, including Islamic ideology, Madrasa education, dress code, and curricula of Islamic textbooks.

During the Covid-19 lockdowns, the effect of anti-Muslim Politics was witnessed with regard to the cremation of COVID-19 burials. Despite all medical and scientific evidence proving that burial was permissible, the government refused to recognize Muslims' (and Christians') religious and cultural rights. At one point, rumours were also spread that Muslims were responsible for the spread of the Covid-19 virus (Saleem 2020a).

Conclusion

In this chapter, we have shown that any discussion on the Sri Lankan Muslim identity cannot treat the community as homogeneous, with the need to be more focused on the intra-group/intersectional ties of geographical perspectives. While there is a lot that has been discussed around Southern Muslims, one cannot ignore the identity discussions of Eastern Muslims. As we outline, the Muslims in the Eastern Province have played and will continue to play pivotal roles in not only the development of the Sri Lankan Muslim identity but, in general, are key catalysts to ensuring that there is a link with the rest of the country. After all, if the Muslims had sided with the LTTE in the 1980s, the conflict would have taken a different turn (Saleem 2020b).

We discuss that as far as Eastern Muslims are concerned, the unique socio-cultural traits and political dynamics intertwined with Islamic religious beliefs play a critical role in developing a consciousness of identity that has evolved to the wider community. The common socio-cultural-political interests shared by Eastern Muslims have also given them solid political activism and the ability to form separate political movements. Although Eastern Muslims are small compared to the country's total Muslim population, they have the platform to create an identity for the Sri Lankan Muslim community through territorial-political enrichment. In the present context, where religious and cultural violence against Muslims has intensified, there is a serious discussion needed of the Muslim identity. The Eastern Muslims' political leaders and civil society have a role to play despite their impact being eroded in recent times. Against this academic discussion, future studies need to unpack this influence in all aspects of Sri Lankan Muslim political life.

Notes

1 Moor is a derogatory term used by the Portuguese to refer to Arabs. They competed with the Portuguese in faith and trade. However, this term was used based on religion (Imtiyaz and Hoole 2011).
2 Memons are Muslim entrepreneurs and humanitarians that originated in the region and settled in India in the 19th century and later migrated to many countries, including Sri Lanka. Bohra's main branch was in Yemen and is known as the Dawood Bohra sect, which is a small but unique community influenced by Yemeni, Egyptian, African, and Indian cultures (Saleem 2019).
3 These are various Islamic movements. Tablighi Jamaat movement originated in India in the mid-19th century and strengthens the Islamic faith and engages Muslims in spiritual activities; while Jamaat-e-Islami is based in Pakistan and seeks to establish Islamic political leadership and focuses on reformations (Saleem 2019). In contrast, McGilvray and Raheem (2007) make the linkages to Tawheed Jamaat and Sufis to religious threads: the former is an organization incorporating Wahhabi and Salafi thought influenced by the Middle East, particularly in Saudi Arabia, while Sufis are a movement that represents a more 'traditional' Islamic thought and practice supporting shrines worship and following the guidance of Sufi teachers.

References

Ali, Ameer (1997) "The Muslim Factor in Sri Lankan Ethnic Crisis" *Journal of Muslim Minority Affairs* 17(2): 253–267

Ali, Ameer (2004) "The Muslims of Sri Lanka: An Ethnic Minority Trapped in a Political Quagmire" *Inter-Asia Cultural Studies* 5(3): 372–383

Ameerdeen, V. (2006) *Ethnic Politics of Muslims in Sri Lanka* Kandy: Centre for Minority Studies

Asad, M.K. (1993) *The Muslims of Sri Lanka under the British Rule* New Delhi: Navrang

Azeez, I.L.M.A. (1956) *A Criticism of Mr Ramanathan's Ethnology of the 'Moors' of Ceylon* Colombo: Sri Lanka Muslim Cultural Center

de Silva, K.M. (1986) "The Muslim Minority in a Democratic Polity-The Case of Sri Lanka: Reflections on a Theme" In *Muslims of Sri Lanka: Avenues to Antiquity* M. Shukri (ed) Beruwala, Sri Lanka: Jamiah Neleemia Institute, pp 443–452

Farook, L. (2009) *Nobody's People: The Forgotten Plights of Sri Lanka's Muslim* Colombo: South Asia News Agency

Faslan, M. and N. Vanniasinkam (2015) *Fracturing Community: Intra-Group Relations among the Muslims of Sri Lanka* Colombo: International Centre for Ethnic Studies

Fowsar, M.A.M., M.A.M. Rameez and A. Rameez (2020) "Muslim Minority in Post-War Sri Lanka: A Case Study of Aluthgama and Digana Violence" *Academic Journal of Interdisciplinary Studies* 9(6): 56–68

Haniffa, Farzana F. (2016) "Sex and Violence in the Eastern Province: A Study in Muslim Masculinity" In *The Search for Justice: The Sri Lanka Papers* K. Jayawardena and K.P. Jayawardena (eds) New Delhi: Zubaan, pp 193–236

Hasbullah, Shahullah and Benedikt Korf (2009) "Muslim Geographies and the Politics of Purification in Sri Lanka 'after' the Tsunami" *Singapore Journal of Tropical Geography* 30(2): 248–264

Hussein, Ameena (2011) "Birth and Death" In *The Muslim Heritage of Eastern Sri Lanka* S.H.M. Jameel and Hussein Asiff (eds) Colombo: Muslim Women's Research and Action Forum, pp 57–74

Imtiyaz, A.R.M. (2007) "The Sri Lanka Muslim Congress: The Logic of Politics" *Sri Lanka Guardian* Available at https://www.sangam.org/2007/10/SLMC.php?uid=2571

Imtiyaz, A.R.M. (2009) "The Eastern Muslims of Sri Lanka: Special Problems and Solutions" *Journal of Asian and African Studies* 44(4): 407–427.

Imtiyaz, A.R.M. (2012) "Identity, Choices and Crisis: A Study of Muslim Political Leadership in Sri Lanka" *Journal of Asian and African Studies* 48(1): 47–63

Imtiyaz, A.R.M. (2021) "Islamic Identity Formation, Madrasas and Muslims in Sri Lanka" *Journal of Security, Governance and Development* 1(2): 1–18

Imtiyaz, A.R.M. and Ranjan Hoole (2011) "Some Critical Notes on the Muslims of Sri Lanka's Non-Tamil Identity and Tamil-Muslim Relations" *South Asia: Journal of South Asian Studies* 34(2): 208–231

Imtiyaz, A.R.M. and Amjad M. Saleem (2022) "Some Critical Notes on Sri Lankan Muslim Religious Identity Formation, Conservatism, and Violent Extremism" *Journal of Asian and African Studies* 58(3): 438–451

Ismail, Qadri (1995) "Unmooring Identity: The Antinomies of Elite Muslim Self-Representation in Modern Sri Lanka" In *Unmaking the Nation: The Politics of Identity and History in Modern Sri Lanka* Qadri Ismail and Jeganathan Pradeep (eds) Colombo: Social Scientists' Association, pp 55–105

Ismail, M., R. Abdullah and M.M. Fazil (2005) "Muslim Perspective from the East" In *Dealing with Diversity: Sri Lankan Discourse on Peace and Conflict* G. Frerks and B. Klem (eds) The Hague: Netherlands Institute of International Relations, pp 151–160

Jameel, S.H.M. (2011) "History of the Muslim Community of the Eastern Province" In *The Muslim Heritage of Eastern Sri Lanka* S.H.M. Jameel and Asiff Hussein (eds) Colombo: Muslim Women's Research and Action Forum, pp 01–32

Klem, Bart (2011) "Islam, Politics and Violence in Eastern Sri Lanka" *Journal of South Asian Studies* 70(3): 730–753

Knoerzer, S. (1998) "Transformation of Muslim Political Identity" In *Culture and Politics of Identity in Sri Lanka* M. Tiruchelvam and C.S. Dattathreya (eds) Colombo, Sri Lanka: International Centre for Ethnic Studies, pp 136–167

McGilvray, Dennis B. (1989) "Households in Akkaraipattu: Dowry and Domestic Organization Among Matrilineal Tamils and Moors of Sri Lanka" In *Society from the Inside Out: Anthropological Perspectives on the South Asian Household* J.N. Gray and D.J. Mearns (eds) London: Sage, pp 192–235

McGilvray, Dennis B. (1998) "Arabs, Moors and Muslims: Sri Lankan Muslim Ethnicity in Regional Perspective" *Contribution to Indian Sociology* 32(2): 433–483

McGilvray, Dennis B. (2003) "Tamil and Muslim Identities in the East" *Marga Journal* 1(1): 79–116

McGilvray, Dennis B. (2008) *Crucible of Conflict: Tamil and Muslim Society on the East Coast of Sri Lanka* Durham: Duke University Press

McGilvray, Dennis B. (2011a) "Celebrations of Maturity and Marriage" In *The Muslim Heritage of Eastern Sri Lanka* S.H.M. Jameel and Asiff Hussein (eds) Colombo: Muslim Women's Research and Action Forum, pp 33–56

McGilvray, Dennis B. (2011b) "Sri Lankan Muslims: Between Ethno-Nationalism and the Global Ummah" *Nations and Nationalism* 17(1): 45–64

McGilvray, Dennis B. and Mirak Raheem (2007) *Muslim Perspectives on the Sri Lankan Conflict* Washington: East-West Center

McGilvray, Dennis B. and Mirak Raheem (2011) "Origins of the Sri Lankan Muslims and Varieties of the Muslim Identity" In *The Sri Lanka Reader: History, Culture, Politics* John C. Holt (ed) Durham and London: Duke University Press, pp 410–419

Mihlar, Farah (2019) "Religious Change in a Minority Context: Transforming Islam in Sri Lanka" *Third World Quarterly* 40(12): 2153–2169

Mohan, V.R. (1987) *Identity Crisis of Sri Lankan Muslims* Delhi: Mittal Publications

Nuhman, M.A. (2004) *Understanding Sri Lankan Muslim Identity* Colombo: International Centre for Ethnic Studies

Nuhman, M.A. (2007) *Sri Lankan Muslims: Ethnic Identity within Cultural Diversity* Colombo: International Centre for Ethnic Studies

Nuhman, M.A. (2016) "Sinhala Buddhist Nationalism and Muslim Identity in Sri Lanka" In *Buddhist Extremists and Muslim Minorities: Religious Conflict in Contemporary Sri Lanka* John C. Holt (ed) New York: Oxford University Press, pp 18–53

Phadnis, U. (1979) "Political Profile of the Muslim Minority of Sri Lanka" *International Studies* 18(1): 27–48

Ramanathan, P. (1888) "The Ethnology of the Moors of Ceylon" *Journal of the Royal Asiatic Society (Ceylon Branch)* 10(36): 234–262

Ruwanpura, Kanchana N. (2006) *Matrilineal Communities, Patriarchal Realities: A Feminist Nirvana Uncovered* India: Zubaan

Saleem, Amjad M. (2019) *Tackling Challenges for the Sri Lankan Muslims in the Wake of the Easter Sunday Attacks* London: The Cordoba Foundation

Saleem, Amjad M. (2020a) "Re-thinking Muslim Political Identities in Sri Lanka" *IIUM Journal of Religion and Civilisational Studies* 3(1): 84–112

Saleem, Amjad M. (2020b) *Muslims in Sri Lanka and the Challenges of Violent Extremism* London: The Cordoba Foundation

Samaraweera, Vijaya (1986) "Aspects of Muslim Revivalist Movement in the Late Nineteenth Century" In *Muslims of Sri Lanka: Avenues to Antiquity* M. Shukri (ed) Beruwala: Jamiah Neleemia Institute, pp 363–384

8
TRANSITIONAL JUSTICE
State of Play in Sri Lanka

Farah Mihlar

Introduction

The United Nations defines transitional justice as a 'full range of processes and mechanisms associated with a society's attempts to come to terms with a legacy of large-scale past abuses, in order to ensure accountability, serve justice and achieve reconciliation' (UN 2010: 2). This could include truth commissions, judicial mechanisms, such as special courts, reparations, state sector reforms, memorialisation, and commemorations. Originating from the Nuremberg trials, transitional justice as we know it today gained strong momentum in the 1980s as several Latin American states shifted from authoritarian to democratic models of governance. Following the creation of international tribunals for the former Yugoslavia and Rwanda in the 1990s, transitional justice began to gain global appeal as a process to seek justice and accountability to reconcile authoritarian regimes after conflict and genocide.

In the last two decades, the field has expanded to now become the 'globally dominant lens through which to approach states addressing legacies of a violent past' (Gready and Robins 2019: 31). Yet transitional justice is itself a contested field, which complicates any review of a particular country context. Though now a global project, implemented on an industrial scale, transitional justice nevertheless is facing a crisis of legitimacy (Nagy 2008; Nesiah 2017). It is heavily critiqued for favouring top-down approaches, marginalising and excluding victims and privileging 'western liberal' perspectives over 'local' ideals of justice (Lundy and McGovern 2008; McEvoy and McGregor 2008; Hazan et al 2010; Kent 2019). Despite being implemented in more than 85 countries, its successes are limited, with few examples of genuine pursuits of accountability, justice, and reconciliation leading to transformation (Loyle and Davenport 2016; Gready and Robins 2019).

Over the last 50 years, Sri Lanka has produced several different processes purportedly aimed at seeking truth and at times aiming to deliver justice and accountability for its legacies of rights violations. The latter include the state suppression of two youth insurgencies (in the 1970s and late 1980s) and the country's armed conflict, against the Liberation Tigers of Tamil Eelam (LTTE) who were fighting for a separate state for ethnic minority Tamils in the north and east. This chapter will consider some of these processes and the country's most recent and comprehensive commitment to transitional justice made through a United Nations Human Rights Council (UN HRC) resolution in 2015. In this resolution, Sri Lanka committed to 'the full range of judicial and non-judicial measures' towards truth-seeking, justice, accountability, reparations, and reconciliation (A/HRC/RES/30/1). I argue that though conceptually far-reaching, this process was also affected by a lack of political commitments and limitations within the field of transitional justice eventually leaving victims feeling dejected. Hence, questions arise about the validity of the globally dominant transitional justice model for a context like Sri Lanka.

This chapter is divided into three sections: the first provides a review of the main national investigations responding to critical periods when gross violations of human rights took place in Sri Lanka. The second section explores whether these investigations could indeed be considered as transitional justice and the final section critically analyses the country's most recent commitment to transitional justice.

Commissions of Inquiries (1990 to Present)

The legacy of human rights violations in Sri Lanka's post-independence history that demand a process seeking justice, accountability, and redress broadly fits into three periods. Though the field of transitional justice has begun to recognise focusing on such specific periods of violations undermines the continuing structural violence and violations, which as in Sri Lanka remained at a 'vast scale' all through the conflict and continues in the post-war context (Amnesty International 2009).

The first noteworthy period in Sri Lanka's independent history was an uprising by the Marxist-influenced *Janatha Vimukthi Peramuna* (JVP) in the early 1970s, which was crushed through a forceful but short military operation, with an estimated 8,000–10,000 people killed (Bush 2003). There is dearth of documented information on the violations that took place during this period, yet existing testimonies indicate several members of the party, including its senior leadership, were arrested, detained, and reportedly tortured in prison (Bush 2003). The release of its leader in the 1980s led to a slow revival of the group and a second uprising in the early 1990s, which was ended through a ruthless military campaign involving a spate of atrocities. More than 40,000 people were believed to have been killed during this period, with human rights groups claiming the number of disappeared was at least three times the figure of 20,000 provided by government commissions (HRW 2008).

More than any other human rights violation enforced disappearances have had the biggest, though still arguably meagre response, in terms of state justice initiatives. From 1990s, successive governments have appointed at least nine 'independent' Commissions of Inquiry (CoI) on this issue, all of which were limited, flawed, and failed to produce adequate results (HRW 2008; Fonseka 2017b). There were also some investigations into other human rights violations, particularly extra-judicial killings during the country's 30-year armed conflict.

Sri Lanka's armed conflict was violently ended in 2009 when the military eliminated the entire leadership of the LTTE after months of intense fighting. In the last stages of the war reports emerged of serious allegations of violations of international human rights and humanitarian law by both parties. The claims were met with blanket denials on the part of the then government, headed by Mahinda Rajapaksa and his brother and Defence Minister Gotabaya Rajapaksa (Klem 2018; Price 2022). The end of the armed conflict had been presented by the Sri Lankan government as a 'humanitarian operation' to save civilians 'trapped' in warfare by the LTTE and promoted as a triumph against terrorism (Klem 2018; Price 2022).

Nevertheless, claims for truth, justice, and accountability for the violations of international law in the last stages of the war remained among international and national human rights groups and victim groups, leading to a UN Secretary General's Panel of Experts (PoE) (United Nations, 2011) investigation, which found 'credible evidence of violation of international human rights and humanitarian laws.' The panel itself was challenged by the Government of Sri Lanka (GoSL) on the grounds that the UN Secretary General did not have the mandate to conduct such an investigation and its report was dismissed (Ratner 2012).

In response, the GoSL appointed a Lessons Learnt and Reconciliation Commission (LLRC) in 2010, which too had a limited mandate, lacked independence and was procedurally problematic. Though challenged on credibility for having whitewashed the country's military in its final report, some other aspects of its recommendations were seen as progressive and constituted the starting framework for accountability within the subsequent international-level action taken on Sri Lanka (ICG 2011).

The latter came in the form of a series of UN HRC resolutions on Sri Lanka. Between 2012 and 2015 these resolutions, boosted by the PoE (United Nations, 2011) and a later Office of the High Commissioner for Human Rights (OHCHR) investigation, were successively strengthened to demand national-level investigations on wartime and other atrocities. In 2015, an unexpected change in government in Sri Lanka and a shift in stance and approach on the larger issue of justice and accountability led to a joint resolution committing to a detailed transitional justice process. In the final section, I discuss the staggered implementation of this process, between the period of 2015–2019 when only two commitments were realised through the establishment of an Office to investigate missing persons and an Office of Reparations (OR).

The return of the Rajapaksa family to government in 2019/20, this time with Gotabaya as President and Mahinda as Prime Minister, closed the door to this transitional justice process though pressure through UN HRC resolution remained. In 2021, the HRC effectively moved some responsibility on transitional justice to the international level by mandating OHCHR, 'to collect, consolidate, analyse and preserve information and evidence, and to develop possible strategies for future accountability processes for gross violations of human rights or serious violations of international humanitarian law in Sri Lanka, to advocate for victims and survivors, and to support relevant judicial and other proceedings' (HRC 2021: 3).

However, in 2022 as Sri Lanka plunged into a humanitarian crisis, precipitated by economic collapse, partly due to poor economic policies by the Rajapaksas', the public in large numbers took to the streets demanding justice and accountability in a manner the country had never seen before. The mass uprising, or *Aragalaya*, consisting of large-scale demonstrations and a permanent sit in protest in the capital city Colombo, was partly seeking a resolution to critical food, medicine shortages, power outages, and a crippling unavailability of fuel but accountability from the ruling elite for driving the country to such a predicament was also demanded.

In two tense months between May and July, the public uprising succeeded in forcing the resignation of Mahinda Rajapaksa as Prime Minister, his brother Basil as Finance Minister and finally Gotabaya Rajapaksa as President. The change was short-lived and Rajapaksa's successor, Ranil Wickremasinghe, a previous Prime Minister and an unelected member of parliament, was elected by fellow MPs as President and went on to violently disband the entire protest movement and arbitrarily arrest many of its leaders (Amnesty International 2022). At the time of writing, it is too early to fully interlink these events and the transitional justice process in Sri Lanka. However, there is little doubt that accountability for human rights violations, even if ethnically divided in nature, remains a major demand of the Sri Lankan people and one that can only be met through structural and systemic changes (Mihlar 2022).

Past Investigative Efforts – Justice Delayed and Denied

I trace some of the past justice initiatives and question their contribution towards transitional justice in this section. Following the violent quelling of the second Marxist uprising, in 1991, the UN Working Group on Enforced Disappearances stated it had received over 15,000 cases and communicated nearly 5,000 of these to the GoSL (HRW 2008). The same year, President Ranasinghe Premadasa (1988–1993), under whose command the violations took place, appointed a 'Presidential Commission of Inquiry into the Involuntary Removal of Persons.' This commission was highly politicised, severely limited in mandate as it only inquired into recent cases ignoring most complaints which had been made in the preceding years, conducted inquiries in secret, and did not proceed to publish its report (Amnesty International 2009; Pinto-Jayawardena 2010).

Aiming to redress this, in the mid-1990s, President Chandrika Kumaratunga (1995–2005) set up three interconnected investigations titled 'Presidential Commission of Inquiry into Involuntary Removal or Disappearance of Persons,' to investigate separate incidents that took place between 1988 and 1994. Comprising three members, each commission investigated crimes within a specific geographical area in the island and after their mandates expired, an 'All Island Presidential Commission on Disappearances,' operating between 1998 and 2000, researched some 10,000 remaining complaints. In total, these commissions received over 20,000 complaints of enforced disappearances. Due to limitations in its mandate and time, the All-Island Commission referred 16,305 cases to the Human Rights Commission of Sri Lanka, which in 1994 started processing these, but by 2006 chose not to pursue investigating them unless directed by the Government (HRW 2008).

Facing strong accusations of serious violations of human rights in the conducting of the country's armed conflict, President Mahinda Rajapaksa (2005–2015) went on to appoint two further CoIs. In 2006, having originally announced an international investigation, Rajapaksa went on to appoint a CoI to investigate 16 specific cases, including the killings of former Foreign Minister Lakshman Kadirgamar, MPs Joseph Pararajasingham and Nadaraja Raviraj and other grave incidents, such as the killing of 17 aid workers of Action *Contra La Faim* in Trincomalee in 2006. Both the LTTE and GoSL had been held separately responsible for many of these incidents. An International Independent Group of Eminent Persons (IIGEP) was appointed by Rajapaksa to 'observe' the work of the CoI. In 2008, the IIGEP resigned in protest citing the GoSL's unwillingness to 'investigate cases with vigour, where the conduct of its own forces has been called into question,' and uncover 'the systemic failures and obstructions' (IIGEP 2008). In its 2008 report Amnesty International framed the CoI as a measure by the GoSL to 'buy time' and 'undermine the systems of accountability.'

In 2013 Rajapaksa appointed the Paranagama Commission to investigate wartime disappearances, which received 24,000 complaints relating to disappearances mostly in the country's north and east (Sri Lanka campaign 2016). The commission was insufficiently resourced with the Centre for Policy Alternatives, one of the country's leading national civil society organisations, estimating that it would have taken the Commission 13 years to purely hear complaints, let alone investigate them (Groundviews 2014).

Fonseka (2017b) suggests that in addition to their 'structural flaws,' these commissions were all often set up under 'external pressure' using tactics to delay genuine truth and justice. Pinto-Jayawardena (2010) raises a host of issues with all these COIs and additional inquiries, including limitations of mandate, independence, lack of cross-examination of perpetrators, and limited public access. The stark gap in normative and legal framework and processes in keeping with international standards have also been raised as a significant issue (Amnesty International 2009; Pinto-Jayawardena 2010; Fonseka 2017a).

Though protracted, the country's 30-year armed conflict was also marked by a portfolio of other violations, including torture, abductions, arbitrary arrest and detention, rape, sexual violations, child recruitment, land appropriation, and acquisition, committed by both parties to the conflict. A few of these have also led to state investigations, which have occasionally delivered justice but generally declined to even provide a clear factual account of what had occurred. Examples of these inquiries include the rape and murder of a Jaffna school girl Krishanthi Coomaraswamy in

1996; the discovery of mass graves of up to 400 persons in Chammani, in Mannar; and other mass killings, such as in Kumarapuram, Trincomalee district, when 24 Tamil civilians were massacred and in Thambalagamam, when 8 Tamils were killed, both by state security personal in retaliation for previous LTTE attacks (Pinto-Jayawardena 2010).

Arguably, the most detailed investigation into violations and atrocity crimes during the armed conflict was conducted by the LLRC. Unlike previous commissions it was deemed a farce from its inception by international and national human rights groups on the grounds that it lacked credibility, impartiality, and independence (Amnesty International 2011). Its investigation was also not backed by a witness and victim protection bill, which limited its potential to gather evidence putting those who provided testimonies to it under significant risk (De Mel 2013). Nevertheless, the LLRC received some 5,000 testimonies, including a large number from women, many from families of disappeared.

The International Crisis Group in an assessment of the LLRC's final report argued that it 'works to exonerate the government and undermine its own limited calls for further inquiry – mostly by accepting at face value the largely unexamined claims of the senior government and military officials who planned and executed the war, and by rolling back well-established principles of international law' (ICG 2011, unpaginated). Despite these criticisms, also held by national and community-based NGOs and groups, there were some positive recommendations from the LLRC report, such as the devolution of political power in the north, return of civilian lands, support for women-headed households and reconciliation between ethnic and religious groups (ICG 2011; De Mel 2013).

CoIs as Truth-Seeking Mechanisms

Though none were created as truth commissions and were grossly inadequate in meeting the objectives of such a commission, including on 'protecting, acknowledging and empowering' victims and influencing change (Gonzalez and Varney 2013), in the face of abject denials of violations and atrocity crimes, these CoIs have contributed to revealing some facts.

Pinto-Jayawardena explains that of the three CoIs appointed by Kumaratunga in the 1990s, from a total of 27,526 complaints 16,800 cases were deemed as enforced disappearances. Statistics, such as this provide forensic truth, which is one of the four typologies of truth amassed in a truth commission (Chapman and Ball 2001: 10). The CoIs also contributed to a narrative truth, on the targeted nature of the crimes, the involvement of police and army in committing the crime and how incidents were covered up (*ibid*: 10). More troublingly, the educational and socio-economic profile of victim in the south of Sri Lanka, 63% were below the age of 30 (Pinto-Jayawardena 2010).

The CoI focusing on the northern province offered a narrative on disputed facts, including on the role of the security forces, which it found responsible for 90% of the disappearances in this province. As these CoIs were not conducted as truth commissions, widely publicised with conversations taking place between victims, witnesses, and perpetrators, they made little contribution to the other two typologies: social or dialogue truth and healing or restorative truth (Chapman and Ball 2001: 10).

Considering that the LLRC was investigating crimes committed by a sitting government, their report too offered important accounts that contributed towards truth-seeking. They referred to the scale and extent of the civilian casualties in the last stages of the war, including the repeated shelling by the government of 'no-fire zones' which contained large civilian populations and presented important detailed information about families of disappeared and war widows in the north and east, including on their economic and social context (LLRC 2011).

The poor treatment of victims and witnesses by these Commissions, particularly the LLRC to which some 5,000 women provided testimonies, has come under much criticism in the literature, highlighting a lack of understanding and sensitivity to the victim suffering and inflamed by their negligent representation of experiences and miscarriages of justice. Recognising victims and addressing their needs and rights are considered critical aims of truth commissions (Hayner 2011). Some of these CoIs did contribute towards formally acknowledging past abuses by starting to discover and clarify such instances and providing, though minimal, some historical record. The Kumaratunga-appointed CoIs also played a marginal role in 'outlining institutional and individual responsibility' (Hayner 2011). Pinto-Jayawardena (2010) states these commissions 'explicitly named the security officers repeatedly implicated in the enforced disappearances but cautioned (as indeed, did the other Commissions) that it could not, on *ex parte* evidence alone, decide on their guilt' (Pinto-Jayawardena 2010: 81). All three reports implicated senior politicians, ministers of Cabinet and so placing the onus on the government for its role and liability (Pinto-Jayawardena 2010).

According to Human Rights Watch (2008) of the many recommendations of the CoIs only two led to some judicial outcome. The first, in 1994, nine suspects were tried for the abduction, torture, and killing of 50 students in an army camp in Embilipitiya, in the southeast of Sri Lanka in 1990. Secondly, in 1999 five soldiers were convicted and sentenced to death for the abduction and rape of Jaffna school girl Krishanthi Kumaraswamy, her mother, brother, and a friend (HRW 2008). The lack of political will to prosecute and weaknesses in the country's legal system are among the factors attributed for the minimal judicial outcomes (Pinto-Jayawardena 2010).

The absence of integrity as a component of transitional justice was clear in all these CoIs, but a few such initiatives led to some form or reparations, though, again, grossly inadequate in relation to the extent and nature of crimes committed in the island nation. In the 1990s under the rule of President Chandrika Kumaratunga, the Registration of Deaths (Temporary Provisions) Act No. 2 and No. 58 simplified the issuing of certification to families of persons, who are presumed dead. Between 1995 and 1999, 15,000 death certificates were issued, which in turn eased access to compensation (HRW 2008). By 2002, over 16,000 families had received compensation (HRW 2008). Fonseka (2017c) also refers to the Commission recognising the right to reparation and some reparatory measures, including compensation for land acquisition, taken through government circulars and programmes and the work of the Rehabilitation of Persons, Properties, and Industries Authorities, though details of these are scant.

One major critique of transitional justice as a field is its state centricity in that the state holds the primary responsibility for meting out justice and accountability. Increasingly, scholars are calling for the recognition of local forms of justice, which are more bottom-up, cognisant of and responsive to local context and victim needs (Hazan et al 2010; Lundy and McGovern 2008; McEvoy and McGregor 2008; Kent 2019). In the absence of formal justice processes, Sri Lankan Non-governmental organisations (NGOs) and community-based organisations (CBOs) have conducted numerous projects premised on the concepts of truth-seeking, justice, and accountability for victims of large-scale human rights violations. Two of these merit mention in this chapter because they served a specific truth-seeking purpose, one about people living in the villages bordering the conflict zone and the second on the forcible eviction of Muslims from the north of Sri Lanka in 1990. Both were civil society-led initiatives, the first a fact-finding mission consisting of civil society activists and academics affiliated with the Movement for Inter-Racial Justice and Equality, while the second was formed from among the northern Muslim displaced community also to investigate and uncover the factors behind the eviction of Muslims by the LTTE and the issues faced by the community after their displacement. The border villages commission did not publish a final report but media coverage of their work revealed some findings particularly on the economic and social difficulties and gender-based violence faced by this specific demography of Muslim, Sinhala, Tamil, and indigenous populations that live on the border of the north and east (Fact Finding Commission 1998). The citizens commission on the expulsion of the Muslims from the northern province presented a landmark final report which for the first time provided documentary evidence of the forcible eviction of this religious group (LST 2011). The findings could provide the basis for a legal investigation on the crime of ethnic cleansing and/or forcible deportation and its recommendations could be developed into specific claims of reparations by the community.

Post-2009 Transitional Justice Commitments

The events around the conclusion of Sri Lanka's armed conflict signified a turning point, even in a country which was known for its legacy of human rights violations. Between the extreme positions of accusations of genocide and assertions of zero-human casualties (Saravanamuttu 2017), the blatant violation of international human rights and humanitarian laws in the last stages of the war by both parties to the conflict was excessive (OHCHR 2015). The early UN HRC resolutions seeking accountability for the end of the war failed to garner support from the GoSL for the implementation of recommendations. The failure to do this confirmed the GoSL's lack of commitment and interest in pursuing justice and accountability for victims and led to stronger resolutions by the Council.

However, by 2015, under a new Government, commitments were made by the GoSL in UN HRC resolution 30/1 towards transitional justice which were far-reaching. In comparison to previous attempts, this was broad-based, as it took into consideration all key aspects of transitional justice initiative – truth, justice, accountability, and reconciliation. Sri Lanka's commitments provided for an Office of Missing Persons (OMP), OR, a truth and reconciliation commission, a hybrid court with prosecuting powers and constitutional reform to deal with the causes of the conflict and ensure non-repetition. The proposed process responded to historic criticisms of Sri Lanka's failures to combat impunity and provided for a judicial mechanism that in its hybrid form would ensure that local limitations would be mitigated through an international presence. No aspect of the transitional justice textbook had been left out apart from the early notable gap on the lack of victim consultation. The GoSL addressed this problem by appointing a civil society-led Consultation Task Force (CTF), which through an extraordinary method of zonal task forces (ZTF) made up of community-level activists engaged in extensive and intense consultations across the country. Though only aimed at consulting on the already proposed mechanisms, based on the reputation of the quest for justice among those involved, the CTF enjoyed some credibility and developed into a process of truth telling, with more than 7,300 submissions made by members of the public. Its final report provided an account of victim experiences, and its recommendations were detailed on the proposed mechanisms and beyond. In his final report on Sri Lanka, UN Special Rapporteur on Transitional Justice, Pablo de Greiff (2020) states, 'In an extraordinarily short period, without pre-existing structures and sometimes with only limited government support, the Task Force has established its presence broadly and deeply, including at the local level. This is the most comprehensive effort to capture the views of victims and others on transitional justice questions.'

One of the prominent critics of the process, Kumaravadivel Guruparan (2017), has distinguished between three visions of transition: one shared by the 'liberal sections of the southern polity' for democracy and good governance, the second by the Tamil polity for 'deep democratisation – a transition to a pluri-national Sri Lanka,' and a third by the majority Sinhala Buddhist community for 'no transition.' Generalising on the standpoint of these groups and excluding other minorities, such as Muslims, Guruparan goes on to present a valid case on the conflict between the Tamil and Sinhala positions within an analytical framing, questioning the very context of transition in view of the then President's alignment with the extreme end of the majority Sinhala Buddhist positioning. Guruparan (2017: 188) concludes that 'the irreconcilable agendas at play' made 'the possibility of a domestic transitional justice process highly unlikely.' In Fonseka's seminal publication on transitional justice in Sri Lanka, Guruparan's co-authors identify several challenges of the transitional justice process including, but not limited to, the ethnic and political contestations, the history of justice failings and concerns regarding the new government's commitments. Despite this the voices represent a position of hope that this process more than any other offers the potential for redress and change.

Nesiah (2017) urges caution from an external perspective through a critical analysis of the field of transitional justice itself. Her concerns are broadly based on the privileging of 'dominant orthodoxy,' that among other factors is 'technocratic,' negligent of 'structural impunity and systemic vulnerability' and focuses on 'western liberal peace' agendas. Nesiah's work contributes to the growing body of scholarly writing on what Sharp (2019: 570) describes as the critical turn in the field of transitional justice; the 'emerging 'fourth generation' of transitional justice scholarship characterised by a willingness to interrogate some of the foundational blind spots and limitations of the field.' Transitional justice in Sri Lanka quite neatly aligns with this critique but prior to this analysis, an assessment of the collapse of the process is necessary.

One of the earliest signs of the government's disinterest in transitional justice came when, in January of 2018, the then President and Prime Minister both refused to accept the final report of their very own consultation task force. In the ensuing year, except for one government minister, all others distanced themselves from the process. Structural issues also jeopardised it, among these being Sri Lanka's constitutional reform process which, though a part of transitional justice, ran separate to it and gained far much more political interest and buy-in from all parties (Lassée 2019). The implementation process was also split between two bodies, the Secretariat for Coordinating Reconciliation Mechanisms (SCRM), which by name avoided referring to justice, and the Office of National Unity and Reconciliation (ONUR), problematically suggesting that peacebuilding and reconciliation were separate to transitional justice (ICG 2017). With continuing international attention on implementation, the GoSL hurriedly rushed through parliament and set up the OMP even before the CTF had completed consultations. The OMP only became operational in late 2018, following which only one more mechanism, the Office of Reparations (OR) was appointed before Sirisena lost his presidency in December 2019.

The year 2019 had seen a major turnaround of events, including a complete breakdown within the coalition government leading to a collapse in relations with the President and Prime Minister. This seriously affected the functioning of the state and compromised the country's security. Consequentially, the government and security apparatus did not act on numerous warnings of an impending coordinated suicide attack by a group of ISIS-inspired militants, which took place on Easter Sunday, killing more than 250 Christian worshippers across the island and guests in Colombo hotels. The attacks, ten years after the end of the war, shook the country deeply affecting inter-ethnic relations with fears of a new threat posed by the country's minority Muslim population. In the following months, Muslim neighbourhoods and places of religious worship came under attack by Buddhist extremist groups in the worst incidents of religious violence witnessed in post-independence history of the country (Mihlar 2021a,b). State complicity offered little or no protection to Muslims bringing in harsh new laws to limit freedom of religion and belief of the group (Mihlar 2021b). The events not only signalled the failure of transitional justice and reconciliation in Sri Lanka but the need for security among the larger population led to the return of the Rajapaksas, with Gotabaya presenting himself as the strongman who having defeated Tamil terrorists would deal with any threat from among Muslims (Mihlar 2022).

Though the Rajapaksas did not disband the OMP and OR, their opposition to the transitional justice was well known, sealing the demise of the process that started in 2015. In 2021, the UN HRC recognised this and, in a resolution, opposed by the GoSL, shifted the responsibility of preserving evidence of crimes to the OHCHR (A/HRC/RES/46/1). There remains a dearth of analysis of the collapse of this latest process of justice. The overwhelming reasoning provided in academic and policy literature is the lack of political will or commitment on the part of the then government.

Lassée (2019) identifies the government's unwillingness to 'fully endorse, promote and implement' its commitment leading to delays and affecting the process. He is also critical of international actors for prioritising consultations despite the extended time it took and for not taking a firmer position against the GoSL on implementation. A small body of literature focuses on the neglect of victim groups, including women and minorities, which consequently affected inclusivity and isolated the process from the larger population. The country's Muslim population, including those who suffered serious atrocities in the north and east, were largely marginalised throughout the process as were the Sinhalese living in the border villages of the conflict zone (Mihlar 2018; De Silva, Fonseka and Mihlar 2019). Efforts to include these populations or research their ideas of justice were minimal. Few publications note the neglect of women and as an extension of gender justice within the process. Women victims of the armed conflict, particularly mothers and wives of disappeared, were instrumental in calls for justice, but the formal process did little to consider their needs and demands and the process evidently fell short of a vision, let alone, the provision of gender justice (ICG 2017).

Though yet to be properly evaluated, Nesiah's early warning based on the larger critiques of the field of transitional justice appears to hold firm in the Sri Lankan case. The country's transitional justice process was internationally construed through 'An industry of praxis…supported by dedicated nongovernmental organizations (NGOs) and large-scale funding from western donors' (Gready and Robins 2019: 31); such knowledge, 'consolidated as a field' becomes 'disseminated' through 'expert technical assistance through UN offices, foreign government agencies or INGOs' (Nesiah 2017: 363). This was not unchallenged, victim groups continued to draw attention to their specific issues. In the absence of national leadership, however, the 'dominant script' prevailed and the promise of another series of mechanisms fitting into the internationally prescribed model of truth-seeking, prosecutions, reparations, etc., had little appeal to victims and survivors. Transitional justice in Sri Lanka was also distant from the larger public imaginary and completely failed to engage with the country's complex ethnic, religious majoritarian nationalism.

During its tenure, Buddhist nationalist extremist groups strengthened leading to a steady increase in racist and violent campaigns against minorities. Arguably, transitional justice was not fully realised in Sri Lanka, but its lack of appeal to victims and its failings even before implementation offer a serious critique of the concept itself and limitations of its most extravagant design. Yet there is no doubt that the Sri Lankan case also complicates the broader critique of the field of transitional justice, especially on the enforcement of international norms on local communities. In Sri Lanka, northern Tamil victims insisted on international involvement, affirming that a solution which is 'exclusively national will not be credible in their eyes' (Saravanamuttu 2017: 56). Even though very embryotic the Sri Lankan case demonstrates that transitional justice as a field requires much more work to reconcile between its international, national, and local objectives as well as in negotiating across identity lines to enable genuine transformative change.

Conclusion

Through deploying a wider lens of what may constitute transitional justice, this chapter considers a range of different mechanisms and processes implemented in modern Sri Lankan history as an attempt to investigate and redress the country's legacy of human rights problems. Though not strictly within the remit of transitional justice and while clearly flawed the vast number of CoIs looking into human rights crisis, particularly enforced disappearances, as this article highlights served some truth-seeking purpose. Yet, there were significant shortfalls in justice and accountability which remained a demand from victim and survivor groups. No doubt the country's 2015 commitments best fitted the transitional justice rubric. Having promised at the least truth, justice, accountability, reparations, and non-repetition measures, it failed to deliver. I have argued that these failing were not limited to the political dynamics of the time but must also be understood in line with the critiques of the field of transitional justice which have been now clearly identified in scholarly work.

The 'Aragalaya' of 2022 critically shows that the Sri Lankan people have potential, though limited, to come together across ethnic, religious divides to bring about change and secondly, that accountability is crucial to any long-term political solution. The crushing of the protest by Rajapaksa's predecessor, Ranil Wickremasinghe, is also indicative that transformation is not based on individuals but on structural and systemic changes. Transitional justice then is ever more important for Sri Lanka and its absence leaves the country lacking peace, stability, and reconciliation.

References

Amnesty International (2022) "Penalized for protesting: Sri Lanka's crackdown on protestors." *Amnesty International* (8 September). Accessed on 28/10/2022. Available at https://www.amnesty.org/en/documents/asa37/5986/2022/en/

Amnesty International (2009) "Twenty years of make believe." *Index Number: ASA 37/005/2009* (11 June). Accessed on 22/04/2022. Available at https://www.amnesty.org/en/documents/asa37/005/2009/en/

Amnesty International (2011) "Sri Lanka's war time inquiry fundamentally flawed." *Amnesty International* (7 September). Accessed on 22/04/2022. Available at https://www.amnesty.org/en/latest/news/2011/09/sri-lanka-inquiry-armed-conflict-fundamentally-flawed/

Bush, Kenneth D. (2003) "Critical Juncture III: 1971 JVP Insurrection and 1987 JVP Resurgence" In ***Intra-Group Dimensions of Ethnic Conflict in Sri Lanka* International political and economy series** London: Palgrave Macmillan

Chapman, Audrey and Patrick Ball (2001) "The Truth of Truth Commissions: Comparative Lessons from Haiti, South Africa, and Guatemala" *Human Rights Quarterly* 23: 1–43

De Greiff, Pablo (2020) *Report of the Special Rapporteur on the Promotion of Truth, Justice, Reparation and Guarantees of non-Recurrence* United Nations (18 June, 2020). Accessed on 22/04/2022. Available at https://www.ohchr.org/en/documents/country-reports/ahrc4545add1-visit-sri-lanka-report-special-rapporteur-promotion-truth

De Mel, Neloufer (2013) *The promise of the LLRC: women's testimony and justice in post-war Sri Lanka* ICES Research paper No 4. Accessed 22/04/2022. Available at https://ices.lk/wp-content/uploads/2013/11/the-Promise-of-the-LLRC.pdf

De Silva, Marisa, Nilshan Fonseka and Farah Mihlar (2019) *The Forgotten Victims of War: A Border Villages Study* Neelan Thiruchilvam Trust (13 October). Accessed on 22/04/2022. Available at https://srilankabrief.org/wp-content/uploads/2019/10/The-Forgotten-Victims-of-War-A-Border-Village-Study-FINAL.pdf

Fonseka, Bhavani (2017a) *Transitional Justice in Sri Lanka: Lessons so Far and the Long Road Ahead* Colombo: CPA

Fonseka, Bhavani (2017b) "Truth-Telling in Sri Lanka: Past Experiences and Options for the Future" In *Transitional Justice in Sri Lanka: Lessons so Far and the Long Road Ahead* Bhavani Fonseka (ed) Colombo: CPA

Fonseka, Bhavani (2017c) "The Importance of Reparations within Sri Lanka's Reform Agenda" In *Transitional Justice in Sri Lanka: Lessons so Far and the Long Road Ahead* Bhavani Fonseka (ed) Colombo: CPA

Gonzalez, Eduardo and Howard Varney (2013) ***Truth Seeking: Elements of Creating an Effecting Truth Commission*** Amnesty Commission of the Ministry of Justice of Brazil. Accessed on 28/10/2022. Available at https://www.ictj.org/publication/truth-seeking-elements-creating-effective-truth-commission

Gready, Paul and Simon Robins (eds) (2019) ***From Transitional to Transformative Justice*** Cambridge: Cambridge University Press

Groundviews (2014) "Infographics: Presidential Commission on Missing Persons." (11 September). Accessed on 22/04/2022. Available at https://groundviews.org/2014/09/11/infographic-presidential-commission-on-missing-persons/

Guruparan, Kumaravadivel (2017) "The Difficulties and Probable Impossibility of a Coherent Conception of Transitional Justice in Sri Lanka" In ***Transitional Justice in Sri Lanka: Lessons so Far and the Long Road Ahead*** Bhavani Fonseka (ed) Colombo: CPA

Hayner, Priscilla (2011) ***Unspeakable Truths: Facing the Challenge of Truth Commissions*** New York: Routledge

Hazan, Pierre, Rosalind Shaw and Lars Waldorf (2010) ***Localizing Transitional Justice: Interventions and Priorities after Mass Violence*** Stanford University Press

Human Rights Watch (2008) "Recurring nightmare: State responsibility for disappearances and abductions in Sri Lanka." Index Number 20,2 (c) (March 2008). Accessed on 22/04/2022. Available at https://www.hrw.org/reports/2008/srilanka0308/srilanka0308web.pdf

International Crisis Group (2011) "Statement on the Report of Sri Lanka's Lessons Learnt and Reconciliation Commission" (22 December). Accessed on 22/04/2022. Available at https://www.crisisgroup.org/asia/south-asia/sri-lanka/statement-report-sri-lankas-lessons-learnt-and-reconciliation-commission

International Crisis Group (2017) ***Sri Lanka's conflict affected women dealing with the legacy of war*** Asia Report No: 289 (28 July). Accessed on 22/04/2022. Available at https://www.crisisgroup.org/asia/south-asia/sri-lanka/289-sri-lankas-conflict-affected-women-dealing-legacy-war

International Independent Group of Eminent Persons (IIGEP) (2008) The final report of the IIGEP (15 April). Available at: http://www.humanrights.asia/wp-content/uploads/2018/07/The-Final-Report-of-the-IIGEP.pdf

Kent, Lia (2019) "Rethinking 'Civil Society' and 'Victim-centred' Transitional Justice in Timor-Leste" In ***Civil Society and Transitional Justice in Asia and the Pacific*** Lia Kent, Joanne Wallis and Claire Cronin (eds) Canberra: ANU Press, pp 22–38

Klem, Bart (2018) "Book Review: War, Denial and Nation-Building in Sri Lanka: After the End by Rachel Soeighe" ***Contemporary South Asia*** 26(3): 363–364

Lassée, Isabelle (2019) "The Sri Lankan Transitional Justice Process: Too Little, Too Late?" ***The Round Table*** 108(6): 709–719

Law and Society Trust (2011) ***The Quest for Redemption: The Story of Northern Muslims***, Second edition, Colombo: LST

Loyle, Cyanne and Christian Davenport (2016) "Transitional Injustice: Subverting Justice in Transition and Postconflict Societies" ***Journal of Human Rights*** 15(1): 126–149

Lundy, Patricia and Mark McGovern (2008) "Whose Justice? Rethinking Transitional Justice from the Bottom Up" ***Journal of Law and Society*** 35(2): 265–292

McEvoy, Kieran and Lorna McGregor (2008) ***Transitional Justice from Below: Grassroots Activism and the Struggle for Change*** Oxford: Hart

Mihlar, Farah (2018) ***Coming Out of the Margins: Justice and Reconciliation for Conflict-Affected Muslims in Sri Lanka*** Colombo: International Centre for Ethnic Studies

Mihlar, Farah (2021a) "Autocratisation, Buddhist Nationalist Extremism and the Muslim Minority in Sri Lanka" In ***Routledge Handbook on Autocratisation in South Asia*** Sten Widmalm (ed) Routledge

Mihlar, Farah (2021b) "Shifting between Desperation and Rejection: Sri Lankan Muslims' Relationship with Demands for Justice and Accountability" In ***Muslims in Post-War Sri Lanka: Repression, Resistance and Reform*** Shreen Saroor (ed) Colombo: LST, pp 121–137

Mihlar, Farah (2022) "Representation of the north and east is critical for a genuinely transformative Aragalaya" ***Daily Financial Times Sri Lanka*** (3 June). Available at https://www.ft.lk/columns/Representation-of-the-north-and-east-is-critical-for-a-genuinely-transformative-Aragalaya/4-735663

Nagy, Rosemary (2008) "Transitional Justice as Global Project: Critical Reflections" ***Third World Quarterly*** 29(2): 275–289

Nesiah, Vasuki (2017) "'Saviours, Victims and Savages' on the Post Conflict Circuit: The Field of Transitional Justice" In *Transitional Justice in Sri Lanka: Lessons so Far and the Long Road Ahead* Bhavani Fonseka (ed) Colombo: CPA

Office of the High Commissioner for Human Rights (OHCHR) (2015). *Report on the OHCHR Investigation on Sri Lanka*. Geneva

Pinto-Jayawardena, Kishali (2010) *Post-War Justice in Sri Lanka: Rule of Law, the Criminal Justice System, and Commissions of Inquiry*. International Commission of Jurists (18 January). Accessed on 22/04/2022. Available at https://reliefweb.int/report/sri-lanka/post-war-justice-sri-lanka-rule-law-criminal-justice-system-and-commissions-inquiry

Price, Megan Frances (2022) "The End Days of the Fourth Eelam War: Sri Lanka's Denialist Challenge to the Laws of War" *Ethics & International Affairs* 36(1): 65–89

Ratner, S. (2012) "Accountability and the Sri Lankan Civil War" *American Journal of International Law* 106(4): 795–808

Saravanamuttu, Paikasorthy (2017) "The Politics of Reconciliation" In *Transitional Justice in Sri Lanka: Lessons Learnt so Far and the Long Road Ahead* Bhavani Fonseka (ed) Colombo: CPA

Sharp, Dustin (2019) "What Would Satisfy Us? Taking Stock of Critical Approaches to Transitional Justice" *International Journal of Transitional Justice* 13(3): 570–589

Sri Lanka campaign for peace and justice (2016) "The Paranagama Commission has done great damage. Now that damage must be repaired." (16 June). Accessed on 22/04/2022. Available at https://www.srilankacampaign.org/paranagama-commission-done-great-damage-now-damage-must-repaired/

The Border Villages Coordinating Committee for Peace and Right to Life and the Movement for Inter Racial Justice and Equality (1998) "Fact finding Citizens' Commission on the border villages in North-East affected by the war." Colombo

The Commission on Lessons Learnt and Reconciliation Commission (LLRC) (2011) The report of the Commission of Inquiry on Lessons Learnt and Reconciliation Commission Available at https://reliefweb.int/report/sri-lanka/report-commission-inquiry-lessons-learnt-and-reconciliation

United Nations (2011) *Report of the UN Secretary General's Panel of Experts on Accountability in Sri Lanka* New York: United Nations. Accessed on 22/04/2022. Available at https://www.securitycouncilreport.org/un-documents/document/poc-rep-on-account-in-sri-lanka.php

United Nations Human Rights Council (2015) "Promoting reconciliation, accountability and human rights in Sri Lanka (A/HRC/RES/30/1)" UN (September 2015). Accessed on 22/04/2022. Available at https://documents-dds-ny.un.org/doc/UNDOC/GEN/G15/239/66/PDF/G1523966.pdf?OpenElement

United Nations Human Rights Council (2021) "Promoting reconciliation, accountability and human rights in Sri Lanka (A/HRC/RES/46/1)" UN (23 March). Accessed on 22/04/ 2022. Available at https://reliefweb.int/report/sri-lanka/resolution-adopted-human-rights-council-23-march-2021-461-promoting-reconciliation

United Nations Secretary-General (2010) "Guidance Note of the Secretary-General: United Nations Approach to Transitional Justice". Accessed on 2204//2022. Available at https://digitallibrary.un.org/record/682111?ln=en

9
CONTEMPORARY GENDER ACTIVISM
Engaging the Law and the State

Kaushalya Ariyarathne and Kiran Grewal

Introduction

Sri Lanka has a long, rich history of gender activism, producing many important feminist scholars, activists and professionals. Gender issues have been at the forefront of much of the human rights activism in post-war Sri Lanka, either directly or indirectly. At the same time there have been numerous other struggles led by women on a diverse range of social and economic issues.[1]

Some recent examples include plantation sector activism in up-country Sri Lanka. In 2013 for the first time a major trade union in the sector – the Red Flag Union – elected a woman (Menaha Kandaswamy) as General Secretary: a significant event in an area historically completely male-dominated and highly patriarchal (Rashid and Rafaithu 2022). The union's struggles and campaigns for higher wages are captured by Jegathesan in this volume; what is significant to note is the mobilisation of women from the Malayaga Tamil community across many sectors. Women's groups across the country have also raised the issue of predatory microfinance schemes and debt: a problem that has disproportionately affected women (Wedagedara 2021). Their non-violent demonstration was held for 55 days until called off due to the Covid-19 pandemic, which de Silva and Wedagedara document in detail in this volume, alongside the issue of indebtedness and land struggles. Finally, groups like the Dabindu Collective, Women's Centre, REHD (Revolutionary Existence for Human Development) and Stand Up have fought to demand decent working conditions and wages for women workers in the apparel sector: covered in chapters by Wickramasinghe and Lingham in this volume.

We will focus on four other gender-related topics that have marked the post-war era and with which we have closely engaged. These topics make important contributions to not just theorising Sri Lankan state and society but general debates about the relationship between social movements and State/formal institutions and the nature of politics itself. The topics are: redress for conflict-related violence, Muslim women's activism for reform of personal laws, women's political participation and the Lesbian, Gay, Bisexual, Transgender, Questioning + (LGBTIQ+) struggle for non-discrimination and the decriminalisation of homosexuality. We will provide a brief introduction to these topics, discuss their contribution to post-war Sri Lanka's socio-political landscape and identify the possible theoretical insights they offer.

First some clarifications of terminology may be helpful. In speaking of 'gender activism' we are conscious that there is a certain vagueness around both terms. We have deliberately retained the vagueness for several reasons. First, in relation to 'gender', we are keen to demonstrate that while gender is often conflated with women, we also want to speak back to this. This is why we have included LGBTIQ+ struggles here: to show how different gendered subjects can and do contribute to challenging the established gender order in Sri Lanka and in the process open up ways of both seeing how gender is deeply entwined with nationalism and how different articulations of citizenship and belonging are also emerging. We also wanted to avoid limiting our discussion to overtly 'feminist' or even 'women's rights' activism. In relation to the first, there is no consensus even among those advocating for women's rights around a 'feminist' position. Many of the women who have engaged in different types of rights struggles explicitly reject or resist the feminist label for various reasons. We also want to capture the ways in which forms of activism that are not narrowly focused on issues of 'women's rights' should nonetheless be seen as gendered.

On the question of 'activism', we also wish to push the boundaries of what sorts of practices and sites can properly be classified as 'political'. In doing this we wish to pick up on a key debate within contemporary Sri Lanka around the boundaries of civil society and the possibilities for recognising political agency outside of the formal public sphere (Grewal 2017, 2021, 2018; Ariyarathne 2020, 2021a; Koens and Gunawardana 2021). This also connects with questions of how different social actors have sought to engage with, through and against the State, formal institutions and the law. By bringing in examples of 'everyday' resistances and engagements with traditionally conceived 'ritual' or 'cultural' (rather than political) spaces, we seek to expand the understanding of social and political action. This we argue allows for a much richer picture of contemporary Sri Lankan politics to emerge as well as a more nuanced and complex understanding of the political.

Redress for Conflict-Related Violence

Given the length and significance of the war to Sri Lankan modern society and politics, it is unsurprising that there is vast literature on the gendered dimensions and impacts of the conflict. In the post-war period, this interest has continued as the after-effects continue to be felt, militarisation remains a significant problem and post-war justice struggles continue to take gendered forms (CEJ 2019).

Since the end of the fighting, women, especially from the Tamil community, have played a particularly visible role in the struggle for truth, accountability and justice. This has been explained in pragmatic terms related to the high rates of disappearance among Tamil men and the ongoing fear of being targeted by security services. As a result, women have been overrepresented in the Families of the Disappeared movement and have also been at the forefront of efforts to work across ethnic and religious communities. They have also been very proactive in organising and presenting submissions to the various fact-finding missions, consultations and commissions that have occurred since 2009. Irrespective of the practical reasons why women may have taken the lead, their activism has resulted in many different conceptualisations of the political that are significant. The tropes they have drawn on have been specifically gendered and brought in dimensions otherwise often excluded from analyses of the political.

A key feature of activism on the issue of disappearance has been the mobilisation of the trope of 'motherhood' (Maunaguru 1995; De Alwis 2002, 2009; Perera-Rajasingham 2008). By using this trope, activists have introduced two interesting contributions on the political. First, the shifting of the focus of politics from the established public sphere into the realm of the domestic, intimate and private opens up a way for reconceptualising the relationship between activism and everyday life. Second, the figure of the grieving mother has allowed for an introduction of the question of emotions into the realm of politics.

Everyday Activism

As Rebecca Walker (2016) captures in her account of human rights work in Batticaloa in the early 2000s, life in situations of extreme violence, precarity and insecurity requires a very different approach to space, voice and practice. In an attempt to disrupt macro-level analyses of conflict and its meaning for subject populations, Walker focuses on the micro-level of ordinary lived experience. Through this she highlights, 'the quiet negotiation and shaping of spaces which are encompassed in the endurance of the everyday' (2016: 189). In many ways, this resonates with work by other feminist scholars who have been similarly critical of the focus on formal, institutional political processes in addressing issues of peace and justice which ignore and/or depoliticise the experiences and perspectives of those most affected by the conflict (Perera-Rajasingham 2007; Grewal 2017, 2021). The failure to engage with the less spectacular, more marginal and more 'mundane' forms of resistance, survival and future-making not only erases subaltern politics – a point also discussed further in relation to LGBTIQ+ politics – it misses vital insights offered on how the political operates and can be conceptualised. Iromi Perera (2021) also describes this in the forms of organising she documents among women forced from *wattes* into high-rise apartment buildings in Colombo (see also Mohideen in this volume).

The Role of Emotion

The role of emotions in politics is a further theme that has been emerging in recent literature on gender activism in Sri Lanka. Researchers both during and after the war have identified themes of grief, mourning and suffering as central to people's lives and politics. Walker argues for a recognition of suffering, '*within* resistance rather than in opposition to it' (2016: 189, emphasis in original). Meanwhile, Malathi de Alwis (2016) uses the theme of mourning to disrupt hegemonic accounts of Tamil masculinity and militarism in her sensitive study of men's experiences in post-Tsunami Batticaloa. De Alwis (2002, 2009) has also offered much to our understanding of the potentiality of grief in conceptualising the political through her decades-long work on the Mothers' movements in both the south and north and east of the country.

Moving beyond grief, the role of emotion more generally in both shaping the political landscape and in relation to activist work is something Grewal and Cegu Isadeen (2022) and Thananjan (2020) have attempted to explore in recent work. In an attempt to make sense of both the regressive turn back to ethno-nationalist politics in the aftermath of Easter 2019 and the efforts over a number of years by activists to create alternative spaces and communities in the face of ongoing inter-communal tension, they turn to the affective dimension of politics and community. Taking up the point by feminist scholar Clare Hemmings that, 'in order to know differently we have to feel differently' (2012: 150), Grewal and Cegu Isadeen discuss their own experiences of building a 'feminist home' as a site of refuge to think, rest, debate and strategise.

This links with Thananjan's reflections (2020) on the emotional labour involved in feminist organising and inter-communal activism. She notes the importance of activists having space to acknowledge their feelings of fear, humour, anger and burnout. While this is true generally for activism, the particular challenges faced by those trying to work across ethnic and religious communities in the context of a highly sectarian political landscape are evident.

There have been many initiatives aimed at using gender as a vehicle for bringing together women from different ethnic communities. As in other post-war contexts, the idea of shared suffering as a way of transcending ethnic divides has been an important organising tool. Various inter-ethnic women's organisations have been established during and after the war, particularly in the East but also in the North. However, this has faced intense challenges. Sinhala and Tamil women's groups have spoken about the suspicion with which they were met by armed forces during the war (Thiruchandran 2012). Most recently, the Easter bombings in 2019 led to frictions below the surface erupting between Tamil and Muslim women in highly disturbing ways. Thananjan documents instances where women who had worked alongside each other for years suddenly became reluctant to sit or eat with each other. Much work has been required to rebuild the fragile relationships although the protests in 2022 have offered new opportunities. Activists' reflections on these emotional dimensions to their work are insightful in the way they allow us to theorise an often-underrepresented aspect of movement building and activism.

The Co-option of Gender

The work of doing 'gender' activism is further complicated by geopolitical factors. Vasuki Nesiah critically analyses the ways in which UN Security Council Resolution 1325 (Women Peace and Security) has 'occupied and constrained the landscape of peace and security in ways that have legitimated a politics of hegemonic internationalism in the name of women affected by conflict' (2012: 156). Doing 'gender' work has been mainstreamed and indeed become 'fashionable' within development and human rights NGOs (Thiruchandran 2012). This has led to a co-option of women's rights in ways that have not necessarily been positive. In one feminist activist's view events like international women's day have largely been taken over by NGOs that do not necessarily adopt particularly progressive approaches to gender.

This brings us back to the question posed by Nesiah (2012) about whether the emphasis on women's inclusion, 'deflects questions regarding the distributive and ideological dimensions of the hegemonic nation-building project… what is foregrounded and what is obscured by it, which issues confronted and which deferred, which social forces empowered and which defeated' (2012: 156). As with the issue of female ex-combatants (Martin 2017) and Mothers of the Disappeared, it seems to point to the pressures to re-establish normative gender order and in turn the dominant social and political order on which they rely (Maunaguru 1995; de Alwis 2002, 2009). Moreover, as Grewal has documented, the emphasis on 'human rights education' and training while ostensibly an agenda of empowerment, has often reproduced the divide between those who 'know, act, think' and those who are forever passive recipients to be disciplined, taught or saved (2017, 2021).

However gender activism has not died as a result. Rather, alongside this governmentality of gender, as critiqued by Nesiah (2012), Grewal (2017, 2021) and others, creative and unconventional forms of gender activism have continued to flourish. On the one hand, the role of the arts has been central, as documented by Jeyasankar (2022). On the other hand, the space of ritual has emerged as significant, not just as a source of solace but also a form of subaltern political expression and space for organising (Vasuki 2012; Grewal 2017, 2018, 2021).

So too in interviews with us many grassroots activists have spoken about the ways in which the trainings and employment opportunities offered by NGOs allowed them space to develop their own critical consciousness and supported their transition into political actors before ultimately moving beyond this constrained space. Similarly, while they are conscious of the limits of many of the formal mechanisms set up following the end of the war, marginalised women have nonetheless chosen to engage with the various commissions and consultation processes.

This is often presented as an act of desperation but our own reading is slightly different. Based on interviews with women activists in Mullaitivu, Batticaloa and Mannar it is evident that they see their engagement as strategic and are pragmatic about the extent to which these formal institutions will produce real results. Their approach is often incremental, concerned with developing their own knowledge, skills, confidence and independence and focused on small-scale material gains alongside larger symbolic claims to justice. Nimanthi (2007) makes similar observations in her description of the Jaffna-based women's shelter *Poorani* during the war. These insights are important in enriching our account of the Sri Lankan political landscape: moving us beyond elite civil society discourse to include subaltern political agency. They are also significant for those of us interested in how human rights operate in practice, adding nuance to both positive and critical accounts of what rights frameworks offer.

Muslim Women's Activism for Personal Law Reforms

While post-war Tamil women's organising has taken a mixed approach to engage the State and formal institutions, Muslim women's activism in recent years has been much more directly focused on enacting law reform. The campaign to reform the Muslim Marriage and Divorce Act dates back to at least the late 1960s. However, it has gained prominence and intensity since the most recent reform initiative was launched in 2005 and the establishment by the Ministry of Justice of a committee headed up by former Supreme Court Justice Saleem Marsoof in 2009. The Marsoof committee took nine years to publish its report but this finally happened in 2018 and since then Muslim women activists have maintained a public campaign demanding a number of essential changes to the laws governing Muslim families. In particular they have called for a minimum age of marriage be specified (in line with Sri Lankan national law), women be allowed to sign their own marriage contract, and that women be allowed to be appointed as Qazis (judges), among other demands.

In making their arguments, activists have made use of a range of resources: highlighting the rights of Muslim women as Sri Lankan citizens, invoking international human rights while also placing the debate within the context of Islamic feminism and challenging patriarchal interpretations of Shariah (Hamin and Cegu Isadeen 2015, 2016).[2] This provides an interesting example of how activists in postcolonial Global South contexts navigate some of the tensions between rights language (often accused of being 'Western' in its focus and framing) and communal claims made in the name of culture and tradition (and indeed in this case religion). As others have also demonstrated in different contexts, this challenge requires further exploration and the case of Muslim women's activism in Sri Lanka thus merits further scholarly research and documentation (Rao 2010; Dave 2012).

This area of activism has also once again highlighted the challenges for marginalised groups to address intra-communal injustices in the context of inter-communal power dynamics. The claim to equal citizenship by Muslim women activists has been complicated significantly by a resurgence in anti-Muslim sentiment and violence. In the post-war years there has been a rise in militant Buddhist groups which have targeted the Muslim community, often with the complicity of the State (Holt 2016). The aftermath of the Easter 2019 bombings led to strange alliances between certain conservative Tamil and Sinhala actors against an apparent 'common enemy' in the form of the Muslim. This led to a range of responses from rumours and boycotts of Muslim businesses, to the detention of some prominent Muslims and the further stigmatisation of ordinary Muslims including the restriction of movement of women wearing forms of Islamic dress.

On the one hand, the construction of the Muslim as a problem has led to a mainstreaming of Muslim women's rights as a discourse mobilised by unlikely allies and provided more political will to abolish the parallel legal framework of Muslim family law, highlighted by Gotabhaya Rajapakse's 'one country – one law' campaign. This track has promoted the perception that it is only Muslim family law that is an aberration, when in fact in Sri Lanka there are several parallel laws in existence – for example Thesawalami. The Islamophobia of the State and mainstream society has also created pressure for Muslim women to not speak against the community for fear of feeding anti-Muslim sentiment. This positioning has made it very difficult for activists to maintain their campaign without being co-opted or silenced. Somehow they have navigated this space, in part through the creative use of social media and the establishment and maintenance of strong friendship networks (see Shenk, de Mel and Wijewardene 2021).

Women's Political Representation

Reforming Electoral Politics

Women's movements for political representation and voting rights in Sri Lanka have a long history dating back to the early 20th century (de Alwis and Jayawardena, 2000). As Jayawardene in Wenona (2002) states, there was not only a women's movement in the 20th century, but there was also a consciousness about women's issues in the 19th-century Sri Lanka. Concerns on women's under-representation in public politics have been rising since the 1990s in Sri Lanka. Women's civil society organisations and individuals have been lobbying the government and major political parties for adequate women's representation in elections. With discussions of local government electoral reforms emerging after 2003, these discussions brought by women's organisations were closely linked with a 25% quota at the local governmental level (Kodikara 2009).

A provision to reserve 25% of seats in the local government for women was included in the draft Constitution of 1997 but was not implemented. In August 2000, the Sri Lanka Women's NGO Forum made a strong appeal that a 25% quota for women should be included in the 2000 draft Constitution, which also did not come into force. Simultaneously, they have been having numerous discussions with political parties and grassroot women's organisations on the issue. Since 2000, there was a proliferation of publications and media presence of the discussion on women's political participation, especially among NGOs. Several obstacles that women face in politics were highlighted in these campaigns: issues of the electoral system itself, party-level reluctance, family and ideological challenges posed by patriarchy, among others (Kodikara 2009; Liyanage 2017).

In 2001, The Women's Political Forum, a collective of 12 women's organisations, drafted a women's manifesto prior to the parliamentary elections in order to highlight a number of critical areas of concern to women in Sri Lanka, including the issue of women's political participation. With the establishment of the Parliamentary Select Committee on Electoral Reform in 2003, women's organisations initiated discussions to ensure that a quota for women would be assured in the event of local government electoral reform. When the Committee called for representations from the public, several NGOs submitted written submissions making a series of recommendations which addressed the problem of women in politics. In 2006, an independent group of 27 women, forming a women-only political party, contested the Kurunegala Pradeshiya Sabha. These campaigns were also followed by awareness programmes at national and grassroots levels, media campaigns, discussions with political parties and submissions to Convention on the Elimination of all forms of Discrimination Against Women (CEDAW) Committee as shadow reports.

As a result, the *Local Authorities Election (Amendment) Act* was enacted in 2017. This Act, as a response to the Constitutional mandate for affirmative action for women, paved the way for a

25% quota for women in the nomination lists by political parties and, therefore, can be considered as a historic moment in the struggle for women's political representation. In the 2018 local government elections, 17,000 women contested out of more than 56,000 candidates. However, due to the practical and structural issues within political parties and the electoral system, women still face challenges in participating in local politics (Munasinghe and Ariyarathne 2019; Ranawana and Brown 2021). In the 2019 Presidential election, there was high visibility of women's issues in political discussions, even though there was less participation of women on political platforms (Commonwealth Parliamentary Association 2019). Each candidate had women's wing's support in elections, while Progressive Women's Collective, the women's wing of the main leftist coalition, National People's Power (NPP) had demanded a minimum of 50% of women's participation in the parliament. During the election period, the Women and Media Collective announced a Women's Manifesto, which was delivered to all presidential candidates, drawing attention to important women's issues. Again, in the 2020 parliamentary elections, there were only 59 women out of 1,082 candidates and the number of elected/nominated women was 12 out of 225.

The Role of Civil Society Activism

It is important to note that the struggle for women's political participation in early 20th Sri Lanka was led by women's wings of political parties and individual women (de Alwis and Jayawardena 2000; Liyanage 2014). More recently it has often been carried out by activists attached to NGO projects. The political parties are influenced and persuaded by women in these spaces, while they engage with the government institutions for lobbying. For example, some of these women's groups have submitted their proposals to the Constitutional Drafting Committee operated during the 2016–2017 period by the then government, demanding women's quota in national elections. Others have engaged in discussions with state institutions, such as the National Committee on Women attached to the Ministry of Women, the Parliamentary Select Committee on Electoral Reform, etc. in order to push the government to make policy changes (Kodikara 2009).

Several others have engaged in challenging patriarchal ideologies which limit women's public roles, which is the most challenging task of all. However, the majority of post-2017 interventions seem not to challenge the patriarchy or the structural inequalities; rather, they focus on short- and medium-term objectives, such as enhancing skills and awareness of women, lobbying with political parties for increased representation, etc. (Munasinghe and Ariyarathne 2019). Also, due to the eventual NGO-isation of social and political mobilisation, the activism had turned towards more developmental oriented interventions (Amarasuriya 2018).

The role of NGOs in Sri Lanka is a complex and controversial issue. Critics have argued NGO-isation has both contributed to and is reflective of a crisis of left politics (Roy 2014). The rise of funded 'gender projects' in the development and human rights field, NGOs have often taken space and resources away from more politically radical activist initiatives (Nesiah 2012; Grewal 2017). The issue of women's political participation has also been affected by the Women Peace and Security agenda, incorporating larger geopolitical agendas. It is a further example of how apparent 'empowerment' initiatives can work to reinforce existing power structures and processes of silencing.

However as we also noted above, the NGO space has also offered opportunities to marginalised actors who otherwise have limited access to the public sphere. Studying political participation among Tamil women in Sri Lanka, Koens and Gunawardana (2021) argue that NGO training have contributed women's coming out for electoral politics in Mannar, North Sri Lanka. Our own research supports this conclusion.

With formal political parties failing to deliver, the shift to using civil society spaces as sites for reimagining and demanding new political arrangements has been important. The current events in Sri Lanka (the protests still ongoing as we write) have further highlighted the disconnect between the possibilities for democratic politics within formal State institutions and the articulation of democracy through popular demands and practices. Thus while civil society cannot be idealised and also requires constant critical engagement of who is excluded and how, it has also offered an important site for democratic politics in a context where liberal democratic institutions have largely failed.

LGBTIQ+ Activism

The Beginnings of a Movement

The first gay rights organisation in Sri Lanka, Companions on a Journey (CoJ), was launched in 1995, with the support of the Dutch government and Alliance London – a UK-based HIV/AIDS support group. Likewise, the majority of LGBTIQ+ rights organisations in Sri Lanka started after 2000s were funded by or even formed as a result of funding provided to prevent global HIV/AIDS programmes. Even after the closing down of several NGOs in the aftermath of the war, there are 14 LGBTIQ+ organisations currently functioning in Sri Lanka (Waradas 2022).

The early activism was mainly focused on healthcare, peer support and networking, while the decriminalisation of homosexuality gradually entered into discussions in the period of 2005–2010. Apart from decriminalisation, there were advocacy programmes run by organisations on several other issues, such as discrimination and gender-based violence against LGBTIQ+ communities, access to healthcare and justice. A number of organisations started submitting shadow reports to the CEDAW Committee after 2010. These reports were compiled not only by LGBTIQ organisations but also by women's rights groups who worked for intersectional justice. These reports highlighted the critical issues faced by LGBTIQ communities in Sri Lanka in relation to the police, healthcare, state and the public.

After 2015, the *Yahapalana* government was generally supportive of LGBTIQ+ communities, since there were non-heterosexual individuals represented in high positions in the government. However, their attempts for decriminalisation were not successful, due to a lack of support and engagement with civil society and citizens. Meanwhile, LGBTIQ groups were constantly engaging with the Human Rights Commission of Sri Lanka (HRCSL) who dedicated one of its nine sub-committees to LGBTIQ issues (Sub Committee on the Rights of LGBTIQ Persons). During the public representations for a new Constitution and reconciliation mechanisms, LGBTIQ groups made written submission to these Committees. The Public Representation Committee (PRC) even suggested the government change the equality clause of the new Constitution. Once again we see that, while institutional mechanisms set up in the post-war period have often failed to deliver major structural reform, they have offered a space for marginalised communities and individuals to come forward and speak. This has both allowed for new political actors to gain access to the public sphere and diversified the political agenda.

Transgender Politics

Meanwhile, transgender individuals have been individually trying to obtain support of the healthcare and document change support by filing individual court cases in District Courts and complaining to the HRCSL. As a result of one such case, a group of activists, HRCSL and the

Ministry of Health collectively conducted a consultation in order to seek possibilities of gender change. This was followed by issuance of Health Ministry circular No. 01-34/2016, allowing psychiatrists to issue of a Gender Recognition Certificate (GRC) to transgender individuals and the Registrar General's Circular No. 06/2016 which allowed transgender people to change their gender in Birth Certificate. With this, several trans-dedicated NGOs were formed, who started supporting transgender individuals for surgeries, hormone treatments and document change. While some scholars argue that GRC paves the way for transgender persons in Sri Lanka to change their legal gender on official documents and for a new life (Ginige and Malalgama 2018; Yutthaworakool 2021), others have highlighted the paradox of recognition of trans persons who are supposed to claim citizenship rights and 'proper' identity through a constant medical gaze (Ariyarathne 2021a, 2021b).

Efforts described above are similar to transgender people in various different contexts, but what is often not remarked upon is the vernacular forms of expression that transgender people have used to both assert their identities in public and to build space for themselves in communities. Ariyarathne (2020, 2021a 2022) has captured some of this in her ethnographic study of transgender people in Colombo. In the process, she has shown that these practices are significant for a number of reasons. First, they allow us to expand our understanding of transgender people beyond stigmatised victims to see them as creative political subjects in their own right. Second, by recognising their actions as a form of politics (again, using every day and 'cultural' forms that have traditionally been excluded from our understanding of the political), our conceptualisation of the contemporary political scene in Sri Lanka is enriched. And finally, she points out that these gender performances allow for a further disruption of the normative gender, sexual and ethnic constructions on which the State and religious and political elites rely.

Intersectional Activism

By 2016, there was a high amount of online presence of LGBTIQ+ activists who were either affiliated to organisations, or worked individually to promote rights. A research study has indicated that to LGBTIQ+ Sri Lankans, the internet has been a significant tool for creating networks, building identities (collectively and individually) as well as community mobilising (WMC 2017). The proliferation of LGBTIQ+-related materials on Facebook and other social media platforms is very much visible since 2015. The use of these online resources for community building and organising mirrors the findings of Shenk et al (2021) regarding the role that social media has played for Muslim women activists (discussed above).

The year 2018 marked an important juncture of intersectional political approach of LGBTIQ+ activism in Sri Lanka. Followed by the then President's homophobic comment on gay politicians in the government and the constitutional coup in 2018, several LGBTIQ+ organisations and individuals in Colombo gathered and demanded to convene the Parliament and restore democracy. As Wanniarachchi (2019) suggests, these protests were very significant in terms of the response of the LGBTIQ+ movement to the President by occupying public spaces with their bodies with signs such as 'Butterflies are also voters', 'Butterfly power'. He argues that the publicness of the butterfly assemblage refused the domesticity into which the State attempted to dispose their bodies. Thus, as with the women's political participation activism, this presented an important challenge to the public/private divide on which the State has long relied. As with the increased attention given to women's issues in the 2019 and 2020 election campaigns, the 'Butterflies' movement during the 2018 parliamentary stand-off created an unprecedented visibility of LGBTIQ people and issues in the mainstream public and political spheres. By calling out the use of homophobic slurs within parliament, this movement both introduced gay rights into mainstream political debate and challenged the heteronormative and patriarchal foundations of the State and formal politics.

The other important aspect of the LGBTIQ+ movement in Sri Lanka after 2015 is their engagement in electoral political campaigns. During the Presidential election in 2019, Progressive Queer Collective (PQC) was formed as a collection of individuals, leftist queer activists, who supported the LGBTIQ+ policy of the NPP. There were several other activists who demanded the inclusion of LGBTIQ policy with other presidential candidates, however, except the NPP candidate, none of the other candidates included LGBTIQ policy in their documents. As a result, PQC campaigned widely across the country for the support of the leftist coalition.

Another important post-war development of the LGBTIQ movement was the emergence of LGBTIQ organisations outside of Colombo, especially in the North and the East. Queer organisations, such as Jaffna Sangam, Anichcham Collective (in the East) and Jaffna Transgender Network, Malayaga Queer Community had initially started with some connection with Colombo-based organisations; however, they have managed to establish their own geographical peripheries of work during the last five years. Importantly, the queer pride events that were initially limited to Colombo are now expanded to Jaffna (online and offline), taken over by Tamil-speaking queer communities. Compared to the LGBTIQ organisations who hide their work behind general human rights titles, Tamil-speaking queer movement has been very much visible in the public sphere, while some of the organisations' (such as Jaffna Sangam and Anichcham Collective) approaches to political issues are intersectional. Even though these organisations have not publicly campaigned for elections, some of them (i.e. Jaffna Sangam, Anichcham Collective) have shown loyalty to national leftist political movements. As Waradas (2022) points out it is important to note that even though these NGOs are dependent on foreign funds, and often painted as pro-neo-liberal, these funds were used to strategically deploy a movement that is rather radical in mainstreaming the LGBTIQ rights in Sri Lanka.

The 2022 *Aragalaya*: The Gendered Dimension of Mass Popular Protest

As we were writing this chapter, a major popular uprising took place across Sri Lanka in 2022. Referred to as the *Aragalaya* (*Porattum* in Tamil, Struggle in English), it led to the then government resigning and was heralded for its non-violent and decentred approach. While protest sites emerged across the country, a large crowd began gathering regularly at Galle Face in the centre of Colombo from late March/early April, which led to the establishment of an encampment that came to be known as *Gotagogama* (Gota Go Village). Other *Gotagogamas* and localised protest sites and movements sprang up in different parts of the country and while there was scepticism expressed about whether the *Aragalaya* could or would really respond to *all* Sri Lankans' struggles, a moment of optimism seemed to open up that a new type of politics and political engagement may be possible. Outside of Colombo the Batticaloa 'Justice March' and 'Justice Village' – primarily established and led by women – continue as active sites of resistance, civic engagement and popular education (Emmanuel 2022).

Within all of this women and queer Sri Lankans have been explicitly present. They have represented different communities (i.e. Malayaga Tamil, women from NGOs, activists from the North and East, women who were seeking disappeared family members, LGBTIQ communities, etc.) and participated not only under the common slogan of Gotagohome, but also used the space to demand broader accountability, economic equality and justice. A women's group called 'Galle Face Aragalaye Kantha Handa' (Women's Voice of the Galle Face) was organised within the larger Organising Committee of the Galle Face and launched separate protests voicing for demands of gender justice. So too the first Pride March in Colombo was held in June 2022 by LGBTIQ+ organisations, activists and allies and walked to the Galle Face protest site demanding equality and justice for gender and sexual minorities. There have also been a wide array of public 'teach outs' at protest sites, which have both sought to raise issues of gender injustice and highlight the gendered effects and impacts of the current political and economic crisis.

In many ways the 2022 protest movement has acted as a microcosm of the broader trends within Sri Lanka in terms of gender activism. The 2022 *Aragalaya* provided a valuable platform to both bring together various struggles and to highlight the intersectional nature of disadvantage, marginalisation and injustice within Sri Lanka. The decentred nature of the protest movement has meant that many different causes have been able to co-exist (in sometimes uncomfortable but nonetheless productive ways) and come together under a common banner. It has also offered a space for the active participation of women and other gendered subjects from all walks of life, as protestors, educators and leaders. At the same time there have been several instances where women activists' suggestions and representations have been either ignored or suppressed by men in the organising committees (authors' personal conversations with activists), once again highlighting the need for broader shifts in political culture and attitudes beyond institutional reform. Many of these issues have been expressly identified in discussions emerging out of the *Aragalaya* such as in the discussions around the People's Council and People's Parliament initiatives.

Engaging the State and Law: Trajectories

Aside from providing rich interventions into post-war Sri Lankan social and political life, the examples of gender activism we have described offer important theoretical contributions that deserve recognition. Through the forms their activism have taken, these groups challenge us to rethink the role of the State, formal institutions and civil society. What we hope has been clear is that the institutional efforts at democratisation have often failed those most marginalised and discriminated. However, that does not mean that there have not been important engagements with these institutions: sometimes in conventional and sometimes unconventional forms. In the process they have both highlighted the failures and opened up new possibilities.

As Vasuki Nesiah has articulated, the framing of law against violence misses the crucial fact that, 'violence and militarism articulate *through* law, rather than *against* law' (original emphasis). This leads her to call for a better analysis of the socio-political meaning of both violence and law in Sri Lanka. Based on the developments in recent years and the insights offered by activists themselves, we would argue that this analysis has been a key feature of activist engagements with law. Rather than appealing to law as the answer to their oppression, activists have treated law as a site of discursive and material struggle. An arena within which they have sought to assert a voice but not necessarily accepted uncritically as having authority or legitimacy. So too in the process of calling on the State to deliver certain types of justice, many of the forms of gender activism we have described above have actually provided valuable critical insights into its patriarchal and heteronormative foundations.

In this sense, while we agree to an extent with Sharika Thiranagama's (2013) interpretation of citizen engagements with processes like the LLRC[3] hearings as desperate but doomed efforts at holding an unresponsive State to account, we also believe there is more going on. Many of the activists in the movements we have discussed above are highly aware of the obstacles to official recognition. Their reasons for engaging with institutions are therefore complex. In some cases, it is a form of empowerment self-education themselves and confidence building. In this sense what the activists describe seems to be a form of 'informed disenchantment' similar to that documented by

Mary Gallagher in relation to Chinese citizens: a paradoxical process by which engagement with the system reduces the faith of individuals in it but empowers them to be more knowledgeable, strategic and creative in making demands in the future (for more see Grewal 2017: 189). This 'life of law' beyond formal institutional logics is important and often under-acknowledged (Grewal 2017).

Finally, what many of the examples we have discussed above have highlighted is that while we are often focused on the spectacular and/or institutionalised aspects of activism, what in fact sustains it is often more mundane: the everyday practices of survival, community and care, the emotional and creative labour dedicated to not just demanding social change but reimagining the social foundations on which that might occur and the tricky negotiations of solidarity across difference. They represent the 'affective infrastructure', feminists like Jasmina Husanovic (2020) have described: the often unrecognised underlying structures which are essential to making institutional and public engagement possible. They also address a gap identified by Harini Amarasuriya (2015), in exploring dissent and resistance beyond the narrow frames of ethnicity and nationalism. And finally, in our view, they provide valuable contributions to broader debates about activism and the nature of the political that may have resonances and significance in other contexts.

Notes

1. Women have also been actively involved in various ways with the different resurgent religious movements (see for example Farzana Haniffa's 2008 work on women's *da'wa* groups), but this is unfortunately beyond the scope of this chapter, which focuses more on rights campaigns.
2. The Muslim Women's Research and Action Forum has produced a range of publications on topics related to women, Islam and Muslim family and personal law: https://mwraf.lk/category/publications/.
3. The Lessons Learnt and Reconciliation Commission, established by the Sri Lankan government immediately after the end of the War in response to calls for investigations into and accountability for serious violations of international human rights and humanitarian law: https://reliefweb.int/report/sri-lanka/report-commission-inquiry-lessons-learnt-and-reconciliation.

References

Amarasuriya, Harini (2015) "Elite Politics and Dissent in Sri Lanka" *The South Asianist* 4(1): 1–22

Amarasuriya, Harini (2018) "Only mothers and daughters? The role of women in left activism during the 1980s" [paper presentation] **AILS conference: "Sri Lankan History: View from the Margins"**, Colombo, Sri Lanka (February 1–2)

Ariyarathne, Kaushalya (2020) "Gaze of Kajal Painted Eyes: Sri Lankan *Jogi* Dance as a Subaltern Political Expression" *Patitha: Socio-Cultural Review* 11(1): 13–37

Ariyarathne, Kaushalya (2021a) *(Un)Framing the Self: Negotiating Transgender Identities in Contemporary Sri Lanka* Unpublished PhD Thesis. Colombo: University of Colombo

Ariyarathne, Kaushalya (2021b) "To be or Not to Be Seen? The Paradox of Recognition among Trans Men in Sri Lanka" *Masculinities: A Journal of Culture and Society* 15(Spring 2021): 66–95

Ariyarathne, Kaushalya (2022) "Priest, Woman and Mother: Broadening the Horizons through Transgender/*Nachchi* Identities in Sri Lanka" *The Sri Lanka Journal of the Humanities* 43(2): 19–39

Centre for Equality and Justice (CEJ) (2019) "Reparations for women in Sri Lanka: What stakeholders say". Accessed on 13/06/2022. Available at https://cejsrilanka.org/wp-content/uploads/Annex-19-Reparations-for-Women-in-Sri-Lanka-2.3.pdf

Commonwealth Parliamentary Association (2019) *Annual Report and Performance Review 2019*. Available at https://www.cpahq.org/media/egjme0w5/cpa-annual-report-2019-final-online-single.pdf

Dave, Naisargi (2012) *Queer Activism in Indian: A Story in the Anthropology of Ethics* Durham: Duke University Press

De Alwis, Malathi (2016) "The Tsunami's Wake: Mourning and Masculinity in Eastern Sri Lanka" In *Men, Masculinities and Disaster* Elaine Enarson and Bob Pease (eds) London: Routledge, pp 92–102

De Alwis, Malathi (2009) "Interrogating the 'Political': Feminist Peace Activism in Sri Lanka" *Feminist Review* 91: 81–93

De Alwis, Malathi (2002) "Ambivalent Maternalisms: Cursing as Public Protest in Sri Lanka" In *The Aftermath: Women in Post-Conflict Transformation*, Meredith Turshen, Sheila Meintjes, and Anu Pillay (eds) London and New York: Zed Books, pp 210–224

De Alwis, Malathi (1997) "Motherhood as a Space of Protest: Women's Political Participation in Contemporary Sri Lanka" In *Appropriating Gender: Women's Activism and Politicized Religion in South Asia* Patricia Jeffrey and Amrita Basu (eds) London and New York: Routledge, pp 185–202

De Alwis, Malathi and Kumari Jayawardena (2000) *Casting Pearls: The Women's Franchise Movement in Sri Lanka* Colombo: Social Scientists' Association.

Emmanuel, Sarala (2022) "The Batti Walk for Justice: A resistance for fundamental system change." *The Morning* (31 July). https://www.themorning.lk/the-batti-walk-for-justice-a-resistance-for-fundamental-system-change/

Ginige, Pabasari and Ayodhya Malalgama (2018) "An Update on Transsexuality" *Sri Lanka Journal of Psychiatry* 9(2): 4–8

Grewal, Kiran K. (2017) *The Socio-Political Practice of Human Rights: Between the Universal and the Particular* London: Routledge

Grewal, Kiran K. (2018) "Politics beyond Institutions: The Creation of New Social Imaginaries in Post-War Sri Lanka" *Social Alternatives* 37(4): 55–59

Grewal, Kiran K. (2021) "Feminist Responses to Conflict: Within, against and beyond the Law" In *Routledge Handbook of Feminist Peace Research* Tarja Väyrynen, Swati Parashar, Élise Féron and Cecilia Confortini (eds) London: Routledge, pp 70–79

Grewal, Kiran K. and Hasanah Cegu Isadeen (2021) "Between the Nationalists and the Fundamentalists, Still We Have Hope!" In *Dystopian Futures: Emotional Landscapes and Dark Futures* Jordan McKenzie and Roger Patulny (eds) Bristol: Bristol University Press, pp 89–103

Hamin, Hyshyama and Hasanah Cegy Isadeen (2016) Unequali Citizens: Muslim Women's Struggle for Justice and Equality in Sri Lanka, Available on https://mplreformsdotcom.files.wordpress.com/2016/12/unequal-citizens-study-hyshyama-hamin-hasanah-cegu-isadeen1.pdf

Haniffa, Farzana (2008) "Piety as Politics amongst Muslim Women in Contemporary Sri Lanka" *Modern Asian Studies* 42(2/3): 347–375

Hemmings, C. (2012) "Affective Solidarity: Feminist Reflexivity and Political Transformation" *Feminist Theory* 13(2): 147–161

Holt, John (ed) (2016) *Buddhist Extremists and Muslim Minorities: Religious Conflict in Contemporary Sri Lanka* Oxford: Oxford University Press

Husanovic, Jasmina (2020) "On Affective Infrastructure" [*public lecture*], Goldsmiths College University of London, London UK (January 27)

Jeyasankar, Vasuki (2022) "A Practitioner's Reflections: Women, Ritual and Community Healing in Sri Lanka" In We are Present: Women's Histories of Conflict, Courage and Survival. Radhika Hettiarachchi (ed) New York: International Coalition of Sites of Conscience, pp 54–97

Kodikara, Chulani (2009) *The Struggle for Equal Political Representation in Sri Lanka* Colombo: UNDP

Koens, Celeste and Samanthi J. Gunawardana (2021) "A Continuum of Participation: Rethinking Tamil Women's Political Participation and Agency in Post-War Sri Lanka" *International Feminist Journal of Politics* 23(3): 463–484

Liyanage, Pulsara (2014) "Left Women and Political Participation" In *Pathways of the Left in Sri Lanka* Marshal Fernando and B. Skanthakumar (eds) Colombo: Ecumenical Institute for Study and Dialogue, pp 135–157

Liyanage, Pulsara (2017) "Women's Representation and Political Engagement in Local Governments: Evidence from Sri Lanka" In *Decentralization and Development of Sri Lanka within a Unitary State* Nawalage Seneviratne Cooray and Sirimal Abeyratne (eds) Singapore: Springer, pp 203–227

Martin, Melissa (2017) "Sri Lanka's Ex-Combatant Rehabilitation Programme: Reconstructing Gendered Identities" *Journal of Peacebuilding and Development* 12(1): 79–84

Maunaguru, Sitralega (1995) "Gendering Tamil Nationalism: The Construction of 'Woman' in Projects of Protest and Control" In *Unmaking the Nation: The Politics of Identity and History in Modern Sri Lanka* Pradeep Jaganathan and Qadri Ismail (eds) Colombo: International Centre for Ethnic Studies, pp 157–172

Munasinghe, Vidura and Kaushalya Ariyarathne (2019) *Quest for Agency: Reflections on Women's Quota in Local Governance* Colombo: Law and Society Trust

Nesiah, Vasuki (2012) "Uncomfortable Alliances: Women, Peace and Security in Sri Lanka" In *South Asian Feminisms* Ania Loomba and Ritty A. Lukose (eds) Durham and London: Duke University Press, pp 139–161

Perera, Iromi (2021) Housing in a Pandemic: Need for New Methods of Engagement. Available on https://www.csf-asia.org/__trashed/

Perera-Rajasingham, Nimanthi (2007) "Feminist Politics beyond the Law: Poorani as a Space for Empowerment and Resistance" In *Feminist Engagements with Violence: Contingent Moments from Sri Lanka* Perera-Rajasingham, Nimanthi, Lisa Kois and Rizvina Morseth de Alwis (eds) Colombo: International Centre for Ethnic Studies, pp 143–172

Perera-Rajasingham, Nimanthi (2008) "The Politics of the Governed: Maternal Politics and Child Recruitment in the Eastern Province of Sri Lanka" In *Constellations of Violence: Feminist Interventions in South Asia* Radhika Coomeraswamy and Nimanthi Perera-Rajasingham (eds) New Delhi: Women Unlimited (Kali), pp 121–148

Ranawana, Kshama and Sanchia Brown (2021) *Women, Quota and Local Councils* Colombo: Women and Media Collective

Rao, Rahul (2010) *Third World Protest: Between Home and the World* Oxford: Oxford University Press

Rashid, Hashim bin and Shafiya Rafaithu (2022) "'Strikes are normal growing up': Plantation politics in Sri Lanka" *Jamhoor* (31 March). Accessed on 14/06/2023. Available at https://www.jamhoor.org/read/plantation-politics-in-sri-lanka-strikes-are-normal-growing-up-in-plantations

Roy, Arundhati (2014) "The NGO-ization of resistance" *Pambazuka News* (23 September) Accessed on 15/06/2022. Available at https://www.pambazuka.org/governance/ngo-ization-resistance

Shenk, Christine, Neloufer de Mel and Shermal Wijewardene (2021) "Negotiating borders within Muslim feminist activism in Sri Lanka after the Easter attacks" [paper presentation] **British Association of South Asian Studies Annual Conference**, Edinburgh, Scotland (April 20–23)

Thananjan, Karththiha (2020) *Lived Experiences of Women Activists in Batticaloa District: Exploring Processes of Negotiation and Confrontation* Unpublished MA Thesis. Colombo: University of Colombo

Thiranagama, Sharika (2013) "Claiming the State: Post-War Reconciliation in Sri Lanka" *Humanity: An International Journal of Human Rights, Humanitarianism, and Development* 4(1): 93–116

Thiruchandran, Selvi (2012) *Women's movement in Sri Lanka: History, Trends and Trajectories* **Colombo** Sri Lanka: Social Scientists' Association

Walker, Rebecca (2016) *Enduring Violence: Everyday Life and Conflict in Eastern Sri Lanka* Manchester: Manchester University Press

Wanniarachchi, Senel (2019) "Of butterfly assemblages and constitutional coups: Invention and intersection of heteromasculinity and class in post-colonial Sri Lanka." *Engenderings: LSE Department of Gender Studies*. Accessed on 13/06/2022. Available at https://blogs.lse.ac.uk/gender/2019/08/26/of-butterfly-assemblages-and-constitutional-coups-invention-and-intersection-of-heteromasculinity-and-class-in-post-colonial-sri-lanka/

Waradas, Thiyagarajah (2022) *Paradox of 'Radical' and 'Non-Radical': Exploring the Origin and Evolution of LGBT NGOs in Sri Lanka* Colombo: Centre for Poverty Analysis

Wedagedara, Amali (2021) "Collective protest by women victimized by Microfinance: A movement with hope for the future" *Karibu Foundation*. Accessed on 14/06/2023. Available at https://www.karibu.no/newsletter/2021/06/collective-protest-by-women-victimized-by-microfinance-a-movement-with-hope-for-the-future/

Wenona, Giles (2002) The Women's Movement in Sri Lanka: An Interview with Kumari Jayawardene, Available on https://btlbooks.com/chapters/feminists_underfire/xhtml/c15.html

Women and Media Collective (2017) *Disrupting the Binary Code: Experiences of LGBT Sri Lankans Online* Colombo: Women and Media Collective

Yutthworakool, Saittawut (2021) "Understanding the Right to Change Legal Gender: A Case Study of Trans Women in Sri Lanka," MA Thesis. Thailand: University of Mahidol, Available on https://repository.gchumanrights.org/server/api/core/bitstreams/b3a9bb49-2da6-4dc8-b29e-0e8c3845e4ef/content

PART IV
Economy and Political Economy

10
SRI LANKA'S FOREIGN DEBT CRISIS
Deep Roots?

Umesh Moramudali

Introduction

On 12 April 2022, for the first time in the country's post-independence history, Sri Lanka defaulted on its foreign debt (with the exception of debt from multilateral agencies) and announced that the country will restructure its foreign debt repayments. The announcement came amidst the most severe economic crisis the country has faced since its independence: with a shortage of essentials; soaring food prices; and daily electricity cuts of up to 13 hours. A week after the announcement of sovereign default, Sri Lanka initiated discussions with the International Monetary Fund (IMF) and reached a staff-level agreement to enter a four-year-long IMF programme under the Extended Fund Facility (EFF) of about US$2.9 billion. In parallel, the Sri Lankan government-initiated debt restructuring negotiations.

Sri Lanka's post-independence development has been significantly driven by foreign loans obtained for investment as well as consumption purposes. This was largely due to a compounding budget deficit and current account deficit, a scenario often referred to as 'twin deficit'. Successive governments continued to borrow to bridge this deficit.

A Brief History

Sri Lanka has been often referred to as a 'donor darling', due to its dependence on concessionary foreign loans and aid (Jayasinghe 2016; CBSL 2016). From 1950 to 1980, Sri Lanka relied on foreign loans for consumption purposes. Such foreign financing assistance played a key role in the country's development as Sri Lanka had a persistent budget deficit. As the country's reliance on foreign loans increased while having a high budget deficit and current account deficit, Sri Lanka faced a Balance of Payment (BOP) crisis. This meant, from time to time Sri Lanka did not have foreign currency to finance imports and make foreign loan repayments. These BOP crises were a frequent phenomenon in Sri Lanka's economic history since 1960. Such crises compelled the country to enter IMF programmes to address short-term foreign currency liquidity issues. Sri Lanka first sought IMF assistance in 1965, and this practice continued at least 16 times despite the changes in government and economic policies.

Sri Lanka was the first country in South Asia to adopt liberalization policies. It did so in 1977 and consequently, Sri Lanka received a large number of foreign loans for development projects

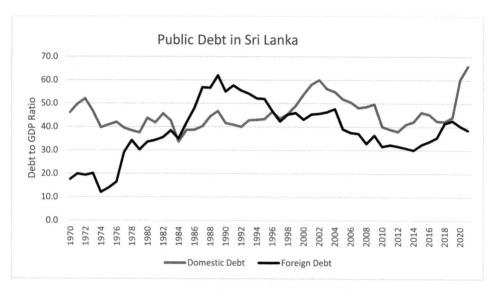

Graph 10.1 Debt to GDP ratio in Sri Lanka (Source: Author constructed based on CBSL data)

that were supported by the World Bank and IMF (Kadiragamar 2018). In 1989, the country's foreign debt stock reached its peak at 62% of GDP, largely caused by the foreign loans obtained to develop infrastructure, such as the Mahaweli accelerated programme, and to compensate for the impact of ethnic conflict which worsened after 1983. Since then, moderate economic growth was the norm, relying more on domestic debt, which led to a reduction in foreign debt stock as a percentage of the GDP (see Graph 10.1). The fact that the country was able to do so through decades of conflict and war is considered remarkable, although the war years also contributed to sluggish growth (Venugopal 2018).

Foreign Debt Dynamics in the Post-War Era

In 1997, Sri Lanka's debt dynamics started to significantly change after upgrading to a middle-income country status. Concessionary loans provided to Sri Lanka by multinational institutions, such as World Bank and Asian Development Bank (ADB), gradually declined after Sri Lanka (De Mel and De Silva 2012). However, despite the constant increase in per capita income, Sri Lanka needed energy infrastructure to provide electricity to all. Furthermore, following the end of the civil war, the government identified hard infrastructure development as the focus of its post-war recovery plans (Chan, Ruwanpura and Brown 2019; Ruwanpura, Rowe and Chan 2020). The country continued to have a high budget and current account deficit. To embark on its post-war infrastructure development plans, Sri Lanka resorted to non-concessional loans from foreign sources.

There are two key aspects to this phenomenon. Firstly, Sri Lanka began to borrow from international capital markets in 2007 by issuing International Sovereign Bonds (ISBs).[1] In July 2007, Sri Lanka issued its' first ISB of USD 500 million maturing in five years (Weerakoon 2017). Since then, ISBs have become the major source of foreign financing for Sri Lanka with the country issuing 13 ISBs worth USD 16 billion (ERD 2022). As a result, by the end of 2021, 36% of Sri Lanka's total outstanding foreign debt stock were ISBs. These market borrowings significantly differ from the concessionary loans provided by multilateral and bilateral development agencies

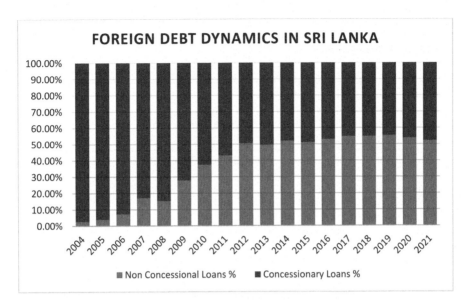

Graph 10.2 Concessionary vs non-Concessionary loans in Sri Lanka (Source: Author constructed based on data from the CBSL and ERD 2022)

in that the latter is tied to a development project, while ISBs are not. The Sri Lankan government, therefore, had complete financial autonomy over how the funds were utilized. These commercial borrowings, however, were extremely costly. For ISBs issued Sri Lanka had to pay interests ranging from 5.5% to 8.5% with a very short payback period of either five or 10 years. Conversely, most concessionary loans were provided at an interest rate ranging from 0.1% to 2% with a payback period of 30–40 years (De Mel and De Silva 2012).

Secondly, since 2005, Sri Lanka heavily relying on non-concessional loans to develop large infrastructure projects (see Graph 10.2). Many of these loans were provided as export credit by Export-Import Banks (EXIM Banks) in several countries, with EXIM Bank of China being the main provider. During 2007–2015, a number of large-scale infrastructure projects were carried out utilizing loans obtained from EXIM Bank of China, including the Colombo-Katunayaka Expressway, which connects the commercial capital Colombo with the major airport in the country, the Norochcholai power plant, the Hambantota Port, Mattala International Airport, an extension of Southern Expressway and many other road constructions. According to the External Resource Department (ERD), during 2007–2015, out of total foreign loan disbursements, 17% was provided by the EXIM Bank of China. While the interest rates of the majority of EXIM bank loans were around 2%, these loans had a shorter grace period and shorter payback period compared to loans obtained from multilateral agencies and other lenders during previous decades. Therefore, Sri Lanka had to start repaying such loans after four to six years of obtaining them and had to complete repayments within 15–20 years.

These two significant changes in the type of foreign loans obtained by Sri Lanka led to a complete shift in the country's foreign debt portfolio. The share of non-concessional debt out of total foreign debt was below 5% in 2006 and, by the end of 2014, it had increased to 52%. The maturity structure of foreign loans also took a complete turn. This meant most of Sri Lanka's outstanding foreign loans had short payback periods, imposing a high annual foreign debt repayment burden (Weerakoon and Jayasuriya 2019).

Table 10.1 Foreign debt repayment for different creditors

Foreign debt repayments of Sri Lanka – 2015–2021

	ISBs	World Bank and ADB	China
Average outstanding debt as a % of total foreign debt	34.2	23.7	17.8
Average debt repayment as a % of total foreign debt repayments	35.6	13.9	18.2
Average interest payments as a % of total foreign debt repayments	20.7	3.1	5.7
Average principle payments as a % of total foreign debt repayments	14.9	10.8	12.4

Source: Author calculations based on the data from CBSL and ERD 2022.

Prior to 2007, a large portion of foreign debt repayments were concessionary loan repayments, which were spread across approximately 30–40 years with low-interest rates (De Mel and De Silva 2012). Having a long repayment period meant that the annual debt repayment burden was manageable (see Table 10.1). However, as the portion of non-concessionary foreign loans continue to rise, it became increasingly difficult to meet foreign debt obligations.

Structural Weaknesses and Foreign Debt

While dependence on foreign commercial borrowing is a common phenomenon among middle-income countries, economic history shows that it has led to severe economic crises. In the 1970s and 1980s, for example, the short-sighted decisions of many Latin American countries to rely on commercial lending from foreign sources led to serious and prolonged economic crises (Devlin and Ffrench-Davis 1995). Research also shows that relying on foreign commercial borrowings and capital market liberalization has proven to contract production, curtail government investment and slow down growth (Stiglitz 2003).

Sri Lanka's decision to rely heavily on non-concessionary foreign borrowings too was short-sighted. The country's economy had not sufficiently developed to absorb the implications of relying on non-concessionary foreign financing. The major reason for this was the unaddressed structural weaknesses of the economy despite Sri Lanka transitioning itself from lower-income status to middle-income status in 1997.

One of the major structural weaknesses of the Sri Lankan economy is its inadequate tax revenue. Sri Lanka's transition to middle-income status as well as the shift to foreign commercial borrowing took place in the context of a continuous fall in tax to GDP ratio (Moramudali 2021). Sri Lanka's tax performance, depicted by the tax-to-GDP ratio, started to decline in the mid-1990s and continued for the next three decades (Moore 2017). From 1990 to 1995, Sri Lanka had an average tax-to-GDP ratio of 18.5%, while from 2010 to 2015, it declined to 11.9%. In contrast, due to the high level of non-concessionary foreign borrowings, the government's interest cost increased significantly. During 1990–1995, interest cost amounted to 34% of tax revenue, it rose to 44% during 2010–2015 and further increased to 54% during 2015–2020. Thus, when Sri Lanka started to repay non-concessionary foreign loans, the country was compelled to borrow heavily to meet debt repayments as the government revenue was not sufficient. As the interest payments for foreign debt increased, the government was compelled to drastically cut back on social spending. Interest payments have been the largest single expenditure item of Sri Lanka, accounting for nearly 25% of total government expenditure (Athukorala et al. 2017).

Over the last two decades, Sri Lanka's reliance on foreign loans has provided a significant part of the required financing for government expenditure. The dependency on foreign debt, therefore, allowed successive governments to continue funding public investment through debt as opposed to taxes. This practice allowed Sri Lanka to boost economic growth in the short term ignoring the need to increase the tax revenue. As the interest cost of public debt rose amid a continuously declining tax ratio, government expenditure on social spending, such as health and education, remained stagnant (Moore 2017). Total government expenditure on education as a share of GDP reduced from 2.5% in 2000 to 2% in 2016. Conversely, interest repayments for foreign debt, which amounted to 0.7% of the GDP in 2000, increased to 1.1% in 2015 and 1.8% in 2020.

Although rising debt servicing cost was a grave concern, keeping low tax rates and providing tax exemptions were crucial to political establishments to satisfy their lobbying groups. In the 2019 Presidential Election, Gotabhaya Rajapaksa pledged to reduce income tax rates and abolish some taxes. The promised tax cuts were provided immediately after the Presidential Election of 2019. This resulted in a significant reduction in government revenue. In 2020, Sri Lanka's tax-to-GDP ratio fell to 8.1% and further decreased to 7.7% in 2021, making it the lowest tax-to-GDP ratio Sri Lanka recorded in the post-independent era (CBSL 2022). This significant reduction of government revenue led to an increase in public debt stock and expanded money printing resulting in credit rating downgrades. The impacts of these tax cuts were severe as Sri Lanka was burdened with massive foreign debt repayments obligations due to the ISB maturities due each year starting from 2020. These factors all contributed to Sri Lanka's sovereign default in 2022.

The other major structural weakness of the Sri Lankan economy was the stagnation of export performances. While Sri Lanka's GDP per capita continued to climb after 2000, the country's export performances continued to deteriorate (Athukorala et al 2017). Exports as a share of the GDP fell from 39% in 2000 to 21% in 2015 (CBSL various years). Given that exports were the major source of foreign currency inflow to Sri Lanka, the continuous weakening of export performances resulted in stagnation of foreign currency inflows to the country. Therefore, Sri Lanka's hasty decision to rely heavily on foreign commercial borrowings while the country's export performance was weakening resulted in a continuous surge of the external debt servicing ratio and a widening of the external finance gap (see Graph 10.3). During 2001–2010, the average external debt repayment ratio (as a percentage of exports) was 13.4% and it increased to 25% during 2011–2020.

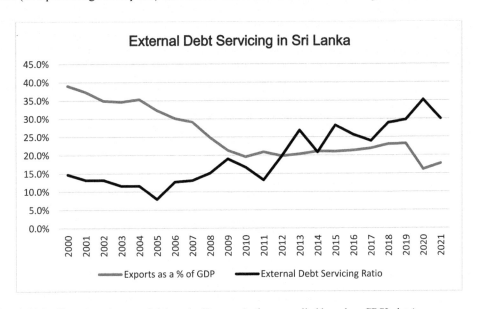

Graph 10.3 Exports and external debt ratio (Source: Author compiled based on CBSL data)

External Vulnerabilities and ISBs

Significant increases in the external debt servicing ratio were caused by three major factors. First, was the increase of ISB repayments, which accounted for more than 30% of total foreign debt repayment during 2015–2021. Second, was a substantial increase in debt repayment for project loans, largely caused by the repayment for project loans obtained during 2005–2010. Third, and more serious, was the structural weakness was Sri Lanka's failure to substantially increase its export earnings. Continuous reduction of the share of export from GDP resulted in a large share of export income spending to meet foreign debt repayment obligations which were rising due to the increasing reliance on ISBs and other foreign commercial borrowings.

ISB repayments adversely affected the external debt ratio and government finances due to several reasons. Firstly, unlike concessional loans, ISBs did not have a grace period, meaning that the country was required to repay interest from the very next year of issuing the ISBs. Secondly, the payment structure of ISBs poses challenges to a debt-distressed country like Sri Lanka due to the maturity structure (De Zilwa and Illanperuma 2021). The principal amount of the ISB is not repaid in instalments, but as a one-off payment in full when the bond matures (at the end of the repayment period). This results in a significant increase in foreign debt repayment, leading to a major outflow of foreign currency, causing an increase in the external debt servicing ratio. Data shows that during the years in which ISBs matured, Sri Lanka recorded a spike in the external debt servicing ratio due to the massive one-off payments. Thirdly, ISBs have high-interest rates ranging from 5.5% to 8.5% requiring repayment within 5–10 years (ERD 2023). Thus, constant reliance on ISBs led to an enormous increase in interest payments to foreign creditors.

The above discussion points to significant changes in debt repayment dynamics compared with concessionary loan repayments, which were obtained at interest rates ranging from 0.1% to 2% with a payback period of 30–40 years (see Table 10.2). The Sri Lankan economy was accustomed to managing concessional loan repayments because the loan repayment burden was not colossal. For example, although the aggregate outstanding debt to ADB and World Bank was approximately 25% of the total outstanding foreign loans in 2021, debt repayments for these loans amounted to only 14% of total foreign debt repayments. In comparison, ISB repayments in 2021 amounted to 47% of total foreign debt repayments even though the outstanding ISB stock was only 36%.

This is not a one-off scenario. Data indicates that sovereign bond repayments have been the largest foreign debt obligations during the last five years (Moramudali and Panduwawala 2022). Calculations by the author based on data from the Ministry of Finance show that during 2015–2021, ISB repayments amounted to 36% of total foreign debt repayments while repayments for loans obtained from two major multilateral agencies were only 14%.

Table 10.2 Maturity, grant element and interest rates of foreign debt – 2020

Category	Grace period (years)	Repayment period (years)	Grant element (%)	Avg. interest rates (% p.a.)
Bilateral	0–21	0–40	0–100	1.81
Multilateral	0–18	0–41	0–100	1.59
Commercial	0–14	0–30	(13)–61	6.05
Export credit	0–18	0–23	(12)–100	3.97
Average				4.04

Source: Ministry of Finance and Central Bank of Sri Lanka.

However, increasing ISBs were not the sole reason for Sri Lanka's foreign debt troubles. Since 2010 – following the end of the war, the increase of debt repayment for large-scale infrastructure project loans obtained from bilateral lenders including China was also a reason for the increase of foreign debt repayment burden.

The Myth of the Chinese Debt Trap

During the post-conflict era, the two major sources of Sri Lanka's foreign debt were international capital markets and China. The latter has emerged as the biggest bilateral lender since 2005. However, out of total foreign borrowings, most loans were obtained through international capital markets through issuing ISBs which accounted for approximately 40% of total foreign loans disbursed to Sri Lanka during 2007–2021. Thus, the largest source of Sri Lanka's foreign lending for Sri Lanka during the post-conflict era is not China, but international capital markets (see Graph 10.4). By the end of 2021, 36% of Sri Lanka's outstanding public foreign debt was ISBs while loans obtained from China only account for 20% (Ministry of Finance of Sri Lanka 2021).

This clarification is important as Sri Lanka's debt problems are often reduced to an issue of Chinese lending. The island nation is frequently portrayed as a victim of the Chinese debt trap in international media as well as in international development discussions (Chellaney 2017; Abi-Habib 2018). The origin of this narrative can be attributed to the misinterpretation of the leasing of Hambantota Port to China Merchant Port Company as a debt-equity swap (Moramudali 2019; Rithmire and Li 2019). As I repeatedly outlined in this chapter, Sri Lanka's foreign debt troubles are a result of foreign commercial borrowings or ISBs, without addressing structural weaknesses which led to BOP issues. The lease of Hambantota Port was one strategy to generate foreign currency inflows and was not a debt-equity swap (Acker, Bräutigam and Huang 2020;

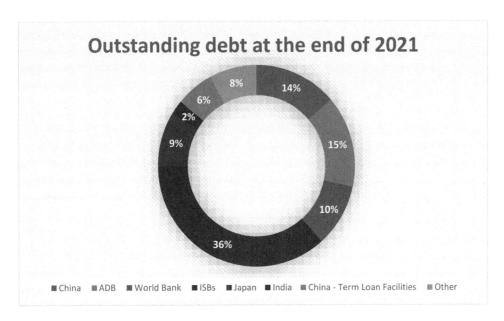

Graph 10.4 Outstanding debt at the end of 2021 (Source: Author developed based on the data from ERD – Data includes State-Owned Enterprise (SOE) loans obtained through the Treasury)

Moramudali and Panduwawala 2022). Thus, narrowing down Sri Lanka's foreign debt troubles as a 'Chinese debt trap' is inaccurate.

During 2010–2021, debt repayments to Chinese lenders including commercial loans obtained from China Development Bank (CDB) amounted to only 14.7% of total foreign loan repayments (Moramudali and Panduwawala 2022). While the Chinese debt trap is an exaggeration and a misinterpretation of Sri Lanka's debt troubles, Chinese lending plays a very crucial role in Sri Lanka's debt landscape, particularly in the context of debt restructuring. The reluctance of Chinese creditors to commit to restructuring debt and delays to provide finance assurances resulted in delays in Sri Lanka obtaining a bailout package from the IMF. Obtaining financing assurance from China was a precondition to receiving the said bailout package, provided in the form of an EFF of USD 2.9 billion in March 2023 (IMF 2023a). In going forward, China continues to play a crucial role in Sri Lanka's debt restructuring process as the largest bilateral creditor. Furthermore, Chinese debt has often been subject to public and scholarly criticism for allegedly facilitating corruption. Some scholars have characterized Chinese lending as quasi-predatory lending or odious debt claiming that projects for which Sri Lanka sought loans lacked an overt public purpose (Sornarajah 2022). While this is up for debate, it is evident that some Chinese lending violated good governance practices. For instance, most of the export credit loans provided by China EXIM Bank lacked transparency and competitive bidding, which resulted in having room for practices of corruption.

Credit, Corruption and Debt

Increased reliance on export credit loans to develop infrastructure also played a key role in worsening Sri Lanka's economic vulnerabilities. These large-scale infrastructure projects – such as the Hambantota port, the Colombo-Katunayake Expressway and the Mattala International Airport – funded through export credit had major room for corruption and very little local value addition other than expanding political power.

These export credit lines were mostly provided by the EXIM Banks of different countries (EXIM Bank of China, EXIM Bank of India, etc.), and the contract to develop the infrastructure is often assigned to a contractor in the lending country. This means infrastructure development projects funded through export credit are often carried out through unsolicited bids, leaving enormous room for corruption and overpricing. Studies show that EXIM Bank loans are often given with conditions, such as the need to hire a contractor from the lending country (Verité Research 2020). The evidence also suggests that projects funded through bilateral credit are tied to contractors domiciled in lender countries, are awarded without competitive bidding, and is highly capital intensive and, therefore, inefficient in terms of capital deployment (Gunaruwan 2016). This indicates that Sri Lanka overspent on its large infrastructure projects resulting in a significant increase in foreign debt stock while the value added to the economy is much lower than the increase in debt.

Although Sri Lanka National Procurement Guidelines stress competitive bidding for awarding contracts for government-funded infrastructure projects, most of these projects were awarded to contractors in lending countries through unsolicited bidding or restrictive bidding. While the guidelines state that deviating from competitive bidding is allowed in exceptional circumstances, with the rise of export credit loans, this exception seems to have become the norm. According to a recent study, 13 out of 35 foreign loans of the highest value obtained through bilateral lending during 2005–2018 were facilitated through unsolicited bidding (Verité Research 2020). Interestingly, out of these 13 bilateral project lending facilitated through unsolicited bidding, 12 loans were obtained from China. For example, the very first loan agreement to construct the Hambantota port states that the contractor for constructing the port was China Harbour Engineering Company (CHEC) and 85% of the contract amount was provided through the loan.[2]

However, it is important to highlight that providing export credit loans with restrictive conditions is not an exclusive phenomenon to China. Other bilateral lenders, such as Japan and India, have also been engaging in providing tied lending to Sri Lanka. During 2005–2018, out of 13 loans provided by Japan, six had tied elements while all loans provided by India had tied elements. In the case of India, two loans provided by India to reconstruct railway lines in Northern Province had restrictions on selecting the contractor. Ircon International Limited (IRCON), a government-owned company, was the contractor for both projects and for one loan the contractor was pre-determined (Verité Research 2020). Therefore, it is clear that unsolicited bidding was a condition for some foreign loans and instituted corruption as a practice. Investigations by journalists revealed that most of the expressway development projects had facilitated corruption through rushed unsolicited bidding or by not selecting the cheapest bidder (Wijedasa 2014, 2020).

Thus, the existing evidence suggests that Sri Lanka's foreign lending has been a contributory factor in promoting corruption as well as lavish government spending, although official reports and numbers are yet to be published. Such practices were facilitated through export credit-based bilateral lending obtained through bypassing competitive bidding. This trend coupled with constant borrowing through ISBs had resulted in island-nation accumulating heavy foreign debt stock without developing the capacity to service its foreign debt. Foreign borrowings during the last two decades facilitated a non-tradable sector-driven, unsustainable growth model instead of expanding manufacturing capacity and exports. A number of foreign loans were obtained for projects that derive short-term political benefits and short-term economic losses. Some scholars have argued that Sri Lanka's debts were accumulated by a government that people allege was steeped in corruption, thus a significant part of Sri Lanka's foreign debt should be considered odious debt (Sornarajah 2022).

IMF Bailouts and Failed Reforms in the Post-Conflict Era

Sri Lanka's continuous BOP crisis is a combination of increases in foreign debt stock and twin deficits. The historical trend of seeking IMF assistance started in 1965 and continues through the post-conflict period. The country continued to fail in fiscal management and in promoting exports, making it vulnerable to global shocks. This led to further deterioration of its twin deficits resulting in Sri Lanka encountering severe BOP vulnerabilities in 2015. The newly elected coalition government resorted to obtaining another IMF bailout package in 2016 through an EFF of USD 1.5 Billion (IMF 2016). This allowed Sri Lanka to avoid a severe BOP crisis and increase foreign reserves thereby allowing it to finance imports without disruption.

The IMF programme in 2016 led to a boost in foreign investor confidence which allowed Sri Lanka to continue borrowing from the international capital market through issuing ISBs. At this point, having the ability to issue ISBs was crucial for the government for two reasons. One was the requirement of foreign currency to meet increasing debt repayments and rollover of previously issued ISBs. Two was the requirement to shift from short-term (less than one year repayment period) risky foreign borrowings to ISBs, which is a less risky, medium-term debt instrument. These short-term risky loans largely consisted of foreign investment in government securities and currency swaps with local banks.

During 2011–2014, on account of the low-interest rates prevailing across the Global North, foreign investors channelled their USD investments to emerging markets seeking higher returns

(Weerakoon and Jayasuriya 2019). Sri Lanka too benefited from this trend, and foreign investors heavily invested in government securities. By the end of 2014, foreign investor holdings of government securities were equivalent to nearly 40% of the country's foreign currency reserves. However, these investments were risky and highly volatile as this type of foreign investment tends to quickly withdraw money in response to global policy changes. After 2015, as the interest rates in developed economies started to rise, foreign investors started to withdraw investment from Sri Lankan government securities. This resulted in a significant increase in foreign currency outflow during a short time span, exerting pressure on exchange rates. At this juncture, Sri Lanka needed to increase foreign currency reserves to offset these outflows and prevent shocks from further outflows (Coomaraswamy 2016). Against this backdrop, issuing ISBs provided Sri Lanka with the required USD to settle most of the short-term foreign currency-denominated borrowings, allowing the government to reduce within a matter of days the risk of encountering significant foreign currency outflows.

Evidence from the recent histories of many East Asian economies suggests that heavy reliance on short-term foreign borrowings exposed them to severe foreign exchange crises (reference). For example, in 1997, one of the major causes of South Korea's economic crisis was the increased reliance on short-term borrowings. Foreign lenders lost confidence in South Korea due to their domestic development, they withdrew their investments, causing a massive outflow of foreign currency and leading to a serious debt crisis (Chang, Park and Yoo 2001).

Sri Lanka's economic indicators pertaining to the external sector have been much worse than South Korea, making it more vulnerable to adverse implications of short-term foreign debt. Thus, curtailing its reliance on short-term foreign debt was critical to minimize the country's economic vulnerabilities. This called for substantial foreign currency inflows ranging from USD 3 to 4 Billion, which were obtained through issuing ISBs resulting in a significant increase in ISB stock.

Foreign Debt and State Sovereignty

There are serious implications for any country with a high level of foreign debt. For developing nations with twin deficits like Sri Lanka, the implications are more adverse, ranging from a reduction of economic growth to severe economic crises. Sri Lanka is currently experiencing a historically unprecedented economic crisis with a sovereign default for the first time since its independence from colonial rule.

As Sri Lanka's foreign debt level rose, its economy became extremely vulnerable to global as well as domestic shocks. Due to inadequate export growth, the country was forced to bridge its external financing gap by borrowing heavily from foreign sources to meet foreign debt repayments. In such a context, any event that affects the country's foreign currency inflows and the ability to borrow from international capital markets can become a big shock to the economy. For example, during the 1997 Asian Financial Crisis, a number of emerging economies in East Asia experienced economic crises because of failing to roll over short-term foreign commercial loans (Hawkins and Turner 2000).

Rising foreign debt has resulted in Sri Lanka compromising its economic sovereignty. This has two aspects. One is the way in which the country was affected by the actions of credit rating. Sri Lanka's (or any country's) ability to borrow from international capital markets as well as the borrowing cost are determined by its credit ratings. Sri Lanka's credit ratings are heavily influenced by both domestic policies and global developments. Thus, its policy decisions are constrained as they could affect the ability to borrow in foreign currency, which holds the key to repaying foreign loans. The scholarship on global finance indicates that emerging market nations' dependency on volatile international capital flows poses threats to economic sovereignty and limits the macroeconomic and regulatory responses (Buckley 2016).

The second aspect is the unfavourable conditions attached to lending. In Sri Lanka's case, it had obtained a number of export credit loans for infrastructure development and credit lines for importing essential items, which often had conditions that largely benefitted the lender. This allowed countries, such as China and India, to dictate terms. Furthermore, conditionalities of the IMF had also intervened with Sri Lanka's fiscal and monetary policy. Scholars are divided on the IMF interventions. While one camp argues that IMF intervention erodes the sovereignty of countries (Balima and Sy 2021; Lee 2003), the other camp argues that IMF intervention establishes financial stability and assists to prevent sovereign defaults in future (Breen 2014). In the case of Sri Lanka, its economic vulnerabilities increased as the country's reliance on foreign commercial borrowings expanded undermining the power of the Sri Lankan state to make economic policy decisions, especially pertaining to finance. In this milieu, there is no doubt that the power has unequivocally shifted to international actors, and global financiers, as well as rating agencies (Moramudali and Naido 2021). Recent studies by Jayathi Ghosh (2022) point out that global investor sentiments often move against poorer countries and rating agencies amplify the problem thereby limiting the power of the 'state' in developing countries. Sri Lanka too was a victim of such global financial dynamics as a result of rushing to heavily rely on global financiers while relying on a non-tradable sector-driven unsustainable growth model.

Sri Lanka's Debt Restructuring

At the time this chapter is finalized, Sri Lanka has had several rounds of negotiations with its creditors along with fulfilling the government's commitment to the IMF programme entered into in March 2023. As per the Debt Sustainability Analysis (DSA) conducted by IMF, Sri Lanka is expected to bring down its debt-to-GDP ratio to 95% by 2032 from 128% in 2022 (IMF 2023b). DSA further states that the foreign debt servicing cost of the Sri Lankan government should remain below 4.5% of GDP in each year over 2027–2032. In order to achieve these goals, US$17 billion in debt service reduction is required, including the arrears accumulated in 2022.

Multilateral agencies, such as ADB and World Bank, maintain preferred creditor status and abstain from providing debt reductions based on the premise that they will provide new finances till Sri Lanka is able to borrow from other sources. This means private creditors and bilateral creditors are required to provide substantial debt relief to Sri Lanka. On May 2023, 17 bilateral creditors of Sri Lanka including Paris Club creditors formally formed an official creditor committee, co-chaired by India, Japan and France, to discuss Sri Lanka's request for debt relief (Paris Club 2023). Previously, on April 2023, a group of ISB holders sent a debt restructuring proposal to the government as well (Reuters 2023). While both bilateral and private creditors had expressed willingness, details of debt restructuring are not finalized. As per the IMF staff report, Sri Lanka is expected to finalize debt restructuring by mid-2024. Literature on debt restructuring indicates that creditor heterogeneity raises issues regarding fair burden sharing in debt restructuring and the bargaining process can be lengthy and often involves domestic and global games (Baqir, Diwan and Rodrik 2023).

Conclusion

Throughout the post-independent era, Sri Lanka's development was largely supported by foreign debt provided on concessionary terms. However, after upgrading to middle-income status, Sri Lanka's foreign debt dynamics took a drastic turn. Costlier non-concessionary loans became the major source of foreign financing for Sri Lanka during the post-conflict era. Sri Lanka's shift to costly non-concessional loans took place in the absence of addressing the long-lasting structural weakness of the economy, including contraction of trade and declining tax revenue. This means, not only did Sri Lanka enter international capital markets prematurely, but the country also over-relied on foreign commercial borrowings. The Sri Lankan economy was not adequately developed nor did subsequent governments have the will and foresight to manage the high cost of commercial borrowings and short maturity structure which imposed higher debt repayments than concessionary loans the country was accustomed to.

Sri Lanka's careless choice to depend on foreign loans during the post-conflict era is linked to large-scale corruption facilitated by a lack of transparency in the foreign financing process. This practice coupled with the lack of fiscal discipline motivated by private sector lobbying had resulted in foreign debt reaching unsustainable levels. That, in turn, resulted in the country experiencing severe economic vulnerabilities, losing economic and political sovereignty, which led to the worst economic crisis in Sri Lanka in post-independence history in 2021–2022. As the crisis exacerbated, Sri Lanka had little choice but to default on its foreign debt repayment and initiate a process of debt restructuring. This demanded that Sri Lanka enter into an IMF programme which was started in March 2023 as Sri Lanka received a bailout package from the IMF. The agreement with the IMF stipulates a number of economic reforms including tax reforms that Sri Lanka must carry out to stabilize the economy.

Debt restructuring is a complex process and Sri Lanka needs significant debt relief in the form of principal haircuts (reduction of debt stock) and maturity extensions to achieve public debt sustainability. However, individual creditors have distinct preferences about the form and extent debt restructuring should take, and such disagreements could potentially be an obstacle to reaching a consensus among creditors. Moreover, given the various types of creditors, the debt restructuring process will inevitably be complex and protracted. China is Sri Lanka's largest bilateral creditor owing approximately 20% of the government's foreign debt.[3] Chinese creditors, however, have historically opposed principal haircuts for their loans. Given the geopolitical dynamics, other creditors, particularly India, have stressed the need for equal treatment in the debt restructuring process. Therefore, Sri Lanka has been drawn into geopolitical rivalry in the debt restructuring process.

Sri Lanka's foreign debt problem has deep roots; long-term and comprehensive policy reforms are imperative if it is to be meaningfully addressed. Merely restructuring debt is not going to resolve the debt issues. It requires enduring tax reforms to increase government revenue, institutional reform built on the principles of equity, good governance, redistribution and a robust system of checks and balances and transparency to combat corruption. The failure to carry out those reforms will inevitably lead to another sovereign default within this decade.

Notes

1 ISB is the term Sri Lanka used for dollar-denominated bonds issued by the country's central bank in international capital markets. In international finance literature, when a country other than USA issues USD denominated bonds, such bonds are called Eurobonds. Throughout this chapter the term ISB is used which refers to a Eurobond issued by added Sri Lanka.
2 Author referred to the original loan agreement obtained through RTI Request.
3 There are different foreign debt classifications. Due to such differences, China's share of Sri Lanka's foreign debt has different numbers. I refer to it as 20% of foreign debt based on calculations in Moramudali and Panduwawala (2022), which considers loans obtained from the Chinese Development Bank (CDB) as a part of China's share of foreign debt. Some other classifications consider CDB lending as market borrowings resulting in a lower number than 20%.

References

Abi-Habib, Maria (2018) *How China Got Sri Lanka to Cough Up a Port*, 15 June. Accessed on June 30, 2022. Available at https://www.nytimes.com/2018/06/25/world/asia/china-sri-lanka-port.html

Acker, Kevin, Deboarh Bräutigam and Yufan Huang (2020) *Debt Relief with Chinese Characteristics.* **Working Paper No. 2020/39. China Africa Research Initiative, School of Advanced International Studies** Washington, DC: Johns Hopkins University

Athukorala, Premachandra, Edimon Ginting, Hall Hill and Utsav Kumar (2017) ***The Sri Lankan Economy – Charting A New Course*** Manila: Asian Development Bank

Balima, H. and A Sy (2021) "IMF-Supported Programs and Sovereign Debt Crises" ***IMF Economic Review*** 69: 427–465

Baqir, Reza, Ishac Diwan and Dani Rodrik (2023) "A Framework to Evaluate Economic Adjustment-cum-Debt Restructuring Packages" Available at https://drodrik.scholar.harvard.edu/files/dani-rodrik/files/a_framework_for_debt_relief_cum_adjustment_packages_010523.pdf

Breen, M (2014) "IMF Conditionality and the Economic Exposure of Its Shareholders" ***European Journal of International Relations*** 20(2): 416–436

Buckley, Ross P. "Reconceptualizing the Regulation of Global Finance." Oxford Journal of Legal Studies 36, no. 2 (2016): 242–271.

Central Bank of Sri Lanka (2016) "Meeting with foreign correspondent association" (Online video). Accessed on March 5, 2022. Available at https://www.youtube.com/watch?v=AR4CQ7at7-U

Central Bank of Sri Lanka (2022) ***Annual Report 2020***, Colombo. Available at https://www.cbsl.gov.lk/en/publications/economic-and-financial-reports/annual-reports/annual-report-2020

Chan, L., K. Ruwanpura and B. Brown (2019) "Environmental Neglect: Other Casualties of Post-war Infrastructure Development" ***Geoforum*** 105: 63–66. https://doi.org/10.1016/j.geoforum.2019.07.010

Chang, H. J., H. J. Park and C. G. Yoo (2001) "Interpreting the Korean Crisis: Financial Liberalization, Industrial Policy and Corporate Governance" In ***Financial Liberalization and the Asian Crisis*** H. J. Chang, G. Palma and D. H. Whittaker (eds) London: Palgrave Macmillan. https://doi.org/10.1057/9780230518629_9

Chellaney, Brahama (2017) 'China's Debt-Trap Diplomacy', *Project Syndicate*, 23 January. Accessed on June 30, 2023. Available at https://www.project-syndicate.org/commentary/china-one-belt-one-road-loans-debt-by-brahma-chellaney-2017-01

De Mel, Deshal and Anneka De Silva (2012) "Trends in Foreign Aid in Sri Lanka" In *Foreign Aid in South Asia* Saman Kalegama (ed) New Delhi: Sage, pp 163–168

De Zilwa, Keneth and Shiran Illanperuma (2021) ***Debt Sustainability and Debt Management in Sri Lanka – a Reflection on the Applicability of Chinese Policy Lessons*** New York, NY: United Nations Conference on Trade and Development

Department of External Resources (n.d.). *Foreign Commercial Borrowings by the Government of Sri Lanka.* Accessed on May 21, 2023. Available at: https://www.erd.gov.lk/index.php?option=com_content&view=article&id=51&Itemid=214&lang=en#details-of-sri-lanka-sovereign-bond-issuances

Department of External Resources (2020) ***Performance Report 2019***, Colombo. Accessed on March 8, 2022. Available at http://www.erd.gov.lk/2020/Performance%202019%20Final.pdf

Devlin, R. and R. Ffrench-Davis (1995) "The Great Latin American Debt Crisis: Ten Years of Asymmetric Adjustment" In ***Poverty, Prosperity and the World Economy*** G. Helleiner, S. Abrahamian, E. Bacha, R. Lawrence and P. Malan (eds.). London: Palgrave Macmillan. https://doi.org/10.1007/978-1-349-13658-2_3

Ghosh, Jayati (2022) "There is a global debt crisis coming – and it won't stop at Sri Lanka" ***The Guardian*** (26 July). Accessed on October 20, 2022. Available at https://www.theguardian.com/world/commentisfree/2022/jul/26/global-debt-crisis-sri-lanka-foreign-capital

Gunaruwan, Lalithasiri (2016) "Economics of Public Capital Expenditure in the Sri Lankan Road Infrastructure Sector" *Sri Lanka Journal of Economic Research* 4(1): 75–90

Hawkins, John and Philip Turner (1999) ***Bank Restructuring in Practice: An Overview*** Basel, Switzerland: Bank for International Settlements. Accessed on July 4, 2023. Available at https://www.bis.org/publ/plcy06a.pdf

International Monetary Fund (2016) ***IMF Completes First Review of the Extended Arrangement Under the EFF with Sri Lanka and Approves US$162.6 Million Disbursement***. Accessed on September 15, 2023. Available at https://www.imf.org/en/News/Articles/2016/11/18/PR16515-Sri-Lanka-IMF-Completes-First-Review-of-the-Extended-Arrangement-Under-the-EFF

International Monetary Fund (2023a) *IMF Executive Board Approves US$3 Billion Under the New Extended Fund Facility (EFF) Arrangement for Sri Lanka.* Accessed on March 23, 2023. Available at https://www.imf.org/en/News/Articles/2023/03/20/pr2379-imf-executive-board-approves-under-the-new-eff-arrangement-for-sri-lanka

International Monetary Fund (2023b) *First Review Under the Extended Arrangement Under the Extended Fund Facility, Requests for a Waiver of Nonobservance of Performance Criterion, Modification of Performance Criteria, Rephrasing of Access, and Financing Assurances Review*—Press release; staff report; and statement by the executive Director for Sri Lanka. Accessed on January 10, 2024. Available at https://www.imf.org/en/News/Articles/2016/11/18/PR16515-Sri-Lanka-IMF-Completes-First-Review-of-the-Extended-Arrangement-Under-the-EFF

Jaysinghe, Uditha (2016) "Budget Inspiration for Private Sector" *DailyFT*, October. Accessed on May 19, 2023. Available at: https://www.ft.lk/article/571043/Budget-inspiration-for-private-sector

Kadiragamar, A. (2020) "Polarization, Civil War and Persistent Majoritarianism in Sri Lanka" in ***Political Polarization in South and South East Asia***, T. Carothers and A. O'Donohue (ed) Carnegie Endowment for International Peace, pp. 53–66

Lee, Catherine (2003) "To Thine Own Self Be True: IMF Conditionality and Erosion of Economic Sovereignty in the Asian Financial Crisis" ***University of Pennsylvania Journal of International Law*** 24(4): 875–904

Ministry of Finance of Sri Lanka (2021) ***Annual Report 2020.*** Accessed on March 5, 2022. Available at https://www.treasury.gov.lk/api/file/0b7d1935-6235-4156-97b6-752d6a8039d0

Moore, Mick (2017) ***The Political Economy of Long-Term Revenue Decline in Sri Lanka*** ITCD Working Paper 65 Brighton: ITCD. Available at https://www.ictd.ac/publication/ictd-wp65/

Moramudali, Umesh (2019) "Is Sri Lanka Really a Victim of China's 'Debt Trap'?" ***The Diplomat*** (14 May). Accessed on March 13, 2022. Available at https://thediplomat.com/2019/05/is-sri-lanka-really-a-victim-of-chinas-debt-trap/

Moramudali, Umesh (2021) "Taxation in Sri Lanka: Issues and Challenges" ***Economy for All***. University of Colombo, Department of Economics, University of Colombo

Moramudali, Umesh and Jervin Naido (2021) "Repositioning Sri Lankan Economy - An International Political Economic Perspective", Sri Lanka Economic Research Conference, Uva Wellassa University of Sri Lanka, 21–22 January 2021, Badulla, Uva Wellassa University of Sri Lanka, pp. 302–309. Available at https://www.slfue.org/images/SLFUE_2020/proceedings/SLERC_2020_Proceedings_2021_04_06_Final_Indes.pdf

Moramudali, Umesh and Thilina Panduwawala (2022) *Evolution of Chinese Lending to Sri Lanka since the mid-2000s-Separating Myth from Reality* Briefing Paper 8. China in Africa Initiative (CARI): Johns Hopkins University. Accessed on December 15, 2022. Available at https://static1.squarespace.com/static/5652847de4b033f56d2bdc29/t/638689771d0e3c4beb14bf2f/1669761400150/Briefing+Paper+-+Sri+Lanka+Debt+-+V5.pdf

Paris Club (2023). Agreement in Principle between the Official Creditor Committee and Sri Lanka. Accessed January 10, 2023. Available at: https://clubdeparis.org/en/communications/press-release/agreement-in-principle-between-the-official-creditor-committee-and-sri

Rithmire, Meg and Yihao Li (2019) "Chinese Infrastructure Investments in Sri Lanka: A Pearl or a Teardrop on the Belt and Road?" ***Harvard Business School.*** Accessed on March 12, 2022. Available at https://www.hbs.edu/faculty/Pages/item.aspx?num=55410

Rosario, Jorgelina Do and Rodrigo Campos (2023) "Exclusive: Sri Lanka's Bondholders Send Debt Rework Proposal to Government, Sources Say" *Reuters* 16 April. Accessed June 18, 2023. Available at: https://www.reuters.com/markets/asia/sri-lankas-bondholders-sent-debt-rework-proposal-government-sources-2023-04-14/

Ruwanpura, Kanchana N, Peter Rowe and Loritta Chan (2020) "Of Bombs and Belts: Exploring Potential within China's Belt and Road Initiative in Sri Lanka" ***The Geographical Journal*** 186(3): 339–345

Sornarajah, M. (2022) "Are Sri Lanka's Debt "Odious"?", *The Island*, 29 May. Accessed on July 20, 2023. Available at: https://island.lk/are-sri-lankas-debts-odious/

Stiglitz, Joseph E. (2003) "Globalization and Growth in Emerging Markets and the New Economy" ***Journal of Policy Modeling*** 25(5): 505–524

Venugopal, R. (2018) ***Nationalism, Development and Ethnic Conflict in Sri Lanka*** Cambridge: Cambridge University Press. https://doi.org/10.1017/9781108553414

Verité Research (2020) "Financing Infrastructure: The (Non)-Concessionality of Concessional Loans" Accessed on July 4, 2023. Available at: https://www.veriteresearch.org/publication/financing-infrastructure-the-non-concessionality-of-concessional-loans/

Weerakoon, Dushni (2017) "Sri Lanka's Debt Troubles in the New Development Finance Landscape" ***Third World Thematic: A TWQ Journal*** 2(6): 744–761. https://doi.org/10.1080/23802014.2017.1395711

Weerakoon, Dushni and Sisira Jayasuriya (2019) "Debt Financing for Development: The Sri Lankan Experience" In ***Managing Domestic and International Challenges and Opportunities in Post-conflict Development*** Dushni Weerakoon and Sisira Jayasuriya (eds) Singapore: Springer Nature, pp 95–112

Wijedasa, Namini (2014) "Unsolicited Projects Open Highway to Corruption" ***The Sunday Times*** (March 16, 2014). Accessed on 04 July 4, 2023. Available at https://www.sundaytimes.lk/140316/news/unsolicited-projects-open-highway-to-corruption-89323.html

Wijedasa, Namini (2020) "Amid Pandemic, Multibillion-rupee Contract Rushed Through for Central Expressway" ***The Sunday Times*** (April 26, 2020). Accessed on July 4, 2023. Available at https://www.sundaytimes.lk/200426/news/amid-pandemic-multibillion-rupee-contract-rushed-through-for-central-expressway-401162.html.

11
THE SRI LANKAN ECONOMY
Hope, Despair, and Prospects

Prema-chandra Athukorala

Introduction

Sri Lanka achieved independence in 1948 with high hopes for economic achievement. The country was favoured with many early advantages not shared by most other Asian countries: a strategic location in the Indian Ocean; an open economy with a vibrant export sector; a relatively good standard of education; a well-developed physical infrastructure; and a broad-based and efficient administrative apparatus staffed largely by locals. The balance of payments position was healthy, backed by large foreign exchange reserves and a sound budgetary position. It was 'an oasis of stability, peace and order, set against the contemporary catastrophes in the rest of the British possessions in the region' (de Silva 1974: 1). It was "Britain's model commonwealth country, carefully prepared for independence" (Lee 2000: 461). These initial conditions justified the expectation that Sri Lanka would prove 'the best bet among all post-colonial nations in Asia' (Jiggins 1976: 26).

At the time of independence, and well into the 1950s, Sri Lanka ranked as one of the most prosperous Asian countries, with per capita income and other development indicators placing it well above its South Asian neighbours and even much ahead of countries, such as Thailand, South Korea, and Taiwan in East Asia (Athukorala et al 2017). Sri Lanka's standards of living, measured by indicators, such as adult literacy, life expectancy, infant mortality, remained well above those of other developing countries. During the ensuing seven decades, the growth of Sri Lanka's per capita income fell way behind the fast-growing East Asian economies, rapidly converging to the levels of its South Asian neighbours. From the late 1960s even the vaunted basic need achievements had become relatively less impressive through time (Osmani 1994; Dunham and Jayasuriya 2000). Given the failure to find a way to make the economy grow fast enough to sustain social progress, Sri Lanka has become a vivid illustration of the limitations of direct approach to problems of social equity: 'a tale of missed opportunities' (Snodgrass 1989). Eventually the country ended up in an unprecedented sovereign debt crisis that culminated in April 2022.

This chapter undertakes an interpretative survey of economic policy and performance of the Sri Lankan economy, with a focus on the economic underpinning of the country's vulnerability to the unprecedented crisis in the wake of the Covid-19 pandemic, and prospects beyond the crisis. The chapter begins with an overview of policymaking during the post-independence era. The next section discusses economic performance with emphasis on how debt-fuelled growth and the resulting debt overhang made the economy vulnerable to the Covid-19 shock. The following two sections examine the unfolding crisis, policy responses, and prospects for economic stabilization and structural adjustment. The final section offers some concluding remarks.

Policy Context: A Historical Perspective

Sri Lanka inherited from the colonial past a classical *export economy* with a system of government, which could already lay claim to being a welfare state (Wriggins 1960; Snodgrass 1966). The economy was heavily dependent on three agricultural export commodities (tea, rubber, and coconut), which directly contributed to nearly a third of the GDP. In addition to its direct contribution to the economy, a host of activities in the services sector depended on the plantation sector. Export earnings from the three crops covered over 95% of the country's imports which accounted for over three-fourth of the total domestic absorption of goods. The period of political transition from colonialism to self-rule in the three decades leading up to independence saw the introduction and gradual expansion of a wide range of welfare measures, including subsidized food, free education from primary through to the university level, free medical care, and subsidized public transportation. During the colonial era, the thriving export industries generated ample surpluses for the state to finance these schemes.

The colonial welfare orientation became the precursor of an extensive welfare system in the post-independence period as the government passed into the hands of leaders with popular mandates. A population boom that began in the late 1940s following a highly successful malaria eradication campaign added to the pressure to widen and deepen the welfare state. The rapid expansion of the welfare state occurred against the backdrop of gradually diminishing fortunes of the traditional export industries because of both supply-side and demand-side reasons. The successive governments of independents Sri Lanka largely failed to match the welfare orientation with a coherent strategy to find new sources of growth through structural diversification of the economy, refurbishing existing export industries, or diversifying into new areas in either agriculture or industry (Snodgrass 1966, 1989; Athukorala and Jayasuriya 1994, 2015).

In the first decade of independence, policymakers perceived periodic export shortfalls as a cyclical phenomenon and maintained the status quo of the colonial economy by financing balance of payments deficits with foreign exchange reserves accumulated during the boom years. There was no coherent strategy to restructure the economy other than continuing a colonization scheme in the dry zone, which specifically focused on expanding paddy cultivation (Snodgrass 1966).

From the late 1950s, a combination of change in political leadership and balance-of-payments difficulties led to the adoption of a state-led import-substitution industrialization strategy. By the mid-1970s, the Sri Lankan economy was one of the most inward-oriented and regulated economies outside the communist bloc, with pervasive state interventions in all areas of economic activity. Widespread nationalization measures, coupled with various economic controls, had effectively marginalized the private sector in the economy. The policy stance during this period vividly demonstrated that a small country was not able to achieve self-sustained growth through the import-substitution development strategy, given the obvious limit to economic expansion within its national boundaries (Snodgrass 1989; Wriggins 2011).

In 1977 Sri Lanka embarked on an extensive economic liberalization process that marked a decisive break with decades of protectionist policies. The reforms, implemented in two stages (during 1977–1980 and in the early 1990s), included lifting almost all quantitative import restrictions and substantially reducing tariffs, opening the economy to foreign direct investment (FDI) and abolishing export duties.

The reform process was, however, incomplete in terms of the standard prerequisites for a market-oriented economy (Levy 1989; Athukorala and Jayasuriya 1994). First, most state-owned enterprises (SOEs) set up during the preceding three decades continued to operate with heavy dependence on budgetary transfers. Second, the promised reforms to achieve greater labour market flexibility were abandoned in face of widespread opposition by the trade unions. Third, and perhaps more importantly, the complementarity between macroeconomic management and trade liberalization required for maintaining the competitiveness of 'tradable production', i.e., production of exportable and import-competing goods and services, which are capable of being traded among countries, was missing in the liberalized economy. The dual exchange rate system, which had been in operation since 1968, was abolished and the new unified exchange rate was allowed to adjust in response to foreign exchange market conditions. However, from about 1979, the Central Bank began to deviate gradually from the original plan and to intervene in the foreign exchange market to use the nominal exchange rate as an 'anchor' to contain domestic inflation. The policy emphasis on fiscal prudence, too, was short-lived because the government embarked on a massive public investment programme side by side with opening the economy. Consequently, the real exchange rate (RER) appreciated, eroding competitiveness of tradable production in the economy.[1]

Reaping gains from liberalization reforms was also seriously hampered by the escalation of the ethnic conflict from the early 1980s (Arunatilake, Jayasuriya and Kelegama 2001). The conflict virtually cut off the Northern Province and large parts of the Eastern Province, which together account for one-third of Sri Lanka's total land area and almost 12% of the population, from the national economy. Even in the rest of the country, the lingering fear of sporadic attacks by the Tamil militants hampered the prospects for attracting foreign investment, particularly in long-term ventures. Nonetheless, the economy continued to be burdened by the massive military expenditure and its consequences for macroeconomic instability.[2] The government's preoccupation with the civil war also caused delays and inconsistencies in the implementation of reforms.

Despite the incomplete reform agenda and the debilitating effect of the civil war, the reforms significantly transformed the economic landscape of Sri Lanka as discussed in the next section. The gains from reforms were substantial enough to set the stage for the continuation of outward-oriented policy orientation well into the early 2000s despite political regime shifts (Moore 1997). By the mid-1990s, Sri Lanka ranked among the few developing countries that had made a clear policy transition from inward orientation to global economic integration (Panagariya 2002).

From about the late 1990s, the reform process suffered a setback because of the pressure for raising additional revenue from import tariffs and a plethora of surcharges on the existing customs duties on imports ('para tariffs') to finance the ballooning war budget. The protectionist tendencies soon received added impetus from the growing discontent among the electorate propelled by the crisis economic conditions as the civil war accelerated. The anti-liberalization lobby begun to portray the failure of reforms to elevate the country to the league of dynamic East Asian economies as an intrinsic flaw of liberalization reforms, while ignoring the constraining effects on the reform outcome of the incomplete and staggered nature of the reform process and the prolonged civil war (Athukorala and Jayasuriya 2015).

The backlash against reforms gained momentum after the country returned to a state of normalcy after the three-decade old civil war ended in May 2009 (Kelegama 2017). The government begun to emphasize the role of the state in 'guiding the markets' to redress perceived untoward effects of market-oriented reforms. During the ensuing years, there were many case-by-case adjustments of duties for several manufacturing imports, which directly compete with domestic production (Athukorala 2012). Rapid infrastructure development and the promotion of small and medium enterprises were the key policy priorities under the new policy. Sri Lanka's emphasis on infrastructure development received added impetus from China's emphasis on geopolitical ascendency through the 'Belt and Road' Initiative (Ruwanpura, Brown and Chan 2019; Ruwanpura, Rowe and Chan 2020; Drehar and Fuchs 2022). The post-civil war period until about 2013 was notable for rapid growth as discussed below, but was predominantly driven by massive infrastructure investment. However, the growth spurt dissipated in the subsequent years with the completion of the massive debt-funded construction projects followed by the government's preoccupation with the impending repayment of accumulated debt.

By the time of the political regime shift in early 2015, the dark clouds of the economic storm were already gathering on the horizon. In 2016, the new government entered a four-year Extended Fund Facility (EFF) programme with the IMF, with a reform programme specifically focussed on fiscal consolidation (Coomaraswamy 2017). The revenue-enhancing fiscal consolidation reforms under this programme managed to reverse the dwindling tax-revenue to GDP ratio in the economy and achieve a modest surplus during 2018–2019 in the primary balance of the budget after several decades. The implementation of the programme abruptly terminated with the regime change in 2019, and the policy pendulum begun to shift in favour of 'guiding the markets' by the state (CBSL 2020).

Economic Performance

Growth Patterns

During the six decades prior to the onset of the Covid-19 pandemic, the Sri Lankan economy grew at an average annual rate of 4.8% (Table 11.1).[3] Given a population growth rate of 1.4%, this translated into a per capita income growth rate of 3.4%, apparently an impressive achievement by 'developing-country' standards. However, annual growth rates have been rather uneven throughout this period. It took almost six decades since independence for Sri Lanka to move from the 'low-income' status to middle-income status in 2007 and another 12 years to become an upper-middle-income country in 2019, in the World Bank's per capita income-based country classification.

During the 1960s and 1970s, per capita income grew at a modest rate of less than 2%. Diminishing fortunes of the traditional export industries and import compression that constrained the expansion of the new import substitution industries, swapped growth dynamism. The economy entered a respectably rapid growth path after the liberalization reforms began in the late 1970s, albeit growth occurred in fits and starts owing to an escalation of the civil war and the Southern youth uprising during the late 1980s. The five years following the ending of the civil war were notable for rapid growth, predominantly driven by debt-funded massive infrastructure investment. However, the growth spurt dissipated in the subsequent years with the completion of the construction projects and the preoccupation of the government with the impending repayment of the accumulated debt.

The structure of production of the economy changed little during the 1960s and 1970s, other than a modest increase in the share of domestic agriculture (mostly paddy production) in the face of a faster decline in the share of plantation agriculture. Manufacturing continued to account for less than 10% of GDP, in spite of the emphasis on import-substitution production, with SOEs playing a dominant role.[4]

Table 11.1 Key economic indicators, 1960–2021

	1960–2019	1960–1969	1970–1977	1978–1994	1995–1904	2005–2009	2010–2014	2015–2019	2020	2021
GDP growth (%)	4.8	4.7	3.1	5.0	4.7	6.0	6.8	3.7	–0.4	3.7
Per capita GDP growth	3.4	2.3	1.1	3.6	4.0	5.3	6.1	2.7	–4.4	3.0
Gross national saving (% of GDP)	18.3	12.2	12.3	16.2	21.2	22.2	29.6	26.9	23.6	23.8
Private	19.0	11.4	12.0	15.8	24.3	24.6	30.7	28.5	31.5	32.9
Gross domestic investment (% of GDP)	23.5	20.4	16.5	25.3	24.5	27.0	33.7	29.4	25.1	27.7
Private	15.4	8.2	9.4	12.2	18.8	21.0	28.6	24.3	21.8	24.3
Government expenditure (% of GDP)	26.2	27.9	31.4	31.3	25.6	26.4	27.0	35.3	35.4	34.0
Govern revenue (% of GDP)	18.4	21.8	25.4	20.6	17.3	18.8	21.0	28.6	24.3	21.8
Primary budget balance (1)	–3.1	–4.7	–4.6	–5.3	–2.1	–2.3	–1.2	–1.2	–4.6	–6.0
Overall budget balance (% of GDP)	–7.8	–6.1	–6.0	–10.4	–8.3	–7.6	–6.0	–6.7	–11.1	–12.2
Government debt (% of GDP)	77.9	52.6	63.0	87.1	97.1	86.3	71.3	81.3	101.0	104.6
Debt service/ government revenue (%)	20.5 (2)	–	–	25.0	28.9	25.5	32.9	45.0	63.7	61.4
Current account balance (% of GDP)	–4.0	–2.7	–1.2	–6.9	–3.1	–4.5	–4.1	–2.5	–1.5	–4.0
External debt (% of GDP)	42.8	6.6	19.5	59.7	57.1	42.7	50.0	59.3	60.3	60.1
Debt service ratio (3) (%)	16.4	4.8	20.5	19.0	13.8	14.8	19.6	27.3	35.2	30.0
Foreign exchange reserves (US$ bn)	2.0	0.1	0.1	0.6	1.8	3.4	7.4	7.2	5.7	3.1
Import months equivalent	3.1	2.1	2.0	2.8	3.6	3.8	5.0	4.2	4.2	1.7

Notes: (1) The difference between government revenue and expeditor excluding interest payment on public debit; (2) average for 1978–2019; (3) amortization of, and interest payment on, external debt as a percentage of earnings from goods and services exports; – Data not available.
Source: Compiled from CBSL (various years).

Following liberalization reforms, there was a notable increase in the share of manufacturing in GDP (from 14% to 18–20% by the mid-2000s). In a notable structural transformation of the economy, the share of manufacturing in GDP begun to surpass that of agricultural from 2005. With the gradual erosion of the role of SOEs, the private sector was largely responsible for economic dynamism in manufacturing (and other sectors) of the country. Disaggregated data (not reported here for brevity) indicate significant export orientation of manufacturing. The share of manufacturing in merchandise exports increased from less than 5% in the 1970s to over 65% by the late 1990s. FDI, mostly in joint ventures with local entrepreneurs, begun to play a pivotal role in export-oriented manufacturing. FDI attracted to Sri Lanka during this period was, however, heavily concentrated in standard light consumer goods industries, predominantly in garments, and also in sport and travel goods, cutting and polishing imported diamonds, and in natural rubber-based industries such as rubber bands, gloves, and automobile tyres. There is evidence that FDI could have played a much more important role in export expansion in labour intensive assembly activities in high-tech industries (such as electronics and electrical goods) if it were not for the political risk resulting from the ethnic conflict (Snodgrass 1998; Athukorala 2022).

The increase in manufacturing share in GDP has not continued into the post-civil war period: it remained virtually unchanged around 20%. The data point to a significant shift in the production structure towards non-tradable sectors reflecting massive investment in infrastructure development and government services. Non-tradable production contributed to over 70% of the increment in real GDP between 2005–2006 and 2018–2019.[5] The relative importance of non-tradables in the economy is relevant for the ensuing discussion on debt servicing capacity of the country. Shifts in the domestic production structure towards non-tradable production result in a compositional shift in domestic aggregate demand towards imports and/or a contraction in exports. This, in turn, contributes to widening the balance of payment deficits and accumulation of foreign debt.

On the expenditure side of the economy, there was a rapid expansion of government expenditure compared to government revenue throughout this period (Table 11.1). Government saving – the difference between government income and current expenditure – turned out to be negative in most years. Government investment was, therefore, financed by relying on capital inflows (foreign aid and borrowing), domestic borrowing, mostly from the central bank ('money financing'). The government failed to diversify the revenue base inherited from the colonial past and to improve the efficacy of the tax administration in face of rapidly increasing government expenditure. Tax revenue as a percentage of GDP declined from over 20% in the 1960s to less than 10% at the end of 2010s, which was one of the lowest in the developing world (Moore 2017).

Private consumption accounted for a disproportionate share of income (Table 11.1). The private savings rate hovered in the range of 8–15% until about the late 1980s. It increased to only about 24% during the ensuing years, which is much lower than the average saving rate of the high-performing East Asian countries (about 35%). The private sector balance – the difference between private expenditure and income, which is equal to the private 'saving – investment' gap – remained positive in most years. However, unlike in the East Asian economies, and also India and Bangladesh in recent decades, the private sector did not generate a substantial surplus to counterbalance the ballooning public sector deficit (Athukorala and Suanin 2022).

The widening gap between government expenditure over government revenue and the meagre private sector surplus meant a persistent gap between aggregate expenditure over aggregate income. This persistent domestic deficit was identical to a persistent deficit in the

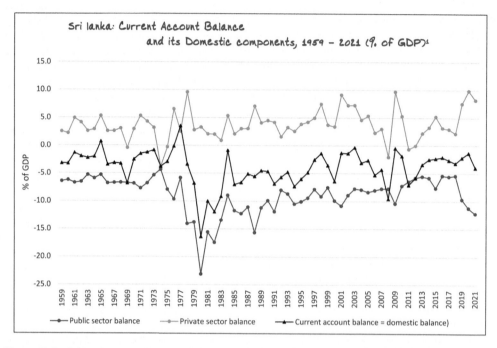

Figure 11.1 Sri Lanka: current account balance and its domestic components, 1959–2021 (% of GDP)

current account of the balance of payments: a country that spends more than what it domestically produces must fill the gap through imports.[6] During 1960–2021, Sri Lanka's current account was in deficit throughout, other than in 1965 and 1977 when there were small surpluses. The current account deficit has closely mirrored the public sector deficit (i.e., the budget deficit). Thus, Sri Lanka is a classic example of a 'twin deficit' economy (*a la* Straiten 1987) throughout this period (Figure 11.1).

Twin Deficits, Debt Overhang, and Vulnerability to the Covid-19 Shock

During the 1950s, the twin deficits were filled largely from accumulated foreign exchange reserves (Snodgrass 1966). During the ensure years until the late 1970s, the government managed to keep deficits within manageable limits with grants and concessional institutional borrowing thorough recourse to import compression (Corea 1971). External financing of government investment increased significantly following liberalization reforms initiated in the late 1970s (Athukorala and Jayasuriya 1994). However, external financing at the time predominantly took the form of grants and long-term loans with concessional interest rates from both individual donor countries and multilateral organizations.

The newfound emphasis of infrastructure investment development during the post-conflict years resulted in increased dependence on foreign financing. Sri Lanka's total external debt amounted to about 65% of GDP by 2019. This number is not excessively high by Sri Lanka's own past records: during 1982–1992, the debt to GDP ratio was around 70%. However, the past-conflict debt-drive growth was underpinned by a notable shift in the composition of debt from grants and conventional concessionary loans to borrowing from more costly market sources, in particular

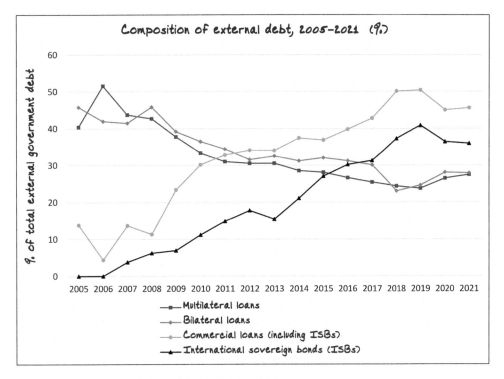

Figure 11.2 Composition of external debt, 2005–2021 (%)

issuing international sovereign bonds (ISBs). Starting with the debut ISB issue of US$500mn in 2007, the share of ISBs in total government foreign debt increased from about 4% in 2007 to over 40% in 2019 (Figure 11.2). Bilateral loans from China, which accounted for over 10% of total stock of external debt by 2019, also generally carried much higher interest rates compared to borrowing from the conventional bilateral donors.

Given the cumulative effect of debt accumulation and the dramatic shift in the debt composition from the conventional multilateral and bilateral debt to more costly borrowing sources, in particular ISB issues, by the late 2010s there were clear signs of debt distress in the economy. By 2019, debt repayments and interest payments accounted for over a third of total earnings from goods and services exports; interest payments on debt absorbed nearly 70% of total government revenue (Figure 11.3). By the end of 2019, the estimated debt service commitment (repayment of debt and interest payment) of the country for the ensuing two years had reached US$5bn.

In November 2019, there was a major policy shift following the change of political leadership that compounded debt distress of the economy: a massive non-funded tax cut that wiped off a third of government revenue in 2020 compared to the previous year, resulting in historically high budget deficit, which was financed with printed money.[7] The drastic decline in revenue seriously cast doubt on the country's ability to service its debt. The three leading credit rating agencies, namely, Moody, Standard and Poor, Fitch, immediately reacted with a downward revision of Sri Lanka's outlook, virtually cutting off the country from global capital markets. In December 2019, the IMF emphasizes the need for a strong commitment to fiscal consolidation for achieving debt sustainability over the medium term (IMF 2019).

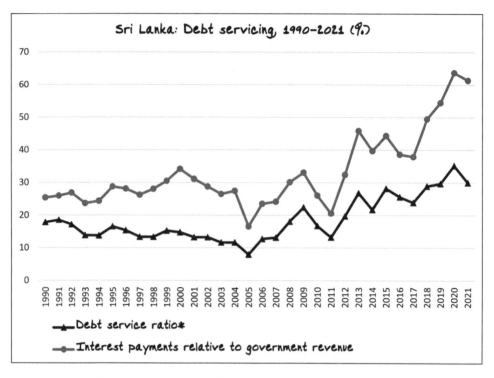

Figure 11.3 Sri Lanka: debt servicing, 1990–2021 (%)

The Covid-19 Shock, Failed 'Home Grown' Response, and Going to the IMF

As discussed, Sri Lanka entered the Covid-19 pandemic with a significant external debt overhang. The onset of the pandemic in March 2020 compounded debt distress. The biggest blow of the pandemic to the balance of payments was the collapse of tourist inflows: total estimated earnings dwindled from about US$4.5bn in 2019 to US$606mn in 2020 and US$50mn in 2021. Merchandise exports declined by about 20% in 2020 from the previous year (from US$12bn to US$10bn), but recovered well in 2021. Inward remittances through the banking system by Sri Lankan migrant workers significantly increased in 2020, reflecting increased family support money transfer during the height of the pandemic. However, the 'official' remittance inflows declined from US$7bn to US$5.4bn in 2021 reflecting diversion to informal channels because of foreign exchange restrictions and fixing of the exchange rate at an overvalued level for several months.

In March 2020, the government approached the IMF for financial assistance under the Rapid Financial Instrument (RFI) facility. However, the IMF rejected the request because it had already assessed Sri Lanka's external debt as unsustainable.[8] The negative response of the IMF was a strong signal for the government to enter into a stabilization programme to achieve debt sustainability and become eligible for IMF balance of payments support. However, the government decided to manage the crisis on its own without seeking IMF support. Sri Lanka had been a 'repetitive' client of the IMF during the previous five decanted with a record of entering into 16 stabilization programmes with the IMF. The governments in both political camps have obtained IMF support (Athukorala 2021). The resistance of the Sri Lankan government to follow this well-traversed path this time was presumably because of the concern that IMF conditionality could close loopholes in fiscal operation that had become a source of political patronage. The populist concern propagated by the government at the time that an IMF programme could involve sacrificing equity and fairness in development policy was not consistent with the IMF's emphasis in recent decades on more inclusive approach to stabilization and structural adjustment reforms.

The government's so-called 'home grown' response to the crisis was an *ad hoc* mixture of import restrictions, artificially fixing the exchange rate, and subsequently floating it, and imposing restrictions on foreign exchange transactions on both current account and capital account transactions.[9] These direct interventions were supplemented with swap agreements with the central banks of India (US$800mn), Bangladesh US$200mn), and China (US$1.5bn), and financing facilities from the governments of India (US$1.5bn) and China (US$1.3bn) to meet debt service commitments and finance necessary imports.

The Covid-19 shock and the uncertainty created by the 'muddling-through' response begun to stifle the economy. In 2020, the economy contracted by –3.6%.[10] The level of GDP recovered to the pre-crisis level in 2021, but contracted by 8.7% in 2022. In July 2020, the World Bank downgraded Sri Lanka from upper-middle to lower-middle income status in its income-based country classification. According to World Bank estimates, between January 2020 and December 2021, population below the poverty line (measured at US$3.20/day) in Sri Lanka had increased by about half a million. A tentative estimate made by combining data on household income distribution by quantiles from the recently released Household Income and Expenditure Survey (DCS 2022) suggests that about 60% of total households in the country are below this poverty line.[11] By July 2022, the headline year on year inflation had reached 66.7%, with food, which accounts for 44% of the national consumer price index (NCPI) basket, recording a rate of 82.5%. The NCPI presumably understates the degree of inflation because of the substantial presence of items subject to price control in the commodity basket.

By early 2022, there was rampant scarcity and price increases of food, fertilizer, gas and fuel, and frequent power cuts. People had to stand in long lines for hours on end to purchase milk powder, kerosene, and cooking gas. Lack of fuel to power plants resulted in more than 12-hour long power cuts by late 2021. Fuel stations had kilometres long lines to purchase rationed quantities for public and private transport as well as agricultural machines. Hospitals had to stop regular surgeries as they ran out of medicines. Protest rallies across the country saw record crowds of all social classes. Thousands camped at the entrance to the Presidential Secretariat for over two months demanding a change in political leadership and constitutional reform. Similar protests started across all major cities. In response, the Prime Minister and the entire cabinet resigned and a new cabinet was formed with some multiparty representation. On July 9, the protesters stormed the president's official residence. The president fled the country and tendered his resignation from Singapore on July 14, 2022. On July 20, the parliament, the Parliament, dominated by the defected president's party, elected a new president (for the remainder of the presidential term that ends in 2024). However, the political stability needed to make progress on an agreement with the IMF remains elusive as the political status quo remain largely unchanged (Wickramasinghe 2023).

Foreign exchange reserves plummet from US$7.6bn at the end of 2019 to about a mere US$50mn (appropriately two-week import requirement of the country) in early April 2022. To make matters worse, a much-anticipated balance of payments support from China was not forthcoming. On April 12, the government declared unilateral suspension of all external debt repayments with effect from 5PM that day. On April 16, 2022, the government started discussions with the IMF.

Extended Fund Facility Programme

In late May 2022, the Sri Lankan government appointed financial and legal consultants for debt structuring and commenced consultation with the IMF. On July 31, 2022 the IMF and the Sri Lankan authorities reached a staff-level agreement for economic adjustment and reform policies with a 48-month Extended Fund Facility (EFF), with a requested access of about SDR 2.286bn (equivalent to US$2.9bn) over a period of four years. The IMF Executive Board approved the staff-level agreement on March 21, 2023.

The key focus of the EFF programme is on near-term policy measures to restore macroeconomic stability and debt sustainability while mitigating the impact of the crisis on the poor and vulnerable (IMF 2023). Structural reforms (for long-term growth) are to be 'sequenced appropriately throughout the programme period, considering the authorities' capacity constraints' (IMF 2023: 26). The reform programme has been structured under five key policy goals: fiscal consolidation accompanied by strong social safety net; public debt restoring to ensure stable functioning of fiscal operations; restoring price stability and rebuilding foreign exchange reserve buffers under flexible exchange rate; ensuring financial sector stability by addressing banking sector vulnerabilities; and reforms to address corruption vulnerabilities.

The economy, as measured by real GDP, is expected to contract by 3% in 202 and 1.5% in 2024, and gradually converge to an average annual rate of 3% by the end of the programme period in 2027. According to these projections, real GDP in 2027 would be about 15% lower compared to the pre-crisis (2019) level. The estimated external resource gap during the programme period is estimated at $25.2bn of which IMF loan ($3bn) amounts to only 12%. The World Bank and the Asian Development are expected to contribute $3.8bn (15%) in the form of budget support. The government is expected to obtain raise $1.5bn (6%) by raising $1.5bn by issuing sovereign bond issues during the final year of the programme. The lion's share of the resource gap (67%) is to come from debt relief obtained through the restructuring of debts to bilateral creditors and private creditors (dominated by ISB holders). Multilateral creditors, specifically the IMF, World Bank, ADB, are treated as 'senior' creditors and are excluded from the debt restructuring process.

The IMF issued the first instalment of the EFF loan ($330mn) immediately after signing the agreement to catalyze external funding from the ADB and the World Bank. The rest of the loan are to be distributed uniformly in four instalments over the period (2023–2027) subject to an assessment of the progress on debt restructuring to restore debt sustainability and of meeting the performance criteria of the EFF programme ('the IMF conditionality'). As noted, anticipated debt relief accounts for over two-thirds of the external resource gap during the programme period. Achieving debt sustainability is also vital for Sri Lanka to re-enter world capital markets.

The IMF Director Board approved the EFF programme on 21 March 2023 after obtaining assurance from the official (bilateral) creditors to bring debt to a sustainable level and expression of reediness to negotiate debt relief by a group that held Sri Lankan ISBs (holding about half of the outstanding Sri Lankan ISBs) (IMF 2023). However, the possibility of the completion of the debate restructuring within the one-year timeframe specified in the EFF agreement remains doubtful. The IMF has warned that 'risk to the program implementation are exceptionally high, given the complex restructuring process' (IMF 2023: ii).

The Paris Club provides an effective forum for negotiations with Western government creditors. However, restructuring of bilateral debt can become a long-drawn process because China, the biggest bilateral creditor of Sri Lanka, is not a Paris Club member.[12] Restructuring debts to private creditors, in particular sovereign bondholders, is even more complicated. This would involve a mixture of a 'haircut' on outstanding bonds and the extension of maturities with a higher coupon rate, to be through voluntary negotiation of bondholders with the government. The experiences of other countries with debt restructuring suggest that the process of negotiating with IBS holders take between six months and over two years, with the time involved in post-default debt restructuring episodes clustering at the upper end (Asonuma and Trebesch 2016; Ams et al 2020). In the Sri Lankan case, the major ISB holders have agreed to participate in restructuring debt, subject to the prior restructuring of the government's domestic debts, which account for over half of its total debt, to their satisfaction. This could possibly prolong debt restructuring.

Concluding Remarks

The unprecedented economic crisis in Sri Lanka is the culmination of debt distress that has been building for over two decades aggravated by more recent policy blunders, contrary to the popular perception that the crisis was caused by the COVID pandemic. When the balance of payment shock of the pandemic triggered debt crises, the authorities believed, as they subsequently admitted, they could manage it on their own without entering into a stabilization arrangement with the IMF. Timely action with IMF support could have helped the government to manage the crises at a lower economic and socio-political cost and avoid a sovereign debt default.

Sri Lanka's policy challenge is to take the unprecedented economic crisis as the springboard for lifting the country to a sustainable growth path and to transform the 'twin deficit' economy, characterized by 'stop-go' growth cycle, into a dynamic, outward-oriented economy that can deliver sustainable and equitably shared growth. This requires achieving a sustainable fiscal position by undertaking government revenue and expenditure reforms, redressing the anti-tradable bias through the monetary, exchange rate, trade and competition reforms, and combining these policy initiatives with a coherent social welfare net as an integral part of the reform process. Given that fiscal operation is the prime source of domestic excess demand, the IMF approach assumes a tight one-to-one link between the budget deficit and the balance of payments deficit, domestic money and credit that drive inflation. Aggregate-demand management is vital for any serious stabilization plan, in the sense of seeking to eliminate domestic demand pressure on the external balance. However, it is necessary to combine stabilization policies with policies to redress anti-tradable bias in the structure of the economy in order to set the economy on a 'new beginning' for a long-term self-sustained development path.

Sri Lanka offers a stark cautionary tale of how flawed economic choices invariably originate in a weak polity characterized by pervasive venality, impunity, and incompetence. In the context of a volatile socio-political setting, economic recovery and structural adjustment cannot proceed without political stability, and popular engagement and legitimacy. There is, therefore, a pressing need for a broad social dialogue aimed at a robust 'listening campaign' behind the shared national objective of inclusive economic recovery.

Notes

1 The *RER* is the nominal exchange rate (NER) (defined here as the price of rupee in terms of a given foreign currency unit) adjusted for the domestic (Sri Lanka's) price level relative to the average price level of the trading partner countries (RP). Appreciation of the RER, that is an increase in NER adjusted for RP, reduces the international competitiveness of tradable production in the economy.
2 Military expenditure increased from 1% to 5% of GDP between 1984 and 2008 (Kelegama 2017).
3 National accounts data are available on a comparable basis only for the period since 1951. For an analysis of economic performance prior to that year see Snodgrass (1966).

4 The data used in this paper, otherwise specifically stated, are from the *Annual Report* and electronic data sources of the Central Bank of Sri Lanka.
5 Sum of value added in transport storage and communication; wholesale and retail trade, banking, insurance, and real estate; ownership of dwellings; public administration and defence; and other (unclassified services) in national income accounts.
6 The current account balance (external balance) is equal to the internal (domestic) balance, which is the sum of the public sector balance (budget balance) and private sector balance (Dornbusch 1980).
7 A tax cut was introduced without accompanying revenue-raising or expenditure-reduction proposals to counterbalance the adverse effect of the tax cut on the overall government budget. Apparently, this policy was based on a misinterpretation of the new monetary theory, which postulates that *a country that borrows in its one currency in a floating exchange rate regime* has no effective limit on its central government debt (emphasis added) (Kelton 2020).
8 According to its Charter, the IMF lends to a member country only if the country's external debt position is sustainable, that is, it has the capability to meet the existing debt servicing commitments.
9 See Athukorala (2024) for details.
10 This contraction was partly due to economic disruption caused by terrorist bombing of three churches and three luxury hotels in Colombo on the Easter Sunday (21 April 2019).
11 The survey was conducted in 2019/20.
12 The Paris Club is a group Western donor countries formed in 1950 to find coordinated solution to developing countries' debt problems. It undertakes non-concessional rescheduling of debt.

References

Ams, Julianne, Reza Baqir, Anna Gelperns and Christopher Trebesch (2020) "Sovereign Default" In *Sovereign Debt: A Guide for Economists and Practitioners* S. Ali Abbas, Alex Pienkowski and Kenneth Rogoff (eds) New York: Oxford University Press, pp 275–327

Arunatilake, Nisha, Sisira Jayasuriya and Saman Kelegama (2001) "The Economic Cost of the War in Sri Lanka" *World Development* 29(9): 1483–1500

Asonuma, Tamon and Christopher Trebesch (2016) "Sovereign Debt Restructurings: Pre-emptive or Post-Default?" *Journal of the European Economic Association* 14(1): 175–214

Athukorala, Prema-chandra (2012) "Sri Lanka's Trade Policy: Reverting to Dirigisme?" *The World Economy* 35(12): 1662–1686

Athukorala, Prema-chandra (2021) "Sri Lanka and the IMF: Myth and Reality" *Daily Financial Times*, Colombo (in three-part article: 30 September 3, and October 1 and 2)

Athukorala, Prema-chandra (2022) "Rethinking Sri Lanka's Industrialization Strategy: Achievements, Lost Opportunities and Prospects" *Asian Economic Papers* 21(2): 14–37

Athukorala, Prema-chandra (2024) "The Sovereign Debt Crisis in Sri Lanka: Anatomy and Policy Options" *Asian Economic Papers*, 23(2) (forthcoming)

Athukorala, Prema-chandra, Edimon Ginting, Hal Hill and Utsav Kumar (2017) *The Sri Lankan Economy: Charting a New Course* Manila: Asian Development Bank

Athukorala, Prema-chandra and Sisira Jayasuriya (1994) *Macroeconomic Policies, Crises and Growth in Sri Lanka, 1969–1990* Washington: World Bank

Athukorala, Prema-chandra and Sisira Jayasuriya (2015) "Victory in War and Defeat in Peace: Politics and Economics of Post-conflict Sri Lanka" *Asian Economic Paper* 14(3): 22–54

Athukorala, Prema-chnadra and Wanissa Suanin (2022) "Saving Transition in Asia: Unity in Diversity" *World Institute of Development Economic Research (WIDER) Working Paper* Helsinki: WIDER. Available at https://www.econstor.eu/bitstream/10419/273960/1/1831055686.pdf

CBSL (Central Bank of Sri Lanka) (2020) *Annual Report* Colombo: CBSL

Coomaraswamy, Indrajith (2017) *Revenue Based Fiscal Consolidation towards Sustainable Growth* Colombo: Central Bank of Sri Lanka. Accessed on 12/07/2022. Available at https://www.casrilanka.com/casl/images/stories/2017/2017_pdfs/full_text_of_oration_by_central_bank_governor.pdf

Corea, Gamini (1971) "Aid and the Economy" *Marga Quarterly Journal* 1(1): 19–54

de Silva, Kingsley M. (1974) "Sri Lanka in 1948" *Ceylon Journal of Historical and Social Studies* 4(1 & 2): 1–19

Department of Census and Statistics (DCS) (2022) *Household Income and Expenditure Survey 2021* Colombo: DCS

Dornbusch, Rudigar (1980) *Open Economy Macroeconomics* New York: Basic Books

Drehar, Alex and Andrew Fuchs (2022) *Banking on Beijing: The Aims and Impacts of China's Overseas Development Program* Cambridge: Cambridge University Press

Dunham, David and Sisira Jayasuriya (2000) "Equity, Growth and Insurrection: Liberalization and the Welfare Debate in Contemporary Sri Lanka" *Oxford Development Studies* 28(1): 97–110

International Monetary Fund (IMF) (2019) *Sri Lanka: Sixth Review under the Extended Arrangement, Staff Report; and Statement by the Executive Director for Sri Lanka* Washington: IMF

International Monetary Fund (IMF) (2023) *Sri Lanka: Request for an Extended Agreement under the Extended Fund Faculty – Press Release, Staff report, and Statement by the Executive Board for Sri Lanka Country report 23/116*. Accessed on 30/04/2022. Available at https://www.imf.org/en/Publications/CR/Issues/2023/03/20/Sri-Lanka-Request-for-an-Extended-Arrangement-Under-the-Extended-Fund-Facility-Press-531191

Jiggins, Janice (1976) "Dismantling Welfarism in Sri Lanka" *Overseas Development Institute Review* 9(2): 84–104

Kelegama, Saman (2017) "The Political Economy of the Rajapaksa Decade in Sri Lanka, 2005-2014: Policy Contradictions and Mal-Governance" In *Managing Globalization in the Asian Century: Essays in Honor of Prema-chandra Athukorala* Hal and Menon Jayant (eds) Singapore: Institute of Southeast Asian Studies, pp 428–456

Kelton, Stephanie (2020) *The Deficit Myth* New Yok: John Murray

Lee, Kuan Yew (2000) *From Third World to First: The Singapore Story: 1965–2000* Singapore: Singapore Press Holding

Levy, Brian (1989) "Foreign Aid in the Making of Economic Policy in Sri Lanka, 1977–1983" *Policy Sciences* 22(3): 437–461

Moore, Mick (1997) "Leading the Left to the Right: Populist Coalitions and Economic Reforms" *World Development* 25(7): 1009–1028

Moore, Mick (2017) "The Political Economy of Long-Term Revenue Decline in Sri Lanka" *International Centre for Tax and Development Working Paper 65* Brighton: Centre for Development Studies

Osmani, S.R. (1994) "Is There a Conflict between Growth and Welfarism? The Significance of the Sri Lanka Debate" *Development and Change* 25(3): 387–421

Panagariya, Arvind (2002) "Trade Liberalization in Asia" In *Going Alone: The Case for Relax Reciprocity in Freeing Trade* Jagdish Bhagwati (ed) Cambridge: MIT Press, pp 219–302

Ruwanpura, Kanchana N., Benjamin Brown and Loritta Chan (2019) "(Dis)connecting Colombo: Situating the Megapolis in Post-war Sri Lanka" *The Professional Geographer* 72(1): 165–179

Ruwanpura, Kanchana N., Peter Rowe and Loritta Chan (2020) "Of Bombs and Belts: Exploring Potential within China's Belt and Road Initiative in Sri Lanka" *The Geographical Journal* 186(3): 339–345

Snodgrass, Donald R. (1966) *Ceylon: An Export Economy in Transition* Homewood: Richard D Irwin

Snodgrass, Donald R. (1989) "The Economic Development of Sri Lanka: A Tale of Missed Opportunities" In *Creating Peace in Sri Lanka: Civil War and Reconciliation* Robert I. Rotberg (ed) Washington: Brookings Institution Press, pp 89–107

Streeten, Paul (1987) "Structural Adjustment: A Survey of the Issues and Options" *World Development* 15(12): 1469–1482

Wickramasinghe, Nira (2023) "A Country in Abeyance: Sri Lanka's Continuing Crisis" *Current History* 122(843): 131–136

Wriggins, W. Howard (1960) *Ceylon: Dilemma of a New Nation* Princeton: Princeton University Pres

Wriggins, W. Howard (2011) "After Forty Years" In *The Sri Lanka Reader: History, Culture, Politics* John Clifford (ed) Durham: Duke University Press, pp 607–617

12
GENDER EQUALITY IN SRI LANKA'S ECONOMY
Persistent Challenges

Dileni Gunewardena

Introduction

Sri Lanka's long-held achievements in gender equality in relation to health and education are accompanied by a dismal record in gender equality in relation to the economy. Women in Sri Lanka have had higher life expectancy than men since the early 1960s and low maternal mortality (Department of Census and Statistics DCS undated). There is gender parity in primary school enrolments and higher secondary and tertiary educational enrolment for girls. Women predominate in the economic sectors that contribute most to the country's foreign exchange earnings, yet the average Sri Lankan woman is engaged in either unpaid or low-paid and segregated work and faces poor working conditions while negotiating a double burden of market and household work.

Female labour force participation (FLFP) has remained low and stagnant between 30% and 37% over the last two decades, and women earn less than their peers in both the private and public sectors (Gunewardena et al 2009; ILO 2016; Seneviratne 2020). As the main caregivers across the generational spectrum, women devote more hours to unpaid care work, contributing to over 86.4% of all unpaid work (DCS 2020). The value of women's contribution to unpaid work is estimated to be between 8% and 34% of GDP, larger than the contribution of the agricultural sector (Gunewardena and Perera 2022).[1]

Driven by economic necessity to work in semi-formal and informal employment, plantation agriculture, export manufacturing and domestic work in Sri Lanka or overseas, women face issues related to precarious employment, exhausting work, and poor living conditions, leading to high turnover and labour shortages in some industries. Women working in non-plantation agriculture and in micro-enterprises, most often as contributing family workers, face issues of invisibility and agency, namely a lack of control over income and productive assets. Women farmers face issues of inequality in access to land and extension services, while women entrepreneurs face inequality in access to training and non-land assets, credit, financing and markets (FAO 2018; de Silva 2020). Women micro-enterprise owners in Sri Lanka receive low or no profits even when capital constraints are eased (de Mel, McKenzie and Woodruff 2009, 2010). Women in Sri Lanka with higher human capital endowments are more likely to be employed in white-collar employment (Gunatilaka 2013; Seneviratne 2019; Gunatilaka and Chandrasiri 2021), but often do not receive equal pay for work of equal value (Gunewardena et al 2009; Seneviratne 2020). Moreover, they must contend with work-family conflict and sexual harassment in the workplace (Kailasapathy and Metz 2012; Adikaram and Kailasapathy 2020).

I begin by providing a comparative overview of the status of gender equality in Sri Lanka. I then review the literature on FLFP in Sri Lanka to offer a critical perspective on women's labour in Sri Lanka, followed by an analysis of the trends and patterns in women's labour force participation (FLP). I conclude with recommendations for the equitable distribution of the burden of care work and unpaid labour.

Women and the Economy in Sri Lanka: A Comparative Perspective

Table 12.1 compares Sri Lanka's gender equality and women's educational and labour force indicators with South Asian neighbours as well as other Asian emerging economies. According to the United Nations Development Programme's (UNDP's) Gender Inequality Index (GII), which measures gender disparities in health, empowerment and the labour market (with usually a higher value indicating a worsening situation), Sri Lanka performs better on gender inequality compared to all its comparators except Malaysia and Thailand. The World Economic Forum (2022) ranks Sri Lanka first among 156 countries in the dimension of health and survival, and first in secondary and tertiary enrolment and sex ratio at birth. However, Sri Lanka does less well in the overall Global Gender Gap Index (GGGI), which draws on economic participation and opportunity, educational attainment, health and survival, and political empowerment (with a higher score indicates a closing of the gap, i.e. an improvement in gender equality); it only exceeds India and Pakistan in the group of comparators in Table 12.1.

The WBL index more specifically looks at how the legal environment promotes gender equality, which is measured by looking at mobility, workplace, pay, marriage, parenthood, entrepreneurship, assets and pension. In this index, Sri Lanka lags behind Nepal and India in the region, and Philippines and Thailand among other comparators – other than in the areas of mobility and marriage (scoring 100%), but does worst in pay and parenthood (World Bank 2022).

Going beyond composite indexes to specific dimensions, Sri Lanka leads in educational attainment, reduced fertility, delayed age at first marriage, life expectancy and financial inclusion, but lags behind in political leadership, FLFP and earned income at a global level. Its absolute and relative FLFP rates and women's labour force shares are higher than several South Asian counties but are lower than other Asian comparators. Its unemployment rate is only lower than that of Malaysia, while its share of women who are not in education, employment or training (NEETs) is lower than neighbouring South Asian countries, but higher than several other of the comparator economies (Table 12.2). Also poor, compared to other economies, especially emerging Asian economies, is women's share of graduates in STEM (Science, Technology, Engineering and Math) subjects.

In contrast, Sri Lanka's share of women in vulnerable employment is lower than many of its neighbours, while its share of women in informal employment is the lowest in the group.[2] Its share of women in agricultural employment is relatively low, but it leads in the share of women employed in industry. Its share of female wage and salaried workers is relatively high, as is its share in senior and middle management. The share of women who receive public sector pensions is also higher relative to other countries in the group, but it has the lowest duration of full-paid maternity leave. Thus, Sri Lanka presents a complex picture of achievements but has several shortcomings compared to emerging Asian comparators.

Table 12.1 Key indicators, Sri Lanka and comparator economies

	Sri Lanka	Bangladesh	India	Nepal	Pakistan	Indonesia	Malaysia	Philippines	Thailand
GII score	0.401	0.537	0.488	0.452	0.538	0.480	0.253	0.430	0.359
GII rank	90	133	123	110	135	121	59	104	80
GGGI score	0.670	0.719	0.625	0.683	0.556	0.688	0.676	0.784	0.710
GGGI rank	116	65	140	106	153	101	112	17	79
Women, Business and Law (WBL) overall score	65.6	49.4	74.4	80.6	55.6	64.4	50.0	78.8	78.1
Educational attainment, at least completed lower secondary, population 25+, female (%) (cumulative)	80.2	50.6	–	51.0	22.1	75.0	–	73.4	47.6
Educational attainment, at least completed upper secondary, population 25+, female (%) (cumulative)	63.0	32.0	–	34.6	10.1	63.0	–	33.2	35.1
Lower secondary completion rate, female (% of relevant age group)	98.1	74.3	86.8	92.7	89.8	87.6	99.4	45.7	89.9
Female share of graduates in Natural Sciences, Mathematics and Statistics programmes, tertiary (%)	56.9	14.9	51.4	74.3	–	70.7	–	62.0	70.7
Age at first marriage, female	23.9	–	21.4	22.4	23.2	–	20.1	23.4	–
Fertility rate, total (births per woman)	2.2	2.0	2.2	2.3	2.5	2.0	1.8	3.4	1.5
Life expectancy at birth, female (years)	80.4	74.9	71.2	74.2	68.5	78.5	72.5	75.6	81.1

(*Continued*)

Table 12.1 (Continued)

	Sri Lanka	Bangladesh	India	Nepal	Pakistan	Indonesia	Malaysia	Philippines	Thailand
Proportion of seats held by women in national parliaments (%)	5.4	20.9	14.4	20.3	20.2	14.9	32.7	28.0	15.7
Labour force participation rate for ages 15–24, female (%) (national estimate)	21.5	26.4	13.0	38.9	19.9	34.9	20.3	23.3	33.2
Labour force participation rate, female (% of female population ages 15+) (national estimate)	34.4	36.3	26.2	53.2	23.5	55.3	26.3	42.5	59.2
Labour force, female (% of total labour force)	33.6	30.4	20.3	39.6	20.2	38.5	55.0	39.3	45.9
Labour force with advanced education, female (% of female working-age population with advanced education)	83.8	56.7	34.2	76.8	36.0	72.7	56.3	56.7	80.6
Ratio of female to male labour force participation rate (%) (national estimate)	47.2	45.1	34.6	65.1	29.5	68.6	48.9	63.6	78.5
Employment to population ratio, 15+, female (%) (national estimate)	31.9	33.9	25.0	51.2	22.0	52.8	22.9	41.4	58.5
Share of youth not in education, employment or training, female (% of female youth population)	29.0	44.5	44.5	26.8	21.5	14.8	46.6	52.5	18.5

(Continued)

Table 12.1 (Continued)

	Sri Lanka	Bangladesh	India	Nepal	Pakistan	Indonesia	Malaysia	Philippines	Thailand
Unemployment, female (% of female labour force) (national estimate)	7.5	6.7	4.4	3.8	6.3	4.7	13.1	2.7	1.1
Vulnerable employment, female (% of female employment) (modelled International Labour Organization (ILO) estimate)	40.2	65.4	75.3	57.1	70.2	27.1	87.5	37.4	48.8
Informal employment, female (% of total non-agricultural employment)	51.3	91.9	76.0	75.9	72.6	–	82.4	–	52.5
Wage and salaried workers, female (% of female employment) (modelled ILO estimate)	58.9	34.0	24.2	41.0	29.7	71.2	12.1	60.4	49.7
Female share of employment in senior and middle management (%)	22.5	11.5	14.8	–	29.3	–	13.9	–	31.0
Employers, female (% of female employment) (modelled ILO estimate)	0.9	0.6	0.6	1.9	0.1	1.7	0.4	2.2	1.4
Employment in agriculture, female (% of female employment) (modelled ILO estimate)	27.6	57.6	54.7	26.4	65.2	5.9	74.1	13.6	28.3

(Continued)

Table 12.1 (Continued)

	Sri Lanka	Bangladesh	India	Nepal	Pakistan	Indonesia	Malaysia	Philippines	Thailand
Employment in industry, female (% of female employment) (modelled ILO estimate)	25.9	17.7	17.4	16.7	16.8	20.0	8.6	9.7	19.8
Employment in services, female (% of female employment) (modelled ILO estimate)	46.5	24.8	28.0	57.0	18.0	74.1	17.3	76.7	52.0
Female migrants (% of international migrant stock)	47.8	48.6	48.8	41.8	47.4	38.9	69.7	48.2	49.8
Length of paid maternity leave (calendar days)	84	112	182	90	112	60	98	105	90
Received a public sector pension in the past year, female (% age 15+)	6.6	2.7	7.2	2.9	0.8	5.6	2.2	6.2	4.8
Account ownership at a financial institution or with a mobile-money-service provider, female (% of population ages 15+)	73.4	35.8	76.6	51.4	7.0	82.5	41.6	38.9	79.8
Debit card ownership, female (% age 15+)	30.7	3.7	22.3	32.4	2.7	67.5	5.9	18.7	58.6
Financial institution account, female (% age 15+)	73.4	31.9	76.6	51.1	6.3	82.1	41.6	35.5	79.5

Source: World Bank Open Data, Gender Statistics, 2015–2021, most recent value; WBL: https://wbl.worldbank.org/en/wbl; GGGI: https://www.weforum.org/reports/global-gender-gap-report-2021/in-full/economy-profiles/; GII: https://hdr.undp.org/en/countries.

Table 12.2 Sri Lanka's relative position in relation to South Asia and emerging Asian economies

Indicator	Compared to South Asia	Compared to other selected Asian countries
Gender Inequality Index	Lower (better)	Lower (exception: Malaysia and Thailand)
GGGI	Lower (worse) (exceptions: Bangladesh and India)	Lower (worse)
WBL	Lower (worse) (exceptions: Bangladesh and Pakistan)	Lower (worse) (exceptions: Indonesia and Malaysia)
Absolute FLFP rate	Lower (exceptions: India and Pakistan)	Lower (exception: Malaysia)
Relative FLFP rate	Higher (exception: Nepal)	Lower (exception: Malaysia)
Female labour force share	Higher (exception: Nepal)	Lower
Unemployment rate	Higher	Higher (exception Malaysia)
NEETs	Lower (exception: Nepal and Pakistan)	Higher (exception: Malaysia and Philippines)
Educational attainment (lower secondary)	Higher	Higher
Lower secondary completion rate	Higher	Higher (exception: Malaysia)
Female share in STEM	Higher (exception: Nepal)	Lower
Youth FLFP	Lower (exception: India and Pakistan)	Lower (exceptions: Malaysia)
Age at first marriage	Older	Older
Women in vulnerable employment	Lower	Lower (exceptions: Indonesia and Philippines)
Women in informal employment	Lower	Lower
Women in wage and salaried employment	Higher	Higher (exceptions: Indonesia and Philippines)
Women in agricultural employment	Lower (exception: Nepal)	Higher (exceptions: Malaysia and Thailand)
Women in industrial employment	Higher	Higher
Women in services	Higher (exception: Nepal)	Lower (exception: Malaysia)
Women's share in senior and middle management	Higher (exception: Pakistan)	Lower (exception: Thailand)
Women who receive public sector pensions	Higher (exception: India)	Higher
Duration of fully paid maternity leave	Lower	Lower (exception: Indonesia)
Fertility	Lower (exception: Bangladesh)	Higher (exception: Philippines)
Female life expectancy	Higher	Higher (exception: Thailand)
Women in parliament	Lower	Lower

Source: Analysis of data in Table 12.1.

Women's Labour Force Participation, Labour Supply and Unemployment

Sri Lanka's LFP gender gap is the 20th largest in the world (World Bank 2022). Low FLFP is a problem common to Asia and in particular South Asia (Table 12.1). Sri Lanka nevertheless ranks below all ASEAN countries and several South Asian countries. Moreover, Sri Lanka faces a declining labour force owing to an ageing population; increasing its FLFP has the potential to mitigate the negative effects on economic growth.[3] Simulations for Sri Lanka show that if gender gaps in LFP are closed in the next 50 years, income gains would be about 21% (Cuberes and Teignier 2016; IMF 2018). In addition to gains in economic growth, women's LFP also improves the education and health of their children and it increases agency and bargaining power (Afridi, Mukhopadhyay and Sahoo 2016; Heath and Jayachandran 2017).

Trends over Time

Historically, women's share in the labour force increased from 22% in 1946 to 25% in 1970. It was 25% in 1980 as well, increasing to 35% in 1995, thereafter it remained stagnant in the range of 30–36%. Concomitantly, women's share in the LFP shifted from a late broad-peak pattern (peaking at age 45–59 in the 1940s and 1950s) to an early peak pattern (ages 20–29) in the 1970s. This pattern also coincided with a shift in FLFP from educated women engaged in the service sector, to a broader expansion of women's LFP in manufacturing and service sectors following economic liberalization in the late 1970s (Kiribanda 1997). However, by 1992, extended participation in schooling had led to an increase in the peak age of participation to 33 years, which further increased to 42 years in 2014. Nevertheless, over this period, the age profile demonstrated a declining concavity; as women aged, they did not leave LFP as quickly as before (Seneviratne 2019).

Age, Education, Marital Status, Ethnicity and Geography

Although FLFP has remained largely constant at the aggregate level over the last three decades, this apparent invariance masks a great deal of variation by age cohort and demographic group. Young women's LFP declined from 37% to 24% between 1992 and 2014 because of increased educational participation, while married women increased their average participation rate by 9.5% points between 1992 and 2014 (Seneviratne 2019). However, by 2019 this had decreased by 7.13% points down to 35.57% (my calculations using Sri Lanka Labour Force Survey 2019 data).

Within these trends too, there is considerable heterogeneity by education and demography. Women with General Certificate of Education (GCE) ordinary level education and above work mainly in white-collar services (public administration, education, finance and health), while women with lower education work mainly in agriculture. Over the 1992–2014 period, there appeared to be a demand for and corresponding engagement in informal, low-wage labour among older women with lower education. Alongside, educated women were retreating from the labour market; the negative income effect for this group strengthened, while prospects for their employment also weakened (Seneviratne 2019). These results are consistent with previous findings that indicate a dip in FLFP in secondary education and a rise in tertiary education but without necessarily securing high-skilled jobs (Gunatilaka 2013; Madurawala 2017; Samarakoon and Mayadunne 2018; Solotaroff et al 2020).

However, further disaggregation shows that this U-shaped pattern is associated with only married women. The LFP of never-married women rises monotonically with their education and is dispersed across many occupations and industries, indicating fewer restrictions on the choice of single women compared to married women; and their substitution effect dominates the income effect as wages rise (Seneviratne 2019). This pattern of falling LFP of married women as their education and income status rise is evident in other countries in the region (Klasen and Pieters 2015). It is often related to the social stigma associated with labour market work and status production activities (Eswaran, Ramaswami and Wadhwa 2013). Between 1992 and 2014, married women with primary and secondary schooling entered manufacturing and low-skilled services (trade, transport, communication, utilities and construction). Their participation rose with wages, implying the domination of the substitution effect over the income effect. However, this participation was in self-employment and informalized work. Overall, married women were shifting into self-employment and contributing to family employment, while single women were shifting into wage employment (Seneviratne 2019).

Ethnicity and geographical location shape LFP. Moor Muslims are less likely to participate in the labour force and Indian Tamil women are more likely (Gunatilaka 2013; Samarakoon and Mayadunne 2018; Seneviratne 2019; Solotaroff et al 2020). Residence in agricultural provinces encourages FLFP, suggesting that the level of economic activity, especially in plantation agriculture, underlies the correlation between geography, ethnicity and FLFP (Gunatilaka 2013; Solotaroff et al 2020).

The FLFP of women with tertiary education is not affected by maternal status, ethnoreligious identity or labour market factors (Samarakoon and Mayadunne 2018). This suggests that they are able to access employment that brings economic returns or sufficient status – or both – in order to overcome the opportunity cost and social norms that are otherwise barriers to FLFP. Fertility decline and male salaried employment contributed to increasing FLFP, while rising household income, demographic ageing and falling agricultural income reduced FLFP (Seneviratne 2019). There is no contradiction between a positive association of FLFP with men's formal employment and a negative association with rising household income. The former effect is likely due to networks – women whose husbands have salaried employment are also more likely to access formal salaried employment. Interestingly, the FLFP (negative) response to household income has been weakening over time, and this finding is also robust to an analysis of birth cohorts, which finds that there is a pattern of falling sensitivity to household economic status with each new generation (Seneviratne 2019).

Job Opportunities

In addition to supply-side factors, limited job opportunities for those who do want to work and the gender wage gap are factors limiting FLFP (Gunewardena et al 2009; Gunatilaka 2013). Opportunity functions explore access to the labour force and find that women are more disadvantaged than men in accessing the labour force and that women in lower deciles are more vulnerable (Madurawala 2017).

The likelihood of a woman participating in the labour force is higher in locations with a better relative share of women than men who are employed in a specific educational category. It indicates that women are encouraged to look for work when there are more opportunities available for educated women (Gunatilaka 2013). In the same study, FLFP also responds to the index of gender segregation by the industrial sector, suggesting that women are more likely to look for or find employment in jobs that are perceived as suitable for women.

Young Women

As noted earlier, the LFP rate for young women (15–24 years) is lower than the national average. It peaked at 37% in 1992 during the post-liberalization period but began declining in the early 1990s, owing to greater participation in education. In 2014 it was 22% and 24% (including and excluding the Northern and Eastern provinces) and remained at 22% in 2019 (Seneviratne 2019; for 1992 and 2014 estimates are my calculations using LFS 2019). That girls stay in school longer is reflected in secondary school and tertiary education enrolments, where girls outnumber boys. However, girls who do not continue in general education lack marketable skills and are under-represented among those who follow technical and vocational training (Gunatilaka 2013; Chandrasiri and Gunatilaka 2015). Women's recruitment into apprenticeships is higher in traditional sectors, such as care and education, but dropout rates are much higher than their male counterparts. Additionally, women who are enrolled in male-dominated fields of study also display even higher dropout rates (Verite 2018). Gender segregation in accessing technical and vocational training may be self-selected, but may also arise as a response to perceptions of employer's gender bias (Samarakoon and Mayadunne 2018). Gunewardena (2015) found that Technical and Vocational Education and Training (TVET) and apprenticeships provided no additional earnings advantage beyond general education.

A new Youth Gender Gap Index developed as part of a youth labour market assessment highlights gender inequality in LFP, wages and occupational roles across Sri Lanka's nine provinces, with no gender parity in any of the five indicators that were examined (Verite 2018). However, 1.5% of employed young women were in managerial positions in 2010, which was higher than that of young men, and an increase from 2006 (Ministry of Youth Affairs and Skills Development 2014). Young women still dominate the apparel industry, where women's share of employment has been 70–80% (Robertson et al 2020). However, turnover is high, particularly after marriage.

The share of the population that is neither in education, employment, or training (NEET) is considered an indicator that addresses a broad array of vulnerabilities, especially among youth. In Sri Lanka, young women are at greater risk of being NEET as are women in ethnic and religious minorities, those with very low levels of education, those belonging to low-income households as well as those who have young children and live in remote areas (Abayasekara and Gunasekara 2019). Representation in STEM subjects is low among girls who continue in general education (Ministry of Youth Affairs and Skills Development 2014).

Older Women

Women's LFP in the older age group (66+ years) has been increasing since the 1990s, from 6.6% in 1992 to 11.8% in 2014 (Seneviratne 2019). However, LFP of older women in Sri Lanka is lower than other countries in the region with the exception of Pakistan and Bangladesh (Vodopivec and Arunatilake 2011). They note how wages for older men and women decline quite steeply in the public sector and more modestly in the private sector. Over half of working elderly people are self-employed or casual workers in the informal sector as skilled workers in agriculture, manufacturing, and wholesale and retail trade, with a large percentage of women in elementary occupations and a smaller percentage as professionals.

Patterns of women's unemployment in Sri Lanka show some indication of having changed in the last decade (Table 12.3). Consistent with Seneviratne's (2019) findings that older women are entering or staying longer in the labour force, Table 12.3 indicates that their unemployment is

Table 12.3 Unemployment rates by sex, age, education and province

Unemployment	2010				2020			
	Sri Lanka	Male	Female	F/M	Sri Lanka	Male	Female	F/M
Sri Lanka	4.9	3.5	7.7	2.2	5.5	4	8.5	2.1
Age group								
15–24	19.4	16.3	24.7	1.5	26.5	22.1	35.1	1.6
25–29	9.2	4.7	17.8	3.8	12	7.9	19.3	2.4
30–39	3.1	1.7	5.8	3.4	3.5	2.2	6	2.7
Over 40	1.1	0.8	1.4	1.8	1.1	0.7	2.1	3.0
Level of education								
Grade 10 and below	3.6	2.8	5.8	2.1	3.3	2.8	4.5	1.6
O/L	6.9	5.4	10.1	1.9	7.2	5.9	9.8	1.7
A/L and above	11.6	7.9	15.8	2.0	9.8	6.2	13.6	2.2
Province								
Western	3.7	2.6	6	2.3	5.5	4.4	7.6	1.7
Central	6.7	5.1	9.6	1.9	6.4	5.6	7.8	1.4
Southern	7.8	5.9	11.6	2.0	7.7	5.9	11.4	1.9
Northern	–	–	–	–	5.2	3.3	10.7	3.2
Eastern	5.3	3.1	11.9	3.8	4.8	2.4	11.8	4.9
North Western	4.8	3.5	7.1	2.0	4.3	2.4	7.6	3.2
North Central	3.6	*	6.4	*	4.1	2.1	7.7	3.7
Uva	4.1	*	7.2	*	4.7	3.3	7.6	2.3
Sabaragamuwa	4.6	3.6	6.1	1.7	5.4	3.9	8	2.1

Source: DCS, Sri Lanka Labour Force Survey Annual Bulletin (2020, 2010).
* Cell sizes were too small to provide statistically significant estimates.

also high relative to men in the same age group while women's unemployment is highest among the youngest age group. Women's unemployment relative to men is also highest among the most educated group and in the Eastern, Northern, North Central and Northwestern provinces. High women's unemployment among those with GCE (advanced level) or higher is consistent with fewer wage employment opportunities for educated women.

Women's Employment in Sri Lanka: Trends and Patterns

In 2020, 2,626,146 women were employed, compared to 5,372,947 men. Sex-specific employment shares comprised 91.5% of the female labour force and 96% of the male labour force, respectively (DCS 2021). The main change observed in the last decade is that the share of women public sector employees has risen, relative to all women employed as well as relative to men in the public sector. The share of both male and female own account workers has risen, but women's own account workers' share has not increased as much as that of men. In contrast, while the percentage of contributing family workers has declined for both men and women, the relative decline for women has been modest.

Tables 12.4 and 12.5 reflect that there is both vertical and horizontal segregation in Sri Lanka's employment. The share of contributing family workers who are women is seven times as high as the share that is men; but just over one-fourth of senior positions as legislators, senior professionals

Table 12.4 Percentage distribution of the employed population by employment status and gender

	2010		F/M	2020		F/M
	Male	Female		Male	Female	
Employee – public sector	12.8	17.3	1.4	12.0	20.5	1.71
Employee – private sector	43.3	37	0.9	44.7	38.5	0.86
Employer	3.5	0.8	0.2	3.4	0.8	0.22
Own account worker	35.9	22.6	0.6	37.5	24.4	0.65
Contributing family worker	4.4	22.4	5.1	2.4	15.8	6.70

Source: DCS (2021), Annual Labour Force Survey Report 2020, p. 18; Department of Census and Statistics (2011) Sri Lanka Labour Force Survey Annual Report 2010 Colombo: p. 16

Table 12.5 Employed population by occupation and gender

Occupations	Shares in female total			Female as a share of total		
	2006	2010	2020	2006	2010	2020
Managers, senior officials and legislators	5.4	6.6	5.3	21.4[a]	23.7[a]	27
Professionals	9.2	10.4	12.9	61.1	61.9	64
Technical and associate professionals	4.9	4.9	9.2	34.1	32.0	34.9
Clerks and clerical support workers	5.3	5.5	6.3	20.3	44.5	54.2
Service and sales workers	8	7.8	8.2	38.8	32.0	28.5
Skilled agricultural, forestry and fishery workers	25	24.5	14.8	39.2	36.7	28.3
Craft and related trades workers	18.9	15.8	12.9	38.7	33.6	27.7
Plant and machine operators and assemblers	2.3	2	4.3	11.3	9.0	15.3
Elementary occupations	20.9	22.7	25.9	33.1	33.6	37
Armed force occupations	–	–	0.2[b]	–	–	11.8[b]
Unidentified	0.1	0.2	–	6.1	7.6	–
Total	100	100	100	35.1	33.4	32.8

[a] These figures relate to senior officials and legislators only.
[b] Figures to be treated with caution due to high coefficient of variation.
Source: DCS (2021), Annual Labour Force Survey Report 2020, p. 19; Annual Labour Force Survey Report 2010, p. 17.

and managers are held by women. Women are a majority in professional and clerical positions. They are over one-third of technicians and associate professionals, but also over one-third of elementary occupations (DCS 2021).

Within industries and firms, men dominate upper management jobs. For example, in export industries senior managers are 84% male and middle-level managers are 62% male, while women dominate operational grades. Among migrant workers, around 86% were housemaids, while 90% of those who have migrated for professional and middle-level jobs are men (Weeraratne 2014). There is evidence that gender segregation of jobs affects women's employment; women tend to work where other women work (Gunatilaka 2013; Samarakoon and Mayadunne 2018).

The gender distribution of employment in the informal sector is biased towards men. The share of informal employment in total employment for women is 61.7%, compared to the comparable figure for men which is 71.3%, which differs from the experience of women in many other countries (World Economic Forum 2021).

Agriculture

Women's role in agriculture is largely unrecognized and undervalued. There is a dearth of research in quantifying women's contribution to agriculture value chains and subsistence agriculture, and in estimating the losses of productivity and reduced economic gains as a result of gender inequality in agriculture (FAO 2018). Despite being engaged in a wide range of agricultural activities and a diversity of employment types, from contributing family workers to self-employed farmers and employees in agricultural companies, they are mainly seen as practising subsistence agriculture. Under the Married Women's Property Ordinance and the Matrimonial Rights and Inheritance Ordinance, men and women have equal ownership and inheritance rights to immovable property, yet only 16% of privately owned land belongs to women. Consequently, women do not have formal access to government-provided water, are not registered in agrarian service centres, and neither own agricultural machinery, nor engage in the rental market for agricultural machinery (FAO 2018).

Constrained by care work and social norms, women primary producers are at the lower end of the agricultural value chain and do not engage in trading or adding value to agricultural produce; as a result, they miss out on training and technology transfer. Women have fewer networks and less access to capital and are, therefore, less involved in commercial agriculture and medium-scale industries (FAO 2018). Gender norms in agriculture, however, vary by ethnicity and location. Prohibitive gender norms around involvement in agriculture were observed in the Muslim community in Ampara, but not among the Tamil community, nor among communities in Hambantota and Polonnaruwa. However, across regions, ethnic groups and religions, a set of widely accepted gender norms around motherhood and duties around social reproduction limited women's participation in agriculture (Gunawardana 2018).

Apparel Industry

About one-fourth of women's employment is in the industrial sector. Of this, the apparel industry plays the most significant role, providing direct and indirect employment to around 300,000 to 600,000 people, respectively, of whom 74% are women (Export Development Board 2017; Robertson et al 2020). Labour force survey data reveal that 764,447 women were employed in 2020 as sewing machine operators (my calculations using LFS 2020).

Employers are more amenable to hiring women because of their perceived better characteristics, such as being more 'manageable', 'flexible' and 'patient', consistent with patriarchal stereotypes of women as being nimble-fingered and docile (Elson and Pearson 1981; Madurawala 2009; Goger 2013). A study of socioemotional skills found that possessing courage increases the odds of paid employment for women in Sri Lanka, while having 'emotional stability' increases their earnings, and somewhat surprisingly, being a 'risk-taker' increases their odds of formal employment (King and Gunewardena 2022).[4] While automation poses a threat to the apparel industry, for instance, up to 90% of sewing operations can be automated, so far workforce numbers have not seen drastic reductions (Fernando et al 2020).

Key reasons for high turnover and labour shortages in the apparel industry include competition from other sectors, mobility issues for rural women and lack of adequate housing and childcare facilities. Moreover, negative social perceptions associated with working in garment factories and changing career aspirations and improved educational qualifications of young women's labour market decisions. also factor in (Lynch 2007; Goger 2013; Gunawardana 2014). Women's gender roles combined with inflexible work models contribute to this high turnover. Some firms provide on-site care centres, although this is not the norm.

Apparel wages are higher than agricultural wages in Sri Lanka, but lower than the economy-wide average and do not make up a living wage (Asia Floor Wage Alliance (2019) "Timeline of Revision: Asia Floor Wage 2017'. https://asia.floorwage.org/our-work/#tab-id-3; Ruwanpura 2022). However, when controlling for characteristics (generally younger, unmarried, less-educated women), working in apparel pays a premium compared to the economy average – even as it falls below the living wage (Robertson et al 2020; see also Asian Floor Wage Alliance 2019; Ruwanpura 2022). Nevertheless, being connected to the global market brings attendant risks. Working conditions in the apparel industry are not ideal although campaigns, such as the Garments without Guilt and Abhimani, have improved working conditions (Ruwanpura 2022).

Service Sector

Teaching professionals and associate professionals are a large proportion of women in the service sector, followed by clerks, sales workers, government social benefits officials and nursing professionals. Over 80% of primary and secondary school teachers, nursing professionals and over two-third of general office clerks are employed in the public sector, as are all government social benefits officials. Women employed as public sector employees in these professions account for approximately 20% of all women employees.

At the lower end of the earnings distribution are domestic and office cleaners and helpers, who account for 2% and 3%, respectively, of all women employees. Comparisons with living wage estimates and minimum wages indicate that domestic workers are paid less than the living wage, but more than the minimum wage despite their precarious work conditions (de Silva 2019). Domestic workers have been excluded from coverage under the minimum wages act of 2016 (de Silva 2019). Legal studies have recommended either that existing labour laws be expanded or amended to include domestic workers or that new legislation be drawn up to specifically include them (de Silva 2019).

Entrepreneurs and Micro-Businesses

The World Economic Forum's gender gap report (2021) indicates that only 26.1% of Sri Lanka's firms have female majority ownership, while the vast majority is male owned (73.9%). The Sri Lankan legal environment does not directly hinder women's entrepreneurship: under the law, a woman can sign a contract, register a business and open a bank account in the same way as a man, and there is no law that prohibits discrimination in access to credit based on gender (World Bank 2022). Yet, of all employed women, 24% are engaged in self-employment as own-account workers, while less than 1% are employers (DCS 2021). A study comparing own account workers with wage workers found that own account workers are older and have lower ability than wage workers on both schooling and tested ability. They also have a strong desire to maintain control of their environment (de Mel et al 2010). Among microenterprise owners, those owned by women were much less likely to add paid employees. These features suggest that many women are entrepreneurs out of 'necessity' rather than because of entrepreneurial ability.

Women microenterprise owners who received a capital grant in a randomized experiment had no returns to capital, compared to men in the same experiment who had large, sustained increases in income, with monthly profits of 9% (de Mel et al 2009). On exploring this issue further, the study found evidence consistent with more efficient outcomes among women enterprises when the enterprise owner has more decision-making power in the household or where the spouse is more cooperative with regard to the management of the enterprise. Re-analysis of the same Sri Lankan data within a household decision-making framework found a significant rise in household income for women entrepreneurs who received capital grants, suggesting that women frequently use their loans or grants to invest in enterprises that they do not own (Bernhardt et al 2019).

While many studies and policy and programmatic efforts have focused on inequality in the endowments of women entrepreneurs, such as skills, expertise and technology, structural barriers, such as social norms that impede networking and marketing as well as the provision of infrastructure are likely to be as or more important (Madurawala et al 2017). In an experiment involving business training provided to two samples of women entrepreneurs, it was found that training hastened entry among potential start-ups and increased profitability. However, neither training nor cash grants had any effect on profits, sales or capital stocks of existing businesses even though it changed business practices (de Mel, McKenzie and Woodruff 2014).

Successful women entrepreneurs appear to have psychological characteristics and entrepreneurial competencies that are similar to those of successful male entrepreneurs and less similar to unsuccessful women entrepreneurs (Ranasinghe 2012). In a study of socioemotional skills, it was found that extraversion increases earnings in self-employment for women relatively more than it does for men in Sri Lanka (King and Gunewardena 2022).

Unpaid Work, Carework and the Way Forward

Sri Lanka's patterns of women's employment and its low and stagnant FLFP have their roots in gender segregation, especially between paid and unpaid work. Sri Lanka's first National Time Use Survey, conducted in 2017, revealed a deep gender divide in both participation in SNA activities, where men vastly outnumbered women, and non-SNA activities, especially unpaid domestic services and unpaid caregiving services where women vastly outnumbered men (DCS 2020). On a given day, the average woman spends one hour and 54 minutes on food and meal preparation and one hour and six minutes on childcare and instruction, while the average man spends 12 minutes on each activity (DCS 2020).

The vast gender gap in time spent on unpaid domestic and care work underlies the gender gap in FLFP and leads to women selecting part-time or self-employment work that facilitates combining paid work with unpaid work, which in turn leads to poorly compensated jobs for women. It is also the source of work-family conflict among employed women, as documented in formal sector work environments (Kailasapathy and Metz 2012; Kailasapathy, Kraimer and Metz 2014). Added to this is the lack of state-supported care services. Most dual-earner couples rely on family networks to assist with unpaid and care work and many women of childbearing age are under pressure to quit their jobs because of the difficulty of balancing domestic and market work (Madurawala 2009; Kailasapathy and Metz 2012).

Increasing the social provision of care in Sri Lanka will remove a significant barrier to access to employment for women, thereby increasing LFP and the potential for economic growth. However, more importantly, it will redesign the social contract, such that just as the benefits of children's capabilities, which are a public good, are enjoyed by all, the costs of social reproduction will be borne not just by parents, and especially mothers, but by all who benefit from it.

Notes

1 Gunewardena and Perera (2022) use an input method, replacement cost approach with a specialist wage and several generalist wages. Valuing women's unpaid work at the minimum wage yields the lowest value of 8% of GDP, while valuing it at the generalist wage of a primary school teacher yields the highest value of 34% of GDP. Valuing it by a vector of specialist wages yields a value of 12% of GDP.
2 Vulnerable employment is defined as the sum of the employment status groups of own-account workers and contributing family workers (World Bank undated).
3 Sri Lanka's old-age dependency ratio is set to increase to 43% in 2050 (ADB 2019).
4 King and Gunewardena (2022) show that in 13 middle income countries, out of a set of ten socioemotional skills, the only skill that consistently showed a statistically significant difference between men and women was that of emotional stability. This supports previous work by Nelson (2015) that demonstrates that despite a popular perception that women are universally risk-averse, this is not the case.

References

Abayasekara, Ashani and Neluka Gunasekara (2019) "Determinants of Youth Not in Education, Employment or Training: Evidence from Sri Lanka" *Review of Development Economics* 23(4): 1840–1862

Adikaram, Arosha and Pavithra Kailasapathy (2020) "Handling Sexual Harassment Complaints in Sri Lanka: Fair Process and Best Practices" *South Asian Journal of Human Resources Management* 7(2): 293–314

Afridi, Farzana, Abhiroop Mukhopadhyay and Soham Sahoo (2016) "Female Labour Force Participation and Child Education in India: Evidence from the National Rural Employment Guarantee Scheme" *IZA Journal of Labor and Development* 5(7) https://doi.org/10.1186/s40175-016-0053-y

Asian Development Bank (2019) *Growing Old before Becoming Rich: Challenges of an Ageing Population in Sri Lanka* Manila: ADB

Bernhardt, Arielle, Erica Field, Rohini Pande and Natalia Rigol (2019) "Household Matters: Revisiting the Returns to Capital Among Female Microentrepreneurs" *American Economic Review: Insights* 1(2): 141–160

Chandrasiri, Sunil and Ramani Gunatilaka (2015) *The Skills Gap in Four Industrial Sectors in Sri Lanka* Colombo: International Labour Organization, ILO Country Office for Sri Lanka and the Maldives.

Cuberes, David and Marc Teignier (2016) "Aggregate Effects of Gender Gaps in the Labour Market: A Quantitative Estimate" *Journal of Human Capital* 10(1): 1–32

de Mel, Suresh, David McKenzie and Christopher Woodruff (2009) "Are Women More Credit Constrained? Experimental Evidence on Gender and Microenterprise Returns" *American Economic Journal: Applied Economics* 1(3): 1–32

de Mel, Suresh, David McKenzie and Christopher Woodruff (2010) "Who Are the Microenterprise Owners? Evidence from Sri Lanka on Tokman vs. De Soto" In *International Differences in Entrepreneurship* J. Lerner and A. Schoar (eds) Chicago: University of Chicago Press, pp 63–87

de Mel, Suresh, David McKenzie and Christopher Woodruff (2014) "Business Training and Female Enterprise Start-up, Growth, and Dynamics: Experimental Evidence from Sri Lanka" *Journal of Development Economics* 106: 199–210

Department of Census and Statistics (2011) *Sri Lanka Labour Force Survey Annual Report 2010* Colombo: DCS

Department of Census and Statistics (2020) *National Time Use Survey 2017 Report* Colombo: DCS

Department of Census and Statistics (2021) *Sri Lanka Labour Force Survey Annual Report 2020* Colombo: DCS

Department of Census and Statistics (undated) "Life Expectancy". Accessed on 07/06/2023. Available at http://www.statistics.gov.lk/Resource/en/Population/Vital_Statistics/LifeExpectancy.pdf

de Silva, Annemari (2019) *An Exploratory Study of Attitudes and Practices towards Domestic Workers in Sri Lanka* Colombo: International Centre for Ethnic Studies

de Silva, Rashmini (2020) *Start Calling Them Farmers* Colombo: Law and Society Trust

Elson, Diane and Ruth Pearson (1981) "'Nimble Fingers Make Cheap Workers': An Analysis of Women's Employment in Third World Export Manufacturing" *Feminist Review* 7: 87–107

Eswaran, Mukesh, Bharat Ramaswami and Wilma Wadhwa (2013) "Status, Caste, and the Time Allocation of Women in Rural India" *Economic Development and Cultural Change* 61(2): 311–333

Export Development Board (2017) *Industry Capability Report – Sri Lanka Apparel Sector.* Colombo: Export Development Board.

Fernando, Karin, Chandima Arambepola, Navam Niles and Anupama Ranawana (2020) *The opportunities and risks for achieving sustainable labour in a global value chain: A case study from Sri Lanka's apparel sector.* Occasional Paper Series No. 65. Southern Voice

Food and Agricultural Organisation FAO (2018) **Country Gender Assessment of Agriculture and the Rural Sector in Sri Lanka** Colombo: FAO

Goger, Annelies (2013) "From Disposable to Empowered: Rearticulating Labor in Sri Lankan Apparel Factories" **Environment and Planning A: Economy and Space** 45(11): 2628–2645

Gunatilaka, Ramani (2013) **Women's Participation in Sri Lanka's Labour Force: Trends, Drivers and Constraints** Colombo: International Labour Organization

Gunatilaka, Ramani and Sunil Chandrasiri (2021) **The Relative Demand for women's Labour in Sri Lanka's Formal Enterprises** Colombo: UN Women

Gunawardana, Samanthi (2014) "Reframing Employee Voice: A Case Study in Sri Lanka's Export Processing Zones" **Work, Employment and Society** 28(3): 452–468

Gunawardana, Samanthi (2018) **Rural Women's Livelihoods in Post-Conflict Sri Lanka Connections between Participation in Agriculture and Care Work Across the Life Course.** Research report. Melbourne: Monash University

Gunewardena, Dileni (2015) "Why Aren't Sri Lankan Women Translating Their Educational Gains into Workforce Advantages?" **The 2015 Echidna Global Scholars** Working Paper Washington: Brookings Institution Center for Universal Education

Gunewardena, Dileni, Darshi Abeyrathna, Amalie Ellagala, Kamani Rajakaruna and Shobana Rajendran (2009) "Glass Ceilings, Sticky Floors, or Sticky Doors? A Quantile Regression Approach to Exploring Gender Wage Gaps in Sri Lanka" In **Labor Markets and Economic Development** Ravi Kanbur and Jan Svejnar (eds) London: Routledge, pp 426–448

Gunewardena, Dileni and Ashvin Perera (2022) "Valuing unpaid care work in Sri Lanka using the National Time Use Survey 2017: first estimates" [paper presentation] *30th IAFFE Annual Conference.* Geneva, Switzerland (June 29–July 1)

Heath, Rachel and Seema Jayachandran (2017) "The Causes and Consequences of Increased Female Education and Labour Force Participation in Developing Countries" In **The Oxford Handbook of Women and the Economy** Susan Averett, Laura M. Argys and Saul D. Hoffman (eds) Oxford: Oxford University Press, pp 345–368

International Labour Organization (2016) **Factors Affecting women's Labour Force Participation in Sri Lanka** Colombo: ILO Country Office for Sri Lanka and the Maldives

International Monetary Fund (2018) **Sri Lanka: Selected Issues** IMF Staff Country Reports 176 Washington: IMF

Kailasapathy, Pavithra, Maria L. Kraimer and Isabel Metz (2014) "The Interactive Effects of Leader–Member Exchange, Gender and Spouse's Gender Role Orientation on Work Interference with Family Conflict" **The International Journal of Human Resource Management** 25(19): 2681–2701

Kailasapathy, Pavithra and Isabel Metz (2012) "Work-Family Conflict in Sri Lanka: Negotiations of Exchange Relationships in Family and at Work" **Journal of Social Issues** 68(4): 790–813

King, Elizabeth M. and Dileni Gunewardena (2022) **Human Capital and Gender Inequality in Middle-Income Countries Schooling, Learning and Socioemotional Skills in the Labour Market** London: Routledge

Kiribanda, B. (1997) "Population and Employment" In **Dilemmas of Development** W. D. Lakshman (ed) Colombo: Sri Lanka Economic Association, pp 223–249

Klasen, Stephan and Janneke Pieters (2015) "What Explains the Stagnation of Female Labour Force Participation in Urban India?" **World Bank Economic Review** 29(3): 449–478

Lynch, Caitrin (2007) **Juki Girls, Good Girls: Gender and Cultural Politics in Sri Lanka's Global Garment Industry** Ithaca: Cornell University Press

Madurawala, Sunimalee (2009) "Labour Force Participation of Women in Childbearing Ages" **Sri Lanka Journal of Population Studies** 11: 1–38

Madurawala, Sunimalee (2017) "Labour Force Participation by Women and Inclusive Growth" **South Asia Economic Journal** 18(2): 214–229

Madurawala, Sunimalee, Dilani Hirumuthugodage, Dharshani Premaratne and Janaka Wijayasiri (2017) *Women-Owned and Led Micro, Small Medium Enterprises in Spice and Coir Sectors of Sri Lanka: Constraints and Policy Options* Colombo: Institute of Policy Studies of Sri Lanka

Ministry of Youth Affairs and Skills Development (2014) *Youth and Development: Realizing the Millennium Development Goals (MDGS) for Sri Lankan Youth* Colombo: Ministry of Youth Affairs and Skills Development

Nelson, Julie (2015) "Are Women Really More Risk-Averse than Men? A Re-analysis of the Literature Using Expanded Methods" *Journal of Economic Issues* 29(3): 566–585

Ranasinghe, Seuwandhi (2012) "Factors Contributing to the Success of Women Entrepreneurs in Sri Lanka" *Sri Lanka Journal of Advanced Social Studies* 1–2: 85–110

Robertson, Raymond, Gladys Lopez-Acevedo and Yevgeniya Savchenko (2020) "Globalisation and the Gender Earnings Gap: Evidence from Sri Lanka and Cambodia" *The Journal of Development Studies* 56(2): 295–313

Ruwanpura, Kanchana (2022) *Garments without Guilt? Global Labour Justice and Ethical Codes in Sri Lankan Apparels* Cambridge: Cambridge University Press

Samarakoon, SJMNG and Geetha Mayadunne (2018) "An Exploratory Study on Low Labour Force Participation of Women in Sri Lanka" *Sri Lanka Journal of Social Sciences* 41(2): 137–151

Seneviratne, Prathi (2019) "Married Women's Labor Supply and Economic Development: Evidence from Sri Lankan Household Data" *Review of Development Economics* 23(2): 975–999

Seneviratne, Prathi (2020) "Gender Wage Inequality During Sri Lanka's Post-Reform Growth: A Distributional Analysis" *World Development* 129: 104878

Solotaroff, Jennifer, George Joseph, Anne Kuriakose and Jayati Sethi (2020) *Getting to Work Unlocking Women's Potential in Sri Lanka's Labor Force* Washington: World Bank

Verite Research (2018) *Youth Labour Market Assessment Sri Lanka* Colombo: Verite Research

Vodopivec, Milan and Nisha Arunatilake (2011) "Population Aging and Labour Market Participation of Old Workers in Sri Lanka" *Journal of Population Ageing* 4(3): 141–163

Weeraratne, Bilesha (2014) *Sri Lankan Female Domestic Workers: Does Recruitment through an Agent Minimize Vulnerability?* Labour Economic Series No. 18 Colombo: Institute of Policy Studies of Sri Lanka

World Bank (undated) *World Development Database*. Accessed on 07/06/2023. Available at https://databank.worldbank.org/metadataglossary/world-development-indicators/series/SL.EMP.VULN.ZS

World Bank (2022) *Women, Business and the Law 2022* Washington: The World Bank Group. Accessed on 07/06/2023. Available at https://wbl.worldbank.org/en/wbl

World Bank, Gender Statistics (2015–2021) *The World Bank Group*. Accessed on 07/06/2023. Available at https://databank.worldbank.org/source/gender-statistics

World Economic Forum (2021) *Global Gender Gap Report 2021* Geneva: World Economic Forum

World Economic Forum (2022) *Global Gender Gap Report 2022* Geneva: World Economic Forum

13
UNVEILING THE MARGINS

Women, Caste, Class, and Post-War Development in Sri Lanka's North and East

Narayani Sritharan

Introduction

In this chapter, I critically examine post-war development in Sri Lanka and its impact on the war-affected districts of the North and East. I pay serious attention to the implicit question in much of the literature: why the North and East of Sri Lanka remain underdeveloped and poor, despite the war ending more than a decade ago? I begin by comparing the economic growth of the North and East with the rest of Sri Lanka and discuss why post-war reconstruction efforts by the Government of Sri Lanka did little to improve the economic conditions of the North and East. By paying special attention to the experiences of women and caste-based communities in the region, I argue why a blanket approach that prioritised infrastructure development did not "trickle down" to the most marginalised groups in the region.

Sri Lanka was embroiled in a protracted ethnic and territorial conflict from 1983 to 2009, oscillating between conflict and war over the independence of Tamil homelands. Both major warring parties – the Liberation Tigers of Tamil Eelam (LTTE) and the state – adopted an ethno-nationalist stance, creating devastating social and gendered consequences for local communities (Tambiah 1992; Ismail and Jeganathan 1995; De Alwis 2002). All nine districts of the North and East were all affected by the war. They are Ampara, Batticaloa, Jaffna, Kilinochchi, Mannar, Mullaitivu, Puttalam, Trincomalee, and Vavuniya and consist of the Northern and Eastern Provinces (Figure 13.1).

Internal strife over horizontal inequality was a major cause of the Sri Lankan conflict with decreased access to education, employment opportunities, disparities in urban development, distribution of benefits, and political exclusion of Sri Lankan Tamils (Langer, Stewart and Venugopal 2012; Venugopal 2012; Stewart 2016). In May 2009 President Mahinda Rajapaksa, having rallied the support of the international society by capitalising on the "global war on terror", ruthlessly defeated the LTTE, with estimates placing around 40,000 civilians killed and 300,000 internally displaced or detained in camps during the last phase of the Sri Lankan conflict (UN 2011).

Despite this violent political backdrop, the Rajapaksa government approached post-war reconciliation through infrastructural development with help from international loans and donors. This approach to conflict resolution side-stepped the root causes of the ethnic conflict by ignoring the basis of the Tamil people's grievances requiring state reform (Thaheer, Peiris and Pathiraja

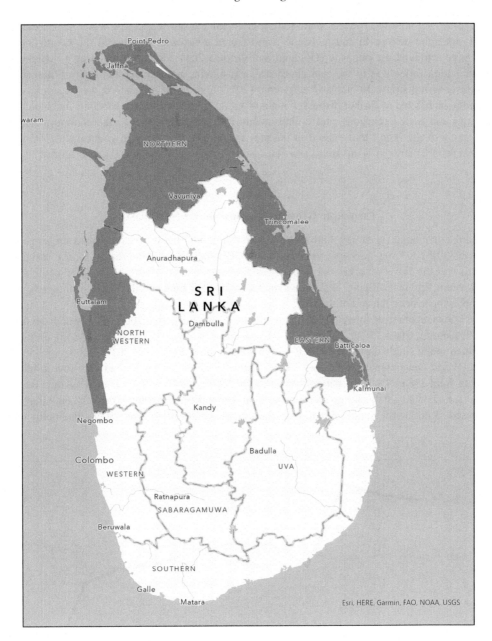

Figure 13.1 War-affected districts

2013; Venugopal 2018; Ruwanpura, Brown and Chan 2020). An important feature of post-conflict Sri Lanka was that the government, led by the Rajapaksa family, moved towards soft authoritarianism, becoming a nepotistic, nationalistic, and militarised state with little regard for minority grievances (Jazeel and Ruwanpura 2009; DeVotta, 2010; Wickramasinghe 2010).[1] It was a watershed moment for Sri Lanka to develop and strengthen democratic systems and institutions was critical; yet it moved towards semi-authoritarianism and state centrality. While reconstruction efforts intended to rebuild and reconcile war-affected areas with the rest of the country, they may have achieved the opposite (Höglund and Orjuela 2011). Reconstruction as a vehicle for reconciliation failed due to the centralised decision-making mechanism and high militarisation in the war-torn districts. In fact, as Kadirgamar (2017) argues, the reconstruction process in war-torn regions has led to further dispossession and social exclusion due to increased indebtedness, religious and caste exclusions, and falling incomes. Consequently, Sri Lanka continues to deal with many of the issues that existed in the pre-war period, such as high youth unemployment, Sinhala resettlements in Tamil areas, and new issues stemming from the end of the conflict.

Economic Growth: Nationwide viz Northeast

Sri Lanka maintained relatively high GDP growth throughout the war years. The average growth from 1983 to 2009 was 5.3% per year. Bastian (2013) suggests that the reason for the sustained growth was the focus on areas not affected by the war; in fact, 49.4% of the GDP came from the Western Province. Figure 13.2 shows the trends for Sri Lankan GDP growth, inflation, and unemployment since the end of the war.

Sri Lanka recorded an average 7.25% growth rate during the period 2009–2013, which declined to 2.8% during 2014–2020. The growth was negative from 2019 to 2020 (–3.6%). Inflation remained in the single digits from 2010 onwards but almost doubled in 2019/2020 from 3.5% to 6.1% (World Development Indicators 2022). Until the 1970s Sri Lanka had very low inflation, varying from 1% to 4%. This pattern has since changed notably, with an annual average rate of 8.5% during 1980–2015 and greater year-to-year variability thereafter. Currently, inflation has increased significantly, mainly due to high food prices (SOE 2019). The official unemployment

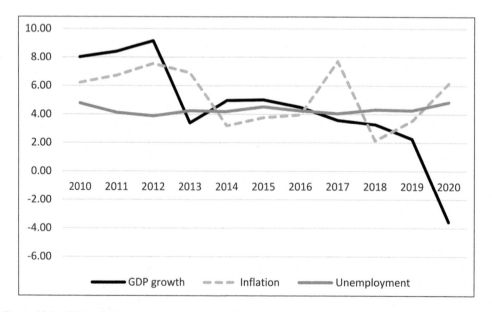

Figure 13.2 GDP, inflation, and the unemployment rate

rate steadily increased from 4.78% in 2010 to 4.84% in 2020. The Gini coefficient increased to 39.3 in 2015.

This Gini coefficient indicates widening inequality even as the country gained status as a middle-income country in 2010. Inequality was also reflected in Sri Lanka's public investment in education, which declined from approximately 2.3% of GDP during the years 2000–2010 to 1.8% of GDP in 2012 (Wickramasinghe 2014). Media freedom – an indicator of a robust democracy – was severely undermined during this time; according to the Reporters Without Borders Press Freedom Index, Sri Lanka dropped from place number 51 in 2002 to 127 out of 180 in 2021. The initial economic growth was caused by massive infrastructural investments and was funded by unsustainable loans from multiple lenders, including international sovereign bonds with China being Sri Lanka's biggest bilateral lender (Moramudali and Panduwawala 2022). In 2022, a combination of the COVID-19 pandemic, soaring global energy and food prices, and irresponsible tax cuts led the economy to collapse.

Initially, the Northeast experienced high growth, like the rest of the country; however, its economic growth slowed down more rapidly than in the rest of the country. The Northern Province's GDP growth rate went from 25.2% in 2012 to merely 4.1% in 2018 (Moramudali 2019). The author investigated the poverty headcount ratio in the country and found four districts with double-digit poverty headcount ratios; all of them were in Northern and Eastern provinces. In 2013, the Uva Province, located in south-central Sri Lanka and consistently considered one of the poorest provinces, recorded the highest poverty headcount ratio of 15.4%, while the Northern Province recorded 10.9% in 2016. However, the poverty headcount ratio for Uva Province subsequently declined to 6.5%, whereas in the Northern Province, the ratio only decreased to 7.7% (Moramudali 2019; Census of Population and Housing 2012).

Does the lack of growth in the Northern Province indicate that the state-driven infrastructure development failed to sustain momentum in the region? How can the discrepancies in development rates be explained? We need to understand the emphasis on infrastructure-led development to answer these questions. The next section describes the limitations of the infrastructural economic model in Sri Lanka since the end of the war.

Infrastructure and Post-War Development

Since 2010, under Rajapaksa's regime, the focus has been on infrastructure development and economic recovery in war-scarred regions of the country. More specifically, the Rajapaksa government developed a "Sri Lankan model" involving a combination of humanitarian action, resettlement, and reconstruction (Goodhand 2010). Post-war economic development in the entire country was driven by massive infrastructural development projects, such as highways, an international airport, a harbour in Hambantota, and Colombo beautification (Sarvananthan 2013; Thaheer, Peiris and Pathiraja 2013; Perera 2014, 2015; Fuglerud 2017; Chan, Ruwanpura and Brown 2019). In the Eastern and Northern Provinces, an international sports stadium in the Kilinochchi district and Magampura Mahinda Rajapaksa Port in the Vanni demonstrate this obsession.

The central issue with a blanket approach to economic development was that the projects did not match the specific circumstances and priorities of local populations (Thaheer et al 2013). One of the enduring challenges is how to tap into and optimise available local resources, including the unemployed, as well as land and sea resources, in developing locally sensitive industries. For instance, there are two primary sources of livelihood in the North: agriculture and fisheries. Agriculture suffers from crop failures and high fluctuations in market prices, while fisheries suffer from Indian trawlers roaming the Sri Lankan waters and destroying the Jaffna fishers' nets, limiting them to shallow waters (Kadirgamar 2017). The Jaffna district provided 20–25% of the total fish production in Sri Lanka before 1983, which had reduced to 3–5% with the end of the war (Thaheer et al 2013). These essential economic issues were regrettably not prioritised by the centrally controlled post-war economic recovery programme. In addition to the economic challenges, issues, such as family and community breakup, alcoholism, trauma, debt burden, ethnic resentments, and caste and gender disparities continue to mediate recovery and reconciliation and livelihood development in general; and yet remain unaddressed (Silva et al., 2018).

Promoting economic development in place of a political solution to the ethnic conflict meant that addressing the grievances of the Tamil people was very low on the political agenda, especially in the Northern provinces. The Rajapaksa regime's priority was to reintegrate Tamils into Sri Lankan society through the spill-over benefits of economic and infrastructural development (Uyangoda 2011; Ruwanpura 2016; see also Lingham 2023, this volume). However, state-sponsored infrastructure projects were contracted to large foreign companies and local companies based in the Western Province that did not utilise human resources from the North and East. Chinese-based companies even imported Chinese labour, while road construction sites in the Northeast contracted workers mostly from the South (Thaheer et al 2013). Hence, the anticipated trickle-down effect on the local people in the Eastern and Northern Provinces regarding employment and profit generation was limited (Sarvananthan 2016).

The Rajapaksa government had, from the beginning, been sceptical of the ethnic dimensions of the conflict. Rather than acknowledge the grievances of the historically marginalised Tamil people of the North and East, it chose to view the conflict as a terrorist threat fuelled by regional underdevelopment. As a result, the regime was resistant to recognising, engaging with, or addressing Tamil grievances through state reforms and mechanisms of accountability. Instead, the government sought to use fast-tracked economic and infrastructure development in the Northeast to win the support of the Tamils and undermine the appeal of ethnic Tamil politics (Venugopal 2018).

After the war ended, infrastructure growth was deemed necessary for economic recovery. However, the relative lack of investment in creating livelihoods has led to joblessness in the post-war period (Kadirgamar 2017). Moreover, infrastructure development has had no impact on livelihood development in the North and East; nor has it addressed the well-being of citizens, namely access to education, quality of education, the care of children, and access to socio-economic opportunities (Thaheer et al 2013; Silva et al 2018).

Another reason for this lack of trickle-down effect is the lack of competent political leaders (Kadirgamar 2017). For example, when I travelled to Vanni in 2017 – one of the most affected areas by the war – I spoke with women who continued to live in houses destroyed by the conflict. They explained that the central government allocated (and continues to allocate) resources to the Northern Province following the end of the war; however, according to them, politicians were unqualified to utilise the budget for job creation, education, or other rebuilding programmes. Therefore, most of the monies were sent back to the Central Government every year. Whether this is true or not is less important than the fact that this is what they *believed* about the allocation of resources in Sri Lanka and the capacity of their own politicians. Their point was corroborated by an activist from Jaffna, who commented that immediately after the first election in the Northern Province for the Northern Province Council (NPC) in 2013, there was a substantial discussion of the NPC's failure to utilise the funds provided to them. As a result, approximately 40% of the funds were sent back to the central government (Sritharan 2022). Thaheer et al (2013) describe how surveyed communities in the conflict-affected areas had similar perceptions of their local politicians and government.

Unveiling the Margins

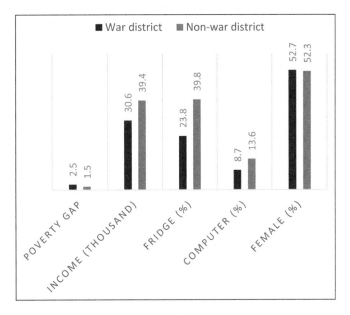

Figure 13.3 Average economic indicators for war and non-war districts, 2009/2010 and 2012/2013

The impact of uneven resource allocation is indicated in Figure 13.3. I compare selected economic indicators for war districts and non-war districts to highlight the economic disenfranchisement of the war-torn districts. The cursory evidence suggests that in conflict-affected districts the poverty gap is higher than in districts not directly affected by war, i.e., poverty levels are more severe, the income levels are lower, and there are fewer percentages of households owning computers and fridges (both of which could be considered non-conventional wealth indicators).[2] There are also more women in the Northeast than in the rest of the country, albeit marginally; reflecting the persistence of women-headed households (Ruwanpura 2004; Lingham, this volume), which I will discuss in detail in the following section.

Women in the Northeast

Although Sri Lanka's population grew from 14,846,274 to 20,277,597 between 1981 and 2012, the population of the Jaffna District fell from 734,474 to 583,071 (Census and Statistics 2012). Compared to a national 1% average annual population growth, the Jaffna district experienced an average annual population decline of 0.74%. This drop in population can be explained by the mass migration of the Tamil community from Sri Lanka. The Tamil diaspora in the West is estimated to be 800,000, with an additional 200,000 people living as refugees in India (Kadirgamar 2017).

The most recent Household and Income Expenditure Survey (2012/2013) indicates that as many as 25% of Sri Lankan households are women headed. Godamunne (2019) finds that the figure is disproportionately higher in the North and East (see also Ruwanpura 2004). According to Sarvananthan (2015), the higher share of women in Jaffna is due to mass migration, (mostly male) disappearances, and war deaths. In fact, UNFPA (2015) found that 90,000 women were left widowed in the North and East due to the war.

In addition to many women being widowed or having their husbands disappear, they also suffer from substantial indebtedness. In the late 1990s, NGOs in Sri Lanka started addressing women's livelihood needs through microfinance. Following the war, the financial sector expanded to include Central Bank-registered banks and new unregulated companies. This led to a substantial microfinance debt crisis, especially in the Northern Province (Kadirgamar and Kadirgamar 2018, 2019; Moramudali 2019). The microfinance loans had effective annual interest rates ranging from 40% to 220%. These massive interest rates created a debt trap where people (particularly women) had to take out new loans from informal lenders to pay back microfinance loans (see de Silva and Wedagedara, this volume). This situation became so dire that in 2019 the Central Bank imposed an interest rate cap of 35% on microfinance loans. According to the Sri Lankan Department of Census and Statistics, the district with the highest percentage of the population in debt was Vavuniya in the Northern Province. In 2016 the district Vavuniya had a population of 80.8% who were indebted. Comparably, the Colombo district only has 51.3% of the population indebted.

In recent years, deep-rooted institutional and socio-cultural barriers to women's upward economic, political, and social mobility persist. For instance, women in the Eastern and Northern Provinces were constrained from realising the benefits of the short-lived post-conflict economic boom. Conservative cultural mores constrain women from actively participating in the formal labour market due to care responsibilities within the family and gendered religious responsibilities, such as administering prayers for the family at the temples. Moreover, women also had security concerns about travelling far from home to work due to high militarisation in the war-affected districts (Thaheer et al 2013; Sarvananthan 2015).

The Eastern Province has the lowest women's labour force participation of the nine provinces in Sri Lanka, followed by the Northern Province, partly due to the direct impact of the war (UNFPA 2015). Furthermore, in 2012 the Northern Province had three districts with the highest women's unemployment rates: Kilinochchi (29.4%), Mannar (21.6%), and Mullaithivu (20.5%). In the other North and East districts, unemployment rates among women were over 10% in 2012. In contrast, unemployment rates among men in the North and East were less than 4% (Sarvananthan 2015: 22–23).

When a group of Jaffna women was asked why they think there is high female unemployment during an open forum in 2011, they identified the following causes: (i) preference for public sector employment; (ii) low-quality knowledge and life skills taught at all educational levels; (iii) caste-based occupational structure; and (iv) the negative impact of foreign remittances (see Sarvananthan 2011 for more).

Class and Caste in the Northeast

Even though the war significantly changed the caste composition, caste continues to divide people in the North and East. The Tamil (and Sinhala) caste system and how it structures access to the economy is severely understudied with limited research regarding the political economy of caste limited to the district of Jaffna. Since the East has a large Muslim population and a higher proportion of Sinhalese people, the caste dynamics differ from Jaffna, which is largely Tamil (see McGilvray 2008). In this section, I provide a historical overview of the caste structure in the North and the impact of the caste-class dynamics.

Class and caste are historically intertwined in Jaffna. While often compared to and conflated with class, a more supple term applies to socioeconomic status, the primary requirement that dictates caste remains relatively rigid and static. Like class hierarchy, the caste system is tied to the division of labour through hereditary occupation (Kuganathan 2022). Although Hinduism is seen as the main purveyor of the caste system whose religious texts sanction systemic inequity and inequality, caste is integral to all communities in Sri Lanka and South Asia, including Christians and Buddhists (Krishan 1998; Mahroof 2000; McDermott 2016).

One major reason for caste and class to be collapsed into a single category is that caste in the North and East of Sri Lanka has actively evaded politicisation. In fact, the mere discussion of caste is taboo (Kuganathan 2014). Particularly disturbing are the institutional efforts that go into caste censorship. For example, Silva et al (2018: 20) report that the University of Jaffna discourages any research on caste. Unlike India's caste system, caste in Sri Lanka is undocumented by the state and remains hidden; yet caste dynamics are salient, particularly in the Tamil-speaking North (Kuganathan 2022).

The caste structure of Jaffna society consists of roughly 20 castes, with the Vellalar caste historically accounting for nearly 50% of the total Tamil population in the region as the undisputed dominant caste controlling land ownership, agriculture, leadership positions, and white-collar employment in colonial and post-colonial settings (see Table 13.1). Brahmins and Saiva Kurukkals are ritually superior to Vellalars, but they are often employed by Vellalar temple trustees, making them economically subordinate to the dominant caste. Except for Karaiyars, Mukkuvars, and possibly Kukkuvars, who were largely self-employed and economically independent, all the other castes historically served hereditary patron families of the dominant caste. The Panchamar castes are identical to Dalits in the Indian context as they are considered untouchable, hence the fifth caste following the Indian model. Except in a few instances, the term "Dalit" is not used for self-identification or as an analytical category in caste research in Jaffna or anywhere else in Sri Lanka. In addition to the term Panchamar, the terms "depressed castes", "depressed classes", or "minority

Table 13.1 Castes in Jaffna Peninsula, 1982

Caste name in Tamil English	*Rendering caste occupation*	*As a % of total Tamil population*
Piraman	Brahmin temple priest	0.7
Saiva Kurukkal	Saiva priest/Priests in non-Brahmin temples	
Vellalar	Land owning caste/Landlord, farmer	50
Pantaram	Garland maker/Temple helper	
Sipacari	Craftsman/Temple sculptor	
Koviar	Domestic worker for Vellalar	7
Thattar	Goldsmith	0.6
Karaiyar	Deep sea fisherman	10
Thachchar	Carpenter/Wood work, roof maker	2
Rollar	Iron work/Blacksmith	
Nattuvar	Musician/Auspicious music	
Kalkular	Weaver/Cantar Oil maker/Sesame oil maker	
Kukkuvar	Potter	
Mukkuvar	Lagoon fisher	
PANCHAMAR CATEGORY		
Vannar	Dhoby	1–5
Ampattar	Barber	0.9
Pallar	Manual worker/Bonded labour	9
Nalavar	Toddy tapper/Toddy tapper and farm worker	9
Paraiyar	Drummer/Funeral Drummer	27

Source: Adapted from de Silva, Sivapragasam and Thanges (2009).

Tamils" have been used to refer to them in scholarly and media discourse (Silva 2020). Vellalars are not only the dominant caste in society but also the social and political elite with property ownership, high levels of education, professional employment, control over temples, and Tamil politics before and since the end of the war. They also had a tight grip over the Panchamars in securing their hereditary caste services, including ritual duties and agricultural labour in farming activities (Silva 2020).

The interethnic war between the LTTE and the various successive Sinhalese government regimes brought about a rupture in intra-Tamil social relations, specifically regarding Vellalar caste dominance. With the rise of Tamil militancy under the leadership of LTTE founder Velupillai Prabhakaran (1954–2009), we saw for the first time a non-Vellalar figure at the wheel of Tamil nationalism (Kuganathan 2022). War and militancy, through the social policy on caste implemented by the LTTE, dramatically modified inter-caste interaction and eliminated overt forms of caste discrimination, enabling some Panchamar castes to escape their previously constrained positions of suppression.

Thiranagama (2018) argues that war profoundly changed the caste composition in the Northeast. There was huge recruitment of the Panchamar castes into the LTTE, many of whom became "martyrs". Massive internal displacement led to the breakdown of caste rules in refugee camps. There were, however, many inter-caste marriages during the war, partly because the living conditions during the war meant greater inter-caste interactions. Parents also allowed children to marry young as married children were not targets for LTTE recruitment. Thiranagama (2018) finds that after the end of the war, many disputes about wartime inter-caste marriages have resurfaced.

Silva's (2020) study of caste blindness that investigates the lingering problem of the IDP population illuminates how caste hierarchy exacerbates the disenfranchisement of oppressed castes in the Northeast. Whereas many of the caste groups had been resettled, a disproportionate percentage of Panchamar people continue to be displaced. This was because historically they had lived on lands in-between Vellalar and Karaiyar settlements and had fragile land rights. These were also the land spaces often acquired by the Sri Lankan security forces to establish high-security zones. Thus, this lower-ranking caste group was more vulnerable to displacements during the war (Pfaffenberger 1982; Räsänen Jeeweshwara 2015). Secondly, the study finds that due to the caste policies and the position of the Panchamar caste in the LTTE, the Panchamar communities became amalgamated, which meant they may have been the targets of anti-LTTE operations during and after the war. Unlike the richer Vellalars who used their own resources and contacts to move to safety, with limited resources at their disposal, the lowest castes relied on their own communities to cope (Thaheer et al 2013). Silva (2020) also uncovers that the Panchamar IDP had become a political token in the power struggle between nationalistic Tamil political parties and the GOSL. Tamil political parties became the quintessential victims of discrimination by the Sinhala State to be showcased.

The educated Vellalar Tamils were traditionally external migrants, who used their extended socioeconomic and educational networks to move out of Sri Lanka. Following the onset of the war in the early 1980s, there was a massive expansion of asylum-seeking migration that resulted in less elite groups leaving the North for overseas destinations (Thiranagama 2014). Nevertheless, migrant destinations were coded. France, Germany, and Norway have greater proportions of non-Vellalars than English-speaking destinations, which are "preferred" by the Vellalar caste. Regardless, chain migration to these destinations continued along caste and kinship lines and often excluded those from the lower caste groups. Those who were unable to leave were also the ones who died due to military recruitment (Thanges Paramsothy 2008). The thousands who died in the last battles between the LTTE and the Sri Lankan state in 2009 were disproportionately those from underprivileged and oppressed castes who had ended up trapped in the Vanni. Most of the Tamil diaspora population comprises an overwhelming majority of the Vellalar (Daniel and Thangaraj 1995; McDowell 1996, 1999). This has changed the traditional demographic proportion of Jaffna and made the Vellalar one of the minorities.

While the LTTE did not eradicate the caste system or eliminate caste discrimination, some social policy initiatives and implementations abolished certain controversial practices and reduced overt caste discrimination in areas under their control (Silva et al 2009). Many of these modifications have carried over into this post-war period, such as the interruption in caste naming as verbal abuse and the transition to a mercantile system of business wherein certain oppressed castes no longer perform their labour at the homes of the dominant caste. However, Kuganathan (2022) shows how various discriminatory practices have resurfaced concerning contemporary temple worship, such as restricting castes from entry at certain rural *kovils* (Hindu temples), perhaps because caste-based discriminatory practices are no longer monitored and policed after the elimination of the LTTE. Overall, however, the war may have reinforced long-term caste inequalities, making different castes vulnerable to the mass displacements, immiseration, and political turmoil of the last 30 years.

Nevertheless, Vellalar domination has consistently remained in Tamil nationalist politics. For instance, Paramsothy (2015) describes how not a single person from an oppressed caste group became a member of the parliament following the parliamentary election in August 2015, even though seven members of parliament from the Jaffna electoral division were selected as qualified members. Additionally, only two people from the Pallar caste out of 38 members became members of the Northern Provincial Council in the election held in September 2013. Hence, even though the oppressed caste groups are higher in numbers now in Jaffna than they ever have, and despite their ability to mobilise themselves upwardly in socioeconomic and educational domains, they are time and again failing to utilise their social capital in their political participation apart from voting for the Vellalar candidates (Paramsothy 2015). This has meant that even as the war changed caste dynamics, the Vellalars remain in political and economic power, leading to the continued exclusion of lower castes from employment, education, and political opportunities (Kadirgamar 2017).

Conclusion

Following the end of the war in Sri Lanka, the entire country witnessed high economic growth, mostly driven by large infrastructural development on large-scale borrowings. The Northeast of the country, which was subject to destruction, displacements, and a controlled economy by the LTTE, also saw an initial boost in their local economies after the war ended. However, the economic growth in those areas could not be sustained for very long. As a result, the families in the Northeast felt less of the economic impact of the reconstruction and felt ostracised from the development process because they were not included in the labour force or considered for any employment opportunities in their homelands. The fisheries and the important agricultural industries in the region were neglected. Nonetheless, the government's infrastructure development drive was recognised and commended. Rather than reconciliation, the post-war development process has bred suspicion because the resettled Tamil people continue to feel marginal to the central government and excluded from the economic and political spheres of power (Thaheer et al 2013).

The war disrupted communities and left many women-headed households in heavily militarised areas with low little access to livelihoods and employment opportunities. These women struggle to make ends meet and face a massive microfinance debt crisis with predatory interest rates (see also de Silva and Wedagedara, this volume). Furthermore, the continued disenfranchisements of lower-ranking caste groups make social mobility even more complicated. They are nevertheless struggling to have a political impact in the Northeast even though they currently outnumber the traditional elite caste. The communities, which once knew how to be together, struggle with how to relate and engage with each other across caste and religion, leading to exclusion from economic opportunities.

Notes

1 In 2022 the country witnessed protests against the Rajapaksa regime that has united people across class and ethnicities.
2 The poverty gap is the ratio by which the mean income of the poor falls below the poverty line. The poverty line is defined as half the median household income of the total population.

References

Bastian, Sunil (2013) *The Political Economy of Post War Sri Lanka* Colombo: International Centre for Ethnic Studies

Chan, Loritta, Kanchana N Ruwanpura and Benjamin Brown (2019) "Environmental Neglect: Other Casualties of Post-War Infrastructure Development" *Geoforum* 105: 63–66

Daniel, Valentine E., and Yuvaraj Thangaraj (1995) "Forms, Formations, and Transformations of the Tamil Refugee' In *Mistrusting Refugees*, E. Valentine Daniel and John Chr. Knudsen (eds) Berkeley: University of California Press, pp 225–256

De Alwis, Malathi (2002) "The Changing Role of Women in Sri Lankan Society" *Social Research: An International Quarterly* 69(3): 675–691

Department of Census and Statistics Sri Lanka (2012) "Census of Population and Housing 2012-Sri Lanka" https://catalog.lib.uchicago.edu/vufind/Record/11400830

Department of Census and Statistics of Sri Lanka (DCS) (2015) "Household Income and Expenditure Survey, 2012/2013 Final Report"

DeVotta, Neil (2010) "From Civil War to Soft Authoritarianism: Sri Lanka in Comparative Perspective" *Global Change, Peace and Security* 22(3): 331–343

Fuglerud, Ø. (2017) "Manifesting Sri Lankan Megalomania: The Rajapakses' Vision of Empire and of a Clean Colombo" *Urban Utopias* Berlin: Springer, pp 119–138

Godamunne, Nayana (2019) *Understanding Women's Livelihood Outcomes and Economic Empowerment in the Eastern Province of Sri Lanka*. Working Papers. Colombo: ICES. Accessed on 9/12/2022. Available at https://ices.lk/publications/understanding-womens-livelihood-outcomes-and-economic-empowerment-in-the-eastern-province-of-sri-lanka/

Goodhand, Jonathan (2010) "Stabilising a Victor's Peace? Humanitarian Action and Reconstruction in Eastern Sri Lanka" *Disasters* 34: S342–S367

Höglund, K. and Camilla Orjuela (2011) "Winning the Peace: Conflict Prevention after a Victor's Peace in Sri Lanka" *Contemporary Social Science* 6(1): 19–37

Ismail, Qadri M. and Pradeep Jeganathan (1995) *Unmaking the Nation: The Politics of Identity and History in Modern Sri Lanka* Colombo: SSA

Jazeel, Tariq and Kanchana N. Ruwanpura (2009) "Dissent: Sri Lanka's New Minority?" *Political Geography* 28(7): 385–387

Jeeweshwara, Räsänen B. (2015) *Caste and Nation-Building: Constructing Vellalah Identity in Jaffna*. Unpublished Dissertation. Gothenburg: University of Gothenburg. Accessed on 25/04/2023

Kadirgamar, Ahilan (2017) *The Failure of Post-War Reconstruction in Jaffna, Sri Lanka: Indebtedness, Caste Exclusion and the Search for Alternatives*. Unpublished PhD Dissertation. New York: City University of New York

Kadirgamar, Ahilan and Niyanthini Kadirgamar (2018) "Reserves for Emancipatory Politics in Post-War Northern Sri Lanka" ERPI Conference Paper. The Hague: International Institute of Social Studies (ISS)

Kadirgamar, Ahilan and Niyanthini Kadirgamar (2019) "Microfinance has been a Nightmare for the global south. Sri Lanka shows that there is an alternative" *Open Democracy* (5 September). https://www.opendemocracy.net/en/oureconomy/microfinance-has-been-nightmare-global-south-sri-lanka-shows-there-alternative/

Krishan, Y. (1998) "Buddhism and Caste System" *East and West* 48(1/2): 41–55

Kuganathan, P. (2014) "Social Stratification in Jaffna: A Survey of Recent Research on Caste" *Sociology Compass* 8(1): 78–88

Kuganathan, P. (2022) "Of Tigers and Temples: The Jaffna Caste System in Transition During the Sri Lankan Civil War" In *Sociology of South Asia: Post-Colonial Legacies, Global Imaginaries* Berlin: Springer, pp 235–265

Langer, Arnim, Frances Stewart and Rajesh Venugopal (2012) "Horizontal Inequalities and Post-Conflict Development: Laying the Foundations for Durable Peace" In *Horizontal Inequalities and Post-conflict Development* Arnim Langer, Rajesh Stewart and Venugopal (eds) Berlin: Springer, pp 1–27

Mahroof, M.M.M. (2000) "A Conspectus of Tamil Caste Systems in Sri Lanka: Away from a Parataxis" *Social Scientist* 28(11/12): 40–59

McDermott, Rachel F. (2016) "From Hinduism to Christianity, from India to New York: Bondage and Exodus Experiences in the Lives of Indian Dalit Christians in the Diaspora 1" In *South Asian Christian Diaspora* Knut A Jacobsen and Selva J Raj (eds) Oxford: Routledge, pp 223–248

McDowell, Christopher (1996) *A Tamil Asylum Diaspora: Sri Lankan Migration, Settlement and Politics in Switzerland* Oxford: Berghahn Books

McDowell, Christopher (1999) "The Point of No Return: The Politics of the Swiss Tamil Repatriation Agreement" In *The End of the Refugee Cycle. Refugee Repatriation and Reconstruction* Richard Black and Khalid Kossler (eds) Oxford: Berghan Books, pp 126–141

McGilvray, Denis B. (2008) *Crucible of Conflict: Tamil and Muslim Society on the East Coast of Sri Lanka* Durham: Duke University Press

Moramudali, Umesh (2019) "Sri Lanka: After the Crisis, What Next? The Immediate Political Crisis Is Over, but the Underlying Fire Is Still Smoldering" *The Diplomat* (7 January)

Moramudali, Umesh and Thilana Panduwawala (2022) *Evolution of Chinese Lending to Sri Lanka Since the mid-2000s-Separating Myth from Reality* SAIS-CARI Briefing Paper No. 8. November 2022

Paramsothy, Thanges (2015) "Political Participation Of Oppressed Castes & The Need For a Progressive Political Tamil Nationalism" *Colombo Telegraph* (5 November). Accessed on 9/12/2022. Available at https://www.colombotelegraph.com/index.php/political-participation-of-oppressed-castes-the-need-for-a-progressive-political-tamil-nationalism/

Perera, Iromi (2014) *Forced Evictions in Colombo: The Ugly Price of Beautification* Colombo, Sri Lanka: Centre for Policy Alternatives. Accessed on 9/12/2022. Available at https://www.cpalanka.org/forced-evictions-in-colombo-the-ugly-price-of-beautification/

Perera, Iromi (2015) *Forced Evictions in Colombo: High-Rise Living* Colombo: Centre for Policy Alternatives. Accessed on 9/12/2022. Available at https://www.cpalanka.org/forced-evictions-in-colombo-high-rise-living/

Pfaffenberger, Bryan (no date) "Caste in Tamil culture: The religious foundations of sudra domination in Tamil Sri Lanka" [Preprint]. Accessed on 25/4/2023. Available at https://cir.nii.ac.jp/crid/1130282268976548480

Pfaffenberger, Bryan (1982) "Caste in Tamil Culture: The Religious Foundations of Sudra Domination in Tamil Sri Lanka" (No Title)

Ruwanpura, Kanchana N. (2004) "Female-Headship among Muslims in Eastern Sri Lanka: A Case of Changing Household Structures?" *Nivedini: A Journal of Gender Studies* 11(x): 1–22

Ruwanpura, Kanchana N. (2016) "Post-War Sri Lanka: State, Capital and Labour, and the Politics of Reconciliation" *Contemporary South Asia: Special Issue on Post-War Sri Lanka: State, Capital, Labour and the Politics of Reconciliation* 24(4): 351–359

Ruwanpura, Kanchana N., Benjamin Brown and Loritta Chan (2020) "(Dis)-connecting Colombo: Situating the Megapolis in Postwar Sri Lanka" *The Professional Geographer* 72(1): 165–179

Sarvananthan, M. (2011) "Sri Lanka: Putting Entrepreneurship at the Heart of Economic Revival in the North, East, and Beyond" *Contemporary South Asia* 19(2): 205–213

Sarvananthan, M. (2013) "Myth of 'No More Minorities': Results of Elections in North and East Sri Lanka" *Economic and Political Weekly*, pp 22–24

Sarvananthan, M. (2015) "Impediments to Women in Post-Civil War Economic Growth in Sri Lanka" *South Asian Journal of Human Resources Management* 2(1): 12–36

Sarvananthan, M. (2016) "Elusive Economic Peace Dividend in Sri Lanka: All That Glitters Is Not Gold" *GeoJournal* 81(4): 571–596

Silva, Kalinga T. (2020) "Nationalism, Caste-Blindness, and the Continuing Problems of War-Displaced Panchamars in Post-War Jaffna Society" *CASTE: A Global Journal on Social Exclusion* 1(1): 51–70

Silva, Kalinga Tudor, M. G. M. Razaak, Dhammika Herath, and Ramila Usoof-Thowfeek. (2018) "Post-war livelihood trends in northern and eastern Sri-Lanka." (2018). https://archive.nyu.edu/bitstream/2451/44167/2/Post-War-Livelihood.pdf

Silva, Kalinga T., M.G.M. Razaak, Dhammika Herath, Ramila Usoof-Thowfeek, S. Sivakanthan and Vikneswaran Kunanayaham (2018) *Post-War Livelihood Trends in Northern and Eastern Sri-Lanka* Background Paper 5. Colombo: ICES and World Bank Group

Silva, Kalinga T., P.P. Sivapragasam and P. Thanges (2009) *Casteless or Caste-Blind?: Dynamics of Concealed Caste Discrimination, Social Exclusion, and Protest in Sri Lanka* Copenhagen: International Dalit Solidarity Network

Sritharan, Narayani (2022) *The Role of Aid on Peace Consolidation in Post-War Sri Lanka* Economics Department Working Paper Series 333 Amherst: University of Massachusetts-Amherst

Stewart, Frances (2016) *Horizontal Inequalities and Conflict: Understanding Group Violence in Multiethnic Societies* Berlin: Springer

Tambiah, Stanley J. (1992) *Buddhism Betrayed? Religion, Politics, and Violence in Sri Lanka* Chicago: University of Chicago Press

Thaheer, Meena, Pradeep Peiris and Kasun Pathiraja (2013) *Reconciliation in Sri Lanka: Voices from Former War Zones* Colombo: International Centre for Ethnic Studies

Thiranagama, Sharika (2014) "Making Tigers from Tamils: Long-Distance Nationalism and Sri Lankan Tamils in Toronto" *American Anthropologist* 116(2): 265–278

Thiranagama, Sharika (2018) "The Civility of Strangers? Caste, Ethnicity, and Living together in Postwar Jaffna, Sri Lanka" *Anthropological Theory* 18(2–3): 357–381

UN (2011) *Report of the Secretary-General's Panel of Experts on Accountability in Sri Lanka: UN Documents: Security Council Report*. Accessed on 9/12/2022. Available at https://www.securitycouncilreport.org/un-documents/document/poc-rep-on-account-in-sri-lanka.php

UNFPA (2015) *Mapping of Socio-Economic Support Services to Female Headed Households in the Northern Province of Sri Lanka.* Accessed on 9/12/2022. Available at: https://srilanka.unfpa.org/en/publications/mapping-socio-economic-support-services-female-headed-households-northern-province-sri

Uyangoda, Jayadeva (2011) "Sri Lanka in 2010: Regime Consolidation in a Post-Civil War Era" *Asian Survey* 51(1): 131–137

Venugopal, Rajesh (2012) "Privatization, Private-Sector Development and Horizontal Inequalities in Post-Conflict Countries" In *Horizontal Inequalities and Post-Conflict Development* Arnim Lager, Frances Stewart and Rajesh Venugopal (eds) Berlin: Springer, pp 108–130

Venugopal, Rajesh (2018) *Nationalism, Development and Ethnic Conflict in Sri Lanka* Cambridge: Cambridge University Press

Weerakoon, Dushni, Harini Weerasekera and Kithmin Hewage. *Sri Lanka State of the Economy (SOE) 2019* Colombo: Institute of Policy Studies of Sri Lanka

Wickramasinghe, Nira (2010) "In Sri Lanka, the Triumph of Vulgar Patriotism" *Current History* 109(726): 158

Wickramasinghe, Nira (2014) "Sri Lanka in 2013: Post-War Oppressive Stability" *Asian Survey* 54(1): 199–205

World Bank (2022) "World Development Indicators 2022" The World Bank

14
HIGHER EDUCATION IN CONTEMPORARY SRI LANKA
Key Topics

Kaushalya Perera

Introduction

A strong education system reflects a country's long-term investment in its people. Educating citizens is not only about literacy, and training for employment per se, but about imparting ethics and values, and the ability to think for themselves and the community. The need for a 'system change' was one of the most visible demands of the *aragalaya* – the protracted agitations by Sri Lankan citizens in the first half of 2022 in response to the political and economic crisis. Eighty years after the establishment of the country's first university, it is telling of the failure of higher education in particular that the *aragalaya* included various projects for 're-educating' the public: a people's library at the main protest site; the active participation of university students and staff in protests; the conducting of 'teach-ins' to educate the general public on the privatization of education, the political-economic foundations of the crisis, memorializing in a post-war context, and so on. Yet, the sheer number of such efforts around the country was also evidence that such efforts had been left too late. Higher education has a significant role to play in rebounding from an economic and political collapse, not only through knowledge, engagement, and interventions but also through reflection. A critical review of contemporary literature on higher education in Sri Lanka is opportune at this moment for that very reason. Following a brief history, the chapter will introduce three key topics that have been the foci of contemporary research: youth unemployment and graduate employability, changes to universities in the face of privatization, and universities as a space of conflict and resistance.

Context

The University of Ceylon opened in 1942 with 904 English-literate students. The state bore all costs of university education, 'free education' having become a pre-election rallying cry prior to that (Jennings 1944). The heated debates at this time included the most suitable space to locate a university ('the Battle of Sites'), the implications and necessity of providing free university education to all undergraduates, and the medium of instruction (Jennings 2005; Wickramasinghe 2005). Since 1947, primary and secondary education was democratized with the introduction of free education in *swabhasha*, or Sinhala and Tamil. Consequently, coinciding with the communal violence and racist language policies in the 1950s and 1960s, large numbers of undergraduates educated in Sinhala and Tamil entered universities, necessitating university education in *swabhasha* too (Gunasekera, Samarasinghe and Vamadevan 1996). By 1970, there were four universities in Sri Lanka, including two converted Pirivenas (Buddhist learning centres).[1]

At present, Sri Lanka has 23 state universities, of which 17 are administered by the University Grants Commission (UGC), functioning under the direction of the Ministry of Higher Education.[2] The expansion of the university system in Sri Lanka has been short-sighted, ensuing as quick responses to public pressure for more higher education opportunities than as planned interventions envisaging the country's needs (see Wickramasinghe 2005). The primary responsibility of state universities is undergraduate education, of which the largest segment is the humanities, social sciences, and management and finance. In 2019, out of approximately 100,000 entrants, one-third (30,867) were humanities and social sciences students, and one-fifth (20,670) in management and finance (UGC 2022). During the last two decades, universities have been reverting to English medium instruction where possible.

While Sri Lanka's state universities are theoretically fully funded by the state, since the 1970s the funds provided have been inadequate, leading to a deterioration in the quality of education (Kaye 2002; Gamage 2014; Samarakoon, Rasnayake and Chandrasekara 2016; Samaranayake 2016). Since 2008, Sri Lankan has rarely spent above 2% of its GDP on education and has needed infusions of grants and loans by international agencies, including the ADB, JAICA, UNICEF, and World Bank.[3]

Since 2000, there has been an intense growth of private higher education institutions, providing external degrees from foreign universities and some local state universities. Statistics of their exact numbers and student enrolment are difficult to come by due to their registration as companies. Unfortunately, both scholarly and public attention on higher education has focused overwhelmingly on state universities. Very little commentary or research exists on private universities and other state institutions of higher education (non-UGC administered universities, teacher training colleges, technical institutes).

Graduates and Employability

A question that has had a direct impact on higher education policy and planning in the past four decades is whether state universities produce students who are employable. A concern over youth unemployment in the 1990s, at first a response to the continuing ethnic conflict and the second JVP insurrection (1987–1989), shifted to a discourse on graduate employability by the late 1990s (Samaranayake 1997; Amarasuriya, Gündüz and Mayer 2009; Ariyawansa 2013; Samarakoon et al 2016). The far-reaching policy changes discussed in the next section were shaped by this discourse on employability.

While one body of literature blames the universities for producing unemployable graduates, another points to the array of noxious factors compounding youth unemployment. The most significant factor is sluggish economic growth (see Samaranayake 2015, 2016). Economic growth and job generation are hindered by "unplanned and ad hoc policy changes by political leaders" (Samarakoon et al 2016: 2), as well as misguided stereotypical beliefs about what types of employment women or rural youth should be engaging in (Amarasuriya et al 2009). Structural impediments to becoming employed have been political patronage, clientelism, ethnic discrimination towards minorities, and bypassing formal processes (Amarasuriya et al 2009; Azmi, Brun and Lund 2013; Gunawardena and Nawaratne 2017). This is especially frustrating as youth who are "monolingual, non-urban, Sinhala- and Tamil-speaking" are already marginalized in terms of social class and regionalism and may not have access to political elites (Amarasuriya et al 2009: 26; see also Samaranayake 2015). For these same groups, the lack of English language proficiency is a barrier to private-sector employment (Amarasuriya et al 2009; Samaranayake 2016). Overall, these discussions show how state policies and public discourses locate the problem with its people and not on bad governance. Claims that unemployment figures are higher for arts graduates, female undergraduates, and graduates from rural areas illuminate how 'facts' are interpreted in the production of discourse (Samaranayake 2016).

Concrete criteria for defining and measuring employment-related concepts are missing despite it being a long-term concern. Employability was defined by a former higher official in the Ministry of Education as "the ability to gain initial employment", with no qualifying or delimiting criteria (Nawaratne 2012: 80). Youth unemployment was defined ambiguously as a "concentration of youth among the unemployed and under-employed categories" (Samaranayake 2016: 17). The reason for graduate unemployability is widely seen as their inability to secure a private sector job (see Senaratne and Sivasegaram 2012), supposedly due to the lack of suitable skills, namely,

> effective communication skills along with English, ability of maintaining interpersonal relationships, ability of leading a team and target achieving within a short time, ability of prioritization of work; initiation of work and intention of its development, open, proactive and pragmatic mind; computer literacy, ability of logical and rational thinking, general knowledge and personal hygiene, office and social etiquette.
>
> *(Samarakoon et al 2016: 23)*

Critical questions can be raised on the superficiality of these criteria, the demand that they be produced through university education, and their actual importance to employment.

Much of the literature on employability is descriptive studies or surveys, with little critical assessment of the loan programme or related activities described. Ranasinghe (2022) asserts in his review of the literature on graduate employability in Sri Lanka that scholars have ignored important factors that contribute to graduate unemployability, such as family and social factors, which makes much of the employability research in Sri Lanka methodologically flawed. Ranasinghe's assertions are of critical consideration since sweeping policy changes with regard to state higher education have been justified by such research. Rather than closely analysing claims of (un)employability or considering its critiques, policymakers have legitimized arguments that "the [state] university system needs to be re-structured, concerned with quality and relevance, and introduce job-oriented programmes" (Samaranayake 2016: 27).

'Fixing' State Universities: The World Bank and the Restructuring of Universities

The demand for 'employable' graduates paralleled demands for systemic changes in state universities which were framed as 'reform'. Loans by the World Bank have been integral to this restructuring, forcing substantive changes in governance and the ethos of universities.

The immediate post-war era, 2009 onward, was one of upheaval in higher education. The then government-initiated programmes were aimed at 'fixing' the problems of state universities. One was to encourage international investment in higher education, with the vision of making Sri Lanka a 'knowledge hub' (Samaranayake 2015). To this end, a bill regulating the foundation and function of state and non-state universities, known as the 'private universities bill', was to be tabled in Parliament in 2010, but was eventually not tabled due to public protests (Senaratne and Sivasegaram 2012; Samaranayake 2016). Another notorious step was a three-week Pre-Orientation Programme (POP) or 'leadership training course' for new university entrants initiated in 2010, conducted by the Sri Lankan military in military camps. This was widely criticized by public interest groups as an instance of the militarization of education (Amarasuriya 2014). While the bill was withdrawn and the leadership course discontinued, other changes continued largely without comment.

The most significant shifts have accompanied projects supported by World Bank loans to higher education, totalling roughly US$180 million since 2000 (Wikramanayake 2015; Perera 2021a). At present, these loans are absorbed into the national budget, thereby becoming indistinguishable from state funds. The conditionalities of all three loan cycles have specific ideological premises. First, they stress the need for efficiency and quality assurance (Perera 2020, 2021a). The keywords 'quality' and 'employability' point to the "overt infiltration of [neoliberal] ideology into Sri Lanka's higher education sector" (Mendis 2021: 37). Efficiency is primarily seen as a centralization of the processes of examination, teaching, and administration, achieved through the incorporation of technology (e.g., using learning management platforms, centralized platforms for uploading exam results) (Perera 2020). Yet, in policy discussions of 'reform', other entrenched problems such as politicization, the lack of dissent within the institution, and a widespread lapse in accountability are ignored (Fernando 2012; Uyangoda 2015; Gunawardena and Nawaratne 2017; Manuratne 2021).

To ensure 'quality', the World Bank's loans facilitated the establishment of the Quality Assurance Council (QAC) and related structures at university and faculty level – an apparatus with far-reaching consequences, not least the permeation of a quality assurance discourse within higher education (Perera 2020). The World Bank loans funded the initial rounds of institutional and programme reviews, which later became institutionalized as periodic reviews (Mendis 2017; Perera 2021a). The reviewers are academics within the same system, which, given the closely networked nature of universities, can lead to partisan or uncritical reviews and consequently reduce the credibility of the process (Mendis 2017). Curriculum changes based on the Sri Lanka Qualifications Framework (SLQF) introduced to streamline all degree programmes into one format have been critiqued for encouraging homogeneity rather than flexibility in degree programmes (Mendis 2017; Perera 2020). In the long term, such changes are transforming universities into places where learning credits are accumulated in rigidly controlled forms of curricula rather than nurturing spaces for flexible and creative forms of learning.

A second ideological premise is that high proficiency in the English language and knowledge of information technology (IT) are integral to the making of an employable graduate. This is a conditionality that has created multiple changes in curricula and dubious opportunities for universities. For example, initiatives were taken for "computer science courses [to be] implemented in all universities of the country, at various levels" (Karunanayaka and Wijeratne 2005: 64). On the one hand, poorly resourced institutions could procure equipment that they "had always dreamed of having but were unable to get due to lack of university funding" and design courses that were considered useful (Ilangakoon 2006: 105; Mendis 2021; Perera 2021a). On the other hand, university administrations frequently saw this as an opportunity to acquire funds and pressurized departments that were hesitant to apply for loan monies to do so (Perera 2021a).

These conditions tie in neatly with existing post-colonial ideologies in Sri Lanka of English as an indicator of more affluent class membership (Kandiah 2010). As previously shown, this has been a tool for discrimination towards poor, rural, or less English-proficient students in the job market (Amarasuriya et al 2009). These conditionalities of World Bank loans, therefore, led to English language programmes being scrutinized, revamped, or newly created (Ilangakoon 2006; Mendis 2021; Perera 2021a). Degree programmes shifted to English medium education swiftly in order to cater to the demand for English medium education, with little regard to the problems this would entail for students or staff lacking in requisite proficiency (Perera and Canagarajah 2010). Problems arising from such ventures could have been circumvented with longer-term planning involving applied linguists and English Language Teaching (ELT) professionals available in universities, but this rarely happens as major decisions are typically taken by non-specialists (Ilangakoon 2006; Mendis 2021). Additionally, the push for English as a deciding link for employment reinforces the link between English proficiency, social class, and employment opportunities instead of uncoupling English language knowledge from other skills and abilities.

In-depth studies evaluating the impact of external funding on higher education in Sri Lanka are lacking. The existing literature is mostly uncritical descriptions of projects, relying on the World Bank's publications themselves for information and supporting arguments that mirror the discourse of the World Bank (see Senaratne and Gunarathne 2010a; Senaratne and Sivasegaram 2012; Wickramasinghe 2018). Additionally, most work on university governance and World Bank loan monies are desk analyses or student surveys, as longitudinal studies are not (e.g., Senaratne and Gunarathne 2010b; Samaranayake 2016).

Encouragingly, however, a critically evaluative body of work is growing (Mendis 2021; Perera 2021a; Wijetunga 2021). This small body of work, using qualitative methodologies and empirical data, presents the impact of the World Bank's loans on universities from the perspective of academics involved in administering such loan projects. Interestingly, the studies reveal deep ambivalence. On the one hand, academics work on these projects due to their commitment to the institution and their students, strategically using the monies as avenues to develop universities (Mendis 2021; Wijetunga 2021). On the other hand, academics struggle with the conditionalities imposed by universities and the World Bank. Such conditionalities significantly constrain the design and implementation of programmes, leading to resentment and cynicism about their effectiveness (Perera 2021a). What these few studies show is a serious need for more work on the role and impact of external aid in higher education.

Privatization of Higher Education

Critics of the recent transformation in Sri Lankan universities see these changes as a continuation of Sri Lanka's post-1978 economic liberalization and a reflection of present-day global shifts towards neoliberal policies in higher education. As Jayawardena (2017) notes, a "university in the neoliberal era can simply be portrayed as a (factory) site in which human resources – employable graduates – are moulded in and for the free market" (2017: 223). In other words, degree programmes are converted into commodities, students are treated as consumers, and competition between institutions is framed as desired practice (Jayawardena 2017; Lecamwasam 2021). Sri Lankan state universities' entry into international university ranking systems, the inculcation of a 'publish or perish' culture into staff and postgraduate student performances, and the entry of fee-levying undergraduates to state universities are framed as measures that will 'internationalize' state universities (Senaratne and Sivasegaram 2012). Such measures have disregarded the critiques of such practices in other parts of the world (see Fitz and Beers 2002).

Understanding the local specificities of privatization of higher education – rarely addressed in scholarly work on Sri Lanka – is, however, important to fully appreciate the many facets of the debate (exceptions are Banda 2011; Perera 2021b). Sri Lankans' desire for 'qualifications' is long-standing, as Little and Evans (2005) show, with an unprecedented growth in the number of foreign-controlled degree awarding bodies in the late 1990s. Despite such institutions being a significant avenue of higher education for a growing portion of the population, there is neither reliable data on the number of students registered in private universities, nor research on their policies, laws, culture, and practices (Ambepitiya 2016; Perera 2021b).

Typically, references to privatization of higher education in public discourse are limited to 'private universities', i.e. companies that facilitate external degrees from foreign universities (see Jayawardena 2017). Yet, what Little and Evans (2005) illustrate is that state institutions too provided 'qualifications' for payment, in the guise of fee-levying courses even before economic liberalization. By the late 1970s, state universities had initiated a series of income-earning ventures including the provision of 'external degrees'. The external degree system is different to education via the Open University of Sri Lanka, the state university mandated to provide degrees in distance education mode for subsidized fees. Universities providing external degrees typically undertake only the registration and examinations of such degrees, leaving the teaching of such degrees to external private institutions (Kaye 2002). They are a major income generator for such universities. Other income-generating staples in state universities include mass-scale postgraduate programmes and other fee-levying courses (e.g., certificate courses), all of which are used to offset expenses unmet by Treasury funds (Kaye 2002; Banda 2011; Karnasuriya 2011).

Despite, or even because of, the complex interplay between state universities and private funds, academics are divided on the topic (see Witharana 2015; Perera 2021b). The affiliation of state-employed academics with private institutions contributes to this conflict (Jayawardena 2017; Perera 2021b). Their divided loyalties make for difficult 'affective positions' and impact state universities in multiple ways (Perera 2021b). One is in the form of support or critique of corporate-like management practices (Lecamwasam 2021). Another is the impact on trade union action. Academic unions have found it difficult to speak out explicitly against privatization given the diverse views on this within its membership (Witharana 2015).

Consequently, resistance against privatization in higher education has been limited to opposition against specific institutions providing higher education (e.g., South Asian Institute of Technology and Medicine). Other forms of privatization – e.g., the proliferation of private universities and the supply of paid qualifications by state institutions – have met with no resistance (Little and Evans 2005), perhaps due to their being recognized as a societal need. Certainly, a wider scholarly discourse on the privatization of higher education is lacking.

Conflict and Resistance: Violence and Well-Being in Universities

State universities are generally seen as harbingers of chaos and conflict. Since the 1960s universities have been 'hotspots' of trouble ('Chronicle' 1967). In January 2012 alone, state universities were featured in 176 items of four Sinhala-language national newspapers, reporting protests, ragging, and other 'problems' relating to undergraduates (Perera 2018). In contrast to their intense inspection in public discourse, ragging, harassment, and political activity in universities are overwhelmingly under-researched, with the exception of a few descriptive and reflexive accounts (Schubert 2012; Gamage 2017).

Ragging (or hazing) is ubiquitous in Sri Lankan public universities. Yet, it is only recently that research on the topic has been available, adding to previous descriptive (and somewhat reflexive) accounts. Recent research is mainly survey-based and qualitative research designs are rare, barring a few exceptions (see: Ruwanpura 2011; Wickramasinghe et al 2022a). Ragging is typically conducted by young men and a smaller percentage of women (Premadasa et al 2011; Lekamwasam et al 2015; Wickramasinghe et al 2022a). Anecdotal accounts indicate that ragging is conducted by second- and third-year undergraduates, though Premadasa et al (2011) found that at times lecturers (mostly female) too ragged new students – a disturbing revelation that calls for further studies into how "victims can become future perpetrators" (Wickramasinghe et al 2022a: 16).

Ragging is a complex sociocultural phenomenon: it is a reflection of hierarchy and violence in the wider Sri Lankan society, is key to political activity and patronage, and is exacerbated by the inertia of institutional authorities (Premadasa et al 2011; Ruwanpura 2011; Manuratne 2021; Wickramasinghe et al 2022b). Even with an anti-ragging act enacted in 1998 after the death of an undergraduate by ragging, studies show that ending ragging needs a more committed, multi-pronged approach. Universities officially prohibit ragging but have shown only sporadic commitment to eradicating it entirely, though individual faculties have succeeded in temporarily suspending the practice. The successful case study of one faculty instituting a cluster of preventive measures, involving multiple groups of concerned parties, can be used by institutions with serious intent towards eradicating ragging (Lekamwasam et al 2015). Yet, as Manuratne (2021)'s analysis shows, ragging is unlikely to end given the continued politicization of university spaces.

The inertia of institutions is surprising considering the cost to students' mental health and institutional culture (Wickramasinghe et al 2022b). Ragging affects students' academic performance due to the stress of continuous harassment as well as its prohibitions over their academic practices, which include puristic linguistic policies (e.g., only speaking in Sinhala/Tamil) and surveillance of in-class interactions (Navaz 2020; Wickramasinghe et al 2022a).

Sexual harassment in higher education is another taboo topic as evidenced by research and non-scholarly accounts (Morley 2006; Ruwanpura 2011; Liyanage and Liyanage 2020). Particularly taboo is the topic of sexual harassment of students by staff, yet to be discussed in public fora or research. Surveys of students show more widespread and intense sexual harassment of male students, in comparison to women students, during ragging, which may continue afterwards (Premadasa et al 2011; Wickramasinghe et al 2022b). A significant publication in recent times is *The Prevalence of Ragging and Sexual and Gender-Based Violence in Sri Lankan State Universities* by the University Grants Commission (2021). The report is indicative of the problems in the system. For example, it refrains from addressing the issue of academic perpetrators of harassment and does not use the term 'rape' in the analysis, using instead "forced to engage in sexual relations" (2021: 52). Research indicates that neither students nor staff, especially if female and junior, have faith in the university administration's ability or will to address ragging or sexual harassment (Premadasa et al 2011). Patriarchal attitudes confirming women's subservience to men and adherence to hierarchies that value seniority continue to prevail among staff and students (Darj et al 2017). The establishment of Gender Cells and a UGC Standing Committee on Gender has had little impact on this aspect of university culture (Liyanage and Liyanage 2020; Kumar 2021).

Given the prevalence of various forms of violence and the general stress of learning in an under-resourced context, the staggeringly high levels of mental health problems in universities are not surprising (Amarasuriya, Jorm and Reavley 2015). Researchers also recognize that underreporting is to be expected in a culture that normalizes violence and offers no institutional support for victim-survivors. In addition, owing to the militarization of the northern and eastern parts of Sri Lanka, Tamil and Muslim undergraduates experience universities as 'unsafe' spaces with little freedom of expression (Azmi et al 2013). Moreover, students' commitment to somehow completing their programme of study may be another contributing factor towards underreporting.

Universities as Politicized Spaces

Universities are politicized spaces that at once replicate and challenge existing power structures and dynamics. Student politics is tightly connected to ragging, where student unions socialize first-year undergraduates into the political culture of the university (Schubert 2012; Manuratne 2021). Schubert (2012) and Ruwanpura (2011) have shown that ragging involves specialized roles by men and women, with women playing a supportive role in political activities. Undergraduates belonging to minority ethnic groups experience the university as a space where they can be more vocal about politics, but feel safer in mono-ethnic groups, signalling the still-fragile state of ethnic relations in the country (Azmi et al 2013).

Politicization is not limited to student politics, as illustrated by the appointments and removals of academics from higher offices of university administration and of political favours granted to academics (see Fernando 2012). From 2010 to 2012, academics in state universities agitated over low-salary scales, low-state expenditure towards education, and political interference in the function of state universities (Witharana 2015). Whereas student protests are seen as emblematic of youth unrest and chaos, protests by academics are framed as resistance or activism calling attention to problems in higher education. This is possibly due to the higher status of academics as well as the lack of overt political affiliations by Federation of University Teachers' Associations (Amarasuriya 2015), whereas student unions are linked to national political parties by reputation. Similar to student politics, political action by academic has received little attention from researchers (exceptions are Amarasuriya 2015; Witharana 2015; Perera 2021b) but deserves study if we are to understand higher education as a space of agency and resistance.

Concluding Thoughts

The large-scale shifts taking place in Sri Lankan higher education in the post-war era in some ways reflect global shifts in higher education. Increased privatization, quantitative measures of quality in teaching and research, and participation in international rankings reflect current neoliberal orientations in higher education across the world. Similar to South America and Africa, they have resulted in changes to structures and systems of management, driven by the support of the World Bank. Yet, some aspects remain locally specific based on the socio-economic and political environment, specifically the manner in which the post-war politico-economic context of Sri Lanka impacts the provision of higher education.

The implications of these changes in Sri Lankan higher education are manifold. Student and academic protests have long signalled the dire straits of public higher education. Less state funds lead to increasing inequity, with poorer families losing access to quality higher education. On the other hand, the reduction of state resources to higher education also means that state education will become a low-quality option for people with fewer means. Left unchecked, large-scale privatization of higher education will lead to larger proportions of the population losing access to quality higher education. Resistance is also dampened by political and economic problems in the country. If the underlying concerns of protests are left unaddressed, phenomena such as ragging, harassment, and politicization of the system will also continue.

Additionally, our knowledge of higher education is limited to state universities, with little awareness of the privatized higher education sector. This results in policies and regulations that are ignorant of the needs and ideologies of a major segment of society. The lack of critical and empirically driven research on crucial aspects of higher education in the country is telling. Higher education is the focus of much public interest, but the dearth of resources is reflected in the gaps in research. Sustained scholarly attention is necessary to understand the changes underway in higher education. Such interest is also vital for informed policies in higher education that can bring about a more democratic, ethical, and humane society.

Notes

1 The University of Ceylon split into two: the campus in Kandy becoming the University of Peradaniya and the Colombo campus becoming the University of Colombo. The two Buddhist learning centres Vidyodaya and Vidyalankara were converted to universities and later renamed Universities of Jayawardenepura and Kelaniya, respectively.
2 Six state universities function directly under the Ministries indicated in parentheses: (i) The General Sir John Kotelawala Defence University (Defence), (ii) Buddhist and Pali University, (iii) the Bhiksu University (Higher Education), (iv) National Institute of Education (Education), (v) University of Vocational Technology (Vocational and Technical Training), and (vi) Ocean University (Skills Development and Vocational Training).
   Note: the information of the universities and their controlling Ministries are as listed in the UGC website (date accessed 15 August 2022). Ministerial portfolios are regularly revised and renamed in Sri Lanka, usually whenever a Cabinet is re-appointed.
3 Trading Economics website: https://tradingeconomics.com/sri-lanka/public-spending-on-education-total-percent-of-gdp-wb-data.html.

References

Amarasuriya, Harini (2014) "Leadership Training for Youth: A Response to Youth Rebellion?" In *Cadjan – Kiduhu: Global Perspectives on Youth Work* Brian Belton (ed) Rotterdam: Sense Publishers, pp 109–131.

Amarasuriya, Harini (2015) "Protests and Counter Protests: Competing Civil Society Spaces in Post-war Sri Lanka" *Economic and Political Weekly* 50: 49–55.

Amarasuriya, Harini, Canan Gündüz and Markus Mayer (2009) *Rethinking the nexus between youth, unemployment and conflict – Perspectives from Sri Lanka*. Accessed on 28/10/2018. Available at https://www.international-alert.org/wp-content/uploads/2021/09/Economy-Youth-Unemployment-Conflict-Sri-Lanka-EN-2009.pdf.

Amarasuriya, Santhushi Devini, Anthony Francis Jorm and Nicola Jane Reavley (2015) "Prevalence of Depression and Its Correlates among Undergraduates in Sri Lanka" *Asian Journal of Psychiatry* 15: 32–37

Ambepitiya, Kalpana R. (2016) "Employability of Graduates of Public and Private Management Education Institutes: A Case Study of Two Institutes in Sri Lanka" *OUSL Journal* 11: 113–133

Ariyawansa, Ranthilaka (2013) "Employability of Graduates of Sri Lankan Universities" *Sri Lankan Journal of Human Resource Management* 2(1): 91–104

Azmi, Fazeeha, Catherine Brun and Ragnhild Lund (2013) "Young People's Everyday Politics in Post-conflict Sri Lanka" *Space and Polity* 17(1): 106–122

Banda, O.G. Dayaratna (2011) *Nidahas vishvavidyala adyapanaya paudgalikakaranayata? [Is Free University Education Being Privatized]* Maharagama: Ravaya Publications.

'Chronicle' (1967) *Minerva* 5(2): 278–282

Darj, Elisabeth, Kumud Wijewardena, Gunilla Lindmark and Pia Axemo (2017) "'Even Though a Man Takes the Major Role, He Has No Right to Abuse': Future Male Leaders' Views on Gender-Based Violence in Sri Lanka" *Global Health Action* 10(1): 1–9

Fernando, Marshall (2012) *Crisis in Education: Focus on a Sri Lankan Experience* [Special Issue] Dialogue (NS): Sri Lanka Ecumenical Institute.

Fitz, John and Bryan Beers (2002) "Education Management Organisations and the Privatisation of Public Education: A Cross-National Comparison of the USA and Britain" *Comparative Education* 38(2): 137–154

Gamage, Siri (2014) "Changing Patterns of Anthropology and Sociology Practices in Sri Lanka in the Context of Debates on Northern and Southern Theory" *Social Affairs* 1(1): 1–29

Gamage, Siri (2017) "Psychological, Sociological, and Political Dimensions of Ragging in Sri Lankan Universities" *Social Affairs: A Journal for the Social Sciences* 1(7): 13–21

Gunasekera, R.G.G.O., S.G. Samarasinghe and V. Vamadevan (1996) *National Language Policy in Sri Lanka – 1956 to 1996: Three Studies in Its Implementation* K. N. O. Dharmadasa (ed) Kandy, Sri Lanka: International Center for Ethnic Studies

Gunawardena, Chandra and Rasika Nawaratne (2017) "Brain Drain from Sri Lankan Universities" *Sri Lanka Journal of Social Sciences* 40(2): 103–118

Ilangakoon, Shivanee (2006) "Designing a Tailor-Made Course for IRQUE at the University of Colombo" In *English for Equality, Employment and Empowerment: Selected Papers of the Sri Lanka English Language Teachers' Association (SLELTA)* Dinali Fernando and Dushyanthi Mendis (eds) Colombo: SLELTA, pp 99–106

Jayawardena, Dhammika (2017) "The "MacBurger", Non-State Universities and the Changing Landscape of Higher Education in Sri Lanka" *Journal for Critical Education Policy Studies* 15(3): 213–240.

Jennings, Ivor (1944) "Race, Religion and Economic Opportunity in the University of Ceylon" *University of Ceylon Reviews* 2(1–2): 1–13. Accessed on 28/12/2014. Available at http://www.dlib.pdn.ac.lk/archive/handle/123456789/1117

Jennings, Ivor (2005) *The Road to Peradeniya: An Autobiography* H.A.I. Goonetileke (ed.) Colombo: Lake House Investments.

Kandiah, Thiru (2010) "'Kaduwa': Power and the English Language Weapon in Sri Lanka" In *English in Sri Lanka: Ceylon English, Lankan English, Sri Lankan English* Siromi Fernando, Manique Gunesekera and Arjuna Parakrama (eds) SLELTA, pp 36–43.

Karnasuriya, Anuruddha P. (2011) *Pawdgalika vishvavidhyala: Vilasithawa saha yatharthaya [Private Universities: Fashion and Reality]* Maharagama: Ravaya Publications.

Karunanayaka, Shironica and Rupa Wijeratne (2005) "Educational Media in Sri Lanka" In *Educational Media in Asia – Perspectives on Distance Education* Usha V. Reddy and Sanjaya Mishra (eds) Vancouver: Commonwealth of Learning, pp 147–162

Kaye, Anthony (2002) *The Current Situation of External Degrees in Sri Lanka.* Accessed on 13/08/2014. Available at http://dspace.col.org/handle/123456789/114.

Kumar, Ramya (2021) "Everyday violence and exclusion at university" *The Island* (22 June) https://island.lk/everyday-violence-and-exclusion-at-university/

Lecamwasam, Hasini (2021) "Not-so-Free Education: State-Citizen Relations in Sri Lanka's Educational Policy Response to the Pandemic" In *Is the Cure Worse than the Disease? Reflections on Covid Governance in Sri Lanka* Pradeep Pieris (ed) Colombo: Center for Policy Alternatives, pp 129–148

Lekamwasam, Sarath, Mahinda Rodrigo, Madhu Wickramathilake, Champa Wijesinghe, Gaya Wijerathne, Aruna De Silva, Mayuri Napagoda, Anoja Attanayake and Clifford Perera (2015) "Preventing Ragging: Outcome of an Integrated Programme in a Medical Faculty in Sri Lanka" *Indian Journal of Medical Ethics* 12(4): 227–230

Little, Angela W. and Jane Evans (2005) "The Growth of Foreign Qualification Suppliers in Sri Lanka: De Facto Decentralisation?" *Compare* 35(2): 181–191

Liyanage, Janethri B. and Kamala Liyanage (2020) "Gender-Based Harassment and Violence in Higher Educational Institutions: A Case from Sri Lanka" In *Gender Mainstreaming in Politics, Administration and Development in South Asia* Ishtiaq Jamil, Salahuddin M. Aminuzzaman, Syeda Lasna Kabir and M. Mahfuzul Haque (eds) Cham: Palgrave Macmillan, pp 61–85

Manuratne, Prabha (2021) "Structural Violence and Ragging in Sri Lankan State Universities: A Case Study of the 1975 V W. Kularatne Report" *Vistas Journal* 14(2): 1–25

Mendis, Dushyanthi (2017) "Assessing Quality in Higher Education" *Professor Manique Gunesekera Memorial Oration*. University of Kelaniya

Mendis, Dushyanthi (2021) "Language Planning and Policy: Negotiating With Global Actors in Local Contexts" *University of Colombo Review (New Series III)* 2(1): 29–41

Morley, Louise (2006) "Hidden Transcripts: The Micropolitics of Gender in Commonwealth Universities" *Women's Studies International Forum* 29(6): 543–551

Navaz, Abdul M.M. (2020) "Ragging and Its Impacts on the English Language Use of the First Year Undergraduate Community: Sri Lankan Perspective" *Asian Journal of Education and Social Studies* 11(1): 11–20

Nawaratne, Sunil J. (2012) "Shifting Paradigms of Higher Education in Sri Lanka" In *Recreating and Re-Positioning of Sri Lankan Universities to Meet Emerging Opportunities and Challenges in a Globalized Environment – Workshop Proceedings* Ranjith Senaratne and Sivanandam Sivasegaram (eds) Colombo: University Grants Commission and Ministry of Higher Education, pp 75–96

Perera, Kaushalya (2018) "The Sri Lankan Undergraduate in the Sinhala Press" *Kalyani [Journal of University of Kelaniya]* XXXII: 83–107

Perera, Kaushalya (2020) "Loka baenku salli saha ape wishwawidyala: Loka baenkuwe naya wya:pruthi saha ra:jya wishwawidyalawala mae:thaka:li:na wiparyasaya [The World Bank's Money and Our Universities: The World Bank's Loan Projects and the Recent Changes in State Universities" *Pravada* 36: 53–75

Perera, Kaushalya (2021a) ""Marrying the Monster": World Bank Loans and English Language Projects in Sri Lankan Universities" *University of Colombo Review (New Series III)* 2(1): 42–60

Perera, Kaushalya (2021b) "Narratives of Privatization: Three Stories of Affect and Position from Public Universities" *Journal of Education Policy* 00(00): 1–19. Advanced online edition

Perera, Kaushalya and Suresh Canagarajah (2010) "Globalization and English Teaching in Sri Lanka: Foreign Resources and Local Responses" In *Globalization of Language and Culture in Asia* Viniti Vaish (ed) London: Continuum, pp 106–119

Premadasa, I.G., N.C. Wanigasooriya, L. Thalib and N.B. Ellepola (2011) "Harassment of Newly Admitted Undergraduates by Senior Students in a Faculty of Dentistry in Sri Lanka" *Medical Teacher* 33(10): e556–e563

Ranasinghe, Athula (2022) "Measuring Graduate Employability: A Critical Assessment of Emplyability Goal in Higher Education Plans" In *National Conference on Celebrating Centenary Year Humanities and Social Sciences in Sri Lanka (1921-2021)*. Accessed on 25/06/2022. Available at https://www.researchgate.net/publication/360513964_Sub-theme_Employability_issues_of_HSS_graduates_Paper_Title_tentative_Measuring_Graduate_Employability_A_Critical_Assessment_of_Employability_Goal_in_Higher_Education_Plans_Athula_Ranasinghe

Ruwanpura, Eshani (2011) *Sex or Sensibility? The making of chaste women and promiscuous men in a Sri Lankan university setting*. Accessed on 3/01/ 2015. Available at http://www.era.lib.ed.ac.uk/handle/1842/6180

Samarakoon, S., S. Rasnayake and D. Chandrasekara (2016) "Youth Aspirations, Social Mobility and Educational Target Achievement in Sri Lanka" *Social Affairs: A Journal for the Social Sciences* 1(4): 1–14

Samaranayake, Gamini (1997) "Political Violence in Sri Lanka: A Diagnostic Approach" *Terrorism and Political Violence* 9(2): 99–119

Samaranayake, Gamini (2015) "Changing University Student Politics in Sri Lanka : From Norm Oriented to Value Orient Student Movement" *Social Affairs: A Journal for the Social Sciences* 1(3): 23–32

Samaranayake, Gamini (2016) "Expansion of University Education, Graduate Unemployment and the Knowledge Hub in Sri Lanka" *Social Affairs: A Journal for the Social Sciences* 1(4): 15–32

Schubert, Andi (2012) "'Thela Bedeema': Examining the Culture of Student Violence within a State University in Sri Lanka" *Dialogue (NS* XXXIX: 259–294

Senaratne, Samanthi and Nuwan Gunarathne (2010a) *A Case of an Accountancy Study Programme in Sri Lanka to Improve Relevance and Quality of Undergraduate Education: a New Dimension on Institutional View ICBI 2010* Colombo: University of Kelaniya, pp 1–20

Senaratne, Samanthi and Nuwan Gunarathne (2010b) "Perceptions of Students on Improving Relevance and Quality of Undergraduate Education : An Organizational Development" *International Research Conference on Management and Finance – University of Colombo* 2010: 293–303

Senaratne, Ranjith and Sivanandam Sivasegaram (eds) (2012) *Re-Creating and Re-Positioning of Sri Lankan Universities to Meet Emerging Opportunities and Challenges in a Globalized Environment - Workshop Proceedings* Colombo: University Grants Commission and Ministry of Higher Education

University Grants Commission (2021) *Prevalence of Ragging and Sexual and Gender Based Violence in Sri Lankan State Universities*. Colombo: University Grants Commission

University Grants Commission (2022) *Sri Lanka University Statistics*. Colombo: University Grants Commission Accessed on 8/15/ 2022. Available at https://www.ugc.ac.lk/index.php?option=com_content&view=article&id=2220%3Asri-lanka-university-statistics-2019&catid=55%3Areports&Itemid=42&lang=en

Uyangoda, Jayadeva (2015) *University Governance in Sri Lanka: A Critique and Ideas for Reform* Colombo: Social Scientist Association

Wickramasinghe, Nira (2005) *University Space and Values: Three Essays* Colombo: International Center for Ethnic Studies

Wickramasinghe, Vathsala (2018) "Higher Education in State Universities in Sri Lanka – Review of Higher Education Since Colonial Past through International Funding for Development" *International Journal of Educational Management* 32(3): 463–478

Wickramasinghe, Ayanthi, Pia Axemo, Birgitta Esse and Jill Trenholm (2022a) "Ragging as an Expression of Power in a Deeply Divided Society; A Qualitative Study on Students Perceptions on the Phenomenon of Ragging at a Sri Lankan University" *PLOS ONE* 17(7): 1–20

Wickramasinghe, Ayanthi, Esse Birgitta, Shirin Ziaei, Rajendra Surenthirakumaran and Pia Axemo (2022) "Ragging, a Form of University Violence in Sri Lanka – Prevalence, Self-Perceived Health Consequences, Help-Seeking Behavior and Associated Factors" *International Journal of Environmental Research and Public Health* 19(2022): 1–13

Wijetunga, Minoli (2021) *Exchanging Ginger for Chilli ?: The Social Ecology of a World Bank-Funded Higher Education Project in Sri Lanka* Oxford: Oxford University

Wikramanayake, Damaris H. (2015) "Donor Aid to the Education Sector in Sri Lanka and the Achievement of Education Goals" In *International Education Aid in Developing AsiaI* Hsuang Cheng and Sheng-Ju Chan (eds) Singapore: Springer Science, Business Media, pp 199–220

Witharana, Dileepa (2015) "The Story of the 6% t-Shirt: the Hundred Day Struggle of the Federation of University Teachers' Association, Sri Lanka" *The South Asianist* 4(1): 1–24

PART V

Work and Life

15
INFORMALITY, MASCULINITY, AND AGGLOMERATION IMAGINARIES

Nipesh Palat Narayanan

Introduction

Discussing the island-ness in the imaginary of Sri Lanka, Jazeel (2009: 400) has argued:

> Like all geographical facts, however, the Sri Lankan island is also a mapping; a way of seeing and imagining space that itself has a representational history. This is not to deny the materiality of island form, but it is to stress that the common-sense reality of Sri Lanka as inviolable, self-contained and unified politico-cultural island space is a fact that has been enabled by particular ways of writing 'Sri Lankan space'.

In this chapter, I refocus on the concerns raised by Jazeel (2009) from the island-ness of Sri Lanka (see also Chapter 1); narrowing it to imageries of agglomerations within this *island* and particular ways of writing this space. Agglomerations in Sri Lanka, as elsewhere, present complex socio-spatial constructs. Everyday life cannot be separated from these socio-spatial constructs where it unfolds. These socio-spatial constructs are most often gendered. The chapter, therefore, aims to engage with literature to argue how the agglomeration imageries (e.g., how a city or village is imagined) are gendered in nature and how it affects work. I will primarily structure the chapter using the construction of ideal village imagery (mostly from the discipline of anthropology) and modern metropolis imagery (mostly from the discipline of geography and development studies), to discuss and outline the discursive construction of agglomerations, using the vantage point of masculinity. Thereafter, I will outline how these imageries impact working lives, especially from the vantage point of informality.

Informality constitutes practices that are not registered by the state (Cirolia and Scheba 2019; Palat Narayanan 2019). However, not all unregistered practices are termed informal, meaning that informality is an academic categorization with its own politics of knowledge. To illustrate: a cluster of houses built without proper permits will fall under informality; however, a luxury condominium with similar status may not necessarily be studied or categorized as informal (Nagaraj 2016; Rasnayake 2019). Or, street vending is informal because it evades direct taxation while app-based taxi services, which also evade taxation, are not informal and are usually categorized as platform/gig economy. Furthermore, informality is studied as a trait present in countries of the Global

South while similar processes in the Global North evade the label of informality (Jaffe and Koster 2019). Without going deeper into discussions on informality and its knowledge politics, I mobilize informality as a category and not a thing in itself.

Rather than informality in general, I will concentrate on informal sector work. The informal sector is a subset of informal practices, which deals with work and employment not registered by the state (thus generally not paying direct taxes). In Sri Lanka, with an unemployment rate of less than 5% in 2010 "… 62.6% of the total employed population worked in the informal sector [as of 2010] … This included 85.6% of agricultural workers and more than half (51.0%) of non-agricultural workers" (Arunatilake 2013: 496). In absolute numbers, informal work in Sri Lanka largely exists in non-agricultural sectors and in urban areas (cf., Gunatilaka 2008).

Governmental regulation and protection of formal sector work in Sri Lanka are far more advanced than elsewhere in the South Asia region (Ruwanpura 2022). Nonetheless, there are two important aspects to informal sector and work. First, informal sector usually avoids direct taxation as informal businesses are not registered, inclining the state to *formalize* informality. Second, as economies grow, there is a general belief that the informal sector contracts (Ihrig and Moe 2004). The latter point is important because state policies take informality as a factor rather than an indicator, i.e., they tend to reduce informality directly to claim a more developed state rather than measuring it to understand the state of the economy.[1] In this process, only some informal works get categorized as informal.

In the following sections, I will first develop how masculine imageries of agglomerations are constructed. Thereafter, I will outline how the categorization of informality is based on these imageries. I will begin by investigating the notion of masculinity and its relation to agglomeration imageries and work, in the next section.

Men and Masculinity

Jani de Silva (2014: 439) has argued:

> Masculinity is, in many ways, tied to the body. Attributes such as valour, violence, aggression, composure, and deference are all inscribed upon the body and acted out through bodily practices, mien and postures. Thus, tropes of masculinity are – openly or subtly – conveyed through bodily demeanour.

Body and gender performativity are linked to the understanding that gender is socially constructed and the body performs these constructs. Within these constructs masculinity is assigned the dominant position. Ariyarathne (2021) has demonstrated how gender stereotypes are performed, either willingly or via socio-statal coercions to gain access to the label of being a man. Furthermore, I have also discussed how gender norms are evoked by *bath* (a rice and curry meal) packet sellers in Colombo to market *good* food, irrespective of their gender identities (Palat Narayanan 2022). These works points how gendered identities are ascribed to certain kinds of activities, and these are socially and spatially dictated. For example, a woman walking alone at night in an upscale shopping mall in Colombo is acceptable, but the same act in some neighbourhoods of the same city would be frowned upon or at worst coercively *corrected*.[2] I focus on the sociocultural basis that not only legitimizes but actively promotes these coercions.

These controls do take larger sociocultural forms. de Mel, Peiris and Gomez (2013) have shown the social acceptance of manhood is dominance and violence, where men need to defend the honour of the house. This arises from the general view of men being responsible for earnings, *disciplining* household members, and engaging in the public sphere.[3] Sri Lankan electoral politics and to an extent the independence movement against British colonialism have been mobilized around defending the honour of the motherland. Taking electoral politics, for instance, the recently deposed president Gotabaya Rajapaksa proposed to discipline the nation in his election manifesto. This evocation is not new, previous presidents have used similar rhetoric, e.g., Ranasinghe Premadasa in the 1990s. I am taking two politicians from opposite ideological spectrums and political parties to point to the social embeddedness of disciplining and its wider public resonance with regard to the masculine positioning of the state.

Connell (2016) has further argued that these socially dictated gender roles, their social embeddedness, and their manifestations need to be historicized, to illustrate the colonial nature of hegemonic masculinity. Further, Mama (1996) has argued that the associations and performativity of gender are not a result of gender relations but constitutive of it. de Alwis (2002: 675–676) in similar lines have argued:

> Sri Lankan women, be they Sinhala, Tamil, or Muslim, continue to be constructed as the reproducers, nurturers, and disseminators of "tradition," "culture," and "nation."

Nation, culture, tradition, etc. are not a result of gender relations, but gender relations and categories of sex, construct them. To understand the masculine imageries in this light, we need to constantly shift scales between the agglomeration and the nation, both of which are interrelated. Nation is constructed by politically articulating its components, and agglomerations of urban, rural, and beyond are one such component. These articulations construct histories, guide development, and outline modalities of control (including on work).

As elsewhere in South Asia, in Sri Lanka too, the colonially imposed notions of gender were internalized and promoted as a code endemic to the culture of the land. Christian sanctity of marriage/sexuality and regimental European classification of sex were legally imposed, primarily to manage land. Therefore, at the core of this colonially imposed gender and sex classification, is control over land and private property (cf., Grossholtz 1984; Mathanaranjan and Swaminathan 2017). Contemporary gender constructs could also be read in a similar manner, one that of the biopolitics of development. In this sense, the state takes on a masculine role for interventions in agglomerations. To do so, the state needs and thus constructs agglomeration imaginaries. These agglomeration imaginaries in turn legitimize intervention, where a crucial aspect is the accepted notions of what bodies should be doing which activity/work.

To illustrate, in the 1990s, the notion of ideal Sri Lankan (Sinhala) village was evoked to convert them to production centres via garment factories. These factories, geared for export, idealized the work by women, the main labour force in these factories, as a contribution to build the nation (Lynch 1999). The idea being that the development of villages will lead to the development of the nation. This conceptualization legitimized exploitation and enforcement of gendered control over women's bodies. Jumping scales to the urban, the Megapolis Plan, which is the plan for urbanization of Western Region, made similar claims, of developing Colombo as leading to development of Sri Lanka (Ministry of Megapolis and Western Development 2016; Palat Narayanan 2020; Ruwanpura, Brown and Chan 2020a). They all point to differently imagined spaces. In the rural construct, particularly relating to the garment factories, women's bodies were imagined as the guardians of Sri Lankan morality and their hard work (and sufferings) as building the nation (Lynch 2007; Gunawardana 2013; Hewamanne 2021). In its urban iteration, they were replaced with masculine entrepreneurial zeal (Ruwanpura et al 2020a; Ruwanpura, Rowe and Chan 2020b; Radicati 2022). A rural-urban distinction has become a frequently invoked category to understand the mobilization of masculine imageries. This is not to say that the distinction is necessary or actual, but the imagination of this difference is important to understand the formation of agglomeration and the work carried out within them. This will become clearer when we look at the rural and urban imageries in the following sections.

Ideal Village and Tameable Bodies

One way to understand the construction of rural agglomerations in Sri Lanka is by juxtaposing two contradictory phases: first, prevalent during British colonization and immediately after independence, the notion of rural backwardness and second, prevalent post the 1950s nationalist revival, the renaissance of the glorious past and ideal village (Brow 1988; Tennekoon 1988). Both these constructs of the village determine the regulation of work by bodies occupying these spaces. I outline how these conceptions could help us in understanding the changing nature of work, agglomeration, and gender relations.

Discussing the colonial nature of Colombo, Perera (2016: 23) has argued that "Ceylon did not produce modern Colombo, but Colombo produced Ceylon." The colonial enterprise resulted from a maritime empire, one that prioritized ports as a means to exploit the *hinterland* (Perera 1998). The British captured Colombo, and it became the keystone of colonial exploitation. The port-centred colonial enterprise had very little understanding of the rest of Ceylon, especially that which was considered rural (Sathananthan 1991). The colonial rendering of the rural was one of underdevelopment. At one level, development meant bringing rural bodies more towards the British ethos of private property. This conceptualization of rural agglomerations of Sri Lanka legitimized the view of development via enabling the rural land holding gentry to *bestow* development alongside mending *backward (native)* ways of living.

Grossholtz (1984) has illustrated how the British colonial government policies were based on the intent to change *backward* ways of living via development. Unwillingness to work in the plantations was considered backward/lazy behaviour and coercive mechanisms were devised to dispose the villagers of their land and force them into wage labour. Much of the labour imports from the south of India to Sri Lanka was also legitimized on the ground of native unwillingness. Taxation on petty landholders and aiding the large holdings was possible, as the rural development was imagined to be provided by large landholders like the plantation owners. This conception, rather than uncovering structural issues leading to problems in rural areas, such as poverty, malnutrition, lack of medical facilities, problematized bodies and their practices, such as lacking work ethics, unhygienic lifestyle, social backwardness, legitimizing the paternalistic role of the state (cf., Sathananthan 1991). This conceptualization of rural Sri Lanka did not change post-independence, in part due to the continuity of actors. D.S. Senanayake (the first Prime Minister of independent Ceylon), who was the Minister of Agriculture and Lands in British Ceylon, had, for instance, proclaimed in 1935 that rural development means re-establishment of rural gentry as a key policy intervention. To recap, the village was imagined as a production site (mainly plantations) and villagers were seen as backward societies that needed to be taught to become productive labour.

Post-independence, in Sinhala majority areas, the government did not engage in active dispossession of small land holders nor coercively force population in rural areas to wage labour. Nonetheless, the rural imagination as backward continued. Out of the multitude of factors, an important facet is the construction of the role of the state and the imagined bodies for which it was acting. Here the state took a paternalistic/masculine attitude, one that must mend backward living manners of rural polity for its own good. This imagination meant that state acted out of good will and the *backward* polity has no agency.[4]

The second phase inverted this imagination to some extent. Intensifying ethnic tensions in Sri Lanka and the rise of nationalist electoral politics changed the notion of rural backwardness in the 1950s. In particular, the 1956 electoral victory of Sri Lanka Freedom Party (SLFP), led by SWRD Bandaranaike, shifted the prevalent imagination of rural Sri Lanka. Bandaranaike's electoral attack on Sir John Kotelawala, the third Prime Minister of Independent Ceylon from the United National Party (UNP), was towards his western modes of life, namely, lavish parties, personal foreign connections, and disregard for Buddhism. This attack necessitated an alternate *native* vision for Sri Lanka, which was largely based on Sinhala Buddhist revivalism (Rambukwella 2018; Venugopal 2022; see also Gamage and Rambukwella, this volume).[5]

SLFP's electoral victory brought political legitimacy to Sinhala Buddhist nationalism, which was largely rural based (Goonewardena 2020; Venugopal 2022). This notion of Sri Lanka and the country's culture imagined as inherently Sinhala was based on an idealized notion that the pre-colonial village that was rich with technical advancements especially around irrigation system, moral superiority of Buddhist ways of life, and social composition where Brahmanical ideals of subservient women safeguarding the purity of house/home were supposedly upheld (Leach 1959; Tennekoon 1988; de Alwis 2002; Jazeel 2009; Udalagama 2021). Furthermore, Haniffa's (2020) work has shown, for example, how agency-less bodies of women were rhetorically mobilized by opposing groups of both the Sinhala nationalist and Muslim elites, in strikingly similar masculine formulations.

The idea that rural bodies need to be *modernized* for development continues albeit the space they occupy evoked a glorious past in the 1950s. This past glory in its contemporary nature usually reinforces patriarchy (cf., de Alwis 2002; Herath 2015). Furthermore, the Sinhala Buddhist notion of rurality also necessitated a state to materialize it. In the post-independence period, UNP governments saw the urban as a locus of civilization, resulting in interventions for changing rural ways of living (Tennekoon 1988). Contrarily, the ideal village which was the epitome of Sinhala civilization could not be rendered in a similar fashion. Thus, the role of the state became to safeguard the *correct* ways of living (Brow 1988). Women's role in safeguarding the home or illustration of *good girls* in the garment industry are emblematic of these socio-spatial constructs (Lynch 1999; de Alwis 2002; Udalagama 2021).

Socio-spatial constructs mobilized by the state had immense impact on the everyday lives of people. The monogamous family unit is the core around which the ideal village is constructed. A rupture to this ideal came with the overseas migration of women as domestic workers. In 2010 the state took policy initiatives to restrict the migration of mothers with children under the age of five and replace it with the migration of men. The rationale of the policy was that the women staying at home would contribute to raising the next generation and building the nation. This move was possible because of the patriarchal notions, where women are carers and men the breadwinners (cf., Samarasinghe 2020). Migration restrictions further pushed women to work in informal sector and domestic work within the country. This is in contrast with the garment factories, where women's labour was rendered as necessary to build the nation, but this time by taking them to the formal sphere. These moments reflect how masculine imaginings control the work and domination of working life.

The evocation of a glorious past perhaps manifests most strikingly in the Mahaweli Irrigation and Development Project, an enormous irrigation planning project affecting around 40% of Sri Lanka's land mass (Tennekoon 1988; Widger and Wickramasinghe 2020). Rice cultivation in the dry zone and repopulation of new villages were possible as a consequence. However, 85.6% of agricultural work is still informal as of 2010 (Arunatilake 2013). Moreover, the past (Sinhala) glory imagery embedded in the Mahaweli development, as Tennekoon (1988) has argued, led to marginalization of ethnic and religious minorities in Sri Lanka.[6] This is a process that demonstrates the deeply entangled nature of agglomeration imageries; of space, work, and state interventions. Let us now turn to see how these imaginations manifest in urban spaces.

Modern Metropolis and Global Workers

The construction of urban also follows a similar pattern as that of rural. These imaginations form the ways through which state intervention affects the majority but often benefits only the elite. Historicization of this pattern is important to understand beyond the upsurge of literature on urban development in post-war Sri Lanka (after the end of the civil war in 2009). This focus is partly for a good reason in that many post-war urban interventions have diluted democracy and violently benefitted only the elite (Correspondent 2013; Godamunne 2015; Ruwanpura et al 2020a; Hewamanne 2021). Additionally, although the urban is thought to be seen by the rural populace as an antithesis of traditional values, the state is engaging to modify this (Moore 1984). The contemporary post-war clustering notwithstanding, these urban interventions are neither new nor uncommon elsewhere in the world.

One of the first *scientific* plans was attempted for Colombo by inviting Patrick Geddes in the 1920s (Perera 2008; Wahab-Salman 2021). The plan argued that the potential for economic growth had to be harnessed by the state using multiple interventions primarily geared towards the expansion of Colombo (Geddes 1921). Reading beyond, the premise which legitimizes this intervention is the imagery of a Colombo-focused development through which the entire country will develop. This imaginary has not changed much ever since. Newer terms like 'world-class city' are now in use, which reiterates the similar need to expand Colombo as foundational for developing the entire country (Nagaraj 2016; Palat Narayanan 2020; Ruwanpura et al 2020a; Radicati 2022).

Colombo has always been (locally) imagined within the global network of capital flows, although the sole focus on foreign direct investment is new. Hennayake (2013) elaborates this point using the local-global discussions, by disassociating it with specific geographies (west, non-west, etc.). Hennayake's (2013) reading of globalization is pertinent in understanding the past renderings of urban agglomeration as well as newer rhetoric of making (at least Colombo) world-class. These imageries of the global from being like Singapore to being a *developed* country are socially produced. Radicati (2022) has further analysed the everyday partaking of different actors like real-estate agents therein. In this imagination, informal work is often rendered as unimportant and undesirable as it is delinked from global capital flows and is reminiscent of (past) rurality. Further, Monteith and Giesbert's (2017) work shows how informal workers in Colombo aspire to be seen (and treated) as legitimate to the city and how they often emphasize the value/legitimacy of their work.

The delegitimization of informality is linked to the discourse around foreign investments and global image/imagery. Although Sri Lankan economy was liberalized in the late 1970s, the neoliberal dispossession at a large scale started much later (Fernando 2008; Nagaraj 2016). Niriella (2017), for example, has argued how the neo-liberalization of housing policy in Sri Lanka is more recent. In the 1970s the UNP government which opened the economy was also responsible for various social housing programmes (both rural and urban) targeting the poor. The projects, named after the target numbers (Hundred Thousand, One Million, and thereafter 1.5 Million houses Program), were discursively based on social welfare. The notion of a welfare state changed after the end of the civil war (2009), when the focus of the state shifted significantly towards economic development.[7] The economic development meant making Sri Lanka modern and thus a *developed* country. The construct of being modern also leads to structural dispossession of the urban poor

(Hennayake 2013; Nagaraj 2016; Abeyasekera et al 2019; Rasnayake 2019). The socio-economic gap which existed before deepened since the early 2000s and accelerated after 2009, which was when the war ostensibly ended. Throughout, Colombo has been the epicentre of economic development and thus that of dispossession, which has led to the marked territorialization of class and ethnicized neighbourhoods leading to the territorialization of informal works like vending (Nagaraj 2016; Niriella 2017; Abeyasekera et al 2019).

When the city is imagined as catalyst for economic growth, modernized notions of work are aligned similarly. It is a two-prong process. First, informal work, which is imagined as an anomaly, is curtailed. Second, any informality within work imagined as modern is overshadowed. A pertinent example of the latter comes from Radicati's (2022) work on real estate agents. The work of real estate agents is highly informal and is based on informal networks and deals. However, their work is neither rendered as informal work nor studied as such, because it deals with high-value property and legitimizes itself with *world-class* entrepreneurial zeal.

Herein, the relationship between Colombo and the rest of urban Sri Lanka also needs to be underlined. Colombo evades the nationalist discourse of being Sinhala. Thiranagama (2011) has shown how even Colombo's elite construct their origins as elsewhere. Similar readings are also offered by Thurairajah, Hollenbach and Alluri (2020) and Chattoraj (2022) to show how the Tamil diaspora understands Colombo as home or becoming home, as opposed to its suspended position in the dominant Sinhala nationalist discourse. Nonetheless, as it is economically and culturally important, the idea of Colombo developing the entire nation fits into the nationalist rhetoric even though Colombo itself evades *being* Sinhala. Colombo, therefore, could easily be ascribed to modernity, a concept that is in conflict with the *traditional* elsewhere in the country (Lynch 1999).

Furthermore, much of urban development in Sri Lanka is envisioned by Urban Development Authority (UDA), a federal body. Apart from the federal patronage, UDA has close links to the University of Moratuwa, which produces the leading planners and architects in the country. This link puts UDA in an advantageous position, both in terms of political mandate and technical expertise. The locational specificity of UDA in Colombo makes imageries of Colombo, the imageries of urban in Sri Lanka, resonating with Perera's (2016) invocation that Colombo shapes Sri Lanka, a contemporary phenomenon. This locational domination of Colombo also reflects in the literature, with considerably reduced number of analyses of/from urban phenomenon elsewhere.

Conclusion

Development of the imagery of authentic Sri Lankan village or that of a world-class city that will change the fate of Sri Lanka exists almost in concurrence. That is, one does not necessarily follow the other. Political movements and resulting academic attention drive certain ideas or critique of those ideas to prominence. I have presented various works which shows the prominence of agglomeration imageries as both masculine and hegemonic.

A large section of literature in Sri Lanka engage with gender formation and its impacts on women. Although more is needed, this centring of body overshadows the larger statal and spatial context in which it unfolds. Key events in Sri Lanka, like the independence (1948), tsunami (2004), end of the civil war (2009), tend to be the anchors around and through which literature on agglomeration is constructed. Historicizing these works, of which my contribution is a modest attempt, presents a larger pattern and diversity of masculine hegemony. We need more work, which looks at the cause, consequence, and mobilization of gender constructs and sexual classification in and beyond the body. Such works in/from Sri Lanka could be path-breaking precedent for understanding cases elsewhere, primarily because of Sri Lanka's (i) high human development index, (ii) free universal healthcare, (iii) free universal education (and high literacy rate), pushes us to move beyond causality and solutions (patronizing discourse of *uplifting* the marginalized) to a more multidimensional understanding of masculinity and hegemony.

To further understand contemporary agglomerations in Sri Lanka, we need to scrutinize the socio-political constructs which legitimize them and makes them physically possible to exist. From the notions of world class to developments in the port city and interventions elsewhere, all follow the masculine imagery, legitimizing violence and dispossession. These imageries also prioritizes and delegitimizes certain forms of work, especially the categorization of informality. I have outlined how the historicity of imageries cannot be overlooked and should be taken as a base on which these interventions on both work and agglomerations are read.

Notes

1 As discussed previously, note that Jaffe and Koster (2019) demonstrate how in the countries of global North, informality is altogether termed as something else, to avoid the connotations associated with informality.
2 Cf., Adikaram and Ratnayake (2021) on cyberbullying in workplaces and Haniffa (2020) on normalization of sexual violence in political rhetoric.
3 There are multitude of factors leading in general a lower level of participation by women in (formal) work force, cf., Karunaanithy (2016) for a quantitative understanding and Samarasinghe (2020) for a case on reversal of this role.
4 I use the term 'backward' as a continuity from the colonial discussions (cf., Sathananthan, 1991). This word/concept has been changing constantly, e.g., to unhygienic, improper, to finally informal.
5 Sinhala Buddhist is a term largely attributed to Anagarika Dharmapala (1864–1933), who linked Buddhism (religion) to Sinhala (ethnicity) and argued for the role of Sri Lanka in safeguarding the religion.
6 On one side the imageries of past Sinhala glory led to creation of new agglomerations and displacements of people to new villages (both displaced by the irrigation project as well as settled by the state for farming the irrigated lands). While on the other side, certain areas like the Jaffna Peninsula seen as a war zone contrarily led to large-scale deforestation and a steady decline of agriculture. Suthakar and Bui (2008) have traced the land-use change in Jaffna, outlining a 70% decrease in number of agriculture land holdings between 1982 and 2002.
7 It should be noted that end of civil war is a marker in the literature. Dispossession of the poor from their land has a longer history, e.g., establishment of Real Estate Exchange (Pvt) Ltd. (REEL) which consolidates *underutilized* land and *shifts* the urban poor to apartment buildings was established before the end of the war (Nagaraj 2016; Abeyasekera et al 2019).

References

Abeyasekera, Asha, Ammara Maqsood, Iromi Perera, Fizzah Sajjad and Jonanthan Spencer (2019) "Discipline in Sri Lanka, Punish in Pakistan: Neoliberalism, Governance and Housing Compared" *Journal of the British Academy* 7(S2): 215–244

Adikaram, A.S. and R.M.D.K. Ratnayake (2021) "Attacked Gender Identities: The Enigma of Cyberbullying in Sri Lankan Workplaces" In *Asian Perspectives on Workplace Bullying and Harassment* P. D'Cruz, E. Noronha and A. Mendonca (eds) Berlin: Springer, pp 153–180

Ariyarathne, Kaushalya (2021) "To Be or Not to Be Seen? Paradox of Recognition among Trans Men in Sri Lanka" *Masculinities Journal of Culture and Society* 15: 66–95

Arunatilake, Nisha (2013) "Precarious Work in Sri Lanka" *American Behavioural Scientist* 57(4): 488–506

Brow, James (1988) "In Pursuit of Hegemony: Representations of Authority and Justice in a Sri Lankan Village" *American Ethnologist* 15(2): 311–327

Chattoraj, Diotima (2022) "Sri Lankan Northern Tamils in Colombo: Broken Memories of Home" *South Asia Research* 42(2): 233–248

Cirolia, L.R. and S. Scheba (2019) "Towards a Multi-Scalar Reading of Informality in Delft, South Africa: Weaving the 'Everyday' with Wider Structural Tracings" *Urban Studies* 56(3): 594–611

Connell, Raewyn (2016) "Masculinities in Global Perspective: Hegemony, Contestation, and Changing Structures of Power" *Theory and Society* 45(4): 303–318

Correspondent, A. (2013) "Cementing Hegemony" *Economic and Political Weekly* 48(34): 22–26

de Alwis, Malathi (2002) "The Changing Role of Women in Sri Lankan Society" *Social Research* 69(3): 675–691

de Mel, Neloufer, Pradeep Peiris and Shyamala Gomez (2013) *Broadening Gender: Why Masculinities Matter: Attitudes, Practices and Gender-Based Violence in Four Districts in Sri Lanka* Ottawa: CARE international

de Silva, Jani (2014) "Valour, Violence and the Ethics of Struggle: Constructing Militant Masculinities in Sri Lanka" *South Asian History and Culture* 5(4): 438–456

Fernando, N. (2008) "Youth Aspirations for Education, Vocational Qualifications and Livelihoods in the Context of Economic Liberalization in Sri Lanka" In *Youth, Peace and Sustainable Development* Siri Hettige and Markus Mayer (eds) Colombo: CEPA

Geddes, Patrick (1921) *Town Planning in Colombo: A Preliminary Report* Ceylon: Government Record Office

Godamunne, Nayana (2015) "Development for Whom? Reimagining Urban Development in Colombo, Sri Lanka" *Journal of Urban Regeneration & Renewal* 8(2): 186–192

Goonewardena, Kanishka (2020) "Populism, Nationalism and Marxism in Sri Lanka: from Anti-Colonial Struggle to Authoritarian Neoliberalism" *Geografiska Annaler: Series B, Human Geography* 102(3): 289–304

Grossholtz, Jean (1984) *Forging Capitalist Patriarchy: The Economic and Social Transformation of Feudal Sri Lanka and Its Impact on Women* Durham: Duke University Press

Gunatilaka, Ramani (2008) *Informal employment in Sri Lanka: Nature, probability of employment, and determinants of wages*. Working paper (15 October). Accessed on 27/04/2022. Available at http://www.ilo.org/newdelhi/whatwedo/publications/WCMS_123348/lang-en/index.htm

Gunawardana, Samanthi J. (2013) "Rural Sinhalese Women, Nationalism and Narratives of Development in Sri Lanka's Post-War Political Economy" In *The Global Political Economy of the Household in Asia* Juanita Elias and Samanthi J Gunawardana (eds) International Political Economy Series. London: Palgrave Macmillan UK, pp 59–74

Haniffa, Farzana (2020) "Sri Lanka's Anti-Muslim Movement and Muslim Responses: How Were They Gendered?" In *Buddhist-Muslim Relations in a Theravada World* I. Frydenlund and M. Jerryson (eds) Berlin: Springer, pp 139–167

Hennayake, Nalini (2013) "Globalization from within: Interplay of the Local and the Global in Sri Lanka" *Sri Lanka Journal of Social Sciences* 33(1–2): 1–14

Herath, S.M.K. (2015) "Displacing Women, Resettling Families: Impact of Landslides on Women's Land Tenure Rights in Sri Lanka" In *Gender and Land Tenure in the Context of Disaster in Asia* Kyoko Kusakabe and R. Shrestha (eds) Berlin: Springer

Hewamanne, Sandra (2021) "Global Worker Protests and Tools of Autocratization in Sri Lanka" In *Routledge Handbook of Autocratization in South Asia* Sten Widmalm (ed) Abingdon: Routledge

Ihrig, J. and K.S. Moe (2004) "Lurking in the Shadows: The Informal Sector and Government Policy" *Journal of Development Economics* 73(2): 541–557

Jaffe, R. and M. Koster (2019) "The Myth of Formality in the Global North: Informality-as-Innovation in Dutch Governance" *International Journal of Urban and Regional Research* 43(3): 563–568

Jazeel, Tariq (2009) "Reading the Geography of Sri Lankan Island-Ness: Colonial Repetitions, Postcolonial Possibilities" *Contemporary South Asia* 17(4): 399–414

Karunaanithy, K. (2016) "Women Entrepreneurship: Can It Be a Driver of Economic Growth in Sri Lanka?" *The Sri Lanka Journal of South Asian Studies* 3(2): 35–46

Leach, Edward R. (1959) "Hydraulic Society in Ceylon" *Past and Present* 15: 2–26

Lynch, Caitrin (1999) "The "Good Girls" of Sri Lankan Modernity: Moral Orders of Nationalism and Capitalism" *Identities* 6(1): 55–89

Lynch, Caitrin (2007) *Juki Girls, Good Girls: Gender and Cultural Politics in Sri Lanka's Global Garment Industry* Ithaca: ILR Press/Cornell University Press

Mama, Amina (1996) "Sheroes and Villains: Conceptualizing Colonial and Contemporary Violence Against Women in Africa" In *Feminist Genealogies, Colonial Legacies, Democratic Futures* Jacqui M. Alexander and Chandra T. Mohanty (eds) Abingdon: Routledge, pp 46–62

Mathanaranjan, P. and M.J. Swaminathan (2017) "Gender Inequality, Land Rights and Socio-Economic Transformation: Historical Studies and Theoretical Analysis of Women's Right to Land under the Law of Thesawalamai" *The Sri Lanka Journal of South Asian Studies* 3(2): 72–90

Ministry of Megapolis and Western Development (2016) ***The Megapolis: Western Region Master Plan*** Ministry of Megapolis and Western Development

Monteith, Will and L. Giesbert (2017) "When the Stomach Is Full We Look for Respect': Perceptions of 'Good Work' in the Urban Informal Sectors of Three Developing Countries" ***Work, Employment and Society*** 31(5): 816–833

Moore, Mick (1984) "Categorising Space: Urban-rural or Core-periphery in Sri Lanka" ***The Journal of Development Studies*** 20(3): 102–122

Nagaraj, Vijay K. (2016) "From Smokestacks to Luxury Condos: The Housing Rights Struggle of the Millworkers of Mayura Place, Colombo" ***Contemporary South Asia*** 24(4): 429–443

Niriella, Nireliege Chandrasiri (2017) "Emerging Social-Spatial Polarisation within the Housing Market in Colombo, Sri Lanka" ***Journal of Urban Regeneration and Renewal*** 11(2): 158–167

Palat Narayanan, N. (2022) "Bath Packets and Multiple Colombo(s): Food and Gendered Urban Experience" ***Anthropology of Food*** 17: 1–14

Palat Narayanan, Nipesh (2019) "The Production of Informality and Everyday Politics: Drinking Water and Solid Waste Management in Jagdamba Camp, Delhi" ***City*** 23(1): 83–96

Palat Narayanan, Nipesh (2020) "World-Class as a Provincial Construct: Historicizing Planning in Colombo and Delhi" ***Planning Theory*** 19(3): 268–284

Perera, Nihal (1998) ***Society and Space: Colonialism, Nationalism, and Postcolonial Identity in Sri Lanka*** Transitions–Asia and Asian America. Boulder: Westview Press

Perera, Nihal (2008) "The Planners' City: The Construction of a Town Planning Perception of Colombo" ***Environment and Planning A: Economy and Space*** 40(1): 57–73

Perera, Nihal (2016) ***People's Spaces: Coping, Familiarizing, Creating*** New York: Routledge.

Radicati, Alessandra (2022) "World Class from within: Aspiration, Connection and Brokering in the Colombo Real Estate Market" ***Environment and Planning D: Society and Space*** 40(1): 118–137

Rambukwella, Harshana (2018) ***Politics and Poetics of Authenticity: A Cultural Genealogy of Sinhala Nationalism*** London: UCL Press

Rasnayake, S. (2019) "The Discourse of 'Slum-Free' City: A Critical Review of the Project of City Beautification in Colombo, Sri Lanka" ***Sri Lanka Journal of Sociology*** 1(1): 87–120

Ruwanpura, Kanchana N. (2022) ***Garments without Guilt?: Global Labour Justice and Ethical Codes in Sri Lankan Apparels*** Cambridge: Cambridge University Press

Ruwanpura, Kanchana N., Benjamin Brown and Loritta Chan (2020a) "(Dis)connecting Colombo: Situating the Megapolis in Postwar Sri Lanka" ***The Professional Geographer*** 72(1): 165–179

Ruwanpura, Kanchana N., Peter Rowe and Loritta Chan (2020b) "Of Bombs and Belts: Exploring Potential within China's Belt and Road Initiative in Sri Lanka" ***The Geographical Journal*** 186(3): 339–345

Samarasinghe, Vidyamali (2020) "When Migrant Women Return: Gender Role Re-Configurations in Sri Lankan Households" ***Asian Journal of Women's Studies*** 26(1): 94–113

Sathananthan, S. (1991) "Rural Development Policy in Sri Lanka, 1935 to 1989" ***Journal of Contemporary Asia*** 21(4): 433–454

Suthakar, K. and E.N. Bui (2008) "Land Use/Cover Changes in the War-Ravaged Jaffna Peninsula, Sri Lanka, 1984–early 2004" ***Singapore Journal of Tropical Geography*** 29(2): 205–220

Tennekoon, Serena N. (1988) "Rituals of Development: The Accelerated Mahaväli Development Program of Sri Lanka" ***American Ethnologist*** 15(2): 294–310

Thiranagama, Sharika (2011) ***In My Mother's House: Civil War in Sri Lanka*** Philadelphia: University of Pennsylvania Press

Thurairajah, Thanuja, Pia Hollenbach and R. Alluri (2020) "Vertical Living: Transnational Urbanisation and Diasporic Returns to Wellawatte/Colombo, Sri Lanka" ***South Asian Diaspora*** 12(1): 73–91

Udalagama, Tharindu (2021) "House Ablaze: A Case Study of Marital Conflict in Rural Sri Lanka" ***Contemporary South Asia*** 29(4): 546–559

Venugopal, Rajesh (2022) "Ethnic Domination under Liberal Democracy in Sri Lanka" ***Journal of Contemporary Asia*** 54(1): 90–109

Wahab-Salman, R. (2021) "Planning Colombo" ***Himal Southasian*** (28 September). Accessed on 28/09/2021. Available at https://www.himalmag.com/planning-colombo-garden-city-2021/

Widger, Tom and U. Wickramasinghe (2020) "Monsoon Uncertainties, Hydro-Chemical Infrastructures, and Ecological Time in Sri Lanka" In ***The Time of Anthropology : Studies of Contemporary Chronopolitics*** E. Kirtsoglou and B. Simpson (eds) Oxford: Routledge, pp 123–141

16
THE WORK AND LIVES OF AGRICULTURAL WORKERS

Cynthia M. Caron

Introduction

The British colonial regime neglected peasant agriculture because of its pre-occupations with the commercial crops of tea, rubber, and spices. Nonetheless, in the early years following Independence, peasants were Sri Lanka's largest occupational group, especially after government investment in large-scale irrigation schemes, such as Gal Oya and Mahaweli that led to the country achieving a 90% self-sufficiency rate in rice (paddy) production by the mid-1980s (Wickramasinghe 2014). Hence, understanding Sri Lanka's agricultural workers requires appreciating agriculture policy, the role that agricultural production plays in household reproduction, and the transformation of peasants and smallholder farmers into agri-entrepreneurs.

The post-colonial state heavily subsidizes agricultural production and, to mobilize nationalist voting constituencies, regularly invokes the idiom of the peasant's toil to feed the nation. While the image of the peasant remains strong, persons working in the agriculture sector are also called smallholder farmers, agricultural workers, and, most recently, agri-entrepreneurs. In general, risk, uncertainty, and low pay characterize the lives of agricultural workers in Sri Lanka.

Who Is the Agricultural Worker in Sri Lanka?

There are several ways to conceptualize the agricultural worker. Agricultural workers are individual men and women who might work on large or small landholdings owned by others as daily wage labourers without a contract. They are also called smallholder farmers, men, and women who cultivate their own landholdings, which may be titled jointly in the names of a husband and wife or titled only in a man's name. Smallholder farmers might work their plots alone, with unpaid family labour, or occasionally hire daily wage workers from nearby villages. Smallholder farmers who own land might enter into agreements with private sector corporations or government entities, forming nodes in their supply chains via out-grower programmes and nucleus farming schemes (Senevirathna 2018). These distinctions are important as they shed light on the fact that not only is agricultural work heterogeneous, but also that there are many entities looking to exploit or develop the agriculture sector in various ways. Therefore, the nature and the range of agricultural work and associated opportunities shape the lives and livelihoods of people who work in agriculture and their families.

Finally, knowledge about people who work in agriculture depends upon who is writing about and analysing the agriculture sector, and how agricultural workers fit into their vision of the sector's future. The Sri Lankan government, I/NGOs, and donor institutions with intentions to improve agricultural productivity for the purposes of economic growth, for example, write about agricultural workers very differently than agricultural scientists trying to find ways to help farmers adapt to the risks presented by climate change (e.g., decreased rainfall and prolonged dry seasons, increased rainfall and flooding, high winds and fluctuating and increased temperatures).

As the country's protracted conflict devastated agricultural infrastructure and livelihoods in the North and East for over 30 years, there is more knowledge about farmers' and agricultural workers' lives in these conflict-affected districts (Klem and Kelegama 2020). Private sector actors, and the donor agencies that support them, analyse the lives of people working in agriculture in instrumental ways as they are interested in finding ways to incorporate workers into markets and value chains.

Overview of the Agricultural Sector

Agriculture is not only a source of income, but a way of life and an expression of cultural heritage. For many people who work in agriculture, it is the only calling that they have the education and skills to pursue. Many factors shape the lives and well-being of agricultural workers in Sri Lanka, such as regional place of residence, land ownership status, and crops cultivated. Even though 77% of Sri Lankans live in rural areas, employment in the service industry is a more important source of income than employment in agriculture. In 2022, 27% of the Sri Lankan population worked in agriculture (World Bank 2022a).

Women outnumber men in the agriculture sector, particularly in their contribution as unpaid family workers (Asian Development Bank 2016). Given gender roles and responsibilities, women working in agriculture contribute a considerable amount of unpaid labour to the agricultural economy. This occurs not only in family-owned and operated farms, but also as subsistence labourers in backyard home gardens as well as the unpaid labour of social reproduction (e.g., cooking, cleaning, and child-rearing), which allows and supports men to pursue paid agricultural work (Gunawardana 2018). While more women than men worked in agriculture in 2019 (27% versus 23%), both men and women are moving away from agricultural work. The highest employment for women in agriculture was 49.7% in 1998; the highest rate for men was 43.8% in 1992.

In 2018, the government classified just over 45% of the country's land as agricultural land up from 27% in 1962. Agriculture contributes 7% to the country's Gross Domestic Product (GDP) (World Bank 2022b). There are sharp regional variations with respect to GDP and agricultural production. The island's most developed and urbanized province, the Western Province, contributes only 3.2% to the island's agricultural productivity whereas more rural provinces, such as Uva, the Northern, and the North Central contribute larger shares to agricultural GDP (30.1%, 24.2%, and 23.3%, respectively; ADB 2016).

Paddy cultivation takes place during both cultivation seasons, Maha (cultivation under rainfed conditions) and Yala (cultivation relying on irrigation water) – where these periods coincide with monsoonal rains and are pivotal in the dry zones of the country. When irrigation waters are too low for paddy cultivation in the Yala Season, farmers will cultivate other field (vegetable) crops, such as cowpea, maize or green gram, or vegetable crops, such as onion, brinjal, and beans. In 2009, paddy cultivation occupied 980,000 ha of cultivated land area island-wide and is an important source of income (Ministry of Primary Industries and Ministry of Agriculture 2016). During the war period, farmers in the Eastern Province maintained their paddy cultivation skills, and young people in the province are interested in agriculture, which bodes well for food security and economic development.

Families that work in the agricultural sector often pursue diversified livelihood strategies. In newly resettled conflict-affected areas of the Eastern Province, for example, women in female-headed households rely on paddy cultivation, either as daily wage labourers or through payment-in-kind towards others. Some women cultivate parcels of paddy land as tenant farmers, using the harvest for their own consumption, seed paddy for the next harvest, and processing into rice for sale in nearby villages during the off-season (Munas and Lokuge 2013).

Informal employment which includes low or unpaid and unregulated work is higher in the agricultural sector than it is in other sectors of the economy, e.g., services, trade, and industry. Informal labour arrangements can create unreliable and unstable incomes for agricultural workers, which increases the vulnerability of their families to social and economic shocks, illness, inflation, weather-related hazards, and their ability to recover from shocks and stressors.

Daily wage work in agriculture falls within the informal sector. There are three general characteristics of informal agricultural work: first, it is based on oral contracts that are not registered with a government authority; second, informal workers do not have union representation, and third, it is seasonal work with payment either in cash or in-kind. Such working conditions create uncertainty for agricultural workers as they are not regulated work environments (Upali 2017; Senevirathna 2018).

There is a gender wage gap between men and women agricultural workers in the informal sector. Men generally make a few hundred rupees more per day than women for the same work and the range of a potential daily wage earning is wider for men than for women. For example, in the Southern Province, a man's daily wage is approximately 31% higher than a woman's (Upali 2017: 347). The undervaluing of women's work and the view of women as dependent on men are among the reasons that men and women hired as daily wage workers in paddy cultivation, highland crop cultivation (vegetable production), banana plantations, and chena cultivation are paid differently. Due to low wages, many agricultural workers in the informal sector earn incomes considered below the poverty line and qualify for government assistance, such as Samurdhi.

Rhythms of the Agricultural Household and the Household Economy

A traditional gender division of labour characterizes agricultural households (Patel and Moore 2017; Caron 2020). Men are considered the breadwinner, engaged primarily in paid work either in their own agricultural fields or outside the home to cover household expenses. Men also participate in unpaid work in diverse, species-rich home gardens, chenas (slash-and-burn agricultural plots), and in the gathering of forest produce. Adult family members spend less time on non-paid work as the extent of their landholding increases.

Women are also engaged in paid work unpaid work as paid work, unpaid work, and care work. care work. While both men and women may spend equal amounts of time in regular and informal paid employment, women spend much more time in care work: preparing meals and caring for children and elderly family members. Men spend very little time on childcare. Adult family members spend less time on non-paid work as the extent of their landholding increases. Overall, women work longer days than men and have less time for leisure (Rathnayaka and Weerahewa 2015). Older children and men with access to bicycles would be more likely to help with domestic chores, such as the collection of water and firewood (unpaid work) if the government improved rural roads.

Agricultural workers do not necessarily have access to modern agricultural technologies, which would connect them to private-sector opportunities that facilitate national economic growth as well as improve household incomes reducing rural poverty (Ministry of Plantation Industries and Export Agriculture and Ministry of Education 2020). Women working in agriculture tend to have less access to capital and are often not able to implement measures suggested by agricultural extension services (Lamontagne-Godwin et al 2017). With respect to the workers' lives and the gender division of labour within agricultural households, women are responsible for the unpaid care work of household reproduction. Men devote few hours to care work within the household, allocating more of their time first to paid labour followed by unpaid work (Rathnayaka and Weerahewa 2015). Women contribute considerable on-farm labour across the agricultural cycle, including planting, weeding, and harvesting, all of which have positive effects on the household economy. However, women are not primary on-farm decision-makers and have limited involvement in local farmer organizations (Lamontagne-Godwin et al 2017). Furthermore, they are rarely considered farmers, as they are not landowners (Kalansooriya and Chandrakumara 2014).

Risks and Uncertainties Facing Agricultural Workers, Livelihoods, and Threats

While several uncertainties and associated risks characterize the lives of agricultural workers and agricultural smallholders, they are also targeted for a range of business, technology, and social science innovations, which can bring risks of their own – including becoming locked into exploitative value chains. The solutions to mitigate risks and cope with contingencies are hence never risk-free. The two greatest threats to agricultural workers' lives and their livelihoods are compromises to their health and natural disasters, and ecological change associated with global climate change.

Health Risks

For over two decades, residents of rural populations including men and women employed in agriculture in Sri Lanka's Northern, Uva, Eastern, and North-Central provinces have suffered from chronic kidney disease of unknown/uncertain etiology or origin (CKDu). Individuals suffering from this degenerative and irreversible kidney disease should visit their local hospital's renal clinic for routine dialysis at least once a week; however, uncertainty characterizes their treatment plans as medical equipment such as haemodialysis machines, medical staff, and related supplies often are limited in rural hospitals. Patients with advanced CKDu and/or end-stage renal failure experience joint pain, swelling of limbs, dizziness, and fatigue making it impossible to work (Senanayake 2022). Farmers often do not use protective gear, such as gloves, masks, or boots, while working with chemicals in the field. Given the diseases' unknown origin, scientists and public health experts continue to study CKDu to better understand if and the extent to which the application of agro-chemicals found in fertilizers and pesticides, agrochemical contamination of groundwater and drinking water, heavy metal exposure, and local geophysical characteristics such as soil type and soil structure are among the origin factors for CKDu.

The availability of pesticides within agricultural households enables self-harm or suicide via ingestion of pesticides. Given the uncertainties and challenges that farming families face such as poverty, debt, and that accompany with associated with stressors economic development (de Silva 2021; Utyasheva and Eddleston 2021), the ingestion of agricultural pesticides that often leads to death is a public health problem. Restricting access to the means or materials to commit suicide or self-harm is an effective preventative measure. Following legislative actions by the Government of Sri Lanka between 2008 and 2011, which banned the use of popular chemical compounds such as dimethoate and paraquat, suicide rates dropped by 70% and without negative effects on agricultural yields (Knipe, Gunnell and Eddleston 2017).

Adapting to Uncertainty: The Risk of Natural Disasters and Global Climate Change

With the effects of global climate change including but not limited to flash flooding, drought, and excessive heat waves, pursuing an agricultural-based livelihood is risky. Farmers need to be able to quickly adapt to a range of unexpected weather conditions and often rely on traditional social and often rely on local ecological knowledge and traditional social institutions to do so. To adapt to changes in temperature and rainfall, farmers plant short-season crops, plant drought-resistant crops, change their crop sowing and planting dates, and plant trees.

Farmers cultivating in the Mahaweli system are working together and practising *bethma*, a traditional drought mitigation technique (Burchfield and Gilligan 2016). Under *bethma*, farmers abandon their individual plots and redistribute all land in the command area (the area adjacent to the irrigation source/dam) among all cultivators. Every farmer will have access to the same sized parcel to cultivate regardless of how much land they own. As a result, some farmers sacrifice private gains so that everyone can cultivate something under drought conditions. Downstream farmers at the tail-end of the command area who would not receive irrigation water due to drought conditions are asked to migrate to the head-end, the command area, to cultivate. In some cases, this requires Tamil-speaking farmers to move temporarily to Sinhala-speaking areas for cultivation. Even though every farmer in the system cultivates less area under *bethma*, farmers prefer this than to have a situation where some farmers are not able to cultivate at all.

Adapting to Uncertainty: Government Policy and Government Decision-Making Power

The Government of Sri Lanka started resettling families from southern parts of the island to the Mahaweli Accelerated Agricultural Development Scheme in the 1950s (Muggah 2008). Today, the Mahaweli Authority of Sri Lanka (MASL) advises farmers to grow soy, maize, or other drought-tolerant crops, such as onion or chillies, as these crops use less water than paddy. However, farmers have little incentive to switch to these crops as the government heavily subsidizes paddy cultivation. To control prices, the Government of Sri Lanka tries to exercise some control over farmer cultivation practices. Its 'one village one crop' approach, for example, ensures that farmers do not overproduce any one crop leading to its oversupply and a lower price point. Farmers may produce multiple crops over a year, but only one crop at a time.

In early 2021, the Government of Sri Lanka banned chemical fertilizers, essentially forcing farmers to pursue organic agriculture. Reducing reliance on imported fertilizer would not only save the cash-strapped government valuable foreign exchange, but then President Gotabaya Rajapaksa argued that the chemical fertilizers posed health and safety risks to agricultural workers (see health risks above). Elevating Sri Lanka on the global stage, as the first 100% organic farming nation and steadfastly protecting citizen rights to non-toxic produce, served as policy justifications for the ban (Presidential Secretariat 2021), not the country's own high level of indebtedness and currency instability (Wipulasena and Mashal 2021). The application of this ban also revealed a double standard, the ban presented an undue hardship on agricultural smallholders whereas large corporations, such as Dole Foods and tea plantation corporations, were exempt (A subsistence farmer 2021).

As a result of this organic turn, crop yields suffered. Nearly 75% of Sri Lankan farmers use chemical fertilizers and could not switch over to organic cultivation techniques quickly enough to produce crops, which subsequently left a considerable amount of arable land uncultivated (Wipulasena and Mashal 2021). In other cases, crops failed without their usual inputs. Lower yields and inability to grow grains and vegetables reduced the country's food supply, leading to food shortages, inflated food prices, and redirecting whatever foreign exchange might have been saved on fertilizer imports to importing rice (estimated at $450 million USD; Nordhaus and Shah 2022).

The government reversed the policy in October 2021, following widespread farmer protests. In early 2022, it agreed to pay compensation to over one million rice farmers who lost crops due to the chemical fertilizer ban (AFP 2022). In addition to the risks and uncertainties discussed in this section, agricultural workers also find themselves as targets of external actors. The targeting of agricultural workers is discussed below.

Agribusiness Networks and Local/Global Value Chains

The lives of agricultural workers and the opportunities that they have, to some extent, depend on where they live and work in the country. As mentioned above, people who work in agriculture are often seen by the government, donor institutions, and private sector entities as instruments to help achieve economic and/or gender equality goals. Given the war's (1983–2009) devastating impact on infrastructure, the Government of Sri Lanka together with international donor institutions, such as the United States Agency for International Development (USAID) and agribusinesses, such as the global entity Land O'Lakes and local Sri Lankan corporation, such as Hayleys and Cargill, are working together to rebuild the conflict-affected agricultural economy of the North and East as well as border areas in the Uva and North Central Provinces (Senevirathna 2018). In the North and East, farmers participate in donor investments in dairy, horticulture (i.e., passion fruit, onion, chilli seed, and mushrooms), and poultry production meant to improve family member nutrition and household incomes through commercialization and strengthen value chains with input suppliers, private sector buyers, and local markets. Financial management, financial literacy, and recordkeeping classes improve their entrepreneurial skills. Donor agencies target women to promote their empowerment and gender equality within the agricultural sector, providing them with improved technologies, such as chicken coops or animal feed, and investment financing. These financing schemes that include microcredit often have adverse consequences for women (de Soysa 2021).[1] Donor agencies also target youth to demonstrate the potential of agriculture as a profitable occupation. Following such interventions, some men indicate their main source of income and occupation has switched from paddy to dairy production.

Over the past decade, smallholder farmers have become increasingly more involved in contract farming arrangements with private sector entities, as global financial and donor institutions promote private sector-led agricultural transformation as a poverty reduction cum economic growth strategy. While such partnerships might improve income and access to markets in the short term, they do not necessarily address the root causes of poverty in rural areas, and they create farmer dependency on the private sector (Senevirathna 2018).

Contract farming provides farmers with access to inputs and market opportunities. It connects rural farmers to global markets by integrating farmers into local value or supply chains. Private sector entities that manage supply chains provide farmers with access to credit, seeds, fertilizer and other inputs, and the provision of such goods and services is important to the country's post-war economic development strategy.

Access to improved technologies could enhance both the earnings of women who earn a living through agriculture and their contributions to value-added production. Women working in agricultural households do not have access to many modern, energy-based household conveniences, such as energy efficient cook stoves, washing machines or refrigerators, which does little to reduce their time spent in household social reproduction and limits their ability to participate in value-added processing of agricultural produce. Reduced access to water pumps, rice husking, and grain milling also limit women's productivity and contribution to their productive tasks in agriculture.

As the government restricts companies from owning large acres of land, local agribusiness companies, such as Hayleys and the local supermarket chain, Cargills, contract rural farmers via out-grower programmes and nucleus farming schemes. As part of these schemes, companies supply farmers with seeds or improved agricultural technology (i.e., drip irrigation or raised beds), training programmes on safe fertilizer and pesticide application, transportation, and a guaranteed market (Senevirathna 2018; Caron 2020). In exchange for these inputs, knowledge and services, farmers sell them their produce, ensuring a continuous supply of produce for these companies' urban consumers (Rathnayake, Gray, Reid and Ramilan 2022).

These corporations establish purchase contracts and provide contracted farmers with techniques to improve crop yields, seed production, and safely apply pesticides. For example, over 1,110 farmers participate in Hayleys Agro Farms (Pvt) Limited, receiving seed paddy as part of the out-grower network (Hayleys 2022). Over 10,000 farmers directly supply Cargills with fresh milk, fruit and vegetables through dozens of collection stations located around the country. Direct contracts with corporate entities, such as Hayleys and Cargills, replace local middlemen that many farmers once relied on for marketing produce. There is little comparative analysis demonstrating the extent to which corporate connections improve the welfare of agricultural workers and their families compared with the general middleman model. Senevirathna's research (2018) shows that corporate partnerships do very little to lift agricultural producers out of poverty, as they tend to work with already-privileged, asset-owning farmers rather than include the poorest of the poor in their projects.

Nestle Lanka is a well-established corporate actor in the dairy sector, guaranteeing a regular income for milk producers and strengthening dairy value chains. Wijayasinghe and Sachitra's (2021) research found that dairy farmers were pleased with the assistance and knowledge received from their corporate buyers and recognized new local employment opportunities along the value chain such as positions at collection and chilling centres, which improve local incomes.

Corporations provide technical assistance, financial support, educational programmes, and infrastructure such as transportation and storage all of which improve production and therefore worker incomes. Corporate field officers encourage and inspire farmers to perform well and assist them through difficult growing conditions. As such, corporate projects transform smallholder farmers and others working in agriculture into agri-entrepreneurs who produce high-end products for both urban consumers and for export.

Targets for Climate-Change Related Agricultural Innovations

Given climate change effects and their implications for national food security and agricultural livelihoods, donor agencies such as the United States Agency of International Development (USAID) and the World Bank are making investments that promote being climate-resilient and climate-smart. These donors and their partners target women's development committees, early-stage entrepreneurs, and market-driven private sector actors with educational and financial resources for climate change adaptation and to manage climate-related risks (USAID 2021). NGOs may compete for donor funds to engage with agricultural communities and deliver goods and services that 'de-risk' (USAID 2022: 4) agriculture livelihoods. Some smallholders receive free seeds, sprinkler systems, and agricultural extension services (World Bank 2021). They are targets of donor-sponsored 'nudging tools (advocacy, demonstration, peer influence and peer pressure)' to encourage the use of 'solar-based irrigation' systems (Lhamtshok 2022).

With new investments in the agriculture sector, farmers will have access to more affordable insurance schemes to protect against crop losses, financial services to invest in climate-smart technology, and climate resilience warehouses to reduce post-harvest losses. Farmers will participate in and benefit from agriculture projects that pilot new climate-smart agriculture technologies and technological applications, such as real-time, agro-meteorological information, precision sensor technology for water management, digitalization of public services, and digital market platforms that link farmers and buyers (USAID 2022; World Bank 2022b).

Targets for Empowerment, Equity, and Inclusions

Women working in agriculture, those living in former conflict-affected areas, and leading women-headed households are targets of international donor agencies and corporate gender equity and empowerment programmes. Nestle Lanka specifically seeks to recruit women into dairy farming, with women in the Northern Province particularly active in that enterprise. In seeking to transform women into agri-entrepreneurs, USAID programmes, for example, seek to move women with small backyard poultry operations into commercial-scale production to supply boiler chickens to local markets and increase their income in the process. Women farmers indicate that direct links between them and private sector buyers via project-facilitated value chains allow them to receive payments directly rather than through men who normally market produce (USAID 2017). Women directly receiving income is a proxy indicator for control over income and an indicator of women's empowerment.

As the older generation moves away from agricultural lifestyles and young people seek jobs in urban areas, the government and donor agencies are finding ways to make agriculture and an agricultural-based lifestyle attractive to young people. Donor agencies target youth in their agricultural programming to develop the sector and appeal to their 'business orientation' and skills by providing Internet-based technical knowledge, hopefully increasing agriculture's share of the national Gross Domestic Product.

Conclusions: Gaps in the Literature

There is a rich ethnographic tradition in Sri Lankan Studies scholarship that focuses on agricultural work, kinship networks, land tenure, and inheritance systems, providing insights into the social, economic, and political contours of rural society (Leach 1961; Gunasinghe 1992). Contemporary scholarship, especially since the end of the war in 2009, tends to focus on the challenges of working in agriculture, the national and internationally sponsored programmes, and interventions created to respond to such challenges as well as local community-based initiatives to cope with climate change. Agricultural workers and their rural-dwelling family members face health risks associated with agrochemical use and chemical contamination of drinking water and economic risks associated with crop failure. With globalization, industrialization, and now climate change effects, men and women pursuing agricultural work continue to consider the opportunity costs of working in agriculture versus working in a free trade zone, migrating to work abroad as unskilled labour, whether to encourage their children to follow in their footsteps or whether to migrate within the country to pursue new agricultural opportunities created in the North and East with the war's end (Caron 2020; Klem and Kelegama 2020).

Researchers and practitioners producing working papers, policy briefs, and other products that constitute the 'grey' literature focus more on production issues and policy formulation to support and increase production. More contemporary ethnographic studies with rich narrative descriptions that introduce readers to the multiple life worlds of agricultural workers from a first-person perspective and resonate with village-level, case study scholarship is needed to balance the instrumental view of farmers that policymakers and donors often take. Important questions to ask about the life worlds of agricultural workers include, but are not limited to: How do farmers grapple with and how to they understand the risks associated with climate change and agriculture-based livelihoods (either slow onset or extreme weather events)? How do farmers and women with 'backyard operations' make decisions about participating in the range of corporate or private-sector programmes created for them or do they consider themselves excluded from private-sector opportunities and if so, why?

There are not many quantitative, sex-disaggregated studies that focus on men's and women's participation in the sector whether as daily wage labourers or as contractors holding longer, fixed-term agreements. With respect to the rise of agri-entrepreneur programmes, agri-business contracts, and the strengthening of value chains, there is a need for robust studies about these programmes that focus on worker or farmer perspective on private sector treatment and working conditions. Such research would not only be in the service of improving private-sector engagement and agricultural worker livelihoods but also shed light on how privatization, neoliberal reforms, and the post-COVID-19 economic crisis are unfolding in Sri Lanka and affecting agricultural smallholders and workers. Most of the information about agri-entrepreneur and agri-business programmes originates in the grey literature such as donor evaluation reports or press releases that tend to profile the model participant and use 'cherry-picked' quotes from beneficiaries to emphasize project success. Lastly, there needs to be follow-up research on donor-funded projects. For example, how does and to what extent can a smallholder who participated in a donor-funded intervention that increased their backyard operations by 537%, moving from 37 to 237 boiler chickens according to (USAID 2017), sustain such enterprises independently, without project support.

The scholarship reviewed here focuses more on production issues and policy formulation to support and increase production. There are very few contemporary ethnographic studies with rich narrative descriptions that take readers into and introduce them to the world of agricultural workers. Important questions to ask about the life worlds of agricultural workers include, but are not limited to: What are the factors that farmers consider about whether to move out of smallholder agriculture and into wage labour or migrate abroad? How do they understand the risks associated with climate change and agriculture-based livelihoods? How do farmers and women with 'backyard operations' make decisions about participating in the range of private-sector programmes created for them or do they consider themselves excluded? These are areas of research that remain to be done by future generations of scholars.

Note

1 One risk associated with such donor interventions is rural indebtedness. Smallholders often find themselves borrowing financial capital to make the required entrepreneurial investments that participation project requires. When entrepreneurial activities fail, smallholders must find some way to settle the debt associated borrowing start-up capital, which often involve taking out another loan (de Silva 2021; de Soysa 2021).

References

A Subsistence farmer (2021) "The Organic Fiasco: A farmer's view" (11 March). Accessed on 21/11/2022. Available at https://groundviews.org/2021/11/03/the-organic-fiasco-a-farmers-view/

AFP (2022) "Sri Lanka to pay $200m compensation for failed organic farm drive" (26 January). Accessed on 19/11/2021. Available at https://www.aljazeera.com/news/2022/1/26/sri-lanka-200-million-compensation-farmers-organic-crops-drive

Asian Development Bank (2016) *Sri Lanka: Gender Equality Diagnostic of Selected Sectors*. Accessed on 19/11/2021. Available at https://www.adb.org/documents/sri-lanka-gender-equality-diagnostic-selected-sectors

Burchfield, Emily K. and Jonathan Gilligan (2016) "Agricultural Adaptation to Drought in the Sri Lankan Dry Zone" *Applied Geography* 77: 92–100. http://dx.doi.org/10.1016/j.apgeog.2016.10.003

Caron, Cynthia M. (2020) "Gendering Work and Labor in the Agriculture Sector, a Focus on South Asia" In *The Handbook of Gender in Asia* S. Huang and Kanchana N. Ruwanpura (eds) Cheltenham: Edward Elgar Publishing, pp 185–202

de Silva, Nedha (2021) "Rural Women Demand Relief from Vicious Cycle of Debt" *Groundviews* (April 2021). Accessed on 23/11/2022. Available at https://groundviews.org/2021/04/03/rural-women-demand-relief-from-the-vicious-cycle-of-debt/

de Soysa, Minoli (2021) "Drowning in Debt, Women Farmers Take a Firm Stand" *Groundviews* (April 2021). Accessed on 23/11/2022. Available at https://groundviews.org/2021/04/06/drowning-in-debt-women-farmers-take-a-firm-stand/

Gunasinghe, Newton (1992) "Transformation and Trajectories of Agrarian Systems in Jaffna and Nuwara Eliya Districts" In *Agrarian Change in Sri Lanka* James Brow and Joe Weeramunda (eds) New Delhi: Sage, pp 131–154

Gunawardana, Samanthi Jayasekara (2018) "Rural women's participation and recognition in sustainable agricultural livelihoods across their life-course, in post-war Sri Lanka" Oxfam-Monash Partnership. Accessed on 10/10/2021. Available at https://www.monash.edu/__data/assets/pdf_file/0010/2482804/rural-sri-lankan-women-in-agriculture-executive-summary-english.pdf

Hayleys (2022) A significant contribution to sustainable farming by Hayleys Agro Farms (Pvt) Limited. Accessed on 06/11/2021. Available at https://www.hayleys.com/a-significant-contribution-to-sustainable-farming-by-hayleys-agro-farms-pvt-limited/

Kalansooriya, C.W. and D.P.S. Chandrakumara (2014) "Women's Role in Household Food Security in Rural Sri Lanka" *International Journal of Multidisciplinary Studies* 1(1): 41–54

Klem, Bart and Thiruni Kelegama (2020) "Marginal Placeholders: Peasants, Paddy and Ethnic Space in Sri Lanka's Post-War Frontier" *The Journal of Peasant Studies* 47(2): 346–365. https://doi.org/10.1080/03066150.2019.1572604

Knipe, Duleeka W., David Gunnell and Michael Eddleston (2017) "Preventing Deaths from Pesticide Self-Poisoning – Learning from Sri Lanka's Success" *The Lancet* 5(7): E651–E652. Accessed on 21/11/2022. Available at https://www.thelancet.com/journals/langlo/article/PIIS2214-109X(17)30208-5/fulltext

Lamontagne-Godwin, Julien, Frances Williams, Willoru Mudiyansele Palitha Thilakasiri Bandara and Ziporah Appiah-Kubi (2017) "Quality of Extension Advice: A Gendered Case Study from Ghana and Sri Lanka" *The Journal of Agricultural Education and Extension* 23(1): 7–22

Leach, Edmund R. (1961) *Pul Eliya A Village in Ceylon: A Study of Land Tenure and Kinship* Cambridge: Cambridge University Press

Lhamtshok, Tshering (2022) *Innovation in Climate-Smart Agriculture.* Asian Disaster Preparedness Center (ADPC). Accessed on 23/11/2022. Available at https://www.adpc.net/cic/index.php/2022/04/15/innovation-in-climate-smart-agriculture/

Ministry of Plantation Industries and Export Agriculture and Ministry of Agriculture (2020) *Environmental Assessment & Management Framework: Agricultural Sector Modernization Project.* Submitted to the World Bank. Accessed on 15/09/2021. Available at https://documents1.worldbank.org/curated/en/135291593168689920/pdf/Environmental-Assessment-and-Management-Framework.pdf

Muggah, Robert (2008) *Relocation Failures in Sri Lanka: A Short History of Internal Displacement and Resettlement* London and New York: Zed Book

Munas, Mohamed and Gayathri Lokuge (2013) *A Livelihood and Market Study of Resettled Communities in the Eastern Province* Colombo: Centre for Poverty Analysis

Nordhaus, Ted and Saloni Shah (2022) "In Sri Lanka, Organic Farming Went Catastrophically Wrong" *Foreign Policy*. Accessed on 05/03/2022. Available at https://foreignpolicy.com/2022/03/05/sri-lanka-organic-farming-crisis/

Patel, Raj and Jason W. Moore (2017) *A History of the World in Seven Cheap Things* Berkeley: University of California Press

Presidential Secretariat (2021) "Importation of chemical fertilizers will be stopped completely" (22 April). Accessed on 18/09/2022. Available at https://www.presidentsoffice.gov.lk/index.php/2021/04/22/importation-of-chemical-fertilizers-will-be-stopped-completely/

Rathnayaka, R.M.S.D. and J. Weerahewa (2015) "An Analysis of Gender Differences in Intra-Household Time Allocation of Rural Farm Families in Sri Lanka" *Tropical Agricultural Research* 26(4): 677–683

Rathnayake, Sanduni, David Gray, Janet Reid and Thiagarajah Ramilan (2022) "The Impacts of the COVID-19 Shock on Sustainability and Farmer Livelihoods in Sri Lanka" *Current Research in Environmental Sustainability* 4: 1–11. https://doi.org/10.1016/j.crsust.2022.100131

Senanayake, Nari (2022) ""We Are the Living Dead", or, the Precarious Stabilization of the Liminal Life in the Presence of CKDu" *Antipode* 54(6): 1965–1985

Senevirathna, Priyan (2018) "Creating Shared Value through Partnership in Agricultural Production in Sri Lanka" *Geoforum* 90: 219–222

Upali, Pannilage (2017) "A Socio-Economic Analysis on the Gender Wage Gap among Agricultural Laborers in Rural Sri Lanka" *American Scientific Research Journal for Engineering, Technology and Sciences* 30(1): 338—335

USAID (2017) *Final Performance Evaluation of USAID/Sri Lanka Supporting Opportunities for Livelihood Development (SOLID) Activity* Washington: USAID. https://pdf.usaid.gov/pdf_docs/PA00N3ZQ.pdf

USAID (2021) *Climate Change Adaptation Sri Lanka*. Accessed on 18/11/2022. Available at https://www.usaid.gov/sites/default/files/2022-05/USAID_Sri_Lanka_EG_11-2021_-_Climate_Change_Adaptation.pdf

USAID (2022) *Annual Program Statement USAID Climate Adaptation Project Sri Lanka (CAP-SL-APS-001)*. Washington: USAID. Accessed on 18/11/2022. Available at https://sharena11.springcm.com/Public/Folder/22197/56005e47-f001-ed11-9c55-ac162d885f33/18f0e818-f901-ed11-9c55-ac162d885f33

Utyasheva, Leah and Michael Eddleston (2021) "Prevention of Pesticide Suicides and the Right to Life: The Intersection of Human Rights and Public Health Priorities" *Journal of Human Rights* 20(1) 52–71. https://doi.org/10.1080/14754835.2020.1850241

Wickramasinghe, Nira (2014) *Sri Lanka in the Modern Age: A History* Oxford and New York: Oxford University Press

Wijayasinghe, Sachin and Vilani Sachitra (2021) "Corporate Citizenhsip Behaviour and Rural Livelihoods: A Study on Multinational Corporations in Sri Lanka" *Vidyodaya Journal of Management* (7)1: 81–104. https://doi.org/10.31357/vjm.v7i1.4910

Wipulasena, Aanya and Mujib Mashal (2021) "Sri Lanka's Plunge into Organic Farming Brings Disaster" *The New York Times* (12 July). Accessed on 01/03/2022. https://www.nytimes.com/2021/12/07/world/asia/sri-lanka-organic-farming-fertilizer.html

World Bank (2021) Result Briefs: Climate Smart Irrigated Agriculture Project Helped Sri Lanka's Smallholder Farmers Weather the COVID-19 Pandemic. Accessed on 20/11/2022. Available at https://www.worldbank.org/en/results/2021/04/19/climate-smart-irrigated-agriculture-project-helped-srilanka-smallholder-farmers

World Bank (2022a) Dataset. Accessed on 20/10/2021. Available at https://data.worldbank.org/country/sri-lanka?view=chart

World Bank (2022b) "Speeches & Transcripts. Knock 2022 Conference: The Doorway to Success with a special theme on Agriculture, Dairy and Fisheries" (15 February). Accessed on 20/10/2022. Available at https://www.worldbank.org/en/news/speech/2022/02/15/knock-knock-conference-2022-the-doorway-to-success-with-a-special-theme-on-agriculture-dairy-and-fisheries

17
THE GENDERED POLITICAL ECONOMY OF WORK IN POST-WAR SRI LANKA

Jayanthi Thiyaga Lingham

The Post-War Political Economy and Its Gendered Dimensions

As the military conflict ended, the Sri Lankan government (GoSL) moved to assimilate the Northern and Eastern Provinces, socially, physically, and economically. This meant that open market reforms implemented across the island at the end of the 1970s were rolled out into the region, as wartime economic embargos had excluded the North and East. Now, as part of the post-war 'transition to peace', the whole island was subjected to deepening neoliberal policies, this time underpinned by financialisation (Kadirgamar 2013). In the North and East, this manifested as a quite abrupt opening of the economy to national and international capital flows, with a concerted drive by the state for large-scale private capital investment. Central state security forces were, and remain, extensively involved in the post-war programme (Government of Sri Lanka 2012; Pieris 2014). With North-South economic relations shifting, reconstruction programmes 'Northern Awakening' and 'Eastern Awakening' were rolled out with selected international assistance and militarised incursions.

One of the stated objectives of these programmes was "the economic advancement of war-affected women" but in practice this meant militarised incursions and selective international assistance (Chandrasiri 2009; Venugopal 2011; Goger and Ruwanpura 2014; Ruwanpura 2018). The government encouraged input from the banking sector via the extension of micro-credit to individuals and small groups for the resumption or expansion of income-generating economic activities. Women-headed households were identified as needing to be "put on the track to self-sufficiency" with credit and technical assistance for "alternative livelihoods" (Government of Sri Lanka, United Nations and Partners 2011). From a feminist perspective, I outline how this focus on women panned out.

Post-War Capital Accumulation and Gendered Dimensions for Women

As broader socio-economic dynamics shifted in these ways in the war-affected territories, so too did their gendered impacts on women. This section looks at literature exploring shifts in the manufacturing and tourist sectors. It is worth noting that these studies mostly focus on the Eastern Province, part of the contested territory during the war but where the socio-political context diverged from the North in several ways. These relate to the differing progression of war in the East and North; differences in wartime, post-war political dynamics and different ethnic, caste, and class dynamics in each province.

Against this backdrop, Goger and Ruwanpura (2014) look at the role of industrial capital and its relationship with the state in the post-war landscape, given the paucity of it. Their study was part of a wider investigation into how power relations, discourses, and practices circulate through elite networks in the garment industry. The apparel-manufacturing workforce across Sri Lanka is overwhelmingly made up of women. Moreover, in the East, matrilineal inheritance patterns and land rights available to women co-exist with uneven impacts of conflict and with patriarchal structures that shape women's livelihoods strategies (Ruwanpura 2006), with patriarchal structures embedded in all dominant ethno-nationalist projects and oppressively pervading the lives of all women (see also de Alwis 2002).

Goger and Ruwanpura (2014) pursued strands of this early scholarship to show how women in this economic niche were being 'produced' and shaped in both gendered and ethnicised ways, as part of the simultaneous processes of primitive accumulation and the state's post-war nation-building efforts. The factory's management structure reproduced ethnic and gender distinctions, along with class, urban/rural, and West/East divisions, rather than challenging them (Goger and Ruwanpura 2014: 11). The study analyses language issues within the factory as almost a microcosm of wider post-war dynamics: there was no focus on teaching Sinhala managers to speak Tamil, although the workforce was Tamil; this demonstrates the silencing of political, war-related, and unresolved tensions (see also Ruwanpura 2022). Moreover, the predominantly male, older managers conceptualised their roles as helping to provide employment to the local, backwards (Tamil) "girls", thus drawing on both ethnonationalist and paternalistic tropes to produce obedient worker-subjects (Goger and Ruwanpura 2014: 12–13). They also argued that targeting women for wage labour in the East was an especially apparent example of the Sri Lankan state's strategy of using rural industrialisation to subdue political unrest. As Lynch (2007) found, it is women's bodies that are disproportionately 'disciplined' and incorporated into a capitalist workforce as part of the state's strategy of development as counterinsurgency. Hence Goger and Ruwanpura (2014) argue for the need to better understand gendered patterns of proletarianisation and, in directly conflict-affected geographies, to consider the gendered ways in which traumatised people are brought into tightly controlled workplaces (2014: 16–19).

Having documented how the state military provided factory owners with lists of local citizens for labour recruitment (Goger and Ruwanpura 2014: 9), Ruwanpura (2018) argued that there is a need to scrutinise how the military (together with capital and the state) also shapes practices on the shop floor. In terms of worker subjectivities, the silence in the factory around the war trauma of mostly young Tamil women operators is about silencing narratives of the past that might challenge or complicate narratives of a unitary Sri Lankan state. Moreover, by 2019, war-affected women in garment factories were articulating, in greater numbers, the need for living wages and for better communication (in Tamil as well as Sinhala) on the factory floor, factors of relevance to business owners who seek global credibility through adherence to codes of labour ethics (Ruwanpura 2022: 124–142).

In tourism too, post-war revival in the directly conflict-affected territories was not only about economic development but also about the transformation of the political landscape and citizen subjectivities. Gunasekara, Philips and Nagaraj (2016) assessed that the development of the East was prioritised over questions of political justice in the post-war period. The development of a luxury resort in Pasikudah on the east coast of Sri Lanka, in Batticaloa district, catered to some of the tens of thousands of foreign visitors who were now coming to the area's high-end resorts

(ILO 2016). Development was underway within a context of "marginalisation, dispossession, accumulation and differentiation in war-affected communities" (Gunasekara, Philips and Nagaraj 2016: 2), and there were multiple and intersecting hierarchies of gender, class, caste, and ethnicity that shaped women's experiences of work here.

While the expansion of tourism disrupted existing, often patriarchal, gender relations, Gunasekara, Philips and Nagaraj (2016) found that this was not necessarily an 'empowering' experience for women because of the economically precarious nature of the work. Women workers experienced this precarity along with shifts in gender norms. Society generally had negative perceptions of women working in hotels, which seem to relate to gendered judgements of women who work outside the home, as opposed to the 'good' woman who stays within the boundaries of the family and the institution of marriage. Additionally, there were fears that women workers would be harassed or attacked by "outsiders" (ibid: 19). Gunasekara, Philips and Nagaraj (2016) argue that this view was invoked as a justification for society to police and control women rather than being based on empirical reality. Yet, given the recent conflict and especially the mass sexual violence committed by the military against Tamil women in the final stages of the war, it would make sense that individuals, households, and communities would have genuine fears, rooted in historical realities of sexual violence from outsiders. The connections between wartime violence and fears of post-war sexual abuse could also partially explain how employment inside the hotels (such as doing laundry, attending to rooms) was perceived as more dangerous for women than work in more public spaces, such as gardening or working in the front office (Gunasekara, Philips and Nagaraj 2016: 18–19). At the end of the war, there were widespread and credible allegations of sexual abuse and assault of Tamil women, committed by the military in closed spaces of detention camps. Collective memories create ongoing fears of future violence; and these fears are often brought to bear on 'outsiders' – where outsiders came from outside the geographic location and ethnic community. The historical thread connecting actual wartime and post-war sexual violence to present-day collective and individual fears is missing from the otherwise nuanced analysis by Gunasekara, Philips and Nagaraj (2016). However, the study demonstrates well how women working or moving in public spaces in post-war encountered gendered violence from within the Tamil community too.

Self-Employment and Livelihoods

Self-employment has been a part of the socio-economic landscape from conflict times. Schemes of this nature typically support individuals through technical skills training and extension of micro-credit to pursue small-scale income generation work. The latter includes home production of goods for the market or opening a home-based retail shop. Targets of such programmes are often women and especially women-headed households, who undertake these activities alongside other work: unpaid social reproductive work, such as caring for children, and/or subsistence farming (Hyndman and de Alwis 2003; Ruwanpura 2007). The programmes are promoted by a multiplicity of actors: local and central state, (I)NGOs, international institutions, such as the World Bank and United Nations Development Programme (UNDP) and diaspora groups (UNSL 2015). Participation is often framed as the opportunity for women to work their own way out of poverty and oppression; and while the activities are heterogeneous, they all fit into 'informal work'.

In the North and East of Sri Lanka, these schemes proliferated with the ending of the war. The wartime economic embargo ended and simultaneously, self-employment or 'self-help' schemes were rebranded as part of the wider drive for "peace through development" to help build the post-war nation-state in a highly militarised context (Kadirgamar 2013; Thaheer, Peiris and Pathiraja

2013; Law and Society Trust 2017; Ruwanpura 2018). The UNDP (2015), for example, documents its post-war support through "stories of people empowered to build a resilient Sri Lanka" and describes self-help groups moving "from trials to triumph" as they transition – smoothly, and largely by themselves – from the trauma of war to the prosperity and progress of peace. Such narratives echo those anticipating an economic 'peace dividend'; for example, the World Bank in 2012 hailed the "historic [economic] opportunity" and "new and abundant promise" afforded by the end of the war (Fonseka, Pinto, Prasad and Rowe 2012).

However, these overtures have drawn attention to the violence immanent in these schemes and linked it to violence embedded in the island's post-war development process. Gunasekara and Nagaraj (2019) illustrate this with a study of self-employed women in the East, where they argue self-employment is a "bottom of the pyramid" development strategy (2019: 38). Rather than fulfilling discourses and expectations of empowerment through entrepreneurship, this kind of work is about survival, through little more than subsistence and diversification of risk. The work is precarious, with low financial returns, often undertaken in dangerous conditions and, for women, necessitates taking on additional gendered risks if they must work in public spaces. Moreover, the typically informal nature of the work means that self-employed workers do not have the legal protections of the state, such as access to a minimum wage or pension support.

Gunasekara and Nagaraj (2019) remind us that the productive and social reproductive spheres are intertwined and by paying attention paid to social reproduction, they also challenge more superficial analyses of women's participation in the workforce based on quantitative measures, such as labour force participation rate. They bring gendered connections between productive and social reproductive work, and the violence inhering through both, to the fore. Home-based production, they argue, is "territorialised differently" from, say, factory work, which occurs in a "physically demarcated zone of exception". In contrast, home-based production consists of "individual women locked into specific privatised household/home-based relations with capital" (ibid: 52). Nonetheless, they note that these varying modes of capital accumulation are 'porous' for workers: for example, a garment factory worker in debt might be driven into sex work. Their intervention challenges the narrative that gendered violence in war is exceptional and crucially highlights continuities of structural violence that extend beyond the temporal (and spatial) boundaries of war.

This focus on the structural violence of these economic relations as part of the neoliberal capitalist phase echoes the findings of other studies. For Jeyasekara and Najab (2016), gendered violence and insecurity are driven by women's dual role in circuits of production and social reproduction. They frame their analysis of women engaged in beedi-making home production in the Eastern Province using social reproduction as an analytical entry point: they note that the women were not restored for production. On the contrary, women had to compromise on basic needs, such as eating and sleeping, to fulfil the labour of both paid work and unpaid household work. They were also exposed to further violence: the structural violence of poverty if they could not generate survival income and domestic violence if they could not meet social reproductive needs. The cost was the severe depletion of women's capacities. The role of the state in perpetuating these violent economic relations also needs underlining. Violence in post-war manifests through institutions and ideologies, and post-war development has essentially "reproduced conditions of violence similar to that of the war" as "development is simply violence by other means" (ibid: 20). They call for a reassessment of transitional justice processes under the Yahapalanaya government, asking what these meant when violent economic relations were simultaneously being advanced. They posit that these debates about justice are "utterly redundant" when considered, for instance, in the light of the lived realities of the beedi workers in the East (Jeyasekara and Najab 2016: 20).

This literature raises questions about what real or substantive post-war justice should consist of, which is covered in the fourth section. The analytical framework does, however, risk erasing the ways in which women might be differentially affected by this structural violence, depending on their proximity to direct wartime conflict. For example, Ruwanpura (2018) points out that worker subjectivities may be different for a war-traumatised population and raises the need for reflexivity, given that the apparel sector entered the region to create jobs.

A range of studies undertaken in 2014 looked at how women in the North and East were able to rebuild their lives in the post-war period and highlighted structural barriers that, together, created a distinctive context for individuals, households, and communities in the directly conflict-affected territories (Women and Media Collective 2014). Unresolved psychological trauma, displacement, the loss of assets, land dispossession, and uncompleted formal education were all common experiences for both men and women, who therefore faced post-war poverty and economic insecurity (Viluthu Centre for Human Resource Development 2014). There were gender-intensified disadvantages for women; however, in these post-war conditions, as women faced additional exploitation and exposure to violence. Women experienced disproportionate exploitation by middlemen; for instance, when seeking employment as migrant workers or when trying to sell products in markets or by money lenders with punitively high-interest rates. Within the domestic sphere, women who (re) negotiated household power relations risked domestic violence (Thaheer, Peiris and Pathiraja 2013; Lingham 2019). The exposure to extreme poverty propelled some women into sex work where they faced additional risks of physical violence and societal stigma. Furthermore, the livelihoods and post-war development programmes deployed in post-war did not recognise or seek to address women's disproportionate roles and time expended in the unpaid care economy (Suriya Women's Development Centre 2014).

These studies on women's lives in the post-war North and East underscore the point that while neoliberal development is structurally violent in gendered ways across the island, it landed and has been experienced in distinctive ways for those in the directly war-affected territories. The next section reviews some of the literature on two groups within the war-affected populations: women heads of households and former Tamil separatist (LTTE) combatants.

Experiences of Women Heads of Households and Ex-Combatants

Women Heads of Households

Studies of both wartime and post-war note the diversity of identity and experience within the broad definition of 'women heads of household' (WHH). The lack of consistent definition has policy impacts: certain groups, such as older women and those not 'obviously' widowed by war, have ended up excluded from access to development and support programmes, despite their socio-economic needs (Ruwanpura and Humphries 2004; Sivachandran 2013; UNSL 2015). Hence, the UN in 2015 argued that WHH in war-affected regions of Sri Lanka "are indeed a distinct demographic group with specific needs, vulnerabilities, and disadvantages, which require special consideration" (UNSL 2015: 1).

Kodikara (2018) examined women's post-war livelihoods strategies through an analysis of in-depth interviews carried out with seven war-affected women in Mullaitivu. They were officially labelled WHH but they "defy easy categorisation", with household arrangements shaped by often unresolved matters from the war (2018: 20–21). Their histories demonstrated their ongoing involvement in both productive work and social reproduction of their households and communities. This, and other research from war times, challenges the narrative that WHH lacks experience in income generation activities (Hyndman and de Alwis 2003; Ruwanpura and Humphries 2004; Ruwanpura 2006; Sivachandran 2013). Nonetheless, the self-employment activities the women were engaging in at the time of research were all "gender-stereotypical" and mainly household-based (Kodikara 2018: 23; see also Hyndman and de Alwis 2003; Ruwanpura 2007; Lingham 2019). Their engagement in these activities was not a 'choice' over waged work driven by the desire to establish themselves as entrepreneurs but, rather, was motivated by their urgent need to survive and ensure the survival of their households, through managing both income-generation activities and social reproductive work. Noting studies that have documented the high failure rate for small/medium enterprises (SMEs) under normal circumstances, Kodikara (2018) questions the logic by which women-headed households affected by war are expected – by a multiplicity of national and international development actors – to succeed as entrepreneurs (see also Hyndman and de Alwis 2003; Ruwanpura 2007). Kodikara (2018) notes how "it was impossible to neatly disentangle their productive labour and their livelihoods from the multiple other labours they were having to perform" (2018: 42–43; Ruwanpura 2007). The labour women were able to expend on income generating activities was severely circumscribed by the need to rebuild their lives in the aftermath of war and having to negotiate traumatic memory. Memory and mourning spilled into the everyday, with intensified trauma for those whose family members had disappeared, at the same time as everyday tasks had to be undertaken and domestic chores continued to be exceptionally time-consuming (see also Walker 2013; Thurnheer 2014).

The affective, spatial, and temporal entanglements of productive and social reproductive labours in conflict-affected areas are echoed in later research (Lingham and Johnston 2024). Using a basic questionnaire, an observational time-use survey, and a narrative interview, we documented the spatial and temporal dimensions of both paid and unpaid labour and took account of historical and current contexts of violence. We found that while women were depleted by social reproductive labour in all research sites, proximity to conflict increased the burdens of social reproduction for women, which included risks associated with social reproduction in militarised geographies and the trauma of pursuing collective justice in the face of unresolved war crimes. We found that the most conflict-affected women were the most lacking in resources to mitigate the effects of physical and psychological depletion.

Post-war livelihoods for war-affected women need, then, to be addressed as an economic justice issue rather than within a neoliberal, "market-based" framework (Kodikara 2018: 43). Issues of economic justice and equality are especially relevant for those WHH whose missing/disappeared husbands were LTTE combatants and who now receive no financial support, unlike state military widows who get the army pension (Lingham and Johnston 2024: 13; see also Women and Media Collective 2014).

Ex-Combatants

Research on the post-war socio-economic experiences of former LTTE combatants living in Sri Lanka is relatively sparse. While surveys have been carried out, they have largely been facilitated by the government and state military (Miriyagalla 2014; Adayalam Centre for Policy Research/ACPR 2022). As such, they need to be treated with caution, given the deeply unequal power relations between state, military, and former Tamil combatants in post-war (see also Satkunanthan 2018). Within Sri Lanka, ex-combatants who speak publicly about any complexity of experience in relation to the LTTE – including post-war experiences shaped by that history – continue to face security risks, which heightened following the changed political administration in 2019.

Wider research on the political economy of work in the post-war North and East is of course likely to include participants who are ex-combatants, even if they are not identified as such.

The most recent and widest-ranging study of the post-war situation for ex-combatants explicitly calls for ex-combatants to be understood as a distinct group with unique needs, given their wartime and post-war experiences (ACPR 2022; see also Satkunanathan 2016).

An overarching theme that emerges is that post-war violence and marginalisation disproportionately shape the socio-economic lives of ex-combatants. This combines with an institutionalised refusal by the state to allow meaningful or complex discussion of the Tamil separatist struggle, including the role and activities of the LTTE. The 'enforced amnesia' and silence about post-war state violence play out in marked, everyday economic ways. For example, many ex-combatants did not complete formal schooling during the war but did undertake sometimes quite extensive education and training within the LTTE. They find that their non-standard qualifications are not recognised by employers, meaning that they struggle to find employment commensurate with their skills and abilities (ACPR 2022). Historical work experiences and skills are discounted if they were gained as a member of the LTTE. This study documents how an ex-combatant was unable to obtain an auto to take up income-generating work as a driver because he had a prosthetic leg, even though when in the LTTE, he drove heavy vehicles with one leg and without even a prosthesis (ACPR 2022: 55).

While socio-economic discrimination due to disability has wider resonance, it emerges as particularly severe for ex-combatants, given the increased likelihood that they sustained disabilities during the war. ACPR (2022) finds that discrimination has extended into post-war work interventions that are supposedly geared towards ex-combatants. For example, garment factories that claimed to actively provide work for ex-combatants refused to employ disabled individuals; Civil Security Defence farms actively recruiting ex-combatants do not provide accessible living facilities for those with disabilities; post-war livelihoods programmes typically fail to consider additional needs of disabled ex-combatants.

Early studies noted the failure of the state rehabilitation scheme to consider the ex-combatants' disproportionate war-related physical and psychological trauma (Home for Human Rights 2014). Furthermore, and significantly, the process of purported rehabilitation itself involved torture and human rights abuses, including sexual abuse of ex-combatants by the state (ACPR 2022). 'Rehabilitation' was, then, a tool of political violence and control and only a nominal means of economic reintegration. Therefore, it is unsurprising that the research available broadly notes that it did not enable ex-combatants to develop sustainable livelihoods.

The refusal by the GoSL to engage with the history of the Tamil separatist struggle results in policies and programmes that do not recognise ground realities. LTTE women challenged traditional expectations: they worked in construction, driving, and administration, for example. In post-war rehabilitation programmes, though they were re-trained in traditional skills in, for example, beauty care and tailoring. A blatant mismatch between previously acquired skills and experiences and the training and limited opportunities given in post-war settings arose (Home for Human Rights 2014). The ACPR (2022) argues that these gendered dimensions of post-war livelihoods support could neutralise women ex-combatants' historical political agency. These issues were compounded by the societal stigma and discrimination faced by all ex-combatants – with added gender dimensions for women – upon their return to civilian life (Satkunanathan 2016, 2018). Women ex-combatants face unique economic marginalisation because they are perceived as "transgressors" and "troublemakers", having challenged patriarchal tropes (Krishnan 2011; Home for Human Rights 2014).[1]

Small loans disbursed by government schemes were insufficient for individuals to be able to start or maintain their own business. This also meant having to find waged work and take further loans on occasion to migrate abroad for work or for another family member to support the household (Miriyagalla 2014). Insufficient income also converged with a multiplicity of war-related constraints: landlessness, lack of political rights, societal stigma, and discrimination and, especially for women, gendered expectations, and vulnerabilities within the household (Miriyagalla 2014; Women and Media Collective 2014; Satkunanathan 2016).

Overall, the literature illustrates immense socio-economic challenges in both productive and social reproductive spheres for ex-LTTE combatants in Sri Lanka. The lasting effects of war trauma combined with the impact of violent post-war 'rehabilitation' schemes, continuing militarisation and everyday military harassment by GoSL forces, societal stigma, and discrimination, and for women, heightened exposure to gendered violence and marginalisation. Economic support is absent, especially for those with disabilities. These factors position ex-combatants as uniquely vulnerable in the post-war political economy. The policy-oriented literature calls for work-related interventions to involve ex-combatants as active participants, rather than mere 'beneficiaries', in the development of livelihood support programmes and highlights small-scale interventions that have done so with some success (ACPR 2022).

New and Emerging Research

In the broader political economy and conflict research studies on Sri Lanka, there is scope for a more consistent exploration of existing debates on the role and significance of social reproduction in the post-war political economy. This is a lacuna common to non-feminist and conflict studies research generally. Feminists have long identified the need to redefine 'work' and the 'economy' when studying socio-economic relations and conflict dynamics by centring social reproduction and social reproductive labour within their analyses. Yet, most studies on the political economy of post-war Sri Lanka all too often continue to exclude social reproduction and social reproductive labour from analyses, even as they acknowledge that conflict-related political economy dynamics have gendered impacts. Consistently conceptualising the economic to include the social reproductive sphere in the first place would go some way to bridging this analytical gap.

Emerging feminist research continues to buck this trend. A previously more International Law and Human Rights oriented strand of literature on post-war justice in Sri Lanka argues that social reproductive rights are central to economic rights and are fundamental to ongoing struggles for post-war justice (Davies and True 2017; Fonseka and Schulz 2018). Fonseka and Schulz (2018) call for 'transformative' rather than 'transitional' justice and draw on the United Nations Women, Peace and Security (WPS) agenda that calls for gender sensitivity in peacebuilding. As part of reparations for civil and political war crimes, they say that socio-economic reparations must pay attention to social reproductive needs, especially social infrastructure – goods and services, such as health and education, to enable communities and households to socially reproduce and individuals to carry out social reproductive work. The nexus between enduring structural gender inequalities and the lack of substantive justice for war-affected communities is a recurring theme. More research on social reproductive needs as central to economic needs among conflict-affected populations could contribute to the development of these debates and policy proposals.

Most recently, and ongoing, studies from the past two years are examining gendered shifts in productive and social reproductive work since the outbreak of the COVID-19 pandemic. These studies have so far mainly focused on other parts of the island than the North and East. They include emerging studies on the consequences of lockdown for social reproductive work in the home (Salman 2021) and on the highly gendered costs of the pandemic for garment sector workers (Ruwanpura and Sarvananthan 2021; Ruwanpura, Gunawardana and Padmasiri 2021). These areas of investigation would benefit from being studied in reference to the North and East and through a feminist conflict lens. Civil society activists and human rights researchers have also focused attention on the deepening militarisation of the pandemic response (Sooka 2020); the impacts of this upon social reproduction for conflict-affected populations would benefit from further study. Finally, it will be incumbent upon future research studies to consider how the heightened economic crisis of 2022 impacts the political economy of the North and East.

Note

1 The feminist literature on the role of women within the LTTE contended that this involvement was both liberating and oppressive (Maunaguru 1995; Coomaraswamy 1997; Rajasingham-Senanayake 2001; de Mel 2003; Thiranagama 2014).

References

Adayalam Centre for Policy Research (2022) *Persecuted and Alone: A Study of Ex-Combatants in Post-War Sri Lanka* Jaffna, Sri Lanka: ACPR

Chandrasiri, G.A. (2009) "The Northern Province Beckons You" *Presentation to International Chamber of Commerce*, Jaffna, Sri Lanka, 30 October. Accessed on 07/01/2019. Available at https://www.defence.lk/

Coomaraswamy, Radhika (1997) "Tiger Women and the Question of Women's Emancipation" *Pravada* 4(9): 8–10

Davies, Sara E. and Jacqui True (2017) "When There Is No Justice: Gendered Violence and Harm in Post-Conflict Sri Lanka" *The International Journal of Human Rights* 21(9): 1320–1336

de Alwis, Malathi (2002) "The Changing Role of Women in Sri Lankan Society" *Social Research* 69(3): 675–691

de Mel, Neloufer (2003) "Agent or Victim? The Sri Lankan Woman Militant in the Interregnum" In *Feminists under Fire: Exchanges across War Zones* Winona Giles, Malathi de Alwis, Edith Klein, Neluka Silva and Maja Korac (eds) Toronto: Between the Lines, 55–73

Fonseka, Bhavani and Ellen Schulz (2018) *Gender and Transformative Justice in Sri Lanka*. Working Paper 18. London: London School of Economics

Fonseka, Dhaminda, Brian Pinto, Mona Prasad and Francis Rowe (2012) *Sri Lanka: From Peace Dividend to Sustained Growth Acceleration* 6192. Washington: World Bank

Goger, Annelies and Kanchana N. Ruwanpura (2014) *Ethical Reconstruction? Primitive Accumulation in the Apparel Sector of Eastern Sri Lanka* Colombo: International Centre for Ethnic Studies. Research Paper No 14

Government of Sri Lanka Presidential Task Force for Northern Province (2012) *From Conflict to Stability – Northern Province Sri Lanka*. Colombo: Government of Sri Lanka Presidential Task Force for Northern Province. Accessed on 18/08/2022. Available at https://www.scribd.com/document/126851924/FROM-CONFLICT-TO-STABILITY-IN-SRI-LANKA

Government of Sri Lanka, United Nations and Partners (2011) *Joint Plan for Assistance Northern Province 2011*. Government of Sri Lanka, United Nations and Partners. Accessed on 18/08/2022. Available at https://reliefweb.int/report/sri-lanka/sri-lanka-joint-plan-assistance-northern-province-2011

Gunasekara, Vagisha, Mira Philips and Vijay Nagaraj (2016) *Hospitality and exclusion: A study about post-war tourism in Passikudah*. London: Secure Livelihoods Research Consortium. Research Report No 13

Gunasekara, Vagisha and Vijay K. Nagaraj (2019) "The Construction of the "Responsible Woman": Structural Violence in Sri Lanka's Post-War Development Narrative" In *The Political Economy of Conflict and Violence against Women: Cases from the South* Kumidhini Samuel, Claire Slatter and Vagisha Gunasekara (eds) London: Zed Books Ltd, pp 29–57

Home for Human Rights (2014) *Female Ex-combatants in post-war Sri Lanka: Experiences from selected regions in Jaffna, Kilinochchi, Mullaitivu, Mannar, Vavuniya, Batticaloa, Ampara and Trincomaloo districts*. Colombo: Women and Media Collective, pp 31–39

Hyndman, Jennifer and Malathi de Alwis (2003) "Beyond Gender: Towards a Feminist Analysis of Humanitarianism and Development in Sri Lanka" *Women's Studies Quarterly* 31(3/4): 212–226

ILO (International Labour Organization) (2016) *Report on value chain analysis of the tourism sector in Ampara and Batticaloa districts*. Local Economic Development through Tourism Project. Colombo: ILO.

Jeyasekara, Prashantha and Nadiya Najab (2016) *The Political Economy of Violence: Women's Economic Relations in Post-War Sri Lanka*. Working Paper 50. London: Overseas Development Institute

Lingham, Jayanthi T. and Melissa Johnston (2024) "Running on Empty: Depletion and Social Reproduction in Myanmar and Sri Lanka", *Antipode*. https://doi.org/10.1111/anti.13016

Kadirgamar, Ahilan (2013) "Second Wave of Neoliberalism: Financialisation and Crisis in Post-War Sri Lanka" *Colombo Telegraph* (28 August). Accessed on 18/08/2022. Available at https://www.colombotelegraph.com/index.php/second-wave-of-neoliberalism-financialisation-and-crisis-in-post-war-sri-lanka/

Kodikara, Chulani (2018) *Doing This and That: Self-Employment and Economic Survival of Women Heads of Households in Mullaitivu*. Research Papers. Colombo: International Centre for Ethnic Studies

Krishnan, Sonny I. (2011) "The Transition of Teenage Girls and Young Women from Ex-Combatants to Civilian Life: A Case Study in Sri Lanka" *Interventions* 9(2): 137–144

Law and Society Trust (2017) *Biting the Bullet – Demilitarising Economic Relations in Post-war Sri Lanka* Colombo: Law and Society Trust

Lingham, Jayanthi T. (2019) *Dispossessing Connections: Women's Working Lives in Post-War Jaffna District, Sri Lanka, 2009–2015*. PhD Thesis Manuscript. SOAS, University of London

Lynch, Caitrin (2007) *Juki Girls, Good Girls: Gender and Cultural Politics in Sri Lanka's Global Garment Industry* Ithaca and London: IHL Press and Cornell University Press

Maunaguru, Sidharthan (1995) "Gendering Tamil Nationalism: The Construction of "Woman" in Projects of Protest and Control" In *Unmaking the Nation: The Politics of Identity and History in Modern Sri Lanka* Pradeep Jeganathan and Qadri Ismail (eds) Colombo: Social Scientists Association, pp 157–172

Miriyagalla, Danura (2014) "Socio-Economic Reintegration of Former LTTE Combatants in Sri Lanka: Self-Employment, Sustainable Incomes and Long-Term Peace" *Global Change, Peace and Security* 26(3): 251–262

Pieris, Ayoma (2014) "Encampments: Spatial Taxonomies of Sri Lanka's Civil War" *Architectural Theory Review* 19(3): 393–413

Rajasingham-Senanayake, Darini (2001) "Ambivalent Empowerment: The Tragedy of Tamil Women in Conflict" In *Women, War and Peace in South Asia: Beyond Victimhood to Agency* Rita Manchanda (ed) New Delhi: Sage, pp 102–130

Ruwanpura, Kanchana N. (2006) *Matrilineal Communities, Patriarchal Realities. A Feminist Nirvana Uncovered* Ann Arbor: University of Michigan Press

Ruwanpura, Kanchana N. (2007) "Awareness and Action: The Ethno-Gender Dynamics of Sri Lankan NGOs" *Gender, Place and Culture* 14(3): 317–333

Ruwanpura, Kanchana N. (2018) "Militarized Capitalism? The Apparel Industry's Role in Scripting a Post-War National Identity in Sri Lanka" *Antipode* 50(2): 425–446

Ruwanpura, Kanchana N. (2022) *Garments Without Guilt? Global Labour Justice and Ethical Codes in Sri Lankan Apparels* Cambridge, New York, Melbourne and New Delhi: Cambridge University Press

Ruwanpura, Kanchana N. and Jane Humphries (2004) "Mundane Heroines: Conflict, Ethnicity, Gender, and Female Headship in Eastern Sri Lanka" *Feminist Economics* 10(2): 173–205.

Ruwanpura, Kanchana N., Samanthi Gunawardana and Buddhima Padmasiri (2021) "Vaccine Inequality and the Cost to Garment Sector Workers" *Groundviews* (22 May). Accessed on 18/08/2022. Available at https://groundviews.org/2021/05/22/vaccine-inequality-and-the-cost-to-garment-sector-workers/

Ruwanpura, Kanchana N. and Jane Humphries (2004) "Mundane Heroines: Conflict, Ethnicity, Gender, and Female Headship in Eastern Sri Lanka" *Feminist Economics* 10(2): 173–205

Ruwanpura, Kanchana N. and M. Sarvananthan (2021) *COVID-19 and Sri Lanka: From Outlier to Uniformity?* Accessed on 18/08/2022. Available at https://www.sps.ed.ac.uk/sites/default/files/assets/BA-GCRF-COVID19%2520Research%2520Brief%2520Sri%2520Lanka.pdf.

Salman, Yumna (2021) "Life at Home during COVID-19" *CEPA Blog* (25 February). Accessed on 17/08/2022. Available at https://www.cepa.lk/blog/life-at-home-during-covid-19/

Satkunanathan, Ambika (2016) "Collaboration, Suspicion and Traitors: an Exploratory Study of Intra-Community Relations in Post-War Northern Sri Lanka" *Contemporary South Asia* 24(4): 416–428

Satkunanathan, Ambika (2018) "The Treatment of Former Combatants in Post-War Sri Lanka" In *Routledge Handbook of Human Rights in Asia* Fernand de Varennes and Christie M. Gardiner (eds) London: Routledge, pp 184–196

Sivachandran, Selvy (2013) *Women Headed Families in the Northern Province* Jaffna, Sri Lanka: Centre for Women and Development

Sooka, Y. (2020) *Sri Lanka's Militarisation of COVID-19 Response*. International Truth and Justice Project. Available at https://itjpsl.com/assets/press/English-ITJP_COVID-19-press-release-Merged-copy.pdf

Suriya Women's Development Centre (2014) *Women, Marginalisation and Poverty in Post War Batticaloa, Sri Lanka*. Colombo: Women and Media Collective, pp 7–18

Thaheer, Meena, Pradeep Peiris and Kasun Pathiraja (2013) *Reconciliation in Sri Lanka: Voices from Former War Zones* Colombo: International Centre for Ethnic Studies

Thiranagama, Sharika (2014) "Female Militancy: Reflections from Sri Lanka" In *Routledge Handbook of Gender in South Asia* Leela Fernandes (ed) London: Routledge, pp 115–128

Thurnheer, Kathrine (2014) *Life Beyond Survival: Social Forms of Coping after the Tsunami in War-Affected Eastern Sri Lanka* Bern: transcript Verlag

UNDP (2015) *Paths to Progress. Stories of Hope, Resilience and Partnerships*. Sri Lanka: United Nations Development Programme. Accessed on 19/08/2022. Available at https://www.undp.org/srilanka/publications/paths-progress.

UNSL (2015) *Mapping of Socio-Economic Support Services to Female Headed Households in the Northern Province of Sri Lanka*. United Nations Sri Lanka. Available at https://srilanka.unfpa.org/sites/default/files/pub-pdf/FemaleHeadedHouseholds.pdf

Venugopal, Rajesh (2011) "The Politics of Market Reform at a Time of Civil War: Military Fiscalism in Sri Lanka" *Economic and Political Weekly* 46(49): 67–75

Viluthu Centre for Human Resource Development (2014) *Situation of Female-Headed Households Post War in Selected Regions of Batticaloa, Jaffna and Vavuniya Districts*. Colombo: Women and Media Collective, pp 20–29

Walker, Rebecca (2013) *Enduring Violence: Everyday Life and Conflict in Eastern Sri Lanka* Manchester: Manchester University Press

Women and Media Collective (2014) *Women claiming rights : using normative frameworks of UNCR 1325 & CEDAW : study on women affected by conflict in post war Sri Lanka : selected cases of marginalisation and poverty; female headed households; female ex-combatants; land rights and domestic violence*. Colombo: Women and Media Collective

18

WORK AND LIFE OF SRI LANKAN GARMENT FACTORY WORKERS

A Gendered Perspective

Shyamain Wickramasingha

Introduction: The Sri Lankan Apparel Industry

The apparel industry took off in Sri Lanka in the early 1980s following market liberalisation in 1977 and favourable trade policies (Kelegama 2004). From what started off as a 2% contribution to total exports in 1977 (CBSL 2009), the industry has grown to account for 48% of the country's total exports by value as of May 2022 (EDB 2022). By 2019, the industry employed around 350,000 people in over 400 apparel factories (BOI 2019). As of 2019, around 70% of the total labour force were women (Wickramasingha 2020), although managers were mostly men (Ruwanpura 2022a). A notable development of the Sri Lankan apparel industry is that it has been relatively successful in upgrading itself from basic products (assembly lines) to providing sophisticated solutions, such as original design and brand manufacturing (Ruwanpura 2022a).

The growth of the Sri Lankan apparel industry is attributed to two factors. First, from 1993 the apparel industry enjoyed the privileges of duty-free inputs, low interest on credit, tax exemptions, tax reductions, tax holidays, and the freedom to repatriate profits. These developments saw the industry enjoying growth of apparel exports from $1.8bn in 1995 to $5.4bn in 2022 (Kelegama 2004; BOI 2022). Second, Sri Lanka benefitted from the grant of a generalised system of preferences plus (GSP+) by the EU in 2005, which provided Sri Lanka zero duty access to EU markets. While GSP+ benefits were removed in 2010 due to the human rights violations associated with civil war casualties, GSP+ status was regranted to Sri Lanka in 2017, based on the positive improvements in human rights indicators. Consequently, Sri Lanka was able to retain its share in major EU and US markets as a 'value-added' manufacturer, which makes it more profitable for the industrial sector to supply to the European region (Goger 2013; Ruwanpura 2016).

However, implications for these developments on workers and their lives are far more contested, as a review of the literature shows in this chapter. Given the industry is highly gendered, the review primarily adopts a gendered perspective drawing on the works of feminist scholars and theories on the global apparel industry. The review is essentially centred on what constitutes work and life for apparel workers. In this context, the chapter is structured around six sections. The second section discusses 'work and life', with attention paid to the embodied experience of labour in working conditions on the shop floor. In the third section, I then review scholarship on the gendered nature of the apparel industry, the devaluation of women's labour, and the social stigma associated with apparel work. This is followed by a review of women workers' agency and the space for unionisation in the industry in the fourth section. The fifth section discusses notable works on global labour governance regimes, in particular, codes of ethics of lead firms and how guilt-free apparel are difficult to sustain. The sixth section concludes the chapter by highlighting key areas to consider in future studies including post-war developments of the industry, climate change and value chain transition, informality of work, and the implications of the Covid-19 pandemic on work and life.

Work and Life-Embodied Experiences

Generally, Sri Lanka self-proclaims as an ethical sourcing destination for apparel with claims of high labour standards (Ruwanpura and Wrigley 2011; Ruwanpura 2012; Goger 2014; Ruwanpura 2022a). Using Jayawardena's (1972) pathbreaking work on the labour history in Sri Lanka, these achievements are also attributed to the welfare state and Sri Lankan labour laws, which were institutionalised and enacted when the country was colonised (Ruwanpura and Wrigley 2011; Goger 2014; Ruwanpura 2022a). As Ruwanpura (2022a) reminds us, it is the organised actions of labour – buttressed by high education standards and the former welfare state – that have made it possible for Sri Lanka to maintain strong labour laws. These laws provide legal protection for workers in areas from economic to social activities, covering worker compensation to termination of employment (Wijayasiri and Dissanayake 2009; Ruwanpura and Wrigley 2011). Additionally, the 'Garments without Guilt' campaign launched by the Joint Apparel Association Forum in the early 2000s promotes workers' rights, education, and personal growth towards alleviating poverty among workers (Goger 2014; Perry, Wood and Fernie 2015; Ruwanpura 2016). With already high labour standards, Sri Lanka then became one of the first countries to adopt the ethical codes initiated by lead firms in the 1990s (Ruwanpura 2016). In this context, it is widely recognised that the overall workplace standards in the Sri Lankan apparel industry are better compared to other apparel producing countries globally (Wijayasiri and Dissanayake 2009).

Having a good reputation for decent work and strong labour laws does not, however, necessarily mean decent work on the Sri Lankan shop floors. In particular, low wages, long working hours, discrimination in many aspects including gender, ethnicity, and formal and informal work arrangement, and the absence of meaningful forms of representation at the workplace afflict the industry (Gunawardana 2007, 2016; Ruwanpura 2016, 2022a; Hewamanne 2017, 2021). Like elsewhere in South Asia, the Sri Lankan apparel industry too is characterised by target-oriented, fast-paced working conditions that exploit women's labour for low wages (De Neve 2009; Ruwanpura 2012, 2016; Carswell and De Neve 2013; Goger 2014; Gunawardana 2014; Hewamanne 2016; Saxena 2020). The Sri Lankan apparel sector usually pays an average wage packet above the minimum stipulated; however, this is still well below a living wage, which Asia Floor Wage Alliance estimates to be at around Rs 94,000.00 (Asia Floor Wage Alliance 2022). In 2020, over 40 years after it was established, the basic salary in the Katunayake Export Processing Zone (EPZ) remained LKR 14,000 per month (about $75 based on 2020 currency exchange rates), although women could earn about LKR 25,000 (about $135) by working overtime especially during busy shipment periods (Hewamanne 2021). Workers seldom make a living wage, and the increments of the Wages Board rarely keep pace with the inflation rate (Ruwanpura 2012, 2022a). Since overtime is a necessity for workers to earn a higher wage packet, national labour regulations are changed to allow excessive work hours (Ruwanpura 2016). Thus, Sri Lankan factories too demand maximum output for minimum wages, contrary to the claims of exceptional labour standards maintained by the Sri Lankan apparel industry (Hewamanne 2016).

This exceptionalism is also observed in the realm of health and safety, where Sri Lanka has not reported catastrophic accidents, such as factory fires and building collapses (Ruwanpura 2014, 2017). Yet, this does not mean that Sri Lankan production regimes protect worker health. Health concerns in the industry involve working with hazardous materials, the repetitive nature of piece-based and hourly work, malnutrition, fatigue, anaemia, and other manifestations of stress (Hewamanne 2017). Attanapola's (2004) study on the health of women workers in the Katunayake EPZ found that in spite of muscular disorders and recurrent headaches, workers normalise illness and poor health preventing them from seeking necessary medical treatment. Amarasinghe (2007), a nutritionist, attributes many such illnesses to nutritional deficits directly linked to the absence of a living wage. Moreover, recurrent overtime encroaches on the time workers have for resting, preparing evening meals, and other daily domestic work. Amarasinghe (2007) argues that these factors explain why apparel sector workers are the population most affected by anaemia and malnourishment.

Struggles over health in the workplace reveal a central paradox in the labour process: employers require healthy bodies, yet they pressure ailing workers from taking time off because of disruption to production (Ruwanpura 2017). With just-in-time production or lean manufacturing becoming the industrial norm, Goger (2013) explains how it has created an extremely competitive atmosphere with a fast-paced and highly stressful production regime. In addition to the absence of leave and holidays, workers have less time for breaks, visit doctors, and recover and recuperate when sick. Even within factory medical facilities, Ruwanpura (2017) found that workers' ability to access treatment in the factory clinic depends on successful negotiation with gatekeepers against whom workers are hierarchically positioned. Consequently, workers carefully assess when and how to access the clinics, while clinicians gauge what kind of health care to provide, and whether workers' claims are genuine and legitimate. Ruwanpura (2017) argues that although there is a visible foundation from which Sri Lanka can boast about its labour standards and facilities, how medical facilities are actually accessed and used by workers suggests that health is more about upholding ethical credentials than protecting worker well-being. The limitations of this technocratic approach already underlined in previous work for a pre-Covid period became pronounced during the recent pandemic, where the initial successes in upholding safety protocols around Covid-19 soon gave way to factory clusters and compounded effects on working bodies (Goger and Ruwanpura 2014; Ruwanpura 2014, 2022b; Wickramasingha and de Neve 2022). Given the conditions that workers must navigate, attention needs to be paid to wider structures that make and unmake healthy working bodies (see also Hewamanne 2008, 2017; Ruwanpura 2019). Such structural conditions also manifest through the highly gendered nature of apparel work, as I outline below.

Gendered Nature of Work, Devaluation, and Social Stigma

Adverse gender stereotypes have contributed to highly unfavourable terms of work for women on the shopfloor (Elson and Pearson 1981; De Neve 2005, 2009; Lynch 2007; Hewamanne 2016, 2017; Mezzadri 2016, 2017; Saxena 2020). Elson and Pearson (1981) early on connected gendered assumptions about 'third world women' and the devaluation of women's labour as disposable. As Wright (2006) argued, this treatment of women's labour as disposable has grown to mythical proportions. Within this disposability myth, young women in developing countries have become over time a 'form of industrial waste that can be discarded and replaced easily' (Wright 2006: 2; see also Mezzadri 2017).

In the Sri Lankan context too, labour scholars have called for a better appreciation of the structures of meaning-making around gender that seeks to attract, retain, and control a highly malleable and disposable women workforce (de Alwis 1999; Lynch 2007; Hewamanne 2008, 2021; Goger 2013, 2014; Ruwanpura and Hughes 2016; Ruwanpura 2022a). Starting with the foundational works of Lynch (2007) and Hewamanne (2008, 2021), feminist scholars highlighted how women workers in the Sri Lankan apparel sector have to navigate complex and stigmatised societal expectations. Indeed, most notable is the social stigma associated with being a 'garment girl' or a 'juki girl' (Lynch 2007), inherently ascribed to the identity of being a woman on the production floor, which continues to prevail (Goger 2013; Wickramasingha 2020; Hewamanne 2021). Hewamanne (2008, 2021, 2016) delineates how apparel factories profit from the devaluation of women's labour, not only through low wages and long hours but also through wider cultural discourses that depict women as disposable and sexualised. The Katunayake EPZ is labelled in pejorative ways (city of women, love zone, whore zone), attracting the attention of local men as well as men in the military, transportation, and shop workers. These findings are consistent with the work of Caitrin Lynch (2007) too for another part of the country. Hewamanne (2020) details numerous social encounters she witnessed near Katunayake, where neighbours, bazaar traders, shopkeepers, and auto-rickshaw drivers used variations of the term 'whore' to refer to apparel workers. The stigma has deepened with exaggerated stories of women living carefree love lives with rampant premarital sex, and discrimination against apparel workers, including sexual harassment and assaults on workers' bodies and possessions (Hewamanne 2021).

Labour shortages in the post-war context have led to initiatives to raise the image of apparel workers in the Sri Lankan apparel industry (Goger 2013; Wickramasingha 2020). This has meant a re-articulation of women workers as empowered as well as devising strategies to attract more men into the industry (Goger 2014; Ruwanpura and Hughes 2016). Notable tactics included cultivating a sanitised image of the apparel industry in Sri Lanka and emphasising its crucial role in post-war nation-building (Ruwanpura 2018, 2022a). As such the proportion of men working for the industry increased from 23% in 2006 to 31% in 2016 (Ruwanpura 2022a). These men are more likely to be supervised and managed by women, suggesting changing shop floor dynamics, which warrants a closer look in future studies. Increasingly, labour has become the motif, rather than gender, speaking to the temporal dynamics affecting Sri Lankan apparel production. By the late 2010s, it was labour, although interlaced with gender, ethnic, and political ideologies, rather than cheap, docile, and dextrous women that employers were increasingly seeking (Goger 2013; Ruwanpura and Hughes 2016; Ruwanpura 2022a). In the next section, I explain how the gendered dynamics of the industry have shaped women's agency and collective activism.

Agency and Freedom of Association

The integration into the global economy has tended to weaken labour power, although workers continue to exert agency through collective action within and outside the shop floor (Kabeer 2002; Biyanwila 2011; Gunawardana 2014; Ruwanpura 2015; Saxena 2020). The existing scholarship on Sri Lanka makes a distinction between the pre-1977 and post-1977 eras in terms of labour activism, with the former being recognised as a period of strong social movements and collective bargaining (see Jayawardena 1972; Gunawardana 2007; Ruwanpura 2022a). Jayawardena (1972) records events in the colonial and immediate post-colonial period wherein Sri Lankan labour did not hesitate to organise themselves against capital and the state even in instances where the odds were against them. The industrial relations landscape of Sri Lanka prior to 1977, Ruwanpura (2022a) explains, was marked by a commitment to social democratic principles.

In the post-1977 context, labour scholars have traced two patterns in the suppression of labour. First, capitalist strategies that sought to de-regulate labour and relax social welfare standards in the industry, with trade unionism, have been under assault legislatively and politically (Gunawardana 2007; Gunawardana and Biyanwila 2008; Biyanwila 2011). Employers reconstructed the notion of trade unionism with alternative mechanisms of organisation at the workplace, first with Joint Consultative Committees (JCCs) and then Employee Councils (ECs) supported by the Board of Investment (BOI) and the labour department. Such JCCs and ECs promoted in the factories resulted in workers and trade unions getting subsumed 'under a paternalist rule of employers' (Biyanwila 2011: 77). Union busting activities have become prevalent among employers – especially among the top manufacturers – where workers are actively discouraged from forming trade unions (Gunawardana 2007; Biyanwila 2011; Ruwanpura 2015; Wickramasingha and Coe 2021). Employers are also quick to spread stories of factory closures associated with unions elsewhere, to cultivate fear of job losses among workers, if unions are to continue (Ruwanpura 2015; Wickramasingha 2020). Indeed, the changes in political regimes in the mid-1990s – with supposedly labour-friendly political leaders coming into power – seemingly relaxed union repression and encouraged trade unionism, but they turned out to be mere lip-service (Biyanwila 2011).

Second, weakening labour activism can be traced back to the inherent structural weaknesses of trade unions themselves. For one, trade unions are highly politicised with an intensification of rivalry between unions (Biyanwila 2011; Wickramasingha 2020). This has led to union fragmentation and a lack of unity on national policy platforms. Party unions are also closely aligned with dominant Sinhala-Buddhist nationalism, with limited space for cross-community labour solidarity. For another, trade unionism in Sri Lanka remains highly gendered – including in the apparel sector. Labour activism is firmly attributed to male-dominated unions, despite the apparel industry predominantly consisting of women workers (Biyanwila 2011; Wickramasingha 2020). Many grassroots-level women activists have found it extremely difficult to be recognised and supported at both national and international platforms, such as the Dabindu Collective, National Workers Congress, and We in the Zone (Jayawardena 2017; Wickramasingha 2020). As noted by the Women's Center (2011), it takes years and generations for women activists to effectively strategise and build momentum on collective activism among workers. Nonetheless, post-1977 has witnessed pivotal moments when trade unions and women workers in the apparel industry exerted their agency even amidst the adverse practices of the state-capital alliance to repress organised labour and eliminate workers perceived to be a threat. One example is the large-scale and impromptu public protests when the EPF (employees provident fund) reforms were attempted by the government in 2011.

Such actions have deviated from previously celebrated union politics and have sometimes taken the form of building cross-border alliances via grassroots social movements and international networks, which have given currency to local labour movements (Gunawardana 2007; Biyanwila 2011; Wickramasingha and Coe 2021; Ruwanpura 2022a). Collective action has also compelled the state and manufacturers to address conditions of work within factories, by bringing labour issues to the forefront thereby shaping the terrain of capitalist evolution within the apparel sector. Some landmark actions include the strikes of the Polytex apparel factory in 1982 and the strike against the Private Sector Pension Reform Bill in 2011 (Biyanwila 2011; Women's Center 2011; Ruwanpura 2013, 2022a).

Equally important to note is the individual everyday agency of workers embedded in the choices and decisions they make (Gunawardana 2014; Wickramasingha and Coe 2021; Ruwanpura 2022a). Gunawardana (2014) demonstrates that in voicing concerns about everyday production and managerial practices, workers exhibited oppositional agency and set about attempting to appropriate control. She argues that the politics of everyday life resonate with worker resistance in both the labour process and how voice develops outside management and state-sanctioned mechanisms, illuminating the importance of worker power. Where structural transformation of working conditions is limited, the agency is significant as it enables workers to prevent the deterioration of existing conditions. Wickramasingha and Coe (2021) outline the way the micro-agency of workers is expressed in many different forms including choosing where to work and when to work (associated with contract work vs regular work), asserting their rights at the production floor, and speaking for others. As Ruwanpura (2022a) notes, the Sri Lankan apparel sector would have found it hard to preserve its ethical sourcing image without the push that came from collective struggles as well as individual acts of agency.

Ethical Sourcing Destination: Global Labour Governance Mechanisms

In this section, I turn to global labour governance regimes to understand the work and life of the apparel industry in Sri Lanka. Codes of ethics (codes) and private regulation have been a cornerstone of ethical trading initiatives since the mid-1990s (Ruwanpura 2016). Such codes are used to ensure worker welfare and promote social justice by forcing suppliers to maintain minimum labour standards. In theory, codes – primarily based on the International Labour Organisation's (ILO) Core Conventions – allow retailers and manufacturers to collectively ensure decent workplace standards (Ruwanpura 2022a). In practice, however, the impact of codes has been uneven with mixed outcomes at the workplace (Ruwanpura 2012, 2022a; Goger 2013; Wickramasingha and Coe 2021), resonating experiences of other countries engaged with the apparel industry (O'Rourke 2006; Hughes, Wrigley and Buttle 2008; Locke, Rissing and Pal 2013). De Neve (2009) notes that private governance mechanisms are a new imperialism that adds to global competitive pressures because these ethical codes shape labour-management processes. Yet, as Goger (2013) and Ruwanpura (2016) note, there are likely to be local inflexions of ethical code practices, highlighting the need to appreciate how local social institutions matter in shaping such codes. By the time the ethical codes came into existence in the mid-1990s, the Sri Lankan apparel sector was already in a strong position to adopt them, given there had been prior political directives to the industry as early as the 1980s requiring employers to adhere to minimum labour standards (Ruwanpura and Wrigley 2011). These laws ranged from paying national minimum wages, zero child labour, and the provision of welfare facilities, including restrooms, toilets, canteens, and locker rooms, which were regularly monitored by the BOI, labour department, and zonal authorities (Gunawardana 2008; Ruwanpura 2022a).

Ruwanpura (2022a) explains the evolution of ethical codes to reveal how global governance mechanisms are shaped by an interplay of institutional, cultural, social, and political economy factors of producing countries. As mentioned before, the existing legislative frameworks and social welfare standards facilitated the implementation of these codes and, more importantly, provided a strong foundation on which to build. Moreover, it is the strong position of labour movements and subsequent struggles of workers, continued primarily by women workers in the post-liberalised years, which has created a political history that safeguards labour rights (see also Jayawardena 1972, 2017; Ruwanpura 2013, 2016). It is this strong foundation – secured by pro-labour market legislation – that has enabled lead firms and manufacturers to capitalise on their ethical sourcing image. Yet, even while the ethical codes make a strong case for social and labour justice (Goger 2013; Ruwanpura 2016), the complex politics around ethical codes on factory floors mean that bold claims for guilt-free apparel are difficult to sustain, as Ruwanpura (2022a) remarks, and I have illustrated throughout this chapter.

Concluding Remarks: Apparel Industry in the Post-Conflict and Post-Pandemic Era

This chapter reviewed the scholarship on the work and life of Sri Lankan apparel workers. It illustrated the breadth and scope of work on the industry since its inception decades ago. The scholarship has produced rich accounts of the embodied experience of working women, gendered dynamics of the industry, agency of labour, and global labour governance mechanisms. Having noted that to broaden our understanding of the industry and its future, it is important to pay attention to six under-explored elements that are likely to have a significant impact on the industry and the way we understand it.

First is the 'militarised capital' coined by Ruwanpura (2018) and its implications on the work and life of apparel workers in the North of Sri Lanka. The end of the 30-year civil war in 2009 marked a turning point for the Sri Lankan apparel industry. While providing much-needed employment and earning opportunities for the ethnic minority labour force in the North, the industry's expansion is mired in tensions and controversies (Goger and Ruwanpura 2014; Ridicki 2015; Sarvananthan 2015; Ruwanpura 2022a). Manufacturers saw nothing anomalous in recruiting workers via the military (Ruwanpura 2022a), although there are no reports of workers being recruited forcibly. Her work underlines how manufacturers were not sensitive to the fact that deploying the military for labour recruitment might amount to forced labour and thus violating the Sri Lankan labour laws and undermining the industry's ethical codes. The potential fear, force, and intimidation that communities in the war-affected regions associate with the military were grossly disregarded because manufacturers saw themselves as the 'saviours' for bringing jobs to the area and facilitating the 'reconciliation' process (Gorger and Ruwanpura 2014; Ruwanpura 2018, 2022a). Many workers, whose lives were ravaged by the war, are still dealing with post-conflict trauma which has not been addressed adequately (Thirangama 2013; Ridicki 2015; Sarvananthan 2015; Lingham 2019, this volume). During and after the Conflict, many experienced disruptions to schooling, grew up in rehabilitation camps that may or may not have been legitimate rehabilitation establishments, and lost their brothers and fathers to the war. They do not leave their social, political, and economic insecurities at the factory gates (Ruwanpura 2022a). Neither do factory managers – most of whom are Sinhalese – cast aside the dominant ethno-nationalist characteristics. The intersection of these contrasting realms and their broader implications on the labour regimes of the industry warrant a closer look.

Second, and related, it is crucial to understand how ethnic identities and social, economic, and political insecurities of Tamil migrant labourers are materialised and negotiated in the EPZs in the South. When the war ended, manpower agencies, brokers, and dealers rapidly reached out to the North, to tap into a willing labour force to work in the South (Ruwanpura 2022a). By luring a previously isolated community with 'fancy and attractive stories about jobs in the South', they encouraged Tamil women workers to fill vacancies in the apparel sector (Women's Center 2013: 39). The urgency was driven by the labour shortage in EPZs (Goger and Ruwanpura 2014; Ruwanpura 2018; Lingham 2019). As with the expansion of the industry in the North, managers' lack of attention to the long-running ethnic tensions, social, economic, and political insecurities of Tamil workers, and their needs are noted. Language discrimination in administrative and production matters on the shopfloors, uneven target distribution between Tamil and Sinhala workers, and unfair pricing tactics engaged by vendors and boarding houses are detailed in the research conducted (Women's Center 2013; Wickramasingha 2020), with segregation or discouraging the association between Tamil and Sinhalese workers considered standard practice (Women's Center 2013; Goger and Ruwanpura 2014; Ridicki 2015; Lingham 2019; Ruwanpura 2022a). Consequently, Tamil workers struggle with feelings of isolation in the factories (Ruwanpura 2022a). A question that needs further exploration is: how do these ethnic politics and racial identities shape the production and labour process?

Third, there is a need to understand climate change and value chain transition in the apparel industry, and its resultant implications for labour. The textile and apparel industries account for around 10% of global CO_2 emissions, and their fast fashion approach consumes large amounts of water and energy in the production and processing stages (GFA 2019). In response, lead firms are now actively using sustainable business practices to help mitigate their environmental footprint. On the one hand, this contributes to the reduction of emissions and waste of resources. On the other hand, this guards firms against reputational risk related to unsustainable sourcing practices, adds to the bottom line, and increases their power in governing value chains (Lund-Thomsen 2020; Ponte 2020). Sustainability is thus becoming mainstream in business conduct and operations.

By 2002, Sri Lankan suppliers had adopted ethical manufacturing processes and promoted environmental accountability in their activities (Goger 2013; Fernando et al., 2019 as cited in Ruwanpura 2022a). Yet, how are such sustainable business practices realised on the ground? Specifically, what economic, social, and legal drivers and barriers exist and how do these drivers and barriers (re)shape work and workers' lives? I emphasise the need to examine the ground realities in implementing a sustainable transition of the Sri Lankan apparel industry, practices of decarbonisation and climate change adaption, and the implications for workers of these intertwined processes.

Fourth, informality in the sector is a major concern especially in EPZs, with persistent labour shortage. Most manufacturers depend on manpower agencies to fill these shortages (Skanthakumar 2019; Wickramasingha 2020; Hewamanne 2021). Manpower agencies have paved the way for a regime of recruitment and employment that operates outside legal frameworks (Skanthakumar 2019; Hewamanne 2021). Manpower workers are not protected by national labour laws as they are not registered as formal workers and do not earn statutory benefits, gratuity, or severance benefits. Manpower workers thus work under extremely precarious conditions. There is thus an urgent need to understand manpower work and growing informalities in the sector, and how such informal work (re)shapes the labour process and its implications for workers.

Fifth, the implications of the Covid-19 pandemic cannot be overlooked. In the two years since the pandemic, the industry in Sri Lanka saw major structural changes. It was affected by the changes in purchasing patterns of global lead firms resulting in withdrawal, delays, cancellation, and price reductions of orders (ILO 2020). Consequently, exports reduced from $5.2bn in 2019 to $3.9 in 2020, a 25% decrease (BOI 2022). A new development in the industry was the transition to manufacturing Personal Protective Equipment (PPE) (Ruwanpura 2022b). This transition was influenced by both the need to stay afloat during the economic downturn and the increased demand for PPEs globally. This shift helped the industry manage the worst effects of the crisis and offered workers continuous employment (Mezzadri and Ruwanpura 2020). Still, the Asia Floor Wage Alliance (2021) reported that only a segment of workers was employed in PPE manufacturing for low wages and long working hours. Moreover, it is not clear how PPE manufacturing has unfolded across the industry, its implication on labour regimes, its contribution to exports, and its long-term sustainability.

Sixth, it is important to understand how the economic crisis in Sri Lanka has affected work and workers. Since early 2022, Sri Lanka has been battling with what is being described as the worst economic crisis since the country's independence in 1948. Without adequate foreign reserves, the government has been struggling for over a year now to provide its citizens with the most basic needs such as fuel, electricity, gas, essential drugs, and food. Inflation has skyrocketed with the prices of essential goods increasing by 200% or more. Indeed, by the end of 2022, the country reported

$5.6bn revenue, a 10% increase from 2021 and a 5.6% increase from 2019, the pre-pandemic context (BOI 2022). However, the initial setbacks of the pandemic – through lockdowns, reduction of orders, and subsequent changes to the production and labour regimes – had drastic economic and social consequences for apparel workers (Workers Rights Consortium 2020; Hewamanne 2021; Ruwanpura 2022b). In addition to the threat to their health and well-being, Sri Lankan apparel workers had to deal with job losses, furlough, wage cuts, loss of incentives and bonuses, loss of overtime, and increased workloads. Against this backdrop, the fate of apparel workers has been a major concern in the post-pandemic context further aggravated by the economic crisis. Thus, future studies of the industry will need to take into consideration the implications of both the pandemic and the economic crisis for the production and labour process with a focus on any short-term and long-term restructuring the industry has undergone.

References

Amarasinghe, N. (2007) "Nutritional Status of the Female Garment Factory Workers in the Katunayake Free Trade One, Sri Lanka" *Labour Gazette – Sri Lanka Department of Labour* 67–72

Asia Floor Wage Alliance (AFWA) (2021) *Money Heist: COVID-19 Wage Theft in Global Garment Supply Chains Report* Bangkok: AFWA

Asia Floor Wage Alliance (AFWA) (2022) *Living wage*. Accessed on 09/05/2023. Available at https://asia.floorwage.org/living-wage/

Attanapola, Chamila (2004) "Changing Gender Roles and Health Impacts Among Female Workers in Export-Processing Industries in Sri Lanka" *Social Science and Medicine* 58(11): 2301–2312

Biyanwila, Janaka S. (2011) *The Labour Movement in the Global South: Trade Unions in Sri Lanka* London: Routledge

BOI (2019) Apparel overview. Accessed on 03/08/2021. Available at http://investsrilanka.com/sectors/apparel-2/

BOI (2022) Apparel exports. Accessed on 29/06/2022. Available at https://investsrilanka.com/apparel-new/

Carswell, Grace and Geert De Neve (2013) "Labouring for Global Markets: Conceptualising Labour Agency in Global Production Networks" *Geoforum* 44: 62–70

CBSL (2009) *Sri Lanka's Socio-Economic Data* Colombo: Central Bank

de Alwis, Malathi (1999) "Millennial Musings on Maternalism" *Asian Women* 9: 151–169

De Neve, Geert (2005) *The Everyday Politics of Labour: Working Lives in India's Informal Economy* New York: Berghahn Books

De Neve, Geert (2009) "Power, Inequality and Corporate Social Responsibility: The Politics of Ethical Compliance in the South Indian Garment Industry" *Economic and Political Weekly* 63–71

EDB (2022) Apparel export performance. Accessed on 30/06/2022. Available at https://www.srilankabusiness.com/apparel/about/export-performance.html

Elson, Diane and Ruth Pearson (1981) "The Subordination of Women and the Internationalization of Factory Production" In *Of Marriage and Markets: Women's Subordination Internationally and Its Lessons* Kate Young, Carol Wolkowitz and Roslyn McCullugh (eds) London: Conference of Socialist Economists, pp 144–166

GFA (2019) Pulse of the fashion industry, Global Fashion Agenda, Copenhagen

Goger, Annelies (2013) "From Disposable to Empowered: Re-Articulating Labor in Sri Lankan Apparel Factories" *Environment and Planning A* 45(11): 2628–2645

Goger, Annelies (2014) "Ethical Branding in Sri Lanka: A Case Study of Garments without Guilt" In *Workers' Rights and Labour Compliance in Global Supply Chains: Is a Social Label the Answer?* Doug Miller, Jennifer Bair and Marsha Dickson (eds) London: Routledge, pp 47–68

Goger, Annelies and Kanchana N. Ruwanpura (2014) *Ethical Reconstruction? Primitive Accumulation in the Apparel Sector of Eastern Sri Lanka*. Working Paper 14, Colombo, Sri Lanka: International Centre for Ethnic Studies

Gunawardana, Samanthi (2007) "Struggle, Perseverance and Organization in Sri Lanka's Export Processing Zones" In *Global Unions: Challenging Transnational Capital Through Cross-Border Campaigns* Kate Bronfenbrenner (ed) Ithaca: Cornell University Press, pp 78–98

Gunawardana, Samanthi (2008) "Meeting Bala Tampoe: A Union Leader Pursuing Social Justice" In *Profiles in Courage: Political Actors and Ideas in Contemporary Asia* Victoria: Australian Scholarly Publishing, pp 92–105

Gunawardana, Samanthi (2014) "Reframing Employee Voice: A Case Study in Sri Lanka's Export Processing Zones" *Work, Employment and Society* 28(3): 452–468

Gunawardana, Samanthi (2016) "To Finish, We Must Finish: Everyday Practices of Depletion in Sri Lankan Export-Processing Zones" *Globalizations* 13(6): 861–875

Gunawardana, Samanathi and Janaka Biyanwila (2008) "Trade Unions in Sri Lanka: Beyond Party Politics" In *Trade Unions in Asia: Balancing Economic Competitiveness in Social Sustainability* J. Benson and Y. Zhu (eds) London: Routledge, pp 177–197

Hewamanne, Sandya (2008) "City of Whores' Nationalism, Development, and Global Garment Workers in Sri Lanka" *Social Text* 26(2): 35–59

Hewamanne, Sandya (2016) *Sri Lanka's Global Factory Workers: (Un)disciplined Desires and Sexual Struggles in a Post-Colonial Society* London: Routledge

Hewamanne, Sandya (2017) "Toward Meaningful Health and Safety Measures: Stigma and the Devaluation of Garment Work in Sri Lanka's Global Factories" In *Unmaking the Global Sweatshop* Rebecca Prentice and Geert De Neve (eds) Pennsylvania: University of Pennsylvania Press, pp 226–249

Hewamanne, Sandya (2020) "From Global Workers to Local Entrepreneurs: Sri Lanka's Former Global Factory Workers in Rural Sri Lanka" *Third World Quarterly* 41(3): 547–564

Hewamanne, Sandya (2021) "Pandemic, Lockdown and Modern Slavery among Sri Lanka's Global Assembly Line Workers" *Journal of International Women's Studies* 22(1): 54–69

Hughes, Alex, Neil Wrigley and Martin Buttle (2008) "Global Production Networks, Ethical Campaigning, and the Embeddedness of Responsible Governance" *Journal of Economic Geography* 8(3): 345–367

ILO (2020). What next for Asian garment production after Covid-19? https://www.ilo.org/wcmsp5/groups/public/—asia/—ro-bangkok/—sro-bangkok/documents/publication/wcms_755630.pdf

Jayawardena, Kumari (1972) *The Rise of the Labour Movement in Ceylon* Durham: Duke University Press

Jayawardena, Kumari (2017) *Labour, Feminism and Ethnicity in Sri Lanka: Selected Essays* Colombo: SailFish

Kabeer, Naila (2002) *The Power to Choose: Bangladeshi Women and Labor Market Decisions in London and Dhaka* New York: Verso

Kelegama, Saman (2004) *Ready-Made Garment Industry in Sri Lanka: Facing the Global Challenge* Colombo: Institute of Policy Studies

Lingham, Jayanthi (2019) *Dispossessing connections: Women's working lives in post-war Jaffna District, Sri Lanka, 2009–2015* PhD Dissertation, SOAS – University of London

Locke, Richard M., Ben A. Rissing and Timea Pal (2013) "Complements or Substitutes? Private Codes, State Regulation and the Enforcement of Labour Standards in Global Supply Chains" *British Journal of Industrial Relations* 51(3): 519–552

Lund-Thomsen, Peter (2020) "Corporate Social Responsibility: A Supplier-Centered Perspective" *Environment and Planning A: Economy and Space* 52(8): 1700–1709

Lynch, Caitrin (2007) *Juki Girls, Good Girls: Gender and Cultural Politics in Sri Lanka's Global Garment Industry* New York: Cornell University Press

Mezzadri, Alessandra (2016) "Class, Gender and the Sweatshop" *Third World Quarterly* 37: 1877–1900

Mezzadri, Alessandra (2017) *The Sweatshop Regime: Labouring Bodies, Exploitation, and Garments Made in India* Cambridge: Cambridge University Press

Mezzadri, Alessandra and Kanchana N. Ruwanpura (2020) "How Asia's Clothing Factories Switched to Making PPE – but Sweatshop Problems Live on" *The Conversation* (29 June). https://theconversation.com/how-asias-clothing-factories-switched-to-making-ppe-but-sweatshop-problems-live-on-141396

O'Rourke, Dan (2006) "Multi-Stakeholder Regulation: Privatizing or Socializing Global Labour Standards" *World Development* 34(5): 899–918

Perry, Patsy, Steve Wood and James Fernie (2015) "Corporate Social Responsibility in Garment Sourcing Networks: Factory Management Perspectives on Ethical Trade in Sri Lanka" *Journal of Business Ethics* 130: 737–752

Ponte, Stephan (2020) "Green Capital Accumulation: Business and Sustainability Management in a World of Global Value Chains" *New Political Economy* 25(1): 72–84

Ridicki, Dan (2015) *Being about people: MAS Holdings journey to the North*. MAS Holdings. https://youtube.com/watch?v=bB_uU6_8eqY

Ruwanpura, Kanchana N. (2012) *Ethical codes: Reality and rhetoric – a study of Sri Lanka's apparel sector*. Working Paper. Accessed on 03/08/2021. Available at https://eprints.soton.ac.uk/337113/1/ESRC-EndofProjectReport2012.pdf

Ruwanpura, Kanchana N. (2013) "It's the (Household) Economy, Stupid! Pension Reform, Collective Resistance and the Reproductive Sphere in Sri Lanka" In *The Global Political Economy of the Household in Asia* Juanita Elisa and Samanthi Gunawardana (eds) London: Palgrave Macmillan, pp 145–161

Ruwanpura, Kanchana N. (2014) "Metal Free Factories: Straddling Worker Rights and Consumer Safety?" *Geoforum* 51: 224–232

Ruwanpura, Kanchana N. (2015) "The Weakest Link? Unions, Freedom of Association and Ethical Codes: A Case Study from a Factory Setting in Sri Lanka" *Ethnography* 16(1): 118–141

Ruwanpura, Kanchana N. (2016) "Garments without Guilt? Uneven Labour Geographies and Ethical Trading - Sri Lankan Labour Perspectives" *Journal of Economic Geography* 16(2): 423–446

Ruwanpura, Kanchana N. (2017) "Limited Leave? Clinical Provisioning and Healthy Bodies in Sri Lanka's Apparel Sector" In *Unmaking the Global Sweatshop* Rebecca Prentice and Geert De Neve (eds) Pennsylvania: University of Pennsylvania Press, pp 203–225

Ruwanpura, Kanchana N. (2018) "Militarized Capitalism? The Apparel Industry's Role in Scripting a Post-War National Identity in Sri Lanka" *Antipode* 50(2): 425–446

Ruwanpura, Kanchana N. (2019) "Imaginary' Illnesses: Worker Occupational Health and Privatized Health Care: Sri Lanka's Story" *Contemporary South Asia* 27(2): 247–258

Ruwanpura, Kanchana N. (2022a) *Garments without Guilt?: Global Labour Justice and Ethical Codes in Sri Lankan Apparels* Cambridge: Cambridge University Press

Ruwanpura, Kanchana N. (2022b) "Doing the Right Thing? COVID-19, PPE and the Case of Sri Lankan Apparels" *Global Labour Journal* 13(1): 111–121

Ruwanpura, Kanchana N. and Alex Hughes (2016) "Empowered Spaces? Management Articulations of Gendered Spaces in Apparel Factories in Karachi, Pakistan" *Gender, Place and Culture* 23(9): 1270–1285

Ruwanpura, Kanchana N. and Neil Wrigley (2011) "The Costs of Compliance? Views of Sri Lankan Apparel Manufacturers in Times of Global Economic Crisis" *Journal of Economic Geography* 11(6): 1031–1049

Ruwanpura, Kanchana N. and the Women's Center (2021) *COVID 19 and made in Sri Lanka: Apparel sector workers making sense of a pandemic* Working paper with Women's Center, Ja-Ela, Sri Lanka

Sarvananthan, M. (2015) "Impediments to Women in Post-Civil War Economic Growth in Sri Lanka" *South Asian Journal of Human Resources Management* 2(1): 12–36

Saxena, Sanchita (2020) *Labour, Global Supply Chains and the Garment Industry in South Asia: Bangladesh after Rana Plaza* Oxford: Routledge

Skanthakumar, B. (2019) *Living for the Day: Contract Workers in Sri Lanka's Free Trade Zones*. Working Paper. Dabindu Collective, Colombo

Wickramasingha, Shyamain (2020) *Labour regimes in global production networks: Comparing the Bangladeshi and Sri Lankan apparel industries* [Unpublished doctoral dissertation]. Singapore: National University of Singapore

Wickramasingha, Shyamain and Neil M. Coe (2021) "Conceptualizing Labor Regimes in Global Production Networks: Uneven Outcomes across the Bangladeshi and Sri Lankan Apparel Industries" *Economic Geography* 98(1): 68–90

Wickramasingha, Shyamain and Geert de Neve (2022) "The Collective Working Body: Rethinking Apparel Workers' Health and Well-Being during the COVID-19 Pandemic in Sri Lanka" *Global Labour Journal* 13(3): 322–339

Wijayasiri, Janaka and J. Dissanayake (2009) "The Ending of the Multi-Fibre Agreement and Innovation in the Sri Lankan Textile and Clothing Industry" *OECD Journal: General Papers* 4: 157–188

Women's Center (2011) *Uprising: Struggle against EPF Daylight Robbery* Ja-Ela: Women's Centre

Women's Center (2013) *Ethnic Discrimination: The Post Armed Conflict Economic Challenges of Tamil Women* Ja-Ela: Women's Centre of Sri Lanka

Workers Rights Consortium (2020) Global survey: Garment workers report widespread hunger during Covid-19. https://www.workersrights.org/press-release/global-survey-garment-workers-report-widespread-hunger-during-covid-19/

Wright, Melissa (2006) *Disposable Women and Other Myths of Global Capitalism* London: Routledge

19
MICROFINANCE, DEBT AND INDEBTEDNESS OF RURAL SECTOR WORKERS IN SRI LANKA

Nedha de Silva and Amali Wedagedara

Introduction

Microfinance and rural credit facilities are often projected as a means for radically improving the livelihoods and living standards of people. In contrast to 'ascribed social statuses' in traditional societies widespread availability of credit was expected to qualitatively transform social status from a 'given' to something 'achievable' for men and women from low-income backgrounds, particularly in the rural areas (Lund 1981). Livelihood-credit approaches or entrepreneurial interventions to rural development became mainstream in the 1980s in line with the modernisation of rural agriculture, poverty alleviation, empowerment of women and mitigation of crises, man-made or otherwise. Pervasive conditions of poverty and indebtedness in contemporary society, particularly indebtedness among rural women driven by microfinance, demand a thorough examination of the narrative of credit-driven entrepreneurialism – a logic in line with self-help/self-reliance, that a small loan could drive a small business and render it profitable by enabling people to lift themselves out of poverty. How does literature on microfinance in Sri Lanka reflect the elements of work and the lives of rural workers? What do they share about livelihoods, the nature of labour, and the lives of rural people? What is missing from the discussion? In this chapter, we aim to respond to some of the broader questions around microfinance, indebtedness, and the rural sector by focusing specifically on the institutionalisation of the practice of microfinance as an entrepreneurial model of development in Sri Lanka and its implementation as a development tool following the crisis.

As such, we begin the chapter with an introduction to entrepreneurship and development in the Sri Lankan context by detailing significant socio-economic changes that have occurred since independence that have directly affected narratives of entrepreneurship. We then proceed to identify microfinance as a development tool specifically targeted at women entrepreneurs. However, we interrogate the role of microfinance as an avenue for self-employment within a backdrop of limited access, opportunities and skills as has been the reality for many rural women in Sri Lanka who are marginalised and made impoverished. We highlight how microfinance, often branded as a tool of poverty eradication, is utilised as a mechanism against all types of crises in the Sri Lankan context by specifically identifying the tsunami and post-war context as examples of instances where microfinance has been promoted. Finally, we emphasise how microfinance, when presented within a broader neoliberal economic policy framework, works as a mechanism that promotes a vicious cycle of poverty, violence, and harassment. We conclude that rather than empowering women, microfinance has empowered capital to extract higher returns by subsuming women's labour.

Entrepreneurship and Development

The ideas of social entrepreneurship, social business, and enterprise have disturbed the traditional notion of work and social status. Apart from attributing a sense of social mobility away from cultural and gender division of labour, entrepreneurship also marks a displacement of collective forms of work, such as *attan*, prevalent in the traditional society as well as the State and formal sector work with regular income, labour safety, and retirement benefits. In Sri Lanka for a long-time self-employment, in contrast to salaried work, was considered as 'residual' in the economy (Perera and Mudalige 1993). Even though generating employment opportunities for the rural poor, especially educated rural youth, became a policy priority in the aftermath of the youth uprising in 1971, termed as 'a rural insurrection' (Morrison 1975; Stokke 1994), the promised increase in employment opportunities by 50% proposed by the Five-Year Development Plan from 1972 to 1976 was linked to import substitution policy of the government (Balakrishnan 1973). Self-employment articulated in the 1972–1976 Five Year Plan was qualitatively different from that mainstreamed after 1977 as it centred around the State and the Cooperatives and was geared towards the promotion of small-scale industries. Even though the overall policy outlook emphasised low-capital and labour-intensive diversification and had an agriculture bias, broadening access to credit was perceived as a core supportive service (Stokke 1994). Nevertheless, loan schemes for non-farm Small and Medium Enterprises were only initiated in 1979 and were limited to established businesses (Hulme, Montgomery and Bhattacharya 1996).

The promotion of self-employment in small enterprises as a policy took off in the late 1980s as large-scale developmental projects encountered obstacles amidst the socio-political instability that prevailed in the country (Perera and Mudalige 1993). Data on self-employment in the late 1980s also illustrates a shift away from the agricultural base to manufacturing, wholesale, retail and construction as preferred sectors to be self-employed. To better comprehend the progress of entrepreneurship development projects in the late 1980s, Perera and Mudalige (1993) propose to distinguish survival-oriented 'self-employment' from capital-intensive micro-enterprises, which form a viable alternative to formal sector employment. The quest to establish connections, specifically in relation to exports, spilt over to small-scale and household-based industries funded through microfinance programmes implemented through regional arms of the government as well as Non-Government Organisations (NGOs) and donor agencies.

Microenterprises and Microfinance

Microfinance models fashioned after the Grameen Bank in Bangladesh in the 1990s as an ideal instrument to promote self-employment were mainstreamed in Sri Lanka as well. Distinct from other rural credit programmes, microfinance caters to low-income women who lack savings, land, or other collateral which excludes them from accessing financial services from the formal sector to invest in income-generating activities. Profitability of microfinance as a tool of poverty alleviation in contrast to traditional mechanisms driven through Universal Safety Nets, state subsidies, aid and public services along with its compliance with neoliberal principles of self-reliance and individualism rapidly expanded and diversified the microfinance industry beyond the State, NGOs, and Community-Based Organisations (CBOs) to finance companies, multilateral creditors like Asia Development Bank (ADB), the World Bank including high-risk investors in the capital markets, such as equity funds, international banks, pension funds, and insurance companies (Mader, Mertens and Zwan 2020).

In line with modernisation ideology, microfinance approaches to microenterprises and social business perceive poverty as a deficiency in factors of production rather than a structural problem connected to relations of production (Stokke 1994). As such it is assumed that enhancing entrepreneurial skills and provision of credit would galvanise the entrepreneurial spirit of individuals and spur development. As in many other developing countries of Asia, Africa, and Latin America, microfinance has been introduced as a neoliberal economic tool of development post 1977. A majority of the literature on microfinance in Sri Lanka upholds this view.

Empowerment of Women

When focusing on the empowerment of women in relation to development, spillovers from the International Decade for Women (1975–1985), increasing visibility of women in the public as a result of equal access to education from the 1940s and the youth uprising in 1971 influenced the government and policymakers to focus on gender inclusive development in Sri Lanka (Jayaweera 1985a). The new interest in women, particularly in their economic well-being, was linked to their disadvantaged status, socio-economically dependent on men. The Women in Development programme for example focused on integrating women into the modern sectors of the economy to make them economically independent (Jayawardena 1997). Apart from the top-down initiatives, such initiatives also opened space for women in local participatory development programmes (Hennayake 2000). However, these initiatives did not examine the negative effects of capitalist economic development on women over the years. Lund (1981) points out that by the late 1970s women had lost the strengths they had in subsistence economies, degenerating their "productive functions in the market economy" (1981: 95). Proposals to empower women did not question dominant patriarchal structures of society and fell short of emancipating women (Jayawardena 1997). Instead of integrating women as equal partners with the ability to contribute to development meaningfully, women were absorbed as cheap labour, secondary earners and were restricted to 'feminine' dependent sectors (Jayaweera 1985b). Over the years, efforts to render women economically active, i.e. enabling them to generate income through their labour, ended up subjecting women to new forms of subordination (Jayawardena 1997; Hennayake 2000; Federici 2018).

Credit-induced self-employment initiatives, especially in agrarian societies, were often used to expand income-generating opportunities for women. A plethora of literature illustrates the feminisation of rural credit through a spectrum of microfinance programmes which sought to expand the availability of credit to promote self-employment. *Janasaviya* implemented in the late 1980s by the Government for low-income earning families could be considered as the first microfinance programme (Tilakaratna, Wickramasinghe and Kumara 2005). The *Samurdhi* programme, which has been implemented since 1995, indicates that *Janasaviya*-like approaches to promote employment-oriented poverty reduction approaches have become a permanent face of the welfare State in Sri Lanka.

Even though self-employment appeared to be a quick answer to the question of high levels of unemployment among women, its ability to enhance their living conditions has been weak, as many of them lack access to technical and managerial skills and are therefore marginalised and trapped in a vicious cycle of poverty (Jayaweera, Sanmugam and Amarasuriya 2004). Fieldwork observations almost a decade later in 2015 pointed out that microfinance has not substantially improved the gendered division of labour or gendered relations of power in the household. Herath, Guneratne and Sanderatne (2015) reveal that even though microfinance programmes have enabled women to build little savings and enhance their self-confidence, women continued to value work by men more than their own and had less control over their wages and household expenditure. In addition, their research also found that in addition to credit, lack of easy access to markets, poor infrastructure and adverse natural environments significantly undermined the success of microenterprises. Moreover, the success of women-owned businesses in terms of increased revenue was determined by the absence of other self-employed people in the household (Bernhardt et al 2019). More than promoting enterprises and facilitating upward social mobility, micro-financialised income generation mechanisms like Samurdhi play a 'protectional role' by providing extra-income financial support (Gunatilaka and Salih 1999: 28). Samurdhi is the only social safety network available to low-income people in Sri Lanka. Explaining failures of Samurdhi-driven projects, they point out that the poor seek the security of wages and not self-employment and argue that supporting large and stable businesses is a better approach to generate wage employment for the extreme poor.

These findings resonate with larger critics of microfinance as a mechanism to sidestep creating decent work with living wages, employment safeguards and protection. Mader (2015) for example has argued that instead of creating livelihoods for the poor, microfinance has created an avenue for financial capital to extract higher returns through poor people's labour. Kodikara's (2018) work on the nature of livelihoods supported by microfinance programmes in the post-war areas substantiates this claim. She points out that microfinance supported "livelihoods is […] a misnomer" (2018: 12). Self-employment activities that microfinance supported women engaged in were subjected to gender division of labour and limited to the domestic sphere. Often, self-employment activities are things women do to get by, "as a routine aspect of their daily struggle for survival" (Kabeer 2012: 19). Rather than liberating women from socio-cultural fetters that hold them back, securing their ownership of means of production, and enabling women to exercise their agency and transcend the gendered division of labour, microfinance has empowered capital to completely subsume labour.

Microfinance as a Crisis Easing Policy

The model of microfinance as a crisis-response tool of economic development has been adopted in Sri Lanka in diverse situations ranging from natural disasters to civil wars. It is believed that in post-crisis contexts, microfinance can act as one among other long-term economic, social, and political recovery tools for communities to achieve economic and social rejuvenation (Poston 2010). As such, it is introduced as a pathway to financial inclusion that secures the livelihoods of the lower-income groups and strengthens communities (Green and Bylander 2019). Similarly, it has been introduced and endorsed in Sri Lanka following varied forms of crisis including natural disasters, conflicts, and pandemics over the past few decades.

In this section, we discuss the implications of crisis-based microfinance as part of long-term recovery, focusing specifically on the post-tsunami recovery plan following the tsunami tidal wave in 2004, post-war reconstruction in 2009, and the Covid-19 pandemic since 2020. Analysing the global anti-microfinance discourse, we also highlight how microfinance introduced to the rural sector under the pretext of increasing financial inclusivity leads to a neoliberal financialisation of the everyday lives of men and women and escalates indebtedness and violence, particularly on women.

Post-Tsunami Recovery

On the 26th December 2004 as the tsunami tidal wave swept across many coastal communities in the Indian Ocean, there was massive devastation in a number of regions in Sri Lanka. Microfinance was introduced as a post-tsunami recovery and development plan with the intention of rebuilding the lives of people (Renuka and Srimulyani 2015). As part of this, income generation activities were introduced both individually and collectively, mostly centring on women. Some of these activities included small businesses such as boutiques, handicrafts, food preparation for sale (such as sweets and snacks), vegetable and banana cultivation and apparel. This was viewed as a significant change when comparing the everyday lives of communities before and after the tsunami.

While the introduction of microfinance is viewed as a strategy for crisis mitigation (Maeda and Takada 2018), it has led to complex issues in the coastal communities, mainly due to a failure to understand the economy of the poor (Kapadia 2014). In Sri Lanka, most institutions involved in microfinance ranging from financial institutions to NGOs introduced microloans based on the assumption that the coastal economy was entrepreneurial and that it could be improved through the provision of assets, training, and financial loans. This is very much reflected in the vast array of assessments, evaluations, and aid agency-created papers (ILO 2005; Karacsony 2005; Parakrama, Scheper and Gunawardena 2006). However, in the coastal belt of Sri Lanka, as most people are engaged in fisheries, entrepreneurship often collided with the everyday economic practices of the people and led to both economic and socio-cultural stresses ranging from higher levels of stress, dissatisfaction, and tensions (Becchetti and Castriota 2010). Moreover, power relations in the communities that were based on patronage and debt were manipulated by the rich through microfinance practices that exploited the poor. Inadvertently, this led to reinforcing the power of the rich and marginalising the poor further in the post-recovery stages (Kapadia 2014). A similar approach to crisis (as has been during the post-Tsunami recovery stage) is visible in the Sri Lankan economic recovery policies targeting the poor in the subsequent crisis, such as the post-conflict recovery where microfinance as a business enterprise is expanded using the metaphor of the crisis.

Post-Conflict Development

With the military victory in 2009, the Sri Lankan government attempted to revive an economic nationalism that was visible in the 1960s and 1970s. The *Mahinda Chinthana: Ediri Dakma* (Mahinda Vision: A Vision for the Future) launched as part of the medium-term development strategy of the country focused on the need to achieve balanced growth with an emphasis on developing the infrastructure of the rural and conflict-affected parts of the country and promoting the small and medium enterprises. However, in the regional development plans launched in the North and East by the government, there was a clear lack of focus on livelihood development in the communities. On the contrary, the government prioritised physical reconstruction and infrastructure development. This led to a mismatch between community needs and the development plans that were carried out which failed to provide opportunities to increase livelihoods, as they were at the centre of attention to enhance the continuity and security of everyday life. It was as a part of this development venture that the Sri Lankan government paved the way for microfinance institutions (MFIs) to enter the war-affected regions with the intention of filling this gap of rebuilding the economic conditions of communities through the promotion of small-scale enterprises through entrepreneurship (Thalpawila 2016; Vithanagama 2018).

Reflecting on the state recovery plan and the livelihood activities of the rural populations of the North and East, Kadirgamar (2013) states that while the civil war had disconnected the regions from the rest of the country and the market, the main traditional livelihood activities including agriculture and fisheries have failed to deliver. Although the state recovery plan has invested in infrastructure development, this has been counterproductive. More efficient transportation has contributed to expanding the market that has undermined the community and regional production as goods can be transported for lower prices from other parts of the country. As such, the state recovery plans have failed to contribute to rural livelihood development and exacerbated indebtedness due to unrestrained access to neoliberal finance.

As Sri Lanka has a long history of similar informal financial practices through programmes, such as Thrift and Credit Cooperative Societies (TCCSs), established in 1911, and the *Janasaviya* programme in the 1980s, the expectation was to rebuild the rural economy by catering to women as agents of rebuilding peace economies. While at the initial stage, microfinance provided people with the opportunity to find the start-up capital to engage in small-scale businesses, with the introduction of commercialised microfinance, institutions started to operate under neoliberal principles where market-oriented reform policies were followed. In the post-war Sri Lankan context, this paved the way to create more havoc in Northern and Eastern regions leading to further impoverishment of the people. As such, women in those regions turned to microfinance as they were denied access to any other formal financial services, giving the microfinance industry a complete monopoly of the everyday financial needs of people. Most of these organisations engage in practices that are harmful to their clients, such as charging extremely high-interest rates (ranging up to 200%) and resorting to harassment and violence upon late payments. However, the issues with microfinance are not limited to the North and East. As articulated by Srinivasan (2020b), high levels of indebtedness are also reported among rural populations in the plantation, agriculture and fisheries sectors from across the country.

Despite the continued critique that the microfinance industry has received for its predatory practices ranging from interest rates to lack of regulation by both local and international organisations (World Bank 2015; OHCHR 2018), the state response has been minimal. The key measures that the government has adopted include an interest cap of 35% and a moratorium of 100,000 Sri Lankan Rupees, both of which have not been enforced effectively. This has resulted in a situation where women, the majority clientele of the microfinance industry, located in the North and East face numerous socio-economic issues the State has largely ignored, despite women's protest and resistance.

Over-Indebtedness and Debt Trap

Research worldwide on microfinance emphasises multiple borrowing and over-indebtedness as common issues faced by microfinanciers. In the rural Sri Lankan context, overt coercion by microfinance officers and fellow microfinanciers in a context of meagre opportunities for economic gain leads many borrowers to continue to take loans from multiple MFIs with the hope of settling their previous debts. This practice of multiple borrowing leads to over-indebtedness that ultimately results in borrowers falling into a debt trap, an economic shock to the household due to rising expenditures ranging from healthcare to consumption needs and unpaid loans and interests (Uddin and Uddin 2021). Based on field research conducted in Moneragala, Mullativu, and Batticaloa, Arambepola and Romeshun (2019) state that the negative effects associated with lending by MFIs have detrimental consequences not only on the women borrowers but also on their families. Practices of multiple borrowing that lead to over-indebtedness are a result of both institutional malpractices and the lack of individual financial literacy.

When focusing on institutional malpractices, what is noticeable is a number of MFIs functioning in the same regions competing for a single group of clients. This leads MFI officers to adopt lending practices that often encourage competitiveness among MFIs with changes to interest rates, loan repayment, and renewal schemes that are implemented as benefits. Such over-competitiveness encourages multiple borrowing. Moreover, the role of the Central Bank as the regulatory body of the microfinance enterprise is called into question by failing to supervise and conduct on-site examinations of MFIs.

In terms of lack of financial literacy, most borrowers fail to comprehend the conditions of their microfinance loan agreements and fail to adhere to the stipulated instalment payments. As a result, most borrowers face issues in loan repayment leading them to view multiple borrowing as a solution. This practice is encouraged by microfinance officers either to renew loans for larger amounts or to take new loans from other MFIs (Wickramasinghe and Fernando 2017).

Additionally, loans are given not only for income generation activities but also for 'consumption smoothing' where the loan is used to pay off medical expenses, education services, and housing when clients experience a shortage of income. Even in pursuit of income generation, most borrowers find it difficult to repay loans due to varied socio-economic reasons that further weaken their economic conditions. This demands an understanding of the borrower as belonging to what is termed a 'vulnerable population'. In the rural sector of Sri Lanka, the general populace can be viewed as vulnerable based on the lack of economic and political opportunities available, poor infrastructure and services that decrease their life chances (Shaw 2001). When this condition of precarity in livelihoods – mostly limited to subsistence agriculture, fishing, and small-scale entrepreneurial activities – is coupled with the malpractices of microfinance, it pushes borrowers to multiple borrowing. As a result, instead of promoting healthy entrepreneurial practices where women can accumulate capital for their businesses, women continuously borrow more money from MFIs to prevent themselves from repayment failure (Wickramasinghe and Fernando 2017). Women then accumulate loan repayments that exceed their repayment capacity, leading to conditions of indebtedness (Srinivasan 2020a).

A further risk is the erosion of savings including both immovable and movable property, such as bank savings, land, and property used for everyday expenses and emergencies. In addition to this, most women who pawn jewellery to repay microfinance loans, not only fall into a debt trap but also fail to save their jewellery. Moreover, studies conducted on the *seettu* system in Sri Lanka, an organic informal financial system mostly involving women, highlight that participation in microfinance reduces women's opportunity to join *seettu* groups as they fail to save even the smallest amount after repayment (Arambepola and Romeshun 2019). Microfinance was purportedly introduced with the aim of reducing the toxic relations that villagers undergo at the hands of local money lenders or loan sharks. However, microfinance borrowers turn to local money lenders to escape the dire realities of microfinance-related indebtedness that have pushed borrowers into a debt trap.

Violence

Empowerment of unbankable populations was an alleged purpose of microfinance. However, studies from across the globe on microfinance emphasise varied forms of violence associated with microfinance practices (Sanyal 2008; Mader 2013; Wada 2018; Elias and Rai 2019; Green and Bylander 2019), including domestic violence (Schuler, Hashemi and Badal 1998; Kabeer 2005; Montgomerie and Tepe-Belfrage 2019), land dispossession (Green and Bylander 2019), and bride price, a concept used to refer to payments associated in marriage quite similar to the dowry system in South Asia (Johnston 2018). In the Sri Lankan context, microfinance borrowers face violence at the hands of the MFIs as well as the community.

When focusing on the first category of microfinance employees, borrowers experience varied forms of exploitation and fraudulent behaviour that led to violence at the hands of microfinance employees. Congruent with the findings of research conducted elsewhere (Mader 2015; Bateman,

Maclean and Galbraith 2017), the lack of access to formal financial services was used as a strategy to seduce rural women into applying for loans. Most borrowers emphasise that given their economic vulnerability, microfinance was the only available financial source open to them. This highlights a clear structural inequality where low-income populations are denied access to formal financial services.

In addition, borrowers face duplicity at all phases of the microfinance loan process. Most loan agreements are in English. As most borrowers come from rural low-income, vulnerable groups, they have not completed school education and have no competence in English. The lack of language competence in English further disadvantages borrowers who fail to comprehend the nature of the agreements and their conditions such as interest rates and instalments, allowing women to be easily exploited by predatory microfinance organisations. At the loan collection phase, microfinance lenders subsequently charged excessively high-interest rates that range even up to 300%, utilising violence and harassment for late or non-payment. These include verbal, sexual, and physical violence against the borrowers. It has also led to an increasing number of suicides among microfinance borrowers since 2016 which has exceeded 200 by 2021 (Wedagedara and de Silva 2021).

In addition to the gendered violence that women face at the hands of microfinance institutions, women also face issues in the community, both within the household and in the larger community. Microfinance debts and late payments can lead to domestic violence from their male partners even in cases where the women have taken the loan with the consent of the partner. Moreover, on the larger community level, as most microfinance loans operate as group loans, if one client fails to pay the instalment on a particular date, the loan officers make the entire group of women wait at the loan collection point until the woman finds the money to complete the payment on that date. This is often used as a strategy to pressurise the client to find money as other women in the group would also be inconvenienced. This leads to an erosion of interpersonal relationships among group members that can escalate to violence. This experience of the borrowers displays how the interpersonal relationships that acted as social capital in the rural economy are reversed by the practices of the microfinance industry (Arambepola and Romeshun 2019).

Conclusion

Experiences with microfinance over the last four decades narrate a story of the development of the market economy in Sri Lanka. As the problems of debt and indebtedness illustrate, it was used mainly as a temporary cushion to accommodate those who fall out of the system as capitalism expands. Strong emphasis is on the income generation aspect of microfinance as well as the denigration of those who default or fail to repay reveal the tension. For example, lack of motivation, mishandling of loans for consumption smoothing, and lack of financial literacy are some of the explanations for failure in microfinance projects (Navarathne 2017). Such failure results in rural populations not only being victims of vicious financial schemes but also experiencing varied forms of violence, harassment, and discrimination. Such responses clearly highlight that in relation to the rural sector of Sri Lanka, adopting a microfinance model of development has brought with it, in line with neoliberal development ideologies, an increasing acceptance that responsibility for an individual's well-being rests on that person's own individual choices, with a corresponding reduction in the responsibilities of the State, which no longer seeing its role includes providing a social safety net for the rural sector.

Through this chapter, we have attempted to present an overview of the experiences of microfinance and its impact on the rural sector using crisis situations in Sri Lanka, such as the tsunami and civil war. However, at the time of writing, this debt-related crisis associated with microfinance has further expanded in light of the Covid-19 pandemic and the ongoing debt crisis provides ample evidence of how the rural sector is made more vulnerable due to the socio-economic challenges that the pandemic presents that go beyond a crisis of health. We emphasise that the Sri Lankan narratives of development have adopted a neoliberal development model that pushes low-income populations into poverty. It also signifies a clear overlook of the relationship between microfinance and practices of consumption and social reproduction as highly significant aspects of everyday work of the rural sector that require further attention.

References

Arambepola, Chandima and Kulasabanathan Romeshun (2019) *Debt at My Doorstep: Microfinance Practices and Effects on Women in Sri Lanka* Colombo: CEPA

Balakrishnan, N. (1973) "The Five Year Plan and Development Policy in Sri Lanka: Socio-Political Perspectives and the Plan" *Asian Survey* 13(12): 1155–1168

Bateman, Milford, Kate Maclean and James K. Galbraith (2017) *Seduced and Betrayed: Exposing the Contemporary Micro-Finance Phenomenon* Albuquerque: University of New Mexico Press

Becchetti, Leonardo and Stefano Castriota (2010) "The Effects of a Calamity on Income and Wellbeing of Poor Microfinance Borrowers: The Case of the 2004 Tsunami Shock" *The Journal of Development Studies* 46(2): 211–233

Bernhardt, Arielle, Erica Field, Rohini Pande and Natalia Rigol (2019) "Household Matters: Revisiting the Returns to Capital among Female Micro-Entrepreneurs" *AER Insights* 1(2): 141–160

Elias, Juanita and Shirin M. Rai (2019) "Feminist Everyday Political Economy: Space, Time, and Violence" *Review of International Studies* 45(2): 201–220

Federici, Sylvia (2018) *Re-enchanting the World: Feminism and the Politics of the Commons*. Kairos: PM Press

Green, Nathan and Maryann Bylander (2019) "The Exclusionary Power of Debt: Over-Indebtedness and Land Dispossession in Cambodia" *Sociology of Development* 7(2): 202–229

Gunatilaka, Ramani and Rozana Salih (1999) *How Successful Is Samurdhi's Savings and Credit Programme in Reaching the Poor in Sri Lanka?* Colombo: Institute of Policy Studies

Hennayake, Nalani (2000) "Participatory Rural Development and the Question of Women's Empowerment in Sri Lanka" In *Gender, Ideology and Development in Sri Lanka*, 1–15. Colombo: CENWOR

Herath, H.M.W.A., LHP Guneratne and Nimal Sanderatne (2015) "Impact of Microfinance on Women's Empowerment: A Case Study on Two Microfinance Institutions in Sri Lanka" *Sri Lanka Journal of Social Sciences* 38(1): 51–61

Hulme, David, Richard Montgomery and Debapriya Bhattacharya (1996) "Mutual Finance and the Poor: A Study of the Federation of Thrift and Credit Co-Operatives (SANASA) in Sri Lanka" In *Finance against Poverty* David Hulme and Paul Mosley (eds) London and New York: Routledge

ILO (International Labour Organization) (2005) *Needs Assessment Survey for Income Recovery (NASIR) in Tsunami-Affected Areas in Sri Lanka* Colombo: ILO

Jayawardena, Kumari (1997) "Feminist Consciousness and Women's Movement in Sri Lanka" *Asian Women* 5(1997): 39–57

Jayaweera, Swarna (1985a) "Integration of Women in Development Planning" In *UN Decade for Women: Progress and Achievements of Women in Sri Lanka* Colombo: Centre for Women's Research, pp 1–19

Jayaweera, Swarna (1985b) "Women and Employment" In *UN Decade for Women: Progress and Achievements of Women in Sri Lanka* Colombo: Centre for Women's Research, pp 87–110

Jayaweera, Swarna, Thana Sanmugam and Harini Amarasuriya (2004) *Gender and Poverty in Selected Locations in Sri Lanka* Colombo: Centre for Women's Research (CENWOR)

Johnston, Melissa Frances (2018) *The political economy of gender interventions: Social forces, kinship, violence, and finance in post-conflict Timor-Leste*. PhD thesis, Murdoch University

Kabeer, Naila (2005) "Is Microfinance a 'Magic Bullet' for Women's Empowerment? Analysis of Findings from South Asia" *Economic and Political Weekly* 40(29 October): 4709–4718

Kabeer, Naila (2012) *Women's Economic Empowerment and Inclusive Growth: Labour Markets and Enterprise Development* SIG Working Paper 2012/1. Vol. SIG Working Paper 2012/1. London, UK: IDRC, DFID

Kadirgamar, Ahilan (2013, Oct 26) "Rebuilding the Post-War North" *Economic and Political Weekly* 48(43). https://www.epw.in/journal/2013/43/web-exclusives/rebuilding-post-war-north.html

Kapadia, Kamal (2014) "Sri Lankan Livelihoods after the Tsunami: Searching for Entrepreneurs, Unveiling Relations of Power" *Disasters* 39(1): 23–50

Karacsony, P. (2005) *On-going and Planned Livelihood Assistance by I/NGOs in Two Tsunami Affected Districts of Sri Lanka: A Rapid Assessment* Colombo: ILO and TAFREN

Kodikara, Chulani (2018) *Doing This and That: Self-Employment and Economic Survival of Women Heads of Households in Mullaitivu* Colombo: International Centre for Ethnic Studies

Lund, Ragnhild (1981) "Women and Development Planning in Sri Lanka" *Geografiska Annaler* 63(2): 95–108

Mader, Philip (2013) "Rise and Fall of Microfinance in India: The Andhra Pradesh Crisis in Perspective" *Strategic Change* 22(1–2): 47–66

Mader, Philip (2015) *The Political Economy of Microfinance: Financialisation of Poverty* London: Palgrave Macmillan

Mader, P., D. Mertens and N. Zwan (2020) *The Routledge International Handbook of Financialization* London: Routledge

Maeda, Masahiro and Mitsua Takada (2018) "The Effect of Microcredit on Life Restoration and Community Formation in Resettlement Households Affected by the Tsunami – A Study on Resettlement with Housing Relocation in Sri Lanka after the Indian Ocean Tsunami in 2004 Part 3" *Japan Architectural Review* 1(2): 259–270

Montgomerie, Johnna and Daniela Tepe-Belfrage (2019) "Spaces of Debt Resistance and the Contemporary Politics of Financialised Capitalism" *Geoforum* 98(May 2018): 309–317

Morrison, Barrie M (1975) "Asian Drama, Act II: Development Prospects in South Asia" *Pacific Affairs* 48(1): 5–26

Navarathne, Kahadawa Appuhamilage Sucharitha (2017) "Challenges Faced by Small and Micro Enterprises in Sri Lanka" *Urban and Regional Planning* 2(6): 34–37

OHCHR (2018) "Sri Lanka: Human rights to dismantle debt trap, says UN expert" *OHCHR*. Accessed on 24/01/2022. Available at https://www.ohchr.org/en/NewsEvents/Pages/DisplayNews.aspx?NewsID=23529&LangID=E

Parakrama, A., E. Scheper and Samanthi Gunawardena (2006) *Impact of the Tsunami Response on Local and National Capacities. Sri Lanka Country Report* London: Tsunami Evaluation Coalition

Perera, Myrtle and R. Mudalige (1993) *Self-Employment Schemes for Women in Sri Lanka: The Macro-Economic Context* Colombo: ILO

Poston, Angus (2010) "Lessons from a Microfinance Recapitalisation Programme" *Disasters* 34(2): 328–336

Renuka, Ruwani and Eka Srimulyani (2015) "Women after the Tsunami: Impact, Empowerment and Changes in Post-Disaster Situations of Sri Lanka and Aceh, Indonesia" *Asian Journal of Women's Studies* 21(2): 192–210

Sanyal, Paromita (2008) *Credit, Capital, or Coalition?: Microfinance and Women's Agency* Cambridge: Harvard University

Schuler, Sidney Ruth, Syed M Hashemi and Shamsul Huda Badal (1998) "Men's Violence against Women in Rural Bangladesh: Undermined or Exacerbated by Microcredit Programmes?" *Development in Practice* 8(2): 148–157

Shaw, Judith (2001) *No Magic Bullet: Microenterprise Credit and Income Poverty in Sri Lanka* Melbourne: Monash University

Srinivasan, Meera (2020a) "In Sri Lanka's rice hub, a tale of rural neglect and mounting debt" *Sri Lankan Brief* (3 August). https://srilankabrief.org/in-sri-lankas-rice-hub-a-tale-of-rural-neglect-and-mounting-debt-meera-srinivasan/

Srinivasan, Meera (2020b) "In Sri Lanka, a people living on borrowed money" *The Hindu* (22 August). https://www.thehindu.com/news/international/in-sri-lanka-a-people-living-off-borrowed-money/article32416399.ece

Stokke, Kristian (1994) "Dynamic Growth or Pauperization? Small-Scale Industries in Hambantota District, Sri Lanka" *Geografiska Annaler* 76B(3): 187–209

Thalpawila, Osantha Nayanapriya (2016) "Post-War Reconstruction in Sri Lanka: Reconstruction and Development of the Socio-Economic Sectors" *International Journal of Liberal Arts and Social Science* 4(5): 43–56

Tilakaratna, Ganga, Upali Wickramasinghe and Thusitha Kumara (2005) *Microfinance in Sri Lanka: A Household Level Analysis of Outreach and Impact on Poverty* Colombo: Institute of Policy Studies

Uddin, S.M. Sohrab and Md Akther Uddin (2021) "Microfinance and Debt Trap: An Ethnographic Evidence From a Village in Bangladesh" *International Journal of Asian Business and Information Management* 12(3): 1–11

Vithanagama, Ranmini (2018) *Exploring women's Empowerment* Colombo: International Centre for Ethnic Studies

Wada, Kenji (2018) "Microfinance : Empowering Women and/or Depoliticizing Poverty?" In *Handbook on the International Political Economy of Gender* Juanita Elias and Adrienne Roberts (eds) Cheltenham: Edward Elgar Publishing, pp 252–264

Wedagedara, Amali and Nedha de Silva (2021) "Stop blaming the victims of the microfinance crisis!" *The Sunday Times* (23 May). https://www.sundaytimes.lk/210523/business-times/stop-blaming-the-victims-of-the-microfinance-crisis-444345.html

Wickramasinghe, Vathsala and Dilshan Fernando (2017) "Use of Microcredit for Household Income and Consumption Smoothing by Low Income Communities" *International Journal of Consumer Studies* 41(6): 647–658

World Bank (2015) *Sri Lanka: Country Snapshot*. Accessed on 24/01/ 2022. Available at https://documents1.worldbank.org/curated/zh/589271468184775424/pdf/100118-WP-PUBLIC-Box393225B-SriLanka-country-snapshots.pdf

PART VI

Environment and Environmental Politics

20
FOLLOWING CURRENTS
Oceanic and Littoral Sri Lanka

Rapti Siriwardane-de Zoysa[1]

> For an island race fishing as a pursuit is inevitable, but it would be interesting to know how far back fishers became a caste. The question becomes all the more interesting because, unlike the fisherman in India, the fisherman in Ceylon is also a *farmer-man*. At one time we must have all been farmers.
>
> (J. Vijayatunga 1935, 28–29; emphasis added)

Introduction

This excerpt, drawn from Jinadasa Vijayatunge's slender volume *Grass for My Feet* (1935), is remarkable in several ways. More biographical than literary, it comprises a collection of vignettes of rural life in Ceylon's deep-south and offers one of the few dedicated chapters on coastal artisanal fishing communities in the early 1900s.[2] While the piece inherently struggles with differentiating the life-worlds of fishing and agricultural farming in rural Ceylonese life, no longer is the sea perceived as a shadowy backdrop in which coastal life unfolds. Except for a few prominent works of literature,[3] the sea and its related littoral worlds hardly remain visible in Sri Lanka unlike in Southeast Asia, awash with its own maritime folklore, micro-histories, and collective identities.

In the same vein, much of the Anglophone writings of historians, explorers, and missionaries in Ceylon's 19th and 20th centuries summarily bypassed the cultural histories of fishing and other maritime community life in favour of an oft-romanticised gaze towards rural farming life. This peculiar land-locked cultural bias was mirrored in postcolonial scholarship, with its emphasis on hinterland communal dynamics firmly embedded within contexts of sedentary agricultural farming and plantation life.

Yet, contemporary writing underlining the distinctiveness of Ceylon/Sri Lanka's littoral life from its hinterland – one that Vijayatunge draws vague de-gendered reference to – has been steadily growing over the past decade and a half. These new writings bring together multi-sited historical work on island geographies and transoceanic connectivities (see Jazeel 2009; Sivasundaram 2013; Fernando 2022), to fine-grained ethnographic forays on coastal lives, natural resource dynamics, and other socio-political transformations that have followed in the wake of both tsunami and wartime (see de Mel 2007; Ruwanpura 2008; Hyndman 2008; de Alwis 2008, 2009; de Mel, Ruwanpura and Samarasinghe 2009). Moreover, the conflation of rurality with littoral life is also questioned, with more attention being paid to the relationality of urban space(s). There is hence a rich splintering of "sea-based" thematic interests and a conjoining of disciplines, where "blue" humanities and the social sciences are rapidly evolving against scholarly currents, such as new thalassology (see Markus Vink 2019; May Joseph and Varino 2021).

The objective of this chapter is twofold. First, it aims to follow thematic currents by tracing recent Sri Lankan writing on and *of* the sea particularly in ways that question and unsettle singularly terrestrial(ised) metanarratives and micro-histories of settler communities and sedentary-ness, whether scholarly, advocacy-led, or policy-centred. Second, it addresses the more conceptual intention of what Peters and Steinberg (2019) frame as thinking through the sea by re-centring the presence of marine life, tidal fluxes, currents, monsoonal winds, and complex meshwork that shape everyday littoral life. To re-piece these writings would also mean privileging underexplored themes of mobility, migration, and flux, also in ways that render new meanings to an island's own sense of its terrestrial boundedness and fixity.

"Fishful" Currents: Littoral Identities, Livelihoods, and Life-Worlds

Historic and contemporary popular writing, literature, and Lankan Anglophone scholarship show bias. Urbanisation and rural land reform, industrial production, nationalisation and socialist reform, paddy cultivation, indentured plantation life, the sociality of taverns and arrack renting and more have been the prime focus. In comparison, coastal collectives have remained indiscernible in postcolonial political life. Moreover, scholars of the littoral have also at the same time remained "fishful" in their thinking, attempting quite the reverse: an overemphasis on coastal life in terms of small-scale fisher livelihoods (see Bartz 1957; Bavinck and van Dijk 1980; Alexander 1982; Bavinck 1984; Stirrat 1988; Tanaka 1997).

Two points are worth raising about Sri Lanka's peculiar "ocean-blindness" – in terms of its geographic area and socioeconomics. For an island with a land area of 65,510 sq. km and a coastline of approximately 1,340 km it holds sovereign rights over a space of approximately 517,000 sq. km of the sea with its Exclusive Economic Zone, together with a further claim of 1,000,000 sq. km under the 1976 United Nations Law of the Sea Convention (Amarasinghe 2009). Over 25% of the island's population live near the coastline while over 70% of the island's industrial and tourist infrastructure has historically been concentrated in its maritime and littoral areas. Furthermore, for an island of its size, small-scale fisheries remain a narrow and shrinking sector, with high-value and high-volume net imports for marine-derived consumables given the importance of seafood as a key source of animal protein in local diets.

The Littoral, Over Time

Early forays into the everyday lives of rural fisherfolk focus on the distinctiveness of their social organisation and forms of production, many of which transcend simple livelihood-based readings.[4] One of the earliest scholarly accounts dedicated to fishing worlds was Fritz Bartz's (1953) German-language monograph on the east coast of the Jaffna Peninsula among ethnically diverse beach seine collectives. In part, his focus was also on technological and socio-economic changes that the coming of beach seining (*Karaivailai*, Tamil) had brought to Ceylon at the end of the 19th century. Higher capital costs, it was argued, also invited new groups of people to show interest like traders and businessmen. The diversity of operations that Bartz identifies is noteworthy, given the mix of "millionaires with several *padu* (seine-plot) owners who were small-time operators (Bavinck 1984: 37).

Paul Alexander's (1982) ethnography *Sri Lankan Fishermen* tracing coastal life in the southeast coast of Ceylon investigated the paradox of why new fishing technology did not conversely lead to an increased scale in productive operations. His was also a critical investigation of Kahn's post-Marxian theory on petty commodity economy, using this lens as a means of explaining the factors that contributed to the growth of small-scale fishing in Sri Lanka despite technological modernisation.

During the same time Maarten Bavinck's ethnography *Small Fry* (1984) on Kadalur, Jaffna sought to examine production types, the conflicts that arose between diverse fisher collectives, and their effect on everyday social organisation in village life. Building on recent work, Bavinck (1984) argued that Ceylonese fishers were not only producing for the market long before the 1940s, but that there were no "ideal-type" subsistence fisher collectives and that unlike agricultural farming groups, fishers could not have sustained a subsistence mode of production living exclusively off their catch. His work was also foundational in putting to question older truisms on territorial rights and customary rulemaking, particularly on how far coastal waters were really open access. His was a steadfast critique on older scholarship that may have also been too purist in considering how people "work the sea", thus omitting a range of other coastal livelihoods with diverse organisational patterns (Bavinck 1984: 9).

Bavinck's early work was also an invitation to more trace diverse forms of social power and dependency that also included the procuring and maintaining of fishing gear, well beyond the gendered realms of capital financing, labour recruitment, and market relations. Stirrat's (1988) ethnography *On the Beach* more finely captures these gendered and caste-based relations of trade and market dynamics, also in conversation with everyday power relations with "petty" financers (*mudalalis*) and the seasonal trajectories of production and indebtedness. Taken together these early works were important in critiquing the notion of small-scale fishing as an enterprise that was timeless. For tracing change around fishing technology and modernity, capital and market relation also revealed how new forms of "artisanal" fishing were iteratively generated during a time of the Indian Ocean's own Blue Revolution with its rapidly mechanising waters. In contrast to these materialist approaches, Masakazu Tanaka's ethnography *Patrons, Devotees and Goddesses* (1997) offers to be taken as refreshing contribution to a historic raft of work on fisher life-worlds through an exploration on everyday relations of power, patronage, and religiosity among Tamil-Hindu collectives.

Wartime Littoral

Scholarly writing that marked the aftermath of Sri Lanka's neo-liberalisation in the 1980s and 1990s paid closer attention to fisheries governance in the context of overfishing.[5] The first was the ubiquity of legal pluralism, and the micro-conflicts thereof about interactions between communal legal systems and newly enforced state regulation since the 1940s (Sivasubramaniam 2009; Bavinck et al 2013). The second emphasis was on the role and efficacy of fisheries cooperative societies despite relatively low membership rates in the 1990s. Yet, the pervasiveness of cooperative societies charactersed a markedly different form of social organisation (from the agricultural hinterlands) and were often conceptualised as nested institutions across scales of production (Lobe and Berkes 2004). These modes of organisation were also studied against notions of social capital for cooperative societies took upon the role of community welfare and the channelling of state resources, while nevertheless being influenced by political patronage and elite capture (Amarasinghe 2009; Amarasinghe and Bavinck 2011).

Against sweeping socio-economic transformations also brought about through the years, the sea arguably remained a shadowy backdrop during the long years of civil war, a territorial space to be fought for and fought over. Charu Gupta's (2008*) Contested Coastlines* offers a harrowing account of conflict intersections over water, with particular emphasis given to everyday precarities faced by both Indian and Sri Lankan fishers who were caught in the interstitial spaces between state actors (both Indian and Sri Lankan) and the LTTE. Here the sea, and particularly the Palk Straits that embodied watery graves, and were lived as spaces of violence and islanded incarceration, a theme that was further excavated by a transcultural group of scholars working between northern Sri Lanka, southern India, and the Netherlands (see Scholtens, Bavinck and Soosai 2012). Wartime dynamics further transformed market relations as Sinhala fishers and traders took control of supply chains in the Eastern Province (Lokuge 2017). In sum, the changing currents of "fishful" thinking against wartime inflections assumed diverse directions, some which approached post-war changes through "older" conflict-centred perspectives and others through more expansive intersectional identity-based and mobility-inspired readings.

Post-war Mobility, Migration, and the Tracing of Littoral Ebbs and Flows

During the war, fishing became entangled in conflict, with much of the contested geography of Sri Lanka remained visibly littoral. Next, with cessation of fishing activity or highly regulated movements on coastal waters, mobility over coastal waters were curtailed as another "counter-insurgency" concern that pattern an illiberal peace (Goodhand and Korf 2010; Spencer 2010). Indo-Sri Lankan conflicts overfishing appeared as one of the more enduring legacies of the war, despite long-standing postcolonial diplomatic contestations over marine territories and islands. New conflicts between Indian and Lankan fisher communities consequently emerged. Built on years of regional fieldwork across the Jaffna Peninsula, the Gulf of Mannar, and southern India, Scholtens (2016) traces the reproduction of fisher marginality through moments of collective action and transboundary conflict implicating Sri Lankan small-scale fishers, economically powerful Indian trawlers, national militaries, state authorities, co-operative societies, and more.

Among the significant shifts seen in recent fisheries-based scholarship is the more attuned emphasis on questions of everyday mobility and gendered relations through more nuanced, intersectional perspectives. In part, this thematic pluralisation could be attributed to the collective efforts of more women scholars, activists, and practitioners co-writing on fisheries – a historically "masculine" field of study in Sri Lanka.

My multi-sited ethnography of fisher life-worlds in the post-war northeast explores chains of interdependence, transversal ties, and hierarchies of patronage between ethno-religiously diverse migrant fisher collectives and local communities (including indigenous *verdar* groups) (Siriwardane-de Zoysa 2015: 2018). Using grounded theorisations of the term *sambandam*, it traces how practices of inter-group co-operation are both effectively routinised and tactically instrumentalised across coastlines and at sea, whether through small-scale "piracy" or through collective rescue missions. Similar work on the nuances of conflict and cooperation brought into question the very nature of rival fisher livelihoods that have been overstressed in traditional fisheries scholarship, through readings on moral economies of reciprocity and exchange (Lokuge and Munas 2018). Using an intersectional analysis, Lokuge (2017, 2019) traces how inequalities are reproduced and structural discriminatory practices subverted among Tamil and Muslim minority women and women (with disparate success) across marketplaces and spaces of religiosity in the Trincomalee District. This work further reveals how Sinhala fishers and traders from the south have exerted local socio-economic dominance and control, having usurped Tamil and Muslim collectives during wartime and its aftermath.

Applying a similar intersectional analysis in exploring gendered identities of caste, ethnicity, and location, Lokuge and Hilhorst (2017) explores how coastal women in Trincomalee experience, reproduce, and subvert power structures in their everyday lives. Subsequent doctoral research by Koralagama, Gupta and Pouw (2017) offers applied institutional pathways through which more inclusive gender-sensitive practices zooming into material, relational, and subjective well-being – particularly alluding to the (selective) erasure of women's participation – might be meaningfully integrated into inclusive small-scale fisheries governance practices. For this recent raft of post-war research, migration and mobility is used as an expansive conceptual lens, an archive of being and belonging, and as a methodology. Using "blue justice" in political ecology (among other perspectives) as a rallying call, Koralagama and Bavinck (2022) explore grounded-theory derived understandings of seasonal mobility and territorial access rights legitimated through a variety of strategies fisher collectives have had at their disposal in the wake of wartime fishing bans (cf. Bavinck 2015).

The post-war revival of "traditional" and newer mobilities that are seasonal is further taken up by Lund et al (2020) and Vitarana et al (2020), in conjunction with Weeratunge et al (2021). The latter is a cross-country project-based monograph, *On the Move*, which explores the many dimensions of understudied seasonal coast-to-coast (internal) migration among fisher communities in the southwest, east coast, and the northwest. Drawing upon an integrative framework of well-being theories, the work detangles the aspirational futures of fisherwomen and men revealing gendered differences in perceiving what a "good life" might entail. Retaining an intersectional lens that brings to the fore a mix of social identity constructions, the collaborative work proves invaluable through the ways in which it draws upon comparisons between fisher and agricultural-based caste and livelihood groups while weaving mythological narratives and micro-histories of place, space, and belonging in collective memory.

Enlivening Currents: A More-than-Human Sea in the Aftermath of Disaster

The Indian Ocean tsunami in December 2004 left an indelible mark in the everyday imaginary of most Sri Lankans, destroying approximately 70% of the island's coastline in its wake. With the tsunami, several scholars traced the long-standing inequalities and inequities that arose from and were a result of shifting power dynamics, in part spurred by international development aid and the oversupply of material resources, such as fishing boats (de Mel 2007; Hyndman 2007; Ruwanpura 2008; de Alwis 2008; de Alwis and Hedman 2009; Hasbullah and Korf 2009; Hollenbach and Ruwanpura 2011; Ruwanpura and Hollenbach 2014). Diverse works ranged from feminist perspectives on post-disaster dynamics, the un/making of post-tsunami widowhood and the temporality of coastal life and disasters (de Mel and Ruwanpura 2006; Ruwanpura 2006, 2008; de Mel 2007; Hyndman 2008; Perera-Mubarak 2012).

Fears over further territorialisation through buffer zones, dispossession, and forced relocation of coastal communities, and the politics of uneven resource distribution and access were also covered in these writings on a profoundly altered coastal line and its everyday rhythms (Hyndman 2007; Ruwanpura 2006; de Alwis 2008; Gamburd 2013; Lehman 2013, 2014; Gunawardena and Baland 2016). Yet, it was more than the coastline that remains perennially altered, materially, symbolically, and metaphysically. For example, Lawrence's (2010) research on everyday littoral life considers changing forms of religiosity and the intersection of precarity and concerns over divine protection implicating protective "mother goddesses" among surviving caste-based fisher families.

Lehman's (2013) invitation to "follow the sea" reveal overlaps between disaster pasts, presents, and futures and can be applied and advanced in the exploration of Sri Lanka's most devastating anthropogenic marine disasters to date. Sailing along one of the world's busiest East-West trading routes, the Singapore-flagged cargo ship M/V *X-Press Pearl* carrying diverse consignments of hazardous chemicals including nitric acid, ethanol, and urea caught fire and sank in 12 days between May and June 2021, approximately 9.5 nautical miles off the west coast of Sri Lanka. Its 1,680 tons of spherical plastic pellets created "an unprecedented complex spill of visibly burnt plastic and unburnt nurdles" (de Vos et al 2021) thus polluting land, sea, and air.

The toxic mass of plastics and invisible chemicals it left in its scorched wake was labelled as a "new kind of oil spill" in a report co-produced by Sri Lanka's Center for Environmental Justice Rubesinghe et al., (2021) and the International Pollutants Elimination Network (IPEN). The catastrophe also coincided with Cyclone Tauktae, which swept over parts of the Indian Ocean at 185 km/hour, further disrupting network connectivity and limiting firefighting capacities. As activists and critics argued, Sri Lanka was not a party to the Convention of Hazardous and Noxious Substances, while its socio-environmental costs were disproportionately borne by degraded marine ecosystems and its wider public, particularly disenfranchised fishing communities (Withanage 2021).

Expanding on the idea of oceanic mobilities (currents, trade winds, vessels, etc.), excavation of the sunken X-Press Pearl would reassemble a host of marine-related political discontents and injustices: the global complexity and complicity of shipping hazardous substances and waste compounded by legal liabilities on ships, multinationals, and nation-states through contested practices, such as flags of convenience and the broader affective and moral geographies of "invasive" species, spills, plastics, waste matter, and more. Interestingly, Sri Lanka's infrastructural port entanglements and recent controversies around playing host to "ships of discard", from medical waste to contaminated soils beg to be taken as an entirely independent topic of study, particularly in relation to broader political ecologies of international shipping and marine pollution.

The last part of this chapter explores conceptual currents and debates in relation to nascent scholarship on the historic and geo-political construction of Sri Lanka's "island" geography, particularly in relation to its placement within formative writing on the Indian Ocean world(s), and through the lens of contemporary transoceanic circulations – of people, species, objects, capital, and neoliberal aspirations.

Unmooring Currents: "islanded" Imaginaries and Transoceanic Circulations

If the (littoral) fieldwork site could be taken as a "political fiction" as Bell (2009) notes, Ceylon/Sri Lanka's self-referential identity as an island nation stands on its own "foundational fictions" (Jazeel and Brun 2009: 10). These fictions remain steadfastly intertwined, melding colonial historiography, archaeological restoration, and colonial racial science amid other processes that have now narrativised Sri Lanka's diverse constructions of its own "islandness". Yet, Jazeel and Brun's (2009) quest is that of spatialising politics beyond notions of territory and territorialising, by exploring practices that co-produce island(ed) sensibilities in everyday life. Sri Lanka's ethnonationalist constructions as a "sacred island" – through islanding imagery in Buddhist mythology – remain as compelling as its geo-strategic imaginary as a connective trading "hub" along pre-colonial maritime crossroads (see Schnepel and Alpers 2017).

These decolonial theorisations are interrogated in Sivasundaram's (2013) seminal work *Islanded*. He argues that "the particularity of the Lankan story also needs to be appreciated and contextualized in relation to the Indian Ocean more broadly …", in which hinterland spaces, such as the Kandyan Kingdom, were neither land-locked nor insular, but sustained manifold trans-regional economic, religious, and other cultural connections. Thus "islanding" and "partitioning" were two related and distinctly colonial (and postcolonial) political projects that were processual, further calling into question the naturalisation of Sri Lanka's geo-political island geography. Resituating this work within broader conversations across Indian Ocean historiographies, he proposes a radical "thinking from the Indian Ocean" that unsettles dualisms between land and sea, coastal belts, and the hinterlands (Sivasundaram 2010). Later studies draw inspiration from these debates and related currents within decolonial island thinking: Radicati (2019) contemplates the complexities of "doing" Indian Ocean studies in ethnographic fieldwork by tracing itinerant urban fisher itineraries in Colombo; Godamunne, Abdeen and Siriwardana-de Zoysa (2022) written in part as a collaborative auto-ethnography, explores postcolonial metaphoric tropes of islandness as witnessed during Sri Lanka's COVID-19 pandemic biopolitics.

Yet, tellingly, much of the writing within the ambit of "Indian Ocean Studies" can be located in its historical works, which explore tensions, contradictions, and dissonances in reference to Sri Lanka's positioning as a historic "nodal point of migration" over its "emphasis on matters of nativeness" (Sivasundaram 2013: 29). Further historic writing continues to trace circulations of people, material objects and artefacts, in ways that have profoundly critiqued contemporary transcultural and transregional understandings of slavery, socio-economic dependence, and religiosity among other aspects (see Blackburn 2015; Schrikker and Wickramasinghe 2020).

One of the more exciting forays in recent marine-related historic scholarship on Sri Lanka has been the focus on underexplored more-than-species entanglements. While excavating Ceylon's lucrative historic pearl fisheries, Fernando's (2022) work implicates not only oysters that "have intersected significantly with human histories" but also takes this exploration "below the waves" extending well beyond human life entangling sharks, boring sponges, parasitic tapeworms, and host of other lively actors that bring their own "animal and ecological histories of the Indian Ocean".

While such work may ply the (historic) depths and voluminalities of the ocean, calling to light other experimental and experiential modes of contemporary underwater ethnography, another emerging body of work on infrastructural futures unsettles the rural-urban dualism that has pervaded littoral writing. Work on the emergence of new coastal infrastructures has been firmly nested within the wider political canvas of China's high-modernist developmental agenda through discourses on Indian Ocean corridorisation (see Radicati 2019; Ruwanpura, Brown and Chan 2019; Alff 2020; Woods 2022). Ruwanpura et al (2019) explore contested trajectories of planning processes with respect to "grand projects", namely the Colombo Port City and the post-war developmental visions and the neoliberal aspirational "wet" dreams of a political class (see also Ruwanpura, Rowe and Chan 2020; Woods 2022). Paradoxically, the socio-materialities of water are conceived in terms of their proclivity to both socially connect and divide. No longer does the remaking of new waterfront spaces offer to be read in terms of a novel kind of forgetting through the layering over the old and the derelict (Siriwardane-de Zoysa and Amoo-Adare 2021). In Colombo, emerging spaces like the promised and highly embattled Port City sit adjoining the old city, stitched together by markedly colonial and ageing landmarks like the Galle Face Green and the Old Parliament House, an adjacent placement (that) recreates new dualisms of place, space, and the urban littoral.

Quo Vadis: Sojourning Farther out to Sea

This chapter began with life-worlds around fishing. Yet, these coasts make more than the sum of a so-called "island's" lively edges and margins, as their trajectories of disaster both reveal and foretell. Yet, to think with the sea, particularly by "following" its conceptual and thematic currents, not only connects various temporalities of the Indian Ocean world; it also ruptures long-standing divisions between urban and rural scholarship, the socio-material coast, and its hinterlands.

Today, the docklands of the colonial port have shrunk in both size and importance. They are no longer associated with mere labour and toil but also with recreation and conspicuous consumption.

Considering infrastructural megaprojects, such as the Port City, what amounts to is the islanding of "high-net-worth-individuals" via the creation of tax havens and its own legal systems, that are materially separated from an ageing urban mainland by water (Ruwanpura et al 2019; Woods 2022). Indeed, political endeavours, such as the Port City, stand as symbols heralding newer visions of metropolitan living, in terms of entirely offshoring urban life. As Kadirgamar, Bin Rashid and Shah (2021) ponder, what new hopes arise for the reorganisation of labour movements and just livelihoods, particularly against an extractive, globally emerging blue economy? The political ecologies of both rural and littoral land use and reclamation, international shipping, extractive mineral mining, multispecies entanglements, the expansion of connective infrastructure, and coastal privatisation (and dispossession) for real estate development all offer to be taken as rich themes for exploration against Sri Lanka's contested futures, amid deepening socio-economic crises and political discontent.

Acknowledgements

Thank you to Nireka Weeratunge, Joeri Scholtens, Dilanthi Koralagama, Hafsa Jameel, Asha de Vos, Vitchitra Godamunne, and the volume editors for their critical feedback on previous drafts.

Notes

1 Rapti Siriwardane-de Zoysa is an environmental anthropologist at the University of Bonn. Her works include *Fishing, Mobility and Settlerhood: Coastal Socialities in Postwar Sri Lanka* (2018), and co-edited volumes *Coastal Urbanities: Mobilities, Meanings, Manoeuvrings* (2022), and *An Anthology of Non-conformism* (2024).
2 Vijayatunge's statement could be read as mistakenly conflating marine fishers into the dominant category of hinterland farmers. He may have been unaware that the origin of diverse Ceylonese fisher castes could be traced to southern India. However, he could also be referring to that morphing borderland between sea and land, and of lagoon spaces inhabited by fisher-farmers, whose livelihoods are based on a dual system of seasonal "harvest" of water and land-based resources. My thanks to Nireka Weeratunge for pointing out nuances in this interpretation.
3 Notable examples include writing such as Martin Wickramasinge's Sinhala-language novel *Karuwala Gedera* (1963).
4 Few trans-local Sri Lankan scholars studied fisher life-worlds for themselves. For example, Michael Roberts' emphasis nevertheless lay in caste-based and elite identity formations against a broader political canvas of postcolonial nationalism alongside some of the earliest wartime writing on the Eastern Province (see Haniffa and Raheem 2005; Ruwanpura 2006).
5 One of the earliest legislation pertained to the Fisheries Ordinance Chapter 212 of 1940 and the Chank Fishery Act of 1953, followed by further legislation that governed the exploitation of spiny lobster and prawn in the 1970s. Further prohibitions came into play on the use of dynamite, poisons, and other stupefying substances for fishing under the Fisheries Amendments Law 20 of 1973, followed by later bans on imports of spear-fishing guns and provisions for marine reserves and fish sanctuaries (Lobe and Berkes 2004; Perera and de Vos 2007).

References

Alexander, Paul (1982) *Sri Lankan Fishermen: Rural Capitalism and Peasant Society* New Delhi: Sterling Publishers

Alff, Henryk (2020) "Negotiating Coastal Infrastructures: An Evolutionary Governance Theory (EGT) Approach to Chinese High-Modernist Development along the Indian Ocean" *Marine Policy* 112(2020): 103545

Amarasinghe, Oscar (2009) "Modernisation and Change: Fishers' Wellbeing and Ecosystem Health in Sri Lanka" Paper submitted for the ESPA Workshop 2, 18–22 July, University of Ruhuna, Sri Lanka

Amarasinghe, Oscar and Maarten Bavinck (2011) "Building Resilience: Fisheries Cooperatives in Southern Sri Lanka" In *Poverty Mosaics: Realities and Prospects in Small-Scale Fisheries* Svein Jentoft and Arne Eide (eds) Dordrecht: Springer, pp 383–406

Bartz, Fritz (1957) *Fischer auf Ceylon: ein Beitrag zur Wirtschafts-und Bevölkerungsgeographie des indischen Subkontinents*. No. 27. Bonn: In Kommission bei F. Dümmlers

Bavinck, Maarten (1984) *Small Fry: The Economy of Petty Fishermen in Northern Sri Lanka*, Antropologische Studies V.U. (Netherlands), No. 5 Amsterdam: VU UitgeverijVU Uitgeverij

Bavinck, Maarten (2015) "Fishing Rights in Post-War Sri Lanka: Results of a Longitudinal Village Enquiry in the Jaffna Region" *Maritime Studies* 14(1): 1–15

Bavinck, Maarten, Derek Johnson, Oscar Amarasinghe, Janet Rubinoff, Sarah Southwold and Kaleekal T. Thomson (2013) "From Indifference to Mutual Support – A Comparative Analysis of Legal Pluralism in the Governing of South Asian Fisheries" *The European Journal of Development Research* 25(4): 621–640

Bavinck, Maarten and F. van Dijk (1980) "The Transformation of a Fishing Economy: The Case of Kadalur, Sri Lanka" *The Transformation of a Fishing Economy: The Case of Kadalur, Sri Lanka* Amsterdam: Vrije Universiteit

Bell, Sharon (2009) "The Distance of a Shout" In *Spatialising Politics: Culture and Geography in Postcolonial Sri Lanka* Cathrine Brun and Tariq Jazeel (eds) New Delhi: Sage, pp 72–100

Blackburn, Anne M. (2015) "Buddhist Connections in the Indian Ocean: Changes in Monastic Mobility, 1000–1500" *Journal of the Economic and Social History of the Orient* 58(3): 237–266

de Alwis, M. (2008) *Double Wounding? Aid and Activism in Post-Tsunami Sri Lanka*. IDRC. Accessed on 12/11/2022. Available at http://hdl.handle.net/10625/42509

de Alwis, Malathi (2009) "'Disappearance' and 'Displacement' in Sri Lanka" *Journal of Refugee Studies* 22(3): 378–391

de Alwis, Malathi and Eva-Lotta Hedman (2009) *Tsunami in a Time of War: Aid Activism and Reconstruction in Sri Lanka and Aceh* Colombo: International Centre for Ethnic Studies

de Mel, Neloufer (2007) "Between the War and the Sea: Critical Events, Contiguities and Feminist Work in Sri Lanka" *Interventions* 9(2): 238–254

de Mel, Neloufer and Kanchana N. Ruwanpura (2006) *Gendering the Tsunami: Women's Experiences from Sri Lanka* Colombo: International Centre for Ethnic Studies

de Mel, Neloufer, Kanchana N. Ruwanpura and Gameela Samarasinghe (2009) *After the Waves: The Impact of the Tsunami on Women in Sri Lanka* Colombo: Social Scientist Association

de Vos, Asha, Lihini Aluwihare, Sarah Youngs, Michelle H. DiBenedetto, Collin P. Ward, Anna P.M. Michel, Beckett C. Colson et al. (2021) "The M/V X-Press Pearl Nurdle Spill: Contamination of Burnt Plastic and Unburnt Nurdles along Sri Lanka's Beaches" *ACS Environmental Au* DOI https://doi.org/10.1021/acsenvironau.1c00031

Fernando, Tamara (2022) "Seeing Like the Sea: A Multispecies History of the Ceylon Pearl Fishery 1800–1925" *Past and Present* 254(1): 127–160

Gamburd, Michele Ruth (2013) *The Golden Wave: Culture and Politics after Sri Lanka's Tsunami Disaster* Bloomington: Indiana University Press

Godamunne, Vichitra, Azhar Jainul Abdeen and Rapti Siriwardane-de Zoysa (2022) "Shored Curfews: Constructions of Pandemic Islandness in Contemporary Sri Lanka" *Maritime Studies* 21(2022): 209–221

Goodhand, Jonathan and Benedikt Korf (2010) "Caught in the Peace Trap?: On the Illiberal Consequences of Liberal Peace in Sri Lanka" In *Conflict and Peacebuilding in Sri Lanka* J. Goodhand, B. Korf and J. Spencer (eds) London/New York: Routledge, pp 17–31

Gunawardena, Asha and Jean-Marie Baland (2016) "Targeting Disaster Aid in Post-Tsunami Sri Lanka" *Development Policy Review* 34(2): 179–195

Gupta, Charu (2008) *Contested Coastlines: Fisherfolk, Nations and Borders in South Asia* New Delhi: Routledge.

Haniffa, Farzana and Mirak Raheem (2005) *Post-Tsunami Reconstruction and the Eastern Muslim Question* Colombo: Centre for Policy Alternatives.

Hasbullah, Shahul and Benedikt Korf (2009) "Muslim Geographies and the Politics of Purification in Sri Lanka after the 2004 Tsunami" *Singapore Journal of Tropical Geography* 30(2): 248–264

Hollenbach, Pia and Kanchana N. Ruwanpura (2011) "Symbolic Gestures: The Development Terrain of Post-Tsunami Villages in (southern) Sri Lanka" *Journal of Development Studies* 47(9): 1299–1314

Hyndman, Jennifer (2007) "The Securitization of Fear in Post-Tsunami Sri Lanka" *Annals of the Association of American Geographers* 97(2): 361–372

Hyndman, Jennifer (2008) "Feminism, Conflict and Disasters in Post-Tsunami Sri Lanka" *Gender, Technology and Development* 12(1): 101–121

Jazeel, Tariq (2009) "Reading the Geography of Sri Lankan Island-ness: Colonial Repetitions, Postcolonial Possibilities" *Contemporary South Asia* 17(4): 399–414

Jazeel, Tariq and Cathrin Brun (2009) "Introduction: Spatial Politics and Postcolonial Sri Lanka" In *Spatialising Politics: Culture and Geography in Postcolonial Sri Lanka* Cathrin Brun and Tariq Jazeel (eds) New Delhi: Sage, pp 1–24.

Joseph, May and Sofia Varino (2021) "Multidirectional Thalassology" *Shima* 15 (1). Accessed on 21/03/2022. Available at chrome extension://efaidnbmnnnibpcajpcglclefindmkaj/https://shimajournal.org/issues/v15n1/15.-Joseph-and-Varino-Shima-v15n1.pdf

Kadirgamar, Ahilan, Hashim Bin Rashid and Amod Shah (2021) "Contesting Agricultural Markets in South Asia: Farmer Movements, Co-operatives and Alternative Visions" *Millennial Asia* 12(3): 277–297

Koralagama, Dilanthi and Maarten Bavinck (2022) "Blue Justice and Small-Scale Fisher Migration: A Case Study from Sri Lanka" In *Blue Justice* Cham: Springer, pp 119–137

Koralagama, Dilanthi, Joyeeta Gupta and Nicky Pouw (2017) "Inclusive Development from a Gender Perspective in Small Scale Fisheries" *Current Opinion in Environmental Sustainability* 24: 1–6

Lawrence, Patricia (2010) "The Sea Goddess and the Fishermen: Religion and Recovery in Navalady, Sri Lanka" In *Tsunami Recovery in Sri Lanka: Ethnic and Regional Dimensions* Dennis McGilvray and Michelle R. Gamburd (eds) Oxford and New York: Routledge

Lehman, Jessica (2014) "Expecting the Sea: The Nature of Uncertainty on Sri Lanka's East Coast" *Geoforum* 52: 245–256

Lehman, Jessica S. (2013) "Relating to the Sea: Enlivening the Ocean as an Actor in Eastern Sri Lanka" *Environment and Planning D: Society and Space* 31(3): 485–501

Lobe, K. and F. Berkes (2004) "The *Padu* System of Community-Based Fisheries Management: Change and Local Institutional Innovation in South India" *Marine Policy* 28: 271–281

Lokuge, Gayathri H.H. (2017) '*Even Fish Have an Ethnicity': Livelihoods and Identities of Men and Women in War-Affected Coastal Trincomalee, Sri Lanka*. PhD dissertation, Wageningen University and Research. Accessed 03/02/2022.

Lokuge, Gayathri and Dorothea Hilhorst (2017) "Outside the Net: Intersectionality and Inequality in the Fisheries of Trincomalee, Sri Lanka" *Asian Journal of Women's Studies* 23(4): 473–497

Lokuge, Gayathri and Mohamed Munas (2018) "Risk, Reciprocity and Solidarity: The Moral Economy of Fishing in Trincomalee, Sri Lanka" In *Social Wellbeing and the Values of Small-Scale Fisheries* Derek S. Johnson, Tim G. Acott, Natasha Stacey and Julie Urquhart (eds) Cham: Springer, pp 243–265

Lund, Ragnhild, Kyoko Kusakabe, Nitya Rao and Nireka Weeratunge (eds) (2020) *Fisherfolk in Cambodia, India and Sri Lanka: Migration, Gender and Well-Being* London: Taylor & Francis

Perera, Nishan and Asha de Vos (2007) "Marine Protected Areas in Sri Lanka: A Review" *Environmental Management* 40(5): 727–738

Perera-Mubarak, Kamakshi (2012) "Positive Responses, Uneven Experiences: Intersections of Gender, Ethnicity, and Location in Post-Tsunami Sri Lanka" *Gender, Place and Culture* 20(5): 664–685

Peters, Kimberley and Philip Steinberg (2019) "The Ocean in Excess: Towards a More-than-Wet Ontology" *Dialogues in Human Geography* 9(3): 293–307

Rubesinghe, C., Brosché, S., Withanage, H., Pathragoda, D., Karlsson, T. (2021) *X-Press Pearl, a 'new kind of oil spill' consisting of a toxic mix of plastics and invisible chemicals*. International Pollutants Elimination Network (IPEN)

Radicati, Alessandra (2019) "Island Journeys: Fisher Itineraries and National Imaginaries in Colombo" *Contemporary South Asia* 27(3): 330–341

Ruwanpura, Kanchana N. (2006) *Matrilineal Communities, Patriarchal Realities: A Feminist Nirvana Uncovered* Ann Arbor: University of Michigan Press

Ruwanpura, Kanchana N. (2008) "Temporality of Disasters: The Politics of Women's Livelihoods 'after' the 2004 Tsunami in Sri Lanka" *Singapore Journal of Tropical Geography* 29(3): 325–340

Ruwanpura, Kanchana N., Benjamin Brown and Loritta Chan (2019) "(Dis)connecting Colombo: Situating the Megapolis in Post-War Sri Lanka" *The Professional Geographer* 72(1): 165–179

Ruwanpura, Kanchana N. and Pia Hollenbach (2014) "From Compassion to the Will to Improve: Elision of Scripts? Philanthropy in Post-Tsunami Sri Lanka" *Geoforum* 51: 243–251

Ruwanpura, Kanchana N., Peter Rowe and Loritta Chan (2020) "Of Bombs and Belts: Exploring Potential within China's Belt and Road Initiative in Sri Lanka" *The Geographical Journal* 186(3): 339–345

Schnepel, Burkhard and Edward A. Alpers (eds) (2017) *Connectivity in Motion: Island Hubs in the Indian Ocean World* Cham: Springer
Scholtens, Joeri (2016) *Fishing in the Margins North Sri Lankan fishers' struggle for access in transboundary waters*. Doctoral Dissertation. University of Amsterdam, Amsterdam. Accessed 04/05/2022. Available at https://pure.uva.nl/ws/files/2797445/177016_Scholtens_Fishing_in_the_margins_Thesis_complete.pdf
Scholtens, Joeri, Maarten Bavinck and A.S. Soosai (2012) "Fishing in Dire Straits: Trans-Boundary Incursions in the Palk Bay" *Economic and Political Weekly*: 87–95
Schrikker, Alicia and Nira Wickramasinghe (2020) *Being a Slave: Histories and Legacies of European Slavery in the Indian Ocean* Leiden: Leiden University Press
Siriwardane-de Zoysa, Rapti (2015) *Sambandam': Conflict, Cooperation and Coastal Lifeworlds in Postwar Sri Lanka*. Doctoral dissertation, University of Bonn, Bonn
Siriwardane-de Zoysa, Rapti (2018) *Fishing, Mobility and Settlerhood: Coastal Socialities in Postwar Sri Lanka* Cham: Springer
Siriwardane-de Zoysa, Rapti and Epifania Amoo-Adare (2021) "The Bi-Polar Waterfront: Paradoxes of Shoreline Placemaking in Contemporary Accra and Colombo" In *Global [Im]-Possibilities: Exploring the Paradoxes of Just Sustainabilities* P. Godfrey and M. Buchanan (eds) London: Bloomsbury, pp 69–87
Sivasubramaniam, K. (2009) *Fisheries in Sri Lanka: Anthropological and Biological Aspects* Colombo: Kumaran Book House
Sivasundaram, Sujit (2010) "Sciences and the Global: on Methods, Questions, and Theory" *Isis* 101(1): 146–158
Sivasundaram, Sujit (2013) *Islanded: Britain, Sri Lanka, and the Bounds of an Indian Ocean Colony* Chicago: University of Chicago Press
Spencer, Jonathan (2010) "Reflections on an Illiberal Peace: Stories from the East" In *Conflict and Peacebuilding in Sri Lanka* Jonathan Goodhand, Benedikt Korf and Jonathan Spencer (eds) London and New York: Routledge, pp 217–228
Stirrat, Roderick L. (1988) *On the Beach: Fishermen, Fishwives and Fish Traders in Post-Colonial Sri Lanka* New Delhi: Hindustan Press
Tanaka, Masakazu (1997) *Patrons, Devotees, and Goddesses: Ritual, and Power Among the Tamil Fishermen of Sri Lanka* New Delhi: Manohar Publishers and Distributors
Vijayatunga, Jinadasa (1935) *Grass for My Feet*: Sketches of Life in a Ceylon Village London: Edward Arnold & Co.
Vink, Markus (2019) "From the Cape to Canton: The Dutch Indian Ocean World, 1600–1800 – A Littoral Census" *The Journal of Indian Ocean World Studies* 3(1): 13–37
Vitarana, Nirmi, Dilanthi Koralagama, Nireka Weeratunge and Ramani Gunatilaka (2020) "Mobilizing for and against Migration: Gendered Networks, Cooperation, and Collective Action in Fishing Communities on the West and East Coasts of Sri Lanka" In *Fisherfolk in Cambodia, India and Sri Lanka* Ragnhild Lund, Kyoko Kusakabe, Nitya Rao and Nireka Weeratunge (eds) New Delhi: Routledge, pp 164–180
Weeratunge, Nireka, Ramani Gunatilaka, Nadine Vanniasinkam, Mohamed Faslan, Dilanthi Koralagama and Nirmi Vitarana (2021) *On the Move: Gender, Migration and Wellbeing in Four Fishing Communities in Sri Lanka* Colombo: International Centre for Ethnic Studies
Wickramasinghe, Martin (1963) *Karuwala Gedara* Colombo: Sarasa Publishers
Withanage, Hemantha (2021) The X-Press Pearl Fire – A Disaster of Unimaginable Proportions. In *Groundviews*. Accessed 03/02/2022. Available at https://groundviews.org/2021/06/03/the-x-press-pearl-fire-a-disaster-of-unimaginable-proportions/.
Woods, Orlando (2022) "A Harbour in the Country, a City in the Sea: Infrastructural Conduits, Territorial Inversions and the Slippages of Sovereignty in Sino-Sri Lankan Development Narratives" *Political Geography* 92: 102521

21
A POLITICAL ECOLOGY OF SRI LANKA'S URBAN AND REGIONAL WETLANDS

Missaka Hettiarachchi

Introduction

In the contemporary times, Sri Lanka's wetlands have undergone vast destruction and degradation, driven by urban sprawl, infrastructure projects, and loss of traditional uses. Politically, this period was characterised by free market economic policies, privatisation, a service and export-oriented economy, civil war (1983–2009), and ubiquitous corruption. It corresponds to the time globally referred to as the "neo-liberal" period by many scholars (Marcuse and Van Kempen 2000; Dasgupta 2007), which was mainly demarcated by the overturning of post-world-war welfare economic policies.

Ecologically, wetlands are defined as transitional ecosystems (ecotones) between terrestrial and aquatic ecosystems (Mitsch and Gosselink 2007). They include a large variety of habitat types, such as freshwater marshes, estuaries, mangroves, swamp forests, salt marshes, inland lakes, and even human-managed systems, such as paddy fields. Vegetation, faunal, hydrological, and soil characteristics of wetlands can change in short periods compared to other ecosystems, making their ecologies highly transient human communities have historically thrived in wetland environments. However, since the emergence of capitalism, wetlands have been seen as dismal landscapes due to their transient unpredictable nature (Purseglove 1988). They are hard to traverse, difficult to cultivate, and often impossible to build on humans have altered and drained wetlands for specific purposes from ancient times. Under capitalism however, grand schemes were launched to tame large swaths of wetlands and convert them to "productive" forms of land use. This perception of wetlands as dispensable barriers to human progress was engraved into development thinking, policy, institutions, education, and the public psyche for nearly two centuries.

In Sri Lanka, this narrative still largely dominates development policies, which decide the fate of wetlands. In colonial times, the wetlands were viewed mainly as wastelands. An excerpt from an early last century report on flood protection of *Colombo* exemplified this view:

> It is, therefore, amazing to find that there should have been allowed to exist up to three square miles of swamp so close into the city, that at various points the swamp approaches to within a mile of the Town Hall.
>
> *(Kitching 1937: 2)*

Despite Sri Lanka gaining independence in 1948, the negative perception of wetlands was passed on to post-colonial development thinking and policy-making. The colonial aspiration of putting the wetlands into "better use" actually came into practice in the 1960s. A 1966 report by the irrigation department on "Reclamation of swamps around the city of Colombo" says:

> there are large extents of marshy land ... abandoned except for a small extent where grass and vegetables are grown ... can be put into beneficial uses.
>
> *(DRD 1966: 39)*

Given the small size of the country (65,610 sq km), Sri Lanka has a significant extent of wetlands, with more than 4,500-km rivers and streams, 20,000 ha of marshes and floodplain lakes, and paddy land covering 12% of the total land area (Van Zon 2004). During the colonial (up to 1948) and post-colonial (1948–1980) periods, urban and peri-urban areas along the Western coast saw large-scale wetland modification. Diking, canalising and change of land management practices have irreversibly changed wetland hydrology and ecologies. Traditional wetland uses for paddy cultivation, fishing, and transportation have almost disappeared with time. Rural wetlands were spared large-scale destruction in the colonial and post-colonial periods. However, the fate of Sri Lankan wetlands dramatically changed after 1980.

The neo-liberal period in Sri Lanka also saw some important milestones in environmental governance. The principal milestone among them was the National Environment Act (NEA) of 1980, which provided an integrated framework for environmental management nationally. Wetlands gained formal recognition in environmental governance after Sri Lanka entered the Ramsar Convention in 1990 (Convention on Wetlands of International Importance). Currently, six Sri Lankan wetland sites are designated under the Convention. However, the efficacy of such normative advancements in environmental governance has been critiqued both in Sri Lanka and globally (Swyngedouw and Heynen 2003; Hettiarachchi, Morrison and McAlpine 2017). They have been clearly inadequate to prevent or even mitigate the unrelenting assaults on nature during the neo-liberal period. Neither have they been able to resolve the grave environmental injustice created by these issues.

Based on contemporary scholarly and grey literature, this chapter characterises the scale and nature of ecological impacts on wetlands in Sri Lanka, after 1980 and their social and economic outcomes. I then analyse the policy and institutional trajectories, which produced these outcomes, and the socio-political resistance they have triggered. The chapter mainly uses a political ecology lens (Robbins 2012), specifically drawing from scholarship on environmental justice, land-grabbing, policy dismantling, and social movements (Pulido 2000; Bebbington 2004; Bauer et al 2012; White et al 2012).

Sri Lanka's Wetlands: Diverse Ecologies and Perceptions

A large array of ecosystems or "wetlands types" come under the Ramsar Convention's definition of wetlands.[1] Sri Lanka's 103 watersheds support many of these wetland types. Wetland types are characteristic of eco-climatic conditions of different regions. They provide different ecosystem services, and are perceived and utilised by the communities accordingly.

The highest prevalence of wetlands in the country is in the wet-zone coastal belt (south-western coast), where the most common wetland type are freshwater floodplain marshes. Characterised by low emergent vegetation (such as grasses) and bog soils, freshwater marshes of the wet zone have supported the livelihoods of coastal communities for many centuries.

Some historical sources, such as the 14th-century poetry tradition called *Sandesha Kavya*, recorded how these magnificent ecosystems were intertwined with social life in pre-capitalist times. They presented vivid poetic renditions of daily life in the marshes – cultivation, fishing, grazing, and recreation. In contrast to capitalist notions of an "intractable landscape," for pre-capitalist coastal communities, the marsh waterways were the principal mode of transport.

Estuarine wetlands, lagoons, and mangroves are the second most common wetland types in the island, found in the lower reaches of all major wet and dry zone watersheds. Being brackish water systems, with salt tolerant plants, and various fish and crustacean species, these wetlands play a major role in estuarine and near shore fishing even today. Both freshwater marshes and estuarine wetlands sustain a vast bio-diversity. Charismatic species, such as saltwater crocodiles, fishing cat, otter, and a plethora of water birds, are often featured by environmentalists to demonstrate the ecological value of these ecosystems.

The interior wetlands of Sri Lanka are dominated by human-managed ecosystems, such as paddy lands and irrigation tanks. Natural lakes, villus (wet grasslands), and swamp forests also form a smaller but important fraction of interior wetlands. These ecosystems have also been extensively used traditionally for farming, fishing, timber harvesting, and for collecting forest products.

The modern scientific study of all wetland types dates from the 19th century. Early natural history works by British bureaucrats and explorers, such as Tennent's Ceylon (1860), have described animal and plant life in the estuarine wetlands and marshes. Later works included more in-depth studies of wetland species, especially water birds and migratory birds. Organisations of nature lovers and naturalists which emerged from the late 19th century, such as the Ceylon Game and Fauna Protection Society (established 1894, later renamed Wildlife and Nature Protection Society – WNPS), also played a role in early wetland studies.

However, these earlier studies were largely confined to individual species or specific sites. Some specifically focused on the hunting and fishing potential in wetlands (e.g. Harry Storey's [1906] book *Hunting and Shooting in Ceylon*, dedicated chapters for water birds hunting and shooting in inland tanks). They did not capture the important role of wetlands as transient ecosystems in landscapes and watersheds. The first integrated wetlands studies in Sri Lanka came after the country's entry into the Ramsar Convention.

A series of systematic wetland status studies were conducted on major wetland systems under the "Wetlands Conservation Project" launched in 1990 by the Central Environmental Authority, where a series of wetlands status reports and management conservation plans were prepared. The studies were based on Ramsar principles and looked into broader ecologies of the wetlands, ecosystem services, social and economic pressures, and patterns of degradation. For the first time, they revealed the alarming state of wetlands, especially the marsh ecosystems on the Western Coast (CEA 1994, 1995).

From the late 2000s, the focus of wetland studies shifted, from environmental status reporting to in-depth analysis of impacts, including reduction of wetland extent, ecological transformation, and fate and transport of pollutants (Priyadarshani et al 2015; Kaleel 2017; Amarasinghe 2019). Studies on socio-economic drivers and consequences of wetland degradation also expanded during this period (Hettiarachchi et al 2017; Nijamir 2017), giving better insights into the differential impacts on different social groups, such as women, the poor, and ethnoreligious minorities. A wetland directory for Sri Lanka was published in 2006 jointly by CEA, the International Conservation Union (IUCN), and the International Institute of Water Management (IWMI).

In the past decade, scientific inquiries on both urban and rural wetlands have substantially broadened and diversified. Wetland scientists have ventured into new areas, such as climate change impacts and wetland ecosystem services driven by global trends (McInnes and Everard 2017;

Katupotha 2018). In addition, the advancement of Geographic Information Systems (GIS)-based studies has enabled a better spatial understanding of the scale of wetland degradation (Gunawardena et al 2015). Studies conducted for the Colombo Wetland Strategy also marked a milestone in these new developments (GoSL 2016).

Perception of wetlands by different stakeholders is as transient as wetland ecologies. The communities traditionally perceived and valued wetlands through their uses and ecosystem services. The scientific understanding of the country's wetlands, which was initially confined to natural history and species conservation perspectives, has broadened after the 1990s to include different aspects of social-ecological interactions. These community and expert perceptions of wetlands did influence wetland governance to some extent. However, broader political and economic dynamics have been more decisive in determining the fate of Sri Lankan wetlands in recent times.

The Changing Tide of Wetlands Governance

The first political interest in Sri Lanka's wetlands was seen in the early 1900s with regard to urban expansion and flood control in Colombo. The Colombo Flood Protection Scheme (DI 1947) modified the hydrology of more than 10,000 ha of wetlands around Colombo in an irreversible way with bunds, deep canals, lock gates, and pump houses. Traditional uses of these wetlands disappeared, and large swaths of marshland were declared flood detention areas.

The vision of filling up and converting the marshes around Colombo into built-up areas was realised in the mid-1960s, initially for building low-income housing schemes (DRD 1966). Colombo District (Low Lying Areas) Reclamation & Development Board (presently Sri Lanka Land Development Corporation – SLLDC) was established in 1968 specifically for this purpose. Informal settlements within the marsh areas, both in and around the city (e.g. Wanathamulla, Meethotamulla, Orugodawatta) were allowed to be reclaimed, and some lands were distributed for housing blue-collar workers of the Municipalities, Railways, and other state-managed industries.

Until the late 1970s, wetland reclamation was predominantly driven by welfare policies, such as providing public housing or common facilities. However, from 1980 onwards, modification and reclamation of wetlands took a distinctly different character. Public welfare schemes faded away and wetlands were seen as a potential space for the expansion of infrastructure and urban real estate (Hettiarachchi et al 2017). The Colombo Master Plan Project of 1978 called for a restructuring of urban space to suit the new free market era. The eradication of slums and the expansion of the city into the eastern suburbs were two major elements of the plan. Impacts of the Development Sector on wetlands from 1980 onwards were largely determined by three policy trends: large-scale wetland acquisition and modification, privatisation of wetlands, and displacement of wetland communities. The impacts of these policies are hard to exactly quantify, however, certain examples provide perspective to their scale.

The first large-scale wetland conversion in Sri Lanka was the construction of the new Parliament House and other government premises in the newly declared capital city of Sri Jayewardenepura. More than 750 ha of marsh and paddy land were dredged or filled. Canal widening, and bank stabilisation work under numerous flood control and drainage improvement projects, from 1990 to the present, further altered the hydrology of wetlands around Colombo. Industrial zones (Free Trade Zones) established along the Western coast were also carved into marsh or paddy lands, and large tourist resorts emerged along estuarine wetlands.

By the mid-1990s, corporate real estate interests entered the wetlands around Colombo. The introduction of new construction technologies, such as bored-piling made construction in the weak wetlands soils much easier. Multi-storey residential and commercial buildings were constructed in or around the marshes, taking advantage of the waterfront views. In 1997, 150 ha of marsh and paddy land in the Kotte area, previously acquired for flood retention purposes, was handed over to a private company for a multi-purpose recreational and property development project. Once worthless, marshlands were becoming a hot commodity in Colombo's real estate market (Hettiarachchi et al 2017).

With this, a trend to "beautify the wetlands" also commenced, where marshes were converted into manicured urban parks with lakes and walking tracks. The beautification trend was later extended to lakes and wetlands outside Colombo. These facilities indeed provided much-needed recreational services welcomed by the urban upper-middle class. However, they were contested by environmental groups as changing the character of wetlands and in some cases tampering with heritage values (Dissanayake 2021).

Beyond 2000, the rural wetlands also could not escape the juggernaut of "development." The main threat for rural wetlands was infrastructure, rather than real estate projects. New expressways were urgently demanded by the tourism and export sectors. However, the main hurdle was acquiring the large extent of land required. Thus the routes were planned through paths of least social resistance, and lowest land value – marshes and paddy lands. The first major Expressway completed in 2014 between Colombo and Galle has nearly half of its course through wetlands (including paddy lands).

In 2009 the 30-year civil war ended in victory for the Sri Lankan government. Mired in an acute economic crisis, the government launched an aggressive campaign to boost investments and growth (Perera 2014). The 2010–2020 marked unprecedented growth in the infrastructure and real estate sectors. More than 250 km of expressways were added to the road network and condominium building floor space grew by 36% annually. In addition to direct conversion, this new phase of construction growth had an additional impact on wetlands in terms of building material extraction, such as sand and clay mining in rivers and flood plains.

Certain institutional and regulatory adjustments were required to realise these policies for the acquisition and privatisation of wetlands. Wetland acquisition was done under the existing Land Acquisition Act (1950) and was often transferred to the Urban Development Authority (UDA) and SLLDC. Both UDA and SLLDC Acts were amended multiple times after the 1980s to strengthen the authority of these agencies. Between 2010 and 2015, the portfolio of Urban Development was taken under the Defence Ministry, and land acquisitions and eviction of communities came under military oversight. This was a manifestation of a broader militarisation of social life during this period (Amarasuriya and Spencer 2015).

The limited protection provided against converting paddy lands for other land uses by the Agrarian Services Act was toothless against powerful development sector agencies. In 2015 a new Ministry (Megapolis and Western Development) was established to coordinate and regulate a faster urban expansion in the Western Province. The Megapolis Western Region Master Plan (2016) envisioned an array of new urban centres and infrastructure projects, with a narrow focus on positioning Colombo as a financial trading hub for South Asia (Ruwanpura, Brown and Chan 2020), which will further deepen the impacts on Western coast wetlands in the years to come.

However, the post-1980 period also marked significant developments in environmental management policy. Before 1980 wetlands had no exclusive protection, and only the wetlands declared as Protected Areas under the Fauna and Flora Protection Ordinance (1937) had any conservation status. However, some post-1980 environmental policies and institutions, such as the NEA of 1980 directly addressed wetland-related issues. NEA introduced numerous provisions for pollution prevention and protection of sensitive ecosystems including wetlands. For example, the Environmental Impact Assessment (EIA) provisions required any development activity involving "reclamation of land, wetland area exceeding four hectares" be approved through an EIA process. NEA also vested the Central Environmental Authority with powers to declare sensitive ecosystems as Environmental Protection Areas (EPAs). CEA did declare numerous wetlands along the Western coast as EPAs, using this provision. The Department of Coast Conservation and Coastal Resource Management was established in 1981 with a special mandate to protect the coastal systems, including estuarine wetlands.

In 2005, a National Wetland Policy (MoE and CEA 2006) was formulated by the CEA. The SLLDC established its own Wetlands Management Unit (WMU) in 2015. Both CEA and WMU commenced wetlands awareness programmes at school, community, and corporate levels. February 4 wetland day celebrations have now become a routine state affair. WMU also secured two urban wetland conservation parks with a wetland education centre, where certain characteristics of the marsh such as native species were restored. In 2016 the Ministry of Urban Development along with SLLDC prepared an exclusive Strategy for Management of Colombo Wetlands (GoSL 2016), with World Bank Funding. In recognition of these positive developments, Colombo was accredited as a "Wetland City" by the Convention on Wetlands in 2019.

Governance of wetlands beyond 1980 clearly had two trajectories. On the one hand, the Development Sector was well and truly at war with wetlands. The colonial vision of taming and sanitising the wetlands took on a new and far more virulent form during this period. On the other, there was a formal expansion of environmental policy, laws, and institutions, which also had specific implications for wetland management. The real outcomes of these two governance trajectories can only be assessed by the impacts they produced on the ground for wetland ecosystems and communities.

Disturbed Ecosystems: Degradation and Ecological Transformation

The policy turn after 1980 to subserviate the wetlands to development projects and market forces brought unprecedented ecological consequences. Arguably the wetlands, including coastal areas, were the most affected ecosystems in Sri Lanka during this period. Especially along the western coast, wetland conversion into non-wetland uses, hydraulic modification, and pollution triggered an overall ecological transformation which permanently changed the ecological character and ecosystem services of the wetlands.

Large extents of marshes along the western coast were converted to non-wetland uses during this period. Hettiarachchi et al (2014) studied a portion of marshes in the northern suburbs of Colombo and estimated that about 14% were filled and converted to non-wetland use between 1980 and 2008. Scattered studies and news reports show that similar trends of direct loss of wetlands are becoming commonplace throughout the country for all wetland types (Gunawardena et al 2015; Kaleel 2017; Amarasinghe 2019). Two of the recent and most alarming incidents were the destruction of 2 ha in a protected mangrove forest in the Kalpitiya peninsula, and the illegal clearing of part of the Anavilundawa wetland reserve (a Ramsar-designated wetland) in 2020, both by private developers under the patronage of local politicians. A newspaper content analysis done by this author revealed that 52% of all the newspaper reports (2010–2020) on wetlands were about loss or reduction of wetland extent.

Large-scale conversion of wetlands for public or private/public partnership development undertakings was indeed the major cause of wetland loss post-1980. However, the impact of gradual and incremental encroachment of wetlands by households is also an important cause. The aerial photographs below show the encroachment of a marsh area Kolonnawa (easter suburbs of Colombo) by informal settlements between 1980 and 2008, where the loss exceeded 80% (see Figure 21.1).

Hydraulic modification, fragmentation, and pollution also had major impacts on wetlands. Hettiarachchi et al (2014) showed how intense canal widening, deepening, and artificial bank

Figure 21.1 Encroachment of a marsh in the Kolonnawa area by informal settlements: (a) 1980 to (b) 2008 (Source: Survey Department of Sri Lanka)

stabilisation in Colombo's wetlands have severely modified the hydraulic patterns. Although not well documented, such hydraulic modifications were seen extensively in all western coast marshes. The hydrological impact of large-scale filling and modification of paddy lands and marshes for expressway projects are yet to be fathomed.

Pollution of wetlands by wastewater and solid waste also rapidly intensified in the post-1980 period. The main sources of pollution shifted from heavy industries, to non-point source pollution from service sector operations and urban expansion. The wetland site reports prepared by CEA (1994) in the 1990s identified the growing pollution issues due to urban sprawl along the western coast. Hettiarachchi, Anurangi and de Alwis (2011) showed the alarming state of water quality in the Colombo wetlands, where key pollution indicators, such as Biochemical Oxygen Demand (BOD), Ammonia, and Phosphate levels were 5–10 times higher than the stipulated ambient standards for healthy aquatic life. The Colombo Wetland Strategy Report (2016) revealed severe nutrient accumulation in water and soils, and Jayawardena et al (2017) demonstrated bioaccumulation of heavy metals in wetland fish.

When environmental pressures, such as habitat conversion, hydraulic modification, and pollution accumulate in a wetland ecosystem, it can be pushed from one ecological state to another. In most cases, these new states are not stable and are referred to as "hybrid ecosystems." Such "ecological transformation" was widespread in the marshes around Colombo, which rapidly transformed from grass-dominated marsh habitat to a shrub habitat with small trees (see Figure 21.2), often dominated by exotic invasive plant species such as *Anonna glabra*.

Wetland ecological transformation was not only limited to changes in vegetation and habitat. The transformation of Colombo's marshes entailed the full spectrum of ecosystem characteristics, such as soil characteristics, hydraulic patterns, water holding capacity, and faunal diversity. The reduction of water holding capacity severely compromised the flood regulation function of the wetlands and caused the rapid increase of flash flood incidents seen in recent times.

Hettiarachchi et al (2014) estimated that about 40–50% of Colombo's marshes transformed this way in the 1980–2010 period. No such quantitative assessments of ecological transformation

Figure 21.2 Transformation of freshwater marshes to shrub wetlands in the Kolonnawa Marsh: (a) marsh habitat and (b) shrub habitat

have been done on rural wetlands. However, a similar proliferation of invasive species has been widely recorded from all wetland types. The ecological impact of development policy on wetlands in this period was staggering, but the social costs were even more devastating with the additional dimension of social-environmental injustice.

Devastated Communities: Dispossession, Disasters, and Resistance

As in the case of ecological impacts, the social issues are also mostly well documented for urban rather than rural wetlands. Before 1980, it was the state-owned wetlands that were converted for public use, such as housing or common amenities. This character changed after 1980, and swaths of smallholder-owned wetlands were acquired in the name of "flood protection" and later transferred to government or corporate development projects.

In addition to such direct dispossession, the appropriation of wetlands also led to the complete elimination of the few remaining uses and livelihoods based on the wetlands such as fishing. By the mid-1990s, most of the wetlands around Colombo were cordoned off with a peripheral canal, which effectively barred public access. Hettiarachchi et al (2017) illustrated that this trend of appropriation of wetlands was akin to the "land grabbing" and "green grabbing" trends recorded from other countries of the Global South, where the land of the poor or marginalised was acquired and allocated for corporate needs.

In the urban areas, appropriation of wetlands for development projects also required mass eviction of the communities settled within or in the vicinity of them. Since colonial times, the wetlands around Colombo have been settled by marginalised peoples (i.e. the poor and caste or ethno-religious minorities). Such informal wetlands settlements exploded in the mid-1990s with Civil War migrants from the North and East. Some settlements were owned by local thugs affiliated with political parties and were rented out to poor families. Most of the settlers did not have legal titles for their lands or houses, in spite of paying taxes and utility bills for many years or decades. They were often loathed as "illegal encroachments" and "incubators of crime." By 2015 there were nearly 70,000 families under threat of eviction in different parts of Colombo (CPA 2014).

Most wetland communities not having defined property rights to their land made wetlands a preferred space for real estate and infrastructure expansion. They were far less contested than other lands with defendable legal titles. Evicting communities from canal banks and wetland peripheries were justified in the name of flood protection and wetland conservation (Dissanaike 1997). The well-being of the communities themselves was often cited as a reason, though most displaced families were either involuntarily relocated to multi-storey low-income housing schemes of poor quality, or given grossly inadequate monetary compensation (Gunasekara 2010; CPA 2014). Some have lived in ramshackle temporary shelters for many years in the hope of resettlement or compensation.

Ecological degradation of urban wetlands also increased the hazards faced by the communities in the vicinity. Floods and diseases are principal among them. A survey by this author in the peripheral areas around Colombo's wetlands (mainly Kolonnawa marsh) showed that between 2000 and 2008, 63% of the households within a 200-m buffer experienced disruptive floods each year. Major flash floods were recorded in 1985, 1989, 1990, 1992, 1994, 2002, 2004, 2005, 2006, 2007, 2008, and 2010, where 35% of households reported vector or waterborne diseases (2000–2008) that can be associated with the ecological transformation and pollution in the wetlands.

The kinds of deep environmental justice issues faced by wetland communities in urban areas of Sri Lanka are in accord with what is described in the environmental justice literature from other regions (Pulido 2000; White et al 2012). The marginalised wetland communities bear the brunt of disasters caused by wetland degradation on the one hand and on the other hand face forcible evictions to make way for the development projects invading the wetlands. Social issues faced by rural wetland communities are far less documented than urban ones. However, with the exponential increase in infrastructure projects and widespread appropriation of rural wetlands, similar reports of social injustice can be expected.

Injustice in the wetlands has not gone unresisted. Wetland acquisition for development projects has been contested both politically and legally by civil society and environmental groups. One successful instance was the Supreme Court ruling in 2008 annulling the transfer of 270 ha of wetlands by the UDA (Sugathapala vs Kumaratunga and others SC 2008) to a private company for the development of a golf course and an entertainment facility. A series of successful court cases by environmental groups against the conversion of wetlands along the Western coast in the early 2000s ultimately resulted in the drafting of the National Wetland Policy in 2005.

However, the most virulent resistance was seen against the forced evictions of settlements around the urban wetlands of Colombo. Fierce resistance was encountered during many attempts of the UDA to forcibly evict low-income communities in the Wanthamulla, Thotalanga, and Meethotamulla areas of Colombo 2010–2019. These protests flared mostly spontaneously and from the downtrodden layers of the community. Sporadic support from political parties was often opportunistic and not sustained. The forms of resistance included demonstrations, sit-ins, and heckling of government officials and politicians. They were always met with violent state repression (Nagaraj 2016).

Conclusions: Wetlands at Crossroads – Towards Resilience, Resistance, or Disaster?

The current state of Sri Lanka's wetlands is best described by the words of the Indian wetlands researcher Shrestha Banerjee (2009):

> wetlands have become sites where the interests of the economy and ecology, authoritarianism and democratic participation, global forces and local communities, meet and clash
>
> *(2009: 194)*

Since colonial times, the net outcome of public policy had been adversarial towards wetlands in Sri Lanka. Assaults on wetlands rapidly intensified after 1980 with the adoption of free-market economic policies. Formerly state-led wetland reclamation projects for urban expansion took a corporate character during this period. They directly served profit interests and were similar to other cases of mass land appropriation in the Global South, now commonly termed "land grabbing" or "green grabbing." This led to disastrous outcomes both ecologically and socially and produced acute environmental injustice.

Development policy wielded a frontal attack, first on urban wetlands, and now rapidly expanding to rural wetlands. The expansion of environmental policy and institutions after 1980, which included formal advancements in wetland management institutions, has clearly failed to curtail or reverse these impacts. Projects to "beautify" wetlands and provide recreational services have served certain sections of society but did not preserve the complex ecological processes or diverse eco-social interactions of the wetlands in any meaningful way.

However, the projects to tame and amend the wetlands (especially urban wetlands) for development purposes have not fully succeeded. Ecologically, wetland conversion and degradation have produced hybrid ecosystems, never predicted or desired by development actors. Flooding has become a much more frequent and untenable problem, severely undermining urban disaster resilience. Socially, the efforts to appropriate wetlands for corporate needs have met with intense resistance from civil society organisations via non-violent legalistic and the communities via peaceful protests and at other times violent forms.

As in the case of many other complex environmental problems, the example of Sri Lanka's wetlands shows that the protection of ecosystems cannot be attained only through normative policy declarations or regulatory provisions. Environmental policy cannot always be reconciled with development policy. Where there are actors with competing interests, gains for some come at the expense of others. Cutting back on corporate and development aspirations through democratic political struggle and social movements becomes necessary for the broader well-being of eco-social systems.

Therefore, all who are concerned about ecological integrity, resilience, and social justice in the wetlands should strive to build alliances of environmental policy advocates, experts, civil society, and communities to overcome the pressures of development policy. Environmental policy advocates can gain the necessary political clout from civil society activism and community struggles, while communities and activists can organise into broader and effective social movements with the guidance of experts and policy advocates.

The advancements in wetland science and management, in the past decades, are indeed remarkable. However, rather than being imposed from above as normative policy directives or regulations, they should be used as guidance for a participatory wetland governance, inclusive of diverse stakeholders, and adaptive to the inherent complexity of wetland ecosystems and their human users.

Acknowledgements

The author would like to acknowledge the support given by Ms. S. Dissanayake, Ms. R.J. Yameen, and Dr. P. Bal.

Note

1 "…areas of marsh, fen, peatland or water, whether natural or artificial, permanent or temporary, with water that is static or flowing, fresh, brackish or salt, including areas of marine water the depth of which at low tide does not exceed six meters." The Convention on Wetlands, Article 1.1 (UNESCO 1971).

References

Amarasinghe, Ankumbure Gedara (2019) "Trends of Wetland Reclamation in Colombo Metropolitan Region in Sri Lanka and Strategies to Minimize Adverse Impact" *Sri Lanka Journal of Advanced Social Studies* 9(1) 18–39

Amarasuriya, Harini and Jonathan Spencer (2015) "With That, Discipline Will Also Come to Them" *Current Anthropology* 56(S11): 66–75

Banerjee, Shreshta (2009) *An evaluation of the political economy of urban ecological sustainability in Indian cities in a globalizing era: A perspective from the east Kolkata wetlands.* PhD Thesis, Newark, DW, USA: University of Delaware

Bauer, Michael, Christoffer Green-Pedersen, Adrienne Héritier and Andrew Jordan (2012) *Dismantling Public Policy: Preferences, Strategies, and Effects* Oxford: Oxford University Press

Bebbington, Anthony (2004) "Movements and Modernizations, Markets and Municipalities: Indigenous Federations in Rural Ecuador" In *Liberation Ecologies* Richard Peet and Michael Watts (eds) London: Routledge, pp 394–421

CEA (Central Environment Authority) (1994) *Wetland Site Report and Conservation Management Plan – Colombo Flood Detention Areas* Colombo: Central Environmental Authority of Sri Lanka

CEA (Central Environment Authority) (1995) *Wetlands Are No Wastelands* Colombo: Central Environmental Authority of Sri Lanka

CPA (Centre for Policy Alternatives) (2014) *Forced Eviction in Colombo: Ugly Price of Beautification* Colombo: Centre for Policy Alternatives

Dasgupta, Kaberi (2007) "A city Divided? Planning and Urban Sprawl in the Eastern Fringes of Calcutta" In *Indian Cities in Transition* A. Shaw (ed) Chennai: Orient Longman, pp 314–341

DI (Department of Irrigation) (1947) *Kelani Ganga Flood Protection Scheme* Colombo: Irrigation Department of Ceylon

Dissanaike, Tharuka (1997) "Colombo's Canals Coming to Life" *Sunday Times* (31 August). https://www.sundaytimes.lk/970831/plus8.html

Dissanayake, Thushara (2021) "Parakrama Samudra: Walking Path Devalues Heritage" *Ceylon Today* (17 September). https://ceylontoday.lk/news/parakrama-samudra-walking-path-devalues-heritage

DRD (Division of Reclamation and Drainage) (1966) *Reclamation of Swamps Around the City of Colombo* Colombo: Division of Reclamation and Drainage (DRD), Irrigation Department

GoSL (Government of Sri Lanka) (2016) *Metro Colombo Wetland Management Strategy*. Metro Colombo Urban Development Project (MCUDP) No. MCUDP/PHRD/03. Colombo: GoSL. Accessed on 30/11/2021. Available at https://www.ramsar.org/sites/default/files/Colombo%20Wetland%20Management%20Strategy.pdf

Gunasekara, Tisaranee (2010) "The Development War – A 'humanitarian operation' against Colombo's Poor" *The Sunday Leader* (12 May): 12

Gunawardena, Ajith, Tamasha Fernando, Wataru Takeuchi, Chathura Wickramasinghe and Lal Samarakoon (2015) "Identification, evaluation and change detection of highly sensitive wetlands in South-Eastern Sri Lanka using ALOS (AVNIR2, PALSAR) and Landsat ETM+ data" In *IOP Conference Series: Earth and Environmental Science 7th IGRSM International Remote Sensing & GIS Conference and Exhibition*, Kuala Lumpur, Malaysia. IOP Publishing Ltd

Hettiarachchi, Missaka, Jayani Anurangi and Ajith de Alwis (2011) "Characterization and Description of Surface Water Quality in the Threatened Urban Wetlands around the City of Colombo" *Journal of Wetland Ecology* 5: 10–19

Hettiarachchi, Missaka, Tiffany Morrison and Clive McAlpine (2017) "Power, Politics and Policy in the Appropriation of Urban Wetlands: The Critical Case of Sri Lanka" *The Journal of Peasant Studies* 46(4): 729–746

Hettiarachchi, Missaka, Tiffany Morrison, Deepthi Wickramasinghe, Ranjith Mapa, Ajith de Alwis and Clive McAlpine (2014) "The Environmental History and Ecological Transformation of the Colombo (Sri Lanka) Urban Wetlands" *Landscape and Urban Planning* 132: 55–68

Jayawardena, Uthpala, Preethika Angunawela, Deepthi Wickramasinghe, Wanigasekara Ratnasooriya and Preethi Udagama (2017) "Heavy Metal-Induced Toxicity in the Indian Green Frog: Biochemical and Histopathological Alterations" *Environmental Toxicology and Chemistry* 36(10): 2855–2867

Kaleel, M.I.M. (2017) "The Impact on Wetlands: A Study Based on Selected Areas in Ampara District of Sri Lanka" *World News of Natural Sciences* 7.16–25

Katupotha, Jinadasa (2018) "Climate Change and Its Impact on Coastal Wetlands" *Wetlands Newsletter* 6(2): 1–7

Kitching, John (1937) **Report on the Proposed Colombo South Drainage and Reclamation Scheme** Colombo: Irrigation Department

Marcuse, Peter and Ronald Van Kempen (2002) "Conclusion; A Changed Spatial Order" In *Globalizing Cities: A New Spatial Order?* Peter Marcuse (ed) Oxford: Blackwell, pp 249–275

McInnes, Robert and Mark Everard (2017) "Rapid Assessment of Wetland Ecosystem Services (RAWES): An Example from Colombo, Sri Lanka" *Ecosystem Services* 25: 89–105

Ministry of Environment (MoE) and Central Environmental Authority (CEA). (2006). National Wetlands Policy and Strategies. Colombo, Sri Lanka: MoE

Ministry of Megapolis and Western Development (MoMWD). (2016). Western Region Megapolis Masterplan: From Island to Continent. Colombo, Sri Lanka: MoMWD

Mitsch, William and James Gosselink (2007) *Wetlands* Hoboken: John Wiley and Sons

Nagaraj, Vijay (2016) "From Smokestacks to Luxury Condos: the Housing Rights Struggle of the Millworkers of Mayura Place, Colombo" *Contemporary South Asia* 24: 429–443

Nijamir, K. (2017) "Socio-Economic Impact of Wetlands: A Study Based on Navithanveli DS Division" *World News of Natural Sciences* 14: 116–123

Perera, Prasanna (2014) "The Political Economy of Post-War Economic Development in Sri Lanka" *International Journal of Business and Social Research* 4(12): 43–62

Priyadarshani, S., W.A.N. Madhushani, Uthpala Jayawardena, Deepthi Wickramasinghe and Preethi Udagama (2015) "Heavy Metal-Mediated Immunomodulation of the Indian Green Frog, Euphlyctis Hexadactylus (Anura: Ranidae) in Urban Wetlands" *Ecotoxicology and Environmental Safety* 116: 40–49

Pulido, Laura (2000) "Rethinking Environmental Racism: White Privilege and Urban Development in Southern California" *Annals of the Association of American Geographers* 90(1): 12–40

Purseglove, John (1988) *Taming the Flood: A History and Natural History of Rivers and Wetlands* Oxford: Oxford University Press.

Robbins, Paul (2012) *Political Ecology: A Critical Introduction* West Sussex: Wiley-Blackwell

Ruwanpura, Kanchana N., Benjamin Brown and Loritta Chan (2020) "(Dis)connecting Colombo: Situating the Megapolis in Postwar Sri Lanka" *The Professional Geographer* 72(1): 165–179

Storey, H. (1906) *Hunting and Shooting in Ceylon* London: Longmans, Green and Co

Swyngedouw, Erik and Nikolas Heynen (2003) "Urban Political Ecology and the Politics of Scale" *Antipode* 35(5): 898–918

Van Zon, J.C.J. (2004) "Wetland Conservation and Management in Sri Lanka: Status Paper" In *IUCN Wetland Conservation in Sri Lanka: Proceedings of the National Symposium on Wetland Conservation and Management Sri Lanka* Colombo: IUCN, pp 2–19

White, Ben, Saturnino Borras Jr., Ruth Hall, Ian Scoones and Wendy Wolford (2012) "The New Enclosures: Critical Perspectives on Corporate Land Deals" *The Journal of Peasant Studies* 39(3–4): 619–647

United Nations Educational, Scientific and Cultural Organization (UNESCO). 1971. Convention on Wetlands of International Importance Especially as Waterfowl Habitat. International Conference on the Wetlands and Waterfowl at Ramsar, Iran: UNESCO

22
SRI LANKA'S ENERGY TRANSITION
One Step Forward, Two Steps Back

Gz. MeeNilankco Theiventhran

Introduction

Sri Lanka has experienced continuous power outages since the 1990s, despite continued assurance from the government of sufficient reserves to produce electricity. The frequency of power outages in the last decade and the inability of the government to address the issue raise questions about Sri Lanka's energy policy and security. The overarching objective of electricity planning is to provide low-cost electricity to stimulate economic growth (Central Bank 2020). By 2019, Sri Lanka had achieved almost 100% electrification and 98% grid connectivity, suggesting higher energy use when compared to other countries with similar per capita GDP, indicating inefficient energy use (Asian Development Bank [ADB] 2019).

For Sri Lanka and elsewhere, the critical challenge for policymakers is to balance the energy 'tri-lemma', involving the interconnected and often competing demands of energy security, sustainability, and equity. Focusing on Sri Lanka, hydropower, the predominant renewable source of electricity until the mid-1990s, has been impacted by climate change in the past decade, which has led to reduced power output (ADB 2015). To ensure an uninterrupted electricity supply, Sri Lanka has relied increasingly on coal and other fossil fuels to back up renewable hydropower. This has implications for the current electricity mix: only around 45% is generated through renewables, including hydro. Limited indigenous fossil fuel supplies mean fossil fuel for electricity is imported and accounts for a considerable portion of Sri Lanka's import spending. Sri Lanka's economy has evolved from a primarily rural agrarian economy to an urbanised one driven by the service and industrial sectors. This economic transformation has led to a rising need for energy and this demand is projected to continue as Sri Lanka seeks economic growth and development. By 2050, Sri Lanka's electricity demand will likely increase fivefold to ~70,000 GWh from ~14,600 GWh in 2019 (Central Bank 2020). Thus, considerable new capacity is needed to fulfil current and future electricity demands.

In 2016, Sri Lanka pledged at the 22nd UNFCCC Conference of Parties in Marrakech, Morocco, as part of the Climate Vulnerable Forum, to reach 100% electricity generation from renewable energy by 2050. Sri Lanka's President Gotabaya Rajapaksa committed to a target of 80% of the country's energy needs to be met via renewable sources by 2030, although this was subsequently reduced to 70% (Daily News 2020). The climatic and spatial setting of Sri Lanka is conducive to

DOI: 10.4324/9781003300991-30

This chapter has been made available under a CC-BY-NC-ND 4.0 license.

harnessing renewables, notably biomass, hydro, solar, and wind energy, but no renewable energy policies are in place. At the same time, amid climate change forecasts on Sri Lanka's energy pathways provide grim readings for renewables. Continued dependence on imported fossil fuels, with almost no fossil fuels identified on- or offshore, played a significant role in the economic crisis that unfolded in 2022, which was aggravated by the debt crisis.

I next outline the present energy status in this chapter. This is followed by an investigation into the contemporary challenges facing Sri Lanka's energy transition. The last section explores the possible trajectories of Sri Lanka's energy transition.

Present Status

The current energy picture in Sri Lanka is captured in Figure 22.1 can be summarised as follows. While renewable energy options, including biomass, hydropower, solar and wind energy (all but biomass), play a minor role, hydroelectricity is now less than 6% of the total national electrical supply. In 2019, petroleum products contributed to around 44% of the primary energy supply, biomass accounted for 33%, and coal accounted for 12% (Sustainable Energy Authority SEA 2020).

In Sri Lanka, domestic and industrial sectors once dominated the electricity market; however, commercial demand has grown significantly in recent years. In 2017, electricity consumption for domestic, industrial, and commercial sectors accounted for 36%, 41%, and 23%, respectively (CEB 2018). In 2021, the domestic sector accounted for 34% of electricity consumed, the industrial sector accounted for 31%, and the commercial sector accounted for 35% (CEB 2022).

Energy Efficiency

Energy efficiency or conservation is intrinsic to any sustainable energy solution. Energy efficiency initiatives can alleviate conflicts between the profit motives of the private sector and the state's

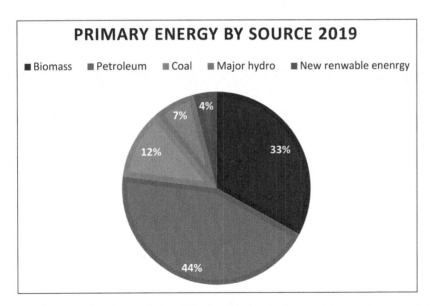

Figure 22.1 Sri Lanka's primary energy by source (Source: Adapted from Energy Balance [Sustainable Energy Authority 2020])

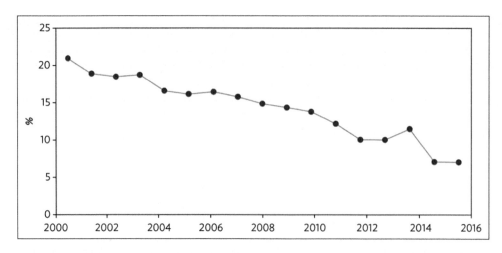

Figure 22.2 Percentage loss in transmission and distribution (Source: ADB [2021])

commitment to sustainable development. Energy efficiency will enhance production while reducing waste and pollution. Sri Lanka has lagged behind its neighbouring countries in the last decade over the implementation of energy efficiency programmes (Wickramasinghe 2010; Shrestha et al 2021). Transportation could potentially be the greatest contributor towards reducing energy consumption reductions between 2030 and 2050, followed by industry (Shrestha et al 2021). ADB (2019) forecasts that if Sri Lanka maintains its current energy resource management practices, greenhouse gas emissions would grow by 1.2 times in 2030 and 4.7 times in 2050. As illustrated below, transmission and distribution losses have decreased over time (see Figure 22.2), but there is still room for improvement.

Main Energy Sources

Primarily used for cooking, biomass is also used for industrial purposes. Agricultural waste accounts for most biomass, in addition to municipal and industrial waste. Hydropower is used mainly to generate electricity. Virtually all the economically feasible large-scale hydropower generation has already been realised. Although solar energy is abundant in near-equator Sri Lanka, there are geographic variations. When compared to locations with mountains, lowland areas receive a greater amount of solar irradiation than mountainous regions. This is primarily due to the persistent occurrence of clouds in mountainous regions and the impact that mountains have of casting shadows on the surrounding area. Sri Lanka enlisted the National Renewable Energy Laboratory in 2003 to build its Wind Resource Map. Significant wind energy resources centred in the country's North-Western coastline region and central highlands were identified. The country's wind energy potential is projected to be 5,600 MW, which is, as with solar, very significant.

Fossil fuels, however, are dominant in Sri Lanka. The country now depends on imported petroleum products for 44% of its energy supply, which is primarily utilised in transportation, electricity production, and manufacturing. Imports have gradually grown during the last several years with around 30% of the country's requirements being met by processing crude oil at the Ceylon Petroleum Corporation (CPC) refinery. Direct imports of refined petroleum products meet the reminder of the need.

Coal supplied 33% of Sri Lanka's electrical demand in 2021 (CEB 2022). The increasing usage of low-cost coal for electricity generation has significantly decreased reliance on oil for power generation – from 62% in 2004 to 16% in 2021 – thereby lowering the cost of electricity generation (CEB 2022). Coal is also utilised in kilns and boilers in some manufacturing industries.

In 2011, Sri Lanka found offshore gas in the Mannar basin North-West of the country (ADB 2019). Exploration lasted until 2015 when two other positive gas finds were made. The discoveries are primarily gas-bearing, with lesser amounts of liquid hydrocarbons. The discovery was not pursued commercially following the departure of the entity holding the exploration and commercialisation rights, and the project was terminated given the global decline in oil and gas prices. In the present context, renewed energy demand and focus on fossil fuels coupled with changing geopolitical landscape could reopen avenues for further exploration.

Institutional Obstacles

The multitude of energy institutions and their non-compatible goals has undermined the energy transition process in Sri Lanka (see Figure 22.3). Sri Lanka's government has four ministries responsible for energy and power. The Ceylon Electricity Board (CEB) is responsible for generating, transmitting, distributing, and retailing electricity. The Sri Lanka Sustainable Energy Authority (SEA) promotes renewable energy and energy efficiency. The Public Utilities Commission of Sri Lanka (PUCSL) regulates the power industry on economic, technical, and safety grounds, while the Climate Change Secretariat (CCS) oversees climate change-related activities.

Lack of coordination, overlapping responsibilities among ministries and departments, lack of innovative thinking, and bottlenecks in policy implementation have contributed to stagnation in energy transitions. Multiple institutions and their different power bases and interests have created institutional inertia, where the operational mechanisms of each institution reinforce the inertia and backtrack the policy initiatives, derail the implantation, and allow politics to be played

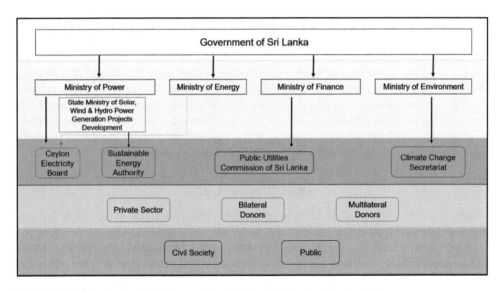

Figure 22.3 Institutional matrix (Source: Adapted from Theiventhran [2022a])

within (Theiventhran 2022a). The complexities of a negotiated consensus across institutions have repeatedly shown how different institutions undermine each other on a sustainable energy transition towards renewables. The result has been competing sectoral agendas or inactivity.

Despite the challenges of weak institutions, carbon lock-in, and individualised sectoral approaches, there are still choices available to plan Sri Lanka's energy future. Sector coupling which involves close integration of major energy consumers, such as the heating/cooling, transportation, and industrial sectors, where the power-producing sector will help to overcome the reliance on fossil fuels. First, it will reduce energy usage; second, sector coupling will bring renewable energy investments to the forefront; third, there will be a reliable and affordable renewable energy market. And finally, it can support research and development with the support of the private sector and through public-private partnerships. Cheap renewable electricity and new technologies can fast start sector coupling and contribute towards energy transition, with several ideas floated by the private sector, research institutions, and external actors on the transition modes, options, and challenges. Eventually, it all depends on Sri Lanka's policy priorities and implementation.

Contemporary Challenges in Sri Lanka's Energy Transition

Sri Lanka's energy debate is centred on three interlinked themes: energy security (availability, affordability, and access), environmental sustainability, and international climate commitments. As noted previously, Sri Lanka has two interrelated goals for renewables achieving carbon neutrality by 2050 and producing 70% of its electricity from renewables by 2030. In February 2022, the Sri Lanka National Audit Office published its findings on renewable energy uptake in the country. It found that the CEB had failed to prioritise renewable energy, which the report described as a violation of national policy and international pledges (National Audit Office 2022). The report highlighted inconsistencies between the government's National Electricity Policy and the CEB's Long-Term Generation and Expansion Plan 2022–2041 (LTGEP). LTGEP's 20-year plans comprise energy security and a least-cost plant mix for each year by analysing and evaluating various technology options. The CEB had not only deviated from the plan but was guilty of non-compliance with cabinet-approved policies. The findings reflect the failure of successive governments to seriously consider renewable energy mainly due to long-term time commitment and the lack of political incentives offered by these projects. Policymakers believe that the nation is not yet financially able to bear the increased costs of electricity generation that would be necessary to finance initial expenditures on clean energy. They argue that due to deficiencies in both technology and infrastructure, as well as funding, many renewable energy projects cannot be brought to fruition, although they would ultimately result in cheaper power. It is also argued that Sri Lanka lacks a suitable distribution network to accept the power from many small-scale rooftop solar panels. Figure 22.4 outlines the trajectory of the Sri Lankan electricity generation mix and its transition from clean energy (primarily hydropower) to fossil-based production.

Affinity towards Coal

Coal has been at the forefront of energy production in the past two decades with LTGEPs favouring coal power plants. The proposed Sampur coal power plant was shut down by the courts in 2016 citing environmental reasons following massive public protests. Interestingly, the plant had obtained the necessary regulatory and legal approvals, including environmental clearance before the court ruling. The discourse around the Sampur coal power plant rests on three arguments. First, the need to build it quickly to address increasing energy demand and avoid an energy crisis. That coal power

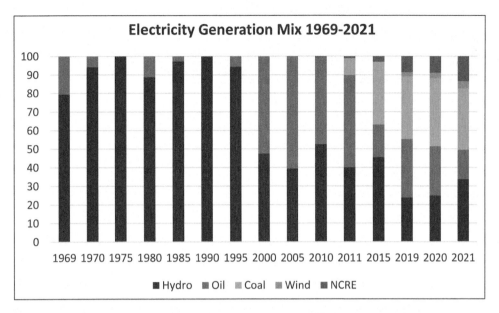

Figure 22.4 Electricity generation mix. Data extracted from the CEB's annual reports NCRE – nonconventional renewable energy – sources including solar and wind power

plants cannot be built quickly was ignored. Second, coal is one of the cheapest energy sources to produce electricity, thus maintaining low electricity prices (Caron and Da Costa 2007). This is simply not true; electricity tariffs via renewable energy have been reduced drastically. Yet in Sri Lanka, the strong coal lobby keeps alive the justification for coal as the 'cheapest source'. The latest data shows a different picture, with Figure 22.5 providing unit costs per energy source as of January 2022. Notably, this data was recorded prior to the major spike in US dollars owing to the economic crisis. According to this, the cheapest energy is major hydro, followed by wind. Solar and coal are in a close race, followed by biomass; by March 2022, however, coal prices surpassed that of solar photovoltaics.

The third argument supporting coal is that the environmental cost of coal power is insignificant. This is also not true, even though the 'clean coal' concept popularised by Japan International Cooperation Agency (JICA) is taken for granted by policymakers. Sri Lanka's consistent refusal to move away from coal has been a major challenge for the energy transition. In September 2021, Sri Lanka signed the 'The No New Coal Compact' pledge initiated by the United Nations to stop building new coal power plants (Farzan 2021). Nevertheless, LTGEP for 2022–2041, approved in October 2021, proposes to build further coal power plants in 2025 and 2028 (CEB 2021).

Social Challenges of Renewable Energy

Sri Lanka's renewable energy uptake has its social challenges. The academic discussion relating to Sri Lanka's transition to renewables mostly focuses on technical solutions and addressing technical hitches in implementation (Kolhe, Ranaweera and Gunawardana 2015; Withanaarachchi, Nanayakkara and Pushpakumara 2015) and on the use of solar and other renewable technologies (Jayaweera, Jayasinghe and Weerasinghe 2018; Almeida, Abeysinghe and Ekanayake 2019;

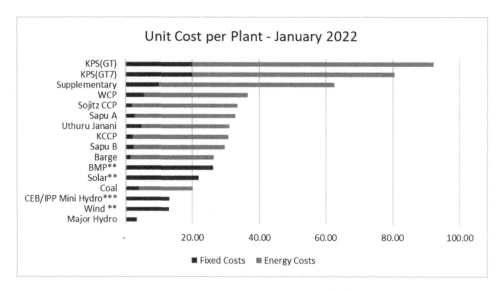

Figure 22.5 Unit cost per electricity plant as of January 2022. (1) Biomass energy sources include waste-to-energy facilities. Since the CEB does not routinely report on all mini-hydro, wind, and solar power, these figures are not totals. (2) Fixed costs are the cost of equipment and construction of the power plant. Energy costs consist of fuel costs. (3) BMP is a Biomass plant, KPS (GT & GT7), Supplementary, WCP, Sojitz CCP, Sapu A&B, Uthuru Janani, KCCP and Barge are oil-fired power plants (Credit: Vidhura Ralapanawe)

Bandara and Amarasena 2020; Silva 2020). However, there is limited literature on non-technical, environmental, and social aspects of Sri Lanka's energy, especially in the post-war context (Caron and da Costsa 2007). In the aftermath of the war, renewable energy projects were seen as 'development projects' in the former war zones. Achieving peace via development is the liberal peacebuilding idea supported by post-war administrations with no real commitment to substantive peacebuilding. Development is viewed as fostering peace, with renewable energy being perceived as one of its main pillars. Energy governance and transition were key to making communities believe that development initiatives are significantly beneficial. Renewable energy projects were included in this development matrix to provide energy security and affordability to war-affected populations. However, the state's discourse has been challenged locally. For different reasons, local people have challenged almost all the renewable energy projects in the former war zones. For example, the wind park in Mannar led to protests and evictions; people in Vavuniya protested against non-consultation regarding the solar farm in their region; and communities in Poonakary worried about the loss of land and livelihood.

I have argued elsewhere, using extensive case studies from renewable energy sites in former war zones, that these sites have also become a battleground for spatial control (Theiventhran 2021). The fluid character of the long-running and still-unresolved conflict results in renewable energy projects viewed as land grabbing from minority communities with renewable energy as a pretext.

Hence, energy equity and justice need to take centre stage in a post-war setting where the memories of conflict and injustice remain fresh (Klem 2014; Klem and Kelegama 2019; Ruwanpura et al 2020). The Sri Lankan experience shows that energy inequity, injustice, and vulnerability are more than simply matters of resource issues; rather, they also involve structural differences that have evolved over time and across space. Energy projects, which are generally sensitive to post-war realities, therefore, can reopen old wounds, potentially create new tensions, and undermine energy transitions if they do not prioritise justice, equity, and democracy.

It is noteworthy that the centre-periphery divide is also evident in new renewable energy projects targeting communities. Sri Lanka launched the rooftop solar power generation project (*Soorya Bala Sangramaya*) in 2016, a community-based power generation project to promote the setting up of small solar power plants on rooftops. Under this project, the loans benefit the industry, commercial establishments, and high-income earners. Low- and middle-income households were denied loan facilities on several grounds, and the project never evolved as a community-based project, as Figure 22.6 indicates, with the number of rooftops and shows clearly the urban-rural divide.

The above figure shows clearly that the urban centres have benefited mostly from the project even though it was intended to benefit the larger population around the country. The economic barriers that were enshrined in the policymaking itself had a major say in the outcome. More than 75% of the total rooftop uptake from the project is from the urban areas and low-income earners were unable to access the project and it outlines the justice questions on the renewable uptake.

Sri Lanka's energy transition pathways since the war ended have both environmental and social impacts. However, social and political issues have generally received little attention in research and academia and even less in policy and practice.

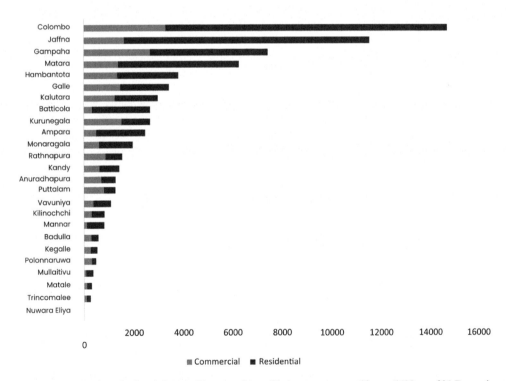

Figure 22.6 District-wise breakdown of the capacities added as per approved loans (kW) as of 31 December 2021, under the rooftop solar power generation project (Source: Sustainable Energy Authority [2022])

Innovation and Investment

Decoupling energy demand growth from economic growth is needed to subsequently decarbonise the residual energy demand. The greater the penetration of renewables, particularly sources, such as solar and wind, the greater the demand for technical solutions supporting the electricity system's flexibility. Several possibilities include batteries or other forms of energy storage, sector coupling, network linkages, demand, and conventional dispatchable power plants. Renewables have become a more competitive component of the energy transition discourse due to technological advancements, increased efficiency, and cost reductions. However, the considerable concern is that the international energy sector has not yet made emerging new technology accessible to Global South nations. Technology must be created within a framework that allows its evolution and maturity into resilient, sustainable technologies capable of bringing about noticeable and reasonable changes that are acceptable to society. Such a context is created within political, economic, social, cultural, and geographic realities and is also entangled in them.

The Sri Lankan energy landscape is handicapped by a lack of innovation in the sector to understand local needs and meet them via tailor-made solutions, which has hindered the energy sector's transition to sustainable energy. Such a transition requires local knowledge production within institutes of higher education and research sectors via specific initiatives, supported by industry. The value chains for energy technology have been increasingly globalised during the last decade. Numerous value chains increasingly drive manufacturing, and this has enabled countries in the Global South to access emerging technology. Nevertheless, political and economic concerns deter private sector firms, particularly energy firms, from investing in projects. This has been the case with Sri Lanka. Sri Lanka's policy failures continue to be aggravated by the country being cut off from global technology transfers. The country's first pilot floating solar project was initiated in Bandaragama in 2018, but it failed to materialise since both the CEB and locals did not welcome it, with locals resisting it as they were inadequately informed about the project. Floating solar brings multiple benefits, including addressing land grab concerns, lower evaporation of water bodies, higher solar panel efficiency due to the cooling effect, and complementarity with hydropower generation and the efficient management of peak hours. A pilot plant was finally established within the university premises in Kilinochchi with the assistance of Norway (Jayatilleke 2020). Despite being a part of Sri Lanka's renewable energy plan since 2018, floating solar power is yet to materialise. This underscores Sri Lanka's renewable energy transition challenges regarding new innovative solutions.

Investment and innovation are critical for Sri Lanka to realise its energy transition while assuring universal access to electricity. The resources available to the government for energy transition will determine the design and direction of the change. Investment has typically favoured large-scale corporations over small-scale or participatory alternatives, which allowed geopolitical actors into the Sri Lankan energy landscape. At the same time, it also allowed large local private sector companies to dictate the transitions, thus disenfranchising and overriding the concerns of local populations.

Geopolitics

During the past two decades, geopolitics has become more salient in the Sri Lankan energy sector as illustrated by the coal power plant. Japan proposed to build the first coal power plant in 2006, although China eventually won the bid (Wignaraja et al 2020). In the same year, India and Sri Lanka signed an agreement to allow India's National Thermal Power Corporation (NTPC) to build a coal power plant in Sampur, Trincomalee. However, this project was stopped in 2016. Instead, the Sri Lankan government promised India that the location would be used to build a Liquefied Natural Gas (LNG) terminal as an alternative to the cancelled coal plant (Economy Next 2016). Finally, in March 2022, NTPC was awarded the contract to build a solar plant in Sampur. India's expression of interest in Sri Lanka's energy sector came soon after a Chinese Company was granted permission to develop a hybrid renewable energy system project on three islands (Delft, Nainatheevu, and Analtheivu) in Jaffna. India did not want the Chinese presence close to its maritime borders and proposed the energy facility in Sampur (Bhaskar 2020; Bagchi 2021). The Chinese project was to be undertaken through an ADB loan. In contrast, India offered Sri Lanka a grant and a small loan component with easy terms for the same project. In December 2021, the Government of Sri Lanka cancelled the Chinese project and awarded the project to India (Srinivasan 2022). It is noteworthy that the Chinese Embassy tweeted that the project was suspended due to a 'security concern' from a third party, openly acknowledging the geopolitical power play.

Since the court ruling against the coal plants, Sri Lanka has been contemplating LNG. Several external actors were interested. For example, India and Japan jointly bided to win the contract for the first LNG regasification terminal in 2017. However, the tender was challenged by China, and the process was dropped (Express News Service 2017; Sebastian 2021). One year later, in 2018, China was awarded the contract to construct the LNG terminal near the Chinese-controlled port and industrial zone in Hambantota (Aneez 2021). Japan financed the CEB to conduct a pre-feasibility study for a coal plant in Foul Point, Trincomalee, and the land acquisition process is ongoing (CEB, 2021). In September 2021, a US-based company signed an agreement with the government of Sri Lanka to construct a new offshore LNG terminal near the capital Colombo. The agreement was signed without cabinet approval, involving energy sales estimated at US$6 billion, which is likely the most significant contract the Sri Lankan government has ever entered with a private entity (Bandarage 2021). In June 2022, when testifying before the Parliamentary Committee on Public Enterprises, the CEB Chairman stated that the Sri Lankan President – Gotabaya Rajapakse – had informed him that the Indian Prime Minister Narendra Modi insisted that a wind power project in Mannar be awarded to India's Adani Group (Basu 2022). Even though it was denied by the President and later by the Chairman himself, the local newspaper *The Sunday Times* carried a story with the details of the communication between the CEB and the Adani group confirming the agreement. India has been pushing Sri Lanka into cross-border electricity grid interconnection since the early 2000s. The initial Sampur coal power plant plan had sections in the agreement to export the electricity generated from the plant to India. The letter sent by the Adani group to the CEB also mentioned that the electricity produced would be exported to India via cross-border transmission lines established by Adani (Wijedasa 2022). In November 2021, the United States Agency for International Development (USAID) announced its new US$19 million, five-year Sri Lanka Energy Program focusing on renewable energy to transform Sri Lanka's power sector into a market-based system.

Energy has become a means for foreign powers to insert themselves into Sri Lanka's affairs. I identify how the energy sector is used for three essential purposes from a geopolitical perspective: (1) territorial control, through the establishment of energy infrastructure in the country by foreign powers; (2) hegemony, as part of grand strategies and initiatives; and (3) influence, to control and counter other actors' influences (Theiventhran 2022b). To channel geopolitics towards further innovation choices and investment possibilities, a coherent and visionary policy is requisite. Effective policymaking is also critical in ensuring that transformation is both practical and possible. Additionally, policymaking must be inclusive and participatory to promote bottom-up energy innovation in ways that benefit the entire population, both as authorities and as consumers/prosumers.

Future Direction of Energy Transition

Sri Lanka's energy future depends on Sri Lanka adopting renewable energy while negating technical, financial, and social challenges. The sustainability of Sri Lanka's energy future depends on the ability of renewable energy to displace fossil fuels, and understanding fossil fuel displacement as a socio-political and spatial process is critical. It is imperative that renewables must supplant fossil fuels financially, institutionally, and discursively. The persistence of fossil fuels in policymaking and institutions, however, has made displacement difficult and limited the role citizens play in influencing energy security (Wood and Baker 2020).

Policymakers typically fail to choose long-term sustainable solutions because energy and climate policy decisions are not just motivated by concerns about overall well-being but are also significantly affected by special interests. These include securing cheap energy costs for political advantage and lobbying by global interest groups. The degree to which such political difficulties obstruct the transition to a clean energy system is context-dependent, shaped by such factors as a country's fossil fuel endowment, its potential for alternative energy sources, its industrial structure, and public attitudes towards change.

Affordable power is a primary goal of energy policy. Low power prices are viewed as critical in ensuring the competitiveness of the domestic (energy-intensive) industry. When policymakers raise electricity costs, they fear protests and losing popularity which could ultimately result in the loss of power. Simultaneously, prices are sometimes insufficient to pay the expenses of the energy system, resulting in implicit subsidies to 'keep the lights on', which frequently have a significant impact on public finances.

Sri Lanka faces significant capital costs. High capital costs of renewables benefit coal, which is less capital-intensive per MW compared to renewables (Schmidt 2014). This bias is exacerbated by policies that favour coal over renewable alternatives, thereby increasing renewable energy risk premiums and capital costs. Promoters of coal promoters also argue that coal outperforms renewables in terms of reliability. Integrating intermittent renewable energy sources into the electric grid presents technical, financial, administrative, and institutional challenges, which impedes renewable energy adoption, especially in Sri Lanka where low institutional and regulatory controls favour coal due to its lower governance requirements.

Climate change mitigation and other environmental problems, such as local air pollution, are critical but do not feature in the debate over energy policy. Ambient air pollution and water consumption appear to receive very little attention in national energy planning unless there is vociferous opposition to specific projects from civil society. Indeed, coal politics is a tale of entangled interests. Independent of the governing framework, vested interests are frequently and inextricably linked to external players and interests. Domestic interests are twofold: (1) The CEB argues that coal is cheaper than any other energy source (except hydro) because it fails to acknowledge associated (external) environmental costs; and (2) coal tenders fall within the intersection of the policymakers-politicians-business nexus, where the procedure has been criticised for corruption and mismanagement. International interests range from building and running coal plants to financial aid, providing technical and policy assistance, and selling coal and impacting energy policies within Sri Lanka. It is noteworthy that Japan's 'clean coal' technology continues to influence Sri Lanka's policymaking considerably.

Conclusions

Adopting low-carbon energy sources is only appealing if they are less expensive than coal. The rapid drop in the cost of renewable energy technology in other parts of the world may contribute to the acceleration of the energy transition in Sri Lanka. Countries in the Global North are phasing out coal due to their technological and financial capabilities to choose from various energy technologies and Due to increasing public actvisim regarding climate change. In Sri Lanka, however, high upfront capital costs and integration of renewables into existing grids face both technological and political impediments. Energy security is commonly used as a pretext for vested interests. However, worries about integrating renewable energy into existing grids and the lack of technical and financial aid for implementing new technologies give established interests the upper hand. Although alternative energy sources are less expensive than coal in the long term, those with vested interests in coal have succeeded in hindering or at least postponing the adoption of renewables. To phase out coal, political reform to reduce the impact of vested interests on policymaking must be combined with a system for compensating those who lose out politically. Continued delays in renewable energy uptake have eroded investor confidence in the energy sector, and a democratic political structure supporting the energy transition is yet to materialise. In other words, the coordination between people, institutions, and academia is yet to take place. Given these constraints, not least the financial ones, it is difficult to see how Sri Lanka can make significant progress towards sustainable energy systems soon, despite the global urgency of the task.

It is also essential to understand energy transition as a multi-scalar process. Bottom-up approaches coupled with top-down initiatives can create carbon-lockout pathways. Talking about energy transition as switching from high-carbon to low-carbon (renewable) energy sources is inadequate. The transition dialogue must incorporate justice and equity when advocating for renewables. Globally, the energy sector is going through titanic shifts that will have localised impacts. It is time to rethink how Sri Lanka can become carbon natural and ensure energy security and equity by considering the following questions:

1. Which mechanisms will contribute to sustainably achieving energy transition at the local, provincial, and national levels?
2. What factors are required to sustain the energy sector?
3. Which models should be used to drive institutions forward?

It is critical that Sri Lanka sees energy justice, security, and climate change through the prism of public values rather than strategic national interests. The energy transition has the potential to re-localise the economy around human-scale institutions that are more directly connected to the communities in which they operate. Internally, this transition should be 'democratised', i.e. a change towards empowerment and ownership, thereby changing end consumers into 'prosumers'. The goal should be to repurpose 'transition arenas' to more open spaces for thought, dialogue, and participation. This is even more important in Sri Lanka due to its post-war political and economic setting.

References

ADB (2015) *Assessment of Power Sector Reforms in Sri Lanka: Country Report* Manilla: ADB
ADB (2019) *Sri Lanka: Energy Sector Assessment, Strategy, and Road Map* Manilla: ADB
ADB (2021) *Energy Efficiency in South Asia: Opportunities for Energy Sector Transformation* Manilla: ADB
Almeida, D.W., A.H.M.S.M.S. Abeysinghe and J.B. Ekanayake (2019) "Analysis of Rooftop Solar Impacts on Distribution Networks" *Ceylon Journal of Science* 48(2): 103–112
Aneez, Shiraz (2018) "Sri Lanka approves $500 million LNG plant near Chinese-controlled port." Reuters. March 5th 2018. Accessed on 09/03/2024 available at https://www.reuters.com/article/idUSKBN1I60GG/
Bagchi, Indrani (2021) "India worked for a year to get China off Lanka projects" *India Times* (4 December). Accessed on 06/07/2022. Available at https://timesofindia.indiatimes.com/india/india-worked-for-a-year-to-get-china-off-lanka-projects/articleshow/88080863.cms

Bandara, U.C. and S.M. Amarasena (2020) "Factors Influencing Solar Energy Technology Adoption by Households in Western Province Sri Lanka" *Vidyodaya Journal of Management* 6(2): 131–152

Bandarage, Asoka (2021) "New Fortress Energy, Sri Lanka, and Planet Earth" *The Island* (5 October). Accessed on 03/07/2022. Available at https://island.lk/new-fortress-energy-sri-lanka-and-planet-earth/

Basu, Nayanima (2022) "Modi blamed for pushing Adani project in Sri Lanka, Gotabaya denies, statement withdrawn" **The Print** (12 June). Accessed on 12/05/2022. Available at https://theprint.in/diplomacy/modi-blamed-for-pushing-adani-project-in-sri-lanka-gotabaya-denies-statement-withdrawn/993507/

Bhaskar, Utpal (2020) "Eyeing China, India plans solar power park in Sri Lanka." mint (22 July). Accessed on 09/07/2022. Available at https://www.livemint.com/industry/energy/eyeing-china-india-plans-solar-power-park-in-sri-lanka-11595419421198.html

Caron, Cynthia and Dia Da Costa (2007) "There's a Devil on Wayamba Beach: Social Dramas of Development and Citizenship in Northwest Sri Lanka" *Journal of Asian and African Studies* 42(5): 415–445

CEB (2018) *Statistical Digest 2017* Colombo: Ceylon Electricity Board

CEB (2021) *Long-Term Generation and Expansion Plan 2022–2041* Colombo: Ceylon Electricity Board

CEB (2022) *Statistical Digest 2021* Colombo: Ceylon Electricity Board

Central Bank (2020) *Annual Report 2019* Colombo: Central Bank of Sri Lanka

Daily News (2020) "Country Must Generate 70% Renewable Energy by 2030 – President" *Daily News* (14 September). Accessed on 16/02/2022. Available at https://www.dailynews.lk/2020/09/15/local/228799/country-must-generate-70-renewable-energy-2030-president

Economy Next (2016) "Sri Lanka hopes for LNG power plant with India in Sampur" *Economy Next* (15 September). Accessed on 08/07/2022. Available at https://economynext.com/sri-lanka-hopes-for-lng-power-plant-with-india-in-sampur-5749/

Express News Service (2017) "India, Japan to build LNG terminal in Sri Lanka" *New Indian Express* (24 May 24). Accessed on 07/07/2022. https://www.newindianexpress.com/business/2017/may/25/india-japan-to-build-lng-terminal-in-sri-lanka-1608779

Farzan, Zulfick (2021) "Sri Lanka pledges to stop building new coal power plants" *News First* (25 September). Accessed on 18/07/2022. Available at https://www.newsfirst.lk/2021/09/25/sri-lanka-pledges-to-stop-building-new-coal-power-plants/

Jayatilleke, Chandani (2020) "Sri Lanka – Norway float solar power plant" *Daily News* (24 January). https://www.dailynews.lk/2020/01/24/finance/209336/sri-lanka-norway-float-solar-power-plant

Jayaweera, Nadeeka, Chathuri L. Jayasinghe and Sandaru N. Weerasinghe (2018) "Local Factors Affecting the Spatial Diffusion of Residential Photovoltaic Adoption in Sri Lanka" *Energy Policy* 119: 59–67

Klem, Bart (2014) "The Political Geography of war's End: Territorialisation, Circulation, and Moral Anxiety in Trincomalee, Sri Lanka" *Political Geography* 38: 33–45

Klem, Bart and Thiruni Kelegama (2019) "Marginal Placeholders: Peasants, Paddy and Ethnic Space in Sri Lanka's Post-War Frontier" *Journal of Peasant Studies* 47(2): 346–365

Kolhe, M.L., K.M.I. Ranaweera and S. Gunawardana (2015) "Techno-Economic Sizing of off-Grid Hybrid Renewable Energy System for Rural Electrification in Sri Lanka" *Sustainable Energy Technologies and Assessments* 11: 53–64

National Audit Office (2022) *Evaluate the Process of Developing New Renewable Energy Sources* Colombo: National audit Office

Ruwanpura, Kanchana N, Loritta Chan, Benjamin Brown and V. Kajotha (2020) "Unsettled Peace? The Territorial Politics of Roadbuilding in Post-War Sri Lanka" *Political Geography* 76: 102092

Schmidt, Tobias (2014) "Low-Carbon Investment Risks and De-Risking" *Nature Climate Change* 4(4): 237–239

Sebastian, Bejoy (2021) "Why Sri Lanka walked back on Indo-Japanese involvement in Colombo Port." *Modern Diplomacy* (6 February). Accessed on 05/07/2022. Available at https://moderndiplomacy.eu/2021/02/06/why-sri-lanka-walked-back-on-indo-japanese-involvement-in-colombo-port/

Shrestha, Ram, Tika Ram Limbu, Bijay Bahadur Pradhan, Amnaya Paudel and Pratik Karki (2021) *Energy Efficiency in South Asia: Opportunities for Energy Sector Transformation* Manilla: ADB

Silva, Kaluthanthiri Patabendi Sepali Darshika (2020) "Opportunities and Challenges of Solar Energy Application in Energy Sector of Sri Lanka" *Bulletin of the Korea Photovoltaic Society* 6(1): 45–55

Srinivasan, Meera (2022) "Indian power projects replace Chinese ventures in Sri Lanka" *The Hindu* (29 March). https://www.thehindu.com/news/international/indian-power-project-replaces-chinese-venture-in-sri-lankas-northern-islands/article65269733

Sustainable Energy Authority (2020) *Sri Lanka Energy Balance 2019* Colombo: Sri Lanka Sustainable Energy Authority

Sustainable Energy Authority (2022) *Rooftop Solar Power Generation Project*. Accessed on 16/06/2022. Available at https://www.rooftopsolar.lk/

Theiventhran, Gz. MeeNilankco (2021) "Energy Transitions in a Post-War Setting: Questions of Equity, Justice and Democracy in Sri Lanka" In *Dilemmas of Energy Transitions in the Global South: Balancing Urgency and Justice* Ankit Kumar, Johanna Höffken and Auke Pols (eds) New York: Routledge, pp 93–110

Theiventhran, Gz. MeeNilankco (2022a) "Emerging Frontiers of Energy Transition in Sri Lanka" In *Energy Policy Advancement: Climate Change Mitigation and International Environmental Justice* Dmitry Kurochkin, Martha J Crawford and Shabliy (eds) Switzerland: Springer Nature, pp 185–210

Theiventhran, Gz. MeeNilankco (2022b) "Energy as a Geopolitical Battleground in Sri Lanka" *Asian Geographer* 1–25

Wickramasinghe, Harsha (2010) *Sri Lanka Country Report on Energy Efficiency Improvement & Conservation* Islamabad: SAARC Energy Centre

Wignaraja, Ganeshan, Dinusha Panditaratne, Pabsara Kannangara and Divya Hundlani (2020) *Chinese Investment and the BRI in Sri Lanka* London: Chatham House

Wijedasa, Namini (2022) "Official letters show CEB Chairman was instructed to facilitate Adani projects" *The Sunday Times* (19 June). https://www.sundaytimes.lk/220619/news/adani-to-expand-still-further-in-sri-lanka-through-wind-and-solar-power-projects-486419

Withanaarachchi, A.S., L.D.J.F. Nanayakkara and C. Pushpakumara (2015) "Are Ready-Made Technology Transfer Solutions Suitable for Developing the Renewable Energy Sector in Sri Lanka?" *International Journal of Scientific and Research Publications* 5(2): 1–4

Wood, Geoffrey and Keith Baker (2020) *The Palgrave Handbook of Managing Fossil Fuels and Energy Transitions* London: Palgrave Macmillan

23
ENVIRONMENTAL PROTECTION IN SRI LANKA
A Critical Legal Approach

Kalana Senaratne

Introduction

The law plays a significant role in environmental protection. Legal interventions often promote a standard set of responses that are nonetheless important: the need to reform existing but ineffective or problematic laws, the need to properly implement existing laws, and/or the need to introduce new laws, based on international, regional, and comparative best practices.

The critical legal approach to the study of environmental protection, proposed in this chapter is interested in a somewhat different set of issues or questions, three of which will be explored below. Firstly, what types of narratives do lawyers and jurists promote when writing about the history of environmental protection in Sri Lanka? And why does paying attention to them matter? Secondly, why is environmental protection in Sri Lanka a continuing challenge in the context of a relatively well-developed legal and institutional framework? Thirdly, what are some of the critical issues that may require further research and study by the legal community?

History

The history of environmental protection in Sri Lanka is often painted in glorious terms, especially by legal scholars and jurists. In examining the numerous works on the law and the environment, we are exposed to a historical narrative that has acquired legitimacy over the years, given its uncritical endorsement by the legal community in particular.

One such prominent narrative was popularized by Judge C.G. Weeramantry, one of Sri Lanka's foremost jurists and a former Vice-President of the International Court of Justice (ICJ). It is a narrative which emerged in the context of a case between Hungary and Slovakia raising important questions about environmental protection and sustainable development. The Separate Opinion of Judge C.G. Weeramantry in that case promoted the view that environmental protection and sustainable development were deeply ingrained in Sri Lanka's traditions (Weeramantry 1997). It is a view that he has repeatedly highlighted in his later works (Weeramantry 2004: 438–444).

The historical account he constructed in his Separate Opinion highlights numerous elements pertaining to ancient Sri Lanka, three of which are prominent. The first concerns the irrigation networks and the irrigation-based civilization, considered to have been constructed by ancient kings (with certain irrigation tanks being developed circa the third-century BC), especially with environmental concerns in mind. Reference is made, for example, to ways in which silting was prevented from interfering with the river systems through the development of erosion control tanks. Weeramantry (1977) also made references to "forest tanks" built in the jungle above the village, to provide water for the animals (1997: 99).

Secondly, the traditional legal system in the country is considered to have promoted environmental protection. Royal decrees as well as ancient customary laws had regulated how irrigation facilities were to be used and protected by the public. There was, for example, a prohibition imposed on the construction of permanent buildings on prime agricultural lands (Weeramantry 1997, 2004).

Thirdly, ancient religious teachings and the work of kings are seen to have given rise to a rich and inspiring body of thought and practice. The philosophy of environmental conservation is supposed to be contained in the ancient chronicles. For example, the famous visit of Arahant Mahinda (a visit which is widely considered to have marked the introduction of Buddhism to Sri Lanka) plays a central role in this narrative. Arahant Mahinda is reported to have reminded the then ruler, King Devanampiyatissa, that animals are to be regarded as equal inhabitants of the land just as all other human beings; and, more famously, that the king is not the owner of the land but merely its trustee (Weeramantry 1997: 102). Another ruler, King Parakramabahu, is regarded to have issued a famous edict to the effect that not a single drop of water should flow into the sea without serving people's interests (Weeramantry 2004: 443).

This narrative about Sri Lanka's commitment to environmental protection was developed with the help of the works of numerous Western scholars, namely Arnold J. Toynbee, H. Parker, Joseph Needham, R.L. Brohier, Edward Goldsmith, and Nicholas Hildyard. Their narratives portray Sri Lanka as a country that has been, since ancient times, deeply mindful of the importance of protecting the environment and committed to a model of development that did not endanger the environment. It is a narrative which has been widely and uncritically embraced especially by the legal community in Sri Lanka, including judges both in their writings on environmental law as well as in judicial decisions (Wimalachandra 2007). Judge Weeramantry, in particular, was seeking to provide historical context in support of the goals of sustainable development and intergenerational equity, which are prominent principles in international environmental law today.

This soothing narrative (especially in the minds of Sri Lankans) raises questions which we often ignore. The mythical past not only promotes a glorified picture of ancient Sinhala-Buddhist traditions and wisdom but also omits and thereby erases the tensions and controversies that may have been prevalent, during ancient times, about matters relating to the environment. We simply do not know, for example, whether the rulers and the people in ancient Sri Lanka interpreted what Arahant Mahinda said in environmental terms. At best, the statements only *resemble* what we today consider to be principles associated with environmental law. In ancient times, these could have meant different things to different people. The attempt to trace the origins of international law principles back to ancient Sri Lanka has also invited the caustic comment that Sri Lankans "have the unfortunate penchant for saying that they knew it all along after a concept is articulated" (Sornarajah 2016–2017: 35).

Importantly, it is not clear whether ancient rulers always had environmental concerns at heart. Take the above illustration involving Arahant Mahinda and King Devanampiyatissa. Did not the need to emphasize the importance of the values of trusteeship and animal protection imply that King Devanampiyatissa was flouting those values? Why would such emphasis be required in a context where those principles were well protected? Also, would not the views expressed by King Parakramabahu (above) suggest the persistence of a very narrow anthropocentric view of the environment? Or, what does it mean to say the same kind of thing today? And how reliable are these edicts, anyway, of a ruler's benevolence? In short, how sure can we be that ancient Sri Lanka was practising sustainable development?

Such questions need to be raised to unsettle some of the comforting historical narratives which many have unquestioningly embraced. While questioning does not amount to rejection, it is well that we entertain the idea that environmental protection may have been a contentious issue in ancient Sri Lanka. In that period too the debate about how best to protect the environment and to what extent these concerns must be taken into consideration when planning developmental activities may have been controversial. Rulers may have adopted policies which were harmful to the environment, which in turn may have been resisted by the people. Having in mind such a complex narrative may make us see contemporary problems with less nostalgia and greater realism. That is important especially if we are to take the current environmental crisis seriously; to awaken us to the reality that serious and urgent attention, at this present moment, is required. Furthermore, narratives which promote a glorious past are foundational to the development of ethno-nationalist projects, the effects of which are extremely problematic in plural societies (Jeganathan 1995). Therefore, one of the important tasks of critical legal thinking is to contest such narratives.

The Legal Framework

Internationally, a vast body of laws, norms, principles, and institutions has developed over many decades, strengthening the legal and institutional framework aimed at protecting the environment and its many aspects. These developments in turn have inspired many local and regional efforts made at protecting the environment through the law (Sands and Peel 2018). Yet, protecting the environment is an immensely challenging task. Therefore, this section will critically examine the broader legal framework to understand how it operates in reality.

There is a developed legal and institutional framework aimed at environmental protection in Sri Lanka (Environmental Foundation Limited 2006: 11–19; Dabare 2009; Nanayakkara 2009a; Gunaratne 2016). In broad terms, this framework includes the constitution, numerous legislative enactments in the form of Acts of Parliament and ordinances, and judicial decisions.

The constitutional framework includes Articles 27 and 28 which state, *inter alia*, that the "State shall protect, preserve and improve the environment for the benefit of the community" and that it is the "duty of every person" in the country "to protect nature and conserve its riches." These principles, set out in Chapter VI, are part of the directive principles of state policy recognized under the Constitution. Also, under the 13th Amendment to the Constitution, the protection of the environment is a subject that comes within List III (Concurrent List), whereby both the central government and the provinces have concurrent jurisdiction. The protection of the environment within the provincial limits is for the respective provincial councils and is therefore listed under List I (Provincial Council List).

There are many laws aimed at protecting different aspects of the environment. Numerous ordinances were enacted during colonial times, yet the modern framework of laws and institutions is a development which began in the 1970s and 1980s (Gunaratne 2016). This was also the period during which one witnessed the significant development of international environmental law. The main law (also known as the "umbrella law") that concerns environmental protection in Sri Lanka is the National Environmental Act of 1980. In broad terms, the Act and its subsequent amendments establish the Central Environmental Authority (CEA), sets out environmental standards that need to be met as well as licensing and project approval procedures and invest the CEA with powers to enforce environmental safeguards.

There are numerous "sectoral laws" which deal with specific aspects of the environment, which have been examined in detail elsewhere (Gomez 2009). Stated briefly, a wide array of topics is covered through such laws; they range from laws aimed at protecting and conserving the forests, national heritage wilderness, plants, and animals, to laws pertaining to the protection and conservation of the soil, the use of pesticides and the protection of the marine environment. A separate set of laws exist to address concerns relating to state lands as well (Nanayakkara 2009a). And on top of these laws, there are judicial decisions which have upheld environmental law principles and the need to protect certain environmental rights. In several decisions the judiciary has upheld the principles of sustainable development, the precautionary and polluter-pays principles, the principle of inter-generational equity and the public trust doctrine (Nanayakkara 2009a; Rajepakse 2009).

One of the most celebrated judicial decisions – in which the above principles (except the public trust doctrine) were recognized – is the Supreme Court's landmark judgement in *Bulankulama v Secretary, Ministry of Industrial Development (Eppawela Case)* (Gunaratne 2000). The case concerned a joint venture between the government of Sri Lanka and Freeport MacMoran Resources Partners of the US to mine the phosphate deposit reserves in the Eppawela region. The Court, in rejecting the proposal, recognized the concept of sustainable development and the need to strike a balance between development and environmental protection. It noted, *inter alia*, that "the human development paradigm needs to be placed within the context of our finite environment as so to ensure the future sustainability of the mineral resources and of the water and soil conservation ecosystems of the Eppawala region, and of the North Central Province and Sri Lanka in general" (Nanayakkara 2009b: 162).

The courts have generally followed the sentiments expressed in the *Eppawela* case and have gone a fair distance in recognizing the importance of reading certain rights into the already existing provisions in the constitution. In broad terms, the Sri Lankan judiciary has been sensitive to environmental concerns and has, in varying degrees, sought to provide redress to the petitioners who have sought judicial intervention when environmental protection was threatened (Rajepakse 2009).

Yet, Sri Lanka confronts numerous environmental challenges. At its most basic and general level, there is the pollution of air, land, water, and the sea, from harmful toxic substances. Climate change continues to alter the weather, rainfall, and temperature patterns. The destruction and conversion of natural habitats, which results from such things as the felling of forests and the destruction of coral reefs, is occurring constantly. There is the extinction of rare species and the loss of biodiversity resulting from over-harvesting. Over-extraction of water has led to impaired water flow, while intensive farming and cultivation have led to the exhaustion of soil and land degradation. There is degradation of the built environment with the encroachment of parks and open spaces, littering of streets and residential areas and unauthorized and unplanned constructions taking place (Environmental Foundation Limited 2006: 5–6).

How does one explain the exploitation of the environment in this way? While a detailed answer to that question is not possible here, four brief observations can be made when viewing the situation through a critical legal lens.

Firstly, the supreme law of the land, the constitution, does not attach much importance to the environment and its protection. The obligations contained in Chapter VI of the constitution (i.e. Articles 27 and 28 mentioned above) are only aspirational. As Article 29 clearly states, the provisions of that chapter "do not confer or impose legal rights or obligations and are not enforceable in any court or tribunal. No question of inconsistency with such provision shall be raised in any court or tribunal." Interestingly, it is the supreme law that negates the legality of certain important obligations; even though the judges could make greater use of directive principles, as their counterparts in India have done (Divan and Rosencranz 2001: 45–46). Therefore, even though many laws exist, there are still no constitutional guarantees enabling the greater protection of the environment. This status quo needs to change.

Secondly, the very expectations we have of environmental law may be misplaced. Environmental law captures a vast body and network of laws and institutions and contains what would be called overarching/umbrella laws and myriad sectoral laws dealing with different aspects of the environment. And environmental laws and treaties are holistic, dealing with not just the environment but with various other interconnected disciplines, such as economics, human rights, science, technology, etc. (Klabbers 2017: 279). Therefore, environmental law's paradox is that it is always cutting into different other areas and fields, while also embracing them at the same time (Philippopoulos-Mihalopoulos 2011: 22). This implies that most problems which we consider to be environmental in character may not be viewed in the same way by others. An ecological setback, such as severe flooding, could be seen as an environmental problem by some, but differently by others. Governments, technical experts, and policymakers may adopt one perspective, while lawyers would tend to approach the question in an entirely different way, with each of these actors bringing different types of biases, prejudices, and interests to the table. This is a broader challenge that environmental law confronts, both globally and locally; and it is one critical factor (out of many) that partly explains why more environmental laws do not always lead, and have not led, to a lessening of environmental problems.

Thirdly, the law's success or failure, as well as its overarching potential, depends on political intervention. On the surface, there is indeed a vast canvass of laws and institutions. However, lawyers and judges cannot do much. It is, perhaps principally, a matter which needs to be tackled by governments and other political actors, who in turn are influenced by people's demands and political struggles for the greater protection of the environment. In other words, environmental protection is largely a political challenge and not always a legal one. And the call for more laws and/or better implementation of the law may not be fruitful on most occasions. Sometimes, very serious systemic changes may be required, which only the law cannot do. There are numerous political, economic, nationalist, and other factors which shape how and when the law operates, to what extent, and for whose benefit.

For example, corruption and political patronage contribute significantly to environmental degradation. As noted by a prominent environmental organization, in relation to Sri Lanka: "Widespread corruption and political patronage allow and encourage misuse of the environment, and the breaking of environmental laws" (Environmental Foundation Limited 2006: 8). The impact of political patronage has been documented by numerous environmental institutions and activists. One case in point is the damage done to the Hakgala Strict Natural Reserve (SNR). Even though the forest has been afforded the highest legal protection, it has been shown that encroachments have destroyed approximately a third of the Hakgala forest, making it a classic case of political patronage devastating one of Sri Lanka's most important and prominent watershed forests (De Mel and Sirimanne 2009: 15). Related to this is the problem concerning forest reserves, which is also a matter widely reported in the newspapers. Political and administrative approval given to carry out private projects and deforestation activity in several forest reserves continue to threaten the environment (Wickramasinghe 2022b). In some cases, the collusion of political actors and public officials ensures that those responsible for the clearance of forests and the resulting environmental degradation are not held accountable. This situation is exacerbated by the lack of foresight shown by politicians and their short-term decisions (Wickramasinghe 2022a).

Ethnic politics is another factor which plays a significant role in matters relating to the environment. The classic case in this regard is the controversy surrounding the Wilpattu forest reserve (Köpke 2021). The dominant concern relating to Wilpattu has been the alleged illegal encroachment of forest land especially by Muslim settlers. This allegation has been directed against a Muslim politician (Rishard Bathiudeen) who was a former Minister for Resettlement in Sri Lanka and is popularly alleged to have facilitated such illegal encroachment. This has been a major battle cry for some Sinhalese, with politicians and activist groups engaging in a virulent anti-Bathiudeen and anti-Muslim campaign in the name of "Save Wilpattu." However, the story is more complex than this politicized narrative, since the resettlement of the Muslim Internally Displaced Persons (IDPs), who fled the Liberation Tigers of Tamil Eelam (LTTE), was allowed through a Presidential Task Force in 2013. Such resettlement was to be done in an area that came within a forest reserve, the limits of which had been demarcated by a gazette notification issued in 2012 by the then Minister of Environment, based on flawed Global Positioning System (GPS) coordinates (Groundviews 2017). In such a situation, even judicial decisions concerning the Wilpattu saga – such as the recently decided "Wilpattu Case" (*CEJ v Anura Satharasinghe & Others, CA Writ 291/2015*) – may not result in a resolution of the inter-ethnic rivalry that has been generated.

Fourthly, it is necessary, therefore, to reflect on the role of the law in matters concerning environmental protection. A critical legal approach would not dismiss the law's relevance because the law plays the important function of resolving disputes while helping in the realization of environmental justice (Atapattu 2019). However, the law is political in that it is shaped, and given effect to, by people with different agendas and interests. The nature of the law, as well as its reach, will be determined by those who are entrusted with the tasks of applying, implementing, and enforcing the law. It follows then that the law has the potential to improve the lives of human beings, but it is never just the law: various other competing and even conflicting economic, scientific, political, rights-related values, and objectives are at play. More critically, legal decisions are almost always decisions based on numerous other values and choices, which is a complexity that even the judiciary needs to contend with. Therefore, to talk about more laws or the better implementation of the law would not take us too far. As Boyle and Redgwell (2021) have noted, if international agreements are seen to be weak it is because states want them to be weak, and redesigning them will only work if governments intend to see them work (2021, 13). This is the case with the domestic legal framework as well: "Ultimately this is a political challenge, not a legal one" (Boyle and Redgwell 2021: 13). It would be politics and political struggle, including decisions taken about economic development, that would decide how legislators think about the environment and how judges think about the disputes that come before them.

Future Research

Viewed from a critical legal perspective, there are a number of issues which need to be explored in order to better understand the challenge of environmental protection and how it can be addressed. Some of these, discussed below, require engagement with the law as well as factors which influence the making and implementation of the law.

Constitutionalizing Environmental Protection

One of the main areas that require close and urgent attention, especially from the legislators and policymakers in Sri Lanka, is the constitutionalization of environmental protection. Fundamentally, this involves the need to ensure that the Constitution recognizes, in more substantive and explicit terms, certain environmental rights. The current constitutional provisions relating to the environment exist in the form of directive principles of state policy which do not create legally binding obligations that can be enforced through the courts (even though the courts have sought to make use of the directive principles on certain occasions). There are numerous facets to the constitutionalization of environmental protection. One is the recognition of environmental human rights. This emerges from the recognition of the inter-relationship between human rights and the environment. The quality of human life is inextricably intertwined with the quality of the environment we inhabit. Human beings cannot flourish without a clean and healthy environment. In the present context of the pandemic and zoonotic diseases, such as the coronavirus, the relationship between human and the environment demands greater attention (Gunaratne 2021: 479–482).

There are several rights that a new constitution could recognize to further promote the effective protection of the environment, even though the mere recognition of such rights would not simply guarantee the realization of environmental protection. Prominent among such rights are the right to life, the right to a clean and healthy environment, the right to health, and the right to water. These rights are recognized in international law as well as in constitutional instruments in different jurisdictions. Their relevance to the protection of the environment and its many dimensions, such as the prevention of water pollution, for example, has been examined (Konasinghe and Edirisinghe 2020). And going beyond the anthropocentric approach, there would also be the need to recognize certain rights of nature by adopting an eco-centric approach. This is already happening in certain jurisdictions, such as Ecuador, Bolivia, and New Zealand, whereby constitutional and legal protections have been afforded to such rights.

Related to this project of constitutionalizing environmental protection is the topic of climate change, which also requires constitutional recognition and attention. There is today the field of "climate constitutionalism," which promotes the need to recognize strong constitutional provisions which address issues of climate change (Jaria-Manzano and Borras 2019; Ghaleigh, Setzer and Welikala 2022). It is a relatively novel field. Proposals for the reformation of the Sri Lankan constitution which consider the need to include provisions concerning climate change have been made (Ghaleigh and Welikala 2022). The proposals are for a separate chapter on climate change in the constitution, which contains a net performance standard (i.e. net zero greenhouse gas emissions by 2060), which provides Sri Lanka sufficient time for the transition into a low-carbon economy.

It is to be seen here, firstly, that the constitutional recognition of environmental human rights corrects an imbalance that exists in the present constitutional framework in Sri Lanka. To that extent, it is a most necessary legal intervention, even though the taming of global warming and addressing the negative impact of climate change on human rights is extremely challenging (Rajamani 2022). Secondly, however, it needs to be stressed that the recognition of these rights would involve a massive shift in the thinking of legislators. Decisions about giving legal recognition to socio-economic rights, including environmental rights, involve the need to give attention to questions about resource allocation and budgetary priorities. Thirdly, this also involves the need to give thought to the role of the judiciary, since the role of the courts is critical to the realization of these rights. However, whether such legal changes can take place and how they could succeed depend on various other factors which lie beyond the immediate grasp of the legal community. To reiterate what has been stated already, the solutions to environmental issues such as climate change could be ultimately political and economic in character and not legal (Adelman 2014). This is not to reject the law; it is rather about realizing the unavoidability of politics and economics.

Development, Investment, and the Environment

In researching about the environment, legal researchers will not be able to ignore the centrality of economic development. Anything to do with the environment is almost always about the economy too. How the state approaches economic development plays a defining role in seeking to understand the nature of the legal interventions required. There is, therefore, the need to grapple with tough questions about the model of economic development pursued, the problems associated with neoliberalism and crony capitalism, and the way issues of consumerism and development are perceived – and how these, in turn, shape the development and reformation of the legal framework.

There is also the related need to study and analyse the extent to which major developmental and infrastructure projects, undertaken by foreign states and investors, have an impact on the environment. Important studies have already been done on the intricate link between foreign direct investments and their impact on human rights and environmental protection (Puvimanasinghe 2007). The rapid expansion and growing influence of global superpowers, including China, would have a critical impact on environmental protection in Sri Lanka. Such concerns have been raised in relation to the development of the Colombo Port-City project (Withanage 2018; Ruwanpura, Brown and Chan 2019). The impact of transnational corporations also requires careful study, especially in a context where the demands for development are great.

In short, the need to balance competing interests – i.e. promoting foreign investments on one hand while protecting the environment and human rights on the other – is not an easy one. However, critical legal interventions cannot avoid considering the foundational role played by economic considerations.

Environmental Movements, Political Parties, and Nationalism

An area that legal researchers are reluctant to tread on concerns the role played by environmental movements, political parties, and nationalist groups in the development and implementation of policies and laws relating to environmental protection. While this is an area that figures prominently in the field of environmental politics (Carter 2007: 115–170), it has been ignored to a large extent in the study of environmental protection in Sri Lanka. Examining the role of movements, individuals and experts is a principal theme in critical legal scholarship (Bianchi 2016: 154–155).

Firstly, as for environmental movements, it is to be noted that non-state actors have played a central and defining role in the development of international environmental law (Spijkers 2021). It is non-state actors, especially in the form of non-governmental organizations (NGOs), which have often been at the forefront of popularizing the environmental harm that is brought about by state and non-state actors. Such organizations have often helped in identifying issues that require serious attention and have played a significant role as expert observers and participants in international negotiations concerning environmental law and policymaking. Therefore, a relationship has developed between the activities of NGOs and the development of international environmental law. The role of the NGOs in the South, however, has been a more marginal one. And in this regard, it has been argued that the role of such NGOs, especially in terms of promoting views and concerns about environmental protection and sustainable development in the South, should be enhanced, an enhancement which would help in bridging the North-South gap (Konasinghe 2020). A local research theme that emanates from this broader theme is the need to examine the role of local environmental movements and their impact on legal and policymaking in Sri Lanka.

Secondly, the role of political parties cannot be ignored. An examination of how political parties in Sri Lanka have approached environmental protection, the extent to which parties can be considered to have gone "green," the legal and institutional policy prescriptions made by parties and their impact require careful study. The work of political parties, such as the United National Party (UNP) in Sri Lanka, for example, would necessarily invite the need to examine the linkage between the development of environmental laws (especially in the 1970s–1990s) and open economic policies pursued during that period.

Thirdly, the global debate about the role of NGOs and activism in the development of environmental law necessitates an examination of the nature of local environmental activism. What is the political character of environmental activism in Sri Lanka? Is there a tendency for environmental activists and policymakers to belong to certain types of political and nationalist forces? To what extent do the political interests and agendas of such activists impact the development of the legal and policy framework relating to environmental protection in Sri Lanka? The politics of environmental activism and activists is, unfortunately, not a well-explored topic in Sri Lanka, even though in recent times, some useful attempts have been made by sociologists to comment on this topic (Amarasuriya 2020). As she notes, the role of individuals has been a prominent one in the different movements that sprang to action in Sri Lanka which focused on the environment, especially in the 1980s and 1990s; and many of the prominent members of these movements have often been associated with the politics of Sinhala-Buddhist nationalism (Amarasuriya 2020: 23–26).

It is interesting to note in this regard that during the past two decades, those representing majoritarian political thought in Sri Lanka have played, by a curious coincidence, a central role in matters relating to environmental protection, institutionally and politically. Of particular interest here is the role of such political figures as Udaya Gammanpila and Patali Champika Ranawaka. Both were once members of the *Jathika Hela Urumaya* (JHU) a political party based on the Sinhala-Buddhist ideology. Gammanpila, who until recently was closely associated with the governments of Presidents Mahinda Rajapaksa and Gotabaya Rajapaksa, was initially the Chairman of the Central Environmental Authority while having also held the post of Minister of Agriculture, Irrigation, Industries and Environment of the Western Provincial Council. Ranawaka, the leader of the JHU, who was also a prominent figure in the Rajapaksa regime (before falling out with the Rajapaksas in 2014), was once the Minister of Environment and Natural Resources.

What these different aspects spell for environmental protection is not an issue that can be discussed here. However, it would be useful to study more closely the link between environmental activism, nationalist politics and the environment, and the subsequent implications of that link on the development and implementation of the law relating to environmental protection.

Conclusion

Practically everything in life depends on how well the environment is preserved and protected (Klabbers 2017: 293). The law will, undoubtedly, play a role in this effort aimed at preserving and protecting the environment. However, the law is of mixed potential. More laws and regulations do not always mean that the environment is better protected. Sometimes, the existence of a large body of legal enactments, regulations, and judicial decisions might act as a smokescreen behind which environmental degradation continues unabated. Therefore, as this chapter suggests, it is necessary to remain vigilant about the role that the law can play in protecting the environment in Sri Lanka. Also importantly, it is necessary to be mindful of those aspects that do not come within the radar of traditional "legal" research in the realm of environmental protection, such as, for example, the narratives we construct about the history of environmental protection, the nature of politics that undergirds environmental activism, the relationship between environmental protection and economic development, and the factors that drive legislatures to constitutionalize environmental protection. To be deeply attentive to such issues is what a critical legal project, which goes beyond the search for yet another legal enactment or a judicial opinion, would entail.

Acknowledgements

I am extremely thankful to Piyumani Ranasinghe and Shalini Samaranayake for their research assistance, and to the reviewers of this chapter – as well as the editors, especially Kanchana N. Ruwanpura – for their helpful and encouraging comments.

References

Adelman, Sam (2014) "Human Rights and Climate Change" Legal Studies Research Paper No. 2014-4 *SSRN* (28 April). Accessed on 15/09/2022. Available at https://papers.ssrn.com/sol3/papers.cfm?abstract_id=2431628

Amarasuriya, Harini (2020) "The Politics of Environmental Movements in Sri Lanka" *Polity* 8(1 & 2): 21–28

Atapattu, Sumudu (2019) "Environmental Justice, Climate Justice and Constitutionalism: Protecting Vulnerable States and Communities" In *Research Handbook on Global Climate Constitutionalism* Jordi Jaria-Manzano and Susana Borras (eds) Cheltenham & Northampton: Edward Elgar, pp 195–215

Bianchi, Andrea (2016) *International Law Theories: An Inquiry into Different Ways of Thinking* Oxford: Oxford University Press

Boyle, Alan and Catherine Redgwell (2021) *Birnie, Boyle and Redgwell's International Law and the Environment* Oxford: Oxford University Press

Carter, Neil (2007) *The Politics of the Environment* Cambridge: Cambridge University Press

Dabare, Ravidranath (2009) *Environmental Law* Colombo: Centre for Environmental Justice

De Mel, Manishka and Nilshantha Sirimanne (2009) "Environmental Challenges and Basic Legal Principles" In *Judges & Environmental Law: A Handbook for the Sri Lankan Judiciary* Mario Gomez (ed) Colombo: Environmental Foundation Ltd, pp 9–71

Divan, Shyam and Armin Rosencranz (eds) (2001) *Environmental Law and Policy in India: Cases, Materials and Statutes* New Delhi: Oxford University Press, 2nd edition

Environmental Foundation Ltd (2006) *Your Environmental Rights and Responsibilities: A Handbook for Sri Lanka* Colombo: Sri Lanka

Gomez, Mario (ed) (2009) *Judges & Environmental Law: A Handbook for the Sri Lankan Judiciary* Colombo: Environmental Foundation Ltd. Accessed on 15/09/2022. Available at https://www.ajne.org/sites/default/files/event/2040/session-materials/judges-environmental-law-a-handbook-for-the-sri-lankan-judiciary-2009.pdf

Groundviews (2017) "Voices from Musali: The real story behind the 'Save Wilpattu' Campaign" *Groundviews* (27 April). Accessed on 15/04/2022. Available at https://groundviews.org/2017/04/27/voices-from-musali-the-real-story-behind-the-save-wilpattu-campaign/

Gunaratne, Camena (2000) "The Eppawela Phosphate Mining Project: Breaking New Ground in Natural Resources Management" *Asia Pacific Journal of Environmental Law* 5(3): 275–289

Gunaratne, Camena (2016) "Overview of the Sri Lankan Environmental Legal Framework" *Asian Judges Network on Environment*. Accessed on 15/04/2022. Available at https://www.ajne.org/sites/default/files/event/7110/session-materials/hcj-workshop-sri-lanka-legal-framework-overview-cameena-gunaratne.pdf

Gunaratne, Camena (2021) "Human Rights and Development: The Need for Indivisibility" In *Perspectives on Constitutional Reform in Sri Lanka* Hiran W. Jayewardene and Sharya Scharenguivel (eds) Colombo: International and Comparative Law Society, pp 468–489

Jaria-Manzano, Jordi and Susana Borras (eds) (2019) *Research Handbook on Global Climate Constitutionalism* Cheltenham & Northampton: Edward Elgar

Jeganathan, Pradeep (1995) "Authorizing History, Ordering Land: The Conquest of Anuradhapura" In *Unmaking the Nation: The Politics of Identity and History in Modern Sri Lanka* Qadri Ismail and Pradeep Jeganathan (eds) Colombo: Social Scientists' Association, pp 106–136

Klabbers, Jan (2017) *International Law* Cambridge: Cambridge University Press, 2nd edition

Konasinghe, Kokila (2020) "NGOs as Loudspeakers: Potential Role of NGOs in Bridging the North-South Gap in International Environmental and Sustainable Development Law Making Process" In *Sustainability and Law: General and Specific Aspects* Volker Mauerhofer, Daniela Rupo and Lara Tarquinio (eds) Switzerland: Springer, pp 355–375

Konasinghe, Kokila and Asanka Edirisinghe (2020) "Protecting Human Rights in the Light of Industrial Water Pollution: Sri Lankan Law and Obligations under International Law" *University of Colombo Review* 1(1): 60–80

Köpke, Sören (2021) "Contested Conservation, Ethnopolitics, and the State: The Case of Wilpattu Forest Complex, Sri Lanka" *Conservation and Society* 19(1): 57–67

Nanayakkara, Anandalal (2009a) "Environmental Laws, Institutions and Mechanisms: An Overview" In *Judges & Environmental Law: A Handbook for the Sri Lankan Judiciary* Mario Gomez (ed) Colombo: Environmental Foundation Ltd, pp 73–97

Nanayakkara, Rukshana (2009b) "Multilateral Environmental Agreements and the Sri Lankan Legal System" In *Judges & Environmental Law: A Handbook for the Sri Lankan Judiciary* Mario Gomez (ed) Colombo: Environmental Foundation Ltd, pp 147–170

Philippopoulos-Mihalopoulos, A. (2011) "Towards a Critical Environmental Law" In *Law and Ecology: New Environmental Foundations* A. Philippopoulos-Mihalopoulos (ed) London: Routledge, pp 18–38

Puvimanasinghe, Shyami Fernando (2007) *Foreign Investment, Human Rights and the Environment: A Perspective from South Asia on the Role of Public International Law for Development* Leiden: Martinus Nijhoff

Rajamani, Lavanya (2022) "Climate Change" In *International Human Rights Law* Daniel Moeckli, Sangeeta Shah and Sandesh Sivakumaran (eds) Oxford: Oxford University Press, pp 644–660

Rajepakse, Ruana (2009) "How Environmental Cases Come Before the Court" In *Judges & Environmental Law: A Handbook for the Sri Lankan Judiciary* Mario Gomez (ed) Colombo: Environmental Foundation Ltd, pp 99–122

Ruwanpura, Kanchana N., Benjamin Brown and Loritta Chan (2019) "(Dis)connecting Colombo: Situating the Megapolis in Postwar Sri Lanka" *The Professional Geographer* 72(1): 165–179

Sands, Philippe and Jacqueline Peel (2018) *Principles of International Environmental Law* Cambridge: Cambridge University Press, 4th edition

Singh-Ghaleigh, Navraj, Joana Setzer and Asanga Welikala (2022) "The Complexities of Comparative Climate Change" University of Edinburgh (School of Law) Research Paper Series No. 2022/06. *SSRN* (3 April). Accessed 15/04/2022. Available at https://papers.ssrn.com/sol3/papers.cfm?abstract_id=4071820

Singh-Ghaleigh, Navraj and Asanga Welikala (2022) "Need for a constitutional and statutory framework on the environment and climate change in Sri Lanka" *The Daily FT* (23 March). Accessed on 15/04/2022. Available at https://www.ft.lk/opinion/Need-for-a-constitutional-and-statutory-framework-on-the-environment-and-climate-change-in-Sri-Lanka/14-715165

Sornarajah, M. (2016–2017) "The Reception of International Law in the Domestic Law of Sri Lanka in the Context of the Global Experience" *Sri Lanka Journal of International Law* 25(3): 03–42

Spijkers, Otto (2021) "Participation of Non-State Actors and Global Civil Society in International Environmental Law-Making and Governance" In *Research Handbook on International Environmental Law* Malgosia Fitzmaurice, Marcel Brus and Panos Merkouris (eds) Cheltenham & Northampton: Edward Elgar, pp 45–61

Weeramantry, C.G. (1997) "Separate Opinion of Vice-President Weeramantry" *International Court of Justice*. Accessed on 15/04/2022. Available at https://www.icj-cij.org/public/files/case-related/92/092-19970925-JUD-01-03-EN.pdf

Weeramantry, C.G. (2004) *Universalising International Law* Leiden and Boston: Martinus Nijhoff

Wickramasinghe, Kamanthi (2022a) "When poor elephants can't fathom political thinking" *The Daily Mirror* (5 February). Accessed on 15/04/2022. Available at https://www.dailymirror.lk/news-features/When-poor-elephants-cant-fathom-political-thinking/131-205161?fbclid=IwAR3qRq-eXvRS-ftyLHZaKkCbJbH1yJWYcPcxuly61ark8qCrw4LI81cCIPE

Wickramasinghe, Kamanthi (2022b) "Looming Environmental Disasters" *Life*. Accessed on 15/04/2022. Available at https://www.life.lk/foodfactor/Looming-Environmental-Disasters/19265/1

Wimalachandra, L.K. (2007) "Legal Framework for Environmental Conservation and Sustainable Development" In *Constitutional Rights and Victims of Crime: Essays in Honour of S.S. Wijeratne* Hector S. Yapa and Rohan Sahabandu (eds) Colombo: Centre for Victims of Crime, pp 93–107

Withanage, Hemantha (2018) "Environmental Damage of the Colombo Port City Project" (26 January). Accessed on 15/04/2022. Available at http://hemanthawithanage.blogspot.com/2018/01/hemantha-withanage-executive-director.html

24
ECOLOGICAL STATES
Nature, Militarization, and Nationalism in Sri Lanka

Vivian Y. Choi

Introduction

In Sri Lanka, post-tsunami reconstruction efforts well illustrate how environmental disasters could be used as political tools to implement state-imposed programmes and policies of national reconstruction and national disaster management. This politicization and militarization of nature and the environment, however, was not necessarily new in Sri Lanka (or beyond). My chapter outlines how nature and the environment are and have been entangled in modern (post-colonial) Sri Lanka's national politics. It is not a comprehensive or exhaustive examination of Sri Lanka's national policies and practices of environmental management, nor does it trace a history of environmentalism on the island. Rather, I provide examples that illustrate how the management of nature and the environment could be instrumentalized by state-sponsored nationalist projects and management. In short, control and management of nature and ecology did not simply result in physical or material forms of state power and violence, but also created and inscribed symbolic and cultural forms of Sinhala hegemony with nature. The chapter ends with a provocation on possible future research endeavours and areas of concern for contemporary Sri Lanka's environmental and ecological politics in the era of the Anthropocene. In summary, the chapter highlights how nature is not an inert backdrop upon which Sri Lankan politics unfolds – following Sivasundaram, it is not to assume Sri Lanka's geography (in his work its "islandness") as "natural" (2013; see also Radicati 2019).

Nature and Nation

In exploring the relationship between nature and nationhood – and in particular, Sinhala Buddhist nationhood – in Sri Lanka, Tariq Jazeel (2013) shows how nature and the environment are political. Nature, often assumed to be apolitical, becomes a mode through which historical narratives and national myths are both produced and sedimented (see also Cederlöf and Sivaramakrishnan 2006). Jazeel illustrates this spatialized production of Sinhala Buddhist nationalism in the creation of national parks, such as *Ruhuna*: The park, with its archaeological ruins, becomes congruent with the Kingdom of *Ruhuna* itself, in turn inscribing into the landscape mythic Sinhala origins (and Tamil invasion). Sinhala Buddhist nationalist zeal around archaeological preservation, and attendant notions of authenticity, and heritage further reveal how nature and landscape can legitimize political, ideological, and cultural claims to nationhood and national belonging. In other words, land and nature, imbued with the past, can legitimize the present ethnonationalist politics of the Sri Lankan state (Fernando 2015; see also Wickramasinghe 2013). To be clear these efforts do not presume a monolithic or stable nationalist hegemony – on the contrary: these efforts illustrate how Sinhala and Sinhala Buddhist hegemony must be constantly maintained through state-sponsored schemes and projects (see Gunatilleke 2018 on the entrenchment of Sinhala-Buddhism in the constitution). As such, this chapter follows how both the politicization and militarization of nature may be enrolled into ongoing productions of Sinhala-Buddhist nationhood and nationalism.

State Sinhalization, Sinhalization of Nature

This section focuses on state-sponsored efforts to manage land, agriculture, and water across Sri Lanka's Dry Zone. An area regaled for its ancient irrigation system, the Dry Zone harkens to the mythical past of the idealized Sinhala peasant (Peebles 1990). Hence, the Dry Zone became a site of cultural and national authenticity and its colonization through agricultural and development schemes in an effort to resurrect Sri Lanka's ancient hydraulic civilization (Tennekoon 1988; Rambukwella 2018). These examples show how nature and the environment, then, become politicized, in turn "naturalizing" Sinhalese and Buddhist claims to the origins of Sri Lanka.

An early post-independence colonization effort of the Dry Zone came under newly elected Prime Minister D.S. Senanayake in 1949, with the Gal Oya Irrigation Scheme. While on the surface these development schemes were aimed to address poverty, agricultural production, and the generation of electricity, they were also used to galvanize Sinhala nationalist sentiments (Tennekoon 1988; Brow 1996). As Mick Moore writes, Senanayake spearheaded "infusing Sinhalese nationalism with the vision that the colonisation of the Dry Zone was a return to the heartland of the ancient irrigation civilisation of the Sinhalese" (Moore 1985: 45). The success of colonization of the Dry Zone could be seen through the changing ethnic demographics in the region. Indeed, the success of these colonization efforts was not measured in financial terms, but in social ones: "The primary purpose of the Senanayake enterprise to colonies Minneriya was social rather than economic. The returns he realized were not to be measures so much in solid rupees, but in the splendid satisfaction of having developed ... rich and fertile lands for Ceylon and her people ..." (Brohier as quoted in Rambukwella 2018). The growth of the Sinhalese population would enable the eventual creation of a separate electoral district for the Sinhalese (Manogaran 1987; Peebles 1990). Gal Oya would also become the site for the first anti-Tamil riots in 1956, after the passing of the Sinhala Only Act (Tambiah 1996).

In the late 1970s the Dry Zone once again staged the realization of state-sponsored nation-building projects. With the election of Sri Lanka's first president, J.R. Jayawardena (who also claimed that he was Sri Lanka's 193rd head of state/King of Sri Lanka) and amidst massive political and economic changes, the Accelerated Mahaweli Development Programme (AMDP) Scheme was also implemented (Tennekoon 1988; Brow 1996). Jayawardena's presidency and development agenda were not restricted to market reforms, foreign investment, and export-processing zones. Instead these progressive moves towards economic liberalization and de-welfarization by the state needed to be legitimated by the implementation of massive rural development schemes, which went hand in hand with an expansion of the state budget and the public sector (Venugopal 2018). AMDP – a $2 billion irrigation and hydroelectric power scheme and Sri Lanka's biggest-ever development project – was the most ostentatious of these measures. The project was originally launched in the 1960s to be phased over 30 years, but in 1978, Jayawardena's United National Party radically "accelerated" the project down to six years.

Serena Tennekoon's work is instrumental in highlighting the AMDP as a modernizing project, which centralized state bureaucracy and privileged science and technology that was not just "compatible with but reincarnated" ancient indigenous, Sinhala Buddhist national culture (Tennekoon 1988: 297). With each opening of a dam, the government performed elaborate Buddhist ceremonies and rituals, harkening to and reconstructing a glorified nationalist landscape of Sinhala hydraulic culture and civilization. Materially and symbolically, state-sponsored nationalist development projects were mechanisms that evoked a Sinhala past while also signifying aspirations for the future. If land and water could be imbued with Sinhala-ness, then Sinhala-Buddhism could be considered inherent and "naturally" foundational to the island. This kind of Sinhala-Buddhist primordialism fed into broader practices of the Sri Lankan state. Buddhism was consecrated in the 1972 constitution. For example, 1978 also saw the development of the Prevention of Terrorism Act (which was then ratified in 1979), a new constitution, a new political majority, the UNP. Year 1978, then, marked the beginning of a gradual expansion of the state that was not inherently Sinhalese, but, as Venugopal (2015) reiterates, became Sinhalized.[1] As such, in the following section, the militarization of nature and disasters after the tsunami further demonstrate how the expansion of the Sinhalized state – through institutionalized mechanisms, such as the National Disaster Management Act – can serve to uphold Sinhala-Buddhist national ideology.[2]

The Militarization of Nature

Militarization is a process; and in Sri Lanka, as Neloufer de Mel (2007a), borrowing from Cynthia Enloe, outlines, militarization occupies a structural position, around which ideologies of militarism are constructed and cohere, in turn legitimizing militant solutions, violence, and terror. Indeed, as anthropologist Catherine Lutz (2002) crucially points out, militarization is not simply an intensification of resources towards military purposes, but also the shaping of institutions congruous with military goals (Ruwanpura 2017; Thiranagama 2020). This section discusses how, following the tsunami, a militarized logic shaped and cohered with the development of national disaster management policies, in which natural disasters became categorized as national threats alongside terrorism.

The militarization of disaster management is a process in Sri Lanka through what I have elsewhere referred to as disaster nationalism (Choi 2015). The tsunami created political openings and opportunities for state-sponsored projects of national and social restructuring. As post-tsunami reconstruction unfolded as the war between the Liberation Tigers of Tamil Eelam (LTTE) and the Sri Lanka government heated up, this section examines the management of the tsunami and its intersection with the war and terrorism – an intersection which illustrates the militarization of nature and the naturalization of threat and terrorism. Connecting state responses of post-tsunami disaster management to previous forms of infrastructural and ecological management, such as the ADMP, for example, moves away from event-focused analyses that can attribute the impacts of the tsunami as simply an act of nature, rather than a protracted disaster that builds upon years of existing social and political conflict and violence (see De Mel and Ruwanpura 2006; Gamburd 2013; McGilvray and Gamburd 2010; Hyndman 2007; Ruwanpura 2008, 2009).

The prevailing discourse of the wreckages of the tsunami resulted in either a foreclosure or erasure of the already ongoing catastrophe of war. De Mel (2007b) tellingly recounts then-president Chandrika Bandaranaike Kumaratunge's 2005 New Year's address in which she described the tsunami as "the worst ever national disaster in living memory" (2007b: 242). That the war was simply the "context" whether ignored for political expediency or overshadowed by the acute shock of the tsunami demonstrates the naturalization of war for many Sri Lankans and, accordingly, the ideology of militarization. With militarization and war naturalized, then, perhaps it is not so curious that war-related attacks should also be included as potential, "ever-present," disaster risk, especially considering that the Disaster Management Centre falls under the purview of the Ministry of Defence (see also Choi, forthcoming).

In this section, I focus on the Sri Lankan state's turn to disaster risk management and Disaster Risk Reduction (DRR) in the aftermath of the tsunami. Influenced by the Hyogo Framework for Action (2005), which was established immediately following the tsunami at the World Conference on Disaster Reduction, a main priority was the development of national strategies and the institutionalization of disaster risk management. Following the devastation wrought by the tsunami, in May 2005, the newly formed Parliamentary Committee on Natural Disasters, tasked with assessing Sri Lanka's levels of preparedness towards disasters, created Sri Lanka's Disaster Management Act No. 13, which provides for a "framework for disaster risk management in Sri Lanka" (Sri Lanka Disaster Management Act 2005). In this risk management approach, the institutional focus is on preparedness over response-based mechanisms – to preemptively reduce potential disaster risks (what is referred to in institutional parlance as "Disaster Risk Reduction").

In the Hyogo Framework, disasters are limited to "disasters caused by hazards of natural origin and related environmental and technological hazards and risks" (2005). Sri Lanka's Disaster Management Act of 2005 definition of disasters is more expansive. It categorizes disasters as "the actual or imminent occurrence [sic] of a *natural or man-made* event, which endangers or threatens to endanger the safety or health of any person or group of persons in Sri Lanka, or which destroys or damages or threatens to destroy or damage any property" (Disaster Management Act 2005, emphasis mine). These "natural or man-made" events include floods; landslides; industrial hazards; tsunami (seismic waves); earthquakes; air hazards; fire; epidemics; explosions; *air raids; civil or internal strife*; chemical accidents; radiological emergency; oil spills; nuclear disaster; urban and forest fire; coastal erosion. Here, terrorist attacks are considered in the same category of risk as tsunamis, to be managed preemptively by the state. This conflation was also outlined by former Minister of Disaster Management and Human Rights, Mahinda Samarasinghe, in 2009, in a speech in Geneva, months after the end of the war:

> My country – Sri Lanka – has just overcome a man-made disaster of a magnitude unparalleled by any similar recent events elsewhere. We have overcome the scourge of terrorism that has beset our island nation for well over two decades …
>
> All our efforts at renewal, rebuilding and resettlement, however will be put at risk if the cause factors of the conflict and terrorism are not addressed and our President has committed himself to evolving a home grown political response to those factors.
>
> **Borrowing from DRR methodology**, our political response will reduce the risk of a renewed human-made disaster, i.e. terrorism and conflict … We do not for a moment think that Sri Lanka's national renewal will be quick or easy.
>
> *There are ever-present threats that we must, and will, guard against, including the threats of new violence and destabilization.*
>
> *(My emphasis)*

According to this institutionalized logic, disasters – both natural and human-made – remain ever possible.

As Benjamin Schnonthal notes, "configurations" of Buddhist nationalism in Sri Lanka, since at least the 1940s, have been organized and motivated by the perception that Buddhism in Sri Lanka is under threat. Tracing three different Buddhist national movements, he stresses that while the movements may seem novel, they are, in short, "new variation[s] of [this] older discursive template" (Schonthal 2016: 98). These are not inevitable nor identical movements and histories, but in Schonthal's configurations, what is emblematic of these nationalist movements – and in these governmental actions after the tsunami – are perceived threats to the territorial sovereignty and stability of the (by May 2009, victorious) Sinhala Buddhist nation. Given an extant militarized logic and long-standing nationalist concerns about the status of Buddhism in Sri Lanka, we might see in the government's national disaster management efforts an articulation of this threat as well. In this preemptive disaster risk management approach, an anxious Sinhala Buddhist nationalist state is perpetually under threat, whether by earthquake, tsunami, or terrorism.

The end of the war did not bring the end of pervasive militarization. Defence spending has steadily increased. Money spent on post-war infrastructural development and "beautification" projects in Colombo, for example, illustrates post-war anxiety and therefore the continued militarization of land and space (Amarasuriya and Spencer 2015; Ruwanpura 2017; Palipane and Peiris 2022). Colombo has never been a predominantly Sinhala Buddhist space, but a "place of minority life," dense with ethnicities (Thiranagama 2011). In 2015, after the re-election of Mahinda Rajapaksa, the Urban Development Authority was formally placed under the Ministry of Defence, led by his brother, Gotabaya. Gotabaya Rajapaksa's vision of Colombo reflects his aggressive militarism (his "short-term expediency") (ibid: S71) and his attachments to Sinhala Buddhist nationalism in conjunction with a broader historical impetus in Sri Lanka linking security to development (Kadirgamar 2013; Nagaraj 2016; Choi forthcoming). The spaces of Gotabaya's "development" projects have "relocated" Muslims where Sinhalese are the minority (Amarasuriya and Spencer 2015). In the Northern and Eastern provinces, the Sri Lankan military's forceful acquisition of land and development of militarized tourist resorts in Panama and Kankasanthurai have further exacerbated conflict-related land grievances and inequities (Ratnayake and Hapugoda 2017; see also Seoighe 2016) The end of one virulent nationalism, the LTTE, continues to strengthen and embolden Sinhalese Buddhist nationalism. Moreover, the focus on infrastructure development, as Chan, Ruwanpura and Brown (2019) point out, comes at the expense of the environment, or without proper evaluation or assessment of environmental impacts. In fact, much also remains understudied regarding the environmental impacts of war (see Dathan 2020; Bohle and Fünfgeld 2007). Sri Lanka remains a contested ecological space, and returning to Tariq Jazeel's (2013) work, its nature is, profoundly, political.[3]

The Securitization of Climate Change? Sri Lanka in the Anthropocene

In 2020 with the election of former Minister of Defense, Gotabaya Rajapakse as President of Sri Lanka, Sharika Thiranagama writes, "The civil war saw the complete militarization of government. The Sri Lankan army had always been subordinate to the president. However, now, Gotabaya Rajapaksa, as a former army man and as the president, symptomizes a collapse that has been a long time coming" (Thiranagama 2020). This collapse included ministries and institutions as well. Indeed, in 2019, under Gotabaya Rajapakse's orders, disaster management was put under the purview of the Ministry of Defense. Acknowledging that the Triforces and police already had an active role in disaster response and rehabilitation, then-Defence Secretary Major General Kamal Gunaratne, stated, "Being cognizant of this vital need, President Gotabaya Rajapaksa has made the decision to synergize all these capabilities which were under different establishments, under the Ministry of Defence to achieve efficiency and effectiveness as a cohesive outfit to face any disaster situation in future" (Prevention Web 2019). Gunaratne, on the same web page, also acknowledged Sri Lanka's vulnerability to climate change: "Climate change makes extreme weather effects more likely than ever before. The average temperature of the globe has already risen by 1°C. Heat waves, droughts, floods, and violent storms could become much more common in the decades to come, making disaster risk reduction even more urgent priority" (Ibid, unpaginated).

Since the implementation of the National Disaster Management Act, Sri Lanka has faced numerous environmental catastrophes, ranging from cyclones, landslides, flooding, and drought. Moreover, the Indian Ocean is warming faster than any other ocean basin in the world (Roxy et al 2014). This observation has recently been reaffirmed in the sixth and latest IPCC report (IPCC 2022), which also projects that rising temperatures will also bring a rise in sea levels, in addition to more volatile climates, extreme temperatures (heat mostly), and increased fluctuations in monsoon precipitation in the Indian Ocean basin. Sri Lanka is uniquely and significantly vulnerable to the rise in sea level and temperature. Human-induced climate change in the age of the Anthropocene, has the potential to severely impact agricultural livelihoods and food security in Sri Lanka (Gunaratne, Radin and Rathnasooriya 2021). As Sri Lanka confronts the social, political, and environmental dimensions of the Anthropocene, how will nature and the environment continue to be politicized?

Conclusions

Given Sri Lanka's long history of militarization and Sinhala Buddhist nationalization of nature, it is easy to see how the logic and ideology of militarization will structure the management of the looming crises of the Anthropocene. The theme of this chapter suggests that militarization has become "naturalized," especially illustrated by the institutionalized logic of the never-ending threats of disaster and now climate change. As environmental disasters and climate change risk management become increasingly streamlined into national development and infrastructural projects, the intersections of state power, nationalism, and climate change will remain salient (on securitization of climate change in Bangladesh, for example, see Cons 2018). Sri Lanka's attempts to rebuild its social, political, and economic life after the momentous and consequential events of 2022 (and has accepted an IMF programme), what might researchers of the environment remain attentive to?

Researchers might focus on Sri Lanka's agricultural recovery after the ban on imported fertilizers wreaked havoc. Given past state colonization practices, would the agricultural collapse enable land grabs or weaken farmers' positions (Ellis-Petersen 2022)? Or perhaps granular studies of infrastructures and large development projects, such as the Colombo Port City (see Radicati 2019; Ruwanpura, Brown and Chan 2019). In line with studies of the Anthropocene, scholars might take a multispecies approach as a way to understand histories of labour and capitalism and nature or discourses of neoliberalism and "habitat loss" (Oriel and Frohoff 2021; Fernando 2022; Ranawana 2022). Studies of environmental movements in Sri Lanka may offer insights into social and political possibilities (see Amarasuriya 2020; Guneratne 2008; Ranawana 2022; Yamane 2009).

In May 2021, in the midst of ongoing COVID-19 restrictions, Sri Lanka also experienced its worst maritime disaster: the MV-Xpress, a container ship carrying 1486 containers, 81 of which were classified as carrying dangerous goods, caught fire, and sunk off the port of Colombo. As toxins oozed out of the ship, an unknown amount of the 1680 tons of plastic pellets called "nurdles," also spilled into the sea, covering Sri Lanka's southern beaches in a startling layer of "plastic snow." The plastic spill is the worst in maritime history (Bourzac 2023). At the moment of writing, the impacts are still being understood, as nurdles continue to be ashore, some in pristine form, others burnt by fire and chemicals. In the months after the ship sunk, over 600 dead turtles were found beached – an ecological tragedy as most of the world's sea turtles visit the Sri Lankan coast at some point in their life cycle. The consequences of the spill are ongoing, with impacts that may not be seen for years. Though the disaster is characterized as Sri Lanka's worst maritime, it is not a local disaster by any means: The ship was owned by a Singapore-based company; the crew of 25 men came from the Philippines, China, India, and Russia; the origins of the chemicals are still under investigation; the nurdles and toxins will be moved by currents to other regions of the world. This, combined with the "existential threats" of climate change in the Indian Ocean, might urge scholars to understand what new forms of governance might look like (Ramachandran 2023). What kinds of novel social and political collaborations and experiments will be required to deal with these "insecurities?" Can environmental management be about more than "security?" What alternatives, human and non-human, can persist under these conditions (Murphy 2017; Liboiron 2021)? This, I believe, offers the possibility to re-imagine Sri Lanka's ecologies and island-space, differently (Jazeel 2007; Sivasundaram 2013).

Notes

1 Some examples of this include conservation efforts in Wilpattu, illustrating how Sinhala Buddhist nationalist framed the resettlement of Muslims in the area as "illegal deforestation," and further, how a "de-ethnicized" or depoliticized environmental movement can also inadvertently enable state action, and further, the link between securitization and environmental protection (Kopek 2021). The conflict in the Eastern province at Deegavapi, in which Buddhist nationalist claim the land and archaeological site as Buddhist, thus disenfranchising a post-tsunami housing settlement for displace Muslims (Silva and Hasbullah 2019).
2 Sri Lanka is not unique, much scholarship denotes how the management and control of nature work in service of state power and national ideologies (see Mitchell 2001; Mukerji 2009; Pritchard 2011).
3 Some other examples of nationalist claims and contestations over land and nature include conservation efforts in Wilpattu and Deegavapi. In Wilpattu, Sinhala Buddhist nationalists framed the resettlement of Muslims in the area as "illegal deforestation," and illustrating how a "de-ethnicized" or depoliticized environmental movement can also inadvertently enable state action, and further, the link between securitization and environmental protection (Kopek 2021). In addition, the conflict in the Eastern province at Deegavapi, Buddhist nationalist claimed the land and archaeological site as Buddhist, thus disenfranchising a post-tsunami housing settlement for displaced Muslims (Silva and Hasbullah 2019).

References

Amarasuriya, Harini (2020) "The Politics of Environmental Movements in Sri Lanka" *Polity* 8(1&2): 21–28

Amarasuriya, Harini and Jonathan Spencer (2015) "'With That, Discipline Will Also Come to Them': The Politics of the Urban Poor in Postwar Colombo" *Current Anthropology* 56(11): 66–75

Bohle, H.-G. and H. Fünfgeld (2007) "The Political Ecology of Violence in Eastern Sri Lanka" *Development and Change* 38: 665–687

Bourzac, Katherine (2023) "Grappling with the Biggest Marine Plastic Spill in History" *Chemical and Engineering News* 101(3)

Brow, James (1996) ***Demons and Development: The Struggle for Community in a Sri Lankan Village*** Tucson: University of Arizona Press

Cederlöf, Gunnel and K. Sivaramakrishnan (2006) ***Ecological Nationalisms: Nature, Livelihoods, and Identities in South Asia*** Seattle: University of Washington Press

Chan, Loritta, Kanchana N. Ruwanpura and Benjamin D. Brown (2019) "Environmental Neglect: Other Casualties of Post-War Infrastructure Development" *Geoforum* 105: 63–66

Choi, Vivian (forthcoming) ***Disaster Nationalism: Tsunami and Civil War in Sri Lanka*** Durham: Duke University Press

Choi, Vivian (2015) "Anticipatory States: Tsunami, War, and Insecurity in Sri Lanka" *Cultural Anthropology* 30(2): 286–309

Cons, Jason (2018) "Staging Climate Security: Resilience and Heterodystopia in the Bangladesh Borderlands" *Cultural Anthropology* 33(2): 266–294

Dathan, Jennifer (2020) "The Environmental Afterlives of Sri Lanka's Civil War" *Jamhoor* 4. Accessed on 18/09/22. Available at https://www.jamhoor.org/read/2020/11/18/the-environmental-afterlives-of-sri-lankas-civil-war

De Mel, Neloufer (2007a) *Militarizing Sri Lanka: Popular Culture, Memory and Narrative in the Armed Conflict* Delhi: Sage

De Mel, Neloufer (2007b) "Between the War and the Sea: Critical Events, Contiguities and Feminist Work in Sri Lanka" *Interventions* 9(2): 238–254

De Mel, Neloufer and Kanchana N. Ruwanpura (2006) *Gendering the Tsunami: Women's Experiences from Sri Lanka* Colombo: ICES

Disaster Management Act No. 13 (2005) Accessed on 22/09/22. Available at https://www.dmc.gov.lk/images/DM_Act_English.pdf

Ellis-Petersen, Hannah (2022) "'It Will Be Hard to Find a Farmer Left': Sri Lanka Reels from Rash Fertiliser Ban" *The Guardian* (20 April). World news. https://www.theguardian.com/world/2022/apr/20/sri-lanka-fertiliser-ban-president-rajapaksa-farmers-harvests-collapse

Fernando, Jude (2015) "Heritage and Nationalism: A Bane of Sri Lanka" *Colombo Telegraph* (30 March). Accessed on 25/04/22. Available at https://www.colombotelegraph.com/index.php/heritage-nationalism-a-bane-of-sri-lanka/

Fernando, Tamara (2022) "Seeing Like the Sea: A Multispecies History of the Ceylon Pearl Fishery 1800–1925" *Past and Present* 254(1): 127–160

Gamburd, Michele (2013) *The Golden Wave: Culture and Politics after Sri Lanka's Tsunami Disaster* Bloomington: University of Indiana Press

Goreau-Ponceaud, Anthony (2018) "Conflict and Environment in Sri Lanka: A Complex Nexus" In *Armed Conflict and Environment: From World War II to Contemporary Asymmetric Warfare* Detlef Brisen (ed) Baden and Baden: Nomos Verlagsgesellschaft mbH & Co. KG

Gunatilleke, Gehan (2018) "The Constitutional Practice of Ethno-Religious Violence in Sri Lanka" *Asian Journal of Comparative Law* 13: 359–387.

Gunaratne, M.S., R.B. Radin Firdaus and S.I. Rathnasooriya (2021) "Climate Change and Food Security in Sri Lanka: Towards Food Sovereignty" *Humanities and Social Science Communications* 8(229): 1–14

Guneratne, Arjun (2008) "The Cosmopolitanism of Environmental Activists in Sri Lanka" *Nature and Culture* 3(1): 98–114

Hyndman, Jennifer (2007) "The Securitization of Fear in Post-Tsunami Sri Lanka" *Annals of the Association of American Geographers* 97(2): 361–372

IPCC (2022) *Climate Change 2022: Impacts, Adaptation, and Vulnerability*. Contribution of Working Group II to the Sixth Assessment Report of the Intergovernmental Panel on Climate Change H.-O. Pörtner, D.C. Roberts, M. Tignor, E.S. Poloczanska, K. Mintenbeck, A. Alegría, M. Craig, S. Langsdorf, S. Löschke, V. Möller, A. Okem, B. Rama (eds) (in press) Cambridge: Cambridge University Press

Jazeel, Tariq (2007) "Reading the Geography of Sri Lankan Island-ness: Colonial Repetitions, Postcolonial Possibilities" *Contemporary South Asia* 17(4): 399–414

Jazeel, Tariq (2013) *Sacred Modernity: Nature, Environment and the Postcolonial Geographies of Sri Lankan Nationhood* Liverpool: Liverpool University Press.

Kadirgamar, Ahilan (2013) "The Question of Militarisation in Post-War Sri Lanka" *Economic and Political Weekly* 48(7): 42–46

Kopek, Sören (2021) "Contested Conservation, Ethnopolitics, and the State: The Case of Wilpattu Forest Complex, Sri Lanka" *Conservation and Society* 19(1): 57–67

Liboiron, Max (2021) *Pollution Is Colonialism* Durham: Duke University Press

Lutz, Catherine (2002) "Making War at Home in the United States: Militarization and the Current Crisis" *American Anthropologist* 104(3): 723–735

Manogaran, Chelvadurai (1987) *Ethnic Conflict and Reconciliation in Sri Lanka* Manoa: University of Hawaii Press

McGilvray and Gamburd, eds. (2010) *Tsunami Recovery in Sri Lanka: Ethnic and Regional Dimensions*. London: Routledge.

Mitchell, Timothy (2001) *The Rule of Experts: Egypt, Techno-Politics, Modernity* Berkeley: University of California Press

Moore, Mick (1985) *The State and Peasant Politics in Sri Lanka* Cambridge: Cambridge University Press

Mukerji, Chandra (2009) *Impossible Engineering: Technology and Territoriality on the Canal du Midi* Princeton: Princeton University Press

Murphy, Michelle (2017) "Alterlife and Decolonial Chemical Relations" *Cultural Anthropology* 32(4): 494–503

Nagaraj, Vijay Kumar (2016) "From Smokestacks to Luxury Condos: The Housing Rights Struggle of the Millworkers of Mayura Place, Colombo" *Contemporary South Asia* 24(4): 429–443

Oriel, Elizabeth and Toni Frohoff (2021) "Affective Ecologies and Multispecies Social Contracts amidst Humans, Elephants, and a Landscape in Sri Lanka." Conference paper: *Composing Worlds with Elephants: Interdisciplinary Dialogues*

Palipane, Kelum and Anoma Peiris (2022) "Reclaiming Neighborhoods through Informal Temporalities: Pettah, Sri Lanka" In *Neighbourhoods and Neighbourliness in Urban South Asia: An Introductory Outloo* Sadan Jha and Dev Nath Pathak (eds) New York: Routledge, pp 56–77

Peebles, Patrick (1990) "Colonization and Ethnic Conflict in the Dry Zone of Sri Lanka" *The Journal of Asian Studies* 49(1): 30–55

Prevention Web. December (2019) Accessed on 22/09/22. Available at https://www.preventionweb.net/news/sri-lanka-bringing-disaster-management-under-defence-ministrys-purview-forms-quick-disaster

Pritchard, Sara (2011) *Confluence: The Nature of Technology and the Remaking of the Rhone* Cambridge: Harvard University Press

Radicati, Alessandra (2019) "Island Journeys: Fisher Itineraries and National Imaginaries in Colombo" *Contemporary South Asia* 27(3): 330–341

Ramachandran, Sudha (2023) "Nilanthi Samaranayake on Indian Ocean Security Dynamics." Accessed on 17/04/2023. Available at https://thediplomat.com/2023/01/nilanthi-samaranayake-on-indian-ocean-security-dynamics/

Rambukwella, Harshana (2018) *Politics and Poetics of Authenticity: A Cultural Genealogy of Sinhala Nationalism* London: UCL Press

Ranawana, Anupama (2022) "Rage against the Port City: Southern Theologies Mobilizing for Climate Justice" *Politics* 43(2): 236–249

Ratnayake, I. and M. Hapugoda (2017) "Land and Tourism in Post-war Sri Lanka: A Critique on the Political Negligence in Tourism" In *Balancing Development and Sustainability in Tourism Destination* A. Saufi, I. Andilolo, N. Othman and A. Lew (eds) Singapore: Springer, pp 221–231

Roxy, M., K. Ritika, P. Terray and S. Masson (2014) "The Curious Case of Indian Ocean Warming" *Journal of Climate* 27(22): 8501–8509

Ruwanpura, Kanchana N. (2008) "Temporality of Disasters: The Politics of Women's Livelihoods 'after' the 2004 Tsunami in Sri Lanka" *Singapore Journal of Tropical Geography* 29: 325–349

Ruwanpura, Kanchana N. (2009) "Putting Houses in Place: Rebuilding Communities in Post-Tsunami Sri Lanka" *Disasters* 33(3): 436–456

Ruwanpura, Kanchana N. (2017) "Militarized Capitalism? The Apparel Industry's Role in Scripting a Post-war National Identity in Sri Lanka" *Antipode* 50(2): 425–446

Ruwanpura, Kanchana N., Benjamin Brown and Loritta Chan (2019) "(Dis)connecting Colombo: Situating the Megapolis in Postwar Sri Lanka" *The Professional Geographer* 72(1): 165–179

Schonthal, Benjamin (2016) "Four Configurations of Buddhist Nationalism in Modern Sri Lanka" In *Buddhist Extremists and Muslim Minorities: Religious Conflict in Contemporary South Asia* John Holt (ed) Oxford: Oxford University Press, pp 97–118

Seoighe, Rachel (2016) "Inscribing the Victor's Land: Nationalistic Authorship in Sri Lanka's Post-war Northeast" *Conflict, Security and Development* 16(5): 443–471

Silva, K.T. and S.H. Hasbullah (2019) "Sacred Sites, Humanitarian Assistance and the Politics of Land Grabbing in Eastern Sri Lanka: The Case of Deegavapi" *Journal of Sociology* 1(1): 62–86

Sivasundaram, Sujit (2013) *Islanded: Britain, Sri Lanka, and the Bounds of an Indian Ocean Colony* Chicago: University of Chicago Press

Tambiah, Stanley (1996) *Levelling Crowds: Ethnonationalist Conflicts and Collective Violence in South Asia* Berkeley: University of California Press

Tennekoon, Serena (1988) "Rituals of Development: The Accelerated Mahaweli Development Program of Sri Lanka" *American Ethnologist* 15(2): 294–310

Thiranagama, Sharika (2011) *In My Mother's House: Civil War in Sri Lanka* Philadelphia: University of Pennsylvania Press

Thiranagama, Sharika (2020) "Figurations of Menace" **SSRC The Immanent Frame**. Accessed on 17/04/2023. Available at https://tif.ssrc.org/2020/04/01/figurations-of-menace/

UNISDR (2005) "Hyogo Framework for Action 2005–2015: Building the Resilience of Nations and Communities to Disasters." International Strategy for Disaster Reduction. Accessed on 22/09/22. Available at https://www.unisdr.org/2005/wcdr/intergover/official-doc/L-docs/Hyogo-framework-for-action-english.pdf

Venugopal, Rajesh (2015) "Democracy, Development and the Executive Presidency in Sri Lanka" *Third World Quarterly* 36(4): 670–690

Venugopal, Rajesh (2018) *Nationalism, Development and Ethnic Conflict in Sri Lanka* Cambridge: Cambridge University Press

Wickramasinghe, Nira (2013) "Producing the Present: History as Heritage in Post-War Patriotic Sri Lanka" *Economic and Political Weekly* 48(43): 91–100

Wijayadasa, K.H.J. and W.D. Ailapperuma (1986) "Survey of Environmental Legislation and Institutions in the SACEP Countries: Sri Lanka" Central Environmental Authority of the Ministry of Local Government Housing and Construction.

Yamane, Akiko (2009) "Climate Change and Hazardscape of Sri Lanka" *Environment and Planning A: Economy and Space* 41(10): 2396–2416

25
SRI LANKA'S ENVIRONMENTAL HISTORY

Sujit Sivasundaram

Introduction

Sri Lanka is a biodiverse island that over the centuries has attracted outsiders and invaders to its shores. One draw among others is the island's species richness and distinct natural zones. It is popularly said that the whole world can be found within it. Yet the global environmental emergency, including the climate crisis but also extinctions, famines, floods and other unprecedented changes, and the age of the so-called 'Anthropocene', present new challenges to Sri Lanka, its public and its scholars. In this context, it is vital to pay serious attention to the physical terrain of the island, which itself has been so changeable, with deforestation, plantation, soil erosion, tourism and infrastructural intervention.

The physical environment of Sri Lanka includes its shores and seas, its air and atmosphere and also what lies beneath the ground. Additionally, it is important to take the many creatures that inhabit Sri Lanka's various habitats, from molluscs to elephants and from snakes to pangolins, into view. Appreciating the ecological richness of the island while contending with the unmaking of this complex of life forms will allow scholars to return to key concerns around labour, ethnicity, gender, state-making and empire from the vantage point of the environment. This will provide one critical route forward, in the decades to come, for research in the humanities and the social sciences specifically in Sri Lankan studies. In this essay, at the invitation of the editors, I bring together my work from across separate projects and publications, to consider what an environmentally attentive strand of Sri Lankan studies might look like.[1]

The first section considers how a variety of sources – that may be classed as colonial, indigenous, classical and modern – represented the environment of the island. I follow an established commitment to avoiding a reification of any of these categories (Sivasundaram 2010). In other words, this essay sees the colonial as imbued with the indigenous and the indigenous as reactive to and responsive to the colonial. They cannot be clinically separated.

There are long environmental legacies in Sri Lankan history, so a case for longue dureé overviews is easily made. The coverage moves for this reason to our present, including the pandemic as also infrastructural intervention. The 'source base' for a study of environmental history cannot be primarily textual; it needs to be visual, physical and embodied in various ways, or else a narrow conception of environmental history will ensue. For this reason, the paper brings maps, art, ballads, material collections and the press together.

Long Narrations of the Paradisiacal Island

Outsiders' maps of the island begin with a fascination with its fabled environment; in tracing these renditions it becomes possible to see cartographers struggling to represent the island's nature and character in two-dimensional form. The gigantically proportioned representation in Claudius Ptolemy's *Geography*, where the island occupies approximately 12 times its current size, is perhaps the best example.[2] In Sebastian Münster's Latin translation of Ptolemy from 1540, this map is marked with mountains, rivers and cities, and the equator is shown running through the island. Alongside the map appears a ferocious tusked elephant as ornamentation. Its angry eyes and serpentine trunk immediately arrest the reader's attention. Ludovico di Varthema who visited Lanka is then quoted as saying the island 'exports elephants that are larger and nobler than those found elsewhere' (Brohier 1951: 22). Taprobane becomes known for its anomalous natural history. The description continues: 'Its yield of the long pepper is likewise richer, indeed wonderful in its abundance' (ibid: 22). The map and the elephant work together to produce the idea of a land which is set apart by its natural curiosities.

This rendering of the 'fabulous island' set the framework for outsiders' accounts of Sri Lanka for several centuries. This is partly because of the impact of classical knowledge on early modern imperialists. Classical topographies were actively used by Portuguese, Dutch and British travellers from the late 15th to the 19th century. Diogo do Couto, the Portuguese historian, for instance, has a section entitled, 'On the various opinions that have existed amongst geographers as to what was the Tapbrobana of Ptolemy: and of the reasons we give for it being the island of Ceilao' (Ferguson 1908: 88). Do Couto provided his readers with an extended commentary drawing on Pliny, Onesicritus and Eratosthenes among others (ibid). The Dutch writer, François Valentijn, followed suit with a similar summary (Arasaratnam 1978: 90). The British period saw the continuation of this bibliographic tradition. For instance, the British chaplain, James Cordiner (1807: 2), notes that the island was 'first discovered' by Onesicritus. He continued: 'It is singular that Pomponius Mela, who wrote in the reign of Claudius, should express a doubt whether Taprobane was an island, or the beginning of a new world, as it was not known to have been circumnavigated'.

Yet the idea of the island as naturally endowed unlike any other did not simply come out of the repetition of a tradition of European scholarship over generations. It is important to note that islanders also pontificated on the nature of the island, its place in the world and its character as a cartographic object. Palm-leaf texts across centuries pay plentiful attention to nature: specific creatures and flora appear in such texts, for instance as sources of cure or harm. Nature also plays a key role in the mural art of the island (Sivasundaram 2013). Simultaneous with the advent of the Portuguese, there was an increased interest in boundaries and this became linked to the use of palm-leaf texts to record the limits of provinces and villages. One set of sources of this kind is the *kadaim-kavi*, literally boundary ballads. In the *kadaim-kavi* there are references, for instance, to a rock from which a king watched a battle; a cave which sheltered a sacred relic; and a mountain which was full of incense. Drawing on the work of Abeyawardana (1999), it is possible to see how some *kadaim kavi* fit into a popular peasant culture of entertainment, by providing riddles that need to be solved by listeners in order to find the way or to set a boundary. The *kadaim-kavi* which describes the boundary of Paranakuru Korale takes this form (ibid: 220):

> Reptiles and snakes gathered in a cloth bag,
> Bloody but sumptuous food kept atop a rock,
> Sweet and tasty betel leaves placed below the rock,
> And old elephants have added their rut to the heap.

This riddle is solved by the realisation that each line contains a pun. For instance, in line two, food (bata) with blood (le) upon the rock (gala) indicates the rock named Batalegala. And so the reply is given as follows:

Friend! I reckon that what you are saying is that,
From Nayiyankada is a difficult climb to Batalegala,
But, there is much fun to sport on the Rahala rock,
Is not the Parana kuruva amidst these three?

This means that where printed texts and two-dimensional representations were used by outsiders, islanders deployed rich and ritualised oral traditions to navigate their way. In their case, knowledge of nature was also tied to notions of piety and good rule, especially by kings as I have argued elsewhere (Sivasundaram 2013). Such knowledge was embodied and open to exchange and dialogue.

Planters, Botanists and an Assault on the Land

There is a rich literature on the plantation system of the island and how it marked an ecological watershed, giving rise to streams of coerced indentured labour.[3] These workers were marginalised and excluded from the makings of the modern Sri Lankan nation. They were often dehumanised, naturalised or made into a resource in colonial schemes of labour. The archive from highland plantations reflects a colonial discourse about 'taming the jungle' and converting it to ordered carpets of crops. It is synchronous with an ideology of disciplining labouring bodies and romanticising machines. All of this constituted a picturesque and 'improved' environment, which was profitable for capitalist empire. Additionally, this transformation was about creating an equivalence between the highlands and the temperate zones of Britain; it was about the creation of a little England. The plantation was tied to a way of life that created inextricable links between humans and environments. From diet to the organisation of the home around ideas of health and on to the articulation of colonial masculinity around hunting, Britishness was reproduced in the interior of the island via the figure of the planter and the planter's bungalow with its orderly gardens.

New interpretations are moving beyond this established narrative to the experiences of workers, and indentured women in particular, and how they sought to create modes of solidarity in such a terraformed space (Jegathesan 2019). There has also been an emphasis on the modes of biopolitical resistance of indentured workers (Duncan 2007). If so, it is also possible to emphasise the failures of this programme of ecological change. For despite the rhetoric of the enhancement of nature, through the introduction of an industrial programme of plantation, in fact the record of the island's plantation is not necessarily triumphal. Turning to another visual medium, photographs of the plantations from the 19th century can oftentimes display the impact of disease and disruption. This is especially the case since photography expanded as a craft just as the coffee leaf disease, *Hemileia vastatrix*, struck the island, first appearing in 1869. This disease arrived in the island through imperial channels, an indicator once again of how supposed 'improvement' could give rise to its diametric opposite in practice. There are various possible causes for the origin of this disease, from Liberian coffee plants imported into the island to colonial troop movements bringing the fungus to Lanka (McCook 2019). As coffee planters went bankrupt, tea eventually took off in the aftermath of this catastrophe. The overcoming of the imperial project by nature and a new assault on nature by imperial planters is one way to read the end of the coffee story in a photograph from the 1880s, 'Cleared land being planted out with tea'.[4]

Thinking more widely with the art of the era, one important departure point is the work of Marianne North, naturalist and lone woman traveller who came to Sri Lanka in 1876–1877. She presents a different eye on the island's nature from that of the male planter's perspective of improving the highlands or the broader programme of ecological transformation and reproduction which linked humans, nature and machines. In North's oeuvre, nature is exuberant, multi-coloured, textured and sexualised. She does not present the plants as specimens for naming, but pictures them in a rich landscape and sometimes set against Lankan people. Note, for instance, 'Ceylon Pitcher Plant and Butterflies'.[5] Supposed accuracy is less important than the feel of the island. In her recollections of the island, after arriving in Galle, she (North 1892: 302) recounts:

> I screamed with delight at the sight of a bright green chameleon with a long tail and scarlet comb which ran over the rocks near. My driver made a noose out of a palm-leaf and caught it for me, but the creature's scarlet comb changed to green, and he wriggled so much that I let him go again.

Her art also presents an opposite perspective to colonial photography from the plantation complex where women, for instance, tea-pluckers, were sexualised as objects of desire, and where workers and nature melded into one. Nature's powerful workings come out more strongly in North's genre of art.

Science, Context and Failure

Behind this colonial invasion, which was often highly imaginative in its power, is a more complex story of Lankan natural knowledge. Colonial scientific knowledge, which was vital to schemes of plantation, did not operate in a tabula rasa. In this section, I locate colonial institutions within an environmental context and also a Lankan intellectual framework.

As I have noted elsewhere, the key botanical garden, the Peradeniya Gardens, outside Kandy, which Marianne North also visited and painted, was built on a historic site, part of which belonged to the *Dalada Maligawa*, the temple of Buddha's tooth relic in the capital of Kandy, and a part of which belonged to another shrine (Sivasundaram 2013). Alexander Moon, the supposed founder of the Peradeniya Gardens, wrote: 'I am of the opinion that the site of the late Kandyan King's Garden at Peradenia is better adapted than any other place for the proposed Botanic Establishment' (ibid: 183). This garden served as a nursery for raising coffee, cocoa and other valuable plants. In one theoretical conception, Enlightenment knowledge is envisaged as a centre acting at a distance (Latour 2007). In this view, Kew Gardens exerts influence over Peradeniya. However, this argument requires substantial reworking. Peradeniya was less an outpost of Kew than an imperial expansion of a pre-existent garden.

Moving to the later 19th century, the inauguration of the Colombo Museum is a good instance of how various sites of science operated within a Lankan landscape. The formation of the Royal Asiatic Society's Ceylon Branch in 1846 had natural history within its vision. For instance, Justice Stark, who addressed the society soon after its formation, noted that everything about Ceylon, from the moral to the natural, came under its purview. The study of nature and the study of people, language and culture were intertwined; orientalism and natural science sat together as related enterprises:

> in moral objects and moral relations, as in the natural, the lofty and the lowly, the rugged, the fascinating and the tame, if they but tell of Ceylon, and hold with the continent and the world, they are all ours, they belong to the Asiatic Society of Ceylon ...
>
> *(Stark 1846: 9)*

It is from this perspective of the inter-relation of disciplines that natural history continued to play a key role in the Colombo Museum, alongside archaeology. The Museum was founded by Governor William Gregory, opening in 1877. The collection of the Royal Asiatic Society was transferred into the new museum. Gregory himself patronised natural historical illustration, bringing together a sequence of watercolours showing the butterflies of the island (McEvansoneya 2017). The museum became a platform from which to view the environment of the island and how it could be utilised. As one guidebook noted, it afforded the visitor 'an extremely interesting opportunity of judging of the character of the natural and manufactured products of the island' (Guide to Colombo 1877: 12). An astonishing 99,490 people visited it in its first year, though numbers declined later. Natural specimens within its walls referenced particular geographical areas of the island; for instance, in the lengthy catalogue on snakes, there was this reference:

17. HAPLOCERCUS CEYLONENSIS, *Günther*

Gthr. Colubr. Snakes, 1858, p. 15. Rept. Brit. Ind., p. 204

A very common snake in the hill districts, at times assuming a dull red colour, when it is known to up-country residents as the 'red-polonga.' It is, however, quite harmless. Observations on the time and cause of this curious change of colour would be very interesting.

(Haly 1886: 8)

Like with Marianne North's art, here too there is attention to changing colours, but the approach is to pin the specimens down within the existent bibliography of snake knowledge and also to locate it within the island. Yet, if there is truth in such an interpretation, one needs to think again. A recourse to islanders' traditions is evidenced in the use of the name 'polanga'. Digging deeper, it is clear that this programme of transporting, preserving and displaying the island's environment within a sterile museological context was not always smooth or successful; the view of a museum, for instance in museum and cultural studies, as a rigid encyclopaedia on the island's environment, should be avoided.

Note for instance the report from *The Ceylon Observer* on what happened with fish specimens from Anuradhapura in 1914, due to be transplanted to Labugama Reservoir in what was evidently a museum-sponsored natural history experiment (Ceylon Observer 1915). A representative of the museum travelled to Anuradhapura with a taxidermist named H.F. Fernando. They caught fish from the tanks in the region. These fish were kept 'in a large barrel and the water was changed almost daily to ensure a good supply of oxygen to the fish'. However, as the fish were transported by train they were jolted and there was a 'high death rate' among the larger fish: '135 lulas, 12 in. to 15 in. long, and 40 carp were found dead'. Plans of improvement met defeat once again. Indeed, within the museum, in this era, there were routine comments on the poor state of preservation and display of natural history.

In the yard of the Colombo Museum, there was also a collection of live animals. The *Ceylon Observer* of 1904 noted that the 'most difficult animals to rear are insectivorous creatures, such as the pangolin or scaly ant-eater …'. Like with other creatures who faced the colonial onslaught, the challenge of the chase fed into a keenness to tame the pangolin. The names of the museum's donors of live specimens of the pangolin were acknowledged in the press in the early 20th century (Ceylon Observer 1903, 1905a–c). Tracking the status of the pangolin in a more animal-centred method is a way of developing the claim that colonial natural manipulation had defined limits.

The way in which the pangolin rolled up into a ball to evade human contact was a continuing theme of its representation. However, James Emerson Tennent, who wrote much on the natural history of the island, pronounced that one of his pangolins was 'gentle and affectionate' (Emerson 1861: 46). Elsewhere, the complaint of pangolins' disinterest reappeared: a 1905 article in the *Ceylon Observer* noted how pangolins did not 'play' (Ceylon Observer 1905d). Slightly earlier, an 1899 correspondent to the same newspaper asked urgently: 'Is it possible to skin the Ceylon Armadillo (Sinhalese *Kabaleewa)*, and is there a specimen of one in the Colombo Museum?' (Ceylon Observer 1899).

The Human and the Animal

Thinking with the Lankan pangolin's disinterest and aversion to human contact is vital as a way of further deepening an environmentally aware historical and social scientific method. In animal studies of Asia, it is increasingly necessary to scrutinise the boundary between the human and the non-human animal, to show how human schemes, ideas and processes rely on the management and organisation of this boundary and also on how other animals respond to such programmes (De Silva and Srinivasan 2019). Before turning back to the pangolin, the obvious subject through which to reflect on animal studies of the island is the elephant.

I have documented how Lankan elephants fed into the colonial structures of the British Raj in India (Sivasundaram 2005). This earlier work emphasised how the East India Company relied on knowledge of the elephant for diplomacy, war and logistics: this included, how to catch an elephant, how to tame it, how to breed it and how to make it work. This knowledge arose partly from the way Britons tapped into prior practices of trading and owning elephants in South Asia, and was linked with the idea that Lanka possessed superior elephants, one that goes all the way back to Ptolemy once more. Modern state-making, both colonial and postcolonial, and their modes of hunting, agriculture and deforestation, have directed extraordinary violence against elephants in Sri Lanka. And this has occurred despite the evidence for how South Asia has been the location for persistent traditions of humanising and anthropomorphising elephants. Indeed the elephant was associated with regal status in Lanka's past.

The colonial fascination with the elephant, however, was often with death, noosing and capture. The subject of the elephant kraal on the island generated a large number of panoramic images of the landscape. Tennent (1876) published a book on Ceylon's elephants, depicting a section of the elephant's head as a means of determining how to fatally shoot an elephant (Lorimer and Whatmore 2009). Yet, elephants have withstood this onslaught and their numbers have recovered from exponential killing on the island in the 19th century, though they are in danger once again. Their agency surfaces in the stories which circulate in the present of wild elephants running 'rampage' through fields which were once their habitat or in the viral images of elephants rummaging through garbage close to human settlements. These contemporary contexts bring us directly to the climate emergency since the category includes future prospects for animals. The pandemic's shadow also haunts this essay.

It was while we were within the pandemic, that my work on Lanka's environmental history took a more decidedly animal-centred approach (Sivasundaram 2020). It also moved from the charismatic elephant, part of a class of creatures which are so often the entry point for animal studies to the evasive pangolin, which was suspected to be an intermediate host for Covid-19, linking bats to humans in the transmission change of the virus. If pangolins were collected by naturalists in Lanka, what is interesting is that prior to colonial structures, Väddā or Wanniyalaeto people also had a tradition of engaging with this creature. Wanniyalaeto men smoked pangolins out of their holes; the creature was an important source of protein, alongside, for instance, bee grubs, terrapins, tortoise, bandicoot rats, porcupine, giant squirrel, hare, jungle fowl, mongoose and freshwater fish and eels (see Chandraratne 2016; Roberts et al 2018).[6] In the early 20th century it was noted that Wanniyalaeto used sharpened sticks to dig pangolins out from their burrows (Parker 1909).

These indigenous peoples were of intense interest to anthropologists, including Charles Seligman (1873–1940). Seligman was chair of ethnology at the London School of Economics and together with his wife, Brenda Zara Seligman (1883–1965), wrote *The Veddas* (1911) about Wanniyalaeto (Seligman and Seligman 1911).

According to Seligman and Seligman (1911), this indigenous community called the pangolin 'bagusa', 'eya' and 'kabelelewa'. The anthropologists noted that the second of these names overlapped with the word for spiny porcupine and that the last was derived from 'shell' (ibid: 443–444). A 1924 Sinhala–English dictionary also gave the pangolin four distinct names: kaballavā, mulkodhu, valdaranayā and æyā denoting how the island's inhabitants were struggling with the creatures' various features in finding a name (Perera and Karawita 2020; Carter 1924). One possibility is that the main name in Sinhala for pangolin, kaballavā combines two words, kabal for skull and æyā for porcupine.[7] The rich traditions that are attached to this creature are also evidenced in Wanniyalaeto oral traditions.

The two extracts below are from a collection of poems which were brought together by Gwladys Hughes Simon, who spent two years in newly independent Sri Lanka between 1951 and 1953. With the support of the US State Department, Hughes Simon worked with women on the island and with Ceylon's Department of Agriculture. The mother of her cook, K.R. Ratnayake, was one source for her riddles; another source was her agricultural students and one other was Mr S.A. Wijayatilake, a principal of a Buddhist school in Kandy.

The first is said to be a Wanniyalaeto lullaby:
Rocked little one,
Crying little one;
Get to sleep little one.

Roasted little one,
Pengolin, little one!
Sleep little one
        (Simon 1955: 261–262)

The second is an exchange between a 'husband' and a 'wife' who are Wanniyalaeto:

The wife asks:
Tell me the name of the little tooth-armed one in the great *Ma-wili ganga*
  [the main river of Sri Lanka];
Tell me the name of the little horn-armed one in the great *Ma-wili ganga;*
Tell me the name of the little one that breaks roots on the red earth mound;
Tell me the name of the little one that overturns stones on the red earth mound.

The husband replies:
The little tooth-armed one in the great *Ma-wili gaga*
Is the little white shark, as was said, say wife;
The little horn-armed one in the great *Ma-wili ganga*
Is the little white catfish, as was said, say wife;
The little one that breaks roots on the red earth mound
The little white pengolin, say its name is, wife;
The little one that overturns stones on the red earth mound
The little wild pig, say its name is, wife
        (Simon 1955: 264–265)

It is worth adding that pangolins feature in other Sinhala proverbs too.[8] These riddles and poems are presented as comic and as indicative of the simplicity of the 'Ceylonese' and in particular the indigenous community of the Wanniyalaeto. There are undoubted biases in the renditions above, including the casting of 'wife' and 'husband' within European norms of gender. Yet it is important to stress that to identify a pangolin with human progeny is a fundamental form of recognition, especially in a community that reveres ancestors. Meanwhile, the cyclicality of rocking and roasting which is part of this chant allows alternative emotions connected to nurture and ingestion to become aligned.

These oral traditions and Wanniyalaeto engagement with the pangolin provide another historical route to engage with nature today; the Wanniyalaeto, like other indigenous peoples in the global South, provide a different pathway through the time of the so-called Anthropocene. Indigenous peoples and their knowledge are now being turned to for ideas and inspiration on how to face the climate emergency and to reanimate our relationship with nature (Chakrabarty 2021; Ghosh 2021; and in this volume, De Zoysa-Siriwardena, Hettiarachchi, Choi and Theiventhran). For arguably, it was from the legacies of imperial science that we arrived at the possibility that pangolins are now the most trafficked mammals on the planet. This last fact is one possible context for a changed wildlife frontier which could cause a global pandemic. If so, we need to return to people like the Wanniyalaeto to learn other relations between humans and animals and to contemplate a more animate and vitalist complex of life that is not human-centred in its utilitarian or classificatory engagement with nature. This means that it is necessary to think like a pangolin too.

Conclusions

This has been a series of dives into the beautiful ecology of the island of Lanka. It is no wonder indeed that naturalists, cartographers and collectors, especially those who were colonial, struggled to name, tame and subjugate the environment of this island (see also Fernando 2022). It is for this reason that they cast it as anomalous and fabulous. What follows from such an insight is the need to dig beneath their voluminous writing, art and narration of the island, to come to the signs of nature. These signs were more evident in traces like those of the Wanniyalaeto and Marianne North, partly because of their indirect placement with respect to structures of power and political expansion. This is not to purify or romanticise any specific engagements with nature on the island, indigenous or colonial, but to take seriously the diversity of natural knowledge and encounters in Lanka.

It is tempting to think that science is the only answer to the crises of the present. If we need to understand a mollusc should we not turn to a scientific article for classificatory information? It is necessary instead to appreciate ways of being with nature which are not about mastery, control and surveillance. It is necessary to cross the human/non-human divide in new ways if we are to live sustainably. Perspectives from the borders of science and from beyond science, from Wanniyalaeto and North for instance, are especially valuable for this. Sri Lanka, given its cultural traditions and natural riches, seems an especially good place from which to mount such a project of reimagining how humans might live in nature while using history for direction and understanding. Indeed, island societies, particularly those prone to sea-level rise, are seen by scholars in other fields to be good places from which to consider human prospects in the climate emergency.[9]

On reading this piece, an emerging scholar in Sri Lankan studies made the valid point that if it is to be possible to move forward in environmental studies of the island, it is the case that we should not limit ourselves to plantations and parks.[10] While work on plantations and parks in crucial, it is imperative now to write about the seas and shores off Lanka and even to find environmental histories within the city or in village gardens. In this vein, I am currently in the midst of working on canals, breakwaters and water management in the city of Colombo as a long-standing environmental project running across the Portuguese, Dutch and British and now into Chinese infrastructure (see Sivasundaram 2022).[11] The idea that Sri Lanka's environment lies in the highlands and not in a place like Colombo has unfortunately made the existent literature spatially uneven in its coverage of the island's environmental past. Meanwhile, rampant urbanisation, remains one of the salient environmental issues facing the island (Radicati 2019; Ruwanpura, Brown and Chan 2020).

Additionally, there are other areas and themes, such as energy history, conservation history, the history of mining and minerals and the history of rivers, which are largely absent in the historiography of Lanka (see Theiventhran, this volume). This essay may then be read as an invitation also to move into these topics, with a wide sense of what constitutes the 'environmental' and also with a flexibility of method, which allows for long dureé and multi-disciplinary analysis. The sources for such scholarship need necessarily to be visual, material and scientific in many ways, as well as textual in a historical sense, and to arise from many different starting points, for the research should aim to make space for nature as much as for subjected peoples. Additionally, like with environmental historiography elsewhere, it will be vital to link scholarship to activism. There may be scope for work in this field to connect with movements around the environment in the island itself, for instance around the Colombo Port Development Project.[12] There is also an urgent need for this scholarship to be characterised by dynamic public engagement.

Notes

1. The article has sections based on or which draw on my previous work. It synthesises them in a new way and also brings in a sequence of new material which is interspersed throughout (Sivasundaram 2005, 2013, 2015, 2020, 2023, 2024).
2. There has been some debate about whether Ptolemy's Taprobane refers to Sri Lanka or Sumatra (for more on this see Bennett 1843; Brohier 1951; Berggren and Jones 2000).
3. For ecology, see Webb (2002); for indenture see, Peebles (2001); for gender and class, see Jayawardena and Kurian (2015); for ethnicity, see Meyer (1990); for colonial settler studies, see McCarthy (2017) and also Rappaport (2017); also see Wenzlhuemer (2008) and Bass (2012).
4. This is a reference to this photograph in the collections of John Ambercromby Alexander: GBR/0115/RCS/Y303E/2. Cambridge University Library. His genre of photographs can be consulted online at: https://cudl.lib.cam.ac.uk/view/PH-Y-00303-E/72, accessed 29 May 2023.
5. This is available to view at this site: https://artuk.org/discover/artworks/ceylon-pitcher-plant-and-butterflies-87756, accessed 29 May 2023.
6. In contrast to these, see the critical work of anthropologist Gananath Obeyesekere on his website devoted to the Wanniyalaeto, <http://vedda.org/obeyesekere1.htm>.
7. I thank Sandagomi Coperahewa from the University of Colombo for this insight.
8. See, for example, John M. Senaveratna, *Dictionary of Proverbs of the Sinhalese* (Colombo, 1936); e.g. 'The pangolin's life is in its head' and 'The pangolin who forcibly occupied the porcupine's hole, swore by his forefathers that he would never leave it'.
9. From the Pacific and its islands, see for instance, Miranda Johnson et al. eds. *Pacific Futures: Past and Present* (Honolulu, 2018).
10. I thank Tamara Fernando for reading this essay and for making thought-provoking comments. This paragraph and the next arise in response to a correspondence with her.
11. For an initial foray in this area, see, Sujit Sivasundaram, 'The Twisted Histories of a Colombo Canal', *History Workshop Online*, https://www.historyworkshop.org.uk/colombo-canal/, accessed 2 September 2022.
12. There is evidence of this happening, at least in the sciences, for instance, Asha de Vos and Ocean Swell, see here: https://oceanswell.org, accessed 2 September 2022 or 'Parrotfish Collective', see here: https://www.facebook.com/parrotfishcollective/, accessed 2 September 2022. It could happen with historical research too.

References

Abeyawardana, H.A.P. (1999) *Boundary Divisions of Mediaeval Sri Lanka* Maharagama: Academy of Sri Lankan Culture
"Address of the Hon. Mr. Justice Stark 4 May 1846", *Journal of the Ceylon Branch of the Royal Asiatic Society* Vol. 1 (1846): 5–12
Arasaratnam, Sinnapah (ed and trans) (1978) *François Valentijn's Description of Ceylon* London: Hakluyt Society
Bass, Daniel (2012) *Everyday Ethnicity in Sri Lanka: Up-Country Tamil Identity Politics* London: Routledge.
Bennett, J.W. (1843) *Ceylon and Its Capabilities* London: W. H. Allen
Berggren, J. Lennart and Alexander Jones (2000) *Ptolemy's Geography: An Annotated Translation of the Theoretical Chapters* Princeton: Princeton University Press
Brohier, R.L. (1951) *Land, Maps and Surveys: Descriptive Catalogue of Historical Maps in the Surveyor General's Office Colombo* Colombo: Survey Department
Carter, Charles (ed) (1924) *A Sinhalese–English Dictionary* Colombo: Baptist Missionary Press
Chakrabarty, Dipesh (2021) *The Climate of History in a Planetary Age* Chicago: Chicago University Press
Chandraratne, R.M.M. (2016) "Some Ethno-Archaeological Observations on the Subsistence Strategies of the Veddas in Sri Lanka" *Social Affairs: A Journal for the Social Sciences* i(4): 2016
Cordiner, James (1807) *Description of Ceylon containing an account of the country, inhabitants and natural productions* (reprinted Colombo 1983, first published Aberdeen, 1807)
Ceylon Observer (26 July 1899)
Ceylon Observer (23 July 1903)
Ceylon Observer (28 April 1904)
Ceylon Observer (22 March 1905a)
Ceylon Observer (4 May 1905b)
Ceylon Observer (10 July 1905c)
Ceylon Observer (2 November 1905d)
Ceylon Observer (13 April 1915)
Anon (1877) *Guide to Colombo: Describing 'what to see and how'* Colombo Times Press.
De Silva, Sunila and Krithika Srinivasan (2019) "Revisiting Social Natures: People-Elephant Conflict and Co-Existence in Sri Lanka" *Geoforum* 102(June 2019): 182–190
Duncan, James (2007) *In the Shadow of the Tropics: Climate, Race and Biopower in Nineteenth Century Ceylon* Aldershot: Routledge
Ferguson, D. (ed and trans) (1908) "João de Barros and Diogo Do Couto's History of Ceylon from the Earliest Times to 1600 A.D." *Journal of the Ceylon Branch of the Royal Asiatic Society* 20(1908): 1–445
Fernando, Tamara (2022) "Seeing Like the Sea: A Multispecies History of the Ceylon Pearl Fishery, 1800–1925" *Past and Present* 254(1): 27–160
Ghosh, Amitav (2021) *The Nutmeg's Curse: Parables for a Planet in Crisis* London: John Murray
Haly, A. (1886) *First Report on the Collection of Snakes in the Colombo Museum* Colombo: Colombo Museum
Jayawardena, Kumari and Rachel Kurian (2015) *Class, Patriachy and Ethnicity on Sri Lankan Plantations: Two Centuries of Power and Protest* New Delhi: Orient Blackswan
Jegathesan, Mythri (2019) *Tea and Solidarity: Tamil Women and Work in Postwar Sri Lanka* Washington
Johnson, Miranda et al (eds) (2018) *Pacific Futures: Past and Present* Honolulu: University of Hawaii Press
Latour, Bruno (2007) *Reassembling the Social: An Introduction to Actor-Network Theory* Oxford: Oxford University Press
Lorimer, Jamie and Sarah Whatmore (2009) "After the 'King of the Beasts': Samuel Baker and the Embodied Historical Geographies of Elephant Hunting in Mid-Nineteenth Century Ceylon" *Journal of Historical Geography* 35(4): 668–689
McCarthy, Angela (2017) *Tea and Empire: James Taylor in Victorian Ceylon* Manchester: Manchester University Press
McCook, Stuart (2019) *Coffee Is Not Forever: A Global History of the Coffee Leaf Rust* Athens: Ohio University Press
McEvansoneya, Philip (2017) "Sir William Gregory and the Origins and Foundation of the Colombo Museum" In *Curating Empire: Museums and the British Imperial Experience* Sarah Longair and John McAleer (eds) Manchester: Manchester University Press, pp 188–206

Meyer, Eric (1990) "Aspects of the Sinhalese-Tamil Relations in the Plantation Areas of Sri Lanka under the British Raj" *Indian Economic and Social History Review* 27(1990): 165–188

North, Marianne (1892) *Recollections of a Happy Life* Vol. 1. London: Macmillan

Parker, Henry (1909) *Ancient Ceylon: An Account of the Aborigines and of Part of the Early Civilization* London: Luzac and Co

Peebles, Patrick (2001) *The Plantation Tamils of Ceylon* London: Leicester University Press

Perera, Priyan and Hasitha Karawita (2020) "An Update of Distribution, Habitats and Conservation Status of the Indian Pangolin (*Manis crassicaudata*) in Sri Lanka" *Global Ecology and Conservation* xxi: e00799

Radicati, Alessandra (2019) "Island Journeys: Fisher Itineraries and National Imaginaries in Colombo" *Contemporary South Asia* 27(2019): 330–341

Rappaport, Erika (2017) *A Thirst for Empire: How Tea Shaped the Modern World* Princeton: Princeton University Press

Roberts, Patrick et al (2018) "Historical Tropical Forest Reliance amongst the Wanniyalaeto (Vedda) of Sri Lanka: An Isotopic Perspective" *Human Ecology* xlvi, 435–444

Ruwanpura, Kanchana N., Benjamin Brown and Loritta Chan (2020) "(Dis)connecting Colombo: Situating the Megapolis in Postwar Sri Lanka" *The Professional Geographer* 72(2020): 165–179

Senaveratna, John M. (1936) *Dictionary of Proverbs of the Sinhalese* Colombo: Times of Ceylon

Seligman, C.G. and Brenda Z. Seligman (1911) *The Veddas* Cambridge: Cambridge University Press

Simon, Gwladys Hughes (1955) "Riddles from Ceylon (Part II)" *Western Folklore* xiv(4): 259–268

Sivasundaram, Sujit (2005) "Trading Knowledge: The East India Company's Elephants in India and Britain" *The Historical Journal* 48(1): 27–63

Sivasundaram, Sujit (2010) "Sciences and the Global: On Methods, Questions, and Theory" *Isis* 10: 146–158

Sivasundaram, Sujit (2013) *Islanded: Britain, Sri Lanka and the Bounds of an Indian Ocean Colony* Chicago: Chicago University Press

Sivasundaram, Sujit (2015) "Imperial Transgressions: The Animal and Human in the Idea of Race" *Comparative Studies of South Asia, Africa and the Middle East* 35(1): 156–172

Sivasundaram, Sujit (2020) "The Human, the Animal and the Prehistory of Covid-19" *Past and Present* 249(1): 295–316

Sivasundaram, Sujit (2024) "The Global and the Earthy: Taking the Planet Seriously as a Global Historian" In *Rethinking Global History* Stefanie Gänger and Jürgen Osterhammel (eds) Cambridge: Cambridge University Press

Tennent, James Emerson (1861) *Sketches of the Natural History of Ceylon* London: Longman

Tennent, James Emerson (1876) *The Wild Elephant and the Method of Capturing and Taming It in Ceylon* London: Longman

Webb, James A. (2002) *Tropical Pioneers: Human Agency and Ecological Change in the Highlands of Sri Lanka, 1800–1900* Athens: Ohio University Press

Wenzlhuemer, Roland (2008) *From Coffee to Tea Cultivation in Ceylon, 1880–1900: An Economic and Social History* Leiden: Brill.

PART VII

Society, Social Systems, and Culture

26
PUBLIC HEALTH SYSTEM OF SRI LANKA

Past, Present, and Future

Shashika Bandara

Introduction

The public health system of Sri Lanka has been recognized as a relatively successful health system within its income category of lower-middle income countries, regionally and also globally more generally (Rajapaksa et al 2021). Yet it has been facing increasing challenges due to the shifting disease burden, changing demographics, and limited fiscal space. The most recent economic crisis has further severely impacted the national health system which was lauded for its low-cost and high-impact model (Perera et al 2019). To better understand the structure, function, and challenges of the public health system in Sri Lanka, I will provide a comprehensive overview situating it within the overall health system and existing epidemiologic, demographic, and socio-economic conditions.

Health indicators for the Sustainable Development Goal (SDG) 3 *Good Health and well-being* show improvement in health over time for countries. Sri Lanka's indicators for maternal mortality, neonatal mortality, and under-five mortality all are comparable with countries that have better health systems in the region (Sachs et al 2021). Sri Lanka has scored 68 on the Universal Health Coverage (UHC) index, which is an average score, yet compared with other lower-middle income countries, Sri Lanka's UHC performance and efforts to improve UHC stand out (Rajapaksa et al 2021).

Sri Lanka's health system is governed by the Ministry of Health under the purview of the Minister of Health. The ministry manages national health services and leads stewardship of health service development and delivery. Healthcare delivery in Sri Lanka remains free at the point of delivery within the public health system and the majority of the services are provided by the state sector and are publicly financed (Kumar 2019; Rajapaksa et al 2021). Regulated health services available to the public include Western allopathic medicine and traditional medicine (e.g., *Ayurvedic, Deshiya Chikitsa*) with Western allopathic medicine dominating in terms of availability and demand (Uragoda 1987; Rajapaksa et al 2021). It is important to recognize the emergence of the private sector providing primary care to tertiary care available at a higher cost, which largely uses out-of-pocket payments – thus limiting accessibility to private healthcare mainly to the affluent. The state and private healthcare services remain largely comparable in terms of quality (Kumar 2019; Perera et al 2019).

Sri Lanka has been successful in eliminating many communicable diseases including polio, neonatal tetanus, filariasis, and most recently Malaria (Rajapaksa et al 2021). Sri Lanka is also making significant progress on eliminating vaccine-preventable diseases listed under the Expanded Immunization Programme of the World Health Organization (WHO) (Gamage, Kapuge, Abeysinghe and Peiris 2021). Gavi, the vaccine alliance, recognizes Sri Lanka's National Immunization Program as one of the success stories (Gavi 2018). As one of the first Asian countries to graduate from Gavi's financing in 2016 Sri Lanka continues its success in achieving high vaccination coverage (Gamage et al 2021). Even when facing the COVID-19 pandemic, despite early policy hiccups, Sri Lanka ultimately managed to achieve vaccination coverage relatively faster than other lower-middle-income countries vaccinating over 75% of the population with at least one dose (Bandara 2021c; World Health Organization 2021; Mathieu et al 2022).

However, with a growing non-communicable disease (NCD) burden and other communicable diseases, such as Dengue, Sri Lanka is facing the challenge of 'double burden of disease' (Remais et al 2013; Ministry of Health, Sri Lanka 2019a).[1] The recent Universal Health Coverage (UHC) strategy of 2018 prioritized strengthening the primary healthcare system and the referral system to improve the functionality of the overall health system (Kumar 2019; Perera et al 2019). Yet the COVID-19 pandemic highlighted the lack of preparedness for surge capacity, and the need to further strengthen facilities outside of urban and tertiary-level hospitals (Bandara 2021a). In addition, non-evidence based and discriminatory policies against religious minorities by the government, such as the 2020 'forced cremation policy', also impacted the trust in the public health system (Bandara 2020; see also Fernando, this volume).

While free healthcare by the state sector remains a key positive feature, Sri Lanka's health system has struggled to expand fiscal space while recognizing the need to develop better health infrastructure, health recording systems, and improving primary care system (Kumar 2019; Rajapaksa et al 2021). The recent economic crisis, caused by poor policies by the current (2022) government that have not prioritized health and education sectors, has also deeply impacted the health system, including an essential medicines shortage (Das 2022; Devi 2022). The following sections will further examine the contemporary strengths and challenges of the health system including what the context and current developments mean for the future of healthcare in Sri Lanka.

Historical Background of Public Health in Sri Lanka

Archaeological and literary evidence point to institutional support for providing healthcare to the public even under monarchical governance structures, including support for the disabled (Uragoda 1987). The roots of indigenous and traditional medicine originate from these systems including current traditional indigenous medical practices, such as *Deshiya Chikitsa, Ayurveda, Siddha, Unani*, and acupuncture (Uragoda 1987). At present, Western allopathic medicine dominates both service availability and demand. Considering the number of patients, in 2017, the government indigenous system provided inpatient services to 36,088 patients, which is just 0.5% of the total patients receiving government Western allopathic inpatient services (6.9 million). For outpatient care, government indigenous services provided services to 4.3 million, which is 7.8% of the total outpatient care provided by the Western allopathic services (55.3 million) (Rajapaksa et al 2021). The Ministry of Health of Sri Lanka oversees and sets standards for both Western allopathic and indigenous medicine practices.

The current Western allopathic health system is built on the foundations of colonial health systems dating back to 1858 and was continued as a government priority from independence in 1948 (Perera et al 2019; Rajapaksa et al 2021). It is notable that Sri Lanka adopted an approach in the 1920s that reflected the principles of 1978 Alma-Ata declaration which identified strengthening primary healthcare as key to achieving health for all (Perera et al 2019).[2] Sri Lanka's first independent government accepted World WHO's concept of health as a human right and this commitment has continued. However health as a human right is not included in the constitution or in the legal code of Sri Lanka, which remains an unfulfilled crucial policy step in achieving health for all (Jayasinghe 2016).

Contextualizing the Public Health System: Demography, Disease Burden, and Financing

Sri Lanka's public health system, like any health system, is impacted by the country's demographic, socio-economic conditions, and epidemiological factors. Demographic and socio-economic conditions, including financing healthcare, impact social determinants of health affecting health-seeking behaviours as well as the capacity for service provision. Epidemiological profile of the country provides an insight into the shifting disease burden of the country (Institute for Health Metrics and Evaluation 2020). All these contextual factors play a significant role in understanding the current and future priorities of the public health system.

Demography

As per 2021 national data Sri Lanka is home to 22.15 million of which approximately 52% are women (Government of Sri Lanka 2021). The population is unevenly distributed with approximately 1/3rd of the population living in the Western Province which consists of most of the urban areas. Districts outside of the Western Province that has over one million people include Galle, Kalutara, Kandy, Kurunegala, and Ratnapura (Government of Sri Lanka 2021). The disparity in the distribution of the population is also reflected in population density statistics: the average national population density is at 347.1 persons per square kilometre, while Western Province has 1705.8 persons per square kilometre (Rajapaksa et al 2021). The average life expectancy has increased over time and currently is 74 years for males and 81 years for women (United Nations Population Fund 2022).

In 2020, 11% of the total population consisted of 65 years or older demographic (Rajapaksa et al 2021). Sri Lanka's population of those 60 years and older is expected to increase in the next decade requiring better targeted healthcare towards the elderly population in terms of infrastructure and service delivery. Projections indicate that the population over 60 years or older will reach 23% by 2024 and by 2052 one in every four persons will be 60 years or older (Rajapaksa et al 2021). While Sri Lanka has a low elderly population compared to high-income countries it exceeds the projected average of South Asia of 21% in 2050 much earlier (United Nations Economic and Social Commission for Asia and the Pacific 2017).

Disease Burden

Sri Lanka has had success in addressing many major communicable disease threats, especially in the last decade. Recording a significant victory, in 2016, Sri Lanka eliminated Malaria with concerted community-level and health system efforts (Senaratne and Singh 2016). Sri Lanka has also eliminated filariasis, polio, and neonatal tetanus. Sri Lanka is nearing the elimination of vaccine-preventable diseases targeted by WHO's Expanded Programme on Immunization. Communicable disease threats are not completely out of the picture for Sri Lanka as dengue, epidemic influenza, and

Table 26.1 Sri Lanka's top ten diseases that causes most deaths in 2009 and 2019

Cause of mortality ranking	Diseases in 2009	Diseases in 2019	Changes in deaths per 100K (2009–2019) for 2019 top ten diseases
1	Ischemic heart disease	Ischemic heart disease	+7.6
2	Stroke	Stroke	–4.1
3	Conflict and terror	Diabetes	+10.2
4	Diabetes	Asthma	–3.0
5	Asthma	Chronic kidney disease	+2.9
6	Chronic kidney disease	Chronic obstructive pulmonary disease (COPD)	+1.6
7	Self-harm	Lower respiratory tract infection	+1.4
8	Chronic obstructive pulmonary disease (COPD)	Self-harm	–1.3
9	Cirrhosis	Cirrhosis	–0.7
10	Lower respiratory tract infection	Alzheimer's disease	+5.3

Source: Institute for Health and Metrics Evaluation (2020).

re-emergence of tuberculosis continue to challenge the health system (World Health Organization 2018; Rajapaksa et al 2021). The COVID-19 pandemic also significantly impacted Sri Lanka during 2020–2022 affecting mortality and morbidity rates in Sri Lanka.

Additionally, it is important to recognize the impact of non-communicable diseases (NCDs) as a major contributor to mortality rates in Sri Lanka both in 2009 and 2019 (Institute for Health Metrics and Evaluation 2020). Eight out of the top ten causes of death are NCDs (see Table 26.1). The top three NCDs, ischemic heart disease, stroke, and diabetes are related to the lifestyle, nutrition, and living conditions of the population. Additionally, conditions, such as asthma, are related to environmental conditions, such as air quality. It is also important to note that self-harm which is related to mental well-being remains in the top ten causes of death in Sri Lanka (Institute for Health Metrics and Evaluation 2020). The ageing population has also had an impact on the disease burden of Sri Lanka (see Table 26.1). One clear example is the rise in Alzheimer's disease between 2009 and 2019 as a cause of death (Institute for Health Metrics and Evaluation 2020). The impact of the conclusion of the armed conflict in Sri Lanka is reflected in the rankings of causes of mortality. Conflict and terror were the third highest cause of death in 2009, and in 2019 it was not listed within the top ten causes for mortality in Sri Lanka (Vos et al 2020).

Considering death and disability using the indicator of disability-adjusted life years (DALY), Sri Lanka's top ten causes in 2019 are diabetes, ischemic heart disease, stroke, self-harm, low back pain, chronic kidney disease, asthma, road injuries, neo-natal disorders, and headache disorders. A decrease in neo-natal disorders by 35.5% from 2009 to 2019 and an increase in diabetes by 34.8% during the same period as causes for death and disability combined stand out among the data. Low back pain and chronic kidney disease have also shown 20.1% and 21% increase, respectively, during the same period (Institute for Health Metrics and Evaluation 2020; Vos et al 2020).

Financing

Government financing via tax revenue and private spending remain the two main financial resource streams for the health sector (Rajapaksa et al 2021). In 2020, Sri Lanka's total expenditure on health (public and private) was 4.07% of its Gross Domestic Product (GDP), an increase from 3.6% in 2019 (World Bank 2022). Sri Lanka's social insurance and other private insurance contribute less than 1% to current health expenditure and external financing has always been approximately 1% of current health expenditure (Rajapaksa et al 2021). Sri Lanka has had a low dependency on external financing for health as domestic financing on average covers 95% of the cost (UNICEF 2022). However, the government is facing challenges due to limited fiscal space for public health and a lack of prioritization.

Over the years although the monetary value of government spending on health has increased, spending as a percentage has remained below 2%. Public financing fluctuated between 1.1% and 1.6% of GDP during 1990–2019 while financing from private sources fluctuated between 1.5% and 2.1% (Amarasinghe et al 2021). While Sri Lanka's public sector financing remains higher than the regional average of approximately 1% of GDP, the government will need to further prioritize health in its budgetary allocations (UNICEF 2022). One competing misallocation is the high spending trend on defence compared to health. For example, the budget for 2023 continued to prioritize defence spending ($1.1 bn) over other sectors such as health ($880 mn) (Parliament of Sri Lanka 2022).

Compounding the challenge of lack of fiscal space to increase public spending on health is the 2022 economic and political crisis that was caused by years of excessive borrowing by successive governments, investments in massive infrastructure development projects without any foreign direct investment in return, and significant policy missteps by the administration since 2019 (Verite Research 2022a). The current (2022) economic crisis has plunged Sri Lanka into an unforeseen health financing crisis with a lack of essential medicines, re-agents for labs, equipment, and power for services, such as surgeries (Bandara and Alwis 2022; Das 2022; Devi 2022).

Contemporary Health System Governance

Government Healthcare

The Ministry of Health is responsible for government health policy formulation, health legislation, and regulating services provided by both the government and private sectors. Additionally, the ministry also directly manages several large, specialized hospitals including the National Hospital of Sri Lanka, teaching hospitals, specialized hospitals, provincial general hospitals, and selected 33 district general hospitals. Overall procurement of medicines and laboratory products is mainly handled by the centre as well (Rajapaksa et al 2021).

The Minister of Health is supported by two deputy ministers and the Secretary of Health who is the administrative lead. The Director General of Health Services (DGHS) is the technical lead in the ministry and is supported by multiple Deputy Directors-General (DDGs) (Rajapaksa et al 2021; Ministry of Health, Sri Lanka 2023). In addition to DDGs, there are also directors for specific national programmes, such as the maternal and child health programme. These directorates which cover both curative and public health sector efforts manage policies, strategies, training, implementation, and other necessary adaptations to address challenges. In addition to the curative and public health sectors, there are several other sectors that cut across the ministry, such as National Authority on Tobacco and Alcohol. Vertical programmes, which include preventive and promotive care, are controlled by the special campaigns and directorates by the ministry. These vertical programmes include maternal and child health, NCDs, mental health, and regional epidemiology.

Since Sri Lanka has a provincial governance system, there are provincial ministries of health (PMoH). PMoHs have provincial directors of health as the technical leads and provincial secretaries of health as administrative leads. They answer to both provincial governance leaders (e.g., the governor) but also to the relevant ministry officials, such as DGHS. The regional and other medical officers and their teams also fall under the purview of provincial directors of health. PMoHs are responsible for the implementation of healthcare services including primary care, secondary care, and preventive services. While health is a devolved subject and provinces are free to formulate their own statutes, they need to abide by national guidelines and policies. However, decentralized decision-making is not common within provinces. The main reasons are the financial dependency of provinces on the centre and the functional control imposed by the centre (Rajapaksa et al 2021).

Private Healthcare

Private healthcare provides primary care, ambulatory care, limited inpatient care, and rehabilitative care (Rannan-Eliya et al 2015; Rajapaksa et al 2021). Payment for private care is out-of-pocket payments (OOP), which are trending upwards in Sri Lanka. The health standards and policies set by the Ministry of Health still apply to private care. However, hospital management and financial management are handled by each respective private companies. Private healthcare providers belong to three categories: first, general practitioners and specialist consultants who are employed in the government service and engage in private practice via consulting services; second, general practitioners with full-time private clinics; third, specialist consultants who are part of private hospitals, such as resident radiologists. The first category has the largest number of healthcare providers, with general practitioners (GPs) usually having a Bachelor of Medicine and Bachelor of Surgery (MBBS). The lack of data from the private sector remains a challenge to assess the exact numbers within these three categories.

Due to the profit-oriented approach, private sector services promise less waiting time, continued care by the same physician, and more privacy. These are some of the reasons that the public is attracted to private healthcare. Additionally, the private sector has an increasing number of pharmacies, and investigative services, such as blood testing and other medical testing (Rajapaksa et al 2021).

Health Infrastructure and Workforce

The government is the largest healthcare provider due to the extensive network and free care at the point of delivery. In 2019, the public sector handled over seven million hospitalizations and over 58 million outpatient visits (Ministry of Health, Sri Lanka 2019a). As the largest healthcare provider, government healthcare infrastructure and workforce play a crucial role in maintaining the quality of care and services available.

In the state sector, outpatient department care is provided by all hospitals and primary medical care units. Those in need of further treatment are directed to inpatient care or to the nearest larger hospitals when facilities are not available at the current healthcare facility. Specialized care is available at the base, district general, provincial general, teaching and selects specialized hospitals. There are also limited outreach clinics by specialists for continuous treatment of identified cases (Rajapaksa et al 2021). In 2019, the state sector provided services through 643 hospitals and had 86,589 hospital beds in total (Ministry of Health, Sri Lanka 2019a). In 2013, Sri Lanka had 624 hospitals with 78,243 hospital beds. Hospital beds per 1,000 population is four and inpatient care beds per 1,000 population is 3.6. In 2013, hospital beds per 1,000 were 3.8 and 3.5 inpatient beds per 1,000 population. The capacity of hospitals has not grown significantly over six years (Ministry of Health, Sri Lanka 2019a). However, 19 hospitals in 14 districts, (Sri Lanka has 25 total districts), recorded over 90% bed occupancy rate with eight of them recording either approximately equal to or over 100% occupancy rate (Ministry of Health, Sri Lanka 2019b). These challenges of bed occupancy rate can be further exacerbated during outbreaks affecting health outcomes and patient care. Sri Lanka's healthcare is considered to have reach in rural areas, while high-level private healthcare facilities are often limited to urban centres, such as Colombo, Kandy, Galle, and other major cities.

As per 2017 statistics, the Ministry of Health employs slightly above 140,000 employees including provincial health ministries. Of the total 140,000, 58% are skilled personnel consisting of medical officers, nurses, midwives, public health inspectors, dental surgeons, medical laboratory technologists, and pharmacists. The estimates of 424 full-time and 4,845 part-time medical officers in the private sector are considered to be an underestimation as there are no clear records of practitioners at private institutes in the Sri Lanka (Rajapaksa et al 2021).

In terms of the overall healthcare workforce, the SDG mid-term review progress of 2020 indicates that Sri Lanka has exceeded the WHO 2006 benchmark of 22.8 doctors, nurses, and midwives per 10,000 population and is close to 25 per 10,000. However, Sri Lanka remains below the revised 2016, 44.5 health workers per 10,000 population. The revised 2016 benchmark is considered critical to achieving the SDGs. Regionally, South-East Asia averages at 26 healthcare workers per 10,000 population (World Health Organization Regional Office for South-East Asia 2020).

Contemporary Challenges for Sri Lanka's Health System

Sri Lanka's health system is facing several contemporary challenges ranging from the need for structural improvement, emerging disease burdens in communicable and NCDs, demographic shifts and issues arising from the current economic crisis. Communicable diseases are impacted the most by the incidence of dengue, epidemic influenza, and re-emerging TB. Lower respiratory illnesses due to communicable diseases are the seventh leading cause of death in Sri Lanka with an approximate 15% increase between 2009 and 2019 (Institute for Health Metrics and Evaluation 2020; Vos et al 2020). Sri Lanka recorded over 105,000 notified cases of dengue in 2019, with the majority of the cases (64,700) affecting those aged 15–49 (Ministry of Health, Sri Lanka 2019a). The cases are not evenly distributed and affect urban areas significantly more than others. The top five districts most affected in 2019 are Colombo (20,718), Gampaha (16,573), Kandy (8,940), Kalutara (8,395), and Jaffna (8,261). Sri Lanka recorded 8,186 cases of TB in 2019, and there is a gap of about 4,000 cases between reported and number estimated for the country (Ministry of Health, Sri Lanka 2019a). With the impact of COVID-19 and its emerging variants Sri Lanka needs to remain vigilant to control current and emerging infectious disease threats.

NCDs are also a significant factor for mortality and are associated with the demographic shift of the increase in the ageing population as well as lifestyle, living conditions, and lack of awareness (Ministry of Health, Sri Lanka 2019a; Institute for Health Metrics and Evaluation 2020). NCDs, including malnutrition, tend to be a significant factor in disability in the population (Institute for Health Metrics and Evaluation 2020; Bandara and Alwis 2022). Therefore, increased focus on managing both disease burdens remains crucial within the country.

Currently, Sri Lanka's health system allows patients to visit any hospital whether it is primary, secondary, or tertiary. Given the options patients choose secondary- or tertiary-level hospitals as opposed to primary healthcare centres. While Sri Lanka's health system utilization is among the highest in the region, the lack of patients at primary healthcare centres means an increased burden on secondary and tertiary hospitals which contributes to the demand and supply imbalance in the healthcare (Ministry of Health, Sri Lanka 2019b; Rajapaksa et al 2021). The disproportionate funding distribution that prioritizes secondary and tertiary care has contributed to the challenge of strengthening the primary healthcare system in Sri Lanka (Rajapaksa et al 2021). Additionally, seeking specialized healthcare is also promoted by the 'one-stop shop' approach provided by private health centres which provide direct access to specialized care for a fee. To manage resources efficiently including healthcare workforce and infrastructure, Sri Lanka will need to strengthen its primary healthcare centres and promote primary healthcare as the first line of healthcare provision. The World Bank is supporting Sri Lanka with a five-year (2018–2023) project that aims to strengthen primary healthcare, including care for NCDs (World Bank 2018). The 2018 UHC strategy of Sri Lanka also aims to strengthen the primary care (Kumar 2019).

Focusing on NCDs, Sri Lanka introduced 'healthy lifestyle centres' and related training to increase screening and diagnostics and lifestyle counselling in order to reduce the NCD disease burden (Ministry of Health, Sri Lanka 2019a). However, the use of these centres remains lower than expected, especially among men. As curative services only become relevant for most NCDs at later and more critical stages of the disease, it is important to strengthen both NCD screening and treatment and build a culture of seeking care early for NCDs including lifestyle changes. The national policy and strategic framework for prevention and control of chronic NCDs (2010) and the multisectoral action plan for prevention and control of NCDs (2016–2020) both are currently being revised (Ministry of Health, Sri Lanka, 2019a). Sri Lanka requires a concerted effort in terms of resources and strategies to build awareness to reduce NCD prevalence.

Stigma and Strengthening Mental Health Services

Recent research indicates approximately one in every five people in Sri Lanka is detected with depression, with higher prevalence among youth (Alwis, Baminiwatta and Chandradasa 2023). Sri Lanka has made some policy progress to improve mental health yet requires effort to implement the policy recommendations effectively and efficiently. A revised National Mental Health Act, drafted with multi-sectoral support is still under deliberation since 2005 (Rajapaksa et al 2021). Most recently the Ministry of Health and Sri Lanka Mental Health Officer's Union were in discussion to amend the 150-year-old act, which is still active (Shantha 2022). The National Committee on Mental Health which was initiated in 2007 to advise the Director of Mental Health is currently headed by the DGHS and convened by the Director of Mental Health. Sri Lanka also improved human resource training related to mental health and set up centres, such as '*mithuru piyasa*', to support those affected by gender-based violence (Ministry of Health, Sri Lanka 2019a, 2019b). In 2007, the main mental health hospital was restructured into the National Institute for Mental Health (Ministry of Health, Sri Lanka, 2019a). In addition to government services, there are also non-profit sector stakeholders that support provisions of mental health services such as suicide hotlines.

Stigma related to seeking services, understanding and awareness related to mental health have significant room for improvement. Stigma at the societal level not only impact patients but also impact service providers where what is acceptable as a mental health illness can be trivialized. Additionally, recognizing the rising number of mental health illnesses in Sri Lanka, the ministry highlights strengthening the workforce as a key factor (Ministry of Health, Sri Lanka 2019a). Sri Lanka also needs to strengthen its service provision and public health communication related to mental health, especially during crises. During COVID-19 the need for promotion of mental health services as an accessible tool for well-being was lacking. Therefore, Sri Lanka has room for improvement in integrating mental health awareness building, improving accessibility of services and de-stigmatization of health seeking behaviours for mental health services by creating safe spaces.

COVID-19 Pandemic

Sri Lanka, like many other countries, faced significant challenges related to the COVID-19 pandemic (Bandara et al 2021). Sri Lanka, as of May 12, 2022, has recorded a total of over 663,000 cases (Ministry of Health, Sri Lanka 2022). While the health system was able to navigate the challenges of the pandemic, there were moments when the health system was facing an impending collapse due to a lack of surge capacity. The pandemic also highlighted the importance of political determinants of health during health emergencies and in general for improving the health sector of a country (Bandara 2021a).

Prior to vaccines becoming available for COVID-19, Sri Lanka used strategies to minimize infection spread, which included a country-wide lockdown to face the first wave, then delayed infection control measures to control the second and the third wave. It is important to recognize direct political interference and push back against public health measures despite warnings from public health experts (Bandara 2021a). Sri Lankan government and ministers many times clashed with public health experts over the need for public health measures. In both instances, during the second and third waves, the government had to abide by the advice given by the public health community and healthcare workers. Another crucial factor was the lack of adequate social support for the vulnerable leaving many at the mercy of altruistic donation services or facing significant food security threats. Political interference was noted at many levels including vaccine approvals and critiquing of an independent panel convened by the WHO Sri Lanka. Lack of transparency related to funds created by the government to support communities and to procure vaccines became a significant cause for concern (Bandara 2021a).

In terms of policy failures, Sri Lanka's forced cremation policy stands out. The forced cremation policy, which required bodies of COVID-19-infected patients to be cremated, was implemented for over eight months. This non-evidence-based policy unfairly affected the Muslim ethnic minority and violated the International Health Regulation commitments of Sri Lanka (Bandara 2021b). Despite repeated requests from the community and statements from experts pointing to the minimal risk caused by burying patients who died due to COVID-19, the government continued the policy. Even though cremation is a violation of the religious rights of the Muslim (and Christian) community, the government initially required all bodies to be cremated including infants, providing a designated land plot in the East of the country far from normal burial grounds (Bandara 2021b, 2021c). After two years, the government finally discontinued the need to use burial grounds in a separate district and allowed normal burials (France 24 2022).

Sri Lanka also took a policy approach where the COVID-19 response was spearheaded by the Army Commander of the country as opposed to public health leaders. Instances of overtly forceful or humiliating means of implementation of public health measures by the military are areas of improvement that Sri Lanka can focus on in future health emergencies. It is also important to recognize that strengthening the healthcare institutions with adequate surge capacity will be more vital than using the military in place of the public health workforce (Bandara 2021a; Ruwanpura 2022; see also Fernando, this volume).

Sri Lanka building on its strong vaccination coverage and know-how managed to vaccinate over 60% of the population with two doses relatively faster than other lower-middle-income countries (Mathieu et al 2020) Sri Lanka used five vaccines, which included Sinopharm, Moderna, Pfizer, Sputnik, and Astra-Zeneca (World Health Organization 2021). Since May 12, 2022 and until June 2, 2023, only 8,756 cases have been reported (Ministry of Health, Sri Lanka 2022). The WHO declared the end of COVID-19 as a global health emergency on May 5, 2023 (United Nations 2023).

Conclusion and Pathways Forward

Sri Lanka's current economic crisis has caused significant damage to the health system. Although Sri Lanka has been lauded internationally as a low-cost-high-impact model the severity of the current economic crisis has left the health system facing severe shortages (Das 2022; Devi 2022). These shortages include essential medicines, re-agents for labs, and personal protective equipment. The shortage became so severe that the health system had to turn to crowdsourcing funds to fill the gaps (Bandara 2022; Wijeratne 2022).

Poor government policies leading up to the crisis and lack of timely responses have characterized both the economic and the health system challenges. Furthermore, Sri Lanka is facing a human resource shortage due to healthcare workers migrating in response to the crisis. The government has facilitated the migration of the healthcare workforce with the short-term goal of gaining more foreign currency (Bandara and Alwis 2022). To ensure the right to health of the population and to continue services, Sri Lanka will need to look for development assistance for health from outside donors at least in the short to medium term.

Sri Lanka will need to continue to ensure that its health system is prepared for the rising NCD burden in addition to communicable diseases. Addressing the increasing demand for healthcare by the ageing population and strengthening preparedness for health emergencies such as pandemics is vital. Reorienting its budget to support public well-being by increasing allocation to health and moving away from high military spending can be beneficial for Sri Lanka. Sri Lanka does have the local expertise and a system that can support recovery if timely policy changes are made to address the current crisis. Understanding and addressing the impact of political determinants of health will contribute immensely to recovering and strengthening the health system.

Acknowledgements

Author would like to acknowledge the expert review input to ensure contextual relevance and accuracy by Professor Neelika Malavige of Sri Jayawardenapura University, Professor Arunasalam Pathmeswaran of University of Kelaniya, and lecturer Inosha Alwis of University of Peradeniya, Sri Lanka.

Notes

1. 'Double burden of disease' is when countries have a high-level communicable disease burden as well as rising non-communicable disease burden.
2. The Declaration of Alma-Ata was endorsed at the Alma-Ata conference in 1978, jointly convened by WHO and UNICEF. The declaration highlighted primary health care as the key to achieving an acceptable level of health throughout the world.

References

Alwis, Inosha, Anuradha Baminiwatta and Miyuru Chandradasa (2023) "Prevalence and Associated Factors of Depression in Sri Lanka: A Systematic Review and Meta-Analysis" *Social Psychiatry and Psychiatric Epidemiology* [Preprint]. Available at https://doi.org/10.1007/s00127-023-02495-z

Amarasinghe, Sarasi Nisansala, H.S.H. Fonseka, K.C.S. Dalpatadu and Ravi P. Rannan-Eliya, (2021) *Sri Lanka Health Accounts: National Health Expenditure 1990–2019*

Bandara, Shashika (2020) "Misguided Policies Damage a Valued Public Health System" *Groundviews* (23 December). Accessed on 28/06/2021. Available at https://groundviews.org/2020/12/23/misguided-policies-damage-a-valued-public-health-system/

Bandara, Shashika (2021a) *Charting a path forward beyond the pandemic for Sri Lanka*. Law and Society Trust. Accessed on 06/05/2022. Available at https://lstlanka.org/images/publications/civic_watch_on_covid/new_Charting_a_path_forward_beyond_the_pandemic_English_1.pdf

Bandara, Shashika (2021b) "Sri Lanka Is Alarmingly Overdue for a Long Term Strategy for COVID-19" *Groundviews* (21 June). Accessed on 28/06/2021. Available at https://groundviews.org/2021/06/21/sri-lanka-is-alarmingly-overdue-for-a-long-term-strategy-for-covid-19/.

Bandara, Shashika (2021c) "Where Is Kindness in Our COVID-19 Health Policy?" *Groundviews* (7 April). Accessed on 28/06/2021. Available at https://groundviews.org/2021/04/07/where-is-kindness-in-our-covid-19-health-policy/

Bandara, Shashika (2022) *Sri Lanka's public health system crippled by the economic crisis is calling out for help, Perspectives on Global Health*. Accessed on 09/05/2022. Available at http://www.perspectivesmcgill.com/opinion/medicineshortagesrilanka

Bandara, Shashika and Inosha Alwis (2022) "Sri Lanka's Health Crisis" *BMJ* 379: e073475

Bandara, Shashika, Soumyadeep Bhaumik, Veena Sriram, Senjuti Saha, Nukhba Zia, Md Hasan Zabir, Neelika Malavige and Drona Rasali (2021) "Stronger Together: A New Pandemic Agenda for South Asia" *BMJ Global Health* 6(8): e006776

Das, Manjulika (2022) "Economic Crisis in Sri Lanka Causing Cancer Drug Shortage" *The Lancet Oncology* 23(6)

Devi, Sharmila (2022) "Sri Lankan Health System Facing Lengthy Shortages" *The Lancet* 399(10336): 1682

France 24 (2022) "Sri Lanka ends widely condemned Muslim burial policy" *France 24*. Accessed on 12 May 2022. Available at https://www.france24.com/en/live-news/20220303-sri-lanka-ends-widely-condemned-muslim-burial-policy

Gamage, Anuji, Yasodhara. Kapuge, Abeysinghe and Sudath Peiris (2021) *Country Case Study: Lessons Learned from Sri Lanka's Experience Transitioning from Gavi Support* Learning Network for Countries in Transition and Institute for Health Policy

Gavi (2018) "Transition twins: Sri Lanka and Timor-Leste team up for sustainable immunisation". Accessed on 06/05/2022. Available at https://www.gavi.org/vaccineswork/transition-twins-sri-lanka-and-timor-leste-team-sustainable-immunisation

Government of Sri Lanka (2021) *Department of Census and Statistics – Sri Lanka, Department of Census and Statistics*. Accessed on 06/05/2022. Available at http://www.statistics.gov.lk/Population/StaticalInformation/VitalStatistics/ByDistrictandSex

Institute for Health Metrics and Evaluation (2020) *Sri Lanka – Country Health Profile, Institute for Health Metrics and Evaluation*. Accessed on 07/05/2022. Available at https://www.healthdata.org/sri-lanka

Jayasinghe, Saroj (2016) "Case for including health as a fundamental human right in new Constitution – Opinion" *Daily Mirror – Sri Lanka* (13 February). Accessed on 06/05/2022. Available at https://www.dailymirror.lk/opinion/Case-for-including-health-as-a-fundamental-human-right-in-new-Constitution/172-105389

Kumar, Ramya (2019) "Public–private Partnerships for Universal Health Coverage? The Future of "free health" in Sri Lanka" *Globalization and Health* 15(1): 75

Mathieu, Edouard, Hannah Ritchie, Lucas Rodés-Guirao, Cameron Appel, Daniel Gavrilov, Charlie Giattino, Joe Hasell, Boobie Macdonald, Saloni Dattani, Dian Beltekian, Esteban Ortiz-Ospina and Max Roser (2022) "Coronavirus Pandemic (COVID-19) – Sri Lanka" *Our World in Data* [Preprint]. Accessed on 21/10/2022. Available at https://ourworldindata.org/coronavirus/country/sri-lanka

Ministry of Health, Sri Lanka (2019a) *Annual Health Bulletin of Sri Lanka – 2019*. Accessed on 06/05/2022. Available at http://www.health.gov.lk/moh_final/english/public/elfinder/files/publications/AHB/2020/AHB%202019.pdf

Ministry of Health, Sri Lanka (2019b) *Annual Health Statistics of Sri Lanka – 2019*. Accessed on 06/05/2022. Available at https://drive.google.com/file/d/1Dyv_y72K1MBO4WCJ0g1vfqyYyutnjXD8/view?usp=drive_link

Ministry of Health, Sri Lanka (2022) *Coronavirus (COVID-19) Sri Lanka – Analytics Dashboard*. Accessed on 12/05/2022. Available at https://hpb.health.gov.lk/covid19-dashboard/

Ministry of Health, Sri Lanka (2023) *Ministry of Health – Sri Lanka*. Accessed on 02/06/2023. Available at https://www.health.gov.lk/top-officials/

Parliament of Sri Lanka (2022) *Presentation of the Appropriation Bill (2023)*. Accessed on 13/11/2022. Available at https://www.parliament.lk/en/budget-2023/presentation-of-the-appropriation-bill-2023

Perera, Susie., Olivia Nieveras, Padmal de Silva, Chatura Wijesundara and Razia Pendse (2019) "Accelerating Reforms of Primary Health Care Towards Universal Health Coverage in Sri Lanka" *WHO South-East Asia Journal of Public Health* 8(1): 21

Rajapaksa, Lalini, Padmal De Silva, Palitha Abeykoon, Lakshmi Somatunga, Sridharan Sathasivam, Susie Perera, Eshani Fernando, Dileep De Silva, Ashok Perera, Usha Perera, Yasoma Weerasekara, Anuji Gamage, Nalinda Wellappuli, Nimali Widanapathirana, Rangika Fernando, Chatura Wijesundara, Seneviratne Ruwanika and Kusal Weerasinghe (2021) *Sri Lanka Health System Review by the World Health Organization* World Health Organization. Regional Office for South-East Asia. Accessed on 06/05/2022. Available at https://apo.who.int/publications/i/item/sri-lanka-health-system-review

Rannan-Eliya, Ravindra P., Nilmini Wijemanne, Isuru K. Liyanage, Janaki Jayanthan, Shanthi Dalpatadu, Sarasi Amarasinghe and Chamara Anuranga (2015) "The Quality of Outpatient Primary Care in Public and Private Sectors in Sri Lanka – How Well Do Patient Perceptions Match Reality and What Are the Implications?" *Health Policy and Planning* 30(suppl_1): i59–i74

Remais, Justin V., Guang Zeng, Guangwei Li, Lulu Tian and Michael Engelgau (2013) "Convergence of non-Communicable and Infectious Diseases in Low- and Middle-Income Countries" *International Journal of Epidemiology* 42(1): 221–227

Ruwanpura, Kanchana N. (2022) "Doing the Right Thing? COVID-19, PPE and the Case of Sri Lankan Apparels" *Global Labour Journal* 13(1)

Sachs, J., C. Kroll, G. Lafortune, G. Fuller and F. Woelm (2021) *Sustainable Development Report 2021*. Accessed on 06/05/2022. Available at https://www.sdgindex.org/reports/sustainable-development-report-2021/

Senaratne, Rajitha and Poonam K. Singh (2016) "Against the Odds, Sri Lanka Eliminates Malaria" *The Lancet* 388(10049): 1038–1039

Shantha, Kumudu U. (2022) "Mental Health Act to Be Amended" *Ceylon Today* (23 August). Accessed on 22/10/2022. Available at https://ceylontoday.lk/2022/08/24/mental-health-act-to-be-amended/

UNICEF (2022) *Budget Brief: Health Sector – Sri Lanka 2021*. Accessed on 22/10/2022. Available at https://www.unicef.org/srilanka/reports/budget-brief-health-sector

United Nations (2023) "WHO chief declares end to COVID-19 as a global health emergency" *UN News*. Accessed on 02/06/2023. Available at https://news.un.org/en/story/2023/05/1136367

United Nations Economic and Social Commission for Asia and the Pacific (2017) *Ageing in Asia and the Pacific: Overview*. United Nations. Accessed on 21/10/2022. Available at https://www.unescap.org/resources/ageing-asia-and-pacific-overview

United Nations Population Fund (2022) *World Population Dashboard – Sri Lanka, United Nations Population Fund.* Accessed 06/05/2022. Available at https://www.unfpa.org/data/world-population/LK.

Uragoda, C.G. (1987) *A History of Medicine in Sri Lanka* Cambridge: Cambridge University Press

Verite Research (2022) "De-Mystifying the Increase in Sri Lanka's Debt" *Verite Research* Available at https://www.veriteresearch.org/publication/de-mystifying-the-increase-in-sri-lankas-debt/

Vos, T. et al. (2020) "Global Burden of 369 Diseases and Injuries in 204 Countries and Territories, 1990–2019: A Systematic Analysis for the Global Burden of Disease Study 2019", *The Lancet*, 396(10258): 1204–1222. Available at: https://doi.org/10.1016/S0140-6736(20)30925-9

Wijeratne, Y. (2022) *The Sri Lankan medical crisis, explained, Watchdog.* (Accessed on 13/05/2022. Available at https://longform.watchdog.team/data-projects/how-to-donate-to-the-sri-lankan-medical-crisis

World Bank (2018) *Sri Lanka: Primary Health Care System Strengthening Project*, *World Bank*. Accessed on 11/05/2022. Available at https://projects.worldbank.org/en/projects-operations/document-detail

World Bank (2022) *Current health expenditure (% of GDP) – Sri Lanka | Data*. Accessed 09/05/2022. Available at https://data.worldbank.org/indicator/SH.XPD.CHEX.GD.ZS?locations=LK

World Health Organization (2018) *Sri Lanka – WHO: country cooperation strategy 2018–2023* Accessed on 06/05/2022. Available at https://www.who.int/publications/i/item/9789290226345

World Health Organization (2021) "Sri Lanka vaccinates 50 per cent of total population, covering over 10 million with both doses". Accessed on 06/05/2022. Available at https://www.who.int/srilanka/news/detail/18-09-2021-sri-lanka-vaccinates-50-per-cent-of-total-population

World Health Organization Regional Office for South-East Asia (2020) *Decade for health workforce strengthening in SEAR 2015–2024, mid-term review*. Accessed on 30/05/2021. World Health Organization. Regional Office for South-East Asia. Available at https://apps.who.int/iris/handle/10665/334226

27
POLITICIZING 'THE VIRTUAL'
Examining the Internet on the Intersections of Gender and Sexuality in Sri Lanka

Senel Wanniarachchi and Zahrah Rizwan

Introduction

The internet has become an important space for the circulation of different forms of speech, from text to audio-visual content; and its proliferation has also generated numerous challenges. Today, various forms of harmful speech, from direct incitements to violence to forms of denigration, including those based on gender and sexuality circulate in the virtual landscape. This has had different and disproportionate implications for women and queer Sri Lankans.[1]

In this chapter, we review existing literature that traces how forms of violence that exist offline permeate into the realm of the virtual. We look at the ways in which majoritarian politics, patriarchy, and heteronormativity surface online and what this means for women and queer Sri Lankans. Additionally, we will also examine the ways in which women and queer Sri Lankans appear to be working on and through these platforms to resist these exclusionary power structures. In doing so, our intention is to highlight the complex ways in which the virtual is characterized by violence, inequality, and injustice (on the downside), as well as community, solidarity, resistance, pleasure, and joy (on the upside). More specifically, we do this, by considering the following questions: In what ways is access to the internet in Sri Lanka mediated by gender and sexuality? How does sexual gender-based violence circulate online and what forms of exclusion does it produce? How do women and queer Sri Lankans negotiate these challenges and use the internet as a space to resist and subvert dominant societal norms?

As there is limited scholarship written on the subject with a focus on Sri Lanka, we also use journalistic and policy accounts in our review. Existing writings largely focus on the Global North, although there are important interventions in India (see Arora and Scheiber 2017; Gupta 2020; Bhandari and Kovacs 2021; Roy and Deshbandhu 2021). We also make the case for the need for similar studies in Sri Lanka.

The Internet as a Site of Inequality

We start by examining anxieties, vilification, and violence faced by women and queer Sri Lankans in the digital world by summarizing key developments and debates about the internet, especially social media, as a site of violence. According to available data, over 50% of Sri Lanka's population uses the internet, is digitally literate, and uses different social media platforms with Facebook and Youtube being the most popular. Meanwhile, the number of sim cards in circulation within the island significantly exceeds the country's population (149.9%), largely due to many people possessing multiple cellular connections (TRCSL 2022). Within such a context, the mobile phone remains the primary device (78%) used to access the internet by Sri Lankans followed by personal computers (12%) (Galpaya, Zainudeen and Amarasinghe 2019). These figures have further risen in the context of the Covid-19 pandemic during which using digital platforms was often needed to access basic services.

Despite these developments, there is a stark 'digital divide' between the 52.6% of the population that has access to the internet and the 48.4% of the population that does not (Galpaya et al 2019; Data Portal 2022). This divide is mediated by, among other factors, class, location, language, gender, disability, age, sexuality as well as levels of education and digital literacy. People occupying multiple disadvantaged subjectivities face the brunt of these disparities in access. For instance, internet usage was lowest among rural elderly women with low levels of income and education (Galpaya et al 2019).

The cost, both of procuring and maintaining digital devices as well as accessing broadband internet, remains the primary factor in determining the degree of access (Galpaya et al 2019). The price of accessing one gigabyte of the internet is not affordable for 60% of Sri Lanka's population (ibid). Further, some Sri Lankans may have fully or partially controlled access to the internet via devices which may be owned by others, including parents, spouses, or places of work. Trans and gender non-conforming Sri Lankans may face additional barriers when procuring and accessing devices and services. For instance, due to stipulated documentary evidence of identity for purchasing new broadband or mobile connections, salespersons may refuse the sale of the same to those whose appearance and gender performance do not 'match' their appearance in their identity documents (Deshapriya et al 2017: 63).

Meanwhile, language, a historically complex political issue which has delineated existing social fault lines in Sri Lanka, is another factor which shapes access to online spaces. The country's Official Language Policy mandates that all state communication be made in Sinhala, Tamil, and English; yet there are significant gaps in the implementation of this policy. This also applies to official government communications made online, including public health messaging during the Covid-19 lockdowns. Further, English proficiency remains important to access and navigate the internet in Sri Lanka despite tools such as Unicode fonts and Google translator has improved levels of access. Some Sri Lankans have navigated these gaps in technology, by resorting to transliterating Sinhala (Singlish) and Tamil (Tanglish) using the English (Latin) script.

Sri Lanka was the first country in South Asia to introduce 4G mobile internet in 2012. President Gotabaya Rajapaksa said he plans to make Sri Lanka 'digitally inclusive' by 2024, including through the development of a high-speed optical transmission system and 5G mobile broadband internet (Vistas of Prosperity 2019). It is important to reflect on what it means for a country to be 'truly' digitally inclusive. Technological expansion needs to be coupled with equitable access to electricity and technology, along with other basic needs, to the most marginalized in our communities. There also need to be efforts to address the underlying forms of marginalization, including poverty, majoritarianism, patriarchy, and heteronormativity. Otherwise, the Sri Lankan case shows that technology, which is often touted as a leveller of existing inequalities, is also an amplifier of these same forms of marginalization, inequality, and injustice.

The Internet as a Site for Violence

Feminist scholarship on technology and the internet has long argued that the online/offline binary is inadequate as online technologies are enmeshed within the inequalities, injustices, and violence pervading our (offline) world (Shaw 2014; Henry and Powell 2015). In recent years, harmful and dangerous speech on social media platforms, including online hate speech, disinformation as well as forms of harassment, have become a pervasive force within Sri Lankan online spaces. Sri Lanka has a history of online hate speech, especially anti-Muslim hate speech, that has led to violence on the ground (Samaratunge and Hattotuwa 2014). How this kind of speech has impacted the country's electoral politics, especially by stifling healthy debate, skewing public opinion on key issues, and generating mistrust between people and communities is well documented. For instance, Hashtag Generation has revealed that coordinated disinformation narratives emerging in online spaces (including from overseas) gained substantive traction among voters in the run-up to and during Sri Lanka's 2019 Presidential Election and 2020 Parliamentary Election (Hashtag Generation 2019, 2020). In Sri Lanka, as elsewhere in the world, much of this type of content is also profoundly gendered and sexualized.

Outspoken women, queer people, politicians, human rights defenders, journalists, and celebrities are disproportionately targeted by online sexual and gender-based violence (SGBV). This represents a major threat to these groups' participation in public life. A study by Hashtag Generation (2022) analysed harmful comments received by 11 women in public life to understand how their participation in public life has put them at a greater risk of harmful speech on social media; found trolling, to be the most common form of harmful speech experienced by these women. In some situations, incessant torrents of abuse prompted some to withdraw from political life and have also deterred others from entering politics. Sri Lanka has some of the lowest rates for women's representation in political office in the world, and there are no openly queer politicians holding elected office (Wickramasinghe and Kodikara 2012).

Online and offline developments often inform, influence and bleed into each other. For example, in May 2021, viral SGBV content circulated online when a group including model Piumi Hansamali was sent in for mandatory quarantine for violating Covid19 quarantine regulations in May 2021 for hosting a birthday party at a luxury hotel in Colombo. An adept, savvy and strategic media user herself, she was extremely vocal about the events on her social media platforms and broadcasted her criticism on a Facebook live video. This video was widely circulated on social media and subsequently resulted in a barrage of sexist and misogynistic language, such as prostitute, porn star, being directed at Hansamali on social media (Hashtag Generation 2021). Research shows that such online conversations inspired by offline developments attract a large amount of attention from Sri Lankan internet users but generally do not last over two weeks (Hashtag Generation 2021).

The most frequent form of harmful speech women public figures faced was trolling, followed by misogynistic and sexist speech, indicating a range in intensity and intentionality of online hate. The harm that women politicians faced most extensively was discrediting comments which were made by men in many cases (Hashtag Generation 2022). The nature and the extent of violence faced by women and queer subjects may also depend on the social media platform in question. For instance, Perera and Wijetunga (2019) have contended that 'when compared to platforms, such as YouTube where gender ambiguity or femme-presentation is often met with heavy hostility, the hostility on TikTok was significantly less'. Despite these differences among platforms, according to the Sri Lanka Computer Emergency Readiness Team (SLCERT), the state institution responsible for cyber security, there has been a 460% increase in the number of complaints related to cyber security breaches received in 2020 in comparison with the previous year (Wanniarachchi 2022).

While SGBV manifests in different forms online, the non-consensual dissemination of intimate content, popularly known as 'leaks', is one of the most widespread forms of online SGBV faced by Sri Lankan internet users. 'Leaks' may include the unauthorized dissemination of images, videos and screengrabs and audio recordings of private conversations. Previous research demonstrates that in Sri Lanka, there is an ecosystem of social media pages and groups created with the explicit intent of routinely collecting and sharing non-consensual intimate images, especially of women, and gender non-conforming people including minors (Hashtag Generation 2022). The dissemination of this type of content, or the threat of dissemination, is often made alongside intimidation and/or 'blackmail' of the subjects that are featured therein and/or their family and friends. The blackmailing comes with specific demands; for example, to grant or not grant a divorce to a spouse or demands for sex or more intimate content to be shared.

A survey by Women in Need (2022), a Sri Lankan NGO focused on responding to gender-based violence, revealed that nearly one in four Sri Lankans 'knew of a friend who experienced online harassment of a sexual nature. Meanwhile, one in five Sri Lankans reported knowing of someone who had edited, doctored or photoshopped images that were subsequently shared on the internet' (2022: 5). This underlines a violent normalization of the dissemination of this type of content in public spaces. Research also shows that while many internet users may not actively 'share' this type of content on their personal social media handles, many still 'view' them (Women in Need 2022: 5).

Deshan, a gay man interviewed for the study, Disrupting the Binary, Experiences of LGBT Sri Lankans Online (Deshapriya et al 2017: 46), shared an experience where he feared having his device repaired:

> I have a tab where the screen broke recently. But I can't give it to be repaired, because it has all the pictures of my vows' ceremony with my partner. I am scared that the pictures will go public if I gave it to someone to repair.

Such fear of potential non-consensual dissemination of an intimate event where Deshan and his partner held a vows ceremony in the presence of their friends and family committing to be with each other is symptomatic of the daily negotiations queer Sri Lankans are forced to make. Partly this reflects how laws from the British Colonial period are often interpreted in ways that criminalize non-heteronormative sex and sex work. Sections 365 and 365A of the country's Penal Code criminalize 'gross indecency' and 'carnal intercourse against the order of nature'. These provisions have been interpreted to criminalize non-penovaginal sex. Meanwhile, the country's Penal Code provisions on 'cheating by personation ... or pretending to be another person' are often used to prosecute and harass its transgender and non-binary residents. These laws and others, such as the Obscene Publications Ordinance, all have a bearing on access and security as many users may decide to reveal and conceal different aspects of their identity due to fear of reprisal and harassment. As Jayasinghe (2021: 5) says, 'in a country like Sri Lanka, where queer identities are criminalized [...] the shadows the internet casts are darker, the elations found therein more intense'.

Women, and queer people, therefore, may be at a higher risk of facing control and regulation when accessing the internet (Deshapriya et al 2017; Women in Need 2020). For instance, in the Women in Need (WIN) study, of the 1533 people surveyed 52.9% of the women respondents said they shared the passwords of their devices with an intimate partner at least once, while 41.3% of men had done the same.[2] Similarly, 44.3% of women had shared the login details of their Facebook account with their intimate partner, as opposed to 31.8% of men who had done the same (Women in Need 2020: 6). While the decision to share access to their online accounts with an intimate partner, may appear a personal one, it is very likely that for many individuals, these decisions are mediated by unequal power relations that exist within intimate relationships, within family and kin.

Many cases of online SGBV reported were perpetrated by an intimate partner. An example cited in the WIN study notes the following:

> Surani's husband had opened her facebook account and given her a smartphone, even though she hardly used it. Her husband eventually used Surani's Facebook account to spread false rumours about Surani having an affair with another man and living a 'free' life. It is ultimately posts, such as these circulated among her friends and colleagues that concern Surani who is a teacher by profession. She is concerned that these pictures and accusations might lead to her losing her job in a leading Provincial school. As a single mother of two young girl children, this was one of her greatest concerns. Because Surani's husband used her own Facebook account to spread these rumours, many of her friends also believed the content
> *(Women in Need 2020: 35–36)*

This form of intimate violence, control, and surveillance are informed by patriarchal notions, such as 'sexual purity', 'familial reputation', 'respectability', and 'marriagability' (de Alwis 2009; Abeyasekera 2021). Seen this way, it becomes apparent that dominant patriarchal and heteronormative frameworks are mediated and re-mediated via technologies, such as the smartphone and social media handles.

Regulation and surveillance enforced within relationships, families, and communities can be read as existing on the same continuum as regulations enforced by the state and large social media conglomerates that profit from these viral interactions. In Sri Lanka, in May 2019, there were at least three internet shutdowns in the aftermath of the Easter Sunday attacks and the anti-Muslim violence that followed, including a nationwide block that lasted nine days (Freedom House 2022). Identity theft, especially in the form of 'fake profiles' on social media platforms, is also common. Contradictorily, attempts to respond to fake profiles also negatively affected transgender and gender non-conforming people whose Facebook profile names may not match the names identified in their official documents, such as National Identity Cards or utility bills. Despite these barriers, queer people prefer to utilize 'fake profiles' to meet and interact with other queer people and potential intimate or romantic partners. For example, Rajesh, interviewed in Deshapriya et al (2017), mentioned how he maintains two profiles – one for his family and another for other queer folks.

Along with the normalization of online SGBV, there is also a culture of 'victim-blaming' that correspondingly arises. The survey by WIN found that 34.2% agreed with the statement that 'both the person who sent the picture as well as the person who shared the picture is to blame', although this was gendered: 43.8% of men agreed as opposed to 34.2% of women (WIN 2020: 38). The results show how patriarchal attitudes manifest across gender differences. The results of the WIN Study are in line with the findings of previous research on gender inequitable attitudes (de Mel et al 2013). In one study, more than 2/3rd of the female respondents affirmed that 'in any rape case, one would have to question whether the victim is promiscuous or has a bad reputation'.

The normalization of online SGBV has also impacted the ways in which social media users interact with each other in online spaces. Studies have found for instance that men (55.6%) are more likely to accept 'friend requests' from a stranger on social media compared to women (17%), send more friend requests to strangers (51.7%) than women (8.9%), and share more personal information with people they meet online (29.2%) than women (19.7%) (Women in Need 2020).

Women and queer people also appear to take various steps to ensure their safety online, including moving between online platforms when the threat to safety is detected, limiting access, or completely restricting family members and relatives from personal profiles, limiting engagement in public conversations related to sexuality and disengaging or not commenting on posts of family members with opposing views (Deshapriya et al 2017: 50).

Along with the normalization of online SGBV as well as the widespread prevalence of victim-blaming and onus put on those at risk, there is also a culture of impunity enjoyed by the perpetrators of this type of violence. One study titled which surveyed 103 Sri Lankans found that 90% of the respondents who faced online SGBV reported the content to the social media platform but did not seek any form of legal redress (Perera and Ibrahim 2021). While legal provisions in the Penal Code and other laws, including the Computer Crimes Act, may be relied on to act against perpetrators, the lack of awareness surrounding these issues, including among law enforcement officials, coupled with a general mistrust in the legal system plus long delays in court proceedings have disincentivized many people from seeking legal action.

Recently, due to advocacy by civil society organizations and global outrage and condemnation, especially in relation to anti-Muslim violence, social media intermediaries, such as Facebook, have taken some action by recruiting more local content moderators and improving automated detection (Wanniarachchi 2022). However, these steps appear to be largely focused on ethnoreligious harmful speech, while moderating gendered and sexualized content does not receive the same level of urgency. This is perhaps because gender and sexuality-based violence often does not erupt in a single moment in the same way that an ethnoreligious riot does and often does not receive the same level of global media coverage and condemnation. Improvements in the enforcement of Community Standards by Social Media intermediaries have also compelled those disseminating SGBV content to seek alternative channels, such as instant messaging services, including Whatsapp.

However, it is important to acknowledge that it is often not possible to distinguish ethnoreligious dangerous speech from gendered and sexualized dangerous speech. As many Sri Lankan feminist scholars have shown, ethnonationalism in Sri Lanka, as is elsewhere, is inherently a gendered project (see de Mel 2001; de Alwis 2004). It is therefore unsurprising that ethnoreligious dangerous speech is often gendered and sexualized. Contemporaneously gendered and sexualized dangerous speech can also circulate based on ethnoreligious grounds. For instance, in March 2021 anti-Muslim conversations, which emerged when the government announced that it intends to ban full-face veils in public places, were simultaneously ethnonationalist and gendered, with Muslim women, the niqab, and hijab often being referred to in derogatory terms.

As new online platforms emerge or as old platforms add new features in their attempts to 'stay relevant', new avenues also emerge for the circulation of harmful and dangerous speech online. Online abuse can elicit feelings of fear, shame, and guilt and can do real and lasting damage to the targets' mental, emotional, and physical health and well-being (Association for Progressive Communications 2017: 4). In the long term, online abuse and violence also work together to buttress forms of inequality and injustice that gendered and sexualized subjects have 'always' faced in Sri Lanka.

The Internet as a Site of Resistance

The previous section discussed how social media has emerged as a site of violence for women and queer Sri Lankans. Yet, this is only a partial analysis of social media's impact on the lives of these groups. Women and queer Sri Lankans are not only victims/survivors of violence, but also use these same spaces to resist, challenge, and contest exclusionary articulations of power, including patriarchy, heteronormativity, and majoritarianism. Thus, in this section, we direct our analytical gaze at the ways in which the internet, especially social media, has been reclaimed by women and queer Sri Lankans as a site of resistance, pleasure, and joy.

We begin with the #MeToo Movement. #MeToo was a campaign that activist Tarana Burke began in 2006 to support women of colour from underprivileged communities who experienced rape or sexual assault. It gained viral momentum globally in 2017 following a tweet made by actress Alyssa Milano calling women who have experienced sexual harassment and/or sexual assault to use the hashtag on their social media platforms (Amarasuriya 2021). This led to conversations on sexual violence receiving 'viral' attention among internet users, especially in, but not limited to, the West. Four years later, a tweet by a Sri Lankan woman journalist sparked conversations on sexual violence faced by Sri Lankan women in the workplace, especially in newsrooms and media institutions (Srinivasan 2021). Her tweet on being subjected to sexual harassment by a male colleague at her workplace induced more women to talk about their own experiences of sexual harassment on social media, especially Twitter (Al Jazeera 2021). These online events stirred offline discussions as well, among policymakers, the media, and civil society.

In response, a statement was issued by the then Government Spokesperson and Minister of Mass Media Keheliya Rambukwella who instructed the Government Information Department to launch an investigation into the reports and to take measures to ensure that women journalists were safe in the newsrooms (de Visser 2021). Further, some digital media organizations, such as Roar Global, and civil society organizations, such as Hashtag Generation, voiced the need for accountability and introspection within media and civil society spaces. In a context where survivors of sexual violence may not receive redress from law enforcement in their workplaces, the internet generated space to bring attention to not only individual experiences of harassment but also the cultures of impunity and patronage that protect harassers.

Additionally, Sri Lankan feminist and queer activists also use social media to join global campaigns on different issues to make transnational connections on experiences of injustice and express solidarity across borders. '16 Days of Activism Against Gender Based Violence' is an example of a global campaign that has piqued interest in Sri Lanka bringing together more institutional actors.[3] Such campaigns bring together grassroots feminist and queer organizations, International Organizations, NGOs, the Government, and the private sector together to raise awareness on SGBV. Advocacy initiatives taken by these actors as part of this campaign have also involved online spaces that utilized poster campaigns, livestreaming (offline) events, webinars, and online discussions. Similarly, 'Take back the Tech' 2022 is another global campaign, initiated by The Association for Progressive Communications – Women's Rights Programme, which specifically focuses on online violence and offers information and tools for those targeted to stay safe online. Research also shows that the internet is used by sexual rights activists for the purposes of 'outreach, community-building, advocacy, and sexual expression of women and queer experiences of pleasure and desire' (Valle 2021: 630).

For queer Sri Lankans, the internet has become a space to learn, meet others like them, express themselves, find a sense of community and access livelihood opportunities (Perera and Ibrahim 2021). It has also provided a space which is used to subvert gender roles and expectations through, among other things, dress, and dance (Perera and Wijetunga 2019). For instance, over 50% of the respondents of the study by Perera and Ibrahim (2021) agreed that 'access to the internet has changed their understanding of gender and sexuality and their perceptions of those of different genders and sexuality' (2021: 10). Furthermore, existing research on the online engagements of lesbian and bisexual women in Sri Lanka shows that online platforms can serve as 'information tools', 'social networking tools', and 'advocacy tools' (WMC 2017: 87). An older gay man who had grown up in a time before the internet, interviewed by the study Disrupting the Binary Code:

Experiences of LGBT Sri Lankans Online, said he was 'completely unaware of homosexuality as a phenomenon', recalling how he had believed for a long time that his same-sex sexual attraction was unique and that he was the 'only person in the world' to be going through the experience. It was only after he stumbled across the entry for 'homosexuality' in an encyclopaedia ... that he came to appreciate the 'commonness' of his nature (Deshapriya et al 2017: 30).

Today, many queer Sri Lankans who can access the internet are more likely to be aware of global and Sri Lankan discourse on LGBTIQ+ rights. An important caveat here is that not all information available online is reliable or accurate, raising important questions on the importance of digital, media, and information literacy.

In Sri Lanka, public spaces where even heterosexual partners can be intimate with each other are often policed. In such a context, queer Sri Lankans have extremely limited safe spaces to meet others like them, especially with the threat of arrest, exposure, and intimidation looming. Many of the spaces that do exist, such as tolerant hotels, also often tend to be classed and may not be accessible to a vast majority of queer people. Countless such spaces may also only be accessible to able-bodied persons.[4] 'Cruising locations' are spaces where queer people, especially gay and bisexual men, meet others like them. However, encounters at such spaces have been described as generally 'hurried, spontaneous, anonymous, with the main (if not the only) purpose of the encounter being the performance of a sexual act' leaving little room for the formation of longer-term relationships and friendships (Deshapriya et al 2017: 46). While there are also many 'community gatherings' organized by NGOs and other organizations, many queer people may not be able or may choose not to attend these for various reasons. Within such a context, the internet, especially social media as well as dating and 'hook-up' applications, have provided spaces to find potential intimate partners and engage in forms of technology facilitate forms of intimacy, such as sexting, sharing erotic images, videos with each other, and so on.

Older queer organizers and activists say that they had to largely rely on snail mail and telephone calls to contact potential participants for their events. These are also largely unsafe options as a family member or housemate could open a letter or pick up a call (Deshapriya et al 2017: 48). Today, queer organizations use social media to disseminate informational content on various issues including human rights and sexual health. Further, in a context where representations of intimacy and desire in the mainstream press are largely heteronormative and cis-normative and the few representations that exist, exist only as further harmful stereotypes about these communities, the internet allows queer people to access information about queer news, history, art, politics, healthcare, and so on and engage in forms of self-representation. Furthermore, women and queer people are also able to strategically use various inbuilt features of social media applications such as privacy settings, unfriending, blocking, reporting breaches to the respective platforms, as well as deactivating or deleting their accounts to ensure their safety, security and as Butler (2022) says 'the liveability of life'.

Conclusion

Through this brief analysis of existing studies and literature, we have attempted to explore the ways in which women and queer people in Sri Lanka work on, with and through the internet. What the analysis demonstrates is that women and queer Sri Lankans are not just mere victims/survivors in distress on the internet. While the internet has reproduced various forms of violence, inequality, and injustice that these subjects also experience offline, this is only half of the story. The reality is a much more complex and ambivalent one where these subjects also use the internet to learn, meet like-minded others, organize themselves around issues that affect them and that they care about, express themselves, expose perpetrators of violence and of course, share laughter, pleasure, and joy with one another.

It is clear then that gender and sexuality have a significant, yet largely under-documented and under-investigated importance to technology broadly and the internet more specifically. Future research could also examine, among other things, the gendered and sexualized dimensions of platform design and infrastructure, algorithms, surveillance, the extraction and commodification of data, monopolistic forms of corporate platform ownership and the use of dating and 'hook-up' applications among other developments.

Notes

1. The term queer has been used as a slur, a theoretical foundation, an identity marker as well as a call to action. In Sri Lanka, the term queer has not received widespread traction, largely because variations of the acronym LGBTIQA+ have been used by NGOs and other policy and human rights actors. We use 'queer' to refer to those with non-normative sexualities and genders to push back on the more dominant LGBTIQA+. However, as we do this, we remain reflexive of the limitations of the term queer itself, especially in relation to questions of translation, activism, and movement building in Sri Lanka and beyond.
2. The sample included nearly equal numbers of men and women (772 women and 761 men).
3. The 16 Days of Activism Against Gender-Based Violence is an international campaign originating from the first Women's Global Leadership Institute 1991 that has since been active between November 25, the International Day Against Violence Against Women, and December 10, International Human Rights Day ("From Awareness to Accountability | Global 16 Days Campaign", 2022).
4. In this study we do not focus on the lived realities of Sri Lankans with disabilities, although there is an important need for further research into this area.

References

Abeyasekera, Asha (2021) *Making the Right Choice Narratives of Marriage in Sri Lanka* New Brunswick: Rutgers University Press

Al Jazeera (2021) "Sri Lanka's belated #MeToo movement starts from its newsrooms" *Al Jazeera* (23 June). https://www.aljazeera.com/news/2021/6/23/sri-lanka-metoo-newsrooms-women-journalists

Amarasuriya, Harini (2021) "Some reflections on the #MeToo movement" *Ceylon Today* (4 September). https://www.aljazeera.com/news/2021/6/23/sri-lanka-metoo-newsrooms-women-journalists

Arora, Payal and Laura Scheiber (2017) "Slumdog Romance: Facebook Love and Digital Privacy at the Margins" *Media, Culture & Society* Thousand Oaks: Sage

Association for Progressive Communications (2017) "Online Gender-Based Violence: A Submission from the Association for Progressive Communications to the United Nations Special Rapporteur on Violence against Women, Its Causes and Consequences" *Association for Progressive Communications (APC)* (20 November). https://www.genderit.org/resources/submissions-united-nations-special-rapporteur-online-violence-against-women

Bhandari, Vrinda and Anja Kovacs (2021) *What's Sex Got to Do with It? Mapping the Impact of Questions of Gender and Sexuality on the Evolution of the Digital Rights Landscape in India*. New Delhi: Internet Democracy Project

Butler, Judith (2022) "A Livable Life? An Inhabitable World? Scheler on the Tragic" *Puncta Journal of Critical Phenomenology* 5(2): 8–27

Data Portal (2022). "Digital 2022: Sri Lanka". Accessed on 02/05/2022. Available at https://datareportal.com/reports/digital-2022-sri-lanka

de Alwis, Malathi (2004) "The Moral Mother Syndrome" *Indian Journal of Gender Studies* 11(1): 65–73

de Alwis, Malathi (2009) "Gender, Politics and the 'Respectable Lady'" In *Unmaking the Nation: The Politics of Identity and History in Modern Sri Lanka* Pradeep Jeganathan and Qadri Ismail (eds) New York: South Focus Press, pp 138–156

de Mel, Neloufer (2001) *Women and the Nation's Narrative: Gender and Nationalism in Twentieth Century Sri Lanka* Lanham: Rowman & Littlefield de Mel, Neloufer (2013) "Broadening Gender: Why Masculinities Matter". Available at https://www.care.org/wp-content/uploads/2020/05/Broadening-Gender_Why-Masculinities-Matter.pdf

de Visser, Shruthi (2021) "Harnessing Sri Lanka's #metoo Moment into a Movement" *Groundviews* (7 September). https://groundviews.org/2021/07/09/harnessing-sri-lankas-metoo-moment-into-a-movement/

Deshapriya, Paba, Michael Mendis, Shermal Wijewardena, Subha Wijesiriwardena, Sepali Kottegoda and Sanchia Brown (2017) ***Disrupting the Binary Code: Experiences of LGBT Sri Lankans Online*** Colombo: Women and Media Collective

Freedom House, Sri Lanka (2022) "Sri Lanka". Accessed on 19/06/2022. Available at https://freedomhouse.org/country/sri-lanka

From Awareness to Accountability | Global 16 Days Campaign (2022) Global 16 Days Campaign.. Retrieved 2 March, 2022, from https://16dayscampaign.org/

Galpaya, Helani, Ayesha Zainudeen and Tharaka Amarasinghe (2019) ***After Access: ICT Access and Use in Sri Lanka and the Global South***. Colombo: Lirne Asia

Gupta, Paridhi (2020) "Art(s) of Visibility: Resistance and Reclamation of University Spaces by Women Students in Delhi" ***Gender, Place & Culture*** 27(1): 86–103

Hashtag Generation (2019) "Findings from the Social Media Monitoring Exercise during the 2019 Sri Lankan Presidential Election". Accessed on 23/08/2022. Available at https://hashtaggeneration.org/wp-content/uploads/2020/01/social-media-monitoring-report.pdf

Hashtag Generation (2020) "Sri Lanka: Social Media and Electoral Integrity. Findings from Sri Lanka's 2020 Parliamentary Election". Accessed 19/07/2022. Available at https://drive.google.com/file/d/1qQKubeK1HtAtom3J5v2BKoQ5hToH9ma_/view

Hashtag Generation (2021) ***Social Media Analysis 2021 Annual Report*** Hashtag Generation

Hashtag Generation (2022) ***Social Media Analysis 2022 Annual Report*** Hashtag Generation

Henry, Nicola and Anastasia Powell (2015) "Beyond the 'sext': Technology-Facilitated Sexual Violence and Harassment against Adult Women" ***Australian & New Zealand Journal of Criminology*** 48(1): 104–118

Jayasinghe, Pasan (2021) "Forward" In ***Somewhere Only We Know: Gender, Sexualities, and Sexual Behaviour on the Internet in Sri Lanka*** Association for Progressive Communications. https://erotics.apc.org/wp-content/uploads/2021/03/Somewhere-only-We-Know-Online

Perera, Sachini and Zainab Ibrahim (2021) "Somewhere Only We Know: Gender, Sexualities, and Sexual Behaviour on the Internet in Sri Lanka". ***Association for Progressive Communications***. Available at https://erotics.apc.org/wp-content/uploads/2021/03/Somewhere-only-We-Know-Online.pdf

Perera, Sachini and Minoli Wijetunga (2019) "How Tiktok is a Platform of Performance and Play for Women in Sri Lanka" ***GenderIt.Org*** (10 May). Available at https://genderit.org/articles/how-tiktok-platform-performance-and-play-women-sri-lanka

Roy, Dibyadyuti and Aditya Deshbandhu (2021) "Anxious Postcolonial Masculinity in Online Video Games: Race, Gender and Colonialism in Indian Digital Spaces" ***Gender, Place & Culture*** 29(1): 104–129

Samaratunge, Shilpa and Sanjana Hattotuwa (2014) "Liking Violence: A Study of Hate Speech on Facebook in Sri Lanka" ***CPA Lanka***. Available at cpalanka.org/wp-content/uploads/2014/09/Hate-Speech-Executive-Summary.pdf

Shaw, Adrienne (2014) "The Internet Is Full of Jerks, because the World Is Full of Jerks: What Feminist Theory Teaches Us about the Internet" ***Communication and Critical/Cultural Studies*** 11(3): 273–277

Srinivasan, Meera (2021) "Sri Lanka's 'Metoo' moment sparks reflection on newsrooms" ***The Hindu*** (26 June). https://www.thehindu.com/news/international/sri-lankas-metoo-moment-sparks-reflection-on-newsrooms/article34949285.ece

Take Back the Tech (2022) ***Take Back The Tech***. Available at https://takebackthetech.net/

TRCSL (2022) "Cumulative Licences Granted". ***TRCSL***. Available at https://www.trc.gov.lk/content/files/statistics/SORQ4202331012024745.pdf

Valle, Firuzeh Shokooh (2021) Turning Fear into Pleasure: Feminist Resistance against Online Violence in the Global South. ***Feminist Media Studies*** 21(4): 621–638. Retrieved from https://doi.org/10.1080/14680777.2020.1749692

Vistas of Prosperity and Splendour (2019) ***Sri Lanka Podujana Peramuna***. Available at http://www.doc.gov.lk/images/pdf/NationalPolicyframeworkEN/FinalDovVer02-English.pdf

Wanniarachchi, Senel (2022) "Consent in the world of the Internet" ***Sunday Times*** (29 May). Available at https://www.sundaytimes.lk/220529/sunday-times-2/consent-in-the-world-of-the-internet-484021.html

Wickramasinghe, Maithree and Chulani Kodikara (2012) "Representation in Politics: Women and Gender in the Sri Lankan Republic" In ***The Sri Lankan Republic at 40: Reflections on Constitutional History,***

Theory and Practice- An Edited Collection of Essays Asanga Welikala (ed) Colombo, Sri Lanka, pp 721–820 Available at http://constitutionalreforms.org/wp-content/uploads/2020/03/Representation-in-Politics1.pdf

Women and Media Collective (2017) "Disrupting the Binary Code: Experiences of LGBT Sri Lankans Online." Available at https://womenandmedia.org/wp-content/uploads/2018/02/Disrupting-the-Binary-Code-_-for-web.pdf

Women in Need (2022) Anti Cyber Violence Initiative: Combatting Tech facilitated Gender based Violence in Sri Lanka USAID. Available at www.wincyberviolence.lk

28
FEMINIST PATHWAYS AND POLITICAL POSSIBILITIES IN SRI LANKAN PLANTATION STUDIES

Mythri Jegathesan

Introduction

I provide a critical review of the literature and debates that represent the English medium scholarly record on Sri Lanka's plantations in the post-war context for the last 50 years. First, I present a brief historical overview of the plantations by tying key strands within plantation studies across the contemporary social sciences and humanities before the end of the war (1971–2009).[1] Second, I discuss how researchers have written about Sri Lanka's plantations' culture, society, and politics in the *post-war context* (2009–2021) across disciplines of history, economics, gender studies, anthropology, sociology, development studies, and political science. I argue that three research arenas have emerged in post-war plantation studies of Sri Lanka: (1) Malaiyaka Tamil heritage and collective memory; (2) gender and social reproduction; and (3) political and labour movements. For each arena, I discuss significant intellectual frames and contributions and conclude with a discussion of future avenues of research that highlight the value of feminist approaches to studying Sri Lanka's plantations. Doing so, I argue, foregrounds the regional and global connections that Sri Lanka's plantations have to broader interdisciplinary debates on the reproduction of gender, politics, labour, and development in plantation studies globally.

A Historical Overview

Scholarship on Sri Lanka's plantations before the end of the war rests on three nodes of critical engagement: (1) the history of the coffee, tea, and rubber plantations with respect to labour, migration, and industrial production; (2) caste, gender, and ethnicity dynamics of social reproduction among Hill Country Tamils; and (3) development research and activities linked to conditions of social and economic marginalisation on the plantations. Each focus area correlates to broader trends in social science and humanities research and writing and is situated within more general shifts in Sri Lankan research to focus on the political conflict and post-colonial formations of Sinhala and Tamil nationalisms, ethnic identity formation, economic development, and sociocultural change.

Sri Lanka's Plantations in History

Since the early 19th century, British capitalists experimented with planting coffee in the Kandyan highlands. Subsequent historical representations of Sri Lanka's coffee and later tea and rubber plantations began tracing both the rapid expansion of the plantation industry and the conditions of its labour force, primarily Hill Country Tamil residents, who migrated from South India during this period or were Ceylon-born descendants of Tamil migrant labourers (Webb 2002). The historical record, however, constituted what Patrick Peebles has called "a palimpsest of interpretations" within Sri Lankan plantation studies (Peebles 2001: 18). Scholars have struggled to fully interrogate the overwhelming presence of the colonial record in their analyses of the history of Tamil migration from India to colonial Ceylon and its extractive motivations and have also struggled to adequately challenge the "colonial construction of Plantation Tamil identity ... as part of Sinhalese nationalist historiography" (Peebles 2001: 19).[2]

Peebles' characterisation of Sri Lankan plantation historiography as "palimpsest" is a productive one, as it draws out the clear roles that scholarly effacement and accommodation had in re-routing Hill Country Tamil histories towards more centrally urgent contemporary narratives of nation, ethnicity, and politics in post-colonial Sri Lanka. In accounts of workers' early migration from Tamil Nadu to Ceylon to those more focused on earlier iterations of bonded and coolie labour, concerns over the contemporaneous sedimentation of ethnonationalist politics effaced broader questions of coalition building and local and regional histories of resistance to ethnonationalism among Malaiyaka Tamils themselves (Wesumperuma 1986; Moldrich 1989).

Notable exceptions to these erasures exist. Select historical accounts note the rise of plantation labour movements and unions, and the ways both reinforced the workings of patriarchy and the consolidation of class differences, alongside concerted efforts of collective bargaining leading up to and immediately following independence (Jayawardena 1972; Sahadevan 1995; Gunawardena and Biyanwila 2008; Kanapathipillai 2009). Documenting politically aligned labour movements, scholars also produced close readings of Malaiyaka Tamil labourer representations in Ceylon. Early iterations of colonial constructions of coolie labour and representations of Malaiyaka Tamils as a distinct ethno-linguistic community also demonstrated that the community was recognised for their distinctive cultural art forms, such as poetry, song, and literature that all centre themes of labour oppression and coolie heritage (Velupillai 1970; Velupillai 1983).

Sri Lanka's Plantations in the Social Sciences

Whereas most historical accounts adhered closely to the trajectories of the colonial record, scholarship outside the discipline of history during this same period filled the gaps of knowledge in the colonial and post-colonial industrial record. Caste, gender, and ethnic difference proved to be useful indicators of understanding social reproduction among Hill Country Tamils living and working on the plantations and in analyses of their interactions with other ethnically identifying communities in Sri Lanka. Between the anti-Tamil riots of 1958 to the island-wide anti-Tamil riots of July 1983, Hill Country Tamils have been uniquely impacted by anti-Tamil discrimination and state-sponsored forms of violence and surveillance due to ongoing forms of socioeconomic marginalisation linked to their statelessness, disenfranchisement, and ongoing forms of caste oppression and social exclusion.

Anthropologists during this time broadened their research approaches to study caste, gender, and ethnicity. Earlier anthropological accounts followed broadly structuralist methodologies, where the single researcher studied community practices using participant observation, household surveys, and structured and unstructured interviews within physically bound estates bound by labour and caste and kin-based relations (Jayaraman 1975; Hollup 1994). These approaches reflected anthropology's predominant directives to produce bound, village studies, and accounts of cultural life and practice during the 1970s through to the mid-1990s. Scholars also revisited the significance of coolie heritage and history and challenged the dualistic representation and myth of the estate "enclave" (Meyer 1992; Daniel 1996).

Emphases on caste continuities have paved the way for future scholars to revisit caste in collaboration with broader, country-wide movements to study across ethnic, religious, and geographically bound communities. While Balasundaram, Chandrabose and Sivapragasam (2009) argue for the need to understand the dynamism of caste relations across generations, labour sectors, gender, and kinship association, they also note the political ellipses of caste due to polarised attention related to the civil war. Following their thesis, caste discrimination and labour segmentation uniquely reveal and confirm the exclusion of Hill Country Tamils from national dialogues on political resolution. The question of ethnicity was also raised as a viable category of study. Social, economic, and political conditions of marginalised and resistance coalesced in the formation of an Up Country or Hill Country Tamil ethnic identity, and they were also grounded in shared histories of diasporic migration and contemporary everyday relations of structural violence and culture work (Bass 2008).

From the 1980s through the first decade of the 2000s, the social sciences began to document and challenge the structurally gendered inequalities that were systemic to the plantation sector. Studies in anthropology, sociology, political science, economics, and gender studies during this period specifically took up how labour segmentation, patriarchal politics, and industrial work practices worked together to enable conditions of gender and socioeconomic marginalisation among Hill Country Tamils before and during the civil war. For these scholars, patriarchy, caste, class, and industrial practices cemented women workers' subordination within the plantation economy (Kurian 1982). This gendered subordination filtered through kinship and reproductive networks through structurally unequal forms of educational access, an unevenness with an interiority that particularly harmed mothers and children on the estates (Gnanamuttu 1979; Little 1999). Following this theme of constriction, gender, and cultural practice on the estates subsequently became slotted as burdens to women's daily lives and roles in work and life but also as impediments to their capacities for work and leadership mobility (Samarasinghe 1993; Kandasamy 2002; Phillips 2003, 2005; de Silva 2005, Balasundaram 2009).

Development Studies on the Plantations

The trajectory of findings above can be linked to *three significant industrial and political shifts* during this period: (1) the 1964 Srimavo Shastri Pact and repatriation scheme and the 1972 and 1973 land reform nationalisation of the plantations; (2) the opening of Sri Lanka's economy in 1977 and 1978; and (3) the reprivatisation of the plantation companies in 1992. Each of these transitions negatively impacted the living and socioeconomic conditions of Tamil workers on the plantations. Their sites of residence and livelihood became key targets for political patronage and state industrial profit accumulation while maintaining their broader states of disenfranchisement and landlessness and uneven forms of access to government services (Caspersz et al 1995; Manikam 1995; Shanmugaratnam 1997). This legal marginalisation was further compounded by years of state-sponsored discrimination and escalating forms of surveillance and violence against Tamil civilians, including the 1977 and 1983 anti-Tamil riots, detention, and disappearances under the Prevention of Terrorism Act (PTA) and waves of displacement and migration of the plantations among Malaiyaka Tamils due to safety fears, poverty, and lack of social mobility (Ajantha 1984; Satyodaya 1984; Institute of Social Development 2016).

In connection with repatriation beginning in 1964 and the impacts of land reform in the early 1970s, SETIK (the Development and Social Justice agency of the Catholic Diocese of Kandy in Sri Lanka) and Satyodaya, two NGOs in Kandy, were created in 1964 and 1972, respectively (Moore 1985;

Hollup 1998). Within the Jesuit tradition, Satyodaya particularly aimed to sustain Marxist Christian and interethnic and religious dialogues around issues of social justice and socialism. However, the group soon shifted to responding to the sustained violence and discrimination experienced by plantation workers during the anti-Tamil riots (Fernando 2007: 140). Other nongovernmental organisations (NGOs), such as PREDO (Plantation Rural Education & Development Organisation), emerged in alliance with Satyodaya in 1987 and focused on children's education and the establishment of sustained Montessori facilities and programmes for preschool children on Sri Lanka's tea plantations.

In 1974, Satyodaya also founded the Coordinating Secretariat for the Plantation Areas (CSPA) amidst Sri Lankan land reforms, statelessness, conditions of poverty, and continued violence against Tamil minorities and dissenting voices more broadly. This alliance was one of the first attempts at building networks of solidarity among the plantation NGOs and trade unions in protest of injustice, inequality, and human rights violations committed against Malaiyaka Tamils on the plantations. Given their collective voice, this network was also able to mobilise on larger Malaiyaka Tamil issues, such as repatriation, the effects of statelessness, wage strikes, and poverty (Dawood 1980); and the targeting of Tamil minorities in Sri Lankan communal violence and emergency rule under the PTA (Satyodaya 1984).[3]

As violence against Tamil minorities escalated in Sri Lanka through the 1970s and into the 1990s, the plantation sector grappled with the opening of the national economy alongside the sustained ethnic conflict (Loganathan 1990; Gunasinghe 2004). The liberalisation of Sri Lanka's markets was most evident in the shift from nationalised plantations to re-privatised ones. During this period of change, many plantation NGOs also suffered major funding crises in direct response to the larger global economic crisis and escalation of civil war and ethnic conflict in Sri Lanka. This crisis of funding compounded with the impact of privatisation also resulted in a research bias of studying living conditions on the tea estates over rubber and coconut plantations in the South and South-Central areas outside Central Province (Uyangoda 1995). Such biases were also influenced by the political agitation of trade unions who were based in the tea growing areas, namely the Ceylon Workers Congress (CWC), National Union of Workers (NUW), Up Country Workers Front (UWF), Democratic Workers' Congress (DWC), and Ceylon Workers' Alliance (CWA) (Thondaman 1994).

During this period, the CPSA also began to dismantle, and several NGOs, including Satyodaya, reduced their activities and number of workers due to the lack of funding from international donors. In CSPA's place, other development networks emerged, including the NGO Forum for Plantation Organisations (NGO members only) in 1994 and Plantation Social Sector Forum (PSSF) (NGOs, CBOs, and trade union members) in 2003, after the Asian Social Forum (de Fontgalland 2004).

The 40-year period marking repatriation through the aftermath of privatisation cemented Sri Lanka's plantations as a site for development organisations and their international donors to address consistent needs. With the shift to company control, responsibility for workers' well-being was entrusted to a tripartite formation of the Sri Lankan government and state, the regional plantation companies, and largely patriarchal, caste-dominant trade unions. Development groups, both local community-based organisations (CBOs), NGOs and international NGOs (INGOs), stepped in to provide communities living on the plantations foreign aid-funded programming for research and social services (Fernando and Heston 1997; Fernando 2007).

Within Catholic (and other Christian denominations) organisations and through their constellations of international donors and religious networks, more tangible forms of development began seeping into forms of charity closely associated with liberation theology and social justice missions. Such movements, while validated on the ground by international donors and donor recipients on the plantations in Sri Lanka alike, sustained an understanding among select donor-dependent organisations that tangible aid would break the cycles of poverty, which had sustained them in the form of bonded labour.

However, other local NGOs traded the "culture of poverty" framework for development programmes that would push for more radical forms of social transformation. After privatisation, NGOs, such as the Institute for Social Development (ISD), Society for Welfare Educational and Awareness Training (SWEAT), Hatton Social Action Centre (later, the Centre for Social Concern, or CSC), UNIWELO (United Welfare Organisation), and Human Development Organisation (HDO) began foregrounding rights-based initiatives that aimed to transform Tamil plantation workers and their families' futures and potential. The rights-based approach involved educational and engaged studies on plantation residents and worker education, and skills-based and vocational training for the unorganised sector and reserve labour force (Vijesandiran 2002; Muralitharan 2003, 2004). They also conducted workshops designed to transform the person from within by discussing the question of human and worker rights and human security (Caspersz 2005). This approach challenged the socioeconomic and political forces that create crisis and insecurity among Tamil workers and resident families (Thambiah 2007; Vijayanathan 2007). This shift in both funding and intervention continued to sustain momentum around workers' rights and political participation in the national arena (Devaraj 2006).

Since the plantation NGO rights-based positions in Sri Lankan civil society contradicted the capitalist objectives of the plantation system, community leaders found themselves challenged in their work because their goals resisted the plantations' structures of labour exploitation and wealth accumulation. As a result, their programmatic strategies often circumvented local and industrial hierarchies of power and focused on internationalist engagements such as International Women's Day, International Children's Day, and the establishment of the first International Tea Day on December 15.

Organisations also worked to build transnational and transregional relationships around questions of poverty and economic marginalisation, women's rights, local governance, and the restructuring of the plantation industry (Kandasamy 2002; Silva and Balasundaram 2007; Vijayanathan 2007; Gunetilleke, Kuruppu and Goonasekera 2008). Such development interventions on the plantations, while integral to the shaping of broader civil and political evaluations and responses to Malaiyaka Tamil claims for national belonging, national and human rights, and political questions of representation, also reveal the limitations and market-driven contours of neoliberal development and its unique harms to labourer and caste-oppressed communities in Sri Lanka. These contours can be seen in the shift of International Tea Day from December 15 to May 21. Originally, worker communities internationally began recognising the day in December 2005 because of a meeting of grassroots union and community leaders from India, Sri Lanka, and other tea-growing countries at the January 2005 World Social Forum. In 2015, the Government of India began petitioning the UN to observe the day through the IGG (intergovernmental group) on tea to support the global tea market and economy. In 2019, the day was officially changed to May 21 by the UN Food and Agricultural Organisation (FAO) vote of approval, erasing the labour-oriented solidarities at its origin.

Post-war Research Arenas

The end of the war in May 2009 provided an opening to reroute Malaiyaka Tamils' scholarship in ways that built and expanded upon the prior scholarly record across three relevant and productive research arenas: (1) Malaiyaka Tamil heritage and collective memory; (2) gender and social reproduction; and (3) political and labour justice. Each arena reflects scholars' deepened attention to the plantations across questions of visibility and materiality, migration and belonging, and the politics of recognition and dignity.

Malaiyaka Tamil Heritage and Collective Memory

The war's end presented an opportunity for Tamil studies scholars particularly to take up questions of collective visibility, memory, and materiality on the plantations. Resisting to be contained within Sri Lanka, vernacular accounts of Indo-Lankan and transregional coalitions and movements between Malaiyaka Tamils and other descendants of coolie, caste oppressed, and unfree plantation labourers particularly brought salience to the need to acknowledge and prioritise the erasure and manipulation of plantation histories within the country. Likewise, questions of home (in Tamil, ūr), migration, and belonging also gained traction (Daniel 2010; Jegathesan 2018; Piyarathne 2019). Previously undocumented histories, such as P. Muthulingam's biography of the 1950s Ceylon Dravida Munnetra Kalagam's (CDMK's) anti-caste leader Ilancheliyan, and Malaiyaka Tamil evaluations and perceptions of the word "coolie", demonstrated the necessity of foregrounding Malaiyaka Tamil language and lived experience (Muthulingam 2011; Nithiyanandhan 2014; Jegathesan 2021b). At the same time, local, post-war Malaiyaka Tamil practices of religious innovation traced the subtle but layered ways in which land and labour dispossession on the estates maintain the plantation as a site of marginalia. Studies on workers' practices of keeping estate and private family shrines and on oral histories of their fluidity of religious affiliations alongside histories of colonial conversion reveal a multiplicity of community experiences that push scholars to view the plantations beyond their position as a footnote to Sri Lanka's broader discourses on religious and community formations (Jegathesan 2015, 2022b; Balasundaram 2022).

Despite logistical limitations for this type of work, such as the preservation of local Tamil language archives, this arena is a particularly compelling site of future research.[4] Scholar's treatment of language, visual archives, and materiality consciously works across disciplines of art and art history, media, and visual anthropology (Arasu 2013; Buthpitiya 2018; Weerarathne 2018; Harris 2021; Jegathesan 2022a). These methodological choices to foreground a multimodal approach to historical consciousness also centre the inscription of Malaiyaka Tamils' collective lived experiences within broader regional and transregional understandings of migration, dispossession, and nation building.

Gender and Social Reproduction

Scholarly attention to gender and social reproduction on the plantations persisted after the civil war. This trend reflects the continued need for scholars to push against the industrial, colonial, and civil society misrepresentations and perceptions of Malaiyaka Tamil women's realities within the industry. The problem of gender injustice on the plantations became a problem of "persistent patriarchy", expanding upon their earlier historical and economic analyses on historical configurations of power and resistance within a nexus of class, ethnicity, and patriarchy on the plantations (Jayawardena and Kurian 2014, 2015). This nexus also appears situated in analyses of gender and social reproduction on the plantations within broader Foucauldian framings of biopolitics, tracking gender inequality in Malaiyaka Tamil women's worlds of work across sites of plantation work, domestic and factory labour, and education (Red Flag Women's Movement 2012; Kandasamy 2014; Vasanthakumary and Arularasi 2015; Neubert 2016; Chandrabose and Logeswary 2019; Ibrahim and Padmasiri 2019).

This body of work on gender and reproduction consents that Malaiyaka Tamil women's experiences of gendered structural violence and inequality are embodied and reproduced through the exploitative patriarchal structure of the plantation system. While this consensus is generative for thinking about questions of persistence and potential for change from within unions and estate communities, the need to foreground the caste-based discrimination, ethnonationalism, and community investments in such exploitative systems remains. Deeper, ethnographic engagements with humanistic and feminist methodologies and contextualising such systemic inequalities within broader questions of political representation, transitional justice and gendered materialities of plantation life and belonging underline this need as well (Sumathy 2014; Jegathesan 2019a; Kamaleswary 2019).

Political and Labour Justice

Alongside research on gender and social reproduction, studies on political and labour movements in and beyond the plantations for Malaiyaka Tamils responded to the historical period of transitional justice but also lingering questions around Malaiyaka Tamils' political irresolution around conditions of landlessness and economic injustice. In this research arena, ethnographic and community-based participatory methods have paved the way for a centring of policy transformation and questions of justice along lines of ethnicity, caste, and human rights.

On the question of Malaiyaka Tamil or Up-Country ethnic identity, Daniel Bass (2013) offers a comprehensive, contemporary English language study of Malaiyaka Tamil politics and ethnic group membership. Building from his early work on rumour and politics during the war, he deftly captures the close and tensely traversed relationship between Malaiyaka Tamil politics and national questions of minority representation and belonging in the context of culture work (Bass 2008). His ethnography is also the first and only study to take up the question of census classification and its direct relationship to the development of ethnic identity affiliations in relation to diasporic attachments. Jegathesan (2019a and c), likewise, employed ethnographic and archival methods to trace workers' desires and aspirations on the plantations as grounded in kinship investment, home-making practices, and realities of women's labour participation beyond the estates.

In contrast, social scientists outside of anthropology – across political science, economics, sociology, and development studies – have used mixed methods to think about questions of economic marginalisation and livelihood, housing and land cultivation, and power sharing and transitional justice mechanisms (Chandrabose and Sivapragasam 2015; Centre for Policy Alternatives 2017; Sinnathamby and Vijesandiran 2018; Muthulingam 2019).

The above works contribute two significant overarching findings. First, they draw necessary attention to the role of consent and collaboration from and with Malaiyaka Tamils in movements for political and labour justice with respect to how scholars represent workers' lived experience and desires. Second, they foreground the necessary cognisance of research ethics and scholarly representation around the politics of naming, scale, policy change, and broader media and global forms of knowledge dissemination about plantation industry.

Conclusion: Feminist Futures and Political Reckonings

The last 50 years of scholarship on Sri Lanka's plantations have revealed that Sri Lanka's plantations are studied sites of colonial and historical forms of misrepresentation and extraction. However, they are also necessary and dynamic spaces to push for the foregrounding of feminist approaches to the production of future knowledge. Here, critical caste and Dalit feminist studies are areas to engage within ongoing studies of the gender, class, caste nexus, converging and competing forms of Sinhala, Tamil, and Hindu ethnonationalism and majoritarian politics, and global histories of enslavement, indentured labour, and racial capitalism (Wickramasinghe and Schrikker 2019; Jegathesan 2021b; Wickramasinghe 2021).

Sri Lanka's 2022 economic crisis cemented the urgency to consider the plantation logics that undergird the country's unresolved political conflict. In 2021, plantation workers finally earned a 1000-rupee wage after the Minimum Wages Board intervened, but soon after plantation companies filed a writ petition arguing to not pay the wage and workers cited a reduction in the number of offered days of work. From wage repression to prevailing cost of living and price hikes on food, medicines, fuel, and other daily items, workers and their families are experiencing higher rates of starvation, school dropouts, and familial debt (Jegathesan 2022c). As 2023 marked 200 years of plantation labour in the country, Malaiyaka Tamil community and political leaders are calling for the Government and industry stakeholders to justly recognise the community and particularly women's contributions to the country. This trajectory also suggests that future research agendas on the plantation will respond to the need to proactively foreground Malaiyaka Tamils' political reckoning in Sri Lanka in the post-war context: to imagine the plantation not as a static place or object of academic study, a development project, or national policy reform, but as a dynamic, dispersive site for ethical groundwork that supports Malaiyaka Tamils' social and economic liberation.

Notes

1 In this chapter, I do not address literatures on tea science and within the natural and biological sciences on tea cultivation in Sri Lanka. While these studies are critical, the scope of this handbook and section are on work, life, society, and culture.
2 Here, Peebles discusses, for instance, the Sinhala nationalist tilt of Malaiyaka Tamil representations in K.M. de Silva's work (1981).
3 Much of CPSA's work has been documented meticulously in their quarterly journal, *The Voice of the Voiceless*, which began in 1972 and continues today under the supervision of Satyodaya.
4 Here, the work of the non-profit, Noolaham Foundation, has been critical to the digitisation of Malaiyaka Tamil local archives in addition to community-led initiatives for material preservation such as the Tea Worker Museum in Pusselawa.

References

Ajantha, B.A. (1984) ***Sri Lanka: July 1983 Violence against 'Indian Tamils'*** S. Sivanayagam (ed) Trans S.A. David. Madras: Tamil Information Centre
Arasu, Ponni (2013) "Karuppi (The Dark Woman)." Filmed May 5, 2013 in Toronto, Canada. YouTube, 28:41. www.youtube.com/watch?v=r1fMgwS-ME
Balasundaram, Sasikumar (2009) *The Structural Violence of Sterilization: Politics of Sterilization in the Plantation Tamil Communities of Sri Lanka*. MA thesis. University of South Carolina
Balasundaram, Sasikumar (2022) "Temples and Deities on Plantations" In ***Multi-Religiosity in Contemporary Sri Lanka*** Mark P. Whitaker, Darini Rajasingham-Senanayake and Pathmanesan Sanmugeswaran (eds) London: Routledge, pp 179–191
Balasundaram, Sasikumar, A.S. Chandrabose and P.P. Sivapragasam (2009) "Caste Discrimination among Indian Tamil Plantation Workers in Sri Lanka" In ***Casteless or Caste-Blind: Dynamics of Concealed Caste Discrimination Social Exclusion and Protest in Sri Lanka*** Kalinga Tudor Silva, P.P. Sivapragasam and Thanges Paramsothy (eds) Colombo: Kumaran Book House, pp 78–96
Bass, Daniel (2008) "Paper Tigers on the Prowl: Rumors, Violence, and Agency in the Up-Country of Sri Lanka" ***Anthropological Quarterly*** 81(1): 269–295
Bass, Daniel (2013) ***Everyday Ethnicity in Sri Lanka: Up-Country Tamil Identity Politics*** New York: Routledge
Buthpitiya, Vindhya (2018) "The Tempest in Your Tea Cup" ***Himal Southasian*** (20 August). Retrieved August 20, 2018. http://himalmag.com/the-tempest-in-your-tea-cup-colonial-tropesin-advertising-sri-lanka/
Caspersz, Paul (2005) ***A New Culture for a New Society: Selected Writings 1945–2005*** Kandy: Paul Caspersz
Caspersz, P., H.K. Wanninayake, S. Vijesandiran, Satyodaya, and Coordinating Secretariat for Plantation Areas (1995) ***The Privatisation of the Plantations*** Kandy: Satyodaya Centre for the Coordinating Secretariat for Plantation Areas

Centre for Policy Alternatives (2017) "This House Is Not a Home: The Struggle for Addresses and Land in the Estate Sector" (17 August). www.cpalankaorg/this-house-is-not-a-home-the-struggle-for-addresses-and-land-in-the-estate-sector

Chandrabose, A.S. and S. Logeswary (2019) "Employable Skills, Higher Education and Livelihood: Outlook for Women in the Tea Plantations" In *Up-Country Tamils: Charting a New Future in Sri Lanka* Daniel Bass and B. Skanthakumar (eds) Colombo: International Centre for Ethnic Studies pp 85–104

Chandrabose, A.S. and P.P. Sivapragasam (2015) *The Red Colour of Tea: Central Issues that Impact the Tea Plantation Community in Sri Lanka* Colombo: Kumaran Book House

Daniel, E. Valentine (1996) *Charred Lullabies: Chapters in an Anthropography of Violence* Princeton: Princeton University Press

Daniel, E. Valentine (2010) "Lost Ūr" In *Village Matters* Diane P. Mines and Nicolas Yazgi (eds) London: Oxford University Press, pp 317–339

Dawood, Nawaz (1980) *Tea and Poverty: Plantations and the Political Economy of Sri Lanka* Kowloon: Urban Rural Mission-Christian Conference of Asia

de Fontgalland, Guy (2004) *The Impact of Globalization on the Plantation Sector in Sri Lanka* Sri Lanka: Plantation Social Sector Forum (PSSF)

de Silva, K. (1981) *A History of Sri Lanka* Oxford: Oxford University Press

de Silva, Mangalika (2005) "Women in the Labour Movement: 'Herstory' of Resistance" In *Excluding Women: The Struggle for Women's Political Participation in Sri Lanka* Morina Perera and Rasika Chandrasekera (eds) Colombo: Social Scientists Association, pp 93–100

Devaraj, P.P. (2006) *Rights and Power Sharing Issues in Sri Lanka with Special Focus on Indian Origin Tamil Community* Colombo: Foundation for Community Transformation

Fernando, Jude and Alan W. Heston (1997) "Introduction: NGOs between States, Markets, and Civil Society" *Annals of the American Academy of Political and Social Science* 554: 8–20

Fernando, Udan (2007) *Uneasy Encounters: Relationships Between Dutch Donors and Sri Lankan NGOs.* PhD diss., Amsterdam Institute for Metropolitan and International Development Studies

Gnanamuttu, George (1979) *Education and the Indian Plantation Worker in Sri Lanka* Colombo: Self-published

Gunasinghe, Newton [1984] 2004. "The Open Economy and Ethnic Conflict in Sri Lanka" In *Economy, Culture, and Civil War in Sri Lanka* Deborah Winslow and Michael Woost (eds) Bloomington: Indiana University Press, pp 98–114.

Gunawardena, Samanthi and Janaka Biyanwila (2008) "Trade Unions in Sri Lanka: Beyond Party Politics" In *Trade Unions in Asia: Balancing Economics Competitiveness and Social Responsibility* John Benson and Ying Zhu (eds) London: Routledge, pp 177–197

Gunetilleke, Neranjana, Sanjana Kuruppu and Susrutha Goonasekera (2008) *The Estate Workers' Dilemma: Tensions and Changes in the Tea and Rubber Plantations in Sri Lanka* Study Series No. 4. Colombo: Centre for Poverty Analysis

Harris, Leila Anne (2021) "Two Leaves and a Bud: Tea and the Body Through a Colonial Lens" *Trans Asia Photography* 11(2). Retrieved on February 6, 2022. https://quod.lib.umich.edu/t/tap/7977573.0011.202?view=text;rgn=main

Hollup, Oddvar (1994) *Bonded Labour: Caste and Cultural Identity among Tamil Plantation Workers in Sri Lanka* New Delhi: Sterling

Hollup, Oddvar (1998) "The Impact of Land Reforms, Rural Images, and Nationalist Ideology on Plantation Tamils" In *Buddhist Fundamentalism and Minority Identities in Sri Lanka* Tessa Bartholomeusz and Chandra de Silva (eds) Albany: State University of New York Press, pp 74–88

Ibrahim, Zainab and Buddhima Padmasiri (2019) "Between the Factory and the Estate: a Reproduction of Exploitative Structures" In *Up-Country Tamils: Charting a New Future in Sri Lanka* Daniel Bass and B. Skanthakumar (eds) Colombo: International Centre for Ethnic Studies pp 137–165

Institute of Social Development (2016) *Inclusion of Hill Country Tamil Community Residing in the Kilinochchi District into the Ongoing Transitional Justice Process* Kandy: Institute for Social Development

Jayaraman, R. Caste (1975) *Continuities in Ceylon: A Study of the Social Structure of Three Tea Plantations* Bombay: Popular Prakashan

Jayawardena, Kumari (1972) *The Rise of the Labour Movement in Ceylon* Durham: Duke University Press

Jayawardena, Kumari and Rachel Kurian (2014) *Persistent Patriarchy: Women Workers on Sri Lankan Plantations*. SSA Pamphlet Series. Colombo: Social Scientists Association

Jayawardena, Kumari and Rachel Kurian (2015) *Class, Patriarchy, and Ethnicity on Sri Lankan Plantations: Two Centuries of Power and Protest* Hyderabad: Orient BlackSwan

Jegathesan, Mythri (2015) "Deficient Realities: Expertise and Uncertainty among Tea Plantation Workers in Sri Lanka" *Dialectical Anthropology* 39: 255–272

Jegathesan, Mythri (2018) "Claiming *ur:* Home, Investment, and Decolonial Desires on Sri Lanka's Tea Plantations" *Anthropological Quarterly* 91(2): 635–670

Jegathesan, Mythri (2019a) *Tea and Solidarity: Tamil Women and Work in Postwar Sri Lanka* Seattle: University of Washington Press

Jegathesan, Mythri (2019b) "State-Industrial Entanglements in Women's Reproductive Capacity and Labour in Sri Lanka" *South Asia Multidisciplinary Academic Journal*. 20 (Online since 18 March 2019] https://doi.org/10.4000/samaj.5095

Jegathesan, Mythri (2019c]) "Visible Grounds: Organising Unorganised Women Workers with the Working Women's Front" In *Up-Country Tamils: Charting a New Future in Sri Lanka* B.B. Skanthakumar (ed) Colombo: International Centre for Ethnic Studies, pp 105–135

Jegathesan, Mythri (2021a) "Nesting Paternalisms: Postwar Indo-Lankan Diplomacies on Sri Lanka's Plantations" *Hot Spots, Fieldsights* (16 March). https://culanth.org/fieldsights/nesting-paternalisms-postwar-indo-lankan-diplomacies-on-sri-lankas-plantations

Jegathesan, Mythri (2021b) "Black Feminist Plots before the Plantationocene and anthropology's "regional closets"" *Feminist Anthropology* 2: 78–93.

Jegathesan, Mythri (2022a) "Plantation Errata" In *Scroll: Projects on Paper: Part 3: 'Language Is Migrant' Colomboscope 2022* Syma Tariq and Aziz Sohail (eds) Placeholder link: https://south-south.art/wp-content/uploads/2022/02/Language-Is-Migrant-Catalog.pdf

Jegathesan, Mythri (2022b) "Conversion, Fixing Faith, and Material Investments on Sri Lanka's Tea Plantations" In *Multi-Religiosity in Contemporary Sri Lanka* Mark Whitaker, Darini Rajasingham-Senanayake and Pathmanesan Sanmugeswaran (eds) London: Routledge, pp 192–203

Jegathesan, Mythri (2022c) "Policing the Patriline: Reading the Current Economic and Political Crisis through the Plantation" *Polity*, Social Scientists' Association. https://ssalanka.org/policing-the-patriline-reading-the-current-economic-and-political-crisis-through-the-plantation-mythri-jegathesan/

Kamaleswary, Letchumanan (2019) "Forgotten Experiences of Up-Country Tamil Women in Transitional Justice" In *Up-Country Tamils: Charting a New Future in Sri Lanka* Daniel Bass and B. Skanthakumar (eds) Colombo: International Centre for Ethnic Studies, pp 53–84

Kanapathipillai, Valli (2009) *Citizenship and Statelessness in Sri Lanka: The Case of the Tamil Estate Workers* London: Anthem Press

Kandasamy, Menaha (2002) *The Struggles Continues: Women's Leadership in Plantation Trade Unions in Sri Lanka* Kandy: Institute for Social Development

Kandasamy, Menaha (2014) *From Plantations to Domestic Labour: The New Form of Exploitation and Political Marginalisation of Women*. SSA Pamphlet Series Colombo: Social Scientists' Association

Kodikara, S.U. (1971) "An Unassimilated Minority – The Case of the Indian Tamils in Ceylon" In *Studies in Asian Development* Ratna Dutta and P.C. Joshi (eds) Bombay: Tata McGraw-Hill, pp 213–231

Kurian, Rachel (1982) *Women Workers in the Sri Lanka Plantation Sector* Geneva: International Labour Office

Little, Angela (1999) *Labouring to Learn: Towards a Political Economy of Plantations, People, and Education in Sri Lanka* New York: St. Martin's Press

Loganathan, Ketheshwaran (1990) *The Plantation System in Sri Lanka and the Search for Sustainable Development* Norway: Agricultural University of Norway Department of Economics and Social Sciences

Manikam, P.P. (1995) *Tea Plantations in Crisis* Colombo: Social Scientists' Association.

Meyer, Eric (1992) "'Enclave' Plantations, 'Hemmed-In' Villages and Dualistic Representations in Colonial Ceylon" *Journal of Peasant Studies* 19(3–4): 199–228

Moldrich, Donovan (1989) *Bitter Berry Bondage: The Nineteenth- Century Coffee Workers of Sri Lanka* Kandy: Coordinating Secretariat for Plantation Areas

Moore, Mick (1985) *The State and Peasant Politics in Sri Lanka* New York: Cambridge University Press

Muralitharan, S. (2003) *Plantation youth in the unorganised sector* Kandy: Institute of Social Development

Muthulingam, Periyasamy (2011) *Ilangai D.M.K. Varalāru [The History of the Ceylon DMK]* Chennai: Nalantha Pathipagam.

Muthulingam, Periyasamy (2019) "Post-war Political Aspirations and Mobilisation of Hill Country Tamils in the North-East" In *Up-Country Tamils: Charting a New Future in Sri Lanka* Daniel Bass and B. Skanthakumar (eds) Colombo: International Centre for Ethnic Studies pp 195–213

Neubert, Christopher (2016) "Power, Everyday Control, and Emerging Resistance in Sri Lanka's Plantations" *Contemporary South Asia: Special Issue on Post-War Sri Lanka: State, Capital, Labour and the Politics of Reconciliation* 24(4): 360–373

Nithiyanandan, M. (2014) *Cooly Thamizh: A Collection of Essays in Tamil* Chennai: Cre-Ā

Peebles, Patrick (2001) *The Plantation Tamils of Ceylon* London: Leicester University Press

Phillips, Amali (2003) "Rethinking Culture and Development: Marriage and Gender among the Tea Plantation Workers in Sri Lanka" *Gender and Development* 11(2): 20–29

Phillips, Amali (2005) "The Kinship, Marriage, and Gender Experiences of Tamil Women in Sri Lanka's Tea Plantations" *Contributions to Indian Sociology* 39(1): 107–142

Piyarathne, Anton (2019) "Life in Pattanam as Āsai: Estate Tamils' Aspiration of Home in Colombo" In *Up-Country Tamils: Charting a New Future in Sri Lanka* Daniel Bass and B. Skanthakumar (eds) Colombo: International Centre for Ethnic Studies pp 169–194

Red Flag Women's Movement (2012) *Women's Leadership: Poverty, Violence Against Women and Women's Leadership in Tea Plantation Trade Unions in Sri Lanka* Kandy: Red Flag Women's Movement

Sahadevan, P. (1995) *India and Overseas Indians: The Case of Sri Lanka* Delhi: Kalinga Publications

Samarasinghe, Vidyamali (1993) "Puppets on a String: Women's Wage Work and Empowerment among Female Tea Plantation Workers of Sri Lanka" *Journal of Developing Areas* 27(3): 329–340

"Satyodaya: Documentation Extract from the Memorandum of the Coordinating Secretariat for Plantation Areas to the Commission to Inquire and Report on the Incidents Which Took Place in the Island between 13 August and 15 September 1977" (1984) *Voice of the Voiceless* 15(1): 6–12

Shanmugaratnam, N. (1997) *Privatisation of Tea Plantations: The Challenge of Reforming Production Relations in Sri Lanka – An Institutional Historical Perspective* Colombo: Social Scientists' Association

Silva, Kalinga Tudor and Sasikumar Balasundaram (2007) *Transition from Tea Worker to Out-Grower? The Impact of an Out-Grower Pilot Scheme on Workers in Selected Tea Plantations in Sri Lanka* Kandy: Institute of Social Development

Sinnathamby, M. and S. Vijesandiran (2018) *Summary Report on Living Wage for the Tea Estate Workers: Context Provided for April – May 2018* Kandy: Institute of Social Development

Sumathy, Sivamohan (2014) "Gendered Fictions: Media and the Making of Malaiyaha Identity in Sri Lanka" *Sri Lanka Journal of the Humanities* 38(1–2): 43–62

Thambiah, E. (2007) "The Hill Country Tamil Nationality" (September 2007). *New Democracy* Colombo: Gowry Printers, pp 3–6

Thondaman, S. (1994) *Tea and Politics* Colombo: Lake House

Uyangoda, Jayadeva (1995) *Life under Milk Wood: Women Workers in Rubber Plantations: an Overview* Colombo: Women's Education and Research Centre

Vasanthakumary, Selvanayagam and Balakrishnan Arularasi (2015) *The Unheard Voice of Plantation Children in Education: Lessons from the Plantation Sector in Matale District* Kandy: Satyodaya Centre for Social Research and Encounter

Velupillai, C.V. (1970) *Born to Labour* Colombo: M.D. Gunasena

Velupillai, C.V. (1983) *Malainaattu Makkal Patalkal* Madras: Kalaignaan Pathipagam.

Vijayanathan, L. (2007) *Development Dilemmas of Indian Origin Tamils in Sri Lanka: Politics and Violence in Relation to Human Security* Colombo: Foundation for Community Transformation

Vijesandiran, Sangaran (2002) *Youth and Development: A Socio-Economic Perspective on the Plantation Community* Kandy: Satyodaya

Vijesandiran, Sangaran (2004) *Alcoholism in the Sri Lankan Plantation Community* Kandy: Satyodaya

Webb, James L.A. Jr. (2002) *Tropical Pioneers: Human Agency and Ecological Change in the Highlands of Sri Lanka, 1800–1900* Athens: Ohio University Press

Weerarathne, Nandana (2018) *Before Memory Dies (Nilaivukal Maranikka Mun)* Kandy: Institute for Social Development

Wesumperuma, Dharmapala (1986) *Indian Immigrant Plantations Workers in Sri Lanka: A Historical Perspective, 1880–1910* Kelaniya: Vidyalankara Press

Wickramasinghe, Nira (2021) *Slave in a Palanquin: Colonial Servitude and Resistance in Sri Lanka* New York: Columbia University Press

Wickramasinghe, Nira and Alice Schrikker (2019) "The Ambivalence of Freedom: Slaves in Jaffna, Sri Lanka, in the Eighteenth and Nineteenth Centuries" *Journal of Asian Studies* 78(3): 497–519

29
CASTE IN CONTEMPORARY SRI LANKA

Dominic Esler

Introduction

On the surface, caste appears to play a marginal and rather obscure role in popular and academic understandings of Sri Lanka, reflecting widespread normative disapproval of caste expressed through the denial of its contemporary social significance and its low prominence in public discussion. This impression is belied, however, by the large amount of caste research produced since Independence that has demonstrated the importance of caste – the closest equivalents of which are *kulǝyǝ* in Sinhalese and *sādi* in Sri Lankan Tamil – in a multitude of different spheres. On the other hand, Sri Lankan caste studies has yet to emerge as an integrated field, particularly as it is divided into research that focuses on caste among either Tamils or Sinhalese. This approach derives from the presumption that Buddhism is antithetical to caste, in contrast to Hinduism, in conjunction with the strong association between these religions and Sinhalese and Tamils, respectively.

In this chapter I provide a brief historical context of caste in Sri Lanka before exploring some of the key themes in contemporary caste research, drawing primarily on recent social scientific studies to do so. This scholarship has been catalysed by a renewed academic interest in caste since the end of the civil war, although new projects are now dwindling, leaving large empirical gaps in a range of issues. Besides addressing these, one of the tasks of future research is therefore to scrutinise Sri Lankan caste scholarship in its totality, which involves asking why, beyond shifts in the research agenda as a result of the civil war, caste has never become more important to local academic attention. As a contribution towards this goal, I finish the chapter by outlining two pressing theoretical and methodological challenges: the need to interrogate both the ethnoreligious divide in Sri Lankan caste research and the relationship between the popular disavowal of and actual caste practice.

Contextualising Caste in Sri Lanka

Sri Lankan caste research has not been heavily influenced by the historical turn, with its attention to power and colonial influence, that has transformed Indian caste scholarship over the past few decades (although see Rogers 2004 and the recent research on slavery discussed below). However, one of the consequences of the presumption of Buddhism's inherent opposition to caste is that Sri Lankan historical research had from an even earlier date emphasised the role of "secular" precolonial state formations in the organisation and maintenance of caste (Pieris 1956: 180–187), particularly the largely caste-based compulsory labour – known as *rājakāriya* in Sinhalese and *ūliyam* in Tamil – due to royal families, temples, and local communities (De Silva 1992/1993). Compulsory labour was maintained by the Portuguese, the Dutch, and – for the first four decades of their rule – the British, although caste distinctions were also enforced and exploited through taxes, the monopolisation of government positions by certain castes – Sinhalese Govigamas (or Goyigamas) and Tamil Vellalars in particular – and customary laws. The most prominent example of the latter was the Thesawalamai, a collection of ordinances applying to Jaffna, which was compiled in 1707 by the Dutch and sanctioned the legal identification of four slave castes.

Major changes occurred in the early 19th century. British attitudes to caste were very different to those in India, and opposition to compulsory labour led to its abolition in 1832, 12 years before the formal abolition of slavery, apart from in certain Kandyan contexts (Kendrick 1992). This decision was accompanied by a perception that caste "was not a legitimate form of social identification" (Rogers 2004: 53), leading to greatly reduced state intervention and little official discussion of caste. Caste was not included in national censuses when they began in 1871, and only sporadic information was collected in colonial publications of the late 19th and early 20th centuries. However, there still remains much to explore in colonial archives (e.g. Meyer 2014), as well as in Christian archives (Balmforth 2020; Esler 2020, 2021).

Caste did not disappear after 1832, however. A key area of historical research has been upward mobility among members of the Sinhalese Durava, Salagama, and Karava castes who took advantage of economic opportunities to become key forces within the emergent local bourgeoisie, expressing their challenge to elite Govigama landowners through varna-based status claims in caste polemics towards the end of the 19th century (Roberts 1982; Kannangara 1993; Jayawardena 2012). From the second half of the 19th century there were also numerous caste conflicts in Jaffna (Saveri 1993; Rogers 2004), largely arising from growing opposition to Vellalar control and exclusion, which continued until the temple entry conflicts of the 1960s (Pfaffenberger 1990). The last sustained public anti-caste activism occurred in Jaffna in the decades immediately before the war but was suppressed by Tamil politicians through a "politics of defensive unity" (ibid.), although within their territories the Liberation Tigers of Tamil Eelam (LTTE) enforced explicitly anti-caste policies that they held up as part of their emancipatory project. However, our historical understanding of the quotidian inter-caste relationships indicated by these dynamics continues to remain shallow in many respects. Social scientific research has contributed more in this regard, although there is still room for greater empirical depth, particularly on caste among Sinhalese. What evidence we do have suggests both the decline of "traditional" caste relationships, specifically those involving caste service, and the perpetuation of caste inequalities in new forms.

The postcolonial state has continued the British policy of officially ignoring caste, as demonstrated by the absence of national quantitative data and caste legislation other than the apparently ineffective 1957 Prevention of Social Disabilities Act, which prohibits caste-based discrimination. The classificatory language of caste is also locally specific, posing complications for both Sri Lankan scholars and those approaching Sri Lanka from other South Asian contexts. Sri Lanka has no official caste categories like those of India – Forward Castes, Scheduled Castes, Scheduled Tribes, and Other Backwards Classes – which are partly shared with Pakistan and Bangladesh as a result of their colonial history. In the absence of a consolidation of the political identity of the low castes (Kadirgamar 2017: 8–9), there is also no comparable popular Dalit, while "Untouchable" seems to have dropped from general use during the war. The question of terminology is most prominent in the north, and today some researchers and Tamil activists use either Dalit or Panchamar ("the fifth", an older Sanskrit term for those who fall outside the four varnas), although neither has wider public purchase. In English, the term "low caste" is sometimes replaced with "oppressed" or "depressed caste". Finally, although it has played a role in Sri Lankan caste ideologies and debates (e.g. Kannangara 1993), varna is unknown by many and less significant than in many areas of the subcontinent.

Key Themes in Contemporary Research

Sri Lankan social scientific caste research can be divided into three broad stages, although the large number of publications and this volume's focus on the contemporary make it impractical to provide a detailed overview here. The first stage spanned the years between Independence and the beginning of the war in the 1980s and produced work that considered caste through a variety of different lenses, but with a focus on either Tamils or Sinhalese that has continued to this day (apart from Yalman 1967). During the second stage, which began with the start of the war, explicit caste research was rare until it returned, focusing largely on Tamils in the north and east, during the 2002–2007 ceasefire. This stage ended with two publications reflecting two quite different approaches to caste research (McGilvray 2008; Silva, Sivapragasam and Thanges 2009a). The third and current stage comprises the research conducted since the end of the war in 2009, which has been largely distinguished by new projects by doctoral students, the majority of whom continue to work with Tamils, although now focused entirely on the north.

Continuity, Change, and Inequality

In response (at least implicitly) to the popular perception that caste is disappearing or unimportant, a central concern of recent research has been whether caste continues to exist and, if so, in what forms. This research has often approached caste as a structure of discrimination, a framework that has become increasingly prominent in Sri Lankan scholarship since Silva et al's (2009a) study of caste discrimination in different areas of the country. Our understanding of what caste change means in practice remains patchy in many respects, due to a lack of data on the relationship between caste, class, dependence, and exclusion – and on experiences and perceptions of caste among people of different caste and class backgrounds. Although Abeyasekera's (2021) study of urban middle-class Sinhalese marriages has made a significant contribution to these issues, the broader absence of research on the higher Sinhalese castes comprises a particularly significant gap. For example, no research has pursued Jiggins's (1979: 26) observation that the directors of rupee companies in Colombo in 1971 were preponderantly high-caste Govigamas and Karavas. Research conducted with Tamils in the north, the east, and the Hill Country tends to provide a more-encompassing sense of contemporary caste inequalities and their perpetuation in new forms. There is also a pressing need to investigate these dynamics more holistically in both rural and urban contexts, as caste also persists in the latter (Silva, Thanges and Sivapragasam 2009c: 97–120; Madavan 2011; Thiranagama 2018).

Despite these caveats, two thematic clusters of research provide substantial insight into these issues. The first comprises studies of primarily low-status specialist castes and their relationships with the occupations attributed to them. Among the Sinhalese, this research has focused on the Kinnara, Berava, Badahäla (also known as Kumbāl), and to a lesser extent Rodiya castes, which are primarily associated with, respectively, weaving household goods with the fibre of the hana plant, ritual dance and drumming, pottery, and begging (Kirk 1992; Simpson 1997; Winslow 2003, 2009; Samuels 2007; Silva, Kotikabadde and Nilanka Chandima Abeywickrama 2009b;

Reed 2010; Uyangoda 2012; Douglas 2017, 2019; Sykes 2018). The findings of these studies cannot be explored here in depth, but they have demonstrated that members of these castes, particularly Kinnaras and Rodiyas, continue to experience stigmatisation and discrimination. Research on Kinnaras and Beravas has also described the incorporation of drumming and weaving into a national culture stripped of caste connotations, which has left these castes in an ambivalent position regarding occupations that many still follow.

Among Tamils, only McGilvray (2008) has dedicated a similar level of attention to individual specialist castes, drawing on research that began in the late 1960s to provide longitudinal insights into the activities of Tattar goldsmiths and blacksmiths, Sandar toddy tappers, Vannar washermen, Navitar barbers, and Paraiyar drummers (also see McGilvray 1983). Silva et al (2009c) have also investigated the highly stigmatised municipal sanitary workers, primarily Tamils of the Paraiyar and Chakkiliyar castes whose ancestors were brought from India by the British in the 19th century, who live as communities in several southern cities; separately, Lall (2015) has discussed the marginalisation of Paraiyar municipal sanitary workers in Jaffna.

The second cluster comprises studies of caste changes among Tamils within the context of specific geographical regions. These include the east coast (McGilvray 2008) and the plantations of the Hill Country (Balasundaram, Chandrabose and Sivapragasam 2009), although the main focus is northern Sri Lanka and Jaffna, which retains a national stereotype of being the most caste-conscious region. A key topic in this latter body of research is the impact of the war, and particularly the LTTE, on caste: while the LTTE were openly hostile to caste in a number of ways (Thanges 2018b), they were hesitant to intervene in certain spheres, particularly religion (Kuganathan 2022), and the overall impact of their actions on caste has been debated (e.g. Kadirgamar 2017: 179).

Another is the question of whether caste has been "returning" since 2009, local responses to which vary (Thanges 2018b: 24; Thiranagama 2018). Some Tamils share the popular "national" view that caste is dwindling, sometimes noting the shared experience of the war as a partial explanation (Esler 2020: 225), although other evidence points to increasingly visible caste activities and the perpetuation of social and economic exclusion in other forms (Kadirgamar 2017; Esler 2021; Kuganathan 2022; Sanmugeswaran 2023), such as the fact that the majority of internally displaced people still living in camps several years after the war's end came from low castes (Silva 2020).

Changes in caste demographics have also become a significant social dynamic in the north, at the village and regional levels. Two factors raise important questions for future research. First, some scholars, such as Thiranagama (2018: 373), have suggested that the greater economic prosperity of the Vellalars in Jaffna resulted in a relatively higher level of emigration during the war, leading to a relative increase in the population of other castes in Jaffna today. However, emigration was not the sole preserve of the Vellalars, and the investment of foreign-earned wealth by Tamils of other castes during and after the war (particularly visible in houses and temples), alongside the formation of a "new middle class", has significant implications (e.g. Thanges 2018b: 86; Hollenbach, Thurairajah and Subramaniam 2020: 18–19). The small amount of research that has investigated the different socio-economic trajectories of Sri Lankan Tamils of different castes in the diaspora, and the ways in which caste has been both maintained and erased, will help to understand this changing context among Tamils in Jaffna and elsewhere in Sri Lanka (Thanges 2018a).

Although yet to be integrated into social scientific approaches, the recent pioneering work of historians on caste-based slavery in Dutch and British Jaffna also makes valuable contributions to analyses of contemporary caste inequalities (Schrikker and Ekama 2017; Wickramasinghe and Schrikker 2019; Balmforth 2020, 2021; Wickramasinghe 2020). However, apart from Balmforth, these researchers have been less interested in caste per se, and a number of related historical topics remain to be addressed. These include the relationship between slavery and other types of caste service, the ownership of slaves by castes other than the Vellalars, and the precise nature of the hierarchical forms of caste dominance that existed before the Dutch codification of slavery and that the Portuguese also referred to as slavery.

Ideology and Ambivalence

Explorations of public denials and disapproval of caste have deepened our understanding of caste ideology and its relationship to practice. On the one hand, caste ideologies are entangled with processes of ethnic differentiation. Rival Sinhalese and Tamil ethnonationalisms have contributed to "caste blindness" – "the deliberate neglect of caste discrimination in public policies" (Silva 2020: 52–53) – although in different ways. Among the Sinhalese, Uyangoda (2000) and Douglas (2017) have described a discourse of modernity that privileges social, democratic egalitarianism while obscuring actual caste practice. Douglas (2017: 13) has also identified the production of castelessness as an upper-caste subjectivity, with caste sometimes considered a characteristic of low-caste Sinhalese per se. M.W.A. de Silva (2018) both describes and replicates this ideological framework in his account of contemporary low-caste adoption of "acaste" (casteless) names, a category in which de Silva includes names that have high-caste connotations. De Silva describes this process as a form of beneficial "assimilation" into a wider society distinguished by urbanisation, modernisation, and individualisation, overlooking the source of the stigmatisation and exclusion that motivate such name changes.

Caste is also, and perhaps more overtly, often considered a characteristic of Tamils by Sinhalese. This stereotype was exploited by Sinhalese politicians before the war to justify opposition to regional autonomy (Pfaffenberger 1990: 86–87). It appeared in a different form in 2017 when the Daily Mirror published (and later retracted) allegations that caste discrimination in Jaffna had led to a shortage of blood donations, which were instead being supplied by Sinhalese soldiers (Colombo Telegraph 2017). Among Tamils themselves, public discussion of caste has been discouraged both by fear of the LTTE and on the grounds that it will undermine Tamil solidarity and the cause of independence (Pfaffenberger 1990). However, the extension of "Tamilness" by the Vellalars to lower castes appears to have been a process that started at the end of the 19th century and was still incomplete in the 1970s (Pfaffenberger 1990: 82–83; Hellmann-Rajanayagam 1993: 256).

On the other hand, normative pronouncements against caste and actual caste practices can be highly divergent, revealing significant ambivalence towards caste, or at least a differentiation between various elements of caste. For example, Abeyasekera (2021: 90) describes middle-class Sinhalese families who prefer caste-endogamous marriages even while considering themselves "modern" and "progressive". Similarly, I have worked with Catholic Tamils in Mannar who see caste as a force of immoral hierarchy and exclusion and a form of beneficial communal solidarity (Esler 2021). Another form of ambivalence is seen, as I have noted above, in the perspectives of Beravas and Kinnaras towards the occupations attributed to them. It is also important to note that the desire to maintain caste identities and boundaries is not solely the preserve of high castes, in part because caste can be harnessed as a form of resistance against discrimination and deprivation.

The deeper ideological bases underpinning the concept of caste itself have received varying levels of attention. While research in Jaffna has largely emphasised Hindu concepts of ritual purity and pollution (e.g. Pfaffenberger 1982), scholars working with Tamils and Sinhalese elsewhere have suggested that these are not the primary manner in which caste is conceptualised (McGilvray 1982; Stirrat 1982; Douglas 2017: 197–198). With regard to the Sinhalese, this topic requires further research, particularly on high-caste understandings of the nature of caste. In contrast, the most developed account of caste ideology has been produced by McGilvray (1982: 35), who argues that caste thinking on the east coast is pervaded by "a strong ideology of chiefly conquest, a system of matrilineal clan rights, and a traditional array of 'marks of honour'", which are all associated with the ideals of "the regional chiefship of the Mukkuvar caste". Similarly, many have noted the prominence of collective memories of duties and honours allocated by the kings of the past (e.g. Spencer 1990: 187; Kendrick 1992: 192), a legacy of Sri Lanka's history of compulsory labour.

Caste Reproduction

Caste scholarship from elsewhere in South Asia has foregrounded marriage and kinship, and food and commensality, as some of the foremost areas in which caste is embodied, produced, and reproduced. While asymmetrical food transactions have often been mentioned in caste studies, for instance by Jegathesan (2021), dedicated research on this subject has not yet been conducted. Marriage has received more attention, and indeed the comment that caste is "only" important at the point of marriage is a common local caveat when emphasising the unimportance of caste (obscuring the fact that marriage is perhaps the key means of caste transmission). Abeyasekera (2021) has recently demonstrated the continuing significance of caste (and class) in Sinhalese middle-class marriages, establishing a valuable point of comparison for studies of marriage in other caste and class contexts. Recent research among northern Tamils has noted that a preference for kin marriages means that caste and kin are often closely intertwined (Bruland 2015; Esler 2020: 129–133), while Thanges (2018b) has investigated the growth in inter-caste marriages during the war. McGilvray's (2008) detailed account of the exogamous, matrilineal *kuḍi* matriclans which shape kinship practices in the east provides an important point of comparison for the apparently less complex patrilineal inheritance of caste elsewhere in Sri Lanka.

Kin and caste boundaries are also mediated by caste associations which, as their membership is voluntary and conditional, are never coterminous with the caste itself. Although caste associations have been largely overlooked, perhaps due to their lack of explicit political activity, they range from business associations – such as the barber and washer associations in Mannar and Jaffna which have regulated labour and prohibited ritual house visits (Thanges and Silva 2009: 76; Esler 2020: 223) – to those that maintain funeral funds and arrange religious events (Esler 2020: 229–242). I have also recently described a relatively public organisation in Mannar dedicated to promoting public devotion to the 16th-century Mannar Martyrs, whose memory plays a central role in local Catholicism, and to improving the socio-economic condition of the Kadaiyars, who claim that the Martyrs were members of their caste (Esler 2021). In the north, at least, association membership often reflects caste patrilineality, as the families of women who marry out are usually ineligible. Other associations exist, even if their activities are not prominent. For example, the appearance in the 2001 census of two new ethnic groups previously considered Tamil castes, Bharatha (also known as Paravar) and Chetty, was an outcome of organised lobbying of President J.R. Jayawardene in the 1980s.

Religion

Quite a large amount of research, although none of it explicitly comparative, has demonstrated that Buddhist, Hindu, and Christian (Catholic and Protestant) ideological and ritual contexts have been key mediums for the production and transformation of caste. However, despite numerous accounts (often historical) of the practices, debates, and conflicts involved in these issues (e.g. Gombrich 1971; Kemper 1980; Saveri 1993 Bastin 1997: 294–317), social scientific approaches, as I will expand upon below, often adopt textual arguments that propound an intrinsic theological opposition to caste in certain religions: Buddhism, Christianity, and Islam – while treating religions as independent actors that exist beyond the activities of their members.

Given this context, it is worth noting that similar caste dynamics have been recorded among members of multiple Sri Lankan religions. In Hindu temples, caste is manifest in struggles around temple rights, particularly participation in festivals, or in complete exclusion from certain temples (Pfaffenberger 1990; Whitaker 1999; McGilvray 2008). In the Sri Lankan Catholic Church, individual churches may be controlled by single and multiple castes, and conflicts over church administration do occur, alongside allegations of discrimination in the Church hierarchy (Esler 2021). However, caste is not a reason for exclusion from the Church or ritual contexts per se. Research on Buddhism has shown that experiences of exclusion have driven some low-caste Buddhists to establish their own temples (Samuels 2007; Uyangoda 2012), while two of the three main *nikāyas*, or monastic lineages, recruit monks on a caste basis (Kemper 1980).

Although it may seem counterintuitive, one of the key comparative questions that this body of research raises is why Sri Lankan Muslims do not practise caste, despite the presence of caste-like groups among them (McGilvray 2008: 308–310). Evidence of caste among Muslims elsewhere in the subcontinent indicates that a theological approach – that Islam is inherently opposed to caste – is not sufficient as an explanation, although McGilvray (2016: 64) has also suggested that the British practice of classifying by "race" rather than caste, in addition to the "the diversity of livelihoods and economic adaptations" in Muslim settlements, may have played a role.

Politics

Although largely absent from public policy discussion and party pronouncements, caste is present in contemporary Sri Lankan politics in "subterranean narratives of group identity and social justice" (Uyangoda 2000: 18). Research on caste in politics – which differs from the topics that I have already mentioned in that it is predominantly comprised of studies focusing on the Sinhalese – has identified several key issues. The first is the preponderance of Sinhalese Govigamas among members of parliament and ministers, and especially among prime ministers and presidents, all of whom, other than President Ranasinghe Premadasa, have been Govigama. Second, caste has become increasingly electorally significant since Independence, particularly after the first-past-the-post parliamentary electoral system was replaced in 1977 with proportional representation – according to which political parties are allocated a number of seats in multi-seat constituencies proportionate to the total local votes that they receive – which gave additional impetus to (often smaller) lower castes to vote collectively (Uyangoda 2000; Peiris and Lecamwasam 2020). Third, Jiggins's (1979) contention that caste plays a central role in political patronage has led to further debate. Jayanntha (1992: 206) has argued that caste is only significant when it is "congruent with a patronage network", while Peiris (2021: 143) has more recently proposed that although caste networks can make patronage more efficient, caste divides the Sinhalese electorate only when politically constructed with that intention. Fourth, in contrast to Tamils, no political movement among the Sinhalese has ever explicitly targeted caste inequality. The presence of caste considerations in politics is not acknowledged publicly, and indeed it is not considered legitimate to do so within the prevailing ideology of social egalitarianism (Uyangoda 2000).

Although no comparable research on contemporary electoral politics has been conducted among Tamils, a handful of scholars have discussed the role of caste, particularly the relationship between the Vellalars and the Karaiyars, in Tamil identity, nationalism, and the development of militant groups, most prominently the LTTE (Pfaffenberger 1990; Hellmann-Rajanayagam 1993;

Jeeweshwara Räsänen 2015). Regarding the last-mentioned theme, this scholarship shows some overlap with less conclusive investigations into caste in the formation and organisation of the Janatha Vimukthi Peramuna, a Sinhalese socialist organisation (now a political party) involved in two armed uprisings against the government in the 1970s and 1980s (Obeyesekere 1974; Moore 2021).

Key Challenges for Future Research

Besides the empirical lacunae indicated above, there is a pressing need to confront two further theoretical and methodological challenges, both of which have emerged at the interface of popular and academic discourses.

Moving beyond Ethnoreligious Caste Systems

Although Sri Lankan caste studies have largely overlooked broader theoretical debates, most research, as Rogers (2004: 51–52) has indicated, has drawn on the popular view of caste as a Hindu phenomenon, according to which other religions are considered inherently antithetical to caste's hierarchical ideology. However, as religion is predominantly viewed as a subcategory of ethnicity in Sri Lanka (Rogers 1994), caste also becomes a subcategory of ethnicity at a further remove, resulting in a conceptual framework of parallel Tamil Hindu and Sinhalese Buddhist caste systems that differ in terms of a generalised notion of caste "strength", Tamils having "stronger" caste than Sinhalese (a perspective reinforced by perceptions of caste-conscious Jaffna). At a higher level, as Sri Lanka is a majority Buddhist country, caste in Sri Lanka as a whole is generalised as non-religious and weak in comparison to the strong, religious caste of "Hindu India", which is sometimes further justified by the absence of a Brahmin-like caste among Sinhalese and the relatively small number of Brahmins among Tamils.

Although usually only sketched briefly in introductions, I suggest that this implicit "ethnoreligious theory of caste" has had three significant impacts on caste research. First, there has been little consideration of the similarities and connections between postulated caste systems, which tend to fragment from ethnoreligious caste systems into regional caste systems at higher levels of detail, despite existing evidence regarding a) the existence of analogous Tamil and Sinhalese castes, b) contexts in which service relationships cross ethnic boundaries (e.g. Ryan 1953: 141; Piyarathne 2018: 158–159), and c) indications that the ethnoreligious framework may not reflect emic perceptions – as seen, for example, in the fact that some Tamil Karaiyars and Sinhalese Karavas previously considered each other to share a caste (Esler 2021: 238). Second, the concept of autonomous caste systems itself, which presupposes static structures of hierarchical relationships arising from ethnicity, has obscured other significant factors such as the historical role of compulsory labour at a national level. Third, the stereotypical representation of the "Indian caste system" reproduced in the theory seems to have largely precluded engagement with caste research from India (and other parts of South Asia), overlooking key debates and comparative data. Finally, moving beyond the assumption of parallel ethnoreligious caste systems permits a reappraisal, not only of caste studies, but of the wider ethnic division in Sri Lankan scholarship – that is, the fact that most research has focused on one ethnic group – of which caste research is a particularly obvious example.

Rethinking Public Caste Discourse and Practice

The second challenge is to interrogate the relationship between the disavowal and silencing of caste in popular discourse and caste as actually practised, while considering the consequences of this context for caste research. Douglas, whose thesis marks the first serious ethnographic attempt to address this topic, notes that many researchers have accepted the principle that caste is disappearing and suggests that this may be responsible for the broader lack of interest in caste (2017: 25). While Douglas is not alone in rejecting this assumption (Uyangoda 1998; Silva et al 2009a; Peiris and Lecamwasam 2020), and researchers working with Tamils have largely avoided it, Douglas argues that silence is not simply a barrier to understanding caste but a central factor in its perpetuation.

Extending this principle, I propose that two other, apparently common-sense assumptions should also be investigated. The first is the extent to which caste *is* invisible in the public domain, and what this means for the category of "public" itself. In fact, caste can be encountered in many everyday forms in Sri Lanka, from cattle brands to marriage ads in mainstream English, Tamil, and Sinhala newspapers, while caste publications also exist in all three languages. However, recognising the presence and role of caste often requires different types of knowledge, from linguistic competence to familiarity with the highly local customs of caste communities (within which knowledge may still be shared unequally, e.g. generationally). How is the distinction between private and public perceived and actively constructed, and what does this mean for Sri Lankan society? Thiranagama's (2019) discussion of "private-public" spheres in the Indian caste context provides a valuable starting point.

The second involves a reappraisal of the position of the caste researcher. Although caste requires a careful approach, taboos must be understood in a relational rather than absolute sense, by considering how research is affected by who is speaking to whom, and about what, and how the purpose and outcomes of the research are viewed. Caste may be easier to pursue via long-term fieldwork that emphasises participant observation and a wider research agenda, rather than a narrow approach reliant on caste-focused interviews and surveys, while having an explicitly political research agenda may be received negatively by some, regardless of the caste in question. It also appears that local researchers are more likely to be considered motivated by ulterior motives (Jeeweshwara Räsänen 2015; Thanges 2018b: 48–49), and foreign researchers as less partial (Jiggins 1979: 7–8; Esler 2021: 243).

Concluding Remarks

In this chapter, which is the first published attempt to provide a comparative analysis of Sri Lankan social scientific caste research, I have described some of the specificities of the Sri Lankan caste context and demonstrated the wide-ranging contemporary significance of caste across numerous different domains. In the hope that these might suggest starting points for future fieldworkers, I have also highlighted empirical lacunae – often related to asymmetrical levels of attention to similar issues among either Sinhalese or Tamils – in the existing scholarship. However, if Sri Lankan caste studies is to become an integrated field in its own right, it will also require a critical examination of the shared theoretical and methodological assumptions about caste that have influenced how research is conceptualised and conducted. Most prominently, this will involve moving beyond the implicit ethnoreligious theory of caste that underpins the ethnic division of caste research, something that I have attempted to do here by bringing together evidence from research among both Tamils and Sinhalese.

Acknowledgements

I would like to thank Dennis McGilvray, John Rogers, Andi Schubert, Hasini Lecamwamsam, Iromi Perera, and the anonymous internal reviewer for feedback on earlier versions of this chapter.

References

Abeyasekera, Asha L. (2021) *Making the Right Choice: Narratives of Marriage in Sri Lanka* New Brunswick: Rutgers University Press

Balasundaram, Sasikumar, A.S. Chandrabose and P.P. Sivapragasam (2009) "Caste Discrimination among Indian Tamil Plantation Workers in Sri Lanka" In *Casteless or Caste-Blind? Dynamics of Concealed Caste Discrimination, Social Exclusion and Protest in Sri Lanka* Kalinga Tudor Silva, P.P. Sivapragasam and Paramsothy Thanges (eds) Colombo and Chennai: Kumaran Book House, pp 97–120

Balmforth, Mark E. (2020) "In Nāki's Wake: Slavery and Caste Supremacy in the 155 American Ceylon Mission" *Caste* 1(1): 155–174

Balmforth, Mark E. (2021) "Blood Red: Slavery, Chintz, and the Dye-Root Diggers of Colonial Ceylon" In *Tradition or Trans/formation? Craft, Practice and Discourse* T. Sanathanan and Abdur-Rahman Ayesha (eds) Jaffna: University of Jaffna, pp 91–103

Bastin, Rohan (1997) "The Authentic Inner Life: Complicity and Resistance in the Tamil Hindu Revival" In *Sri Lanka. Collective Identities Revisited, Volume I* Michael Roberts (ed) Colombo: Marga Institute, pp 385–438

Bruland, Stine (2015) *Under the Margosa Tree: Re-creating meaning in a Tamil family after war and migration.* PhD thesis, Norwegian University of Science and Technology

Colombo Telegraph (2017) "Shortage of Blood in Jaffna: Daily Mirror Accused of Planting Fake Story to Boost Army" (14 June). Accessed on 10/07/2023. Available at https://www.colombotelegraph.com/index.php/shortage-of-blood-in-jaffna-daily-mirror-accused-of-planting-fake-story-to-boost-army/

de Silva, M.W.A. (2018) "Do Name Changes to "acaste" Names by the Sinhalese Indicate a Diminishing Significance of Caste?" *Cultural Dynamics* 30(4): 303–325.

De Silva, M.U. (1992/1993) "Land Tenure, Caste System and the Rājakāriya, under Foreign Rule: A Review of Change in Sri Lanka under Western Powers, 1597–1832" *Journal of the Royal Asiatic Society of Sri Lanka* 57: 1–57

Douglas, Aimée (2017) *Caste in the Same Mold Again: Artisans and the Indignities of Inheritance in Sri Lanka.* Unpublished PhD thesis, Cornell University

Douglas, Aimée (2019) "Heritage for Whom? Caste and Contestation among Sri Lanka's Dumbara Rata Weavers" In *Heritage Movements in Asia: Cultural Heritage Activism, Politics, and Identity* Ali Mozaffari and Tod Jones (eds) New York and Oxford: Berghahn, pp 147–179

Esler, Dominic (2020) *Under the Giant's Tank: Village, Caste, and Catholicism in Postwar Sri Lanka* Unpublished PhD thesis, University College London

Esler, Dominic (2021) "Claiming the Mannar Martyrs: Catholicism and Caste in Northern Sri Lanka" In *Multi-Religiosity in Contemporary Sri Lanka: Innovation, Shared Spaces, Contestation* Mark P. Whitaker, Darini Rajasingham-Senanayake and Sanmugeswaran Pathmanesan (eds) London: Routledge, pp 233–245

Gombrich, Richard F. (1971) *Precept and Practice: Traditional Buddhism in the Rural Highlands of Ceylon* Oxford: Clarendon Press

Hellmann-Rajanayagam, Dagmar (1993) "The Jaffna Social System: Continuity and Change under Conditions of War" *Internationales Asienforum* 24(3–4): 251–281

Hollenbach, Pia, Tanuja Thurairajah and Jeevasuthan Subramaniam (2020) "Gift of a Temple: Socio-Economic and Cultural Changes Around Diasporic Engagement in Jaffna Peninsula, Sri Lanka" *Contemporary South Asia*: 1–24

Jayanntha, Dilesh (1992) *Electoral Allegiance in Sri Lanka* Cambridge: Cambridge University Press

Jayawardena, Kumari (2012) [2000] *Nobodies to Somebodies: The Rise of the Colonial Bourgeoisie in Sri Lanka* Colombo: Social Scientists' Association and Sanjiva Books

Jeeweshwara Räsänen, Bahirathy (2015) *Caste and Nation-Building: Constructing Vellalah Identity in Jaffna.* Unpublished PhD thesis, University of Gothenburg

Jegathesan, Mythri (2021) "Watching for Caste, Commensality, and Compatibility on Sri Lanka's Tea Plantations" *General Anthropology* 28(2): 6–9

Jiggins, Janice (1979) *Caste and Family in the Politics of the Sinhalese, 1947–1976* Cambridge: Cambridge University Press

Kadirgamar, Ahilan (2017) *The Failure of Post-War Reconstruction in Jaffna, Sri Lanka: Indebtedness, Caste Exclusion and the Search for Alternatives.* Unpublished PhD thesis, City University of New York

Kannangara, A.P. (1993) "The Rhetoric of Caste Status in Modern Sri Lanka" In *Society and Ideology: Essays in South Asian History Presented to Professor K. A. Ballhatchet* Peter Robb (ed), in collaboration with K. N. Chaudhuri and Avril Powell (eds) Delhi: Oxford University Press, pp 110–141

Kemper, Steven (1980) "Reform and Segmentation in Monastic Fraternities in Low Country Sri Lanka" *Journal of Asian Studies* 40(1): 27–41

Kendrick, Andrew (1992) "Landholding and Service in a Temple Village in the Kandyan Highlands" In *Agrarian Change in Sri Lanka* James Brow and Joe Weeramunda (eds) New Delhi: Sage, pp 191–228

Kirk, Colin (1992) "Perceiving Agrarian Change: Past and Present in Ratmale, a Sinhalese Potter Village" In *Agrarian Change in Sri Lanka* James Brow and Joe Weeramunda (eds) New Delhi: Sage, pp 389–422

Kuganathan, Prashanth (2022) "Of Tigers and Temples: The Jaffna Caste System in Transition during the Sri Lankan Civil War" In *Sociology of South Asia: Postcolonial Legacies, Global Imaginaries* Radhakrishnan Smitha and Vijayakumar Gowri (eds) London: Palgrave Macmillan, pp 235–265

Lall, Aftab (2015) *Access to Water and Sanitation in Jaffna, Sri Lanka: Perceptions of Caste* Colombo: Centre for Poverty Analysis.

Madavan, Delon (2011) "Socio-Religious Desegregation in an Immediate Postwar Town" *Carnets de Géographes* 2: 1–22

McGilvray, Dennis B. (1982) "Mukkuvar Vannimai: Tamil Caste and Matriclan Ideology in Batticaloa, Sri Lanka" In *Caste Ideology and Interaction* Dennis B. McGilvray (ed) Cambridge: Cambridge University Press, pp 389–422

McGilvray, Dennis B. (1983) "Paraiyar Drummers of Sri Lanka: Consensus and Constraint in an Untouchable Caste" *American Ethnologist* 10(1): 97–115

McGilvray, Dennis B. (2008) *Crucible of Conflict: Tamil and Muslim Society on the East Coast of Sri Lanka* Durham and London: Duke University Press

McGilvray, Dennis B. (2016) "Rethinking Muslim Identity in Sri Lanka" In *Buddhist Extremists and Muslim Minorities: Religious Conflict in Contemporary Sri Lanka* John Clifford Holt (ed) Oxford: Oxford University Press, pp 54–77

Meyer, Eric (2014) "Historical Aspects of Caste in the Kandyan Regions with Particular Reference to the non-Goyigama Castes of the Kägalla District" *The Sri Lanka Journal of the Humanities* 40: 21–54

Moore, Mick (2021) "The Insurrectionary JVP and the Sri Lankan State" *Polity*. Accessed on 12/03/22. Available at http://ssalanka.org/insurrectionary-jvp-sri-lankan-state-mick-moore/

Obeyesekere, Gananath (1974) "Some Comments on the Social Backgrounds of the April 1971 Insurgency in Sri Lanka (Ceylon" *The Journal of Asian Studies* 33(3): 367–384

Peiris, Pradeep (2021) *Catch-All Parties and Party-Voter Nexus in Sri Lanka* Singapore: Palgrave Macmillan

Peiris, Pradeep and Harini Lecamwasam (2020) "Caste-Based Differentiation in Sinhalese Society: Role of Buddhism and Democracy" *Economic & Political Weekly* 8 August 2020: 6–3.

Pfaffenberger, Bryan (1982) *Caste in Tamil Culture: The Religious Foundations of Sudra Domination in Tamil Sri Lanka* Syracuse: Syracuse University

Pfaffenberger, Bryan (1990) "The Political Construction of Defensive Nationalism: The 1968 Temple-Entry Crisis in Northern Sri Lanka" *The Journal of Asian Studies* 49(1): 78–96

Pieris, Ralph (1956) *Sinhalese Social Organisation: The Kandyan Period* Colombo: The Ceylon University Press Board

Piyarathne, Anton (2018) *Constructing Common Grounds: Everyday Lifeworlds beyond Politicised Ethnicities in Sri Lanka* Nugegoda: Sarasavi Publishers

Reed, Susan (2010) "Performing Respectability: The Beravā, Middle-Class Nationalism, and the Classicization of Kandyan Dance in Sri Lanka" *Cultural Anthropology* 17(2): 246–277

Roberts, Michael W. (1982) *Caste Conflict and Elite Formation: The Rise of a Karava Elite in Sri Lanka, 1500–1931* Cambridge: Cambridge University Press

Rogers, John D. (1994) "Post-Orientalism and the Interpretation of Premodern and Modern Political Identities: The Case of Sri Lanka" *The Journal of Asian Studies* 53(1): 10–23

Rogers, John D. (2004) "Caste as a Social Category and Identity in Colonial Lanka" *The Indian Economic and Social History Review* 41(1): 51–77

Ryan, Bryce (1953) *Caste in Modern Ceylon: The Sinhalese System in Transition* New Brunswick: Rutgers University Press

Samuels, Jeffrey (2007) "Monastic Patronage and Temple Building in Contemporary Sri Lanka: Caste, Ritual Performance, and Merit" *Modern Asian Studies* 41(4): 769–795

Sanmugeswaran, Pathmanesan (2023) "How Are Tamil Villages Reconstructed? Ethnography of Place-Making in Post-War Reconstruction in Sri Lanka" In *Rebuilding Communities after Displacement* Mo Hamza, Dilanthi Amaratunga, Richard Haigh, Chamindi Malalgoda, Chathuranganee Jayakody and Anuradha Senanayake (eds) Cham, Switzerland: Springer Nature, pp 269–288

Saveri, Nicholapillai Maria (1993) *A Catholic-Hindu Encounter: Relations between Roman Catholics and Hindus in Jaffna, Sri Lanka, 1900–1926* Jaffna: Centre for Performing Arts

Schrikker, Alicia and Kate J. Ekama (2017) "Through the lens of Slavery: Dutch Sri Lanka in the Eighteenth Century" In *Sri Lanka at the Crossroads of History* Zoltán Biedermann and Alan Strathern (eds) London: UCL Press, pp 178–193

Silva, Kalinga Tudor (2020) "Nationalism, Caste-Blindness and the Continuing Problems of War-Displace Panchamars in Post-War Jaffna Society, Sri Lanka" *Caste* 1(1): 51–70

Silva, Kalinga Tudor, P. Kotikabadde and D.M. Nilanka Chandima Abeywickrama (2009b) "Caste Discrimination in Sinhala Society" In *Casteless or Caste-Blind? Dynamics of Concealed Caste Discrimination, Social Exclusion and Protest in Sri Lanka* Kalinga Tudor Silva, P.P. Sivapragasam and Thanges Paramsothy (eds) Colombo and Chennai: Kumaran Book House, pp 29–49

Silva, Kalinga Tudor, P.P. Sivapragasam and Paramsothy Thanges (eds) (2009a) *Casteless or Caste-Blind? Dynamics of Concealed Caste Discrimination, Social Exclusion and Protest in Sri Lanka* Colombo and Chennai: Kumaran Book House

Silva, Kalinga Tudor, Paramsothy Thanges and P.P. Sivapragasam (2009c) "Urban Untouchability: The Condition of Sweepers and Sanitary Workers in Kandy" In *Casteless or Caste-Blind? Dynamics of Concealed Caste Discrimination, Social Exclusion and Protest in Sri Lanka* Kalinga Tudor Silva, P. P. Sivapragasam and Paramsothy Thanges (eds) Colombo and Chennai: Kumaran Book House, pp 97–120

Simpson, Bob (1997) "Possession, Dispossession and the Social Distribution of Knowledge among Sri Lankan Ritual Specialists" *The Journal of the Royal Anthropological Institute* 3(1): 43–59

Spencer, Jonathan (1990) *A Sinhala Village in a Time of Trouble: Politics and Change in Rural Sri Lanka*. Delhi: Oxford University Press.

Stirrat, R.L. (1982) "Caste Conundrums: Views of Caste in a Sinhalese Catholic Fishing Village" In *Caste Ideology and Interaction* Dennis B. McGilvray (ed) Cambridge: Cambridge University Press, pp 8–33

Sykes, Jim (2018) *The Musical Gift: Sonic Generosity in Post-War Sri Lanka* New York: Oxford University Press

Thanges, Paramsothy (2018a) "Caste within the Sri Lankan Tamil Diaspora: Ūr Associations and Territorial Belonging" *Anthropology Matters Journal* 18(1): 51–82

Thanges, Paramsothy (2018b) *Conflict-induced Migration and Shifting Caste Relations: Resisting and Reproducing Hierarchies in Post-war Sri Lankan Tamil Space*. Unpublished PhD thesis, University of East London

Thanges, Paramsothy and Kalinga Tudor Silva (2009) "Caste Discrimination in War-Affected Jaffna Society" In *Casteless or Caste-Blind? Dynamics of Concealed Caste Discrimination, Social Exclusion and Protest in Sri Lanka* Kalinga Tudor Silva, P.P. Sivapragasam and Paramsothy Thanges (eds) Colombo and Chennai: Kumaran Book House, pp 50–77

Thiranagama, Sharika (2018) "The Civility of Strangers? Caste, Ethnicity, and Living Together in Postwar Jaffna, Sri Lanka" *Anthropological Theory* 18(2–3): 357–381

Thiranagama, Sharika (2019) "Respect Your Neighbour as Yourself: Neighbourliness, Caste, and Community in South India" *Comparative Studies in Society and History* 61(2): 269–300

Uyangoda, Jayadeva (1998) *Studies in Caste and Social Justice in Sri Lanka, Vol. 1: Caste in Sinhalese Society, Culture and Politics* Colombo: Social Scientists Association

Uyangoda, Jayadeva (2000) "The Inner Courtyard: Political Discourses of Caste, Justice and Equality in Sri Lanka" *Pravada* 6(9–10): 14–19

Uyangoda, Jayadeva (2012) "Local Democracy and Citizenship in the Margins. In Reframing Democracy: Perspectives on the Cultures of Inclusion and Exclusion" In *Contemporary Sri Lanka* Jayadeva Uyangoda and Neloufer De Mel (eds) Colombo: Social Scientists Association, pp 29–89

Whitaker, Mark P. (1999) *Amiable Incoherence: Manipulating Histories and Modernities in a Batticaloa Hindu Temple* Amsterdam: VU University Press

Wickramasinghe, Nira (2020) *Slave in a Palanquin: Colonial Servitude and Resistance in Sri Lanka* New York: Columbia University Press

Wickramasinghe, Nira and Alicia Schrikker (2019) "The Ambivalence of Freedom: Slaves in Jaffna, Sri Lanka, in the Eighteenth and Nineteenth Centuries" *The Journal of Asian Studies* 78(3): 497–519

Winslow, Deborah (2003) "Potters' Progress: Hybridity and Accumulative Change in Rural Sri Lanka" ***The Journal of Asian Studies*** 62(1): 43–70

Winslow, Deborah (2009) "The Village Clay: Recursive Innovations and Community Self-Fashioning among Sinhalese Potters" ***Journal of the Royal Anthropological Institute (N.S.)*** 15: 254–275

Yalman, Nur (1967) ***Under the Bo Tree: Studies in Caste, Kinship, and Marriage in the Interior of Ceylon*** Berkeley, Los Angeles, and London: California University Press

30
DYNAMICS OF LOW-INCOME SETTLEMENTS IN COLOMBO, SRI LANKA

Mohideen M. Alikhan

Introduction

Cities are vibrant social spaces that bring different people together, increasing their diversity and providing an experience of living near these differences (Stephanie et al. 2009). Migration and natural increases stimulate the urban population's rapid growth in the global south (UN-Habitat 2016). According to Seabrook (2007), the expansion of slums in many cities in the global south is significantly attributed to internal movement because of various forms of mobility. The physical and social contexts of these low-income neighbourhoods mean that they are widely seen as problematic, unsafe, and rife with dystopian characteristics. These unfavourable conceptions of low-income neighbourhoods fail to appreciate the beneficial aspects of this group, such as the diversity and coexistence of their inhabitants (Datta 2012). While urban governance struggles to tackle diverse issues caused by rapid urbanization, urban residents also face numerous challenges in everyday urban life.

The cultural landscape of Sri Lanka reflects the geographic distribution of Sri Lankan ethnic groups; in most places, people tend to live within the same ethnic, religious, and language groups. However, low-income neighbourhoods in Colombo (known locally as *watta*) are unusual in this regard and have a mixture of people from diverse cultural backgrounds (Silva and Athukorale 1991; Silva 1994; Alikhan 2021, 2022). These settlements are in specific geographic areas with distinct cultural patterns for living with differences. These settlements are not concentrated in any specific area but are spread all around the city. Although inhabitants face many socioeconomic difficulties, one of the most interesting and important elements of these settlements is that diverse cultural groups live together. Ethnically and religiously diverse people have lived together in these settlements for centuries; thus, multiculturalism is an identifying characteristic of these communities (Kottegoda 2004; Ruwanpura 2006, 2008; Alikhan 2021, 2022). In addition, slum residents are vulnerable in terms of housing, living conditions, livelihood, land ownership, the threat of eviction, and the physical environment. leading to the spread of disease and a lack of security resulting from a concentration of criminal activity (Lakshman et al 2016; Lakshma, Alikhan and Azam 2020). These conditions make slum residents rely on the government and other agencies to improve the situation in slums.

I divide this chapter into four sections that provide an overview of the past and contemporary situation of low-income settlements in Colombo. The first section of this chapter provides a brief description of the origin and evaluation of low-income neighbourhoods in Colombo. The second section focuses on the housing-related issues in these neighbourhoods. The next section examines the importance of gender and social networks in everyday interactions and how this interaction helps with various activities of women in the *watta*. The last section focuses on how post-war urban development and eviction affect the low-income residents of Colombo.

Evolution of Low-Income Neighbourhoods in Colombo

Like many places in the global south, a significant proportion of low-income settlements in Colombo emerged during the colonial period, and rapid expansion took place in the post-independence era (Sevanatha 2003; Perera 2008). The expansion of Colombo port in 1883 and its associated industries were a primary instrument that stimulated the rise of a particular clustering of working-class tenements. The introduction of railways in the 1860s, and the expansion of communication networks, facilitated rural-to-urban migration, resulting in substantial numbers of rural youths migrating to Colombo to seek opportunities in the new modes of the economy (Perera 2008). As the population demands increased, the city's supply of housing began to lag. Consequently, people began to encroach on marginal areas, such as canal banks, along railroad lines, marshy areas, and paddy fields abandoned due to economic constraints. These areas offered easy access to workplaces, stimulating the growth of low-income settlements.

These types of poor housing in Colombo generally fall into two categories: slums and shanties (Sevanatha 2003; Perera 2008). Slums are old buildings constructed from permanent materials, overcrowded, and poorly serviced. Most slums are in the inner city and were built in the 1930s for labour migrants. By contrast, shanty communities emerged after 1948 to accommodate the excess population from slum areas and new migrants to the city and are collectives of small, single units built of impermanent materials (Perera 2008). In addition to these types of dwellings, the other type of dwelling was self-built housing, which added a new dimension to the landscape of Colombo. A common solution to the lack of affordable dwellings was the construction of single-story, mostly detached, small housing units using less durable materials found in urban environments. Building their own houses with the materials available and using self-help methods to do so represents the transfer of rural housing methods to the city (Sevanatha 2003). These low-income dwellings, which spread across areas, such as Maradana, New Bazaar, Kotahena, Slave Island, Kochchikade, and Gintupitiya, housed a large proportion of the working class (Perera 2008). These areas were under the "Colombo Municipal Council" (CMC) limits.

Since shanties are built on vacant land in the city, most inhabitants do not have legal rights (Silva and Athukorala 1991; D'Cruz, McGranahan and Sumithre 2009). Although significant upgrades were made to these settlements over time, most of them are still congested and have a high density. Contemporary migration from the rural and plantation sectors to Colombo also significantly contributes to the spread of low-income settlements (Dias 1976; Arularasi and Alikhan 2015). Due to the lack of affordable housing in the city, rural migrants move into slums and shanties, which are often located on expensive land in inner cities (Kottegoda 2004; Perera 2008). Currently, migrant labourers and their families live in these areas, in addition to generations of original residents. In the local context, low-income settlements are generally referred to by different names, such as *Mudukku, Peli Gewal, Pelpath*, however, the most common word is "watta," which means "garden" (Kottegoda 1991; Silva and Athukorala 1991; Sevanatha 2003). Since the term *watta* is commonly used to refer to all kinds of low-income settlements, I use the term to describe all low-income neighbourhoods in Colombo in this chapter.

Overcrowded Housing

Control over low-income neighbourhoods is one of the oldest unsolved issues in the country and can be traced to the British period (Perera 2008). British colonial officers made Colombo a hub of economic and administrative functions, which increased employment opportunities. Since its establishment in 1865, the unhealthy and overcrowded living standards of the working class in low-income settlements have attracted the attention of the CMC. Since then, the CMC has carried out several strategies and initiatives to address the problem of high-density housing in low-income neighbourhoods. However, most of the interventions to eradicate overcrowding and poor-quality housing in low-income neighbourhoods in both colonial and post-colonial periods did not provide sufficient opportunities for these underprivileged communities to participate in policy formation and implementation. Different city designs had been developed by local and international planners to alleviate the overcrowding and improve the quality of life for slum inhabitants. Some of these plans include Sir Patrick Geddes (1921), Clifford Holiday (1940), Sir Patrick Abercrombie (1949), the Colombo Master Plan (1978), the Colombo Development Plan by the Urban Development Authority (UDA in 1985), the Colombo Metropolitan Regional Structural Plan (CMRSP in 1998), and most recently the Western Region Megapolis Planning Project (WRMPP) and the Urban Regeneration Project (URP) (Sevanatha 2003; Abeyasekera et al 2019).

In Sri Lanka, urban areas, particularly the country's capital city of Colombo, have a considerably higher tendency to have acceptable housing (Samaratunga and O'Hare 2013, 2014). According to the 2012 census, 1.5% of Sri Lanka's housing structures fit the criteria of shanties, and 1.3% of residents are residing there unlawfully (Department of Census and Statistics 2012). A thorough analysis of urban housing reveals that the distribution of housing and its affordability are more skewed in urban areas, even though at the national level, the average housing condition is not yet apparent as a significant issue in terms of affordability, home ownership, and housing characteristics (Weeraratne 2020).

A report by Sevanatha (2003) highlights that more than half of the people in Colombo live in low-income settlements that lack essential services. In relation to the low-income housing, inhabitants in these settlements have been facing a few issues, such as types of housing, size, inner-outer atmosphere, tenure, and fear of eviction. Slums are blighted by a lack of durable housing, insufficient living space, a lack of clean water, inadequate sanitation, etc. Due to the informal nature of their settlements, slum-dwellers often lack tenure security, which makes them vulnerable to forced evictions, threats, and other forms of harassment (Silva and Athukorala 1991; D'Cruz et al 2009). While these residential areas have the common features of having a very high population density (approximately 820 persons per hectare), or four times the average of the city of Colombo) and congested housing (with each block averaging 1.5 perches), it is the chronic condition of the services and infrastructure available to the residents that give them the term "underserved settlements" (Gunetilleke, Cader and Fernando 2004). Based on a 2001 survey by the Sevanatha Urban Resource Centre along with the CMC, 77,612 families live in 1,614 low-income settlements in Colombo, which contain nearly half of the city's population (Sevanatha 2003: 10). With this figure, Sevanatha notes that low-income neighbourhoods are an important vote bank for politicians who contest elections on the local and national levels.

Authorities – national or local – are often reluctant to extend basic services to slums precisely because they are informal. Informality is one of the challenges that slum residents face when trying to access essential services through formal channels. For example, due to the absence of land ownership and voting rights in the city, they struggle to access electricity, water, education, and employment. Since there is a lack of opportunity to obtain services formally, these people tend to do so informally. The previous housing policies, including slum and shanty upgrading projects, did not bring substantial change to the housing situation. Past slum and shanty upgrading programmes mainly helped relatively better-off families, those who are the core sector of the urban labour force. Since the liberalization of the economy has occurred, new demand for office space, warehouses, shopping facilities, etc., has resulted in spiralling ground rents on the "free" land market. Davis (2007: 86) emphasizes that "property values in Colombo increased a thousand-fold during the 1970s and 1980s, pushing a large number of older, poorer residents into peri-urban areas." Low-cost housing policies only helped the better off and had no impact on the housing problems of the poor. Blanket programmes of modernization and upgrading will only result in the expulsion of the population and its shift to the next slum and shanty area.

Gender, Social Networks

Studies on women in low-income areas have provided significant evidence of how essential it is to retain domestic duties while also contributing to the household economy as part of their socio-culturally prescribed position (Kottegoda 1991, 2004; De Alwis 2002; Ruwanpura 2006, 2008, 2009; De Mel 2009; Perera 2015, 2016; Lakshman et al 2016; Abeyasekera et al 2019). Most of these studies concentrate on the close-knit social relationships that are facilitated by diverse social networks in low-income settlements, which are essential to their daily lives and where people are closely connected via multiple relationships that produce dense informal social networks among residents. These social networks and kin relationships help residents enjoy many resources and provide an essential space for different groups to interact (Kottegoda 1991, 2004; Ruwanpura 2008). White (2002: 261) defines social networks as "a web of social relations or resources that surrounds Individuals, groups or organisations and the characteristics of their ties." Social networks strengthen and expand social capital, according to Carpenter, Daniere and Takahashi (2004: 855), who state that "social capital is a resource available to individuals that emanate from group contact because of trust, reciprocity, and cooperation." These networks could increase the collective actions and cooperative behaviour to yield community actions (White 2002). The types and sizes of social networks help people in many ways, such as financial, material, and emotional support (Kottegoda 1991, 2004; Ruwanpura 2008; Matthews and Besemer 2014). Low-income settlements are thus unique geographic locations that enhance the reciprocal relationships between different groups in everyday engagement.

Since households are part of wider social interactions and realities and because their structure is influenced by the social context, Ruwanpura (2007) notes that "households are not the same everywhere. Gender roles are thus influenced by a variety of social, cultural, political, and economic settings" (2007: 525). Socially constructed gender roles and a lack of political engagement are common among women in Sri Lanka more generally. "Sri Lankan women, be they Sinhala, Tamil, or Muslim, continue to be constructed as the reproducers, nurturers, and disseminators of tradition, culture, community, and nation" (De Alwis 2002: 676). According to Kottegoda (1991), the domestic life cycle of the household and anticipated household role responsibilities and obligations influence women's choice of income-generating work. Further evidence of how ethnic identification and cultural views of women affected the types of networks, as Kottegoda (2004) elaborates (see also Ruwanpura 2006).

Women in low-income areas typically want to take up flexible jobs that allow them to manage household responsibilities. According to Kottegoda (1991), the domestic life cycle of the household and anticipated domestic role responsibilities and obligations influence women's choice of an income-generating profession. As a result, people rely heavily on social networks to find good employment prospects. Additionally, studies show that the diverse social networks that women interact with daily in low-income settlements offer these women a variety of psychological and material assistance. Kottegoda (1991) highlighted three crucial areas where women receive support through these networks: (a) finding out information regarding work opportunities; (b) sharing childcare and other domestic responsibilities; and (c) obtaining financial loans (Kottegoda 1991: 29). Women maintain reciprocal exchanges with neighbours or others from their ethnic groups as a form of survival. Ruwanpura (2008) emphasizes how ethnic differences in low-income neighbourhoods coexist with strong similarities. These networks are crucial for the well-being and survival of women (2008: 414). According to Kottegoda (2004), networks of social ties function at several layers, such as those between neighbours, kin groups, and ethnic groups (Kottegoda 2004: 123).

The geographical layout and economic marginalization are two significant factors strengthening social networks in the Watta community. It is difficult to avoid interacting with others in the *watta* setting because of the limited space and dense population. Most of the houses in the neighbourhood range in size from 350 to 450 square feet, comprising room(s), living space, kitchen, bathroom, and toilet. This narrow domestic space encourages children to play in open public spaces, which are also limited in the *watta*. When children play in these public spaces, they meet children of similar ages from different ethnic and religious backgrounds. Gradually, they develop strong relationships with each other and maintain them throughout their lives. Some peer groups in the *watta* have held close relations since their childhood. These groups' social networks become an essential element among the members because of the multiple supports they accumulate from their peers.

Residents in these settlements have strong social networks with kin, neighbours, and friends, which enhance the "private support system" (Kottegoda 1991, 2004: 120). People use their social networks for multiple reasons, such as childcare, finding jobs (particularly in the informal labour market), accessing instant loans, getting support in emergencies, and organizing religious festivals and New Year celebrations. The nature of social life and social networking among the *watta* residents undoubtedly impacts their sense of belonging to the community. People who were born and grew up in the *watta* have a strong understanding of their neighbours and their cultural practices through social learning since childhood. In low-income neighbourhoods, the space for socialization with others is impossible to avoid because of much higher population densities. These social networks help enhance trust among residents in the community to take collective action in more productive ways, increase reciprocal trust, and ultimately improve support for tackling differences in everyday life.

The role of women in marginalized communities is much more important as women spend more time in the community and engage in a wide variety of both family and community activities (Kottegoda 1991, 2004; Alikhan 2022). Compared with men, interaction among women in everyday life is reasonably high in the *watta*. Generally, men go out of the neighbourhood for work in the morning and return in the evening. Thus, their interaction with other men in the *watta* happens at a specific time, mostly once they return from work. In contrast, most women spend most of their time in the neighbourhood from the morning until night (Kottegoda 2004). In some families, women are engaging in various livelihoods, such as cooking fast food, being vegetable vendors, and running small grocery shops within the settlement, to earn supplementary income for their families.

Further, some of these regular interactions often happen in public places, such as collecting water from the communal tap, purchasing groceries for daily grocery shopping needs, disposing of garbage, and picking up children from preschool and tuition classes. These neighbours also meet for mutual assistance, including childcare, borrowing money, kitchen help, and spending spare time together. Members of the community have a mechanism enabling these women to cope with *watta* culture. This support may help new migrant women overcome psychological marginality in a culturally diverse space. Migrant women generally receive most information about *watta* resources and services from their immediate neighbours, while their spouses are mainly concerned about employment. These neighbours are typically not from the same ethnic or religious groups; nevertheless, they form strong bonds through their everyday interactions. The discussion so far indicates that women, as both income earners and homemakers, spend more time in the neighbourhood than their male partners, which allows them to interact with other women in the *watta*.

These interactions help them share information and receive help; beyond that, talking to their neighbours also serves a valuable psychological function by helping relieve stress. Since the spouses of women are out most of the day, they do not have anyone to share their everyday life difficulties with. Most migrants' parents, siblings, and relatives are in their hometown, and only their neighbours can share and care for them. When these women have spare time, mainly after lunch, they visit neighbouring homes and talk about many topics, including gossip about the *watta* people. Thus, the engagement between women in the *watta* plays a significant role in gradually constructing a mutual understanding for each other regardless of ethnicity, religion, and language.

Nevertheless, socio-cultural norms that reinforce women's unequal status persist in the *watta* and limit women's ability to engage in the public sphere. Public life of the *watta* community is often dominated by men, and, consequently, women lack influence in political, economic, or social contexts as compared with men. Although some women engage in livelihood activities, their income source is dependent primarily on livelihood activities and is typically an extension of socially constructed gender roles. Although women engage with other women through informal talks, culinary culture, and especially during emergencies, their voices are not equal to those of men in decision-making for the entire community.

Thus, individually and at the community level, women are expected to adhere to socially constructed, gendered roles. They face many challenges in retaining relationships constructed with culturally diverse groups. Any conflicts among men in the public space directly impact the household, and women mostly must obey their husbands. As a result of conflict between men, women may lose the opportunity to spend time with their neighbours. Thus, the engagement of women in the neighbourhood is fragile and partly outside of women's control; therefore, the next generation also loses social learning opportunities, and this contributes to gradual, long-term change in the *watta*.

Social networks provide an ideal space for diverse groups to mingle together. These informal networks are essential for the kind of support that leads to an improved understanding of differences. People who were born and grew up in low-income settings construct networks with friends from their childhood and remain in them for long periods of time (Kottegoda 2004; Perera 2015, 2016; Lakshman et al 2016; Abeyasekara et al 2019). While these networks provide the multiple forms of support discussed, it is a key factor that ensures the mingling of people from diverse cultures. However, many people are eager to move away from the *watta* because of increasing environmental disturbances, such as flash floods, garbage, and drainage issues, and unpleasant local characteristics, such as rising drug-related problems, conflict with some people, and using foul language. As both in and out-migration are increasing rapidly, this could affect social networks, which are generally established through long-term relationships and understanding. The nature of these networks also informs social norms from one generation to the next. However, since a significant number of people are waiting for an opportunity to move because of increasing social and environmental issues, they do not try to develop close relationships with the remaining people in the *watta*. The in-between situation of people reduces interaction between people and eliminates the space needed to establish effective social networks (Alikhan 2022).

Post-war Development and Eviction

In Sri Lanka, new initiatives supported by the national government to reshape the urban environment and revitalize the national economy also provide a substantial challenge for individuals living in low-income neighbourhoods. In 2009, the Sri Lankan government forces defeated the Liberation Tigers of Tamil Eelam (LTTE) and brought 30 years of civil war to an end. Soon afterwards, the government took various steps to develop the country, with particular attention being paid to Colombo. The government used urban development as a strategy to attract foreign investors to Colombo. To attain this goal, selected low-income settlements located on some of the most valuable lands in the city were relocated so that the vacant land could be used for economic purposes (Perera 2015; Nagaraj 2016; Abeyasekera et al 2019). Some of these evictions were carried out forcibly with the support of military forces, and people who lived in these areas scattered to various places (Amarasuriya and Spencer 2015).

The WRMPP, sometimes known as "Megapolis," was created to attract significant international investment to the country. The proposed project includes three districts in the western region, namely Colombo, Gampaha, and Kalutara. This proposal also includes the most controversial "Port City" project and targets completion within 15 years. The aim of the project was to help Sri Lanka raise its per capita gross domestic product to a level appropriate for a high-income developed country by 2030. Much of the framing and conceptualization of the megapolis, therefore, appears derived from and caught in the grip of dominant templates and ideas about development and urbanization spun by powerful global actors and capital (Nagaraj 2016).

Nearly 50% of urban dwellers are living in so-called underserved settlements in the Colombo city area (Sevanatha 2003). According to the UDA, these people occupied around 900 acres of prime land, which can be utilized for economic activities (Nagaraj 2016). The government has constructed high-rise towers, many of which will be between 12 and 15 stories. Although the Megapolis plan has a criterion for the size of the house, the actual size will be decided by the land developers. The minimum amount for a two-bedroom flat will be one million rupees, which is difficult to bear for low-income dwellers. According to Bresnick's (2016), the investors say that they have already approached private banks to create loan facilities that will help buy new apartments. Also, they point out that all these strategies to create a denser housing model will allow for space to be used more efficiently. Bresnick cited an official who said that the government will use one-third of the land for the slums located on government land and develop buildings for the people. The remaining two-third will be offered for mixed development to private businesses. The government will fund the creation of the new structures through these transactions. It demonstrates that those with low incomes must seek out other housing if they are unable to pay for a "new flat."

Most recently, to "beautify" the city by eliminating "slums" and relocating residents into "modern dwellings," the URP moved a sizable number of the working class into high-rise apartments. According to the URP framework, upgrading underserved communities in the city of Colombo through private developers and liberating prime areas for commercial operations are two important objectives of urban development (Abeyasekera et al 2019: 223). Some of the evictions took place forcibly (Amarasuriya and Spencer 2015). Most of these people were relocated to high-rise condominiums, which shifted their social lives from horizontal to vertical. Little literature suggests that the significant consequences of this eviction and relocation can undermine the unity, relationships, and networks that low-income residents have maintained for a long period. Relocated people in new settlements do not actively participate in community organizations due to their weak sense of belonging, which is the most significant challenge facing relocated communities. The robust social network in their previous low-income settlements was mostly shattered due to the individualized lifestyle introduced by condominium living (Lakshman et al 2016; Collyer, Amirthalingam and Jayatilaka 2017). Low-income neighbourhoods in Colombo have become an important site for post-war urban development as they occupy some of the most valuable lands in the country. With the support of international donor agencies and private investors, the government relocates low-income residents to condominium apartments. This top-down slum uplift approach has caused adverse social and economic implications due to the absence of victims in decision-making. More importantly, this kind of project could harm the socioeconomic and mental well-being of relocated communities.

Low-income settlements are generally located in the inner city and occupy some of the most valuable lands. Most residents in these settlements do not have proper documents to indicate the ownership of their land and houses. Thus, people who live in low-income settlements fear eviction when the land is needed for development by the government (Alikhan 2022). Although residents claim legal ownership of their homes through various documents, they understand they will have to move if the government requires the land. Residents with permit cards and deeds feel more protected against forcible evictions. Even if it were to happen, they expect to be able to seek compensation or a suitable substitute dwelling in a nearby location. Residents who hold other forms of documentation are concerned about their security because of their tenure type. As a result, those with higher tenure rights feel safer than those with less or no tenure rights. Thus, although most people live in permanent homes with access to services like water, electricity, and drainage, they are not mentally at ease since they fear being evicted by the government in the future as has occurred in other locations with comparable characteristics.

Conclusion

Low-income neighbourhoods in Colombo have a long history dating back to the colonial era. These settlements are exceptional in terms of cultural diversity when compared to many other areas of the country. Because of the informality and geographical setting of the area, working-class groups representing a variety of religious and ethnic backgrounds have been living together in the *watta* community since its inception. Although there are positive aspects of cultural diversity among *watta* residents, the settlements' widespread reputation as problematic places prevents outsiders from appreciating their rich and significant diversity. Besides, additional pressure comes from day-to-day issues such as high density, inner-outer atmosphere, a lack of long-lasting housing, insufficient living space, a lack of clean water, poor sanitation, the surrounding environment, and service accessibility.

However, residents, particularly women, benefit from strong social networks through which they receive financial, material, and emotional assistance. Women in low-income communities frequently seek flexible positions that let them handle domestic duties. Women's choice of an income-generating career is influenced by the home life cycle of the household and projected domestic roles, responsibilities, and obligations. People therefore heavily rely on social networking to find promising employment opportunities. Additionally, these diverse social networks offer women a variety of psychological and material assistance.

At present, one of the key challenges most residents in these settlements face is development-related relocation, which sometimes happens in the form of forced eviction. The government used urban development as a strategy to attract foreign investors to Colombo. Since many low-income settlements are located on prime land in the city centre, selected low-income settlements in the city were relocated so that vacant land could be used for economic purposes. Recently, some of these evictions were carried out forcibly with the support of military forces, and people who lived in these areas were scattered to various places. Considering the majority of those who reside in these communities lack the required documentation proving they are the owners of their houses and land. Hence, in addition to the ongoing socioeconomic and environmental difficulties they have long faced, they also live in constant fear of eviction.

References

Abeyasekera, Asha, Ammara Maqsood, Iromi Perera, Fizzah Sajjad and Jonathan Spencer (2019) "Discipline in Sri Lanka, Punish in Pakistan: Neoliberalism, Governance, and Housing Compared" *The British Academy* 7(s2): 215–244

Alikhan, Mohideen (2021) "Watta Culture: A Study of Subaltern Cosmopolitanism in Low Income Neighbourhoods of Colombo" [paper presentation] **7th National Geography Conference (NGC-2021)** University of Peradeniya (October 29)

Alikhan, Mohideen (2022) Conviviality, tension, and everyday negotiations: subaltern cosmopolitanism and governance dynamics of low-income neighbourhoods in Colombo, Sri Lanka [Doctoral thesis, University of Sussex] *Sussex Research Online*. Accessed on 15/12/2022. Available at http://sro.sussex.ac.uk/id/eprint/109012

Amarasuriya, Harini and Jonathan Spencer (2015) "With That, Discipline Will Also Come to Them: The Politics of the Urban Poor in Postwar Colombo" *Current Anthropology* 56(S11): S66–S75

Arularasi, Balakrishnan and Mohideen Alikhan (2015) "Plantation to Urban: Phenomenon and Causes of Youth Migration in the Pitakanda Estate, Matale" [paper presentation] *Peradeniya University International Research Session* University of Peradeniya (13–14 December)

Bresnick, Sam (2016) *Where do we go from here? Daily News* (19 September). https://archives1.dailynews.lk/2016/09/19/features/93484

Carpenter, Jeffrey, Amrita Daniere and Lois Takahashi (2004) "Social Capital and Trust in South-east Asian Cities" *Urban Studies* 41(4): 853–874

Collyer, Michael, Kopalapillai Amirthalingam and Danesh Jayatilaka (2017) "The Right to Adequate Housing Following Forced Evictions in Post-Conflict Colombo, Sri Lanka" In *Geographies of Forced Eviction* Katherine Brickell, Melissa Arrigoitia and Alexander Vasudevan (eds) London: Palgrave Macmillan, pp 47–69

D'Cruz, Celine, Gordon McGranahan and Upali Sumithre (2009) "The Efforts of a Federation of Slum and Shanty Dwellers to Secure Land and Improve Housing in Moratuwa: From Savings Groups to Citywide Strategies" *Environment and Urbanization* 21(2): 367–388

Datta, Ayona (2012) "Mongrel City: Cosmopolitan Neighbourliness in a Delhi Squatter Settlement" *Antipode* 44(3): 745–763

Davis, Mike (2007) *Planet of Slums* New York: Verso

De Alwis, Malathi (2002) "The Changing Role of Women in Sri Lankan Society" *Social Research* 69(3): 675–691

De Mel, Neloufer (2009) "The Production of Disaster: Contextualizing the Tsunami and Its Impacts on Women in Sri Lanka" In *After the Waves: The Impact of the Tsunami on Women in Sri Lanka* Neloufer De Mel, Kanchana Ruwanpura and Samarasinghe Gameela (eds) Colombo: Social Scientists' Association, pp 3–16

Department of Census and Statistics (2012) *Census of Population and Housing – 2012* Colombo: Department of Census and Statistics

Dias, Erika (1976) *A Study of Slums and Shanties in the City of Colombo* Colombo: University of Colombo

Gunetilleke, Neranjana, Azra Cader and Mariam Fernando (2004) *Understanding the Dimensions and Dynamics of Poverty in Underserved Settlements in Colombo* Colombo: Centre for Poverty Analysis/ Colombo Municipal Council

Kottegoda, Sepali (1991) The role of women in household survival strategies: A case study from an urban low-income settlement in Colombo, Sri Lanka [Doctoral thesis, University of Sussex]. Accessed on 21/02/2018. Available at https://sussex.primo.exlibrisgroup.com/discovery/delivery/44SUS_INST:44SUS_VU1/12234940690002461

Kottegoda, Sepali (2004) *Negotiating Household Politics: Women's Strategies in Urban Sri Lanka* Colombo: Social Scientists' Association

Lakshman, Iresha, Mohideen Alikhan and Abdulla Azam (2020) "Finding 'Reasons to Stay' Amidst Issues of Well-Being: A Case Study of Two Underserved Communities in Colombo" *European Scientific Journal, ESJ* 16: 94–94

Lakshman, Iresha, Dammika Herath, Mohideen Alikhan and Asela Ekanayake (2016) *Experiences of Relocated Community in Colombo: Case Study of Sinhapura, Wanathamulla* Colombo: International Centre for Ethnic Studies

Matthews, Peter and Kirsten Besemer (2014) "Poverty and Social Networks Evidence Review" *STORRE* (3 September). Accessed on 11/10/2020. Available at https://dspace.stir.ac.uk/handle/1893/21042

Nagaraj, Vijay (2016) "From Smokestacks to Luxury Condos: The Housing Rights Struggle of the Millworkers of Mayura Place, Colombo" *Contemporary South Asia* 24(4): 429–443

Perera, Iromi (2015) "Forced Evictions in Colombo: High-Rise Living" *Centre for Policy Alternatives* (12 May). Accessed on 22/07/2022. Available at https://www.cpalanka.org/forced-evictions-in-colombo-high-rise-living/

Perera, Iromi (2016) "Living It Down: Life after Relocation in Colombo's High Rises" *Centre for Policy Alternatives* (1 December). Accessed on 04/08/2022. Available at https://www.cpalanka.org/living-it-down-life-after-relocation-in-colombos-high-rises/

Perera, Nihal (2008) "The Planners' City: The Construction of a Town Planning Perception of Colombo" *Environment and Planning A* 40(1): 57–73

Ruwanpura, Kanchana N. (2006) *Matrilineal Communities, Patriarchal Realities: A Feminist Nirvana Uncovered* Ann Arbor: University of Michigan Press and Delhi: Zubaan Books

Ruwanpura, Kanchana N. (2007) "Shifting Theories: Partial Perspectives on the Household" *Cambridge Journal of Economics* 31(4): 525–538

Ruwanpura, Kanchana N. (2008) "Separating Spaces? Ethno-Gendering Social Networks" *Contemporary South Asia* 16(4): 413–426

Ruwanpura, Kanchana N. (2009) "Waves of Reality: Spatial and Temporal Dynamics of Post-Tsunami Development in Sri Lanka – A Gender Analysis" In *After the Waves: The Impact of the Tsunami on Women in Sri Lanka* Neloufer De Mel, Kanchana Ruwanpura and Samarasinghe Gameela (eds) Colombo: Social Scientists' Association, pp 65–83

Samaratunga, Thushara and Daniel O'Hare (2013) "Reflections on Over 100 Years of Urban Housing Policies in Sri Lanka" *Social Sciences* 2: 14

Samaratunga, Thushara and Daniel O'Hare (2014) "'Sahaspura': The First High-Rise Housing Project for Low-Income People in Colombo, Sri Lanka" *Australian Planner* 51(3): 223–231

Seabrook, Jeremy (2007) "Slums" In *Cities: Small Guides to Big Issues* Jeremy Seabrook (ed) London: Pluto Press, pp 66–82

Sevanatha (2003) "Understanding Slums: Case Studies for the Global: The Case of Colombo, Sri Lanka" *University College London*. Accessed on 23/05/2017. Available at UN-Habitat. http://www.ucl.ac.uk/dpu-projects/Global_Report/cities/colombo.htm

Silva, Tudor (1994) "Ethnicity, Multiculturalism and Violence among Urban Poor in Sri Lanka" *Sri Lanka Journal of Social Sciences* 17(1 & 2): pp 79–93

Silva, Tudor and Athukorala, Karunatissa (1991) *The Watta-Dwellers: A Sociological Study of Selected Low-Income Communities in Sri Lanka* Lanham: University Press of America

Stepehenie, Donald, Kofman Eleonore and Kevin Catherine (2009) "Processes of Cosmopolitanism and Parochialism" In *Branding Cities: Cosmopolitanism, Parochialism, and Social Change* Stepehenie, Donald, Kofman Eleonore and Kevin Catherine (eds) New York: Routledge, pp 1–13

UN-Habitat (2016) "Governance" (25 April). Accessed on 05/05/2017. Available at https://unhabitat.org/governance/

Weeraratne, Bilesha (2020) "Urban Housing in Sri Lanka" In *Urbanization and Regional Sustainability in South Asia: Socio-Economic Drivers, Environmental Pressures and Policy Responses* Sumana Bandyopadhyay, Ranjan Pathak and Tomaz Dentinho (eds) Cham: Springer International Publishing, pp 109–33

White, Leroy (2002) "Connection Matters: Exploring the Implications of Social Capital and Social Networks for Social Policy" *Systems Research and Behavioral Science* 19(3): 255–269

PART VIII

Moment of Flux, Looking Ahead

31
COVID-19
Sri Lanka's Moral Test

Santhushya Fernando

Introduction

Contemporary Sri Lankan society was forced to examine its underbelly during the COVID-19 pandemic. By 2021 the SARS-CoV-2 virus (COVID-19) had affected 221 countries and was the leading cause of death in the USA and some Latin American and European nations. The first case of COVID-19 in Sri Lanka was reported by a Chinese national on 27 January 2020 and the first Sri Lankan patient was reported on 10 March 2020 (Jeewandara et al 2021). From 2020 and early May 2023, the total number infected was estimated as 672,227, and a total of 16,849 deaths were attributed to COVID-19 (WHO 2023). During the three-year haul of Sri Lanka, the COVID-19 pandemic affected all crucial sectors of society, such as governance, politics, economy, health, and education exposing disturbing disparities.

Sri Lanka prides itself on having one of the most cost-effective healthcare systems in the region. World Health Organization's publication, Sri Lanka Health System Review (2021), indicates while regional counterparts are lagging in many health indicators, the country has been occupying a high ground on public health, where the state strives to provide universal health coverage to all citizens amidst vast challenges (Rajapaksa et al 2021). The past four decades have seen the rapid growth of the private sector, especially in curative care at clinics and hospitals.

The COVID-19 pandemic in Sri Lanka was marked by three significant waves. The first wave lasted from January to September 2020 peaking with a Sri Lanka Navy Base cluster beginning on the 22 April 2020. The Navy personnel were presumably infected during preventive work related to COVID-19 contacts in a detection centre for drug dependents in Kandakadu (Jeewandara et al 2021; Wijesekara et al 2021). At the same time, another cluster was found in April 2020, in a densely populated underserved settlement, namely, Bandaranayakawatta in Colombo (Jeewandara et al 2021; Wijesekara et al 2021). This wave was largely contained with intense mobility restrictions and succeeded until the end of September 2020 (Jeewandara et al 2021).

The second wave originated in late September 2020 in a garment factory in Minuwangoda, about 40 km from Colombo that went undetected. Personal interviews with apparel industry workers' rights activists and news reports revealed instances where allegations were raised that the workers were forced to continue working despite having fevers. Later into the epidemic, the disease rapidly spread into their overcrowded boarding houses and the community and to a fish market and the main harbour (Arambepola et al 2021). The likely causes were also a lack of agency in the people to seek healthcare, and delays in the detection of symptomatic COVID-19 cases (Arambepola et al 2021; Wijesekara et al 2021). Others, in contrast, have pin-pointed factory corporate entities, including the Sri Lankan factory of Brandix, a global apparel organization, which were implicated in the community spread of the virus (Hewamanne 2021; Puviharan 2021; Ruwanpura 2022). The third wave propagated steadily due to the relaxation of stringency measures in April 2021, just prior to the Sri Lankan New Year celebrations – which usually bring family and friends together – resulting in a 'New Year cluster' (Jayasinghe, Weerawarana and Jayaweera 2021).

Complex Path to Success

By May 2022 there were 664,000 cases of COVID-19 and 16,510 deaths (Ministry of Health 2022). Compared to similar international settings, these health metrics are remarkably successful (Jayasinghe et al 2021). The first wave was controlled by travel restrictions, lockdown of high-transmission areas, aggressive contact tracing, hospitalization of all cases and quarantine of contacts and overseas arrivals (Arambepola et al 2021). Whilst instrumental in controlling the spread of the disease, they were implemented with little sensitivity towards the plight of daily wage earners and common citizens who fell to depths of poverty and hunger (Centre for Policy Alternatives 2021). The government initiated the distribution of Rs 5,000.00 and a 'relief goods bag' to those financially affected by the economic impact of the COVID-19 pandemic (The World Bank 2021).

The significant contact tracing involved tapping patient information via mobile phone data by the intelligence services and sharing them with the Ministry of Health without the consent of the owner. The punitive nature of implementing the quarantine process often shown in the media led to the stigmatization of the patients, families, and contacts. In some instances, only a few minutes were given for the infected to gather their belongings before they were driven to quarantine centres hundreds of kilometres away (CPA 2021). The upshot was that the stigmatization that came with contracting COVID-19 meant that there also developed an aversion to being tested. Moreover, the media reported suicide attempts upon receiving COVID-19 positive status indicating the intensity of stigmatization. They showed scant respect for ethics often revealing the identities of patients and featuring dramatic scenes of them being hauled to quarantine centres (Jayakody et al 2021).

Due to the higher incidence of case detection in some of the areas densely populated by the Muslim community, unethical and unsubstantiated narratives were spun, connecting ethnicity and infection spread (Jayakody et al 2021). The most high profile incident connected to this phenomenon was the arrest of Hejaz Hizbulla, an activist lawyer who was arrested, allegedly under the pretext of COVI-19 contact tracing. This event highlights how the extensive involvement of the military for disease surveillance was used to abuse the system (Amnesty International 2020). The height of ethnoreligious discrimination was the forced cremations enforced by the government on those dying of COVID-19 (CPA 2021). Despite credible scientific data disproving this stance.

For certain professional groups, the government forced cremations amidst intense legal, social, and political outcry supported by a small group of health professionals and scientists. It contravened WHO protocols for the disposal of the dead and violated human rights. Most notorious was the forced cremation of a 20-day-old Muslim infant (British Broadcasting Corporation 2020). Moreover, the inhumane and callous manner in which the forced cremations were implemented, allegedly giving little or no time for emotional preparation, performing safe rituals and grieving compounded the undesirable experience of forced cremations. During the pandemic, visuals of 'callous cremations' where incineration of PPE including boots that were used by staff being thrown onto the burning casket were common.

Militarization of Healthcare Services

The heavy involvement of the military in the control of the epidemic was observed from the beginning. The armed forces were instrumental in maintaining lockdowns, distribution of relief goods, crowd control and contact tracing. Initially, most of the government quarantine centres were manned by the military. They also provided the human resources for building more than 40 quarantine centres almost overnight (Jayawardane 2020). Four salient institutional structures were established to tackle the pandemic. The main implementation arm was the National Operation Centre for Prevention of COVID-19 Outbreak (NOCPCO) in March 2020, chaired by the Army Commander.

There were three other Presidential Task Forces formed:

1. To direct, coordinate and monitor the delivery of continuous services for the sustenance of overall community life formed via the Gazette Extraordinary No. 2168/8 in March 2020
2. To study and provide instructions on measures to be taken by all Armed Forces to prevent Coronavirus infection among members of the Tri-Forces formed via Gazette Extraordinary No. 2173/4 in April 2020
3. For National Deployment and Vaccination Plan for COVID-19 Vaccine formed via Gazette Extraordinary No. 2208/33, in December 2020

These task forces were heavily manned or chaired by officers of the Sri Lanka Army (Centre for Policy Alternatives 2021). For the better part of the pandemic, the Commander of the Sri Lanka Army appeared before the media as the spokesman on health and civil matters related to COVID-19. There was also disruption to the organized health service response when the popular Director General of Health Services (DGHS) was promoted to Secretary to the Ministry of Environment. This left a vacuum as the post was handled by an Acting DGHS. The curative services continued largely under the Ministry of Health's control. The government hospitals contributed to almost 90% of beds, providing comprehensive care at zero user charge. Patients were not refused admission. As a result, the hospitals effectively responded and helped control excess mortality and morbidity.

Migrant Workers' Plight

The justice gap of the quarantine process was evident with regard to repatriating Sri Lankans with the impending border closure as a COVID-19 control measure (Weeraratne 2020). As the epidemic spread, the Sri Lankan immigrant workers belonging to the poorest sections of society were given the least priority in the repatriation process. Discrimination against migrant Middle East during repatriation resulted in an estimated 89 migrant workers dying in the Middle East during the pandemic (Ranasinghe 2022).

These migrant workers from the Middle East, the major pillar on which the country's economy rests, were forced to pay for a government-enforced repatriation package that included relatively high prices for air tickets, hotel quarantine and testing practically preventing them from repatriating (Weeraratne 2020). In contrast, the more affluent returnees were able to afford higher-quality quarantine facilities. Reports of significant confusion regarding the facilities included in the government-mandated 'repatriation packages' and corruption linking Sri Lankan diplomatic mission staff surfaced (Weeraratne 2020).

Injustices within: Antigen Tests, Vaccines and Quarantine

The plans for vaccination were determined centrally by the Ministry of Health. The initial batches of vaccines were used for frontline health staff and vaccination of the public began in early March 2021. Within two weeks, 103,269 people were vaccinated. In the City of Colombo, the initial group to receive the vaccine was over 30 in 19 of the 47 municipal wards. These wards were selected based on having an excessive disease burden and high death rates. On 18 March 2021 vaccination of those over 60 began (Hettiarachchi et al 2021).

The selection of groups to be vaccinated was contrary to the WHO guidelines. The ad hoc way they were selected created panic among the public who assumed vaccine scarcity. The demand for vaccines was high, giving an opportunity for politicians and healthcare workers to use it for their supporters, associates, friends and relatives. Beyond the associates of politicians inoculation centres for influential members of society, celebrity sportsmen, and artists were reported. The Government Medical Officers Association (GMOA) was accused of obtaining vaccines for family members (The Island 2021). Few irregular vaccination centres were set up in in temples, government offices, military institutions and even private homes.

The Criminal Investigation Department (CID) initiated an investigation following media reports that the spouse of the former Minister of Health was conducting a private vaccination clinic for VIPs and political allies in an office on the Ministry of Health premises (Andrews 2021). Many political leaders across the world waited their turn and made public their vaccination to promote the COVID-19 vaccines. In contrast, the dates of vaccination of the Sri Lanka First family and their extended family remain a mystery to the public. To date, no audit reports are available to the public on the vaccine roll-out. However, there were no reports of vaccine discrimination based on ethnicity or religion. Social media and television highlighted controversies regarding vaccine quality (especially regarding the Chinese vaccines) and potential side effects of the Pfizer vaccine. These reports unfortunately encouraged vaccine hesitancy and several deaths among vulnerable populations. With increasing vaccine availability, the inequities in supply waned and a large proportion of the population received the vaccine. In the midst of a global scarcity of vaccines and local delays in vaccine procurement Sri Lanka faced a shortage of the booster dose for a variety of COVID-19 vaccines. The complexities of the vaccine deployment coupled with allegations of corruption and misuse of the system created panic regarding the availability of the booster doses. To date, there is no comprehensive audit report on the usage of vaccines during the pandemic.

There were credible reports that close supporters of the government were given the right to import antigen kits and ivermectin. The latter is a safe drug that had weak evidence of efficacy against COVID-19, but was promoted extensively in the USA, Brazil and India as an alternative to vaccination. These importers, retailers and hoteliers also reaped large profits by establishing paid quarantine facilities (Hettiarachchi 2020; Ranasinghe 2020). Media reports highlighted instances of those returning to Sri Lanka, unknowingly being shunted to these expensive quarantine centres.

Threads of Inequality

The effect of the infection on the loss of income, social isolation, mental health issues and restricted access to health and vaccine were all heightened in the poor and the marginalized (Centre for Policy Alternatives 2021). Both school and university education were compromised with schools being closed for nearly two years even though the economy opened. The premise for closing the schools for over one year was predominantly, the fear that opening schools would trigger large outbreaks in the communities. Alternative education through online modes was inaccessible to those without devices and internet connections (United Nations Children's Fund 2021). However, later in the pandemic, Sri Lankan television channels initiated voluntary telecasts of 'school' educational programmes for homebound children. The confinement of children in their homes resulted in a disruption in their psychological well-being. In some instances, children were victims of domestic abuse and violence and became 'captive' in their own homes with perpetrators.

The two-year presence of children within households without formal schooling posed a burden on the livelihoods of the females. Women's labour force participation rates fell from 34.5% to 32.1% between 2019 and 2020 plummeting domestic economies, food security and independence of women (Department of Census and Statistics, Sri Lanka 2020; Weerasinghe, Silva and Sewwandi 2021). In the context of worsening poverty and lockdowns, violence and abuse of children and women increased (Ministry of Health 2020).

A New Social Morality?

The widening inequalities and responses by the government have given a new opportunity for citizens to re-evaluate their socioeconomic reality. COVID-19, at a superficial glance, appeared to be a 'social equalizer' affecting all strata of power, class, wealth and status locally and globally. Disproportionate numbers of morbidity, mortality and the inequalities and human suffering experienced by the poor and the disempowered such as women, children, LGBTQI community has probably forced society to reinvent and reimagine a social conscience and an ethical standpoint (Rodriguez 2022). The author has personal experience working together with community groups that supported feeding and providing essential medicines and rent for those affected by restricted ability and loss of work such as commercial sex workers, HIV-infected individuals and vulnerable groups in the LGBTQI community.

The use of technology and the liberal use of online platforms to share ideas and knowledge has, in part, softened knowledge flow hierarchies and opened opportunities to engage with global knowledge. The suffering ignited the flame of questioning authority and demanding transparency. Exposes of COVID-19-related corruption were done mostly by courageous whistle-blowers and common citizens. Sri Lankan society that is almost stepping into its post-COVID-19 age is more damning, fearless and tempered in pain. Although not directly related, the exposure to the inequality-filled experience of the pandemic has perhaps set the mood for Sri Lankans to demand a better-governed country, as we have witnessed via the *Aragalaya* (the struggle) that manifested as public protests.

Concluding Reflections: Emergence of a New Order?

Following COVID-19 and the resulting social awakening, Sri Lankan society began to experience a series of protests in early 2022. The government's abrupt decision to stop importation of fertilizer and pesticides led to falling agricultural outputs and financial catastrophe for farmers. Their protests were compounded by striking teachers demanding resolution of salary anomalies that merged with mass protests against economic hardships. The latter were due to inflation, fuel and gas scarcities, and power cuts, attribute to massive corruption and economic mismanagement.

As a result, Sri Lanka experienced an unprecedented period of protests, and political chaos including the resignation of its President. It continued to see levels of protests and massive mobilization of activists with a diversity of political views. The educated youth were at its forefront and many declined to be aligned to the traditional political parties. Social media were the main portal of sharing views calling for the resignation of the President and the government, and a complete overhaul of the political system and its corrupted values. Sri Lanka may truly have come of age due to COVID-19 and may be at the cusp of a new identity as a nation about to redefine a new social morality-tinged political consciousness.

References

Amnesty International (2020) *On Hejaaz Hizbullah: The latest victim of Sri Lanka's draconian Prevention of Terrorism Act*. Accessed on 13/05/2023. Available at https://www.amnesty.org/en/latest/news/2020/07/sri-lanka-on-hejaaz-hizbullah-and-the-prevention-of-terrorism-act/

Andrews, Grusha (2021) "How Pavithra was kicked out" (17 August). **Colombo Telegraph.** Accessed on 01/05/2022. Available at https://www.colombotelegraph.com/index.php/how-pavithra-was-kicked-out/

Arambepola, C., N.D. Wickramasinghe, S. Jayakody, S.A. Hewage, A. Wijewickrema, N. Gunawardena, S. Dhanapala and S. Prathapan (2021) *Sri Lanka's Early Success in the Containment of COVID-19 through Its Rapid Response: Clinical and Epidemiological Evidence from the Initial Case Series*. PLoS One 16(7): e0255394. https://doi.org/10.1371/journal.pone.0255394

British Broadcasting Corporation (2020) *Covid-19: Sri Lanka forcibly cremates Muslim baby sparking anger* (December 2020). Accessed 15/05/2022. Available at https://www.bbc.com/news/world-asia-55359285

Centre for Policy Alternatives (2021) *A Commentary: Legal and Policy Issues Related to the COVID-19 Pandemic in Sri Lanka Centre* Colombo: Policy Alternative (CPA)

Department of Census and Statistics, Sri Lanka (2020) *Labour Force survey – First Quarter 2020* (March 2020). Accessed 10/5/2022. Available at http://www.statistics.gov.lk/Resource/en/LabourForce/Bulletins/LFS_Q1_Bulletin_2020

Hettiarachchi, Kumuduni (2020) "Mixed views on the controversy surrounding rapid antigen test kits" *The Sunday Times* (15 November). Accessed 12/05/2022. Available at https://www.sundaytimes.lk/201115/news/mixed-views-on-controversy-surrounding-rapid-antigen-test-kits-422483.html

Hettiarachchi, Kumuduni, Deane Rugyyah and Rathnayake Maleeza (2021) "Community vaccination drive: Special measures for vaccination rollout for elderly in Colombo city" *The Sunday Times* (21 March).

Hewamanne, Sandhya (2021) "Pandemic, Lockdown and Modern Slavery among Sri Lanka's Global Assembly Line Workers" *Journal of International Women's Studies* 22(1): 54–69

Jayakody, S., S.A. Hewage, N.D. Wickramasinghe, R.A.P. Piyumanthi, A. Wijewickrama, A.N.S. Gunewardena, S. Prathapan and C. Arambepola (2021) "'Why Are You Not Dead Yet?' – Dimensions and the Main Driving Forces of Stigma and Discrimination among COVID-19 Patients in Sri Lanka" *Public Health* 199(2021): 10–16

Jayasinghe, S., S. Weerawarana and D.T. Jayaweera (2021) "Addressing COVID-19 in Resource-Poor Settings: Comparing the Experiences of Vietnam and Sri Lanka" *American Journal of Public Health* 111(3): 387–389

Jayawardane, T.V.P. (2020) "Role of Defence Forces of Sri Lanka During the Covid-19 Outbreak for Nations Branding" *Journal of Management* 15(2): 47–64

Jeewandara, C., D. Guruge, D. Jayathilaka, P.A. Deshan, P.D. Madhusanka, P.D. Pushpakumara, S.T. Ramu, I. Sepali, Aberathna, D.R. Saubhagya, Rasikangani Danasekara, T. Pathmanathan, B. Gunatilaka, S. Malavige, Y. Dias, R. Wijayamuni, G.S. Ogg and G.N. Malavige (2021) "Transmission Dynamics, Clinical Characteristics and Sero-Surveillance in the COVID-19 Outbreak in a Population-Dense Area of Colombo, Sri Lanka April–May 2020" *PLoS One* 16(11):e0257548. https://doi.org/10.1371/journal.pone.0257548

Ministry of Health (2020) *Violence against children and women during COVID-19* (10 October). Weekly Epidemiological Report. Vol. 47 No. 42 10–16 October 2020. Accessed on 13/05/2022. Available at https://www.epid.gov.lk/web/images/pdf/wer/2020/vol_47_no_42-english.pdf

Ministry of Health (2022) *Covid 19 – National Epidemiological Report* Epidemiology Unit (14 May). Accessed on 12/05/2022. Available at https://www.epid.gov.lk/web/index.php?option=com_content&view=article&id=225&lang=en

Puviharan, Ravindran (2021) "The Impact of COVID-19 on Sri Lanka Economy" (21 August). Accessed on 25/05/2023. Available at http://dx.doi.org/10.2139/ssrn.3909017

Rajapaksa, L., P. De Silva, A. Abeykoon, L. Somatunga, S. Sathasivam, S. Perera et al. (2021) *Sri Lanka Health System Review* New Delhi: World Health Organization Regional Office for South-East Asia

Ranasinghe, Imesh (2020) "Opposition Questions the Import of Antigen Tests for Covid without Due Process" *EconomyNext* (November 2020). Accessed on 10/05/2022. Available at https://economynext.com/opposition-questions-the-import-of-antigen-tests-for-covid-without-due-process-75779

Ranasinghe, Imesh (2022) "89 Sri Lankans in the Middle East Have Died of COVID-19: Labour Minister" *Talking Economics* (January 2021). Accessed 12/05/2022. Available at https://economynext.com/89-sri-lankans-in-the-middle-east-have-died-of-covid-19-labour-minister-77688/

Rodriguez, Diego Garcia (2022) *Research on the Impact of COVID-19 on LGBT+ Individuals in Indonesia, Nigeria, and Sri Lanka* Westminster Foundation for Democracy. Accessed on 13/05/2023. Available at https://www.wfd.org/sites/default/files/2022-11/the_impact_on_covid-19_on_lgbt_individuals_in_indonesia_nigeria_and_sri_lanaka_0.pdf

Ruwanpura, Kanchana N. (2022) "Doing the Right Thing? CoVID-19, PPE and the Case of Sri Lankan Apparels" *Global Labour Journal* 13(1): 110–121

Sangakkara, Arundathie (2021) "Vaccine Thieves of Sri Lanka" *Colombo Telegraph* Accessed on 05/05/2022. Available at https://www.colombotelegraph.com/index.php/vaccine-thieves-of-sri-lanka/

The Island (2021) "GMOA declares inoculation of family members received necessary approval". Accessed on 13/05/2023. Available at http://island.lk/gmoa-declares-inoculation-of-family-members-received-necessary-approval/

The World Bank (2021) "Who We Are? In Sri Lanka Cash Transfers Give Essential Support to People Hit Hardest by COVID-19". The World Bank. Accessed on 13/05/2023. Available at https://www.worldbank.org/en/news/feature/2021/07/11/cash-transfers-give-essential-support-to-people-hit-hardest-by-covid19-in-srilanka

United Nations Children's Fund (2021) *Situation Analysis on the Effects of and Responses to COVID-19 on the Education Sector in Asia. Sri Lanka. Case Study* (August 2021). Accessed on 13/05/2022. Available at https://www.unicef.org/srilanka/reports/situation-analysis-effects-and-responses-covid-19-education-sector-sri-lanka

Weeraratne, Bilesha (2020) "COVID-19 and Migrant Workers: The Economics of Repatriation" *Talking Economics* (December 2020). Accessed on 13/05/2022. Available at https://www.ips.lk/talkingeconomics/2020/12/16/covid-19-and-migrant-workers-the-economics-of-repatriation/

Weerasinghe, T.W.M.K.K., K.N.N. Silva and T.A.D. Sewwandi (2021) "Employees Perception Towards Job Security during COVID-19 Pandemic: A Case Study among Private Sector Employees in Sri Lanka" *Applied Economics and Business* 5(2): 47–61

WHO (2023) Sri Lanka Situation. https://covid19.who.int/region/searo/country/lk

Wijesekara, N.W.A.N.Y., N. Herath, K.A.L.C. Kodituwakku, H.D.B. Herath, S. Ginige, T. Ruwanpathirana, M. Kariyawasam, S. Samaraweera, A. Herath, S. Jayawardena and D. Gamge (2021) "Predictive Modelling for COVID-19 Outbreak Control: Lessons from the Navy Cluster in Sri Lanka" *Military Medicine Research* 8(1): 31. https://doi.org/10.1186/s40779-021-00325-4

32
PEOPLE IN THE PALACE[1]

Dinesha Samararatne

Introduction

A mother carrying a young infant, a university student sporting a black bandana, which reads 'GotaGoHome,' an elderly couple, a group of young schoolgirls, and a father pushing a wheelchair with his son caught my eye on July 9, 2022, at the *Aragalaya* (roughly translated as the struggle) in Sri Lanka. At some point, I pass around packets of biscuits that a home-bound elder had sent through us, to distribute at the protest. I hand them out and they are accepted, not with mere gratitude but with a sense of solidarity.

For more than two weeks Sri Lanka has had an acute shortage of fuel, but it is estimated that more than 500,000 people flocked to Colombo to peacefully compel their President and Prime Minister to step down. Ironically this President was elected with 52% votes in 2019. People walked, rode trucks, carpooled, cycled, and boarded tightly packed trains and buses to be there. I came back home that night confronted by what I had experienced that day and with more questions than answers about Sri Lanka's democracy and what that means for constitutional governance. That day, the President promised to resign by July 13 and the Prime Minister also promised to resign. After much uncertainty, the death of a protestor, and much more struggle and pain, the resignation of the President was officially announced today (July 15). The hitherto impenetrable Executive Presidency has now fallen. We can finally hope that this office will be abolished from our Constitution and from our political imagination.

From Protest to Imagined Community

This is Sri Lanka's moment of re-democratization. In 1931, Sri Lanka was the first to receive a universal franchise in Asia, but it is in 2022 that the People are coming to the foreground as a democratic force. Before this, it was the minorities and workers who were on the streets, making normative demands of the state. When the rural youth made such demands collectively, they did so with violence. However, these movements remained on the fringes of a society, which suffered from many ailments, including dynastic politics, corruption, and ethnonationalism. In 2022, island-wide peaceful protests have built up. *Aragalaya* is now a real and imagined community, demanding accountable governance and a better future. Questions about representation within and by the *Aragalaya* come up frequently. The recent occupation of the Presidential Secretariat, the official residences of the President and the Premier, and the Prime Minister's office have raised concern among the public, particularly among the middle class. As of yesterday, the protestors have vacated these buildings, except the Presidential Secretariat.

Through these disruptions and chaos, Sri Lanka is experiencing something new and unexpected. The multitude is speaking, and they can be and are being heard. They (we) are exposing the crisis of representation in Sri Lanka and offer a compelling critique of the status quo, including of constitutional governance as we have experienced it thus far. At some point the normative demands made by the public ought to be translated into a reform agenda. The proposed 21st Amendment of the Opposition captures some of that. However, for a more complete realization of these demands, we require a democratic process which involves some measure of expertise as well. Yet in my view, in Sri Lanka, we are still at the stage where we are seeking to understand the implications of our re-democratization. I outline four such implications below.

The People are critiquing the national security discourse. Sri Lanka has a history of the militarization of law and order as well as an ethnonationalist security discourse. As a result, national security was often interpreted to mean the security of the government. Today, that is being challenged by the People. At public protests, people openly invite the police and the army to join the *Aragalaya*. Arbitrary arrests and police/army brutality against protestors are being challenged by lawyers acting in the public interest and are being condemned by the Bar Association of Sri Lanka (BASL). When the Inspector General of Police declared a police curfew the day before the planned protest on July 9, 2022, the pushback was immediate. The BASL issued a statement declaring it to be illegal (Bar Association Sri Lanka 2022).

The People are reviving the discourse on economic inequality. From July 9 up to July 14 protestors occupied the President and the Prime Minister's official residences. Powerful images and videos are being shared via social media by people who visit these premises. Average citizens use the plush furniture, marvel at the swimming pool, and use the gym. Memes are being made and shared about the inequalities between representatives and the represented.

The inclusion and representation of women is another striking feature of the People's movement. Sri Lanka's political sphere has been male-dominated and patriarchal despite the granting of universal suffrage in 1931. Women's representation in Parliament has never been beyond 12%. In the protests, however, women are at the forefront and are an integral part of it. Women have been extremely vocal and taken the initiative as politicians in the Opposition, as journalists, and as activists.

It is clear then that the demands of *Aragalaya* are for 'a system change.' One that involves, but is not limited to, structural change. The demand is for a new political order based on values of accountability, transparency, and responsiveness. The need for such a call is made obvious by an Executive President, who is now on the run, who held an entire nation to ransom until his personal safety was secured.

Yet, I cannot help but notice the limits or blind spots of *Aragalaya*. To date, it has fallen short of bringing within its discourses the question of the self-determination of Sri Lankan Tamils or the discrimination experienced by Muslims. However, at least on the fringes of the *Aragalaya*, the discourse about discrimination against minorities is alive and abounds. Moreover, even if the *Aragalaya* is a moment of re-democratization, it is a precarious moment. It is a leaderless, spontaneous, and nebulous mass of people. That has been its strength, but it is also its risk. Only time will tell.

Challenging the Constitution

What does this mean for constitutional governance and the rule of law? The Aragalaya is most clearly a critique and rejection of the concentration of executive power and of the Executive

Presidency. The repeated and wilful refusal to repeal the Executive Presidency by numerous governments is now coming back to haunt the political class. Beyond that, it is also a critique of electoral representation. People have had enough of the abuse of power by elected representatives, they have had enough of political parties that fail to channel and modulate people's needs into government policymaking and resource allocation. The *Aragalaya* is a powerful critique of the rule of law that fails to punish corruption, reclaim stolen wealth, and prevent the kind of crisis that Sri Lanka is faced with. It is also a critique of political leaders, public institutions, professionals, and experts that fail to recognize human suffering, empathize, and respond appropriately.

What insights can comparatists gain from this story? It is a given that all these developments affirm the limits and risks of court-centric scholarship. This is not to say by any means that it is not useful, but rather, to point to the need to meaningfully bracket its significance. It reveals the need to modulate electoral representation with other forms of representation, such as a representation of democratic norms through a guarantor branch (fourth branch/integrity branch). As I have noted on this blog previously, one of the progressive developments that have emerged from Sri Lanka's current crisis is the consolidation of the support for a guarantor branch among a range of political actors (Samararatne 2022).

The Sri Lankan story also points to the risks associated with a presidential system and illustrates its potential to undermine democracy from within. In Sri Lanka's past, the Executive President maintained legitimacy despite the internal armed conflict, despite targeted discrimination against Muslims and even despite allegations of corruption and family rule. Only a minority of voices called for the office to be abolished. What has changed now is that the economic crisis is catastrophic, it has spared no one and it is material. This critical and new event has created a new moment in Sri Lanka's political discourse. It made the unimaginable possible: the deconstruction of the narrative of charismatic political leadership for Sinhala-Buddhists, delivering Singapore-type economic development. This is an encouraging but also a cautionary tale, one which tells us that in an era of catastrophic events, including the climate crisis, the unimaginable might be possible in other parts of the world too.

The most challenging insight to emerge from this story is the critique of the current Constitution and even the very idea of constitutional governance. Sri Lanka's current Constitution is problematic: it concentrates power on the executive president, prohibits judicial review of legislation and even provides means to pass laws that are unconstitutional. Many perceive this Constitution to be not only part of the problem but increasingly also a root cause. Therefore, many question its capacity and legitimacy to guide Sri Lanka out of this crisis. Many see this document as indifferent and as promoting systemic abuse of power, human suffering at a large scale, and preserving and advancing economic inequality. The People see constitutional governance as failing to deliver on the promise of the sovereignty of the People and as failing to compel the state to promote human flourishing. These are hard questions and questions that constitutional law scholars and practitioners are perhaps not equipped to respond to. That itself is another crisis, a crisis of 'expertise.'

There is more to be said, about emotions, location, belonging, suffering, hope, exhaustion, mentoring others through a crisis, care, and what all of this means for scholarship. I leave that task for another day. For today, I will rest and raise a glass to my fellow citizens. Come what may, we now have a Sri Lankan story of democratization that we can talk of, for generations to come.

Note

1 This is a reproduction of a guest editorial published by Verfassungsblog on July 15, 2022, available at https://verfassungsblog.de/the-people-in-the-palace/, accessed on 29 June, 2023, Verfassungsblog. This piece was written at a time of acute crisis in Sri Lanka and offers a short commentary on the implications of the peoples protests of 2022 for constitutional governance.

References

Bar Association Sri Lanka (2022) "Statement on the declaration of purported police curfew by the Inspector General of Police" https://www.lankaxpress.com/basl-statement-on-the-igp-declaring-police-curfew/ (8 July) accessed 12 March 2024.

Samararatne, Dinesha (2022) "Constitutional Ping-Pong: Sri Lanka's Crisis and the Rediscovery of Political Agency" VerfBlog. Accessed on 12/03/2024. Available at https://verfassungsblog.de/constitutional-ping-pong/.DOI: 10.17176/20220505-182407-0

33
AFTER *ARAGALAYA*
Moving beyond the Status Quo?

Oliver Walton

The *Aragalaya* protests which engulfed Sri Lanka in 2022 represented the dramatic culmination of a wave of crises that followed the ending of the war in 2009. The mass street protests, which ended with the dramatic storming of the presidential residence, were unprecedented: never before had a relatively spontaneous collection of citizens demanded fundamental reforms of the political system or had a people's movement succeeded in bringing down a President.

While the protests promised long-lasting impacts on Sri Lankan politics, the period since Gotabaya Rajapaksa's resignation in July 2022 has seen the gradual restoration of the status quo. This pattern mirrored the aftermath of the shock 2015 presidential election defeat of Mahinda Rajapaksa, when a new coalition promised political transformation but ultimately failed to move beyond majoritarian and patronage politics. Following Gotabaya Rajapaksa's resignation, a coalition of status-quo actors (the Sri Lanka Podujana Peramuna (SLPP) or Sri Lanka People's Front, United National Party (UNP)) and the military-police establishment) have worked together to shore up their positions. This process of restoration began with a crackdown on dissent, using emergency regulations and the provisions of the Prevention of Terrorism Act (PTA) to intimidate protestors and curb further demonstrations. The Wickremasinghe-led government subsequently postponed local elections scheduled for 2023 and has increasingly sought to exploit ethnic and religious tensions for political gain ahead of presidential elections due to take place in 2024.

Beyond calls for the resignation of President Gotabaya Rajapaksa and his government, the *Aragalaya* protestors made a series of demands including the provision of temporary relief to all citizens, for the recovery of illegally earned resources from the corrupt political class, and political reform including the abolition of the executive presidency and a new constitution.

While the political energy and political imagination generated by the *Aragalaya* stemmed from its spontaneity, the movement's relatively uncoordinated structure and leaderless character generated a divided response to the President's resignation. A more liberal strand of the movement was relatively supportive of the new interim President's efforts to stabilise the economy, whereas the left remained highly critical of International Monetary Fund (IMF) support (Gunawardena 2023a; Kadirgamar and Gunawardena 2023). Some were also critical of the movement's failure to fashion a truly inclusive movement which incorporated the key demands of the minority communities (Satkunanathan 2022).

Despite the inherent difficulties of adapting a spontaneous protest into a sustainable movement, there are some aspects of the current juncture which appear more promising. Party politics since the war has been characterised by fragmentation and flux, with the two dominant parties – the SLFP and the UNP – collapsing and being replaced by two new parties, the SLPP and the Samagi Jana Belawegaya (SJB) or United People's Power. While the direction of the old and new parties is uncertain and the barriers to overcoming the existing political settlement are high, the fluid nature of the current juncture presents greater opportunities for third parties or new coalitions to challenge the status quo or to shift prevailing political narratives. The movement has the potential to breathe new life into an established civil society which has often been criticised for being too cautious and too close to political elites. The *Aragalaya* has also succeeded in mobilising young people, which in turn has provided space for campaigns by feminist groups and sexual and gender minorities to gain momentum. There is hope that these new forms of engagement may support broader shifts in political culture.

Perhaps the most daunting barriers to transformation, however, are the economic and social challenges facing the country. The poverty rate has more than doubled between 2019 and 2022, generating severe long-term impacts on health, including a sharp rise in malnourished children. Inflation has come down slightly since the $2.9 billion IMF package was agreed but remains extremely high and cost of living pressures have risen further as subsidies on electricity have been removed.

The structural backdrop is also dire. Sri Lanka's tax-to-GDP ratio has declined from around 20% in the 1970s to around 7% in 2023. Spending on health and education as a percentage of GDP has fallen sharply since the end of the war. While the government has committed to some structural reforms, it remains unwilling to address high levels of spending on the military or the high level of unproductive and politically motivated public sector jobs. Efforts to reform social welfare benefits through the introduction of the *Aswesuma* programme and proposals to cut pensions have already sparked protests and disquiet around the bearing on working-class communities (Gunawardena 2023b). Rates of migration (including skilled workers such as doctors or IT professionals) have reached record levels.

These economic challenges create fertile ground for a 'second phase' of the people's movement (Uyangoda 2022). However, at the same time, they limit the space for opposition mobilisation by underpinning the claims to power of President Wickremasinghe, which are rooted in his capacity to generate political and economic stability. At least in the short term, there are signs that Wickremasinghe's approach is working, with government approval ratings rising from 10% to 21% between February and June 2023 (Verité Research 2023). Recent opinion polls show a sharp decline in support for the National People's Power (NPP)/Janatha Vimukthi Peramuna (JVP) or People's Liberation Front) (from 43% to 23%) over the same period and a steady rise in support for the SLPP (4–10%) and for the UNP (4–13%), with SJB's support broadly hovering around 28% (IHP 2023).

As is clear from these developments, there is no guarantee that the energy and widespread commitment to political transformation generated during the *Aragalaya* protests will be sufficient to bring about meaningful change in the next elections or beyond. There is hope, however, that a narrow reliance on ethnonationalism and authoritarianism will prove less electorally sustainable in the years ahead. This may present opportunities for political parties and civil society groups to build an alternative vision that is more squarely focused on the growing needs of the poor and a commitment to more radical democratic reform espoused by protesters in 2022.

References

Gunawardena, Charith (2023a) "IMF deal: Facts behind the hype" ***Daily Financial Times*** (23 March). Available at https://www.ft.lk/columns/IMF-deal-Facts-behind-the-hype/4-746642

Gunawardena, Charith (2023b) "DDO: Irresponsible, irrational and inequitable" *Daily Financial Times* (18 July). Available at https://www.ft.lk/columns/DDO-Irresponsible-irrational-and-inequitable/4-750715

IHP (Institute for Health Policy) 2023 "IHP MRP General Election Voting Intentions Update May 2023". Available at https://ihp.lk/news/pres_doc/IHPPressRelease202306301.pdf

Kadirgamar, Ahilan and Devaka Gunawardena (2023) "Sri Lanka's great IMF lie" *Himal Southasian* (20 February). Available at https://www.himalmag.com/sri-lanka-imf-development-food-insecurity-debt-economic-crisis/

Satkunanathan, Ambika (2022) "The Tamil Struggle, the Aragalaya and Sri Lankan Identity" *Groundviews* (15 May). Available at https://groundviews.org/2022/05/15/the-tamil-struggle-the-aragalaya-and-sri-lankan-identity/

Uyangoda, Jayadeva (2022) "Bringing Democracy Back Through People's Power" *Groundviews* (16 June). Available at https://groundviews.org/2022/08/16/bringing-democracy-back-through-peoples-power/

Verité Research (2023) "Mood of the Nation" (June 2023). Available at https://www.veriteresearch.org/insight/mood-of-the-nation-june-2023/

34
CONSOLIDATING A DANGEROUS CONSENSUS

The Failure of Sri Lanka's Public Policy Complex in 2019

Kusum Wijetilleke

"How did the Sri Lankan post-war development story collapse in such spectacular fashion?" has been a recurring theme in the local commentariat since the country's first sovereign debt default in March 2022 (Kidd and Nayana 2022). The dominant consensus across the political spectrum in the country suggests a combination of unforeseeable external events, decades of untreated structural weaknesses and ill-considered shifts in economic policy (Das 2023; Perera 2023; Ranasinghe 2022). The 2019 Easter Attack was one such unforeseeable external event, devastating for economic growth, particularly, the foreign exchange-generating tourism industry (Mallawarachchi 2019). The October 2018–2019 constitutional crisis was both a precursor and contributor to the failures of the national security and intelligence apparatus on Easter Sunday 2019. The political power struggle within the Government was another key contributor to this security lapse (Aneez and Sanjeev 2019; Khalil 2019). Both events preceded the election of Gotabaya Rajapaksa and his administration.

Other external shocks emanating from the Russian invasion of Ukraine, including energy and food price fluctuations and supply shortages, accelerating realignments, as well as the Covid19 pandemic, impacted countries across the world and throughout the developing world especially (Wignaraja 2021; Younus 2021; Newswire 2022). Was Sri Lanka uniquely impacted?

Structural weaknesses in the economy have been observed for decades; yet, similar flaws exist in many developing economies (World Bank 2015; Rafi and Wong 2022; Das 2023). During the peak of inflation in 2022, Sri Lanka was among the countries with the highest rates of year-on-year inflation, resulting directly from the overnight "free float" of the Sri Lankan Rupee against the US Dollar (Colombage 2022; Neufeld 2022). Sri Lanka also had USD 7.6 billion in foreign exchange reserves or equivalents when the Gotabaya Rajapaksa administration took over the Treasury in late 2019 (Fitch Ratings 2021). Balance of Payments and Fiscal deficits and exposures to volatility in energy markets are commonplace among lower-middle income countries including those in the Southeast Asian region (Bhowmick 2022). Yet Sri Lanka suffered a uniquely deep and intense economic crisis by every meaningful measure, while the UNDP (2022) identified at least 53 other countries that would be undergoing debt distress, 2022 Sri Lanka had one of the world's worst-performing currencies and highest rates of inflation (Babali 2022; O'Neill 2023).

A sequence of decisions that began in 2019 set the economy on a path to imminent collapse and the tax reforms specifically are difficult to reconcile with the data. The policy agenda was accepted by a majority of the political and business class and was passed without resistance from the mainstream media, business press, various think tanks and business chambers. In many instances, the tax cuts were even championed by much of this cross section. More than the fact of the sovereign debt default, it is the incoherence of the rationale behind policymaking that is most damaging to the reputation of Sri Lanka's governance systems (CPA 2021).

The foreign exchange shortage and accompanying volatility were directly linked to the deteriorating external credit profile of Sri Lanka's Treasury (Fitch Rating 2021). A drastic reduction in the Government's revenue projections caused by the tax cuts produced a shock to sovereign bondholders proposed large-scale infrastructure developments signalled the intent for fresh borrowings; all of which was sufficient for Ratings Agencies to downgrade Sri Lanka (Sen 2021; BBC 2022; Maki 2022).

President Gotabaya Rajapaksa's historic victory in the 2019 Presidential Election victory led to the implementation of his manifesto: "Vistas of Prosperity and Splendor". The manifesto was regarded by the economic commentary as being a mixture of supply-side business-friendly policies with significant State involvement (Singapulli 2019; Wijewardena 2020). Foundational to the claim of being "business-friendly" was a new tax structure: "the prevailing tax system has contributed to the collapse of the domestic economy by entirely discouraging domestic entrepreneurs. We would instead introduce a tax system that would help promote production in the country" (Ministry of Finance n.d.). This new "tax system" would reduce the tax net drastically, increase thresholds for tax payments and reduce tax rates across the economy estimated to cost the Treasury between Rs. 600 and 800 billion in lost tax revenue annually (Bhowmick 2022; NDTV 2022). Tax cuts are theoretically supposed to increase disposable income and thereby improve economic output through the increase in money circulation. The "Vistas" manifesto was described by the Ceylon Chamber of Commerce (CCC) as "business-friendly, production-oriented and demonstrative of policy continuity" (EconomyNext 2020).

Multilateral organizations, including the World Bank, have suggested that successive Sri Lankan Administrations have failed to make sufficient investments in the health and education sectors (Ada Derana 2019; Schafer 2021). Moreover, the Sri Lankan State also spends less overall than its peers relative to their incomes and this is because the State does not generate adequate revenue through income taxes; revenue is predominantly generated through indirect taxes that are usually regressive (IMF 2022). The 2015 Administration, headed by current President Ranil Wickremesinghe, sought to introduce a programme of fiscal consolidation on the advice of the International Monetary Fund (IMF), with which that Government signed a fresh agreement for the 16th time with an Extended Fund Facility (EFF) in 2016 (IMF 2016a).

The World Bank country report for Fall 2016 notes that Sri Lanka's "budget 2016 presented in November 2015 included a few promising business-friendly measures in relation to the overall policy direction" (The World Bank 2016: 6). However, it did not signal the necessary fiscal consolidation with the fiscal deficit only marginally below the preliminary estimate of 6% of GDP for 2015. "The main drivers of revenue were an increase of the Nation Building Tax rate and a revision of fees while there were proposals that effectively reduce the collection of VAT, personal income tax and corporate income tax. Further, the proposed strengthening of indirect taxes while relaxing income taxes seemed to deviate from the announced government policy" (World Bank 2016: 7). The report concludes that the 2016 budget would increase both the deficit and the debt.

The World Bank (2016) report also provides no justification for the continuation of a regressive ratio of indirect-to-direct taxes:

Although the Prime Minister announced that the current ratio of indirect-to-direct taxes of 81:19 was expected to change to 60:40 in the medium term, the budget plans would have led to a ratio of 85:15 for 2016. The budget proposed to raise the personal income tax (PIT) threshold from LKR 500,000 to LKR 2.4 million while unifying the rate at 15 percent. The new threshold would be about 5 times the per capita income, and as such it could further erode the tax base of PIT. The changes to corporate income tax (CIT) were also expected to reduce revenue.

(2016: 7)

During its period in administration, the 2015 regime did manage to increase overall tax revenue as a percentage of GDP. However the increase in total revenue was largely inadequate and the effects of the tax structure were regressive; high income earners and corporate entities were not contributing proportionately to total tax revenue (IMF 2016b, c). The shortfall was addressed through indirect taxation.

In an IMF review dated June 2018, there was once again a focus on "further revenue-based fiscal consolidation" noting also that tax revenue was unlikely to reach the Indicative Target (IT) of the agreement, a common occurrence with IMF programmes (IMF 2018). The Government responded to public pressure by reducing the import duty on fuel imports but also enacted new legislation to update the tax structure. The "Inland Revenue Act (IRA) which came into force on April 1st, 2018 [...] creates a predictable, stable, and transparent income tax system [...] Notable features include the removal of tax exemptions to broaden the tax base; a modernized legal framework ... introduction of a capital gains tax on immovable property; increased taxes on dividends and interest income; and a transparent set of investment-based tax incentives" (IMF 2018: 21).

During a subsequent review in May 2019, the administration had fallen short of the IT on revenues again but did improve the primary balance in the year prior. The "shortfall reflects weaker growth, the delay in implementing the 2018 budget measures, and an underperformance in trade tax collections due to import duty waivers" (IMF 2019: 69). There was no critique of corporate taxation specifically and the review repeats the exact wording from June 2018: "Notable features include: removal of tax exemptions to broaden the tax base; a modernized legal framework" (IMF 2019: 69).

The IMF also considers the economic consequences of the Easter Attacks of April 2019 as well as the "political crisis" of October 2018, noting the "weaker domestic demand ... an underperformance in trade tax collections ..." (IMF 2019: 69). In November 2019, the IMF once again reiterates their concerns around fiscal policy and the lack of revenue-based consolidation, which they note as likely to elevate public debt (IMF 2019). At this stage, post Gotabaya Rajapaksa's election as President and the implementation of aspects of his manifesto, the economy began to shift away from the policy path of the previous government, which was informed by the IMF programme although was shy on revenue raising through progressive taxation. The IMF review from a few months earlier specified "a primary surplus for 2020 of 0.7% of GDP, to be achieved mostly through new revenue measures [...] Revenue mobilization through greater reliance on broad-based indirect taxation [...]" (IMF 2019: 70). Thus, in the lead up to November 2019 and the "Vistas" manifesto, the major multilateral institutions, including the IMF, had specifically noted the importance of revenue mobilization, a path that was abandoned by the Gotabaya Rajapaksa administration.

After the tax cuts, there were major windfalls to some of Sri Lanka's largest corporate entities, especially among diversified conglomerates and financial institutions (Gunadasa 2021; Ekanayake 2022). The presupposition has always held that as the business and corporate sectors grow and succeed in increasing profitability, ostensibly through improvements in productivity, it creates a net positive for the economy. In 2022, Sri Lanka's corporate sector was burgeoning against the backdrop of food rationing and queues for milk powder, a reflection of Statecraft that prioritizes industry with relevant protective incentives but considers a programme of subsidized meals for low-income citizens, a "price distortion".

In the aftermath of the shock of readjustment, under the conditionality of another IMF programme, the Administration seeks to perform an overhaul of the entire structure of Sri Lanka's economy (Srinivasan 2022). Sri Lanka has proud a tradition of social welfare protections. Economist Ronald J. Herring's (1987) essay titled "Economic Liberalization Policies in Sri Lanka" encapsulates two distinct periods of this economic history. The first begins in 1948, whereby increased State intervention was utilized as the solution to economic challenges and the second, where this intervention was viewed as a contributor to these challenges. Herring describes the period leading up to 1977 as an "expansion of the functional scope of government in the economy [...] resulting in a very heavily taxed, tightly regulated system" (Herring 1987: 125).

The early literature from development research suggests that Sri Lanka was an example of the connection between "premature welfarism" and stunted growth (Herring 1987). In 1948, half the staple food (rice) requirement was imported and yet Ceylon also adopted several social welfare policies that were disproportionate to its per capita income. Some consider that it was a classic case of diverting resources away from investment and into social welfare, while others hailed Sri Lanka as low-growth, high social development model (Dunham and Jayasuriya 2000; Sen 2021). In the 1970s, however, the World Bank along with other developmental organizations began to shift their emphasis away from aggregate growth towards alternative criteria. It was an implicit acceptance that a focus on rapid aggregate growth may not trickle down and hence create marginalization (Gunadasa 2021). Based on these new sets of criteria, while showing stagnant growth on one side, Ceylon – as it was known then – was also showing significant improvements in social well-being and was recognized as a positive development model in the post-1970s literature (Herring 1987).

Sri Lanka had a literacy rate of 85% when China's was 66% and India's was 36%. GNP per capita for 1977 showed Sri Lanka at $200 while India ($150), Pakistan ($190) and Bangladesh ($90) were lower. Sri Lanka also outperformed these nations and many others on Infant Mortality and Life Expectancy rates (Macrotrends n.d.). To underline these achievements, Herring (1987) focuses on the Physical Quality of Life Index (PQLI), which is a composite of literacy, infant mortality and life expectancy. He states that "Sri Lanka's PQLI of 82 [...] came closer to that of Sweden (97) or to the United States (95), than to that of India (42) or Afghanistan (17)" (ibid: 325). Around 25% of the Government of Sri Lanka's (GOSL) expenditures went towards social security and welfare in the mid-1970s, while India and Pakistan were at low single-digit levels (2% and 3%, respectively). This is cited as evidence of "relatively effective mediation between national poverty and individual well-being in Sri Lanka [...] sustained by extensive public intervention in economic processes, with specific politically driven priorities" (ibid: 325).

The conclusion follows that the post-independence welfare state in Sri Lanka, while expensive and administratively complex, was largely successful, especially compared to others in the region. Sri Lanka's structural dependencies on international markets and the commodity-based export mix, however, would consistently leave it vulnerable to external shocks. As the terms of trade deteriorated throughout the 1960s and for much of the 1970s, the policy became more reactionary and ultimately untenable as Junius Richard Jayawardene launched the liberalization program (CBSL 1975; Dunham and Kelegama 1994). Sri Lanka by then had a legacy of successful welfare schemes, but also an extensive regulatory framework. In this post-economic collapse context Sri Lankan policy must resist the over-correction of introducing an agenda of unrestrained liberalization, risking Sri Lanka's unique history of safeguards for the poor.

David Dunham and Saman Kelegama (1994) note that policy in the 1980s "was preoccupied with infrastructural development" and that the resulting "losses to the poor were not offset by higher incomes. On the contrary, the limited available evidence suggests that the benefits of reform were distributed unequally, heavily concentrated amongst the top 10% of income receivers" (Dunham and Kelegama 1994: 15). They conclude that "in Sri Lanka, the factor reallocation costs that accompanied the post-1977 liberalization package resulted in increasing social and regional disparities … dove-tailing liberalization and stabilization measures proved extremely difficult" (ibid: 28).

The Sri Lankan state and the people must reckon with the aforementioned sequence of and rationale for policy decisions taken in 2019. How did the insistence of multilateral agencies for Sri Lanka to embark on "revenue-based fiscal consolidation" translate into a programme of tax cuts? Why did that very same programme enjoy such wide acceptance among the political, business and think tank groups with no material resistance from the very mature complex of media, institutions and professionals whose job it was to critically evaluate such policy on its merits?

There is still little focus on previous failures to generate adequate tax revenues and no emphasis on the need for more radical changes to the tax structure if the Government is serious about meeting the ITs on revenue for the IMF (Rafi and Wong 2022; Moore 2023). The Sri Lankan political class and bureaucracy must acknowledge the hubris of 2019 and consider the failures of bureaucracy and of wider society, including institutional failures, during the period of implementation of policies including the tax cuts and policies that seem to reject clear data points, implemented with an ideological bias without adequate resistance, this then might be considered among the primary drivers of Sri Lanka's uniquely dramatic economic collapse.

References

Ada Derana (2019) "World Bank directs Sri Lanka to Invest in health and education of People to Unlock Its Productive Potential" (30 September). Available at http://bizenglish.adaderana.lk/world-bank-directs-sri-lanka-to-invest-in-health-and-education-of-people-to-unlock-its-productive-potential/

Aneez, Shihar and Miglani Sanjeev (2019) "Suicide bombing intelligence row stokes political tension in Sri Lanka." *Reuters* (24 April). Available at https://www.reuters.com/article/us-sri-lanka-blasts-intelligence-idUSKCN1S00NN

Babali, Babak (2022) "Worst performing currencies of 2022." *The Business Year* (25 October). Available at https://thebusinessyear.com/article/worst-performing-currencies-of-2022/

BBC (2022) "Sri Lanka debt default has begun, says rating agency" (14 April). Available at https://www.bbc.co.uk/news/business-61102495

Bhowmick, Soumya (2022) "Understanding the Economic Issues in Sri Lanka's Current Debacle." Observer Research Foundation Occasional Papers. (21 June). Available at https://www.orfonline.org/research/understanding-the-economic-issues-in-sri-lankas/

Central Bank of Sri Lanka (CBSL) (1975) "A review of the Sri Lankan economy: 1950–1975." *Central Bank of Ceylon 1950–1975*. Available at https://www.cbsl.gov.lk/sites/default/files/cbslweb_documents/publications/otherpub/25th_anniversary_review_of_the_economy_of_sri_lanka.pdf

Centre for Policy Alternatives (2021) *Sri Lanka's Vistas of Prosperity and Splendour: a Critique of Promises Made and Present Trends*. Colombo: CPA. Available at https://www.cpalanka.org/wp-content/uploads/2021/07/Sri-Lankas-Vistas-of-Prosperity-and-Splendour-A-Critique-of-Promises-Made-and-Present-Trends.pdf

Colombage, Sirimevan (2022) "Managed exchange rate floating unlikely to rescue the falling rupee." *DailtyFT* (18 May). Available at https://www.ft.lk/columns/Managed-exchange-rate-floating-unlikely-to-rescue-the-falling-rupee/4-734939

Das, Shaktikanta (2023) "South Asia's current macroeconomic challenges and policy priorities." Bank for International Settlements (BIS) (23 January). Available at https://www.bis.org/review/r230110c.htm

Dunham, David and Sisira Jayasuriya (2000) "Equity, Growth and Insurrection: Liberalization and the Welfare Debate in Contemporary Sri Lanka" *Oxford Development Studies* 28(1): 99–100

Dunham, David and Saman Kelegama (1994) Economic liberalization and structural reforms: The experience of Sri Lanka, 1977–93. *ISS Working Paper Series/General Series*, 163, 1–37. Available at https://pure.eur.nl/ws/portalfiles/portal/70868771/wp163.pdf

Dunham, David and Saman Kelegama (2007) "Stabilization and Adjustment: A Second Look at the Sri Lankan Experience, 1977–93" *The Developing Economies* 35(2): 166–184

EconomyNext (2020) "Ceylon Chamber of Commerce welcomes Sri Lanka's budget, calls for consultations." (18 November). Available at https://economynext.com/ceylon-chamber-of-commerce-welcomes-sri-lankas-budget-calls-for-consultations-76129/

Ekanayake, Samson (2022) "Get the super-rich to payback: Impose a windfall gain tax and a wealth tax." *DailyFT* (6 June). Available at https://www.ft.lk/columns/Get-the-super-rich-to-payback-Impose-a-windfall-gain-tax-and-a-wealth-tax/4-735773

Fitch Ratings (2021) "Fitch Affirms Sri Lanka at 'CCC'" (June 2021). Available at https://www.fitchratings.com/research/sovereigns/fitch-affirms-sri-lanka-at-ccc-14-06-2021

Gunadasa, Saman (2021) "Sri Lanka big business reaps huge profits during pandemic." *The Island* (5 September). Available at https://island.lk/sri-lanka-big-business-reaps-huge-profits-during-pandemic/

Herring, Robert J. (1987) Economic Liberalisation Policies in Sri Lanka: International Pressures, Constraints and Supports. *Economic and Political Weekly* 22: 325–333.

International Monetary Fund (2016a) "IMF Reaches Staff Level Agreement with Sri Lanka on Three-Year $1.5 Billion EFF." Press Release 16/190 (28 April). Available at https://www.imf.org/en/News/Articles/2015/09/14/01/49/pr16190

International Monetary Fund (2016b) "Sri Lanka." IMF Country Report No. 16/150 (08 June). Available at https://www.imf.org/external/pubs/ft/scr/2016/cr16150.pdf

International Monetary Fund (2016c) "Sri Lanka: Staff Report for the 2016 Article IV Consultation and Request for a Three-Year Extended Arrangement under the Extended Fund Facility." (14 June). Available at https://www.elibrary.imf.org/view/journals/002/2016/150/article-A001-en.xml

International Monetary Fund (2018) "IMF Country Report No. 18/175" (20 June). Available at https://www.imf.org/-/media/Files/Publications/CR/2018/cr18175.ashx

International Monetary Fund (2019) "Country Report No. 2019/335" (4 November). Available at https://www.imf.org/en/Publications/CR/Issues/2019/11/04/Sri-Lanka-Sixth-Review-Under-the-Extended-Arrangement-Under-the-Extended-Fund-Facility-and-48787

International Monetary Fund (2022) "Mobilizing Revenue in Sri Lanka" (11 November). Available at https://www.elibrary.imf.org/view/journals/002/2022/341/article-A001-en.xml?rskey=Q6dghY&result=428

Jensen, Lars (2022) "Avoiding 'Too Little Too Late' on International Debt Relief." United Nations Development Programme – Development Futures Series Working Papers. Available at https://www.undp.org/sites/g/files/zskgke326/files/2022-11/UNDP-DFS-Avoiding-Too-Little-Too-Late-on-International-Debt-Relief-V4.pdf

Khalil, Lydia (2019) "Sri Lanka's Perfect Storm of Failure" *The Foreign Policy* (23 April). Available at https://foreignpolicy.com/2019/04/23/sri-lankas-perfect-storm-of-failure-bombings-government-mistakes-terrorism/

Kidd, Stephan and Mansoor Nayana (2022) "How can Sri Lanka escape crisis with IMF's $2.9 billion?" *Daily Financial Times*. (5 September). Available at https://www.ft.lk/columns/How-can-Sri-Lanka-escape-crisis-with-IMF-s-2-9-b/4-739459

Macrotrends (n.d.) "Sri Lanka Literacy Rate 1981–2023." Available at https://www.macrotrends.net/countries/LKA/sri-lanka/literacy-rate

Maki, Sydney (2022) "Sri Lanka Credit Rating Cut by Moody's as Looming Default to Bring Losses." *Bloomberg* (18 April). Available at https://www.bloomberg.com/news/articles/2022-04-18/sri-lanka-slashed-by-moody-s-as-looming-default-to-bring-losses#xj4y7vzkg

Mallawarachchi, Bharatha (2019) "Easter Bombings damaged Sri Lanka's economy beyond tourism." *The Diplomat* (31 July). Available at https://thediplomat.com/2019/07/easter-bombings-damaged-sri-lanka-economy-beyond-tourism/

Ministry of Finance, Economic Stabilization, and National Policies (n.d.) "People-centric economy." Available at https://www.treasury.gov.lk/national-policy#policy_4

Moore, Mick (2023) "Making the IMF Work for Sri Lankans." Sri Lanka Brief (23 April). Available at https://srilankabrief.org/making-the-imf-work-for-sri-lankans-part-2-1-mick-moore/

NDTV (2022) "Bankrupt Sri Lanka Hikes Taxes, Rolling Back Rajapaksa Cuts." (31 May). Available at: https://www.ndtv.com/world-news/sri-lanka-economic-crisis-bankrupt-sri-lanka-hikes-taxes-rolling-back-rajapaksa-cuts-3027206

Neufeld, Dorothy (2022) "Mapped: Which Countries Have the Highest Inflation?" Visual Capitalist (5 December). Available at https://www.visualcapitalist.com/mapped-which-countries-have-the-highest-inflation/

Newswire (2022) "Sri Lanka becomes first Asia-Pacific country in decades to default on foreign debt." *Newswire* (19 May). Available at https://www.newswire.lk/2022/05/19/sri-lanka-becomes-first-asia-pacific-country-in-decades-to-default-on-foreign-debt/

O'Neill, Aaron (2023) Statista.com (11 May). Available at https://www.statista.com/statistics/268225/countries-with-the-highest-inflation-rate/

Perera, Ayeshea (2023) "Sri Lanka: Why is the country in an economic crisis." *BBC* (29 March). Available at https://www.bbc.com/news/world-61028138

Rafi, Talal and Brian Wong (2022) "The Deep Roots of Sri Lanka's Economic Crisis." *The Diplomat* (15 July). Available at https://thediplomat.com/2022/07/the-deep-roots-of-sri-lankas-economic-crisis/

Ranasinghe, Shivanthi (2022) "Economic Downturn and External Role: Defusing foreign interferences and influences." *Daily News* (26 October). Available at https://archives1.dailynews.lk/2022/10/26/features/289855/defusing-foreign-interferences-and-influences

Schafer, Hartwig (2021) "The climb ahead: Making the case for human capital investments in Sri Lanka." World Bank Blogs (3 November). Available at https://blogs.worldbank.org/endpovertyinsouthasia/climb-ahead-making-case-human-capital-investments-sri-lanka

Sen, Amiti (2021) "India announces $400 million line of credit for infrastructure in Sri Lanka." *The Hindu* (6 December). Available at https://www.thehindubusinessline.com/news/want-to-take-ties-with-india-to-very-high-level-sri-lankan-president-gotabaya-rajapaksa/article30113811.ece

Singapulli, Waruna (2019) "Gotabaya manifesto: What's good and what's missing." *DailyFT* (29 October). Available at https://www.ft.lk/Columnists/Gotabaya-manifesto-What-s-good-and-what-s-missing/4-688491

Srinivasan, Meera (2022) "Ranil presents crucial Budget aimed at 'recovery and reform' of Sri Lankan economy" *The Hindu* (14 November). Available at https://www.thehindu.com/news/international/ranil-presents-crucial-budget-aimed-at-recovery-and-reform-of-sri-lankan-economy/article66136718.ece

The World Bank (2015) "South Asia Grows Strongly but Fiscal, Financial Weaknesses Remain." Press release (4 October). Available at https://www.worldbank.org/en/news/press-release/2015/10/04/south-asia-grows-strongly-fiscal-financial-weakness-remain

The World Bank (2016) "Sri Lanka development update." Washington: The World Bank. Available at https://documents1.worldbank.org/curated/en/622841476967944601/pdf/109372-REVISED-PUBLIC-SLDU-fv9.pdf

Wignaraja, Ganeshan (2021) "Four Stylised Facts about Covid-19 Impacts in Sri Lanka." South Asia@LSE. (18 October). Available at https://blogs.lse.ac.uk/southasia/2021/10/18/four-stylised-facts-about-covid-19-impacts-in-sri-lanka/

Wijewardena, W.A. (2020) "Budget 2021: A Reversion to JR Jayewardene Policies of the 1940s?" *Colombo Telegraph* (30 November). Available at https://www.colombotelegraph.com/index.php/budget-2021-a-reversion-to-jr-jayewardene-policies-of-1940s/

Younus, Uzair (2021) "The Impact of COVID-19 on South Asian Economies." United States Institute of Peace (3 August). Available at https://www.usip.org/publications/2021/08/impact-covid-19-south-asian-economies

35
THE 'DREARY PILLAGE OF PRIVACY', TALKING ECONOMICS IN COLOMBO'S TOWER BLOCKS

Michael Collyer

I first met Ishva in 2018. After a standard interview with her, the conversation took an awkward turn, one of the moments when as a researcher I was forced to respond to the many difficult questions posed about the act of research. These questions are partly post-colonial and are therefore most acute in my own case, a white, middle-class British man conducting research with low-income residents in Colombo. But I am keen to get beyond my own experience, to the extent that that's possible, to reflect more broadly on what it is we do when we do research and how that is understood.

The urban transformation of Colombo, and to a lesser extent other cities has been one of the major changes in Sri Lanka's post-2009 landscape. This has involved evicting residents of Colombo's many pockets of low-income, informally built housing, or *wattas*, and selling or developing the vacated areas to create amenities appealing to a predominantly upper-middle-class constituency. Former residents have usually required some coercion or even direct physical force to move. The large, purpose-built blocks of flats in marginal areas of the city where they have been rehoused contrast very markedly to the extremely expensive blocks of luxury apartments that have multiplied over the same period.

After years of research with *watta* residents, Ishva's story was familiar. She had recently been forced to leave the *watta* where she had spent most of her life in the home built by her husband on a plot of land he had found vacant in 1993. This home was scheduled for demolition to accommodate a new road. Ishva had been allocated a small flat in one of Colombo's new blocks of low-income housing. My friend and colleague Mohideen Alikhan, who has a chapter in this volume himself, had got to know her in the *watta*. I had travelled to Sri Lanka for a workshop and I joined Ali to visit her and find out how the move had gone.

Colombo's new housing blocks were built as cheaply as possible. The construction of these blocks is embedded in webs of international finance and many new residents arrive to discover they owe mortgages. Flats have deteriorated rapidly. Lifts have broken, lightbulbs in common areas are stolen and not replaced and drugs have quickly become a problem. The cramped, bare concrete boxes piled 12 stories high have generated very little enthusiasm, particularly amongst their residents. Ishva was no exception and was deeply unhappy there. She had been promised more than other residents, since she had been the guardian of a *kovil* in her *watta*, which was also in the part of the *watta* that was demolished. She had expected a place to re-establish the *kovil*, but this hadn't been provided when we first visited.

The *kovil* statues had come with her. Her tiny front room, barely 12 square metres, was unfurnished but dominated by four large wooden statues from the *watta kovil*. There was just space for the three of us to sit on the floor between the statues. The only light came from a single bare bulb hanging overhead, casting shadows over the peeling colours of the statues' paintwork. Ishva's dedication to the transfer of the *kovil* to this new site was clear.

We discussed the *kovil* relocation extensively. Ishva reported that she had been promised a new site. The government had made a public commitment to religious provision at the new tower block locations. The Buddhist temple was clearly visible, and the public broadcast of monks' chanting was audible around the flats as we spoke. Yet there was no space for a *kovil*, despite the significant proportion of Hindu residents in this block. The failure of religious provision for anyone not following Buddhism has characterised the government's brand of religious nationalism since the formal end of the civil war in 2009. The promises made to Ishva and not kept mirrored a much larger issue.

Ishva sought our support and we discussed who we could speak to about it, though she had already approached everyone we suggested. We were keen to stress that we had no more influence in dealings with these officials than she did, though she plainly didn't believe us. As our discussion of her situation in general and the *kovil*, in particular, drew to a close, I asked if she had any questions for us, a standard end-of-interview check. Ishva addressed me directly 'How long are you here for?' I explained that I had come for a research meeting and I was only in the country for five days. She was obviously shocked and I agreed that it was a short trip. 'What does the airfare cost from the UK?' I knew it wasn't going to sound good, but there was no choice but to admit 'about a lakh', despite knowing that 100,000 Sri Lankan rupees was almost as much as Ishva saw in a year. At the time it was about £700 – five years later it is worth £250, a sign of the deterioration of the Sri Lankan economy since then.

Amongst recent analyses of post-colonial politics of knowledge production, there is usually little discussion of the straightforward economics of doing research. The financial costs of research are a particularly tangible example of the imbalance of power between Ishva and I. 'You know, with that money, I could pretty much sort out this *kovil*' – Ishva was clearly taken aback by the sum of money I had at my disposal for such a short trip. She continued to stare unsmilingly at me, 'How about next time you think of coming for a few days, you send the money to me instead?'.

Explanations of the restrictions placed on expenditure from research grants were irrelevant. This was about the resources that each of us could call on, about how we valued those resources and about how the cost of a trip I had made could have been spent on something of dramatically more significance to her. Ishva was also highlighting a further imbalance. For me, this was a job, I was being paid and I had the resources of a well-funded university behind me. The subject of our discussion for the previous hour or so was her life, not something she could step in and out of as she chose.

My discomfort in this situation must be familiar to anyone doing this kind of research. Vikram Seth, an economist before he made his name as a novelist, captured this perfectly in the poem Research in Jiangsu Province, a copy of which I have on my office wall: 'On the obnoxious, dreary pillage/Of privacy, imperfect knowledge/Will sprout ....' As so often when faced with the direct, uncomfortable reality of what I was doing, I floundered.

The instrumentalised, transactional nature of much research encourages an instrumental response from those invited to be involved. Co-produced research, working directly with community organisations from the planning phase and orientating the research around explicitly activist goals, is an ideal scenario, but it still does not avoid the politics of knowledge production. There are few community organisations with the support of an entire neighbourhood. And the priorities of community organisations rarely translate directly to the frameworks required for competitive funding, so some kind of negotiation and compromise is always necessary. In a recent well-funded project, we worked through community organisations and had the resources to pay everyone who took part in recognition of the time they devoted to the research. Even in this instance, however, the distribution of resources provoked some criticism (Ali and Collyer 2023).

Ishva was the first person interviewed in this project who was interested in analysing the financial side of things, and I could only admit to her that the situation made no sense. I have regularly thought about this conversation since then. Ishva's first question, asking how long I had been there, was based on her observation that I was not from there and I would one day leave – it was only the brevity of my visit on that occasion that shocked her, but five days, months or years, there was no doubt that I was a temporary visitor.

In his provocative and unforgiving book *Abiding by Sri Lanka*, Qadri Ismail (2005) sought to replace the accepted 'insider/outsider' distinction with a notion of 'abiding' by Sri Lanka. He highlighted the Oxford English Dictionary's definition of 'abide', picking out, amongst other things '"wait, stay"; "pause, delay"; "tarry over"; "remain (after others have gone)"' (2005: xxx). I am certain that Ishva had not come across Ismail's book, yet one of the strengths of her critical insight (and, it must be said, of the book) is that Ismail's central point was immediately obvious to her. In both Ishva's and Ismail's terms I was definitely not abiding by Sri Lanka.

I last saw Ishva almost a year later, in 2019. Ali had visited her more regularly in the intervening year so I knew she was still sharing her small flat with the huge wooden statues. She reported that these religious representations brought her a degree of comfort and she was unwilling to let them go until she could share them with a wider Hindu community. After the long pandemic-induced pause, I went back again with a community group in 2023, but there was no answer from her mobile phone or at her door, although we confirmed that more than five years after she moved in there was still no kovil in the area.

The obvious improvements enjoyed by certain sectors of Colombo society since 2009 resulted in little but suffering for Ishva and many *watta* dwellers in her position. The dominant religious nationalist stance of the government has ensured that for too many, the absence of conflict has not brought peace. In recent years, the rapid deterioration in the country's financial situation has impacted the urban poor most severely (Colombo Urban Lab 2023). And the Hindu residents of Ishva's flats complex still have no opportunity for collective worship.

The question remains about the value of research in these contexts, more specifically, the value of my short exchanges with Ishva over the years. The very different positions we occupied in terms of power relations were immediately obvious to Ishva though she understood the research process largely in economic terms. Our exchanges have had no impact at all on her material living conditions, in fact, these conditions have deteriorated since we first spoke. The only impact I can claim is to have borne witness to the consequences of her forced eviction and to have recognised the illegitimacy of the treatment she had received.

It is easy to say that such critique has very little legitimacy, due to my position outside Sri Lanka, and I have been told as much by representatives of the Sri Lankan government. From a research perspective, I am open to similar critiques. Tariq Jazeel (2007) has pointed out that, contrary to broader post-colonial approaches, Sri Lankan studies is centred in Sri Lanka, specifically in the South-East of the country, and to be located elsewhere is to be partially marginalised in that field. There are good reasons for this, and much of my legitimacy as a researcher from Ishva's perspective depended on Ali's more regular visits.

In writing about Sri Lanka, I am implicated in the production of place, as both Ismail and Jazeel have argued. Yet to suggest that that place is rigidly bounded by the national borders of Sri Lanka would overlook the significance of international networks that have such an influence on the lives of people living there. The ongoing financial crisis is only the latest example of these connections. From the markets for the tea that Ishva picked as a young woman to the financing of the house where she now lives, we need to understand how Sri Lanka, just like any other place, is embedded in particular global networks, often in unfavourable ways.

My own research is part of these networks, the economics of which Ishva drew my attention to. And although I would not claim to abide by Sri Lanka in the same way that Ali, or indeed Ishva herself has done. I think there is value in research which bears witness to the operation of these networks that go far beyond Sri Lanka, while attempting to remain centred on the experience of those, like Ishva, who bear the brunt of the power disparities which these networks enact.

References

Ali, Ali and Michael Collyer (2023) "Paying Participants for Research: Ethical and Practical Questions" Paper presented at the RGS-IBG annual conference 2023, London

Colombo Urban Lab (2023) "Borrowing to Eat: The Impact of Sri Lanka's Economic Crisis on Colombo's Working Class Poor". Accessed on 5/3/2024. Available at https://www.csf-asia.org/wp-content/uploads/2024/02/CUL-September-2023-Policy-Brief.pdf

Ismail, Qadri (2005) **Abiding by Sri Lanka: On Peace, Place and Postcoloniality** Minneapolis: University of Minnesota

Jazeel, Tariq (2007) "Awkward Geographies: Spatializing Academic Responsibility, Encountering Sri Lanka" **Singapore Journal of Tropical Geography** 28: 287–299

INDEX

Note: Page references in *italics* denote figures, in **bold** tables and with "n" endnotes.

The 16 Days of Activism Against Gender-Based Violence 367, 369n3
22nd UNFCCC Conference of Parties in Marrakech, Morocco 300

Abdeen, Azhar Jainul 283
Abercrombie, Sir Patrick 398
Abeyasekera, Asha L. 385, 387, 388
Abeyawardana, H.A.P. 336
Abeysekara, Ananda 100
Abiding by Sri Lanka (Ismail) 432
academia 13, 25–26
Accelerated Mahaweli Development Programme (AMDP) Scheme 326–327
acupuncture 350
Adani Group 309
Adayalam Centre for Policy Research (ACPR) 247
Adikaram, A.S. 228n2
agency 19, 45, 46, 131, 134, 176, 183, 214, 224, 225, 248, 254, 256–258, 259, 267, 268, 340
agglomeration imaginaries 19, 221–228
Agrarian Services Act 292
agribusinesses 236, 237
agribusiness networks and local/global value chains 236–238
agricultural household 233–234
agricultural innovations 237–238
agricultural sector: agricultural household/ household economy 233–234, 237
agricultural workers: empowerment 238; equity 238; gaps in literature 238–239; and government decision-making power 235–236; and government policy 235–236; health risks 234–235; inclusions 238; livelihoods 234–236; risk of natural disasters/global climate change 235; risks/uncertainties facing 234–236; in Sri Lanka 231–232; threats 234–236; uncertainty, adapting to 235–236; work and lives of 231–239
agriculture: bias 265; commercially oriented 97; daily wage work in 233; domestic 165; employment 188; organic 235; smallholder 239; subsistence 188, 270; women in 188, 232–233, 238
Alexander, Paul 279
All Ceylon Tamil Congress 85
Alliance London 137
All-Island Commission 121
Alluri, R. 227
Alma-Ata conference 351, 358n2
Amarakeerthi, Liyanage 94
Amarasekara, Gunadasa 94, 96, 99
Amarasuriya, Harini 141
ambivalence: caste 387; and ideology 387
Anderson, Benedict 38–39
animals 21, 114, 236, 278, 283, 290, 315, 317, 339–342
Anonna glabra 294
Anthropocene 325, 329, 330, 335; Sri Lanka in 329–330
antigen tests 412
anti-Moor pogrom (1915) 68
anti-Muslim violence/rhetoric: and Bodu Bala Sena 61–62; post-war period 75; on social media 75
anti-Tamil pogroms 46, 56, 71, 73–74, 95; of 1958 97; of 1983 56

Index

anti-Tamil riots 30, 98–99, 326, 373–375
Anti-Terrorism Bill 23, 90
Anurangi, Jayani 294
apparel industry 185
  employment in 188–189; in post-conflict era 259–261; in post-pandemic era 259–261; women in 185, 188–189
Aragalaya 7–11, 23–25, 26n2, 63n1, 75, 90, 120, 127, 139–140, 207, 413, 416–418, 420–421
Aranthalawa massacre (1987) 74
Ariyarathne, Kaushalya 15–16, 138, 222
Ashraff, M.H.M. 113
Asia Development Bank (ADB) 16, 148, 152, 157, 172, 208, 266, 302, 309
Asia Floor Wage Alliance 254, 260
The Association for Progressive Communications – Women's Rights Programme 367, 369
Attanapola, Chamila 255
authoritarian politics 13; and capitalist development 47–49; and colonial legacies 43–44; and ethnic conflict 44–46; and post-war militarization 44–47; in Sri Lanka 43–49
auto-coup 60, 62
Ayurveda 96–97, 350
Azeez, I.L.M. Abdul 108

Balasundaram, Sasikumar 374
Bandaranaike, S.W.R.D. 70–71, 73, 84, 97, 225; assassination 97
Bandaranaike-Chelvanayagam Pact 71, 97
Banerjee, Shrestha 296
Bar Association of Sri Lanka (BASL) 417
Bartz, Fritz 278
Bass, Daniel 378
Bastian, Sunil 196
Bavinck, Maarten 279, 281
Bawa, Geoffrey 39
'Belt and Road' Initiative 165
bethma 235
Bin Rashid, Hashim 284
Blackburn, Anne 69, 100
Blue Revolution 279
Bodu Bala Sena (BBS) 61, 74
botanists 337–338
Boyle, Alan 319
Bresnick, Sam 402
British colonialism 45, 223; 224, 231, 364, 398; and capitalism 45; categorisation of populations 69; and ethnicity 44; Madrasa education system 109; project 100; Sri Lankan Muslim identity 108
British Emergency (Defence) Acts 44
British India 36–37
Brohier, R.L. 97, 315
The Broken Palmyra (Hoole, Somasundaram and Thiranagama) 99
Brun, Cathrin 282

Buddhism 43, 55, 57–59, 61, 72, 74, 85, 100, 225, 228n5, 315, 326–329, 383, 389, 431
Buddhist 'noise worship' 70
Bui, E.N. 228n6
Bulankulama v Secretary, Ministry of Industrial Development (Eppawela Case) 317
Burke, Tarana 367
Buthpitiya, Vindhya 75
Butler, Judith 368

capital accumulation: and gendered dimensions for women 242–245; post-war 242–244, 262
capitalist development: and authoritarian politics 47–49; and colonial policies 47
care work 176, 188, 190, 233
Carpenter, Jeffrey 399
caste: 11, 18, 22–23, 55–57, 61, 68, 72, 74, 76, 100, 194, 196, 198; in contemporary Sri Lanka 383–391; contextualising 383–385; continuity/change/inequality 385–387; ethnoreligious caste systems 390; future research 390–391; ideology and ambivalence 387–388; key themes in contemporary research 385–390; in Northeast 200–203, **201**; politics 389–390; public caste discourse and practice 390–391; religion 388–389; reproduction 388; structure of Jaffna society 200–201, **201**; Tamil (and Sinhala) 200; Vellalar 202–203
casteism 10
caste politics 23
Cegu Isadeen, Hasanah 132
Central Environmental Authority (CEA) 290, 293–294, 316
Certificates of Absences 89
Ceylonese folk culture 39, 40
Ceylon National Congress 70, 84
The Ceylon Observer 339–340
Ceylon Reform League 70
Ceylon Workers' Alliance (CWA) 375
Ceylon Workers Congress (CWC) 85, 375
Chan, Loritta 329
Chandrabose, A.S. 374
change: caste 385–387; and continuity 385–387; and inequality 385–387
Chank Fishery Act of 1953 284n5
Chattoraj, Diotima 227
Chelvanayagam, S.J.V. 71
China Development Bank (CDB) 155
China Harbour Engineering Company (CHEC) 155
Christianity 56, 389
Chronic Kidney Disease of Unknown Etiology (CKDU) 99
Citizenship Act of 1948 85
civil society activism 136–137
Claessen, George 39

435

class 9–12, 16, 18, 24, 43, 47–48, 55, 57, 68, 72–73, 75–76, 96–98, 107–108, 111–112, 171; in Northeast 200–203, **201**; structure of Jaffna society 200–201, **201**; Tamil (and Sinhala) 200; Vellalar 202–203
class-based conflict 71–73, 76n2
class-based identity 72
Cleghorn, Hugh 37
climate change: 18–21, 232, 234–235, mitigation 310; related agricultural innovations 237–238; securitization of 329–330
Climate Vulnerable Forum 300
coal: 300, 301, 303, affinity towards 304–305; energy transition 304–305
collective memory 281, 372, 376, 377
Colombo, Sri Lanka: low-income neighbourhoods in 397; overcrowded housing 398–399; post-war development and eviction 402–403; tower blocks 430–433
Colombo Development Plan by the Urban Development Authority (UDA) 398
Colombo Flood Protection Scheme (DI 1947) 291
Colombo Master Plan Project of 1978 291
Colombo Metropolitan Regional Structural Plan (CMRSP) 398
Colombo Museum 338–340
Colombo Wetland Strategy 291
Colombo Wetland Strategy Report 294
colonial Ceylon 36–37, 40, 373; *see also* Sri Lanka
colonialism 36–37, 97; British 45, 223; and ethno-religious group 69
colonial legacies 43–44
Colors of the Robe (Abeysekara) 100
Commissions of Inquiry (CoI) 119–120; as truth-seeking mechanisms 122–124
community-based organisations (CBOs) 123, 265, 375
community/ies: devastated 295–296; imagined 38, 416–417; LGBTQI 413; Sinhala (*see* Sinhala communities); *watta* 400–402, 403, 430–431
Companions on a Journey (CoJ) 137
Computer Crimes Act 366
conflict: class-based 71–73; contemporary Sri Lanka 68–76; ethnic 44–46; ethnopolitical 55–59, 61; and nation/nationalism 55–57
conflict-related violence: co-option of gender 133–134; everyday activism 132; gender activism 131–134; role of emotions 132–133
Connell, Raewyn 223
contemporary health system governance 353–355
Contested Coastlines (Gupta) 279
continuity: caste 385–387; and change 385–387; and inequality 385–387
contract farming 236–237
Convention of Hazardous and Noxious Substances 282

Convention on the Elimination of all forms of Discrimination Against Women (CEDAW) Committee 135
Coomaraswamy, Krishanthi 121–122
Coordinating Secretariat for the Plantation Areas (CSPA) 375, 379n3
Cordiner, James 336
corruption: of capitalism 12, 17; and debt crisis 154–155; in post-conflict era 158; systemic 83
Cosgrove, Denis 38
Counter Terror Bill 90
COVID-19 pandemic 22, 25, 48, 55; antigen tests 412; burials, cremation of 114; complex path to success 410–411; emergence of new order 413–414; injustices within 412; migrant workers' plight 411–412; militarization of healthcare services 411; new social morality 413; political dynamics of 62–63; public health system 357; quarantine 412; and Sri Lankan economy 162–163, 168–171; threads of inequality 412–413; vaccines 412
credit-induced self-employment initiatives 266
credit loans 154–155, 157
Criminal Investigation Department (CID) 412
culture 22–23; Ceylonese folk 39–40; Sri Lankan Muslims 108–109; *watta* 23
currents: enlivening 281–282; "fishful" 278–281
Cyclone Tauktae 282

Dalada Maligawa 338
Daniere, Amrita 399
de Alwis, Ajith 294
de Alwis, Malathi 132, 223
debt: and corruption 154–155; and export credit loans 154–155; restructuring 157, 158; trap 269–270
debt crisis 10, 12, 17, 20, 22, 162, 200, 203, 272, 301; foreign (*see* foreign debt crisis)
Debt Sustainability Analysis (DSA) 157
Declaration of Alma-Ata 358n2
degradation 288, 290, 317; of disturbed ecosystems 293–295; environmental 8, 318, 322; wetland 290–291, 296–297
De Mel, Neloufer 222, 327
democracy 11–15, 46, 83, 96, 124, 137–138, 197, 226, 307, 416, 418; illiberal 59–60
Democratic Workers' Congress (DWC) 375
demography 124, 183; and public health system 351
De Neve, Geert 258
Deshiya Chikitsa 350
de Silva, Jani 222
de Silva, K.M. 96
de Silva, Minnette 39–40
de Silva, M.W.A. 387
de-territorialization 40–41

devaluation 253, 255–256
devastated communities: disasters 295–296; dispossession 295–296; resistance 295–296
development: and entrepreneurship 265; and environment 320–321; and investment 320–321; post-conflict 268–269; studies on the plantations 374–376
De Votta, Neil 60
Dharmadasa, K.N.O. 98
Dharmapala, Anagarika 95–96, 100
diaspora groups 244
digital media 22–23, 367–368
Disaster Management Act No. 13 328
disasters: devastated communities 295–296; wetlands 296–297
disease burden, and public health system 351–352, **352**
dispossession: devastated communities 295–296; and disasters 295–296; and resistance 295–296
disturbed ecosystems: degradation 293–295; ecological transformation 293–295
diverse ecologies and perceptions 289–291
Domestic Debt Optimization (DDO)/Domestic Debt Restructuring (DDR) 11
donor darling 147
Donoughmore constitution 57
'double burden of disease' 350, 358n1
Douglas, Aimée 387, 391
Dunham, David 427

'Eastern Awakening' 242
Eastern Muslims 15, 106–115; overview 106–107; political dynamics 110–113; post-war complexities 114; socio-cultural dimension 110–112; Sri Lankan Muslim identity 107–110
Easter Sunday bomb blasts of 2019 7, 62, 89–90, 114, 125, 133
East India Company 36–37, 340
ecological states 325–331; militarization of nature 327–329; nature and nation 325–326; overview 325; securitization of climate change 329–330; Sri Lanka in Anthropocene 329–330; state Sinhalization/Sinhalization of nature 326–327
ecological transformation 290, 293–296
economic crisis 9–11, 17, 158, 173; authoritarian politics 43; South Korea's 156; systemic changes 83; work conditions 19
"Economic Liberalization Policies in Sri Lanka" (Herring) 426
economic policies 16; JVP insurrection 72–73; Rajapaksas' 120; Sri Lanka 48–49
economy/economic growth 16–18; from 1983–2009 196; from 2009–2013 196; public investment inequality 197
ecosystems, disturbed 293–295

Edirisinha, Rohan 59
Edney, Matthew 37
education *see* higher education
electoral politics 135–136, 223, 225, 363, 389
Elson, Diane 255
emotions: conflict-related violence 132–133; and gender activism 132–133
employability: defined 209; and graduates 208–209
employment: agriculture 188; in apparel industry 188–189; vulnerable 177, 191n2; women, in Sri Lanka 186–190, **187**
empowerment 20, 133, 136, 140, 177, 236, 238, 245, 311; of women 264, 266–267
energy efficiency 301–303
energy sources 302–303, 305, 310–311
energy transition 300–311; affinity towards coal 304–305; contemporary challenges in 304; energy efficiency 301–302; future direction of 310; geopolitics 308–309; innovation and investment 308; institutional obstacles 303–304; main energy sources 302–303; overview 300–301; present status 301; social challenges of renewable energy 305–307
enlivening currents 281–282
Enloe, Cynthia 327
entrepreneurs 111, 115n2, 167, 176, 189–190, 231, 237–239, 247, 264
entrepreneurship 177, 189, 245, 264, 268; and development 265
environment 20–21; and development 320–321; and investment 320–321
environmental history 335–343; human and the animal 340–342; long narrations of Paradisiacal Island 336–337; overview 335; planters/botanists and assault on land 337–338; science, context and failure 338–340
Environmental Impact Assessment (EIA) 292
environmental movements: and nationalism 321–322; and political parties 321–322
environmental politics 20–21, 321
environmental protection 314–323; constitutionalizing 319–320; development/investment/environment 320–321; environmental movements 321–322; future research 319–322; history of 314–316; legal framework 316–319; nationalism 321–322; overview 314; political parties 321–322
Environmental Protection Areas (EPAs) 293
equity 44, 158, 162, 171, 201, 214, 238, 300, 307, 311
estuarine wetlands 290–293
ethical sourcing destination 254, 258
ethnic conflict 8, 14, 44–47, 71, 84, 107, 148, 164, 167, 194, 198, 208, 375
ethnic identity 56, 106, 111; formation 98; Muslim 13, 113; Tamil 374

ethnicity 11; ideologies in Sri Lanka 56; labour force participation (LFP) 184; preoccupation in Sri Lanka 69
ethnic politics 56, 260, 318–319
ethnic violence and riots 8–9, 12
ethnocracy 24, 60
ethno-linguistic conflict: anti-Tamil attacks and pogroms 73–74; in post-independence period 70–71; 'Sinhala Only' language policy 70–71
ethnonationalism 9, 55–56, 58, 61, 366, 373, 378, 387, 416–417, 421
ethnopolitical conflict 55–57, 61; historiography of 57–59
ethnoreligious caste systems 390
ethno-religious conflict: ethno-religious identity 68–69; re-emergence of 74–75; in Sri Lanka 68–70
ethno-religious identity 68–69
Evans, Jane 211–212
ex-combatants 247–249
EXIM Bank of China 149, 154
Expanded Immunization Programme of the World Health Organization (WHO) 350
Extended Fund Facility (EFF) programme 165, 172–173

Families of the Disappeared movement 131
Federal Party of Sri Lanka 85
female labour force participation (FLFP) 176–177; gender gap in 190; job opportunities 184; low, in Sri Lanka 183; rates 18; in secondary education 183; with tertiary education 184
feminist futures and political reckonings 378–379
feminist pathways in plantation studies 372–379
Fernando, H.F. 283, 339
financing: capital 279; external 168; foreign 148, 150, 158, 168; investment 236; money 167; and public health system 352–353
First Republican Constitution 85–86
Fisheries Amendments Law 20 of 1973 284n5
Fisheries Ordinance Chapter 212 of 1940 284n5
"fishful" currents: life-worlds 278–281; littoral identities 278–281; livelihoods 278–281
Fonseka, Bhavani 121, 123, 125, 249
foreign debt crisis: Chinese debt trap 153–154; corruption 154–155; credit loans 154–155; debt 154–155; failed reforms 155–156; history 147–148; IMF bailouts 155–156; ISBs 148–149, 152–153; overview 147; in post-war era 148–150, **150**; state sovereignty 156–157; structural weaknesses 150–151

Galgodaaththe Gnanasara Thero 74
Gallagher, Mary 141
'Galle Face Aragalaye Kantha Handa' (Women's Voice of the Galle Face) 139–140

Gal Oya Irrigation Scheme 326
Gammanpila, Udaya 322
Gamperaliya (Uprooted) (Wickramasinghe) 97
'Garments without Guilt' campaign 254
Gavi 350
Geddes, Sir Patrick 226, 398
Geertz, Clifford 10
gender 377–378; inequality in LFP 185; Internet on intersections of sexuality and 361–369; social networks 399–402; in Sri Lanka 15–16, 43–49; *see also* women
gender activism: conflict-related violence 131–134; co-option of gender 133–134; and emotions 132–133; LGBTIQ+ activism 137–139; Muslim women's activism 134–135; overview 130–131
gendered dimensions for women 242–244
gendered nature of work 255–256
gendered political economy of work 242–250
gender equality: overview 176–177; in Sri Lanka's economy 176–190
Geography (Ptolemy) 38–39, 336
geopolitics 8, 12, 48, 308–309
Ghosh, Jayathi 157
Giesbert, L. 226
global capitalism 12, 43
global climate change 234, 235
Global Gender Gap Index (GGGI) 177
global labour governance mechanisms 258
global value chains 236–238
global workers 226–227
Godamunne, Nayana 199
Godamunne, Vichitra 283
Goger, Annelies 243, 255, 258
Goldsmith, Edward 315
Gomez, Shyamala 222
Gotagogama (Gota Go Village) 139
governance: health system 353–355; wetlands 291–293
government decision-making power 235–236
government healthcare 353–354
Government Medical Officers Association (GMOA) 412
government policy: agricultural workers 235–236
Grameen Bank (Bangladesh) 265
Grass for My Feet (Vijayatunge) 277
Gregory, William 339
Grewal, Kiran K. 132, 133
Grossholtz, Jean 224
Gunananda, Migetuwatte 69
Gunaratne, Kamal 329
Gunasekara, Vagisha 243–245
Gunasekera, Valentine 39
Gunawardana, R.A.L.H. 98
Gunawardana, Samanthi J. 136
Gunawardena, Philip 97
Guneratne, Arjun 68–69

Guneratne, L.H.P. 266–267
Gupta, Charu 279
Gupta, Joyeeta 281
Guruparan, Kumaravadivel 124–125

Hakgala Strict Natural Reserve (SNR) 318
Haniffa, Farzana F. 113, 225, 228n2
Hashtag Generation 363, 367
Hayleys Agro Farms (Pvt) Limited 237
healthcare 22, 137, 269, 355–356, 358, 368, 410; free 350; government 353–354; institutions 357; private 349, 354; services, militarization of 411; universal 228
health infrastructure and workforce 354–355
health risks 234–235, 238
health system governance: government healthcare 353–354; health infrastructure and workforce 354–355; private healthcare 354
Hemileia vastatrix 337
Hennayake, Nalini 226
Herath, H.M.W.A. 266–267
Herring, Ronald J. 426
Hettiarachchi, Missaka 293, 294–295
Hewamanne, Sandya 256
higher education 18, 207–214; free education 207–208; graduates and employability 208–209; overview 207; private higher education institutions 208; privatization of 211–212; sexual harassment in 213; state universities 209–211; *swabhasha* 207–208; violence and well-being in universities 212–213
Hildyard, Nicholas 315
Hilhorst, Dorothea 280
history, of Sri Lankan plantations 372–373
History and the Roots of Conflict (Spencer) 98
Holiday, Clifford 398
Hollenbach, Pia 227
Hoole, Ranjan 109
household economy 233–234, 399
Hughes Simon, Gwladys 341
human and the animal 340–342
Human Rights Commission of Sri Lanka (HRCSL) 137
Human Rights Watch 123
Hunting and Shooting in Ceylon (Storey) 290
Husanovic, Jasmina 141
Hyogo Framework for Action 328

Iberian imperialism 38
Ibrahim, Zainab 367
ideal village 19, 224–226
identity: ethnic (*see* ethnic identity); political 109–110; religious 108; Sri Lankan Muslims 107–110
identity politics 14, 83, 91, 98; ethno-religious conflict 70; forms of 13; homogenized 10

ideology 14, 44, 57, 68, 75, 76; and ambivalence 387–388; caste 387–388; Islamic 114; *jathika chinatnaya* 99; Marxist 71–72; of militarization 328, 330; modernisation 266; political 72; separatist 74; Sinhala-Buddhist 322, 327
"If I was President" (Kabir) 3–6, 7
"illegal deforestation" 331n1, 331n3
illiberal democracy 59–60
imaginaries: agglomeration 19, 221–228
imagined communities 38, 416–417
Imtiyaz, A.R.M. 109, 112
inclusions 133, 238, 417
"Indian Ocean Studies" 283
Indian Ocean tsunami (2004) 62, 227, 267–268, 281, 327–329
Indian Peacekeeping Force (IPKF) 72, 74
indignation 9
Indo-Lanka Accord 57, 113
inequality: caste 385–387; and change 385–387; and continuity 385–387; COVID-19 pandemic 412–413; Internet as a site of 361–362
informal employment 176–177, 187, 233
informality 19; as academic categorization 221; delegitimization of 226; and EPZs 260; formalize 222; in Global North 222, 228n1; and slum residents 398–399
infrastructure 154, 197–199; affective 141; agricultural 232; coastal 283; communication 36; economic 18; healthcare 22, 350, 354–355; physical 162; and and post-war development 197–199; social 249; tourist 278
Inimage Ihalata (Up the Ladder) (Amarasekara) 94
In My Mother's House (Thiranagama) 57
innovation: climate-change related agricultural 237–238; energy transition 308; and investment 308; social science 234
institutional obstacles: energy transition 303–304
institutions: democratic 13, 44, 60, 137; media 367; microfinance 268–269, 271; multilateral 12, 16, 425; multinational 148; private higher education institutions 208; public 73, 418; religious 58; social 235; in Sri Lanka 14–16; state 91, 130, 134, 136–137, 208, 212, 258
inter-ethnic solidarity 11
inter-generational equity 315, 317
International Conservation Union (IUCN) 290
International Crisis Group 122
International Independent Group of Eminent Persons (IIGEP) 121
International Institute of Water Management (IWMI) 290
International Labour Organisation (ILO): Core Conventions 258

International Monetary Fund (IMF) 17, 420–421, 424–427; bailouts and Sri Lankan debt crisis 155–156, 170–171; Extended Fund Facility programme 165; intervention 157
international NGOs (INGOs) 126, 375
International Pollutants Elimination Network (IPEN) 282
International Sovereign Bonds (ISBs) 148–149; and external vulnerabilities 152–153; use of term in Sri Lanka 158n1
International Women's Day (IWD) 7–8
Internet: on intersections of gender/sexuality 361–369; as site for violence 363–366; as site of inequality 361–362; as site of resistance 366–368
intersectional activism 138–139
investment: and development 320–321; energy transition 308; and environment 320–321
Ircon International Limited (IRCON) 155
Islam 56, 69, 106, 109, 111–112, 389; ideological pre-occupations surrounding 75; religious distinctiveness of 108; religious identity of 106
Islamic revival 69, 75, 111
Islamic State 62
Islamophobia 62, 101, 135
Islanded (Sivasundaram) 100, 282
"islanded" imaginaries 282–283
islandness, Sri Lanka 34–41
Ismail, Qadri 34, 41, 69, 107, 432

Jaffe, R. 228n1
Janasaviya programme 266, 269
Janatha Vimukthi Peramuna (JVP) 45, 48, 56, 71–72, 390; independent history 119
Japan International Cooperation Agency (JICA) 305
Jathika Chinthanaya (JC) 45, 99
Jathika Hela Urumaya (JHU) 61, 322
Jayanntha, Dilesh 389
Jayawardena, Dhammika 211
Jayawardena, Kumari 47, 76n2
Jayawardene, J.R. 98, 254, 294, 326, 388, 427
Jazeel, Tariq 221, 282, 325, 329, 432
Jegathesan, Mythri 130, 378, 388
Jeyasekara, Prashantha 245
Jiggins, Janice 385, 389
Joint Apparel Association Forum 254
justice: labour 258, 376, 378; political 8, 11, 243, 378

Kabir, Sarah 3–6, 7
kadaim-kavi 336
Kadirgamar, Ahilan 196, 268, 284
Kadirgamar, Lakshman 121
Kaliyugaya (Age of Kali) (Wickramasinghe) 97
Karunaanithy 228n3

Karuwala Gedera (Wickramasinge) 284n3
Kelegama, Saman 427
Kemper, Steven 100
Keyt, George 39, 40
King Devanampiyatissa 315
Klem, Bart 58, 108
Knighton, William 95
Kodikara, Chulani 246–247, 267
Koens, Celeste 136
Koralagama, Dilanthi 281
Koster, M. 228n1
Kotelawala, Sir John 225
Kottegoda, Sepali 399–400
Kuganathan, P. 203
Kumaraswamy, Krishanthi 123
Kumaratunga, Chandrika 121, 123, 327
kurulu hadawatha (The Bird's Heart) (Amarakeerthi) 94

labour activism 256–257
labour force participation (LFP): ethnicity 184; gender inequality in 185; in manufacturing and service sectors 183; of married women 184; in older age group 185–186; rate for young women 185; women 183–186
labour justice 258, 376, 378
lagoons 290
language: 'Sinhala Only' language policy 70–71, 84; Sri Lankan Muslims 108–109
Lassée, Isabelle 126
Lawrence, Patricia 281
legal framework 41, 58, 88, 91, 121, 135, 260, 425; and environmental protection 316–319
Lehman, Jessica 281
Lesbian, Gay, Bisexual, Transgender, Questioning + (LGBTIQ+) 130–131, 369n1; activism 137–139; community 413; intersectional activism 138–139; rights 368; transgender politics 137–138
Lessons Learnt and Reconciliation Commission (LLRC) 120, 122–124, 140, 141n3
Liberation Tigers of Tamil Eelam (LTTE) 33, 35, 41, 45, 86, 99, 101, 194, 247–249, 250n1, 319, 327, 329, 384, 386, 402; defeat of 60–61, 119; emergence of 74; Indo-Lanka Accord 113; woman warrior 47
The Life and Times of an Asian Woman Architect (de Silva) 40
life-worlds 277, 278–281
Little, Angela W. 211–212
littoral: ebbs and flows 280–281; identities 278–281; over time 278–279; wartime 279–280
livelihoods 278–281; agricultural workers 234–236; self-employment and 244–246
Local Authorities Election (Amendment) Act 135–136

local value chains 236–238
Locations of Buddhism (Blackburn) 100
Lokuge, Gayathri 280
low-income settlements 396–404; gender, social networks 399–402; low-income neighbourhoods 397; overcrowded housing 398–399; post-war development and eviction 402–403
Lutz, Catherine 327
Lynch, Caitrin 243, 256

Mader, Philip 267
Madrasa education system 109
Mahajana Eksath Peramuna (MEP) 96
Mahaweli Accelerated Agricultural Development Scheme 235
Mahaweli Authority of Sri Lanka (MASL) 235
Mahinda, Arahant 315
Mahinda Chinthana: Ediri Dakma (Mahinda Vision: A Vision for the Future) 268
Malaiyaka Tamil heritage and collective memory 377
Mama, Amina 223
mangroves 288, 290
Married Women's Property Ordinance 188
Marsoof, Saleem 134
Marxist ideology 72
masculinity 19, 47, 132, 221; colonial 337; and men 222–224
Matrimonial Rights and Inheritance Ordinance 188
Maunaguru, Sidharthan 58
McGilvray, Dennis B. 110–111, 386, 388, 389
Memons 115n2
memory, collective 372, 376, 377
men, and masculinity 222–224
Mendis, G.C. 96
mental health services 356
Metallic Modern (Wickramasinghe) 100
#MeToo Movement 367
micro-businesses 189–190
microenterprises and microfinance 265–266
microfinance 20, 130, 200, 203, 265–266; as a crisis easing policy 267; debt/indebtedness of rural sector workers 264–272
microfinance institutions (MFIs) 268–270
migrant workers 19, 109, 170, 187; COVID-19 pandemic 411–412; plight 411–412
migration 199, 202, 225, 278, 280–281, 358, 372–374, 377, 397, 421
Milano, Alyssa 367
militarization 20–21, 43, 330; and apparel sector 48; of education 210; of healthcare services 411; of nature 325, 327–329; post-war 44–47, 62
Mishra, Pankaj 10
modern metropolis 19, 221, 226–227
Modi, Narendra 309

Monteith, Will 226
Moon, Alexander 338
Moore, Mick 72, 97, 326
Mudalige, R. 265
Münster, Sebastian 336
Muslim Marriage and Divorce Act 134
Muslim Moors 69–70, 107, 115n1, 184
Muslims: conflicts between Tamils and 110; Eastern Province 15; ethnic chauvinism 55; right-wing 9; women's activism 134–135; *see also* anti-Muslim violence/rhetoric; Sri Lankan Muslims
Muthulingam, P. 377

Nagaraj, Vijay K. 245
Najab, Nadiya 245
National Committee on Mental Health 356
National Disaster Management Act 327, 330
National Environment Act (NEA) 289, 292, 316
National Mental Health Act 356
National Operation Centre for Prevention of COVID-19 Outbreak (NOCPCO) 411
National People's Power (NPP) 136, 139, 421
National Thermal Power Corporation (NTPC), India 308–309
National Thowheed Jamath (NTJ) 75
National Union of Workers (NUW) 375
nation/nationalism: and conflict 55–57; and constitutional order 55–57; and environmental movements 321–322; and nature 325–326; and political parties 321–322; Sinhala Buddhist (*see* Sinhala Buddhist nationalism); spatial dimensions of 13; in Sri Lanka 13–14, 55–57; Tamil 13
natural disasters 234, 235, 267, 327–328
nature: militarization of 327–329; and nation 325–326; Sinhalization of 326–327
Navalar, Arumuga 69, 96
Navaratnam, V. 85
Needham, Joseph 315
Nesiah, Vasuki 125–126, 133, 140
Nestle Lanka 237
new social morality 413–414
Niriella, Nireliege Chandrasiri 226
non-communicable diseases (NCDs) 352–353, 355–356
non-governmental organizations (NGOs) 89, 122–123, 133, 135–139, 200, 238, 265, 268, 321–322, 367–368, 375–376
Noolaham Foundation 379n4
North, Marianne 338–339
North-East Provincial Council 113
Northeast Sri Lanka: class and caste 200–203, **201**; women in 199–200
'Northern Awakening' 242
Nuhman, M.A. 111

"ocean-blindness" 278
Office for Reparations 15, 88
Office of Missing Persons 15, 124
Office of National Unity and Reconciliation (ONUR) 125
Office of the High Commissioner for Human Rights (OHCHR) 120, 126
Office on Missing Persons (OMP) Act 88
Official Language Act 71
On the Beach (Stirrat) 279
On the Move 281
overcrowded housing 398–399
over-indebtedness 269–270

Paddy Lands Act 97
Paradisiacal Island 336–337
Paramsothy, Thanges 203
Pararajasingham, Joseph 121
Paris Club 172, 174n12
Parker, H. 315
Parliamentary Committee on Natural Disasters 328
Patrons, Devotees and Goddesses (Tanaka) 279
Pearson, Ruth 255
Peires, Ivan 39
Peiris, Pradeep 222
Perera, Myrtle 265
Perera, Nihal 35, 36, 39, 224, 227
Perera, Sachini 363, 367
personality-led politics 44–45
pervasive militarization 329
Peters, Kimberley 278
Philips, Mira 243–245
Physical Quality of Life Index (PQLI) 426
Pieris, Anoma 35
Pinto-Jayawardena, Kishali 121, 122–123
Plantation Social Sector Forum (PSSF) 375
plantation studies 22–23, 372–379
planters 337–338
political Buddhism 55, 61–62
political ecology 20, 281; of urban/regional wetlands 288–297
political economy 8, 10, 13, 16–18, 19, 23–24, 48, 96–97, 200; post-war 242, 249
political justice 8, 11, 243, 378
political parties 61, 87, 89, 109, 135–137, 296, 389, 414; and environmental movements 321–322; and nationalism 321–322; Tamil 202
political possibilities in Sri Lankan plantation studies 372–379
political violence 56; religious sphere 58; state rehabilitation scheme 248; and women 47
politics: authoritarian (*see* authoritarian politics); caste 22–23, 389–390; environmental 20–21, 292–293, 297, 321; personality-led 44–45; in Sri Lanka 14–16
Ponnambalam, G.G. 84–85

post-conflict development 268–269
post-tsunami recovery 267–268
post-war: capital accumulation 242–244; development 197–199; militarization 44–47; mobility 280–281; political economy 242, 249–250
post-war transition: memorial practices 60; in Sri Lanka 60–61
Pouw, Nicky 281
Prabhakaran, Velupillai 202
PREDO (Plantation Rural Education & Development Organisation) 375
Premadasa, I. G. 212
Premadasa, Ranasinghe 121, 223, 389
Pre-Orientation Programme (POP) 210
'Presidential Commission of Inquiry into Involuntary Removal or Disappearance of Persons' 121
Prevention of Social Disabilities Act 384
Prevention of Terrorism (Amendment) 90
Prevention of Terrorism Act (PTA) 23, 45, 89–91, 327
private healthcare 349, 354
privatization of higher education 18, 211–212, 214
Progressive Queer Collective (PQC) 139
protest 416–417
Ptolemy, Claudius 38–39, 336
public caste discourse and practice 390–391
public health system 22, 349–358; contemporary challenges for 355–357; contemporary health system governance 353–355; contextualizing 351–353; COVID-19 pandemic 357; demography 351; disease burden 351–352, **352**; financing 352–353; historical background of 350–351; overview 349–350; stigma and strengthening mental health services 356
public policy complex 423–427
Public Security Ordinance (PSO) 89
Public Utilities Commission of Sri Lanka (PUCSL) 303

Quality Assurance Council (QAC) 210
quarantine 363, 410–412
Quo Vadis: sojourning farther out to sea 283–284

race 45, 47, 55, 74, 389; and preoccupation 69
Radicati, Alessandra 226, 227, 283
ragging 18, 212–214
Raheem, Mirak 110–111
Rajapaksa, Gotabaya 24, 49, 90, 119–120, 223, 300, 309, 322, 329, 362, 420, 423–424; income tax rates 151; 'one country – one law' campaign 135
Rajapaksa, Mahinda 33–34, 36, 41, 45, 100–101, 119–120, 322, 329; appointment of CoIs 121; defeated LTTE 194; International Independent Group of Eminent Persons (IIGEP) 121

Rajapaksa family regime: centralization of executive power 60; infrastructure 197; populist authoritarianism 46; populist politics 46; soft authoritarianism 195
Rajasingham-Senanayake, Darini 99
Ramanathan, Ponnambalam 69, 108
Rambukwella, Keheliya 367
Ramsar Convention in 1990 (Convention on Wetlands of International Importance) 289
Ranasinghe, Athula 209
Ranawaka, Patali Champika 322
Ratnayake, K.R. 341
Ratnayake, R.M.D.K. 228n2
Raviraj, Nadaraja 121
Real Estate Exchange (Pvt) Ltd. (REEL) 228n7
reconstruction 60, 194, 196–197, 203, 242, 267–268, 325, 327
Redgwell, Catherine 319
Rehabilitation of Persons, Properties and Industries Authority (REPPIA) 88
religion 58–59, 69, 74, 85, 125, 134, 188, 383, 386; caste 388–389; Sri Lankan Muslims 108–109
renewable energy 21, 300–311
replacement cost approach 191n1
Reporters Without Borders Press Freedom Index 197
resilience, wetlands 296–297
resistance 10, 16, 22, 44–49, 131–132, 139, 258, 373–374; against privatization in higher education 212; and conflict 212–213; devastated communities 295–296; Internet as a site of 366–368; wetlands 296–297
restructuring of universities 209–211
re-territorialization 40–41
right-wing Muslims 9
risks: facing agricultural workers/livelihoods 234–236; of natural disasters 235
Roar Global 367
Roberts, Michael 284n4
Rogers, John D. 95, 390
Roy, Arundhati 9
Royal Asiatic Society 339
Ruhuna 325
Ruwanpura, Kanchana N. 19, 214, 243, 246, 254, 258, 329, 399–400

Said, Edward 35
Saleem, Amjad M. 112
Samarasinghe, Mahinda 328
Samarasinghe, Vidyamali 228n3, 255
Samurdhi 233, 266–267
Sanderatne, Nimal 266–267
Sandesha Kavya 290
Sarachchandra, Ediriweera 97
Saratchandra, E. R. 40
Sathkunanthan, Ambika 9

Satyodaya 374–375
"Save Wilpattu" 319
Schiller, Nina Glick 95
Schnonthal, Benjamin 328–329
Scholtens, Joeri 280
Schubert, Andi 214
Schulz, Ellen 249
science: context and failure 338–340; social *see* social sciences
Seabrook, Jeremy 396
Secretariat for Coordinating Reconciliation Mechanisms (SCRM) 125
securitization of climate change 329–330
security laws 83–84, 89–91
self-employment 18–20, 184, 265–267; and livelihoods 244–246; women in 189, 190
Seligman, Brenda Zara 341
Seligman, Charles 341
Senanayake, D.S. 97, 224, 326
Senevirathna, Priyan 237
SETIK (the Development and Social Justice agency of the Catholic Diocese of Kandy in Sri Lanka) 374
Sevanatha 398
sexual and gender-based violence (SGBV) 363–366, 367
sexual harassment 18, 367; in higher education 213; in workplace 177, 256
sexuality 15; Christian sanctity of 223; Internet on intersections of gender and 361–369
Shah, Amod 284
shelling of the Shrine of Our Lady of Madhu (1999) 74
Siddha 350
Silva, Kalinga T. 202, 385
Sinhala-Buddhist 228n5; chauvinism 45; consciousness 9; extremism 61–62, 114; hegemony 326; ideology 322; national culture 327; primordialism 327; revivalism 225
Sinhala-Buddhist nationalism 13, 44, 55, 225, 257, 325; and JVP's programme 72; and material inequalities 47; victim narratives 68, 70–76; and women 46
Sinhala civilizational state 45
Sinhala communities 15, 86, 100–101; collective fears of 97; numerical superiority of 96; violence against Tamils 9
Sinhala national cultural form 96–98
Sinhala nationalism 56; and anti-Tamil riots 98–99; contemporary life of 100–102; methodological nationalism 95–96; overview 94–95; post-war Sri Lanka 99–100; Sinhala national cultural form 96–98; Sri Lanka's political landscape 14–15
Sinhala Only Act 85, 112, 326
'Sinhala Only' language policy 70–71, 84

The Sinhalese Folk Play and The Modern Stage (Saratchandra) 40
Sinhalization of nature 326–327
Sirimavo Bandaranaike/Sri Lanka Freedom Party (SLFP) 34, 72, 225, 421
Sirisena, Maithripala 60, 62, 125
Siriwardane-de Zoysa, Rapti 283, 284n1
Sivanandan, Ambalavaner 45
Sivansundaram, Sujit 36–37
Sivapragasam, P.P. 374
Sivasundaram, Sujit 100, 282
Skanthakumar, B. 11
SLLDC Acts 292
Small Fry (Bavinck) 279
social challenges of renewable energy 305–307
social reproduction 19–20, 188, 190, 232, 237, 245–247, 249–250, 372–373, 377–378
social sciences 95, 208, 234, 278, 335; in Sri Lankan plantations 373–374
social stigma 184, 253, 255–256
social systems 22–23
society 22–23; civil society activism 136–137; Jaffna society 200–201, **201**
socio-economic discrimination 248
Soulbury Commission 84
sovereign mimicry 58
Sri Lanka, the ethnic conflict: Myths, realities and perspectives 98
Sri Lanka at the Cross-roads of History 100
Sri Lanka Computer Emergency Readiness Team (SLCERT) 363
Sri Lanka Freedom Party (SLFP) 34, 72, 109, 225, 421
Sri Lanka Health System Review 409
Sri Lanka Muslim Congress (SLMC) 110, 113
Sri Lankan apparel industry *see* apparel industry
Sri Lankan constitution 14, 55, 86; challenging 417–418; and environmental protection 319–320
Sri Lankan economy: and Covid-19 168–171; debt overhang 168–169; debt servicing *170*; economic performance 165–169, **166**; Extended Fund Facility (EFF) programme 165, 172–173; 'home grown' response 171; IMF bailout 170–171; liberalization reforms 164–165, 167–168; overview 162–163; policy context 163–165; twin deficits 168–169
Sri Lankan Fishermen (Alexander) 279
Sri Lankan garment factory workers: agency and freedom of association 256–258; apparel industry in post-conflict/post-pandemic era 259–261; devaluation 255–256; ethical sourcing destination 258; gendered nature of work 255–256; global labour governance mechanisms 258; social stigma 255–256; work and life-embodied experiences 254–255; work and life of 253–261

Sri Lankan identity 13; constitutional dimensions of contested 84–87; overview 83–84; security laws 89–91; transitional justice and reforms 87–89
Sri Lankan Muslims 106–109, 111, 114, 389, 410; culture 108–109; identity 107–110; language 108–109; political identity 109–110; religion 108–109; religious identity of 108
Sri Lankan plantations: development studies on 374–376; feminist futures and political reckonings 378–379; gender and social reproduction 377–378; historical overview 372–376; in history 372–373; Malaiyaka Tamil heritage and collective memory 377; overview 372; political and labour justice 378; post-war research arenas 376–378; in the social sciences 373–374
Sri Lankan plantation studies: feminist pathways in 372–379; political possibilities in 372–379
The Sri Lankan Republic at 40 59
Sri Lanka Qualifications Framework (SLQF) 210
Sri Lanka Sustainable Energy Authority (SEA) 303
Sri Maha Bodhi Shrine massacre (1985) 74
Srimavo Shastri Pact (1964) 374
Srinivasan, Meera 269
state: -regulated economic system 72–73; Sinhalization 326–327; in Sri Lanka 14–16
state-owned enterprises (SOEs) 164, 165, 167
Steinberg, Philip 278
stigma: and apparel work 253–254; labour market work 184; social 184, 253, 255–256; and strengthening mental health services 356; women ex-combatants 248–249
Stirrat, Roderick L. 279
Storey, Harry 290
Sufi Muslims 112
The Sunday Times 309
Suntharalingam, C. 85
Sustainable Development Goal (SDG) 3 349
Suthakar, K. 228n6

Tablighi Jamaat 61, 111–112, 115n3
Takahashi, Lois 399
'Take back the Tech' 2022 campaign 367
tameable bodies 224–226
Tamil nationalism 13, 55, 56, 60, 71, 96, 98–99, 101, 202, 372
Tamil United Liberation Front (TULF) 85–86
Tanaka, Masakazu 279
'Taprobane' 38, *38*
Tawheed Jamaath 61–62
Tennekoon, Serena N. 225, 327
Tennent, James Emerson 95, 339–340
Thananjan, Karththiha 132
Thanges, Paramsothy 388
Thiranagama, Sharika 57, 58, 140, 202, 227, 329, 391

Thirteenth Amendment 87, 91n6
Thiruvarangan, Mahendran 10, 11
Thongchai Winichakul 38–39
Thrift and Credit Cooperative Societies (TCCSs) 269
Thurairajah, Thanuja 227
Toynbee, Arnold J. 315
tradable production 164, 167
Tramway Strike of 1929 71
transgender politics 137–138
transitional justice/reforms 87–89; Commissions of Inquiry (CoI) 119–120, 122–124; overview 118–119; past investigative efforts 120–122; post-2009 transitional justice commitments 124–126
transoceanic circulations 282–283
Trincomalee massacres 74
Truth and Reconciliation Commission 89, 124

Unani 350
unemployment 196, 200; educated 73; rates by sex, age, education and province 177, 185–186, **186**; women 183–186, 266; youth 207–209
UNICEF 208, 358n2
Unitary State 9, 45, 85, 86–87
United National Party 45, 73, 109
United Nations (UN): Food and Agricultural Organisation (FAO) 376; Human Rights Council Resolution 88; Indian Government's lobbying of 376; 'The No New Coal Compact' pledge 305
United Nations Development Programme (UNDP) 9, 177, 244–245, 423
United Nations Law of the Sea Convention (1976) 278
United Nations Women, Peace and Security (WPS) agenda 249
United States Agency for International Development (USAID) 236–239, 309
Universal Health Coverage (UHC) index 349–350, 356
universities: as politicized spaces 213–214; restructuring of 209–211; state 209–211; violence and well-being in 212–213
University Grants Commission (UGC) 208
University of Ceylon 207, 215n1
Unmaking the Nation (Jeganathan and Ismail) 98
unmooring currents 282–283
'Unmooring Identity' (Ismail) 69
unpaid work 176, 190, 233–234
Up Country Workers Front (UWF) 375
Urban Development Authority (UDA) 227, 292, 296, 398
Urban Regeneration Project (URP) 398, 402
urban/regional wetlands: devastated communities 295–296; disturbed ecosystems 293–295; diverse ecologies and perceptions 289–291; political ecology of 288–297; resilience/resistance/disaster 296–297; wetlands governance 291–293
Uyangoda, Jayadeva 387

vaccines 357, 412
Vaddukoddai Resolution 85
Valentijn, François 336
Varthema, Ludovico di 336
The Veddas (Seligman and Seligman) 341
Vellalar caste 201–203, 384
Vijayatunge, Jinadasa 277, 284n2
Vijay Nagaraj 243–245
violence 8–12, 15, 22, 70, 72–73, 87, 89, 124–125, 270–271; anti-Tamil 98, 374–375; class-based 75; conflict-related 131–134; ethno-religious 68, 74; gender-based 15, 124, 137, 356, 361, 363–364; Internet as a site for 363–366; political (*see* political violence); state 44–46; structural 119, 245–246, 374, 377; in universities 212–213; *see also* anti-Muslim violence/rhetoric
vulnerable employment 177, 191n2

Walker, Rebecca 132
Wanniarachchi, Senel 138
wartime littoral 279–280
watta community 396–397, 400–402, 403, 430–431; culture 23
Weeramantry, C.G. 314–315
Wendt, Lionel 39, 40
Western Region Megapolis Planning Project (WRMPP) 398, 402
wetlands: at crossroads 296–297; diverse ecologies and perceptions 289–291; estuarine 290–293; governance 291–293, 297; towards resilience, resistance, or disaster 296–297; *see also* urban/regional wetlands
Wetlands Conservation Project 290
Wetlands Management Unit (WMU) 293
Wickramasinge, Martin 284n3
Wickramasingha, Shyamain 258
Wickramasinghe, Martin 96, 97
Wickramasinghe, Nira 36, 69, 72, 100
Wickremasinghe, Ranil 9, 12, 120, 127, 420–421
Wijayalath, Ayesha 14
Wijayatilake, S.A. 341
Wijetunga, Minoli 363
Wimmer, Andreas 95
Witharana, Dileepa 102
women: in agriculture 188, 232–233, 238; anti-Tamil attacks and pogroms 73–74; in apparel industry 188–189; and economy 177, **178–181**; and employment 186–190, **187**; empowerment of 266–267; entrepreneurs 189–190; heads of households 246–247; labour force participation

183–186; labour supply 183–186; marginal status of 18; in Northeast 199–200; political representation 135–137; and political violence 47; post-war capital accumulation 242–244; in service sector 189; and Sinhala Buddhist nationalism 46; unemployment 183–186, 266; working life chances of 19
Women in Need 364–365
Women's Center 257
Women's Global Leadership Institute 369n3
Women's Political Forum 135
Woods, Orlando 41
working life 19–20, 225
work/workforce: gendered nature of 255–256; gendered political economy of 242–250; and health infrastructure 354–355; and life-embodied experiences 254–255; and life of garment factory workers 253–261; and lives of agricultural workers 231–239; in post-war Sri Lanka 242–250
World Bank 16, 19, 148, 152, 157, 171–172, 209–211, 214, 237, 244, 245, 266, 356, 424–425, 426
World Conference on Disaster Reduction 328
World Health Organization (WHO) 355, 357, 358n2, 410, 412; Expanded Immunization Programme of 350; Expanded Programme on Immunization 351; *Sri Lanka Health System Review* 409

Xpress Pearl disaster 8

youth quotas 73
Yuganthaya (End of an Era) (Wickramasinghe) 97